Negotiation

Readings, Exercises, Cases

fifth edition

Roy J. Lewicki
The Ohio State University

Bruce Barry
Vanderbilt University

David M. Saunders
Queen's University

McGraw-Hill Irwin

Boston Burr Ridge, IL Dubuque, IA Madison, WI New York
San Francisco St. Louis Bangkok Bogotá Caracas Kuala Lumpur
Lisbon London Madrid Mexico City Milan Montreal New Delhi
Santiago Seoul Singapore Sydney Taipei Toronto

McGraw-Hill Irwin

NEGOTIATION: READINGS, EXERCISES, AND CASES

Published by McGraw-Hill/Irwin, a business unit of The McGraw-Hill Companies, Inc., 1221 Avenue of the Americas, New York, NY, 10020. Copyright © 2007 by The McGraw-Hill Companies, Inc. All rights reserved. No part of this publication may be reproduced or distributed in any form or by any means, or stored in a database or retrieval system, without the prior written consent of The McGraw-Hill Companies, Inc., including, but not limited to, in any network or other electronic storage or transmission, or broadcast for distance learning.

Some ancillaries, including electronic and print components, may not be available to customers outside the United States.

This book is printed on acid-free paper.

2 3 4 5 6 7 8 9 0 DOC/DOC 0 9 8 7 6

ISBN-13: 978-0-07-297310-5
ISBN-10: 0-07-297310-2

Editorial director: *John E. Biernat*
Senior sponsoring editor: *Ryan Blankenship*
Editorial coordinator: *Allison J. Belda*
Senior marketing manager: *Lisa Nicks*
Marketing coordinator: *Jared Harless*
Senior media producer: *Damian Moshak*
Lead project manager: *Christine A. Vaughan*
Senior production superviosr: *Rose Hepburn*
Senior designer: *Adam Rooke*
Media project manager: *Joyce J. Chappetto*
Cover design: *Joanne Schopler*
Typeface: *10/12 Times New Roman*
Compositor: *GTS—New Delhi, India Campus*
Printer: *R. R. Donnelley*

Library of Congress Cataloging-in-Publication Data

Negotiation : readings, exercises, and cases / [edited by] Roy J. Lewicki, Bruce Barry,
    David M. Saunders.—5th ed.
      p. cm.
    Includes bibliographical references and index.
    ISBN-13: 978-0-07-297310-5 (alk. paper)
    ISBN-10: 0-07-297310-2 (alk. paper)
    1. Negotiation in business. 2. Negotiation. 3. Negotiation—Case studies. I. Lewicki, Roy
J. II. Barry, Bruce, 1958-III. Saunders, David M.
HD58.6.N45 2007
658.4'52—dc22   2005057677

www.mhhe.com

We dedicate this book to all negotiation, mediation, and dispute resolution professionals who try to make the world a more peaceful and prosperous place.

About the Authors

Roy J. Lewicki is the Dean's Distinguished Teaching Professor and Professor of Management and Human Resources at the Max. M. Fisher College of Business, The Ohio State University. He has authored or edited over 30 books, as well as numerous research articles. Professor Lewicki has served as the president of the International Association of Conflict Management, and received the first David Bradford Outstanding Educator award from the Organizational Behavior Teaching Society for his contributions to the field of teaching in negotiation and dispute resolution.

Bruce Barry is Professor of Management and Sociology at Vanderbilt University. His research on negotiation, influence, power, and justice has appeared in numerous scholarly journals and volumes. Professor Barry is a past president of the International Association for Conflict Management and a past chair of the Academy of Management Conflict Management Division.

David M. Saunders is Dean of the School of Business at Queen's University, Canada. He has coauthored several articles on negotiation, conflict resolution, employee voice, and organizational justice. He has taught at Duke University, People's University in Beijing, China, and at McGill University in Montreal and Tokyo. Professor Saunders in currently Chair of the Canadian Federation of Business School Deans, a member of the Board of Directors of AACSB International, and member of the Board of Trustees of the European Foundation for Management Development (EFMD).

People negotiate every day. During an average day, we may negotiate with

- The boss, regarding an unexpected work assignment.
- Subordinates, regarding unexpected overtime.
- A supplier, about a problem with raw materials inventory management.
- A banker, over the terms of a business loan.
- A government official, regarding compliance with environmental regulations.
- A real estate agent, over the lease on a new warehouse.
- Our spouse, over who will walk the dog.
- Our child, over who will walk the dog (still an issue after we lose the previous negotiation).
- The dog, once out, as to whether any "business" gets done.

In short, negotiation is a common, everyday activity that most people use to influence others and to achieve personal objectives. In fact, negotiation is not only common, it is also essential to living an effective and satisfying life. We all need things—resources, information, cooperation, and support from others. Others have those needs as well, sometimes compatible with ours, sometimes not. Negotiation is a process by which we attempt to influence others to help us achieve our needs while at the same time taking their needs into account. It is a fundamental skill, not only for successful management but also for successful living.

In 1985 Roy Lewicki and Joseph Litterer published the first edition of this book. As they were preparing that volume, it was clear that the basic processes of negotiation had received only selective attention in both the academic and practitioner literature. Scholars of negotiation had generally restricted examination of these processes to basic theory development and laboratory research in social psychology, to a few books written for managers, and to an examination of negotiation in complex settings such as diplomacy and labor–management relations. Efforts to draw from the broader study of techniques for influence and persuasion, to integrate this work into a broader understanding of negotiation, and to apply this work to a broad spectrum of conflict and negotiation settings were only beginning to occur.

In the past 21 years this world has changed significantly. Several new practitioner organizations (such as the Society for Professionals in Dispute Resolution and the Association for Conflict Resolution) and academic professional associations (such as the Conflict Management Division of the Academy of Management and the International Association for Conflict Management) have devoted themselves exclusively to facilitating research and teaching in the fields of negotiation and conflict management. Several journals (*Negotiation Journal, International Journal of Conflict Management, International Negotiation*) focus exclusively on research in these fields. Finally, through the generosity of the Hewlett Foundation, a number of university centers have devoted themselves to enhancing the quality of teaching, research, and service in the negotiation and conflict management fields. Many schools now have several courses in negotiation and conflict management—in schools of business, law, public policy, psychology, social work, education, and natural resources. Development has occurred on the practitioner side as well. Books, seminars, and training courses on negotiation and conflict management abound. And, finally, mediation has become an extremely popular process as an alternative to litigation for handling divorce, community disputes, and land use conflicts. In pragmatic terms, all of this development means that as we assembled this fifth edition, we have had a much richer and more diverse pool of resources from which to sample. The net result for the student and instructor is a highly improved book of readings and exercises that contains many new articles, cases, and exercises, which represent the very best and most recent work on negotiation and the related topics of power, influence, and conflict management.

A brief overview of this book is in order. The readings in this book are organized into seven sections: (1) negotiation fundamentals, (2) negotiation subprocesses, (3) negotiation contexts, (4) individual differences, (5) negotiation across cultures, (6) resolving differences, and (7) a summary.

The rest of the book presents a collection of role-play exercises, cases, and self-assessment questionnaires that can be used to teach about negotiation processes and subprocesses. Complete information about the use or adaptation of these materials for several classroom formats is provided in our accompanying Instructor's Manual, which faculty members may obtain from their local McGraw-Hill/Irwin representative, by calling (800) 634-3963, or by visiting the McGraw-Hill Web site at http://mhhe.com/business/management/lewickinegotiation/.

For readers who are familiar with the earlier editions of this book, the most visible changes in this edition are to the book's content and organization, as follows:

- The content of this edition is substantially new. About half of the readings are new to this edition, and there are approximately eight new exercises and cases. Almost all exercises and cases have been revised and updated.

- We have reorganized the readings into seven sections. These sections parallel the seven sections and 20 chapters of the completely revised textbook, *Negotiation,* 5th edition, by Lewicki, Saunders, and Barry, also published by McGraw-Hill/Irwin. The text and reader can be used together or separately. A shorter version of the text, *Essentials of Negotiation* (3rd ed.) by Lewicki, Saunders, Barry, and Minton, can also be used in conjunction with this readings book; a fourth edition of *Essentials* should be available in late 2006. We encourage instructors to contact their local McGraw-Hill/Irwin representative for an examination copy (call 800-634-3963, or visit the Web site at http://mhhe.com/business/management/lewickinegotiation/).

This book could not have been completed without the assistance of numerous people. We especially thank

- The many authors and publishers who granted us permission to use or adapt their work for this book and whom we have recognized in conjunction with specific exercises, cases, or articles.

- The many negotiation instructors and trainers who inspired several of the exercises in this book and who have given us excellent feedback on the previous editions of this book.

- The staff of McGraw-Hill/Irwin, especially our current editor, Ryan Blankenship, and our previous editors: John Weimeister, John Biernat, Kurt Strand, and Karen Johnson; Allison Belda, an editorial coordinator who can solve almost any problem; and Christine Vaughan, a tireless project manager who helps turn our confusing instructions and tedious prose into eminently readable and usable volumes!

- Our families, who continue to provide us with the time, inspiration, opportunities for continued learning about effective negotiation, and personal support required to finish this project.

Roy J. Lewicki
Bruce Barry
David M. Saunders

Contents

Cases

Questionnaires

Negotiation Fundamentals

Reading 1.1

Three Approaches to Resolving Disputes: Interests, Rights, and Power

William L. Ury
Jeanne M. Brett
Stephen B. Goldberg

It started with a pair of stolen boots. Miners usually leave their work clothes in baskets that they hoist to the ceiling of the bathhouse between work shifts. One night a miner discovered that his boots were gone.[1] He couldn't work without boots. Angry, he went to the shift boss and complained, "Goddammit, someone stole my boots! It ain't fair! Why should I lose a shift's pay and the price of a pair of boots because the company can't protect the property?"

"Hard luck!" the shift boss responded. "The company isn't responsible for personal property left on company premises. Read the mine regulations!"

The miner grumbled to himself, "I'll show them! If I can't work this shift, neither will anyone else!" He convinced a few buddies to walk out with him and, in union solidarity, all the others followed.

The superintendent of the mine told us later that he had replaced stolen boots for miners and that the shift boss should have done the same. "If the shift boss had said to the miner, 'I'll buy you a new pair and loan you some meanwhile,' we wouldn't have had a strike." The superintendent believed that his way of resolving the dispute was better than the shift boss's or the miner's. Was he right and, if so, why? In what ways are some dispute resolution procedures better than others?

In this reading, we discuss three ways to resolve a dispute: reconciling the interests of the parties, determining who is right, and determining who is more powerful. We analyze the costs of disputing in terms of transaction costs, satisfaction with outcomes, effect on the relationship, and recurrence of disputes. We argue that, in general, reconciling interests costs less and yields more satisfactory results than determining who is right, which in turn costs less and satisfies more than determining who is more powerful. The goal of dispute systems design, therefore, is a system in which most disputes are resolved by reconciling interests.

Three Ways to Resolve Disputes

The Boots Dispute Dissected

A dispute begins when one person (or organization) makes a claim or demand on another who rejects it.[2] The claim may arise from a perceived injury or from a need or aspiration.[3] When the miner complained to the shift boss about the stolen boots, he was making a claim that the company should take responsibility and remedy his perceived injury. The shift boss's rejection of the claim turned it into a dispute. To resolve a dispute means to turn opposed positions—the claim and its rejection—into a single outcome.[4] The resolution of the boots dispute might have been a negotiated agreement, an arbitrator's ruling, or a decision by the miner to drop his claim or by the company to grant it.

In a dispute, people have certain interests at stake. Moreover, certain relevant standards or rights exist as guideposts toward a fair outcome. In addition, a certain balance of power exists between the parties. Interests, rights, and power then are three basic elements of any dispute. In resolving a dispute, the parties may choose to focus their attention on one or more of these basic factors. They may seek to (1) reconcile their underlying interests, (2) determine who is right, and/or (3) determine who is more powerful.

When he pressed his claim that the company should do something about his stolen boots, the miner focused on rights—"Why should I lose a shift's pay and the price of a pair of boots because the company can't protect the property?" When the shift boss responded by referring to mine regulations, he followed the miner's lead and continued to focus on who was right. The miner, frustrated in his attempt to win what he saw as justice, provoked a walkout—changing the focus to power. "I'll show them!" In other words, he would show the company how much power he and his fellow coal miners had—how dependent the company was on them for the production of coal.

The mine superintendent thought the focus should have been on interests. The miner had an interest in boots and a shift's pay, and the company had an interest in the miner working his assigned shift. Although rights were involved (there was a question of fairness) and power was involved (the miner had the power to cause a strike), the superintendent's emphasis was on each side's interests. He would have approached the stolen boots situation as a joint problem that the company could help solve.

Reconciling Interests

Interests are needs, desires, concerns, fears—the things one cares about or wants. They underlie people's positions—the tangible items they *say* they want. A husband and wife quarrel about whether to spend money for a new car. The husband's underlying interest may not be the money or the car but the desire to impress his friends; the wife's interest may be transportation. The director of sales for an electronics company gets into a dispute with the director of manufacturing over the number of TV models to produce. The director of sales wants to produce more models. Her interest is in selling TV sets; more models mean more choice for consumers and hence increased sales. The director of manufacturing wants to produce fewer models. His interest is in decreasing manufacturing costs; more models mean higher costs.

Reconciling such interests is not easy. It involves probing for deep-seated concerns, devising creative solutions, and making trade-offs and concessions where interests are opposed.[5] The most common procedure for doing this is *negotiation,* the act of back-and-forth communication intended to reach agreement. (A *procedure* is a pattern of interactive behavior directed toward resolving a dispute.) Another interests-based procedure is *mediation,* in which a third party assists the disputants in reaching agreement.

By no means do all negotiations (or mediations) focus on reconciling interests. Some negotiations focus on determining who is right, such as when two lawyers argue about whose case has the greater merit. Other negotiations focus on determining who is more powerful, such as when quarreling neighbors or nations exchange threats and counterthreats. Often negotiations involve a mix of all three—some attempts to satisfy interests, some discussion of rights, and some references to relative power. Negotiations that focus primarily on interests we call "interests-based," in contrast to "rights-based" and "power-based" negotiations. Another term for interests-based negotiation is *problem-solving negotiation,* so called because it involves treating a dispute as a mutual problem to be solved by the parties.

Before disputants can effectively begin the process of reconciling interests, they may need to vent their emotions. Rarely are emotions absent from disputes. Emotions often generate disputes, and disputes, in turn, often generate emotions. Frustration underlay the miner's initial outburst to the shift boss; anger at the shift boss's response spurred him to provoke the strike.

Expressing underlying emotions can be instrumental in negotiating a resolution. Particularly in interpersonal disputes, hostility may diminish significantly if the aggrieved party vents her anger, resentment, and frustration in front of the blamed party, and the blamed party acknowledges the validity of such emotions or, going one step further, offers an apology.[6] With hostility reduced, resolving the dispute on the basis of interests becomes easier. Expressions of emotion have a special place in certain kinds of interests-based negotiation and mediation.

Determining Who Is Right

Another way to resolve disputes is to rely on some independent standard with perceived legitimacy or fairness to determine who is right. As a shorthand for such independent standards, we use the term *rights.* Some rights are formalized in law or contract. Other rights are socially accepted standards of behavior, such as reciprocity, precedent, equality, and seniority.[7] In the boots dispute, for example, while the miner had no contractual right to new boots, he felt that standards of fairness called for the company to replace personal property stolen from its premises.

Rights are rarely clear. There are often different—and sometimes contradictory—standards that apply. Reaching agreement on rights, where the outcome will determine who gets what, can often be exceedingly difficult, frequently leading the parties to turn to a third party to determine who is right. The prototypical rights procedure is adjudication, in which disputants present evidence and arguments to a neutral third party who has the power to hand down a binding decision. (In mediation, by contrast, the third party does not have the power to decide the dispute.) Public adjudication is provided by courts and administrative agencies. Private adjudication is provided by arbitrators.[8]

Determining Who Is More Powerful

A third way to resolve a dispute is on the basis of power. We define power, somewhat narrowly, as the ability to coerce someone to do something he would not otherwise do. Exercising power typically means imposing costs on the other side or threatening to do so. In striking, the miners exercised power by imposing economic costs on the company. The exercise of power takes two common forms: acts of aggression, such as sabotage or physical attack, and withholding the benefits that derive from a relationship, as when employees withhold their labor in a strike.

In relationships of mutual dependence, such as between labor and management or within an organization or a family, the questions of who is more powerful turns on who is less dependent on the other.[9] If a company needs the employees' work more than employees need the company's pay, the company is more dependent and hence less powerful. How dependent one is turns on how satisfactory the alternatives are for satisfying one's interests. The better the alternative, the less dependent one is. If it is easier for the company to replace striking employees than it is for striking employees to find new jobs, the company is less dependent and thereby more powerful. In addition to strikes, power procedures include behaviors that range from insults and ridicule to beatings and warfare. All have in common the intent to coerce the other side to settle on terms more satisfactory to the wielder of power. Power procedures are of two types: power-based negotiation, typified by an exchange of threats, and power contests, in which the parties take actions to determine who will prevail.

Determining who is the more powerful party without a decisive and potentially destructive power contest is difficult because power is ultimately a matter of perceptions. Despite objective indicators of power, such as financial resources, parties' perceptions of their own and each other's power often do not coincide. Moreover, each side's perception of the other's power may fail to take into account the possibility that the other will invest greater resources in the contest than expected out of fear that a change in the perceived distribution of power will affect the outcomes of future disputes.

Interrelationship among Interests, Rights, and Power

The relationship among interests, rights, and power can be pictured as a circle within a circle within a circle (as in Figure 1). The innermost circle represents interests; the middle, rights; and the outer, power. The reconciliation of interests takes place within the context of the parties' rights and power. The likely outcome of a dispute if taken to court or to a strike, for instance, helps define the bargaining range within which a resolution can be found. Similarly, the determination of rights takes place within the context of power. One party, for instance, may win a judgment in court, but unless the judgment can be enforced, the dispute will continue. Thus, in the process of resolving a dispute, the focus may shift from interests to rights to power and back again.

FIGURE 1 | Interrelationships among Interests, Rights, and Power

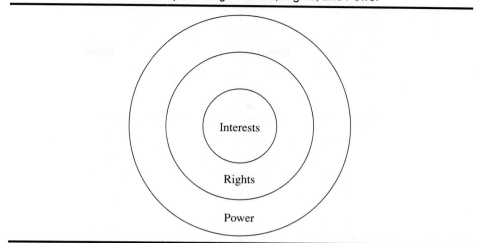

Lumping It and Avoidance

Not all disputes end with a resolution. Often one or more parties simply decide to withdraw from the dispute. Withdrawal takes two forms. One party may decide to "lump it," dropping her claim or giving in to the other's claim because she believes pursuing the dispute is not in her interest, or because she concludes she does not have the power to resolve it to her satisfaction. The miner would have been lumping his claim if he had said to himself, "I strongly disagree with management's decision not to reimburse me for my boots, but I'm not going to do anything about it." A second form of withdrawal is avoidance. One party (or both) may decide to withdraw from the relationship, or at least to curtail it significantly.[10] Examples of avoidance include quitting the organization, divorce, leaving the neighborhood, and staying out of the other person's way.

Both avoidance and lumping it may occur in conjunction with particular dispute resolution procedures. Many power contests involve threatening avoidance—such as threatening divorce—or actually engaging in it temporarily to impose costs on the other side—such as in a strike or breaking off of diplomatic relations. Many power contests end with the loser lumping her claim or her objection to the other's claim. Others end with the loser engaging in avoidance: leaving or keeping her distance from the winner. Similarly, much negotiation ends with one side deciding to lump it instead of pursuing the claim. Or, rather than take a dispute to court or engage in coercive actions, one party (or both) may decide to break off the relationship altogether. This is common in social contexts where the disputant perceives satisfactory alternatives to the relationship.

Lumping it and avoidance may also occur before a claim has been made, thus forestalling a dispute. Faced with the problem of stolen boots, the miner might have decided to lump it and not make a claim for the boots. More drastically, in a fit of exasperation, he might have walked off the job and never returned.

Which Approach Is "Best"?

When the miner superintendent described the boots dispute to us, he expressed a preference for how to resolve disputes. In our language, he was saying that on the whole it was better to try to reconcile interests than to focus on who was right or who was more powerful. But what does "better" mean? And in what sense, if any, was he correct in believing that focusing attention on interests is better?

What "Better" Means: Four Possible Criteria

The different approaches to the resolution of disputes—interests, rights, and power—generate different costs and benefits. We focus on four criteria in comparing them: transaction costs, satisfaction with outcomes, effect on the relationship, and recurrence of disputes.[11]

Transaction Costs For the mine superintendent, "better" meant resolving disputes without strikes. More generally, he wanted to minimize the costs of disputing—what may be called the *transaction costs*. The most obvious costs of striking were economic. The management payroll and the overhead costs had to be met while the mine stood idle. Sometimes strikes led to violence and the destruction of company property. The miners, too, incurred costs—lost wages. Then there were the lost opportunities for the company: a series of strikes could lead to the loss of a valuable sales contract. In a family argument, the costs would include the frustrating hours spent disputing, the frayed nerves and tension headaches, and the missed opportunities to do more enjoyable or useful tasks. All dispute resolution procedures carry transaction costs: the time, money, and emotional energy expended in disputing; the resources consumed and destroyed; and the opportunities lost.[12]

Satisfaction with Outcomes Another way to evaluate different approaches to dispute resolution is by the parties' mutual satisfaction with the result. The outcome of the strike could not have been wholly satisfactory to the miner—he did not receive new boots—but he did succeed in venting his frustration and taking his revenge. A disputant's satisfaction depends largely on how much the resolution fulfills the interests that led her to make or reject the claim in the first place. Satisfaction may also depend on whether the disputant believes that the resolution is fair. Even if an agreement does not wholly fulfill her interests, a disputant may draw some satisfaction from the resolution's fairness.

Satisfaction depends not only on the perceived fairness of the resolution, but also on the perceived fairness of the dispute resolution procedure. Judgments about fairness turn on several factors: how much opportunity a disputant had to express himself; whether he had control over accepting or rejecting the settlement; how much he was able to participate in shaping the settlement; and whether he believes that the third party, if there was one, acted fairly.[13]

Effect on the Relationship A third criterion is the long-term effect on the parties' relationship. The approach taken to resolve a dispute may affect the parties' ability to work together on a day-to-day basis. Constant quarrels with threats of divorce may seriously weaken a marriage. In contrast, marital counseling in which the disputing partners learn to focus on interests in order to resolve disputes may strengthen a marriage.

Recurrence   The final criterion is whether a particular approach produces durable resolutions. The simplest form of recurrence is when a resolution fails to stick. For example, a dispute between father and teenage son over curfew appears resolved but breaks out again and again. A subtler form of recurrence takes place when a resolution is reached in a particular dispute, but the resolution fails to prevent the same dispute from arising between one of the disputants and someone else, or conceivably between two different parties in the same community. For instance, a man guilty of sexually harassing an employee reaches an agreement with his victim that is satisfactory to her, but he continues to harass other women employees. Or he stops, but other men continue to harass women employees in the same organization.

The Relationship among the Four Criteria   These four different criteria are interrelated. Dissatisfaction with outcomes may produce strain on the relationship, which contributes to the recurrence of disputes, which in turn increases transaction costs. Because the different costs typically increase and decrease together, it is convenient to refer to all four together as the *costs of disputing*. When we refer to a particular approach as *high-cost* or *low-cost*, we mean not just transaction costs but also dissatisfaction with outcomes, strain on the relationship, and recurrence of disputes.

Sometimes one cost can be reduced only by increasing another, particularly in the short term. If father and son sit down to discuss their conflicting interests concerning curfew, the short-term transaction costs in terms of time and energy may be high. Still, these costs may be more than offset by the benefits of a successful negotiation—an improved relationship and the cessation of curfew violations.

Which Approach Is Least Costly?

Now that we have defined "better" in terms of the four types of costs, the question remains whether the mine superintendent was right in supposing that focusing on interests is better. A second question is also important: when an interests-based approach fails, is it less costly to focus on rights or on power?

Interests versus Rights or Power   A focus on interests can resolve the problem underlying the dispute more effectively than can a focus on rights or power. An example is a grievance filed against a mine foreman for doing work that contractually only a miner is authorized to do. Often the real problem is something else—a miner who feels unfairly assigned to an unpleasant task may file a grievance only to strike back at his foreman. Clearly, focusing on what the contract says about foremen working will not deal with this underlying problem. Nor will striking to protest foremen working. But if the foreman and miner can negotiate about the miner's future work tasks, the dispute may be resolved to the satisfaction of both.

Just as an interests-based approach can help uncover hidden problems, it can help the parties identify which issues are of greater concern to one than to the other. By trading off issues of lesser concern for those of greater concern, both parties can gain from the resolution of the dispute.[14] Consider, for example, a union and employer negotiating over two issues: additional vacation time and flexibility of work assignments. Although the union does not like the idea of assignment flexibility, its clear priority is additional vacation. Although the employer does not like the idea of additional vacation, he cares more about gaining flexibility in assigning work. An agreement that gives the union the vacation days it seeks and the employer flexibility in making work assignments would likely be satisfactory to both. Such joint gain is more likely to be realized if the parties focus on each side's interests. Focusing on who is right, as in litigation, or on who is more powerful, as in a strike, usually leaves at least one party perceiving itself as the loser.

Reconciling interests thus tends to generate a higher level of mutual satisfaction with outcomes than determining rights or power.[15] If the parties are more satisfied, their relationship benefits, and the dispute is less likely to recur. Determining who is right or who is more powerful, with the emphasis on winning and losing, typically makes the relationship more adversarial and strained. Moreover, the loser frequently does not give up, but appeals to a higher court or plots revenge. To be sure, reconciling interests can sometimes take a long time, especially when there are many parties to the dispute. Generally, however, these costs pale in comparison with the transaction costs of rights and power contests such as trials, hostile corporate takeovers, or wars.

In sum, focusing on interests, compared to focusing on rights or power, tends to produce higher satisfaction with outcomes, better working relationships, and less recurrence, and may also incur lower transaction costs. As a rough generalization, then, an interests approach is less costly than a rights or power approach.

Rights versus Power   Although determining who is right or who is more powerful can strain the relationship, deferring to a fair standard usually takes less of a toll than giving in to a threat. In a dispute between a father and teenager over curfew, a discussion of independent standards such as the curfews of other teenagers is likely to strain the relationship less than an exchange of threats.

Determining rights or power frequently becomes a contest—a competition among the parties to determine who will prevail. They may compete with words to persuade a third-party decision maker of the merits of their case, as in adjudication; or they may compete with actions intended to show the other who is more powerful, as in a proxy fight. Rights contests differ from power contests chiefly in their transaction costs. A power contest typically costs more in resources consumed and opportunities lost. Strikes cost more than arbitration. Violence costs more than litigation. The high transaction costs stem not only from the efforts invested in the fight but also from the destruction of each side's resources. Destroying the opposition may be the very object of a power contest. Moreover, power contests often create new injuries and new disputes along with anger, distrust, and a desire for revenge. Power contests, then, typically damage the relationship more and lead to greater recurrence of disputes than do rights contests. In general, a rights approach is less costly than a power approach.

Proposition

To sum up, we argue that, in general, reconciling interests is less costly than determining who is right, which in turn is less costly than determining who is more powerful. This proposition does not mean that focusing on interests is invariably better than focusing on rights and power, but simply means that it tends to result in lower transaction costs, greater satisfaction with outcomes, less strain on the relationship, and less recurrence of disputes.

Focusing on Interests Is Not Enough

Despite these general advantages, resolving *all* disputes by reconciling interests alone is neither possible nor desirable. It is useful to consider why.

When Determining Rights or Power Is Necessary

In some instances, interests-based negotiation cannot occur unless rights or power procedures are first employed to bring a recalcitrant party to the negotiating table. An environmental group, for example, may file a lawsuit against a developer to bring about a negotiation. A community group may organize a demonstration on the steps of the town hall to get the mayor to discuss its interests in improving garbage collection service.

In other disputes, the parties cannot reach agreement on the basis of interests because their perceptions of who is right or who is more powerful are so different that they cannot establish a range in which to negotiate. A rights procedure may be needed to clarify the rights boundary within which a negotiated resolution can be sought. If a discharged employee and her employer (as well as their lawyers) have very different estimations about whether a court would award damages to the employee, it will be difficult for them to negotiate a settlement. Nonbinding arbitration may clarify the parties' rights and allow them to negotiate a resolution.

Just as uncertainty about the rights of the parties will sometimes make negotiation difficult, so too will uncertainty about their relative power. When one party in an ongoing relationship wants to demonstrate that the balance of power has shifted in its favor, it may find that only a power contest will adequately make the point. It is a truism among labor relations practitioners that a conflict-ridden union–management relationship often settles down after a lengthy strike. The strike reduces uncertainty about the relative power of the parties that had made each party unwilling to concede. Such long-term benefits sometimes justify the high transaction costs of a power contest.

In some disputes, the interests are so opposed that agreement is not possible. Focusing on interests cannot resolve a dispute between a right-to-life group and an abortion clinic over whether the clinic will continue to exist. Resolution will likely be possible only through a rights contest, such as a trial, or a power contest, such as a demonstration or a legislative battle.

When Are Rights or Power Procedures Desirable?

Although reconciling interests is generally less costly than determining rights, only adjudication can authoritatively resolve questions of public importance. If the 1954 Supreme Court case, *Brown v. Board of Education* (347 U.S. 483), outlawing racial segregation in public schools, had been resolved by negotiation rather than by adjudication, the immediate result might have been the same—the black plaintiff would have attended an all-white Topeka, Kansas, public school. The societal impact, however, would have been far less significant. As it was, *Brown* laid the groundwork for the elimination of racial segregation in all of American public life. In at least some cases, then, rights-based court procedures are preferable, from a societal perspective, to resolution through interests-based negotiation.[16]

Some people assert that a powerful party is ill-advised to focus on interests when dealing regularly with a weaker party. But even if one party is more powerful, the costs of imposing one's will can be high. Threats must be backed up with actions from time to time. The weaker party may fail to fully comply with a resolution based on power, thus requiring the more powerful party to engage in expensive policing. The weaker party may also take revenge—in small ways, perhaps, but nonetheless a nuisance. And revenge may be quite costly to the more powerful if the power balance ever shifts, as it can quite unexpectedly, or if the weaker party's cooperation is ever needed in another domain. Thus, for a more powerful party, a focus on interests, within the bounds set by power, may be more desirable than would appear at first glance.

Low-Cost Ways to Determine Rights and Power

Because focusing on rights and power plays an important role in effective dispute resolution, differentiating rights and power procedures on the basis of costs is useful. We distinguish three types of rights and power procedures: negotiation, low-cost contests, and high-cost contests. Rights-based negotiation is typically less costly than a rights contest such as court or arbitration. Similarly, power-based negotiation, marked by threats, typically costs less than a power contest in which those threats are carried out.

Different kinds of contests incur different costs. If arbitration dispenses with procedures typical of a court trial (extensive discovery, procedural motions, and lengthy briefs), it can be much cheaper than going to court. In a fight, shouting is less costly than physical assault. A strike in which workers refuse only overtime work is less costly than a full strike.

The Goal: An Interests-Oriented Dispute Resolution System

Not all disputes can be—or should be—resolved by reconciling interests. Rights and power procedures can sometimes accomplish what interests-based procedures cannot. The problem is that rights and power procedures are often used where they are not necessary. A procedure that should be the last resort too often becomes the first resort. The goal, then, is a dispute resolution system that looks like the pyramid on the right in Figure 2: most disputes are resolved through reconciling interests, some through determining who is right, and the fewest through determining who is more powerful. By contrast, a distressed dispute resolution system would look like the inverted pyramid on the left in Figure 2. Comparatively few disputes are resolved through reconciling interests, while many are resolved through determining rights and power. The challenge for the systems designer is to turn the pyramid right side up. It is to design a system that promotes the reconciling of interests but that also provides low-cost ways to determine rights or power for those disputes that cannot or should not be resolved by focusing on interests alone.

FIGURE 2 | Moving from a Distressed to an Effective Dispute Resolution System

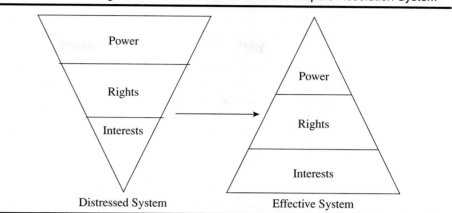

Endnotes

1. In order to steer between the Scylla of sexist language and the Charybdis of awkward writing, we have chosen to alternate the use of masculine and feminine pronouns.

2. This definition is taken from W. L. F. Felstiner, R. L. Abel, and A. Sarat, "The Emergence and Transformation of Disputes: Naming, Blaming, Claiming." *Law and Society Review 15* (1980–81), pp. 631–54. The article contains an interesting discussion of disputes and how they emerge.

3. See W. L. F. Felstiner, R. L. Abel, and A. Sarat, "The Emergence and Transformation of Disputes: Naming, Blaming, Claiming." *Law and Society Review 15* (1980–81), pp. 631–54.

4. In speaking of resolving disputes, rather than processing, managing, or handling disputes, we do not suggest that resolution will necessarily bring an end to the fundamental conflict underlying the dispute. Nor do we mean that a dispute once resolved will stay resolved. Indeed, one of our criteria for contrasting approaches to dispute resolution is the frequency with which disputes recur after they appear to have been resolved. See S. E. Merry, "Disputing Without Culture," *Harvard Law Review 100* (1987), pp. 2057–73; A. Sarat, "The 'New Formalism' in Disputing and Dispute Processing," *Law and Society Review 21* (1988), pp. 695–715.

5. For an extensive discussion of interests-based negotiation, see R. Fisher and W. L. Ury, *Getting to Yes* (Boston: Houghton Mifflin, 1981). See also D. A. Lax and J. K. Sebenius, *The Manager as a Negotiator* (New York: Free Press, 1986).

6. S. B. Goldberg and F. E. A. Sander, "Saying You're Sorry," *Negotiation Journal 3* (1987), pp. 221–24.

7. We recognize that in defining rights to include both legal entitlements and generally accepted standards of fairness, we are stretching that term beyond its commonly understood meaning. Our reason for doing so is that a procedure that uses either legal entitlements or generally accepted standards of fairness as a basis for dispute resolution will focus on the disputants' entitlements under normative standards, rather than on their underlying interests. This is true of adjudication, which deals with legal rights; it is equally true of rights-based negotiation, which may deal with either legal rights or generally accepted standards. Since, as we shall show, procedures that focus on normative standards are more costly than those that focus on interests, and since our central concern is with cutting costs as well as realizing benefits, we find it useful to cluster together legal rights and other normative standards, as well as procedures based on either.

8. A court procedure may determine not only who is right but also who is more powerful, since behind a court decision lies the coercive power of the state. Legal rights have power behind them. Still, we consider adjudication a rights procedure, since its overt focus is determining who is right, not who is more powerful. Even though rights, particularly legal rights, do provide power, a procedure that focuses on rights as a means of dispute resolution is less costly than a procedure that focuses on power. A rights-based contest, such as adjudication, which focuses on which disputant ought to prevail under normative standards, will be less costly than a power-based strike, boycott, or war, which focuses on which disputant can hurt the other more. Similarly, a negotiation that focuses on normative criteria for dispute resolution will be less costly than a negotiation that focuses on the disputants' relative capacity to injure each other. Hence, from our cost perspective, it is appropriate to distinguish procedures that focus on rights from those that focus on power.

9. R. M. Emerson, "Power-Dependence Relations," *American Sociological Review 27* (1962), pp. 31–41.

10. A. O. Hirschman, *Exit, Voice, and Loyalty: Responses to Declines in Firms, Organizations, and States* (Cambridge, MA: Harvard University Press, 1970). Exit corresponds with avoidance, loyalty with lumping it. Voice, as we shall discuss later, is most likely to be realized in interests-based procedures such as problem-solving negotiation and mediation.

11. A fifth evaluative criterion is procedural justice, which is perceived satisfaction with the fairness of a dispute resolution procedure. Research has shown that disputants prefer third-party procedures that provide opportunities for outcome control and voice. See E. A. Lind and T. R. Tyler, *The Social Psychology of Procedural Justice* (New York: Plenum, 1988); and J. M. Brett, "Commentary on Procedural Justice Papers," in R. J. Lewicki, B. H. Sheppard, and M. H. Bazerman (eds.), *Research on Negotiations in Organizations* (Greenwich, CT: JAI Press, 1986), pp. 81–90.

   We do not include procedural justice as a separate evaluation criterion for two reasons. First, unlike transaction costs, satisfaction with outcome, effect on the relationship, and recurrence, procedural justice is meaningful only at the level of a single procedure for a single dispute. It neither generalizes across the multiple procedures that may be used in the resolution of a single dispute nor generalizes across disputes to construct a systems-level cost. The other costs will do both. For example, it is possible to measure the disputants' satisfaction with the outcome of a dispute, regardless of how many different procedures were used to resolve that dispute. Likewise, it is possible to measure satisfaction with outcomes in a system that handles many disputes by asking many disputants about their feelings. Second, while procedural justice and distributive justice (satisfaction with fairness of outcomes) are distinct concepts, they are typically highly correlated. See E. A. Lind and T. R. Tyler, *The Social Psychology of Procedural Justice* (New York: Plenum, 1988).

12. O. E. Williamson, "Transaction Cost Economics: The Governance of Contractual Relations," *Journal of Law and Economics 22* (1979), pp. 233–61; and J. M. Brett and J. K. Rognes, "Intergroup Relations in Organizations," in P. S. Goodman and Associates, *Designing Effective Work Groups* (San Francisco: Jossey-Bass, 1986), pp. 202–36.

13. For a summary of the evidence of a relationship between procedural and distributive justice—that is, satisfaction with process and with outcome—see E. A. Lind and T. R. Tyler, *The Social Psychology of Procedural Justice* (New York: Plenum, 1988). Lind and Tyler also summarize the evidence showing a relationship between voice and satisfaction with the process. For evidence of the effect of participation in shaping the ultimate resolution beyond simply being able to accept or reject a third party's advice, see J. M. Brett and D. L. Shapiro, "Procedural Justice: A Test of Competing Theories and Implications for Managerial Decision Making," unpublished manuscript.

14. D. A. Lax and J. K. Sebenius, *The Manager as Negotiator* (New York: Free Press, 1986).

15. The empirical research supporting this statement compares mediation to arbitration or adjudication. Claimants prefer mediation to arbitration in a variety of settings: labor-management (J. M. Brett and S. B. Goldberg, "Grievance Mediation in the Coal Industry: A Field Experiment," *Industrial and Labor Relations Review 37* (1983), pp. 49–69), small claims disputes (C. A. McEwen and R. J. Maiman, "Small Claims Mediation in Maine: An Empirical Assessment," *Maine Law Review 33* (1981), pp. 237–68), and divorce (J. Pearson, "An Evaluation of Alternatives to Court Adjudication," *Justice System Journal 7* (1982), pp. 420–44).

16. Some commentators argue that court procedures are always preferable to a negotiated settlement when issues of public importance are involved in a dispute (see, for example, O. M. Fiss, "Against Settlement," *Yale Law Journal 93* (1984), pp. 1073–90), and all agree that disputants should not be pressured into the settlement of such disputes. The extent to which parties should be encouraged to resolve disputes affecting a public interest is, however, not at all clear. See H. T. Edwards, "Alternative Dispute Resolution: Panacea or Anathema?" *Harvard Law Review 99* (1986), pp. 668–84.

Selecting a Strategy

Roy J. Lewicki
Alex. Hiam
Karen W. Olander

After you have analyzed your own position and that of the other party and have looked at the contextual issues of the negotiation, you are ready to select a strategy to use in negotiating with the other party. This lengthy preparation allows you to negotiate strategically, adopting a style and plan that are best suited to the situation. As we have noted before, most people skip this preparation; as a result, they negotiate blind. The right strategy greatly improves your odds of a successful outcome.

In this chapter, we will look at five basic strategies that can be used for negotiation. Each strategy applies to a particular set of circumstances and has its own advantages and disadvantages. If you have done your homework, you will be well prepared for selecting the appropriate strategy or combination of strategies for a particular negotiation situation. Note that we say *combination* of strategies. Most negotiations involve a mixture of issues, and each may be best handled with a different strategy. There is usually no single "best" strategy. Variations in the positions of the parties and the context of the negotiation will affect each negotiation differently. And as negotiations continue over time, each side will make adjustments that may call for shifts or changes of strategy by the other side.

Key Factors That Determine the Types of Strategies

The five basic types of negotiating strategies depend on your combination of preferences for two basic concerns: the *relationship with the other negotiator* and the *outcome of the negotiation itself.* The strength or importance of each of these two concerns, and their relative priority, should direct the selection of the optimal negotiation strategy. The other party may select a strategy in a similar manner. If they do not, you will want to give serious consideration as to whether you should share this strategic negotiating model with them. Your chances of a good outcome are often better if both parties agree to play by the same rules. The interaction of the two parties' choices will further influence the negotiation process that actually occurs, and this will have dramatic impact on the outcomes. We will now describe each of these concerns.

Relationship Concerns

First, how important is your past and future *relationship* with the other party? How have the two of you gotten along in the past, and how important is it for the two of you to get along, work together, and like each other in the future? Perhaps it is very important. Perhaps it does not matter at all. Perhaps it is somewhere between these extremes. If maintaining a good relationship with the other party is important to you, then you should

Source: From Roy J. Lewicki, A. Hiam, and K. W. Olander, *Think before You Speak* (New York: John Wiley, 1996), pp. 54–75. Used with permission.

negotiate differently than if the relationship is unimportant, or if it is unlikely that you can repair the relationship.

The importance of the relationship between the two parties will be affected by a number of factors: (1) whether there is a relationship at all; (2) whether that relationship is generally positive or negative (whether the two of you have gotten along well or poorly in the past); (3) whether a future relationship is desirable; (4) the length of the relationship and its history, if one exists; (5) the level of and commitment to the relationship; (6) the degree of interdependence in the relationship; and (7) the amount and extent of free, open communication between the parties.

For example, if you are negotiating the purchase of a new car, you may never have met the salesperson before and may not expect to have a continuing relationship. Therefore, your relationship concerns are low. However, if your business uses a fleet of cars and you expect to work with this person on deals in the future, your relationship concerns are high, and this will affect negotiations. Or if you are buying the car from your neighbor, and want to continue to have a good relationship with that person, you may negotiate differently than if you are buying it from a stranger.

In the case of a party with whom you have an ongoing relationship, it may be congenial, or it may be antagonistic if earlier negotiations have been hostile. If it is a congenial relationship, you may wish to keep it that way, and avoid escalating emotions. If the relationship has a history of hostility, you may prefer not to negotiate, or you may want to lower the emotional level in the negotiations. This is important if you expect the relationship to continue in the future.

Outcome Concerns

The second factor affecting negotiating strategy is the importance of the *outcome* of the negotiation. How important is it for you to achieve a good outcome in this negotiation? Do you need to win on all points to gain the advantage? Or is the outcome of only moderate importance? Or does the outcome not really matter in this negotiation? For example, let us return to the car-buying example. If you are buying a car from a dealer, price may be the most important factor, and you may have absolutely no interest at all in the relationship. If you are buying the car from your neighbor, and you want to keep a good relationship with your neighbor, then you might not press as hard to get a good price. Finally, if you are buying the car from your mother simply so that she doesn't have to worry about it any more, you probably are most concerned about the relationship and care very little about the outcome.

Most of the planning and preparation described in the earlier chapters have focused on the outcome. Hence we will not say much more about outcome concerns here. The important message in this chapter, however, is that the priority of each of the two negotiating concerns, relationship and outcome, will direct the strategy you choose to use for a particular negotiation. The relationship may be your top priority, especially if there is a relationship history and you want to maintain the relationship. In contrast, in many other negotiations, the outcome is the most important factor, as in the example of buying a car. Or relationship and outcome may *both* be important. This will require working together with the other party in some fashion to effect a result. If the relationship concerns have a strong influence on the

FIGURE 3 | Negotiation Strategies

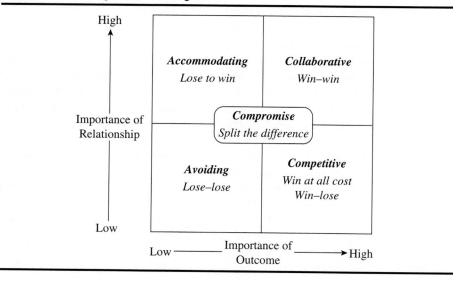

matter at hand, and you decide to emphasize them over the outcome, then you will select a different strategy than you would select where the outcome is more important.

If we show the relationship and outcome concerns on a graph, with high and low priorities for each represented, it looks like Figure 3. The vertical axis represents your degree of concern for the relationship, and the horizontal axis represents your degree of concern for the outcome. When we look at the various quadrants created by different levels of concern for relationship and outcome, five distinctly different strategies emerge:

1. *Avoiding (lose–lose):* This strategy is shown in the lower left of the diagram. In this strategy, the priorities for both the relationship and the outcome are low. Neither aspect of the negotiation is important enough for you to pursue the conflict further. You implement this strategy by withdrawing from active negotiation, or by avoiding negotiation entirely.

2. *Accommodating (lose to win):* This strategy is represented in the upper left of the diagram, where the importance of the relationship is high and the importance of the outcome is low. In this situation, you "back off" your concern for the outcome to preserve the relationship; you intentionally "lose" on the outcome dimension in order to "win" on the relationship dimension.

3. *Competitive (win–lose):* The lower right of the diagram represents high concern for the outcome and low concern for the relationship. You use this strategy if you want to win at all cost, and have no concern about the future state of the relationship.

4. *Collaborative (win–win):*[1] The upper right part of the diagram defines a strategy where there is a high priority for both the relationship and the outcome. In this strategy, the parties attempt to maximize their outcomes while preserving or

enhancing the relationship. This result is most likely when both parties can find a resolution that meets the needs of each.

5. *Compromising (split the difference):* In the middle is an area we will call a compromising, or "satisficing," strategy. It represents a combination approach that is used in a variety of situations. For example, it is often used when the parties cannot achieve good collaboration, but still want to achieve some outcomes and/or preserve the relationship. Thus, for example, if the parties cannot achieve good collaboration but do not want to pursue the outcome and abandon the concern for the relationship (or vice versa), then a compromising strategy can be effective. It is also often used when the parties are under time pressure and need to come to a resolution quickly. Each party will give in somewhat to find a common ground.

These brief descriptions are ideal or "pure" negotiating situations where there may be only one issue at stake. In contrast, most real-life negotiation situations are frequently complex, and thus are often best addressed by using a mix of strategies. Remember, too, that the other party will be formulating a negotiating strategy. You will find your analysis of the other party helpful when you are selecting the appropriate strategy for a particular situation, because you may want to adjust your strategy choice based on what you expect the other to do. If the parties are able to agree on one strategy, negotiations will be easier. In real-life situations, however, each party may start with a different strategy.

We now look at the five basic negotiating strategies in detail. Although you may be inclined to use one particular strategy, it is a good idea to study the components of each strategy carefully. In this way, you can be prepared for the other party's moves, if they use a different strategy than you anticipated.

Avoiding Strategy (Lose–Lose)

The avoiding strategy is used infrequently, but has merit in certain situations. Our nickname of this strategy is actually a misnomer, since an active choice of an avoiding strategy is not necessarily a "loss" on either the relationship or the outcome. However, since we tend to refer to the more active pursuits of relationship and outcomes as "winning," we will call the avoiding strategy a "loss" in terms of the outcome and the relationship.

Why would one choose an avoiding strategy? Because negotiations can be costly (in time, money, and relationships) and there are many cases where negotiators would have been better off to drop the matter entirely! The person employing an avoiding strategy basically sees negotiation as a waste of time—or not worth pursuing. This person may feel that his or her needs can be met without negotiating. In addition, this person may decide that the outcome has very low value and that the relationship is not important enough to develop through the negotiation. As a result, the party reasons that neither the relationship nor the outcome is sufficiently important (at least compared with the costs) and so takes no action or simply refuses to negotiate.

If the "avoider" refuses to negotiate when the other party wants to, this may have a negative effect on the relationship. Even when the outcome is unimportant, many people will prefer to avoid angering the other party. A more moderate method of avoidance may be to not raise any objections to the proceedings, or simply to not show up. If the other party insists on negotiations, and it is important to preserve the relationship, then you might switch to an accommodating strategy.

The avoiding strategy also is a possibility when a party can pursue a very strong alternative outcome. If a strong alternative is available, the person may choose not to negotiate. For example, if you are looking at two different houses to buy, and both meet your needs, you may choose not to negotiate with one seller because you feel the price is too high and the person is inflexible. So you simply select your alternative and pursue an avoiding strategy in the first negotiation.

Alternatives can provide you with bargaining power in other situations, as we will see. If you have no alternatives, or only weak ones, you may also choose not to negotiate. We will discuss alternatives in more depth later in this chapter.

Accommodating Strategy (Lose to Win)

An accommodating strategy is used when the relationship is more important than the outcome of the negotiation. The person using this strategy may prefer to primarily concentrate on building or strengthening a relationship. Since other people are usually happy when we give them what they want, we may simply choose to avoid focusing on the outcome and give it to the other side, thus making them happy. A second reason is that we may want something else in the future. Since many social relationships are built on rather informal expectations and rules of exchange,[2] giving something away now may create the expectation that they need to give us what we want later on. So we give them their preferences now to obtain a better future outcome. A short-term loss is exchanged for a long-term gain.

For example, in a manager–employee relationship, the employee may want to establish a good relationship with the boss now to have a good evaluation, a raise, or a better position in the future. The employee may choose an accommodating strategy and not push for a salary increase now, at her three-month review, if it is expected that this will put her in a better position for a raise at the six-month review.

The accommodating strategy may be used to encourage a more interdependent relationship, to increase support and assistance from the other, or even to cool off hostile feelings if there is tension in the relationship. If the relationship is ongoing, then it may be particularly appropriate to "back down" now, to keep communication lines open and not pressure the opponent to give in on something that they do not want to discuss. In most cases, this strategy is *short term*—it is expected that accommodation now will create a better opportunity to achieve outcome goals in the future. For example, a manager might not urge an employee to take on an extra task right now if the employee is overloaded with projects and the manager can find another person to complete the task, especially if the manager knows that a big project is coming next week, and everyone is going to have to put in overtime.

In a long-term negotiation or over a series of negotiations, it may happen that one side constantly gives in. This precedent may be noted by the other side and seen as accommodating behavior (which it is). It should not be construed as an invitation to the other party to be competitive. But sometimes it is. If this happens to you, the other party will begin to compete and take advantage of your guard being down. You will need to learn how to use damage control and reconnection strategies to overcome these problems.

The accommodating strategy is not usually considered a formal strategy in negotiation. Many negotiation books do not even mention accommodation as a viable strategy; however, most of these books also are based on "high outcome concern" strategies (competing or collaborating) and spend less time on specific strategies to improve or strengthen the relationship. There are two important times to consider an accommodating strategy: first, if the outcome is not very important to you, or pursuing the outcome is likely to create too much tension and animosity, and second, if your primary objective is to improve the relationship. In addition, you might decide to switch to an accommodating strategy during negotiations, particularly when they reach a point where you no longer wish to press for a resolution.

Competitive Strategy (Win to Lose)

When many people think of negotiation and bargaining, this is the strategy they think of. The competitive strategy is used frequently, so it is important to understand how it works, even if you do not plan to use it yourself.

In a competitive strategy, the outcome of the negotiation is more important than the relationship. Because the outcomes (resources, gains, profits, etc.) are seen as finite and limited in amount or size, the person engaging in a competitive strategy wants to get as much of those outcomes as possible. (We will use the term *competition* to denote the person using the competitive strategy.) We call this strategy *win to lose* because it is likely that while competitors may gain on the outcome, they strain and endanger the relationship between the parties. The thinking and goals in this strategy are short term: to maximize the magnitude of the outcome right now, and to not care about either the long-term consequences of this strategy or the relationship. The relationship with the other party does not matter, for one of several reasons: (1) this may be a one-time negotiation with no future relationship, (2) the future relationship may not be important, (3) the relationship exists, but was poor to begin with, or (4) the other party may have a reputation for hard bargaining or dishonesty, and this strategy is adopted for defensive reasons. At any rate, this strategy is undertaken with the assumption that the future relationship with the other party is unimportant, but the specific outcome *is* important.

The competitive strategy tends to emphasize the differences between the parties, promoting a "we/they" attitude. Thus the relationship during negotiation in a competitive situation will be characterized by lack of trust and even by conflict. This contrasts with the collaborative strategy in which differences are minimized and similarities emphasized.

The goal in the competitive strategy is to get the other party to give in, and thus to satisfy the competitor's needs now. It is based on the "I win, you lose" concept. The competitor will do anything to accomplish the objectives and obtain as much of the pie as possible. This can include a variety of behaviors, including hardball tactics.

Critical Factors In a Competitive Strategy

A Well-Defined Bargaining Range   In a competitive strategy, each side has a bargaining range, which consists of a *starting point,* a *target,* and an *ending point* or walkaway. Bargaining occurs because the line bargaining range for each party is different. During bargaining, you attempt to bring the two ranges into overlap so that each party is satisfied.

The *starting point* is announced or inferred as the negotiations begin. Starting points will be different for the two parties. In new car negotiations, for example, the buyer will have a lower starting point, the seller, a higher one. Usually the buyer makes gradual concessions upward, while the seller will make gradual concessions downward, with the expectation that the two will be able to meet somewhere in the middle. In labor negotiations, labor is usually expected to ask "high" and management to offer "low," again with the expectation that concessions on each side will result in finding a meeting ground.

Both parties will have a walkaway point, which is the cutoff point, beyond which they will not go. The walkaway point of the other party is usually not known, and is not stated. In fact, they will actively try to keep you from learning their walkaway point, because if you knew it, you would offer them something slightly above it and expect that they would agree! If talks break off because this point has been reached, then you may surmise that the walkaway point of the other party was probably close to, or at, the last offer that the other side made. If this point is not reached, and the parties agree to a resolution, this point may never be known. In future chapters, we will explore ways of discovering competitors' walkaway points and learn how to turn this knowledge into better outcomes.

As long as the bargaining range for one party in some way overlaps with that of the other party, then there is room for bargaining. (By *overlap,* we mean that the most the buyer is willing to offer is above the least the seller is willing to accept.) If the ranges do not overlap (and this may not be known at the beginning of the negotiations), then there may be no successful negotiation. The parties will need to decide whether to adjust their bargaining ranges, or to end negotiations.

A Good Alternative   An alternative or BATNA[3] (best alternative to a negotiated agreement) is an option that can be pursued if the current negotiation fails. It is an outcome outside the scope of the negotiation with this other party, and can be pursued if it appears more attractive than any potential outcome from this negotiation. Alternatives are good to have because they can be weighed against the value of any particular outcome from this negotiation, to decide which is most advantageous. Not only is an alternative an evaluative tool, it is also a power tool that can be introduced into negotiations in the manner of "I have this alternative that is equally good and costs less. Can you improve on what I will get if I pursue my alternative?"

Alternatives interact with walkaway points to influence the choices you make. For example, say you currently make $25,000 in your job and you are job hunting. You decide that you want to find a job making at least $30,000. What do you do if you find a job you like, but it pays only $28,000? Do you take it or not? If there are no other such jobs available (no alternatives) because the economy is sluggish, then you might take the $28,000 job. However, if many alternative jobs are available for the taking, then you may hold out for a higher salary. On the other hand, suppose you lose your $25,000 job and you are offered $24,000 for another similar job. Will you take it? Perhaps under these circumstances, you will be more likely to do so. In any negotiation, it is wise to be well-informed of your alternatives and, wherever possible, to use them to your advantage.

Tactics   The competitive strategy is also characterized by a number of tactics calculated to enhance the competitor's position and place the other party at a disadvantage. These include behavioral tactics such as bluffing, being aggressive, and threatening, which can give the competitor power over the other party. While these tactics work sometimes, they also have the problem that they can potentially backfire on the person using them, so they must be employed carefully.

Results and Drawbacks of Using a Competitive Strategy

The competitive strategy can be successful, in spite of being one-sided. People using this strategy usually come away from a negotiation with the belief that they obtained the best that they could.

Negotiations that rely on a competitive strategy can be costly and time-consuming, especially if each party holds out for all its demands. Much time is spent researching, pressuring, and "psyching out" the other party. Further time is consumed making moves and countermoves, trying to figure out what the other party will do. Competitive strategies are often compared with strategies used in chess, military warfare, and other tactical, competitive battles. The time spent in these activities is very different from alternative uses of that time; for example, in the collaborative model, this same time could be spent on mutual exploration of issues, sharing of information, and an attempt to find mutually acceptable solutions.

Time and goodwill may also be lost if the competitor anticipates that the other party will be competitive and prepares a competitive strategy. If the other party had not intended to be competitive, they may switch strategies when they discover that you have decided to be competitive, thus escalating emotions and increasing conflict. Not only do you lose time, but you may have alienated the other party, hurt the relationship, and toughened them so that they are now willing to give you far less than they might have on the outcome dimension.

A major problem with the competitive strategy is that it is frequently used by inexperienced or untrained negotiators who believe that competition is the only viable strategy. They may be missing opportunities by automatically selecting the competitive strategy. It is important to select a strategy only after thorough investigation of the issues, an understanding of what strategy the other party is likely to pursue, and some clear decisions about the relative importance of the outcomes and the relationship with the other party.

Likewise, it is possible to underestimate the other parties in a competitive situation. Remember that they, too, have adopted the mission to win at all costs. When using a competitive strategy, we tend to underestimate the strength, wisdom, planning, and effectiveness of the other party and assume that even though they are preparing to be competitive too, we can beat them at their game! If you do not pay close attention to their behavioral and verbal clues, you may set yourself up for manipulation by the other party.

Finally, we need to beware of something called the *self-fulfilling prophecy*. A self-fulfilling prophecy is something we believe so strongly that we actually make it come true. It often happens in negotiation when one party expects the other to behave in a particular way, and as a result, actually makes the party behave that way. This tends to come true if the other party is using the competitive strategy because they think you are. Anticipating that the other is going to be competitive, we prepare to be competitive ourselves. The cues we give off in this preparation—our language, tone of voice, gestures, and behaviors—let the other party believe that we intend to be competitive. So they behave competitively, which only assures us that our initial assumptions were right.

The Collaborative Strategy (Win–Win)

A collaborative strategy is one in which both parties consider the relationship and the outcome to be equally important. This strategy is also referred to as cooperative or win–win.[4] In a collaborative strategy, the parties to the negotiation either begin with compatible goals or are willing to search for ways to pursue their goals so that both can gain. This is in sharp contrast to the competitive strategy, in which the parties believe their goals are mutually exclusive, and only one side can win. The relationship between the parties is very likely an ongoing one, with some established history of give-and-take, so that the parties trust each other and know that they can work together. In addition, collaborative strategies are often initiated when the parties know that they want to establish long-term goals for particular outcomes and for the relationship. For example, many local governments are finding that they simply cannot sustain the operating costs of the past, especially in view of the voters' unwillingness to accept higher taxes. Knowing that city budgets have to be cut, departments need to work collaboratively, with *each* department taking a cut, and try to find creative ways to help each other stay in the black or at least minimize the red.

To make this strategy work, *both* parties to the negotiation must be willing to use the collaborative strategy; if only one side employs it, and the other uses a different one, the chances are that both parties cannot achieve both an optimal outcome and preserve or enhance their working relationship. A collaborative strategy is particularly appropriate within an organization, when two parties have common ground, or in situations where two parties have the same customers, same clients, same suppliers, or same service personnel. In any of these cases, the parties have or want to establish a working relationship, and to keep it working smoothly.

For a collaborative strategy to work, there must be a high degree of trust, openness, and cooperation. The parties look for common needs and goals and engage in mutually supportive behavior to obtain them. Both parties realize that they are interdependent and that their cooperative effort can solve the problems and meet the needs of both sides.

In collaboration, communication between parties is open and accurate. This contrasts greatly with the competitive strategy, in which the negotiators have a high level of distrust and guard information carefully to prevent the other side from obtaining the advantage.

The parties in a collaborative endeavor have support from their constituencies. The constituencies trust the parties to find common ground and support them in doing so.

Doing so may mean not achieving absolutely everything the constituency wanted on the substantive issues, and the constituency has to accept this as valid. In contrast, in the competitive strategy, the constituencies usually push the negotiator to get everything he or she can, regardless of the future of the relationship.

Collaborating parties respect deadlines and are willing to renegotiate the time frame if necessary to achieve their goals. Contrast this with the competitive strategy, where time is used as an obstacle or as a power ploy to accomplish one's own ends.

The collaborative strategy is hard work, but the results can be rewarding. It takes extra time and creativity to build trust and to find win–win solutions. But the outcome and relationship results are usually better for both parties.

Keys to Successful Collaboration

The collaborative strategy has traditionally been underutilized, because most people do not understand the fine points of the strategy and because it is less familiar than the competitive strategy. Many negotiations are based on the competitive model, which is the way most people view negotiation—as a competitive situation where one is better off being suspicious of the other, and the fundamental object is to get all the goodies.

Of key importance in a collaborative strategy is commitment. Both parties need to be committed to (1) understanding the *other* party's needs and objectives; (2) providing a free flow of information, both ways; and (3) finding the best solution(s) to meet the needs of both sides.[5]

Understanding the other party's goals and needs is critical to the collaborative strategy. We suggested that this is important in competitive strategy as well, but for very different reasons. In a competitive strategy, you may know or think you know what the other party wants; but your objective in learning this is to facilitate your own strategy development, and also to strategize how to beat the other side by doing better than them or denying them what they want to achieve. In a collaborative strategy, your objective is to understand their goals and needs so that you can work with them to achieve their goals as well as your own. Good collaboration frequently requires not only understanding their stated objectives, but their underlying needs—*why* they want what they want. In the collaborative strategy, both parties must be willing to ask questions and *listen carefully to the answers,* to learn about the other's needs.

Second, to provide a free flow of information, both parties must be willing to *volunteer* information. The information has to be as accurate and as comprehensive as possible. Both sides need to understand the issues, the problems, the priorities, and the goals of the other. They need to fully understand the important context factors in the negotiation. Compare this with the competitive strategy, in which information is closely guarded, or, if shared, often distorted.

Finally, having listened closely to each other, the parties can then work toward *achieving mutual goals* that will satisfy both parties. To do this, the parties will need to minimize their differences and emphasize their similarities. They will need to focus on the issues and work at keeping personalities out of the discussions. Collaborative goals differ from competitive goals. In competition, the goal is obtaining the largest share of the pie, at any cost, without giving away any information or conceding on any issue. In collaboration, each party must be willing to redefine its perspective in light of the collaboration, knowing that the whole can be greater than the sum of the parts. In this light, having a strong knowledge of the problem area is a definite advantage. While a lack of information can be overcome, starting out with the knowledge is definitely an asset.

To achieve success, each party *from the beginning* must send signals to the other that will help build trust between and among those negotiating.

Obstacles to the Collaborative Strategy

Both parties to a negotiation must be willing to collaborate if this strategy is to be successful. It will be difficult, if not impossible, to employ collaborative strategy under the following circumstances:

- One party does not see the situation as having the potential for collaboration.
- One party is motivated only to accomplish its own ends.
- One party has historically been competitive; this behavior may be hard to change.
- One party expects the other to be competitive and prepares for negotiation based on this expectation.
- One party wants to be competitive and rationalizes this behavior.
- One party may be accountable to a constituency that prefers the competitive strategy.
- One party is not willing to take the time to search for collaborative items.
- The negotiation or bargaining mix may include both competitive and collaborative issues. (Sometimes, the two parties can collaborate on collaborative issues and compete on competitive issues. Our experience, however, is that competitive processes tend to drive out collaborative processes, making collaboration harder to achieve.)

Most of the foregoing obstacles reflect a conflict between the parties' preferences for strategy. It may be possible to get the other party to take a different stance if it appears to be desirable in light of the information. Communication is of major importance when you are trying to establish a collaborative relationship.

Compromising Strategy

Ultimately, most negotiating situations are mixed; some bargaining elements are competitive in nature, and others can be approached collaboratively. There are times when the relationship is only somewhat important, and the outcomes are only somewhat important. This is where the fifth strategy comes in.

The compromising strategy may be thought of as an "adequate for most occasions" approach to negotiation. In this strategy, each side will have to modify its priorities for the relationship and for the preferred outcome(s). In both cases, the parties are making a decision that compromising is preferred because, on the one hand, *both* parties gain something (an advantage over accommodation or competition), both parties gain *something* (as opposed to nothing—an advantage over avoiding), and yet compromising does not require all the intentional effort required for collaboration. For example, if a manufacturing facility has a mandate to contain costs, the union and the factory representatives (whose relationship is usually competitive) will want to find an acceptable way to achieve this. The union will want to avoid layoffs. The company may propose a wage freeze. So the two parties may agree on a small wage increase offset by a decrease of the labor pool by attrition rather than layoffs; this is a compromise.

While negotiators usually don't start off planning a compromise (particularly if a competitive or collaborative strategy is possible), compromising is often seen as an acceptable "second choice." There are three major reasons to choose a compromising strategy (particularly as a "default" alternative to other strategies):

1.   A true collaborative strategy does not seem to be possible. One or both parties don't believe that true win–win can be achieved because it is simply too complex or too difficult. Or the relationship may already be too strained for the parties to work together in a manner that fosters and supports good collaboration.

2.   The parties are short of time or other critical resources necessary to get to collaboration. Compromising is usually quick and efficient. While it may be suboptimal on the quality of the outcomes achieved, the trade-off between achieving a great outcome and the time required to do it may force one to pick time over quality.

3.   Both parties gain something (or don't lose anything) on both dimensions. As opposed to pursuing a competitive strategy (and maximizing outcomes at the expense of the relationship) or an accommodating strategy (and sacrificing outcomes for the relationship), compromising assures some gain on *both* the outcome and relationship dimensions.

When to Choose Which Strategy

Now that we have reviewed the five basic strategies, we come to an important part of this chapter: how to decide which strategy you should use for a negotiation. There are two key factors to consider:

1.   How important is the outcome to be gained from this negotiation?

2.   How important is the past, present, and future relationship with the opponent? The following paragraphs describe ways to decide about these two questions and other factors to consider in answering them.

Situation

Look at the *situation* and try to figure out which strategy might be best in those circumstances. Do I care a lot about the outcomes in this situation? If I do, am I willing to sacrifice my relationship with the other person? Or, conversely, is the relationship so important that I am unwilling to endanger it by pursuing the outcome? Alternatively, consider the conditions under which each strategy is most effective (see Figure 3 on page 16). Which of these conditions apply to the present situation?

Remember that each strategy has both advantages and disadvantages. One strategy is more or less appropriate depending on the type of conflict and the situation.

Preferences

Analyze your personal *preferences* for the various strategies. You will probably be more successful using a strategy that feels comfortable. Research has shown that people in conflict have distinct *preferences* for employing certain strategies in conflict situations.[6] These preferences lead individuals to develop distinct *styles* with which they approach many situations. Based on past experience and history, some people have strong biases toward being competitive, collaborative, compromising, accommodating, or avoiding in conflict situations. The stronger your preference for a particular conflict management strategy (style), the more often you will choose it, the more "biased" you become in seeing it as an advantageous strategy, and the more likely you will be to see that strategy (style) as appropriate in a variety of situations. Thus, if you normally respond to conflict (and negotiation) situations in a competitive manner, then you are more likely to see the competitive strategy as widely appropriate—even when it may not be. Similarly, the less likely you are to avoid conflict, the more likely it is that you will not choose the avoiding strategy—even when it may be the most appropriate thing to do. Therefore, understanding your preferences and "biases" is critical, because they will affect your tendency to overselect or underselect strategies in particular situations.

Your preferences for a particular strategy are also influenced by subtle issues such as your *values and principles.* These may be harder, in some ways, to define than your goals, priorities, or limits. But how you evaluate the following will have a great impact on your willingness to use (or not use) certain strategies:

- How much do you value truth, integrity, manners, courtesy?
- Is respect an important issue for you?
- How important is fair play? (And, for that matter, how do you define *fair*?)
- How much of your ego is involved in this—your reputation, your image? How concerned are you about how you will see yourself—or others will see you—if you get what you want, or don't get what you want?

Experience

Next, consider your *experience* using the various strategies. The more experience you have, the better you become at using that strategy—and, probably, the more likely you are to use it. Experience is one of the key factors that works to shape your *preferences.*

Style

Think about your own style as it interacts with the *other party's style,* and consider the possible consequences. What will be the effect of such a combination? For example, two competitive parties might have more conflict in their negotiation than a competitive party negotiating with a party that usually yields. While it would be too complex to explore all the possible interactions between each of your five possible styles and the styles of the other in detail, we have summarized the possible combinations in Table 1. (Some of the cells in the left side are blank because the information is contained in the "matching cell" on the right side.)

TABLE 1 | Likely Interactions between Negotiators of Different Styles

	Avoiding	Accommodating	Competing	Collaborating	Compromising
Avoiding	Both parties avoid pursuing their goals on the issues, and do not take any action to endanger the relationship.	Accommodator shows strong concern for the avoider, particularly the relationship; avoider attempts to minimize interaction.	Competitor will dominate or avoider will escape. Avoider attempts to minimize interaction, while competitor tries to "engage."	Collaborator shows strong concern for both issues and the relationship while avoider tries to escape. Collaborator may give up.	Compromiser shows some concern for both issues and relationship; avoider tries to escape. Compromiser may give up or avoider may engage.
Accommodating		Both parties avoid pursuing their goals on the issues, give in to the others goals, and try to smooth over relationship concerns.	Competitor pursues own goals on the issues, while the accommodator tries to make the competitor happy. Competitor usually wins big.	Collaborator shows strong concern for both issues and relationship; accommodator tries to make the collaborator happy. Relationship should be very strong, but the collaborator may achieve better outcomes.	Compromiser shows some concern for both issues and relationship; accommodator tries to make the compromiser happy. Relationship will improve, compromiser may entice the accommodator to pursue some issue focus.
Competing			Both parties pursue their goals on the issues and ignore any concern for the relationship; create conflict, mistrust, hostility.	Collaborator shows strong concern for both issues and relationship, while competitor only pursues issues. Competitor usually "wins" and both parties become competitive.	Compromiser shows some concern for both issues and relationship, while competitor only pursues issues. Competitor usually "wins" and both parties become competitive.
Collaborating				Both parties pursue their goals on the issues, show strong concern for the others' goals *and* sustaining trust, openness, and a good relationship.	Compromiser shows some concern. Collaborator shows strong concern for both issues and the relationship. Minimally, good compromise or better.
Compromising					Both parties pursue their goals on the issues in a limited way and attempt to "do no harm" to the relationship.

27

Perceptions and Past Experience

Consider your *perceptions and past experience* with the other party. How you feel about the other party, and what you want to have happen in that relationship in the future, will drive your strategy. How well do you like each other? How much do you communicate? How much do you need to work with the other party in the future because you are dependent on what they can do for you? How much do you trust them? Your level of trust with the other party will be based on your past experience with them, and on the history and results of other negotiations they have conducted with you or with other parties in the past.

Other Factors

Finally, there are other factors that may affect the selection of strategy but that might be less in your control. Nevertheless they should be part of the planning process. These reflect the following situational or context issues:

- Is this negotiation voluntary or imposed? Are both parties going into it willingly, or has it been assigned by a manager or some other constituency whose voice and support are influential?

- Is the situation highly structured? Are there rules, laws, and management mandates that will direct the negotiation?

- Is the agenda already established? (Can it be changed if necessary?)

- Finally, realize that the setting plays an important part in the proceedings and in the results. Consider not only the physical environment but elements of the psychological setting, including the players, both individuals and groups; their cultures and behavior; and established norms, standards, and processes.

Can You Make a "No Strategy" Choice?

Some people whom we have taught in negotiation have argued that it is possible to adopt *no strategy:* You refuse to make an explicit strategic choice, and "let the chips fall" to determine what you will do next. This allows you "maximum flexibility" to adjust your approach based on what your opponent does first, or as the proceedings change.

This approach has some distinct advantages. You get a chance to find out how your opponent wants to negotiate first, which may tell you a lot about your opponent. It also keeps you from making a commitment to a strategy that may not work or get completed—for example, to be accommodative while the other is being competitive? However, a "no strategy" choice is often the lazy negotiator's way of avoiding a key part of the planning and preparation process. We do not think this is a good choice! While a "no strategy" choice may give you some negotiating leeway, it could also put you in a precarious position if you have not planned well. The result will be that the opposition gains an advantage over you before you realize what is going on!

If you know that you care about the relationship, or the outcome, or both (or neither), select a strategy and begin to plan around it. If you are proactive about strategy choice, you are much more likely to get what you want than if you wait for the other to initiate action. As we have pointed out, you can always adapt your strategy later as necessary.

Moving Forward

As with planning a trip, it is wise to know *where* you want to go and *how* to get there. It is important to have a well-developed plan that includes specific moves and counter-moves. Your game plan can be modified as needed. Modifications will be based on what the other party says and does. Plans start with a strategy.

Endnotes

1. G. T. Savage, J. D. Blair, and R. L. Sorenson, "Consider Both Relationships and Substance When Negotiating Strategically," *Academy of Management Executives 3,* no. 1 (1989), pp. 37–48.

2. G. C. Homans, *Social Behavior: Its Elementary Forms* (New York: Harcourt, Brace & World, 1961).

3. R. Fisher and W. Ury, *Getting to Yes* (Boston: Houghton Mifflin, 1981); R. Fisher, W. Ury, and B. Patton, *Getting to Yes: Negotiating Agreement without Giving In,* 2nd ed. (New York: Penguin Books, 1991).

4. R. E. Walton and R. B. McKersie, *A Behavioral Theory of Labor Negotiations: An Analysis of a Social Interaction System* (New York: McGraw-Hill, 1965); A. C. Filley, *Interpersonal Conflict Resolution* (Glenview, IL; Scott, Foresman, 1975); R. Fisher, W. Ury, and B. Patton, *Getting to Yes: Negotiating Agreement without Giving In,* 2nd ed. (New York: Penguin Books, 1991); D. G. Pruitt, *Negotiation Behavior* (New York: Academic Press, 1981); D. G. Pruitt, "Strategic Choice in Negotiation," *American Behavioral Scientist 27* (1983), pp. 167–94; P. J. D. Carnevale and D. G. Pruitt, "Negotiation and Mediation," in *Annual Review of Psychology,* M. Rosenberg and I. Porter (eds.), Vol. 43 (Palo Alto, CA: Annual Reviews, Inc., 1992), pp. 531–82; D. G. Pruitt and P. J. D. Carnevale, *Negotiation in Social Conflict* (Pacific Grove, CA: Brooks-Cole, 1993).

5. Fisher and Ury, *Getting to Yes.*

6. K. Thomas and R. Killman, *The Conflict Mode Inventory* (Tuxedo Park, NY: XICOM, 1974).

Making Strategic Moves

Deborah M. Kolb
Judith Williams

Effective advocacy hinges on getting into a good position in the shadow negotiation and staying there. Usually that objective involves some deliberate maneuvering on your part. You want the other person to be receptive to your demands—or at least grant them a hearing. But just because you are primed to negotiate is no guarantee that your counterpart is anxious to meet you halfway.

Ready to sit down with a boss, a colleague, or a client, you may find that you have a reluctant bargainer on your hands. She stalls or ignores you, refusing to meet. Phone calls go unanswered. That important talk keeps being postponed. Even if you succeed in arranging a meeting, the negotiation never gets off the ground. He pays lip service to your ideas and immediately skips to his own agenda or changes the subject. Somehow you never manage to get a two-way conversation going. He has made up his mind before you open your mouth. She thinks that if she holds out long enough, you may relax your demands or stop bothering her.

It's perfectly normal to encounter resistance in negotiation. A good part of every bargainer's job is to persuade others to take his or her proposals seriously. It may seem obvious, but your first task is to get the other person to the table. Equally important, you must then convince him or her to engage in a process of give-and-take. Not all the giving or the taking can come from one side. Strategic moves are the means you use to coax reluctant bargainers to the table and ensure that the give-and-take goes both ways.

A willingness to negotiate is at some basic level a confession of mutual need. People negotiate when you have something they want and they cannot count on your falling in with their plans without getting something in return. These perceptions of mutual need play out in the shadow negotiation. When you seem to need the other person more than he or she needs you, the balance in the shadow negotiation can tilt dramatically against you. Differences in power or position, for example, can stymie fruitful exchange. Subordinates generally pay acute attention to a superior's demands, but they can encounter real difficulty in persuading a boss to listen to their demands. Managers who are in the minority due to their race or gender can find themselves excluded from important networks. They may have neither the personal clout and experience nor the organizational standing to convince others that talks should be started.

Even when bargainers are in a position to press their demands, they can find them being discounted. This happens for a lot of reasons. Some people acquire a reputation for going along so that others don't really expect them to voice strong objections. Their style of communicating may get in the way as they cloak their arguments in diffidence. Accustomed to working within a rigid chain of command, they may have hesitated to speak up in the past. Most bosses will keep piling on the work so long as an employee

Source: From Deborah M. Kolb and Judith Williams, *Everyday Negotiation* (San Francisco: Jossey-Bass, 2003).

silently goes about completing the assignments on time without recognition or reward. Clients and colleagues, suspecting that someone is not likely to buck the system, will be tempted to press for concessions.[1] Bargainers can be left out of the informal discussions where the issues are really decided. By the time they offer their opinions, what they have to say is irrelevant. It's not just that they are not heard. Their ideas no longer count. Little by little, without conscious recognition on the bargainer's part, his or her bargaining power may have slipped away.

More than persuasive coaxing is needed when you bump up against attitudes like these in the shadow negotiation. You must bring the people you negotiate with to the point where they realize that they have to deal with you seriously and fairly. Just as there are steps you can take so that you come to the table with confidence, there are strategic moves you can make to convince other people to heed your demands. These moves convey exactly why they need to meet you halfway. Any reluctance they might have to negotiate with you fades once they are forced to admit that they will be better off if they deal with you *and* worse off if they don't.

Getting into a Good Position

Strategic moves employ both the carrot and the stick to improve your negotiating position. Using incentives, the carrots, you make other people aware of the *benefits* of dealing with you. You point out the value they get in return, how negotiating with you works to their advantage. So long as the loan officer at the bank senses that you don't fit the profile of a good customer, and many single proprietorships in service industries do not, he or she is going to think twice about setting up a credit line for your new business. It is always safer to say no, after all. Denied loans don't appear on the bank's monthly watch list of troubled accounts. For the application to warrant more than a perfunctory review, the loan officer must be convinced that there are clear advantages (and precious little risk) in approving the loan.

Sticks operate in reverse. By exerting pressure on the other party, you underscore the *costs* to her if she continues to ignore you or to him if he persists in giving you a hard time. If they see few reasons to discuss your needs, you supply them by raising the stakes. Increased pressure may be in order when the prospect of negotiation holds some real disadvantages for the other party. He or she may be quite content to let things drift along as they are. A boss accountable to management for the department's cost cutting may be reluctant to give you a raise until you tell him you have another job offer. Business as usual is more comfortable than introducing an alien voice (yours) into the decision-making apparatus already in place—until, that is, the others realize you have a much-needed piece of information. A coworker who has been successful in persuading you to produce those late-night projections has a vested interest in not revisiting the issue, but may become far more amenable after you leave promptly several nights in a row.

Establishing your voice *as a negotiator* in the negotiation is no small task. Your credibility will be questioned and your resolve tested. In situations where you are not the only one involved in making the decision, the other party must understand that you have the authority to commit your organization. A supplier will always defer to the person in the firm he thinks has the final say and controls the checkbook. It doesn't matter that the account is your responsibility and you are the one making the sales calls. Your opinions won't carry any weight so long as he doubts your authority to make decisions or put his requisition through.

At times it can be awkward to use carrots and sticks on your own or they may not be enough to compel someone to negotiate with you. Strategic allies can pave your way by putting their credibility behind you. It also pays to plan ahead when you know an important negotiation is coming up. You can then move to influence its outcome by shaping the process. By anticipating resistance and lobbying behind the scenes, you can position your ideas and issues so that they are heard positively once the negotiation actually gets under way. Here's a quick summary of strategic moves you can use:

- *Hold out incentives:* In any negotiation, the other party controls something you need—more money, more time, more cooperation, better communication, an opportunity. That's why you want to negotiate in the first place. But your needs alone won't get anyone to the table. Your counterparts must recognize that you have something of value to them. Incentives make that value visible.

- *Step up the pressure:* The incentives you hold out may not convince someone to negotiate with you. He or she may be perfectly content to let things continue the way they are—in which case you have to raise the costs of not dealing with you. You can increase the stakes by letting him know you have other alternatives and don't have to go along with his plans. You can bring people to the table by convincing them that taking no action on your demands is not an option. Things are going to change even if they continue to stall.

- *Establish your authority:* Unless the other party recognizes your authority, she will resist dealing with you. To have any control over the negotiating process, you must establish your credibility and, when others are involved in the decision-making process, your right to speak for them.

- *Enlist support:* In many circumstances, what you can accomplish on your own is limited. You can reinforce your efforts to influence the other party by enlisting allies. Strategically placed allies can ensure you get a favorable hearing. They can also bring pressure to bear on your behalf.

- *Exert control over the process:* You can move to structure the negotiation process by planting seeds for your ideas and gathering support for your agenda. Besides increasing your chances of encountering a positively disposed bargainer, behind-the-scenes efforts can prevent opposition from gaining momentum and make it less likely that your proposals will be rejected prematurely.

Laid down in black and white, these strategic moves seem very formal and premeditated, manipulative even. It is easy to slip into the mistake of thinking you can hold them in reserve, just for those big negotiations. You are not, after all, planning a major merger. You merely want to lower the decibel level at the weekly staff meeting. Just once it would be nice if you could make the arrangements with your client without discovering later that he has double-checked them with your boss. With all the cutbacks at work, you don't mind picking up some of the overload. But you would like to participate in the discussions over who is going to do what. None of these situations seems to call out for a strategic campaign. But unless you change the way the other party looks at them and at you, nothing about the situation will change for you in the shadow negotiation.

Strategic moves help you shape the game. They provide the means to increase your influence over a negotiation's course. They help you bring the other party to the table and even the odds once the real bargaining starts.

Fiona's Campaign

Fiona Sweeney faced a negotiation that turned out to be a pivotal point in her career. She had joined an international computer company when she graduated from college. Over the next 11 years, she steadily moved up the ranks. Calm, pragmatic, and thoughtful, she attributed her success to diligence. Her coworkers in the Albany plant singled out her intuitive feel for organizations. Her businessman father thought it was his doing.

Suddenly Fiona was promoted to controller of operations and transferred to Palo Alto. Never "one of the boys" in a predominantly male environment and a newcomer to the division, Fiona found California a jolting experience. Accustomed to thrashing out ideas with long-time colleagues, she felt isolated. And then her new boss gave her what seemed to be an impossible task. He charged her with negotiating a change in the company's decision-making processes. Despite a professed goal of customer satisfaction, the company was a series of fiefdoms, with little coordination even on major accounts. Even though the system almost guaranteed a constant level of customer dissatisfaction, the sales managers had no inclination to change. Instead, to protect commissions and their valued customers, they exerted pressure on production and quality control.

Fiona, new on the scene and ripe for testing, needed all the strategic moves at her disposal to carry out her assignment. First and foremost, she had to convince the various departments to take her seriously. Only then could she begin to negotiate the significant changes demanded by any real shift in an organization's decision making. Once we explore the individual moves that contribute to an effective advocacy, we will return to Fiona's story to show how she integrated them into a strategic campaign.

Hold Out Incentives

Incentives entice people to deal with you. These strategic moves can take many forms, but they have one purpose. They convince other parties that negotiating with you is in their best interest. You cannot just tell them that you have something valuable to offer; you have to *show* them. This demonstration requires coming up with the right incentives, and those, in turn, depend on the specific circumstances.

You can have the best product or service in the world, a long list of talents you have scrupulously inventoried, but you won't get far in a negotiation if the other person is not in the market for what you are selling. Value must be perceived as valuable before you can turn it into an advantage. Your customer says she can get comparable services from other vendors, and she won't pay a premium for yours. If you want that premium, you have to make clear what you provide that other suppliers don't. The product launch comes off ahead of schedule. If no one knows that you made that happen, your contribution goes unnoticed. To be rewarded for it, you have to make it visible in the shadow negotiation. Even when your value is apparent to the other person, he or she may be tempted to discount it simply to maintain the upper hand in your relationship. When you let that happen, you shortchange your contribution and severely penalize yourself.

Make Sure You Have Something the Other Person Needs.   Just because you are motivated and see clear benefits in what you offer, that doesn't mean you can be sure the other party will jump to the same conclusion. No matter how versatile the talents or services are that you bring, if the other party doesn't need them, then he won't have an incentive to deal with you. Your incentives must have some resonance with his needs. If you want his attention, you have to create that need.

At 40, Molly was a month away from finishing her MBA. Although she had begun her job search early, her prospects were not bright. Her age worked against her, but so did her résumé. Her entire work experience consisted of teaching English as a foreign language when her husband was stationed in Germany. "I was a blank page," she comments, "with a young daughter." Molly did, however, have considerable motivation: a need for financial security.

> I never expected to work full time. But then my husband died suddenly. I went to business school to make sure that I could afford to send my daughter to college.

Molly also had a game plan. She wanted to carve out a niche for herself in mergers and acquisitions. But after several chilly interviews it was apparent that no one was going to sign her up on a promise to work hard.

Molly decided she needed something concrete to bring to the negotiations. She went back to the drawing boards and developed a matrix of Internet software firms. She analyzed what niche each company filled in the emerging market. She then looked for synergies with established companies. With this work in hand, she wangled her way into three investment banking firms. None was interested in hiring her, but one found her project promising enough to give her a trial as a researcher—without pay or any staff support.

After getting her foot in the door, Molly faced the daunting task of creating a perception of value for what she was giving away and translating her trial period into a job. Only when her research began to yield real results did she approach the managing partner.

> Joel didn't even realize how tentative our arrangement was. I told him I could not continue to work for free and had begun a job search. He had no idea they weren't paying me.

Her focus on a hot new market gave Molly leverage, an incentive for the managing partner to deal with her. Her research was just starting to produce results and he couldn't afford an interruption. Keeping her on was easier than training someone new. Once he came to this conclusion, Molly could negotiate terms. She had established her value.

Creating value is a key move in negotiation. Once you figure out what the other party actually needs, you can tailor your incentives so that they respond to those needs. You suddenly appear more useful than he or she realized. You don't always have to create this value out of whole cloth the way Molly did. But you do have to demonstrate it. You cannot leave it up to the other party to puzzle through how and where your talents or product might be useful. You have to make that connection yourself. The trick comes, as Molly discovered, in knowing what the organization values (or will value in the future) and then making it easy for the other person to see that you can do that valued work or provide the needed service. He or she then has a reason to negotiate with you.

Make Your Value Visible.   After assessing your situation, you may conclude, quite rightly, that you have a lot of value to offer. But somehow that value does not seem to be gaining you much ground in the negotiation. Generally it is not working to your advantage because it is invisible. Value can be discounted on both sides of the table. Not only do you have to be aware of your value. You must make sure that it is firmly implanted in the other person's mind.

The value of the work you do disappears unless you claim it. The conference goes off without a hitch. If no one knows about the long hours you put in to make that happen, your contribution goes unnoticed. Unnoticed, it goes unrewarded. If you want to change that situation, you need to make your value visible.

Frequently the people we negotiate with must be reminded of our contributions. Rather than continue to be taken for granted, you can deliberately jostle their awareness. It does not take much to remind someone of what you do. You can interrupt your services for a bit. Toni was a partner in a growing architectural practice. Gradually, she had taken over the responsibility for making sure the office ran smoothly, clients paid promptly, and bills went out on time. She assumed these duties largely by default. Her partner had no interest in anything other than design. Before long he gave no credit to the effort and time Toni spent keeping the office on an even keel. Then Toni was invited by an old friend to give a talk in London.

About to prepare "instruction" sheets for her partner, Toni held off. She thought he might at least be curious about the procedures she had put in place. He wasn't. At the last minute, she asked if he wanted to go over them, but he just smiled. "No problem," he assured her. "I'll take care of everything." After a few days, in the course of which he had to make an emergency run to the bank to transfer funds, he had a good picture of what went on behind the scenes in his own office. The work Toni had been doing was no longer invisible. The experience left him with a new appreciation of the burden Toni had been carrying. He was now prepared to talk about sharing responsibilities so that they were both freer to get on with what they really enjoyed—designing.

For your value to influence a negotiation, you must take steps, however subtle, to ensure that it is right there on the table for both of you to see. We cannot stress this point enough. When your work disappears, so do your influence and your bargaining power.

Make Certain the Other Party Pays for Your Value.   The person you are negotiating with may, in fact, have a good idea of your value. He or she may even appreciate the work you do. The sticky problem comes not in making your value visible but in making sure you get credit for it. The negotiation turns into a tug-of-war in which you are pushed to retreat on your demands. You want a promotion; she pushes you to settle for praise and a pat on the back. You need incentives at hand to convince the other person that being valued means having your value rewarded.

Chris, a television executive, knew exactly what she contributed at the station. But she still faced two major obstacles when she decided to ask for a raise. She worked in an industry notorious for underpaying and overworking backroom people, and she reported to a boss, a lawyer by training, who prided himself on his reputation as an aggressive negotiator. "Al likes everyone to think he eats nails for breakfast. He would not hesitate to cram a take-or-leave-it proposition down my throat."

To get the raise she wanted (and deserved), Chris had to force Al to admit that she played a critical part in the station's operations and that she should be paid accordingly.

Chris drew on her flair for the dramatic and a rather puckish sense of humor to orchestrate the interview. She thought out each detail with a feeling for the dynamics in the shadow negotiation.

> Al loved the exercise of power. He always conducted salary negotiations from behind a huge desk. The supplicants sat opposite him on a couch that sank to the ground, making them feel inconsequential. I brought one of the high stools we use in the studio with me to the meeting. From that perch, I wasn't swallowed up in a bottomless couch. I looked down on Al.

The negotiation began amicably. Al agreed to all but one of her requests. He gave her another week of vacation, a company car, and a first-class seat when she had to fly to the network's West Coast offices. But he would not budge on her demand for more money.

As they went back and forth, Chris's value to the station became abundantly clear.

> I timed the meeting to occur during the busiest part of the day in the newsroom—at deadline when my presence was crucial. I purposely let producers interrupt us. They broke into the meeting several times to tell me about stories, tape editing, and satellite shots.

Despite these timely interruptions, Al remained adamant: No raise. Chris got off her stool and looked at Al.

> After a long silence, I said I hoped there would be no hard feelings. I thought he valued my work. Then I told him I had to get the newscast on the air and walked out of the office.

When Chris left Al's office, she was not bluffing. She knew her value, Al knew her value. If he wanted to keep her, he was going to have to pay her a fair wage. Al sent his secretary after Chris. When she walked back into his office, he was sitting on the couch. "Let's talk money," he said.

Each of us brings different skills and expertise to bear in a negotiation. But, like Al, other people may discount what we offer in a negotiation, generally for a simple reason. They are going to have to pay for it—by giving us more money, or time, or cooperation. You can help them over this hurdle, but you have to do it in a way they understand and appreciate. Chris's high stool and the interruptions she prompted were symbolic actions that Al immediately read. Toni's trip to London jolted her partner, and they were able to come up with more equitable ways to share the office burdens. And Molly's project provided the managing partner with tangible evidence of the future contributions she could make to a firm engaged in mergers and acquisitions. The incentives you hold out, to be effective and increase your influence in a negotiation, must be recognizable and worth something to the other person.

Step Up the Pressure

Negotiation inevitably involves change. You open talks because you want something to be different. That something might be a salary, or a job, or a relationship. The right incentives can prompt your counterparts. The obvious advantages to them may make them amenable to negotiating that change with you. But holding out a carrot is not always enough. Caught in inertia and a dislike of change in any form, they may not mind passing up some possible advantage. Things are just fine the way they are. Why risk unsettling the situation? Abba Eban, Israel's former foreign minister, once observed that diplomats have "a passionate love affair with the status quo" that stills any forward movement.[2] That love affair carries over into ordinary negotiations. Often to get them off the ground, you have to unfreeze the situation by making the status quo less attractive.[3] The pressures you exert raise the cost of business as usual. As the other party weighs her choices, she begins to see that things cannot remain the same. She will be worse off if she doesn't deal with you.

These pressure levers run the gamut from outright threats to gentle prods and must be used carefully. Blurting out a threat to go over your boss's head is likely to escalate the tensions and might get you fired. Sometimes you can get your point across simply by letting the other person know that you *can* increase the costs to him or her. You don't necessarily have to act on that warning. Once he suspects that the current arrangements are going to change whatever he does, he is likely to be more willing to negotiate. That way he ensures that he has a voice in any decision. Alternatives can also be used as a pressure lever. If the other party seems reluctant to meet your demands, you make sure he knows you have other options that do.

Issue a Credible Threat. Threats are the most obvious means of forcing the other person to admit that maintaining the status quo is not an option. A threat commits you to a course of action if the other person does not respond in a particular way. Threats can be a powerful tool, but to apply real pressure, the threat has to be real. You must be prepared to follow through on it. If your bluff is called and you don't, you are the one who will be worse off, not the other party. The negotiation tips in your counterpart's favor if you issue an ultimatum on the minimum salary you will accept and then quickly revise that figure downward at the first sign of resistance.

Abby was more than ready to act on a threat. She and her reporter fiancé had planned an idyllic getaway in the Bahamas before he left on assignment for the Middle East. Abby wanted the long weekend to be perfect and did not even shop around for a bargain. The couple paid top dollar for a suite steps away from the ocean. Both had pulled long hours in exchange for the time away and they arrived, exhausted, at the resort. Instead of being shown to their room, they were told the hotel was overbooked. They soon found themselves shuttled off to a dismal lodging house miles from the ocean. They stayed the night and flew back home the next morning.

An irate Abby promptly called her travel agent to complain. She wanted a full refund for the hotel and airfare. The travel agent just as promptly denied any responsibility. He had no control over the resort's booking policies. Nonsense, Abby responded. There was no way he could compensate her for the lost weekend, but he could make her whole financially. If he didn't, she was going to make sure other clients were spared a similar experience. Either she heard from him by 5:00 or she would file a complaint with the consumer protection agency and post a reprise of her weekend on the Internet. For good measure she also mentioned that her fiancé was a reporter and friendly with the newspaper's travel editor.

The travel agent couldn't have cared less about a complaint at the consumer protection agency. It would take years for the agency to get to it. But much of his business came from referrals. Any bad press would be a disaster. He didn't need until 5:00 to settle with Abby. He agreed right then to credit her MasterCard account in full. Had Abby's travel agent suspected she was bluffing, he might have tried to stonewall her, but he could not take the risk. His bookings might suffer.

Abby had nothing to lose by threatening the travel agent. That is not always the case. In most business situations you need to give yourself and the other person room to maneuver. You might couple a threat with a conciliatory move that makes it clear you would prefer not to go down that path. Rather than issue an ultimatum from which you cannot back off, you can talk about what you will be forced to do if your counterpart does not move on your demands. Say, for example, a coworker resents being assigned to your team and is being less than cooperative. You can threaten to go to the vice president, but cushion the warning with an assurance that you would prefer for the two of you to settle the problem.

Force a Choice on the Other Party.   Threats can be masked and issued subtly, but the risk of retaliation remains. Letting the other person know you have other alternatives carries less risk and can be just as effective in persuading her to negotiate with you. Once she realizes you are not captive to her plans or her schedule, she is forced to move on your demands. Karen leveraged her alternatives in order to push a boss who was stalling on her raise.

Karen had been promoted from administrative assistant to department manager, but without an increase in pay. Her old position was never filled, so she wound up doing two jobs. Karen didn't mind the long hours, but she resented the flat salary. Her boss, a nice guy, procrastinated on any decisions that might cause dissension. "He never makes waves. He's not a coward," she says, "but he avoids conflict." When she complained about her salary, he was sympathetic and agreed she deserved a raise. "I'll see what I can do." Every few weeks, he would reassure Karen. "Don't worry. I'm working on it." But nothing changed. Patience was not one of Karen's virtues. Already in a slow burn over the delays, she heard about a similar job in another agency.

After several interviews, she decided the other agency was not a place she wanted to work. The offer did, however, provide her with the leverage to unfreeze the talks with her boss. She told him an opportunity had come up that paid 30 percent more than her current salary. She preferred to stay, but only if he could match that figure. Given her boss's obvious tendency to procrastinate, she set a deadline. He had to let her know by the end of the week so she could give the other agency an answer.

Karen used her alternative to raise the cost to her boss of doing nothing. He could no longer delay and maintain the status quo. It was the prod (and the justification) he needed to argue forcefully on her behalf with his boss and with human resources.

Often the people you are negotiating with do not have complete authority to make the decision. They must squeeze the resources you want out of a superior. Rather than become embroiled in a contest with a higher-up, they take the path of least resistance. It is easier to stall and see how things play out. To speed the process along, you have to provide them with the ammunition they require to get what you want from their boss.

Make the Consequences Tangible to the Other Person.   Big sticks like the one Karen wielded are often not at hand and might not work if they were. An indirect approach can exert subtle, less overt pressure and be as effective in the long run. Caroline had always been willing to pick up the extra work that needed doing around the office. Resources were tight, and everyone was stretched. Usually Caroline accepted the extra assignments gracefully, but she had reached her limit. She couldn't take on any more work without producing a shoddy product. When her boss approached her with yet another project, she was ready. She was not going to let herself be positioned as a slacker in the shadow negotiation. On her white board she had listed all her projects and their due dates. She was happy to take on this new work, but she wondered which projects he wanted her to drop or delay. The move immediately shifted the focus in the shadow negotiation from her dedication to her unreasonable schedule. She forced her boss to make a decision. Rather than give the assignment to someone else or delay Caroline's other work, he hired an assistant for her.

Peter, recently hired as director of engineering at a telecommunications firm, saw early on that delays in getting systems up and running were causing problems. He tracked the source of the difficulties to Alex, the chief engineer. Only by making the business consequences of Alex's performance clear to corporate could he convince them to take his concerns seriously.

Peter's boss had known Alex a long time; he had watched his progress from technician to chief engineer. Downplaying Peter's worries, he encouraged Peter to coach Alex. Peter tried, but despite his efforts, he could see no improvement. Worse, Alex failed to inform Peter when problems came up, and these were beginning to reflect badly on Peter. To get his boss to take his concerns seriously and negotiate the problem the chief engineer posed, Peter gave a presentation on the financial ramifications of the delays and poor quality. If things continued as they were, the division would experience significant losses. Once Peter's boss saw the consequences in black and white, he was willing to negotiate. They transferred Alex to R&D, returning him to the bench work where he excelled. When incentives do not get the other party's attention, you need to make these kinds of strategic moves to increase the pressure. Otherwise the other party will predictably remain satisfied with things as they are. By making the current situation less comfortable, you shake up the other person's complacency. When the other person realizes the costs attached to doing nothing, he or she will be far more receptive to negotiating with you.

Establish Your Authority When You Are Negotiating for Others

When you are negotiating for yourself with another person, you can direct your strategic moves to him or her. Once you establish your credibility, you are all set. But if others are involved in the decision-making process and you are speaking for them, there is another level of complexity to consider. Not only do you have to be credible in your own right, you must also convince the other side that you have the backing of the group you represent. Whatever incentives you hold out or pressures you bring to bear, it is impossible to get a negotiation off the ground if the other side questions that support. Generally, they consider negotiating with you a waste of time and prefer to deal with the real decision makers.

Whenever you speak for a larger group or represent your organization in a negotiation, the other side needs to understand just how much latitude you have to make a decision or commit your organization. No lawyer in his right mind will allow you to make changes to a joint venture agreement unless he is convinced you can act for your partners. He wants some proof. Your customer must know whether your boss fully approves of the precedent-breaking agreement you have offered. Unless he has that assurance, he won't care about the terms you offer, however attractive. He is going to entertain quite reasonable fears that the final agreement will be far less favorable once those with real authority get involved.

Secure Explicit Authorization.   Certain elements almost guarantee that your authority will be questioned. If the other parties involved have never negotiated with you before, they naturally want reassurance about your ability to commit. Big differences in status, age, or background can generate unease and sometimes outright suspicion. For example, Dora, treasurer of a utility in the Northeast, looked at an upcoming negotiation and knew she would have to establish her authority before any meeting took place. Dora's assignment was difficult enough. She was to extricate the utility from a partnership with a Kentucky coal company that had not worked out.

> I was going to be negotiating our withdrawal with a bank chairman and the president of the coal company. They were angry about how the partnership turned out to begin with. When my CEO told them I was going to handle the negotiations, they took it as an insult, another example of their shabby treatment. They felt quite justified in being offended. I was young enough to be their daughter. They were from the South, I was a Northerner. They were heads of their organizations; I was a couple reports short of being boss.

To establish her authority to negotiate the financial disentanglement, Dora drafted a letter for her CEO's signature. The letter was conciliatory, but succinct. Dora had been chosen to conduct the negotiations because she was the person in the organization who knew most about the partnership. She enjoyed the full confidence of the board and had complete authority to act on its behalf. As Dora suspected, the president of the coal-mining operation attempted to bypass her and called her boss directly. The CEO simply referred back to "his" letter.

By establishing her authority ahead of time, Dora got the negotiations off on the right foot. The others involved in the negotiation recognized that they had no choice but to deal with her. At times you will not have the clear and complete backing that Dora enjoyed, in which case you need to establish the authority you do have. Clarity here serves two purposes. You won't be tempted to overstep your bounds and promise more than you can deliver. And the other party has a better sense of what he can legitimately expect to negotiate with you.

Maintain the Backing of Your Side.   The ability to negotiate effectively often depends on perceptions, and when you are negotiating on behalf of others, the impressions that influence the shadow negotiation multiply. You must address your opponent across the table *and* maintain the continued confidence of your own constituency.[4] Real authority is not necessarily conferred by a title or a corner office. It comes from the continued support given your efforts and your approach. Without express backing from your side, the other parties involved invariably doubt your control and your ability to commit. Are you really leading the negotiation? Can they trust what you say?

Debra and her boss decided they could no longer postpone office renovations. They badly needed their space rewired in order to upgrade their systems. Since Debra had just finished a major project, the timing was perfect. She had the time to handle all the supervision of the changeover. But the engineering contractor was uncomfortable taking orders that involved intricate systems decisions from a woman. He kept calling Debra's boss on the pretext of sounding out his ideas. What he really wanted was authorization. Debra's boss thought nothing of talking to the contractor. He enjoyed discussing the new fiber technologies. It never occurred to him that he might be undermining Debra—until she protested. So long as her boss took the contractor's calls, the contractor would cut her out of the loop and refuse to deal directly with her. Once Debra worked through this hidden consequence with her boss, he stopped taking the calls. Their united front also conveyed their commitment to the terms of the original contract. That front came in handy when problems developed with the project and the contractor wanted to make change orders.

Consider Authorization An Ongoing Activity.   Even when you can count on your side's full support, your authority will be tested in negotiation. If those involved in the direct negotiations sense that you enjoy less than enthusiastic backing from the people who count in your organization, they will pick up on these doubts and use them. The testing intensifies, and your own constituents, watching this performance play out, become uneasy. They begin to wonder whether you are the right person to manage the negotiations for them. Soon you are in danger of losing credibility on all sides. To break this cycle, you have to confront challenges to your authority as they happen.

Fran, director of human resources in a research center, moved to stop the erosion of her authority on both fronts in the aftermath of a merger. Soft-spoken, with a self-deprecating sense of humor, Fran radiated approachability—one of the reasons she was so good at her job. She was a great believer in consensus building, and she went into the talks determined that they not be adversarial. She saw them as an opportunity to build strong working relations.

> Confrontation goes against my grain. With good will on both sides, I thought we could find a way to work together on the challenges we faced in meshing two very different cultures.

Across the board, existing benefits at Fran's center outstripped those offered by their new partner. As head of human resources Fran was charged with working out the discrepancies. At the start, she had to set at rest suspicions within the center that she was not "tough enough" to stand up to the other side's team of negotiators. "Some of our people were openly nervous," she says. "Envisioning Bambi coming up against Rambo, they were afraid I would cave when the stakes got high or the pressure mounted and give away their benefits."

These doubts spread through the center's grapevine. Inevitably, they reached the other company's negotiators. Sensing little widespread support for Fran's collaborative approach, they began to distrust anything she said as nothing more than lip service, lacking any real force. Their lead negotiator was already gleeful about facing her. Now he became openly scornful of Fran, writing off her collaborative overtures as so much "Zen mumbo-jumbo."

Fran's ability to negotiate—collaboratively or otherwise—depended on her colleagues' confidence in her and her strategy. To gain their active support, she set up an advisory group with representatives from all departments, including human resources. The meetings of this group furnished Fran with ample opportunities to calm worries. When talks stalled, she explained why she refused to make a concession or what steps she was taking to restart discussions.

Fran next consolidated her authority to speak for the center. "I was getting challenges from the legal counsel and from my own boss," she says. "I couldn't work that way, constantly guarding my back." She went to the centers managing director and asked him point-blank, Who has the last word? He said she did. This request for explicit authorization became key. The director was on record as supporting Fran, and she was beholden to him to deliver.

As Fran discovered, an "official" assignment does not automatically convey the backing necessary to carry it out. Without obvious backing from her side, Fran would have lacked the legitimacy needed to negotiate the benefits schedule for the merged companies. To get that authorization, she moved to dispel worries within her company that she might be too soft for the job. At the same time, she put in place monitoring mechanisms that prevented doubts from resurfacing later during the negotiations.

Sometimes your credibility will be challenged when you negotiate, as Fran's was. Because this questioning is seldom set permanently to rest, it is essential to think about your authority in terms of the strategic moves that you can make—not just to establish credibility but to keep it. Explicit and ongoing authorization from someone with real power gives you visible support that means something to your own team. It also drives home a necessary point to the other party. Attempts to circumvent you and go over your head will achieve nothing. The other side must deal with you. You are in charge of the negotiations.

Enlist Support

At times, the strategic moves you make on your own fall short. The other side does not see sufficient benefits in what you offer, and the costs you have raised are not high enough to force a change of mind. No matter what you do you cannot seem to attract his attention or get her to take your demands seriously. If you don't think you have the resources to move the negotiation forward on your own, you can call up reinforcements and enlist the support of others. Just by sheer numbers, strategic allies can add credibility to your cause. Their confidence in you is what convinces the other party to negotiate with you. When an ally's opinion counts with that person, the extra influence often tips the shadow negotiation in your favor.

The roles strategic allies play range from modest to critical. Their interventions can simply open doors for you. A timely phone call from a mentor adds a personal note to a letter of recommendation and can shift your résumé to the top of the pile. An opportune word from a well-placed friend can coax a larger check from a contributor hesitant to support your agency, As allies become more actively engaged, they alter the dynamics in the shadow negotiation even more profoundly. They become, in effect, strategic partners and broaden your impact, particularly if they complement your strengths with other skills or give you access to different spheres of influence.

Allies can also wield sticks you may not want to use and apply overt pressure on the other party. He or she may think twice about incurring a boss's displeasure, alienating a prominent figure, or disappointing a valued colleague or an important client. Resistance tends to evaporate when it carries a penalty.

When enlisting strategic allies, you have to consider two points. The most obvious is whether the potential ally actually supports you and how firmly. The second is the relationship he or she enjoys with the person you are negotiating with. Does he have the clout to make a difference? Does the other party value her opinions?

Use Allies as Intermediaries. Acting as intermediaries, allies can intervene in a negotiation. They can troubleshoot a proposal ahead of time and ensure that its hearing is biased in your favor. When you involve them in the early drafting stages, they have a chance to contribute to the proposal's final shape. Once their suggestions are incorporated, the proposal carries their stamp of approval. In effect, they become its sponsors. Liv's boss June served as a critic and buffer during Liv's work/family negotiations.

Liv started from scratch when she carved out a niche for public-interest counseling at a major East Coast law school. With the birth of her first child, Liv had shifted to a 70 percent schedule, trading flexibility to work at home for actual hours. Pregnant with her second child, Liv wanted to bring in a codirector to job-share with her.

Liv was not breaking new ground when she requested a part-time schedule. A job-share, on the other hand, would be a first. For Liv and for the dean who would have to approve the request, the stakes were higher. A job-share could jeopardize the counseling office, which was universally regarded as Liv's creation. At the same time, it could establish a potentially troublesome precedent in a milieu that was not particularly hospitable to creative work arrangements.

Liv's boss—June, an associate dean—would have loved to work half-time. Identifying as she did with Liv's situation, she acted as a sponsor for Liv. She reviewed Liv's proposal, identifying points where it might provoke the dean's resistance. Just as important, June raised the issue with the dean. That broad-brush and informal discussion colored the dean's first impressions. He respected June and valued her judgment. Not only was he persuaded to consider the proposal, he took seriously June's warning that Liv would resign if something could not be worked out.

> It was very important to have a buffer between the dean and me. Eventually I had to argue my own case, but June prepared the way. I did not have to go in to the dean cold. And I did not have to threaten him with leaving.

Intermediaries like June position you favorably before talks even begin. At a minimum, their confidence primes the other party to listen to what you have to say. Their support can he particularly important when you are not in a good position to do the negotiating directly.

Dan, a senior navigator in the navy, faced a double problem when his ship's home port moved from Southern California to Washington. The captain's standing orders stipulated watch rotations and specified that full teams had to man the bridge during any maneuvers in sight of land or in the presence of other shipping. In California, the ship would leave port and head straight out to sea, clearing land at once and rarely seeing another vessel. In Washington, it still operated where there was little merchant traffic, but land was always in sight. Under the current standing orders, the on-duty time effectively doubled with the change in home port.

Any alteration to the standing orders required the captain's consent. But Dan hesitated to approach the captain directly, as he would be jumping several ranks and wondered whether his suggestions would be taken seriously given his relative lack of experience. In addition, Dan had a reputation for caring too much about his people, of putting concerns for his own team above the operational mission of the ship.

All watch bills had to be signed by the senior watch officer and the executive officer, number two and number three in the ship's hierarchy of command. Dan approached both with his concerns. If his navigation team had to be at full force, he could not stand watch as officer of the deck. This conflict made the senior watch officer a natural ally since he absolutely needed Dan on that rotation. Readiness, a prime concern for the executive officer, could be compromised by doubling rotation times on deck, so the number two officer was open to brainstorming possible changes in the standing orders.

Eventually Dan, not the executive officer or the senior watch officer, argued the case for change, but these allies prepared the way. They not only helped him to anticipate possible objections the captain might raise on certain points; they also mentioned to the captain the difficulties that the ship's new venue caused in the rotations. By the time Dan presented his solution, the captain already recognized that the problem warranted his attention. Dan's motivation and credibility never came into question, and only the merits of his solution were discussed.

Use Allies as Strategic Partners. Certain allies are positioned—through personal relationships or status alone—to influence a negotiation. Others bring specific skills that complement yours and increase your value in the eyes of the other party. Anna, the executive director of a social service agency in a depressed New England mill town, drew on allies for both influence and skills. Increasingly troubled by her agency's dependence on state allocations and the United Way, Anna was determined to broaden the agency's financial base. She was especially concerned that the agency secure sufficient funding for its expanding community health programs. Private foundations seemed the logical place to go.

> I became a cheerleader for what my agency could do for the community. I had a specific agenda. I wanted to be known and respected in the private foundation world. That was where the new money was coming from in health care, and I wanted to establish my agency as a "credible vendor."

Anna soon encountered a major stumbling block in this plan. The foundations were not interested. The agency's rapid growth made foundation officials wonder whether she and her staff could handle the larger budgets involved. She also suspected they weren't overly impressed with her. "I just don't come over as a player," she says.

Anna decided she needed to shore up her agency's image. A disconnect existed between what the agency could accomplish and what outsiders thought it could do. At first Anna was baffled. Then she realized her board could provide a bridge to the wider community and to greater legitimacy. To access professional strategic advice on health initiatives, Anna invited the head of the school of public health and a respected surgeon to join the board. To give depth to the agency's financial planning, she sought out two prominent members of the business community and put them in charge of overseeing the finance and budget committees.

Anna's new board members became strategic partners in the agency's expansion. Anna never went alone to critical foundation presentations. She always arranged to have the appropriate board member accompany her. These moves increased foundation confidence in her programs, and they began to work with her on grants.

Allies are important resources in the shadow negotiation. They can be critical when you encounter difficulties in establishing your credibility. Their support makes your incentives more tangible precisely because they can trumpet your value in a way that you cannot.

Use Allies as Sources of Pressure.   Allies are not restricted to working on the bright side, extolling your virtues and the benefits of negotiating with you. They can also bring pressure to bear. Their influence on the other party raises the costs of not dealing with you forthrightly. Not incidentally, it is often easier for them to be the bearer of bad news. June, as an associate dean, could let the dean know that Liv might resign unless a job-share could be worked out. Had the comment come from Liv, he would have given it far less credence. He might have dismissed it altogether as a hollow threat.

During an intense negotiation, it is easy to forget that other people besides you and the person you are negotiating with have a stake in the outcome. These stakeholders represent potential sources of influence. When your interests coincide with theirs, it is not difficult to persuade them to become vocal or exert pressure behind the scenes.

Roni deliberately sought out such a stakeholder when she negotiated a part-time schedule. While serving as director of development for the symphony of a large city in the Midwest, she was getting her master's in public policy at night. She found the pace toward her degree frustratingly slow. When her contract with the symphony came up for renewal, she proposed cutting back on her hours in order to finish earlier. The symphony's general manager responded with two options. One: Go on a part-time schedule until she completed her degree requirements. The general manager made this option contingent on her commitment to remain with the symphony, full-time and in the same position (that is, for the same salary) for two years after graduation. Two: Leave the symphony when her contract expired.

Neither option was acceptable to Roni. She suggested other possibilities, but the general manager refused to discuss them. Not wanting to leave, but unwilling to commit to two years at a flat salary, Roni tendered her resignation. She then turned to the conductor. His plans for a series of celebrity concerts and a European tour hinged on securing corporate support, an effort Roni was spearheading. When Roni told him of her resignation, his concern was obvious. "My alliance with the conductor was a natural," she says. "I knew what a high priority he placed on fund-raising at that moment."

Although Roni never requested the conductor's intervention, she was not surprised when he asked the general manager to extend her contract and allow her to work part-time until the corporate fund-raising was safely launched. After talking with the conductor, Roni did not press her boss. Instead, she proceeded as if she were departing when her contract expired. She was actually waiting for the general manager to come to her. And he did.

Roni capitalized on her good relationship with the conductor. The mutual interest they shared in the uncompleted fund-raising effort raised the costs to the general manager of her leaving. By accepting her resignation, he would jeopardize the conductor's good will. It is important to note how carefully Roni employed this strategy. She avoided the appearance and the fact of exploiting the conductor. At the same time, she protected the general manager from any loss of face. Neither he nor the rest of the organization was ever aware that she had gone "over his head." Rather than bring public pressure to bear, she gave him room to change his mind.

Certain stakeholders are natural allies. But enlisting their aid implies a quid pro quo. Your strategy must take into account their interests as well as your own. These do not always dovetail so perfectly as Roni's and the conductor's. Moreover, the issue of enlisting outside support often has a hidden catch-22. Calling on allies, instead of being interpreted as a sign of strength—that you have powerful people behind you—is read as weakness. You obviously need someone to bail you out or fight your battles. The danger can be real, but the benefits of such help so frequently outweigh the costs that it pays to consider ways of offsetting any negative impressions. By enlisting the conductor's support indirectly and informally, for example, Roni maintained the public impression that she was negotiating on her own.

Allies even the odds at the table. Strategically chosen, they set the stage for a favorable hearing. They also alter the consequences for the other party. It is not so easy for her to ignore you or for him to treat your demands casually when that behavior carries the added risk of offending people whose goodwill and opinions have long-term value.

Exert Control over the Process

Incentives and pressures increase your influence over a negotiation. Incentives pull the other party into the negotiation. You demonstrate just what you can do and are doing for them. Pressures push them into dealing with you. They come to see that their situation will only deteriorate if they don't. You—what you offer or can cost them—are the focus. In this sense, incentives and pressures are highly personal and can generate highly personal reactions. The advantages you are demonstrating are your advantages; the threats, however subtle, are threats you are making. The allies defending or supporting you are your allies.

It is not always possible to use these direct methods. There may be personal reasons. The moves, even when they can be deftly employed, don't fit your negotiating style. Promoting your value seems too blatantly self-serving and exerting pressure too heavy-handed. Or, worse, you suspect the remedy will do more harm than good and provoke resistance or retaliation. These circumstances call out for a different approach. Rather than attempt to influence the negotiation directly by holding out incentives and stepping up the pressure—moves that always carry a personal dimension for you and for the person you are negotiating with—you can center your moves on the negotiation process itself.

Process-oriented moves, while they do not directly address your interests, do directly affect the hearing those interests get. The agenda, the sequence in which ideas and people are heard, the groundwork you lay ahead of time—all these structural elements influence how receptive others will be to your opinions. When your suggestions surprise or shock, you can almost bank on a negative reaction. If a boss or coworkers think you are trying to manipulate them or surreptitiously gain an advantage, they will see any effort you make as a challenge. Working behind the scenes, indirectly, you can plant the seeds of your ideas so that no one is taken by surprise or put on the defensive. Before an agenda gets fixed in anyone's mind, you can build support for your ideas. You may even be able to engineer consensus so that your agenda frames the discussion.

Anticipate Reactions.   How you present your ideas can be as important as what you say. To make sure your suggestions get a fair hearing, you must pay attention to the process leading up to their presentation. The insights you glean from scouting information refine your reading of the situation, and that knowledge can be put to work. Once you discover where and how your ideas are likely to encounter opposition and, conversely, what kinds of proposals generally meet with approval, you can shape the process to your advantage.

Harry, the director of a university research program, wanted to expand the fellows program in terms of both numbers and diversity. In the past most of the fellows worked in labs supervised by two faculty members. Since the current arrangement benefited them, Harry anticipated that the two would resist any expansion of the fellows program. He also expected that he would be challenged about the quality of the fellows and the willingness of other faculty to supervise them. Anticipating these reactions, Harry instituted an evaluation process that had all the faculty members assess the candidates. When names came up, he brought out the evaluation forms. He had also secured commitments from other faculty members to supervise the fellows. During the meeting, he handed out a grid that showed which fellows would work with which faculty members. By anticipating obstacles, Harry was able to structure the meeting so that his agenda could move forward. Sometimes it is possible to move strategically, as Harry did, to reframe the process.

Over the past year, Marcie's group had taken on several large projects. To staff them, the group had recruited talent from other departments and added new hires. Their current quarters were cramped, with most people doubled up in cubicles meant for one person. Despite these crowded conditions, Marcie was not optimistic when the annual negotiations over space were scheduled. If past experience was any guide, a high degree of gamesmanship would govern the discussions. Extra room typically went to those who pushed the hardest or protested the loudest. The previous year Marcie had stated her actual needs and been penalized for her candor. The negotiations proceeded according to a hidden rule: to get what you wanted, you had to exaggerate your needs by at least 30 percent.

Marcie believed that there were real costs attached to this process. The company was growing at a rapid pace, yet with the other group leaders pressing inflated figures on the administrator, she was unable to assess the company's actual space requirements. Several weeks before the scheduled negotiations, Marcie invited the administrator over for a tour of her group's facilities. As they walked around, the administrator could see that the group was bursting at the seams. But, more important, Marcie found out from a chance comment that the administrator was tired of the game that the other groups played. Not only could she not allocate space fairly and efficiently, she could not plan where future needs were likely to develop.

Sensing the administrator's frustration, Marcie proposed changing the process. Rather than allocate space in a series of discrete negotiations with group heads, why didn't they develop criteria for assessing need? They could come up with a formula that took the guesswork and gamesmanship out of the decision-making process. The administrator embraced the idea with relief. There would be heated arguments over the criteria, but it was a step in the right direction. Without any pressure on Marcie's part, she found herself chairing the committee that the administrator created to develop more objective criteria.

Marcie's work behind the scenes allowed her to take control of a process that had previously put her at a disadvantage. The shift in process that she initiated changed the game. Not only had she put herself in a position to initiate a more realistic policy for space planning, under the new guidelines her group moved to another floor where it had almost twice as much room.

Plant the Seeds of Your Ideas.   At times people simply shut down. They don't listen. Whatever the reason, they screen out certain comments or certain people. Being ignored in a negotiation is not always a question of saying too little or saying it too hesitantly—a common diagnosis when people lose their impact in meetings. When ideas surprise or shock, they are likely to provoke negative, defensive reactions. Also, bargainers screen out the familiar. If they expect to be pressured, forcefulness too loses its impact. Maybe they have heard the speech before, or a close variant, and they stop paying attention. Working behind the scenes, it is possible for negotiators to influence a negotiation in ways that make it easier for ideas to be heard. Planting seeds of an idea ahead of time relieves the burden of pushing ideas once you're into a meeting. These seeds remain in the back of everyone's mind and become part of the agenda.

Pat was a talker and an aggressive one in meetings. In the past, her fellow managers had tuned her out during annual staff reviews—not because she was hesitant, but because they felt she pushed too hard. Being heard was no small matter for Pat or for the members of her department. Merit increases reflected the managers' collective assessment of what individual engineers contributed to the firm. They were also widely regarded as signs of whether a particular manager was doing a good job.

This year, Pat vowed, the performance reviews were going to be different. No effort on her part was suddenly going to transform her into a shrinking violet—she was too commanding a personality. She could, however, prepare the ground ahead of time so that she would not feel so compelled to dominate the review sessions. Over many lunches in the weeks before the reviews, she casually asked other managers about openings in their departments. On each occasion she slipped in a mention of her star employees, saying it was too bad they weren't available. They had precisely the skills and attitude the managers needed.

Once the actual reviews started, the other managers had already heard of her stars. That name recognition saved Pat from overselling. By lobbying for team members informally, Pat was able to make herself heard without belaboring her case—an objective that had previously eluded her. Preliminary work like this allows you to build receptivity where an aggressive or direct approach might offend. Once you have planted the seeds, however firmly attached others are to their own agendas, those seeds cannot help but influence their view of the situation.

Build Support Behind the Scenes.   Even when we seem to be in control of the agenda, that control is seldom complete. Individual members of the new product team need to be persuaded to go along with a development plan. A majority of the board members of a nonprofit organization must be convinced before they agree that the funding guidelines must be revised.

Generally these negotiations take place either in a meeting where the group makes the decision or in stages, through back-and-forth consultations. This process has a good deal of room for slippage, and it is risky to leave issues you care about to a process that you may be unable to control. Hidden agendas can surface unexpectedly. Groupthink can overtake substance so that consensus becomes a matter of who shouts loudest or whose voice customarily dominates. Or you may discover that a decision has been reached without your input.

Lobbying behind the scenes provides a potential antidote to these dangers. You can build consensus before matters come to a head. Backstage efforts provide opportunities to gather momentum behind your agenda. As that support grows, it isolates the blockers, making continued opposition harder and harder for them. Moreover, once agreement has been secured privately, it becomes more difficult (although never impossible) for a supporter to defect publicly.

Lynn, a public health expert in her early forties, left a job in a large teaching hospital to become head of a struggling community hospital in a suburb outside Baltimore. Lynn moved quickly to establish control over the direction the hospital's turnaround would take, but she kept this private agenda to herself. Each department head thought his or her budget should be the last to be cut, and Lynn could not afford to watch months of valuable time being consumed by departmental infighting.

> Before I came on board, I crawled all over the place. Once I got here, I met with key leaders of the board, the medical staff, and management in the first six or eight weeks. I did those all one-on-one. These sessions are time-consuming, but they are also what I call "clean encounters." When you are pushing an agenda, it's important that your initial interactions not be contentious.

Lynn's private talks linked the multiple agendas in play with specific people. They provided her with a strategic map. She discovered where she would find support and where she was likely to be blocked.

Lynn paid particular attention to the order in which she approached people in her next round of talks. She began with the most supportive player—the medical chief of staff. Not only had he been instrumental in bringing her to the hospital, he had publicly backed the kinds of changes she envisioned. Together they came to a basic understanding on his role in the hospital's turnaround. Next she met with the vice president of finance and administration, who, she thought, would probably go along with her plan provided she had a voice in its development. Cutbacks would take a heavy toll on the nurses, however, and before Lynn approached the head of nursing, she worked with the chief of staff and the finance vice president to keep the burden on nursing to a minimum. She saved the head of surgery for last, anticipating that he would be the most obstinate. But by that time she had everybody else on board, and he had little choice but to go along with her ideas.[5]

Lynn's private talks, and the way she gradually built support, got the key players to commit, one by one, to her reading of the agenda before any opposing factions could develop. That danger was real. Had the heads of the various services coalesced, they could have blocked her efforts. Her "clean encounters" fixed the agenda for the hospital's turnaround on her terms. When the various parties considered their options, they did so within the framework she proposed.[6] Lynn's consensus building also positioned her as a fellow collaborator. Having built commitment privately, she did not have to rely on her formal position to dictate terms when the department heads met to work on the budget.

In today's leaner organizations, bargainers frequently find themselves negotiating without direct authority to impose their will on an agreement.[7] When you anticipate resistance, as Harry did, you can structure the process to defuse the challenges. You can move behind the scenes to foster agreement on objectives so the goals of the negotiation align with your goals, as Marcie did when she defused the established gamesmanship previously embedded in the process of negotiating office space. If you are concerned that your interests will be ignored, as Pat was during the performance reviews, you can plant the seeds of your ideas so that the other party will be more receptive to them.

Even when you do have the authority to control a negotiation, as Lynn did, exercising it preemptively may interfere with a longer-term goal—that of building cooperation and a cohesive team. Behind-the-scenes efforts draw others into the consensus-making process that takes place within any group negotiation. Not only do these "clean encounters" allow you to identify and deal with any resistance before it hardens, they ensure that your views shape any agenda that emerges.

Step by Step: Planning a Strategic Campaign

Any of these strategic moves will position you to advantage in negotiation and increase your influence over how the issues come to be weighted and decided. But your choice of moves must be made against a realistic appraisal of what you can legitimately expect to take on all at once. The more complex the negotiation, the less likelihood there is that it can be brought to closure overnight. A single strategic move seldom carries the day.

The negotiation can, however, be broken down into segments. What cannot be achieved in one giant step can often be accomplished through a series of strategic moves. Approaching a complicated negotiation in stages, isolating benchmarks, gives you manageable goals. Not all the resources you need to create incentives or pressure the other person to pay attention to you are immediately available. They must be marshaled over time by building credibility, support, and respect. Thoughtful and well-planned strategies combine multiple moves that create incentives, apply pressure, and exert control over the process. As your value increases in the negotiation, so does the cost to the other party of not coming to terms over the issues. To illustrate how strategic moves can be used, singly and together, we return to Fiona Sweeney and follow her as she negotiates the change in decision making mandated by her boss.

Fiona's negotiations, if successful, would improve coordination between sales and production. With the current system of commissions, sales managers pursued any and all sales opportunities with little regard for the company's capacity to deliver. In turn, production was blamed for delays and cost overruns. Although the lack of cooperation hurt profits and left customers disgruntled, Fiona soon discovered that the attitudes behind it were firmly entrenched.

> The formal culture at the company supports consensus decision making. The reality is totally different. Sales dominates everything, and the compensation system encourages short-term, opportunistic behavior. There is a disconnect between the official goals of quality and customer satisfaction and the informal operational realities.

Sales routinely ignored the company's procedures for coordinating with production and quality control, and neither Fiona's predecessor nor the head of production had ever challenged the sales managers on their decisions.

> The sales managers had been running the business for a long time. Each was outstanding in his own right, strong-minded and competitive, with zero tolerance for weakness. All relished a good fight and were accustomed to winning.

Fiona viewed her assignment as a staged campaign. She had no authority to order sales and production to cooperate. She was new to the division and the players involved saw no reason to deal with her beyond their perfunctory interactions.

To encourage sales and production to work with her on improving coordination, she needed to be credible to both. "I turned myself into an asset by filling unmet needs," she says. "These efforts gave me visibility and started my relationships with the various departments off on the right foot."

First, Fiona made adjustments to the billing process that cut the error rate over a three-month period from 7.1 percent to 2.4 percent. The increased billing efficiency raised her standing with all the departments. Customers were no longer calling sales to complain about erroneous bills, and production had an accurate accounting of its output. The move also positioned her as a potential ally.

Next, she appealed directly to sales and made them aware of her impact on their daily lives where it counted most to them—their expense accounts. She reduced turnaround time on expense report processing from 40 days to 3. This was a simple task in computer programming, but its results got the attention of the entire sales force.

Fiona also needed to raise the costs of business as usual for the sales division. The people in sales were more than satisfied with the current state of affairs. All the informal reward systems—and many of the formal ones—worked to their benefit. Having brought greater efficiency to the billing systems, Fiona started talking about a bonus system that penalized sales if the department oversold and production could not deliver. She stopped short of acting on this threat and merely floated it as a possibility.

At the same time she took steps to make the lack of cooperation from sales more broadly known. For over two years the company had been surveying its customers about satisfaction. Nobody paid any attention to the findings until Fiona started posting them on the cafeteria bulletin board. Comments began appearing in the employee e-mail system, and it soon became apparent that customer discontent was a major problem, not a figment of Fiona's imagination.

Having planted the idea that something would have to change in the sales department, she mobilized allies in production and quality control. Their departments were directly affected by what sales did. Every time sales made a promise to a customer, production had to adjust its scheduling and quality slipped. Fiona proposed forming an operations subgroup with the heads of quality control and production. "The three of us had different areas of expertise," she says. "Pretty soon a common agenda emerged and we had a real impact in full staff meetings." Together, they began to work to isolate sales in the staff meetings. In one staff meeting, for example, Fiona proposed that a low priority be assigned to orders that had not been cleared by the operations subgroup. Quality control and production roundly supported the suggestion. Fiona no longer faced the prospect of confronting sales on her own.

When Fiona's boss gave her the task of negotiating a change in behavior in sales, he more or less dumped the problem in her lap. If she succeeded, fine. If not, he avoided being drawn into a contest of wills with the fiercely independent sales division. But Fiona soon reached an impasse. To make additional headway, she required, if not the general manager's active involvement, at least his visible backing.

To build support with her boss, Fiona kept him apprised of progress on her primary assignment, all the time soliciting his ideas privately. Working closely with him ensured that she would not be second-guessing his intentions. As his confidence in her judgment grew, he began to send more tangible signs of his backing.

> Whenever he was out of the office on a trip, he delegated general manager authority to me and required that I approve all exceptions to production specs. This caused howls from sales, but made the point.

Moreover, the general manager started to think that the change in decision making he wanted might actually be possible. He let key people know that he backed Fiona's proposal to base bonuses on profits, not revenues. This change would affect everyone, but especially sales. For the first time sales managers began to question how long they could conduct business as usual.

With the general manager's visible support (and the veiled threat of impending changes), Fiona was positioned to deal directly with sales. She joined the division's quality improvement team. The big project in development was a new pricing and profit model to be used as a sales tool.

> I became the local guru on this model and made myself available to sales for consultation and support. They began to want me to be involved in their decisions.

Fiona's gradual moves brought sales to the table. The sales force now trusted her, but they also realized she had the resources to enforce changes in the decision-making process if she had to. Only then was she in a position to negotiate those changes with sales. By working incrementally, she was able to demonstrate the benefits of new systems and how counterproductive resistance was for everyone. Increased internal coherence, communication, and efficiency raised profits and tightened quality control. Sales actually made more money with improved quality, and production no longer had the burden of delivering on the unrealistic promises made by the sales force. Customers and the general manager were extremely pleased.

Strategic moves increase your influence in a negotiation. They work not only to bring people to the table but also to ensure that they take you seriously once you are there. But influence is not static in a negotiation or from one negotiation to another. Strategic moves begin before any exchange takes place and do not end when an agreement is reached. Present encounters exert an impact on the influence you carry over to future negotiations. Parity, once reached, is not always stable, and credibility cannot be taken for granted. Authority earned in one situation does not transfer automatically to another. A banker spoke to us of the persistent need to "prove up." With each promotion, credentials had to be established. This proof takes place in the shadow negotiation, where you manage the perceptions other people have of you.

As the stories in this chapter show, you do not have to be in a great bargaining position starting out. With strategic moves, marshaled collectively and over time, you can shift the dynamics in your favor.[8] Strategic moves position you in the negotiation, but staying positioned is a continuous process.[9]

Endnotes

1. In "Bargaining and Gender," Carol Rose contends, for example, that it does not matter whether women are or are not more inclined to cooperation and accommodation in their negotiations. The assumption that they are makes the job of getting people to the table more difficult and the pressure to make concessions, once there, almost inevitable. This assumption holds broadly whenever the other party perceives a bargainer as being accommodating.

2. Abba Eban, *Diplomacy for the Next Century.*

3. *Unfreezing* is a concept developed, among others, by Kurt Lewin, *Resolving Social Conflicts; Field Theory in Social Science.*

4. Negotiations to secure the backing of a bargainer's own side are so critical to success in the main negotiation that they have been called the "second table." See Thomas Colosi, "Negotiation in the Public and Private Sectors"; Ray Friedman, *Front Stage, Backstage: The Dramatic Structure of Labor Negotiations;* and Richard Walton and Robert McKersie, *A Behavioral Theory of Labor Negotiations.*

5. See David Lax and James Sebenius, "Thinking Coalitionally."

6. "Clean encounters," conducted one-on-one privately, have another benefit. A negotiator may be willing to explore controversial issues or concessions in private but feel constrained in a more public forum.

7. On making change without explicit authority, see Allan R. Cohen and David L. Bradford, "Influence without Authority: The Use of Alliances, Reciprocity, and Exchange to Accomplish Work." Peter Bachrach and Morton S. Baratz differentiate between direct and indirect uses of power in "The Two Faces of Power."

8. Influence in negotiation is relational. It is not fixed, as the notion of bargaining power implies; it is fluid, malleable. It can, within limits, be increased through strategic moves. For this reason, we prefer the concept of *positioning*—the active bettering of your odds at the table—to the static notion of *bargaining power.* On the intersection of power relations and gender relations, see Joan Scott, *Gender and the Politics of History;* Jane Flax, "Postmodernism and Gender Relations in Feminist Theory"; and *Thinking Fragments: Psychoanalysis, Feminism, and Postmodernism in the Contemporary West.*

9. On using strategic moves to get negotiations off the ground, see also Deborah Kolb and Judith Williams, "Breakthrough Bargaining."

Reading 1.4

Six Habits of Merely Effective Negotiators
James K. Sebenius

Global deal makers did a staggering $3.3 trillion worth of M&A transactions in 1999—and that's only a fraction of the capital that passed through negotiators' hands that year. Behind the deal-driven headlines, executives endlessly negotiate with customers and suppliers, with large shareholders and creditors, with prospective joint venture and alliance partners, with people inside their companies and across national borders. Indeed, wherever parties with different interests and perceptions depend on each other for results, negotiation matters. Little wonder that Bob Davis, vice chairman of Terra Lycos, has said that companies "have to make deal making a core competency."

Luckily, whether from schoolbooks or the school of hard knocks, most executives know the basics of negotiation; some are spectacularly adept. Yet high stakes and intense pressure can result in costly mistakes. Bad habits creep in, and experience can further ingrain those habits. Indeed, when I reflect on the thousands of negotiations I have participated in and studied over the years, I'm struck by how frequently even experienced negotiators leave money on the table, deadlock, damage relationships, or allow conflict to spiral.

There are as many specific reasons for bad outcomes in negotiations as there are individuals and deals. Yet broad classes of errors recur. In this article, I'll explore those mistakes, comparing good negotiating practice with bad. But first, let's take a closer look at the right negotiation problem that your approach must solve.

Solving the Right Negotiation Problem

In any negotiation, each side ultimately must choose between two options: accepting a deal or taking its best no-deal option—that is, the course of action it would take if the deal were not possible. As a negotiator, you seek to advance the full set of your interests by persuading the other side to say yes—and mean it—to a proposal that meets your interests better than your best no-deal option does. And why should the other side say yes? Because the deal meets its own interests better than its best no-deal option. So, while protecting your own choice, your negotiation problem is to understand and shape your counterpart's perceived decision—deal versus no deal—so that the other side chooses *in its own interest* what you want. As Italian diplomat Daniele Vare said long ago about diplomacy, negotiation is "the art of letting them have your way."

This approach may seem on the surface like a recipe for manipulation. But in fact, understanding your counterpart's interests and shaping the decision so the other side agrees for its own reasons is the key to jointly creating and claiming sustainable value

Source: From *Harvard Business Review,* April 2001, pp. 87–95. Used with permission.

from a negotiation. Yet even experienced negotiators make six common mistakes that keep them from solving the right problem.

Mistake 1: Neglecting the Other Side's Problem

You can't negotiate effectively unless you understand your own interests and your own no-deal options. So far, so good—but there's much more to it than that. Since the other side will say yes for its reasons, not yours, agreement requires understanding and addressing your counterpart's problem as a means to solving your own.

At a minimum, you need to understand the problem from the other side's perspective. Consider a technology company, whose board of directors pressed hard to develop a hot new product shortly after it went public. The company had developed a technology for detecting leaks in underground gas tanks that was both cheaper and about 100 times more accurate than existing technologies—at a time when the Environmental Protection Agency was persuading Congress to mandate that these tanks be continuously tested. Not surprisingly, the directors thought their timing was perfect and pushed employees to commercialize and market the technology in time to meet the demand. To their dismay, the company's first sale turned out to be its only one. Quite a mystery, since the technology worked, the product was less expensive, and the regulations did come through. Imagine the sales engineers confidently negotiating with a customer for a new order: "This technology costs less and is more accurate than the competition's." Think for a moment, though, about how intended buyers might mull over their interests, especially given that EPA regulations permitted leaks of up to 1,500 gallons while the new technology could pick up an 8-ounce leak. Potential buyer: "What a technological tour de force! This handy new device will almost certainly get me into needless, expensive regulatory trouble. And create P.R. problems too. I think I'll pass, but my competition should definitely have it." From the technology company's perspective, "faster, better, cheaper" added up to a sure deal; to the other side, it looked like a headache. No deal.

Social psychologists have documented the difficulty most people have understanding the other side's perspective. From the trenches, successful negotiators concur that overcoming this self-centered tendency is critical. As Millennium Pharmaceuticals' Steve Holtzman put it after a string of deals vaulted his company from a start-up in 1993 to a major player with a $10.6 billion market cap today, "We spend a lot of time thinking about how the poor guy or woman on the other side of the table is going to have to go sell this deal to his or her boss. We spend a lot of time trying to understand how they are modeling it." And Wayne Huizenga, veteran of more than a thousand deals building Waste Management, AutoNation, and Blockbuster, distilled his extensive experience into basic advice that is often heard but even more often forgotten. "In all my years of doing deals, a few rules and lessons have emerged. Most important, always try to put yourself in the other person's shoes. It's vital to try to understand in depth what the other side really wants out of the deal."

Tough negotiators sometimes see the other side's concerns but dismiss them: "That's their problem and their issue. Let them handle it. We'll look after our own problems." This attitude can undercut your ability to profitably influence how your counterpart sees its problem. Early in his deal-making career at Cisco Systems, Mike Volpi, now chief strategy officer, had trouble completing proposed deals, his "outward confidence" often mistaken for arrogance. Many acquisitions later, a colleague observed that "the most important part of [Volpi's] development is that he learned power doesn't come from telling people you are powerful. He went from being a guy driving the deal from his side of the table to the guy who understood the deal from the other side."

An associate of Rupert Murdoch remarked that, as a buyer, Murdoch "understands the seller—and, whatever the guy's trying to do, he crafts his offer that way." If you want to change someone's mind, you should first learn where that person's mind is. Then, together, you can try to build what my colleague Bill Ury calls a "golden bridge," spanning the gulf between where your counterpart is now and your desired end point. This is much more effective than trying to shove the other side from its position to yours. As an eighteenth-century pope once noted about Cardinal de Polignac's remarkable diplomatic skills, "This young man always seems to be of my opinion [at the start of a negotiation], and at the end of the conversation I find that I am of his." In short, the first mistake is to focus on your own problem, exclusively. Solve the other side's as the means to solving your own.

Mistake 2: Letting Price Bulldoze Other Interests

Negotiators who pay attention exclusively to price turn potentially cooperative deals into adversarial ones. These "reverse Midas" negotiators, as I like to call them, use hard-bargaining tactics that often leave potential joint gains unrealized. That's because, while price is an important factor in most deals, it's rarely the only one. As Felix Rohatyn, former managing partner of the investment bank Lazard Frères observed, "Most deals are 50 percent emotion and 50 percent economics."

There's a large body of research to support Rohatyn's view. Consider, for example, a simplified negotiation, extensively studied in academic labs, involving real money. One party is given, say, $100 to divide with another party as she likes; the second party can agree or disagree to the arrangement. If he agrees, the $100 is divided in line with the first side's proposal; if not, neither party gets anything. A pure price logic would suggest proposing something like $ 99 for me, $1 for you. Although this is an extreme allocation, it still represents a position in which your counterpart gets something rather than nothing. Pure price negotiators confidently predict the other side will agree to the split; after all, they've been offered free money—it's like finding a dollar on the street and putting it in your pocket. Who wouldn't pick it up?

In reality, however, most players turn down proposals that don't let them share in at least 35 percent to 40 percent of the bounty—even when much larger stakes are involved and the amount they forfeit is significant. While these rejections are "irrational" on a pure price basis and virtually incomprehensible to reverse Midas types, studies show that when a split feels too unequal to people, they reject the spoils as unfair, are offended by the process, and perhaps try to teach the "greedy" person a lesson.

An important real-world message is embedded in these lab results: people care about much more than the absolute level of their own economic outcome; competing interests include relative results, perceived fairness, self-image, reputation, and so on. Successful negotiators, acknowledging that economics aren't everything, focus on four important nonprice factors.

The Relationship   Less experienced negotiators often undervalue the importance of developing working relationships with the other parties, putting the relationships at risk by overly tough tactics or simple neglect. This is especially true in cross-border deals. In much of Latin America, Southern Europe, and Southeast Asia, for example, relationships—rather than transactions—can be the predominant negotiating interest when working out longer term deals. Results-oriented North Americans, Northern Europeans, and Australians often come to grief by underestimating the strength of this interest and insisting prematurely that the negotiators "get down to business."

The Social Contract   Similarly, negotiators tend to focus on the economic contract—equity splits, cost sharing, governance, and so on—at the expense of the social contract, or the "spirit of a deal." Going well beyond a good working relationship, the social contract governs people's expectations about the nature, extent, and duration of the venture, about process, and about the way unforeseen events will be handled. Especially in new ventures and strategic alliances, where goodwill and strong shared expectations are extremely important, negotiating a positive social contract is an important way to reinforce economic contracts. Scurrying to check founding documents when conflicts occur, which they inevitably do, can signal a badly negotiated social contract.

The Process   Negotiators often forget that the deal-making process can be as important as its content. The story is told of the young Tip O'Neill, who later became Speaker of the House, meeting an elderly constituent on the streets of his North Cambridge, Massachusetts, district. Surprised to learn that she was not planning to vote for him, O'Neill probed, "Haven't you known me and my family all my life?" "Yes." "Haven't I cut your grass in summer and shoveled your walk in winter?" "Yes." "Don't you agree with all my policies and positions?" "Yes." "Then why aren't you going to vote for me?" "Because you didn't ask me to." Considerable academic research confirms what O'Neill learned from this conversation: process counts. What's more, sustainable results are more often reached when all parties perceive the process as personal, respectful, straightforward, and fair.[1]

The Interests of the Full Set of Players   Less experienced negotiators sometimes become mesmerized by the aggregate economics of a deal and forget about the interests of players who are in a position to torpedo it. When the boards of pharmaceutical giants Glaxo and SmithKline Beecham publicly announced their merger in 1998, investors were thrilled, rapidly *increasing* the combined company's market capitalization by a stunning $20 billion. Yet despite prior agreement on who would occupy which top executive positions in the newly combined company, internal disagreement about management control and position resurfaced and sank the announced deal, and the $20 billion evaporated. (Overwhelming strategic logic ultimately drove the companies back together, but only after nearly two years had passed.) This episode confirms two related lessons. First, while favorable overall economics are generally necessary, they are often not sufficient Second, keep all potentially influential internal players on your radar screen; don't lose sight of their interests or their capacity to affect the deal. What is "rational" for the whole may not be so for the parts.

It can be devilishly difficult to cure the reverse Midas touch. If you treat a potentially cooperative negotiation like a pure price deal, it will likely become one. Imagine a negotiator who expects a hardball, price-driven process. She initiates the bid by taking a tough preemptive position; the other side is likely to reciprocate. "Aha!" says the negotiator, her suspicions confirmed. "I *knew* this was just going to be a tough price deal."

A negotiator can often influence whether price will dominate or be kept in perspective. Consider negotiations between two companies trying to establish an equity joint venture. Among other issues, they are trying to place a value on each side's contribution to determine ownership shares. A negotiator might drive this process down two very different paths. A price-focused approach quickly isolates the valuation issue and then bangs out a resolution. Alternatively, the two sides could first flesh out a more specific shared vision for the joint venture (together envisioning the "pot of gold" they could create), probe to understand the most critical concerns of each side—including price—and craft trade-offs among the full set of issues to meet these interests. In the latter approach, price becomes a component or even an implication of a larger, longer-term package, rather than the primary focus.

Some negotiations are indeed pure price deals and only about aggregate economics, but there is often much more to work with. Wise negotiators put the vital issue of price in perspective and don't straitjacket their view of the richer interests at stake. They work with the subjective as well as the objective, with the process and the relationship, with the "social contract" or spirit of a deal as well as its letter, and with the interests of the parts as well as the whole.

Mistake 3: Letting Positions Drive Out Interests

Three elements are at play in a negotiation. *Issues* are on the table for explicit agreement. *Positions* are one party's stands on the issues. *Interests* are underlying concerns that would be affected by the resolution. Of course, positions on issues reflect underlying interests, but they need not be identical. Suppose you're considering a job offer. The base salary will probably be an issue. Perhaps your position on that issue is that you need to earn $100,000. The interests underlying that position include your need for a good income but may also include status, security, new opportunities, and needs that can be met in ways other than salary. Yet even very experienced deal makers may see the essence of negotiation as a dance of positions. If incompatible positions finally converge, a deal is struck; if not, the negotiation ends in an impasse. By contrast, interest-driven bargainers see the process primarily as a reconciliation of underlying interests: you have one set of interests, I have another, and through joint problem solving we should be better able to meet both sets of interests and thus create new value.

Consider a dispute over a dam project Environmentalists and farmers opposed a U.S. power company's plans to build a dam. The two sides had irreconcilable positions: "absolutely yes" and "no way." Yet these incompatible positions masked compatible interests. The farmers were worried about reduced water flow below the dam, the environmentalists were focused on the downstream habitat of the endangered whooping crane, and the power company needed new capacity and a greener image. After a costly legal stalemate, the three groups devised an interest-driven agreement that all of them considered preferable to continued court warfare. The agreement included a smaller dam built on a fast track, water flow guarantees, downstream habitat protection, and a trust fund to enhance whooping crane habitats elsewhere.

Despite the clear advantages of reconciling deeper interests, people have a built-in bias toward focusing on their own positions instead. This hardwired assumption that our interests are incompatible implies a zero-sum pie in which my gain is your loss. Research in psychology supports the mythical fixed-pie view as the norm. In a survey of 5,000 subjects in 32 negotiating studies, mostly carried out with monetary stakes, participants failed to realize compatible issues fully half of the time.[2] In real-world terms, this means that enormous value is unknowingly left uncreated as both sides walk away from money on the table.

Reverse Midas negotiators, for example, almost automatically fixate on price and bargaining positions to claim value. After the usual preliminaries, countless negotiations get serious when one side asks, "So, what's your position?" or says, "Here's my position." This positional approach often drives the process toward a ritual value-claiming dance. Great negotiators understand that the dance of bargaining positions is only the surface game; the real action takes place when they've probed behind positions for the full set of interests at stake. Reconciling interests to create value requires patience and a willingness to research the other side, ask many questions, and listen. It would be silly to write off either price or bargaining position; both are extremely important. And there is, of course, a limit to joint value creation. The trick is to recognize and productively manage the tension between cooperative actions needed to create value and competitive ones needed to claim it. The pie must be both expanded and divided.

Mistake 4: Searching Too Hard for Common Ground

Conventional wisdom says we negotiate to overcome the differences that divide us. So, typically, we're advised to find win–win agreements by searching for common ground. Common ground is generally a good thing. Yet many of the most frequently overlooked sources of value in negotiation arise from differences among the parties.

Recall the battle over the dam. The solution—a smaller dam, water flow guarantees, habitat conservation—resulted not from common interests but because farmers, environmentalists, and the utility had different priorities. Similarly, when Egypt and Israel were negotiating over the Sinai, their positions on where to draw the boundary were incompatible. When negotiators went beyond the opposing positions, however, they uncovered a vital difference of underlying interest and priority: the Israelis cared more about security, while the Egyptians cared more about sovereignty. The solution was a demilitarized zone under the Egyptian flag. Differences of interest or priority can open the door to unbundling different elements and giving each party what it values the most—at the least cost to the other.

Solving Teddy Roosevelt's Negotiation Problem

Theodore Roosevelt, nearing the end of a hard-fought presidential election campaign in 1912, scheduled a final whistle-stop journey. At each stop, Roosevelt planned to clinch the crowd's votes by distributing an elegant pamphlet with a stern presidential portrait on the cover and a stirring speech, "Confession of Faith," inside. Some 3 million copies had been printed when a campaign worker noticed a small line under the photograph on each brochure that read, "Moffett Studios, Chicago." Since Moffett held the copyright, the unauthorized use of the photo could cost the campaign one dollar per reproduction. With no time to reprint the brochure, what was the campaign to do?

Not using the pamphlets at all would damage Roosevelt's election prospects. Yet, if they went ahead, a scandal could easily erupt very close to the election, and the campaign could be liable for an unaffordable sum. Campaign workers quickly realized they would have to negotiate with Moffett. But research by their Chicago operatives turned up bad news: although early in his career as a photographer, Moffett had been taken with the potential of this new artistic medium, he had received little recognition. Now Moffett was financially hard up and bitterly approaching retirement with a single-minded focus on money.

Dispirited, the campaign workers approached campaign manager George Perkins, a former partner of J. P. Morgan. Perkins lost no time summoning his stenographer to dispatch the following cable to Moffett Studios: "We are planning to distribute millions of pamphlets with Roosevelt's picture on the cover. It will be great publicity for the studio whose photograph we use. How much will you pay us to use yours? Respond immediately." Shortly, Moffett replied, "We've never done this before, but under the circumstances we'd be pleased to offer you $250." Reportedly, Perkins accepted— without dickering for more.

Perkins's misleading approach raises ethical yellow flags and is anything but a model negotiation on how to enhance working relationships. Yet this case raises a very interesting question: why did the campaign workers find the prospect of this negotiation so difficult? Their inability to see what Perkins immediately perceived flowed from their anxious obsession with their own side's problem: their blunders so far, the high risk of losing the election, a potential $3 million exposure, an urgent deadline, and no cash to meet Moffett's likely demands for something the campaign vitally needed. Had they avoided mistake 1 by pausing for a moment and thinking about how Moffett saw his problem, they would have realized that Moffett didn't even know he had a problem. Perkins's tactical genius was to recognize the essence of the negotiator's central task: shape how your counterpart sees its problem such that it chooses what you want.

The campaign workers were paralyzed in the face of what they saw as sharply con-flicting monetary interests and their pathetic BATNA. From their perspective, Moffett's only choice was how to exploit their desperation at the prospect of losing the presidency. By contrast, dodging mistake 5, Perkins immediately grasped the importance of favor-ably shaping Moffett's BATNA perceptions, both of the campaign's (awful) no-deal op-tions and Moffett's (powerful) one. Perkins looked beyond price, positions, and common ground (mistakes 2, 3, and 4) and used Moffett's different interests to frame the photog-rapher's choice as "the value of publicity and recognition." Had he assumed this would be a standard, hardball price deal by offering a small amount to start, not only would this assumption have been dead wrong but, worse, it would have been self-fulfilling.

Risky and ethically problematic? Yes . . . but Perkins saw his options as certain disaster versus some chance of avoiding it. And was Moffett really entitled to a $3 mil-lion windfall, avoidable had the campaign caught its oversight a week beforehand? Hard to say, but this historical footnote, which I've greatly embellished, illuminates the intersection of negotiating mistakes, tactics, and ethics.

Even when an issue seems purely economic, finding differences can break open deadlocked deals. Consider a small technology company and its investors, stuck in a tough negotiation with a large strategic acquirer adamant about paying much less than the asking price. On investigation, it turned out that the acquirer was actually willing to pay the higher price but was concerned about raising price expectations in a fast-moving sector in which it planned to make more acquisitions. The solution was for the two sides to agree on a modest, well-publicized initial cash purchase price; the deal included complex-sounding contingencies that virtually guaranteed a much higher price later.

Differences in forecasts can also fuel joint gains. Suppose an entrepreneur who is genuinely optimistic about the prospects of her fast-growing company faces a potential buyer who likes the company but is much more skeptical about the company's future cash flow. They have negotiated in good faith, but, at the end of the day, the two sides sharply disagree on the likely future of the company and so cannot find an acceptable sale price. Instead of seeing these different forecasts as a barrier, a savvy negotiator could use them to bridge the value gap by proposing a deal in which the buyer pays a fixed amount now and a contingent amount later on the basis of the company's future performance. Properly structured with adequate incentives and monitoring mechanisms, such a contingent payment, or "earn-out," can appear quite valuable to the optimistic seller—who expects to get her higher valuation—but not very costly to the less optimistic buyer. And willingness to accept such a contingent deal may signal that the seller's confidence in the business is genuine. Both may find the deal much more attractive than walking away.

A host of other differences make up the raw material for joint gains. A less risk-averse party can "insure" a more risk-averse one. An impatient party can get most of the early money, while his more patient counterpart can get considerably more over a longer period of time. Differences in cost or revenue structure, tax status, or regulatory arrangements between two parties can be converted into gains for both. Indeed, conducting a disciplined "differences inventory" is at least as important a task as is identifying areas of common ground. After all, if we were all clones of one another, with the same interests, beliefs, attitudes toward risk and time, assets, and so on, there would be little to negotiate. While common ground helps, differences drive deals. But negotiators who don't actively search for differences rarely find them.

Mistake 5: Neglecting BATNAs

BATNAs—the acronym for "best alternative to a negotiated agreement" coined years ago by Roger Fisher, Bill Ury, and Bruce Patton in their book *Getting to Yes*—reflect the course of action a party would take if the proposed deal were not possible. A BATNA may involve walking away, prolonging a stalemate, approaching another potential buyer, making something in-house rather than procuring it externally, going to court rather than settling, forming a different alliance, or going on strike. BATNAs set the threshold—in terms of the full set of interests—that any acceptable agreement must exceed. Both parties doing better than their BATNAs is a necessary condition for an agreement. Thus BATNAs define a zone of possible agreement and determine its location.

A strong BATNA is an important negotiation tool. Many people associate the ability to inflict or withstand damage with bargaining power, but your willingness to walk away to an apparently good BATNA is often more important. The better your BATNA appears both to you and to the other party, the more credible your threat to walk away becomes, and the more it can serve as leverage to improve the deal. Roger Fisher has dramatized this point by asking which you would prefer to have in your back pocket during a compensation negotiation with your boss: a gun or a terrific job offer from a desirable employer who is also a serious competitor of your company?

Not only should you assess your own BATNA, you should also think carefully about the other side's. Doing so can alert you to surprising possibilities. In one instance, a British company hoped to sell a poorly performing division for a bit more than its depreciated asset value of $7 million to one of two potential buyers. Realizing that these buyers were fierce rivals in other markets, the seller speculated that each party might be willing to pay an inflated price to keep the other from getting the division. So they made sure that each suitor knew the other was looking and skillfully cultivated the interest of both companies. The division sold for $45 million.

Negotiators must also be careful not to inadvertently damage their BATNAs. I saw that happen at a Canadian chemical manufacturing company that had decided to sell a large but nonstrategic division to raise urgently needed cash. The CEO charged his second-in-command with negotiating the sale of the division at the highest possible price.

The target buyer was an Australian company, whose chief executive was an old school friend of the Canadian CEO. The Australian chief executive let it be known that his company was interested in the deal but that his senior management was consumed, at the moment, with other priorities. If the Australian company could have a nine-month negotiating exclusive to "confirm their seriousness about the sale," the Australian chief executive would dedicate the top personnel to make the deal happen. A chief-to-chief agreement to that effect was struck. Pity the second-in-command, charged with urgently maximizing cash from this sale, as he jetted off to Sydney with no meaningful alternative for nine endless months to whatever price the Australians offered.

Negotiators often become preoccupied with tactics, trying to improve the potential deal while neglecting their own BATNA and that of the other side. Yet the real negotiation problem is "deal versus BATNA," not one or the other in isolation. Your potential deal and your BATNA should work together as the two blades of the scissors do to cut a piece of paper.

Mistake 6: Failing to Correct for Skewed Vision

You may be crystal clear on the right negotiation problem—but you can't solve it correctly without a firm understanding of both sides' interests, BATNAs, valuations, likely actions, and so on. Yet, just as a pilot's sense of the horizon at night or in a storm can be wildly inaccurate, the psychology of perception systematically leads negotiators to major errors.[3]

Self-Serving Role Bias   People tend unconsciously to interpret information pertaining to their own side in a strongly self-serving way. The following experiment shows the process at work. Harvard researchers gave a large group of executives financial and industry information about one company negotiating to acquire another. The executive subjects were randomly assigned to the negotiating roles of buyer or seller; the information provided to each side was identical. After plenty of time for analysis, all subjects were asked for their private assessment of the target company's fair value—as distinct from how they might portray that value in the bargaining process. Those assigned the role of seller gave median valuations more than twice those given by the executives assigned to the buyer's role. These valuation gulfs had no basis in fact; they were driven entirely by random role assignments.

Even comparatively modest role biases can blow up potential deals. Suppose a plaintiff believes he has a 70 percent chance of winning a million-dollar judgment, while the defense thinks the plaintiff has only a 50 percent chance of winning. This means that, in settlement talks, the plaintiff's expected BATNA for a court battle (to get $700,000 minus legal fees) will exceed the defendant's assessment of his exposure (to pay $500,000 plus fees). Without significant risk aversion, the divergent assessments would block any out-of-court settlement. This cognitive role bias helps explain why Microsoft took such a confrontational approach in its recent struggle with the U.S. Department of Justice. The company certainly appeared overoptimistic about its chances in court. Similarly, Arthur Andersen likely exhibited overconfidence in its arbitration prospects over the terms of separation from Andersen Consulting (now Accenture). Getting too committed to your point of view— "believing your own line" —is an extremely common mistake.

Partisan Perceptions   While we systematically err in processing information critical to our own side, we are even worse at assessing the other side—especially in an adversarial situation. Extensive research has documented an unconscious mechanism that enhances one's own side, "portraying it as more talented, honest, and morally upright," while simultaneously vilifying the opposition. This often leads to exaggerated perceptions of the other side's position and overestimates of the actual substantive conflict. To an outsider, those caught up in disintegrating partnerships or marriages often appear to hold exaggerated views of each other. Such partisan perceptions can become even more virulent among people on each side of divides, such as Israelis and Palestinians, Bosnian Muslims and the Serbs, or Catholics and Protestants in Northern Ireland.

Partisan perceptions can easily become self-fulfilling prophecies. Experiments testing the effects of teachers' expectations of students, psychiatrists' diagnoses of mental patients, and platoon leaders' expectations of their trainees confirm the notion that partisan perceptions often shape behavior. At the negotiating table, clinging firmly to the idea that one's counterpart is stubborn or extreme, for example, is likely to trigger just that behavior, sharply reducing the possibility of reaching a constructive agreement.

As disagreement and conflict intensify, sophisticated negotiators should expect biased perceptions, both on their own side and the other side. Less seasoned players tend to be shocked and outraged by perceived extremism and are wholly unaware that their own views are likely colored by their roles. How to counteract these powerful biases? Just knowing that they exist helps. Seeking the views of outside, uninvolved parties is useful, too. And having people on your side prepare the strongest possible case for the other side can serve as the basis for preparatory role-playing that can generate valuable insights. A few years ago, helping a client get ready for a tough deal, I suggested that the client create a detailed "brief" for each side and have the team's best people negotiate for the other side in a reverse role-play. The brief for my client's side was lengthy, eloquent, and persuasive. Tellingly, the brief describing the other side's situation was only two pages long and consisted mainly of reasons for conceding quickly to my client's superior arguments. Not only were my client's executives fixated on their own problem (mistake 1), their perceptions of each side were also hopelessly biased (mistake 6). To prepare effectively, they needed to undertake significant competitive research and reality-test their views with uninvolved outsiders.

From Merely Effective to Superior Negotiation

So you have navigated the shoals of merely effective deal making to face what is truly the right problem. You have focused on the full set of interests of all parties, rather than fixating on price and positions. You have looked beyond common ground to unearth value-creating differences. You have assessed and shaped BATNAs. You have taken steps to avoid role biases and partisan perceptions. In short, you have grasped your own problem clearly and have sought to understand and influence the other side's such that what it chooses is what you want.

Plenty of errors still lie in wait: cultural gaffes, an irritating style, inadvertent signals of disrespect or untrustworthiness, miscommunication, bad timing, revealing too much or too little, a poorly designed agenda, sequencing mistakes, negotiating with the wrong person on the other side, personalizing issues, and so on. Even if you manage to avoid these mistakes as well, you may still run into difficulties by approaching the negotiation far too narrowly, taking too many of the elements of the "problem" as fixed.

The very best negotiators take a broader approach to setting up and solving the right problem. With a keen sense of the potential value to be created as their guiding beacon, these negotiators are game-changing entrepreneurs. They envision the most promising architecture and take action to bring it into being. These virtuoso negotiators not only play the game as given at the table, they are masters at setting it up and changing it away from the table to maximize the chances for better results.

To advance the full set of their interests, they understand and shape the other side's choice—deal versus no deal—such that the other chooses what they want. As François de Callières, an eighteenth-century commentator, once put it, negotiation masters possess "the supreme art of making every man offer him as a gift that which it was his chief design to secure."

Endnotes

1.   W. Chan Kim and Renée Mauborgne, "Fair Process: Managing in the Knowledge Economy," *HBR,* July–August 1997.

2.   This and other studies illustrating this point can be found in Leigh Thompson's *The Mind and Heart of the Negotiator* (Prentice Hall, 1998).

3.   See Robert J. Robinson, "Errors in Social Judgment: Implications for Negotiation and Conflict Resolution, Part I: Biased Assimilation of Information." Harvard Business School, 1997; and Robert J. Robinson, "Errors in Social Judgment: Implications for Negotiation and Conflict Resolution, Part II: Partisan Perceptions," Harvard Business School, 1997.

Reading 1.5

Successful Negotiating
Julia Tipler

Preparation

All negotiations have a life cycle—a series of stages to be traveled to ensure that the criteria for a good agreement are met. Applying a structure to the negotiation process can help you avoid potential dangers and address all your requirements, as well those of the other party, in detail. Before entering into any negotiation, you should consider the following five questions:

1. What Is Your Objective?

- What should a good agreement include?
- What must you have?
- What are your expectations of the other party in the negotiation?

2. What Are Your Limits?

- What level of authority do you have?
- Will you need to get clearance prior to final agreement?
- What is nonnegotiable ?

3. Whom Are You Negotiating with?

- What do you know about them already?
- What can you find out about them?
- What might their requirements be?
- Will they bring any nonnegotiable areas to the discussion?

4. Are You Dealing with the People Who Can "Sign Off" the Deal?

- Will they have the authority to sign the contract?
- Will they have any limits on what they can agree to?
- Will they need to get clearance from someone else before they can sign an agreement?
- If so, how can you help them to recommend the deal?

Source: From *Successful Negotiating: The Essential Guide to Thinking and Working Smarter,* by Julia Tipler. Copyright © 2000 by AMACOM, New York, NY.

5. What Would Be Unacceptable?

• At what point would you walk away from the deal?

• At what point would any short-term benefits of the deal be outweighed by the long-term costs?

Why?

The first of the critical analysis questions, "Why?," actually should be broken down into two questions: "Why am I doing this?" and "Why me?"

Why Am I Doing This?

You need to be quite clear what your desired outcome is for the negotiation. If you haven't identified clear objectives for the discussion, the probability of your needs being met is diminished. You also should have specific requirements for the deal. For example, you may be meeting with a supplier to secure a lower price for your regular order because the market for the particular product has changed and you could get it more cheaply elsewhere. In such a case it would be essential to know how much of a reduction you want and what you would be prepared to accept.

Why Me?

The second question to ask yourself is "Why am I the best person to conduct this negotiation?" Think about the skills, experience, or knowledge that you will bring to the negotiating table. Does your relationship with the person you will be dealing with make you particularly suitable? For example, have you dealt successfully with this person before, or will you be responsible for the agreement during its implementation?

When answering this second "why" question, you should also consider the limits of what you can achieve. Consider whether other people would be able to help. Would it be helpful to have other people there during the negotiation? Are there other people with whom it would be useful to consult prior to the final agreement? Who will need to be informed once the agreement has been reached?

Who?

You may be entering into a negotiation with someone you have encountered before or with someone who has no history with you or your company. Either way, you should take the time to find out something about the person or people with whom you will be dealing.

Know Your History

If there is an established relationship with the other party, do all you can to find out about them and what they are likely to bring to the negotiation. Know whom you are dealing with.

- What do you know about them, or what can you find out?
- Whom should you ask? Is your source's view likely to be colored by personal concerns?
- What are the interests, needs, and concerns of this person?
- What is the history of the relationship?

If there have been problems in the past, it may be wise to acknowledge these openly in the beginning. Stress that you have taken steps to avoid similar problems in the future, rather than hope that they don't bring them up. On the other hand, if they have had a good business relationship with one of your colleagues, acknowledge that relationship and stress that your intention is to continue it.

Do Some Detective Work

If the person you are dealing with is a prospective new customer or supplier, it is still worth trying to find out something about them. Any information could help to strengthen your position.

- If they are a potential customer, are they approaching you as an alternative to any existing suppliers you might have?
- If they are a supplier, who are their existing customers? Does their customer base inspire confidence?
- Have they been given any industry awards or has there been any favorable press coverage about them recently? Most people are flattered by the fact that you have taken the trouble to find out something like this.
- Do you know, or can you find out, anything about them on a personal level? People like to be treated as individuals. It doesn't have to be anything very personal; just knowing what football team they support, for example, could help break the ice.

Where?

Location may not seem like a very important issue, but it can be crucial. The fundamental question is "Your place or mine?"

Your Place

The general rule is, if you are selling, you should go to the customer. You should be seen as the one making the most effort.

This is not simply a matter of courtesy. Visiting customers on their own territory can work in your favor. Surprisingly, people are usually easier to sell to when they are on their home ground. They feel more comfortable and relaxed and are, therefore, more receptive.

People are also inclined to be more polite when you are a guest in their office or home. This is why many financial services agents prefer to visit you at home.

Many people think—incorrectly—that the best thing to do is to invite prospective customers to their location so that they can show them hospitality. This is advisable for the second meeting but rarely for the first one.

My Place

When you are the customer or are asked for your cooperation, you should expect the other party to come to you. Remember, though, that they are guests on your territory and treat them accordingly. Whether you decide to do business with them or not, the way you deal with them reflects on you and your company. You do not want to develop a reputation for being an uncourteous person with whom to do business.

Neutral Territory

If you feel that there are grounds for conflict, it may be better to meet on neutral ground. High-level diplomatic negotiations, for example, are often held in neutral countries. Internal negotiations may be an exception to the "your-place/my-place" rule. Booking a meeting room can ensure that neither side feels at a disadvantage.

When?

Timing can be crucial. The best time for the negotiation to begin is when everybody has been fully briefed and knows what to expect. Make sure that you, your colleagues, and the other party have all been given a brief outline of the issues you will want to cover, and let them know when you intend to call or meet with them. If you are dealing internationally, remember to take the time difference into consideration.

What Time?

Even a detail, such as the time of day when the meeting takes place, can make a difference. Don't be tempted to play the power game of asking for breakfast meetings at impossibly early times, just to give the impression that you are extremely important and busy. This will irritate everyone else.

Schedule meetings for a time when everyone is relaxed and at their best; midmorning is usually a good time. If the discussions are likely to be complex, don't try to fit them all into one meeting, as people's concentration will start to flag. Allow plenty of time for breaks in an all-day meeting, and remember that people will not be at their most alert after a heavy lunch.

Ready or Not?

Do not be pressured into a negotiation before you have had time to prepare. Reschedule if you are not ready. Equally, you should resist the urge to pressure the other side just because you are ready. This is particularly important if you are negotiating over the phone: Always check that it is convenient for the other person to deal with the matter at that time. If you interrupt them or catch them unprepared, it can make them less inclined to cooperate.

What?

The next question in your critical analysis is, What do you want to achieve? The answer to this may be simple— "I want a stereo system with reasonable sound for less than $300"— or it may be more complex, involving issues of cost, quality, variety, delivery, and more.

What Do I Need?

If your negotiation is of the more complex kind, make a checklist of what you need from the agreement. For example, suppose a shoe retailer is looking for a supplier of women's fashion shoes. Concerns might include

- Price.
- Profit margin.
- Quality.
- Wide range of styles.
- Wide range of sizes.
- Ability to fulfill orders on short notice.
- Discounts for large orders.
- Guaranteed delivery dates.
- Guaranteed stock availability.

What Is Most Important to Me?

The next step is to prioritize your checklist into what you must have, what would be useful to have, and what would simply be nice to have.

These will depend on the situation. In the case of the shoe retailer, a "nice-to-have" term might be the ability to fulfill orders at short notice. However, if they were buying sandals, and sales varied from one week to the next according to the weather, then that issue might be more important, even becoming a "must-have."

What Am I Prepared to Give?

An additional area to think about is what you are prepared to concede in order to do the deal. You might decide that discounts are not a crucial factor, and that you would be able to forgo them in return for something—perhaps a guarantee that prices would not rise before a certain date or an earlier delivery date.

How?

The last of your critical analysis questions is "How?" There are so many means of communication now that you have more choices than ever before. You can negotiate

- Face-to-face.
- Over the phone.
- In writing—by letter, fax, or e-mail.

Face-to-Face

Meeting face-to-face can provide you with vital evidence about how the person you are dealing with feels about the situation. This evidence—provided by tone of voice, facial expression, and body language—is missing in any other form of communication.

Over the Phone

Because nonverbal signals are missing when you talk to someone on the telephone, it may be best to reserve this method for negotiating with people you know well. It is usually helpful, however, to supplement face-to-face discussions with telephone calls, just to confirm details or check progress.

In Writing

Face-to-face dialogue may be best, but written communication still plays a vital part in negotiations. Written briefs, summaries of proposed agreements, and minutes of meetings all have their role to play.

A disadvantage of written communication, however, is that your tone can easily be misinterpreted. For example, if the recipient has had a bad day, he may take offense at a message that you believed to be neutral in tone when you wrote it.

Nonnegotiable Items

The phrase "everything is negotiable" is not really true. In any deal you need to be clear that there may be certain restrictions. Some things cannot be offered within a negotiation, because negotiating around them at the outset will lead to problems later.

Standards

Such nonnegotiable items are often known as *standards*. Standards are objective criteria that bring independent measures of fairness, efficiency, or scientific merit to the process of the negotiation. Ideally, they should exist independently of the negotiating parties and be both legitimate and practical. It is vital that you recognize these standards prior to your negotiation, and it may be helpful to express them explicitly at the opening stages of the discussion.

Legal Requirements

A contract may have to follow a specific format to be legally binding. Sometimes certain licenses or permissions need to be obtained prior to agreement. For instance, a firm that prints T-shirts could not undertake to produce shirts with the image of a copyrighted character without obtaining the necessary permissions first from the copyright holder. A contract that required one of the parties involved to break the law would be invalid. For example, it would be illegal for a recruitment agency to enter into a contract that required them to discriminate against certain groups, where the law forbids it.

Health and Safety

Contravention of safety requirements could lead to prosecution or personal liability claims and make any insurance policy invalid. For example, a transport company could not offer delivery schedules that would involve their drivers working longer than the legal maximum shift. As another example, a toy company could not offer to cut costs by modifying their toys in a way that would compromise their ability to meet safety standards.

Overhead Costs

Some overhead, such as the costs of materials or labor (particularly if there are minimum wage agreements) may be unalterable. Time—for example, the staff time required to service a deal—is often forgotten as an overhead cost.

Professional Codes of Conduct

Many professions and industries have regulatory bodies that establish codes of conduct. Practices that break these codes could leave an individual or company open to prosecution or steep fines.

For instance, a hospital might agree to sell information on its use of drugs to a pharmaceutical firm carrying out market research, but it could not provide any patient details, as that would break confidentiality. To cite another example, a builder might have to refuse to install stairs or a bathroom in a particular space because it would not comply with building regulations.

Market-Value and Market-Rate

The perceived value of goods and services is often a matter of opinion and subject to change or the laws of supply and demand. However, in some cases, values may be determined by an external body that decides what is fair and reasonable and widely accepted within an industry. In such cases, it will become nonnegotiable.

Ethics

Very few people would be prepared to enter into an agreement that involves what they would consider improper practices. These could include breaking the law, betraying confidentiality, undercutting competitors, deception, endangering people's safety, or unfair treatment of employees.

The Escape Hatch

Having considered all of the critical analysis questions, you should consider the point at which you might decide that agreement will not be reached. When would the cost/benefit equation not make sense for you? What stipulations in the contract might make delivery very difficult or impossible?

It may seem negative to think about what would kill the deal, but preparing for it and having your "fall-back" position ready can help you to feel and behave more confidently.

Prepare a "Parting Shot"

If you reach deadlock in a negotiation, your main objective should be to exit with dignity. You should leave the other party with the message that, even though doing business is not possible at this time, you would be happy to try again at a later date.

Even if you feel that your time has been wasted, you will need to keep your cool; a display of temper or sulking is unlikely to create the desired effect. If the other party has behaved badly and you feel you never want to do business with them again, you should still treat them with respect. Remember that your behavior should reflect well on you and on your company.

Prepare a "Fall-Back" Position

As well as deciding what would be unacceptable, you should also have a plan in case the negotiation breaks down. If you are the customer, consider whether

- There are other suppliers who could meet your needs.
- You could strengthen your position by talking informally to them prior to the negotiation.

    If you are the supplier, consider whether

- There are other markets for your goods or services.
- You can recoup any investment made in researching or preparing your proposal by using your knowledge to approach potential customers in the same sector.

The Negotiation Checklist

Tony Simons
Thomas M. Tripp

Preparation increases your chance of success, whether in combat, sports, or negotiations. The well-prepared negotiator knows the playing field and the players, is seldom surprised, and can promptly capitalize on opportunities. This article offers a tool for use in effectively negotiating important transactions and disputes.

Making deals is a key part of being effective in business. Managers and executives negotiate constantly over issues as varied as hiring decisions and purchases, corporate resource allocations, and labor contracts. One could argue that the American system of government is based on an ongoing process of negotiation, which is sometimes successful and sometimes not.

The "negotiation checklist" that we present in this article is a systematic way to make sure you are well-prepared before you walk into your next negotiation. It is based on proven principles of negotiation that are taught at several of North America's top business schools. The techniques we describe apply whether you are getting ready for a labor negotiation, a negotiation with a supplier, or a negotiation with a customer. This checklist is not a formula for easy success in negotiations. Rather, it is a methodical approach that requires significant work. The amount of time and effort you spend answering the questions should depend on the importance of the negotiation and on the resources you have available. The payoff for your efforts emerges from the confidence and information that you gain from preparation.

The Negotiation Checklist

The negotiation checklist (in the accompanying box) is a guide for thinking about an important, upcoming negotiation. The pages that follow describe and explain the items on the list.

A. About You

1. What Is Your Overall Goal? Start with the big picture. What basic need will an agreement address? Why are you talking to this person or this company? What do you hope to accomplish? Understanding your main goal helps put all the other aspects of the negotiation into perspective. Most people begin and end their negotiation planning by determining their overall goal. We suggest that it is just the beginning.

Negotiation Checklist: A systematic way to ensure you are well-prepared before your next negotiation

☑ *Item accomplished*

A. About You

❑ 1. What is your overall goal?

❑ 2. What are the issues?

❑ 3. How important is each issue to you?

Develop a scoring system for evaluating offers:

    ❑ (*a*) List all of the issues of importance from step 2.

    ❑ (*b*) Rank-order all of the issues.

    ❑ (*c*) Assign points to all the issues (assign weighted values based on a total of 100 points).

    ❑ (*d*) List the range of possible settlements for each issue. Your assessments of realistic, low, and high expectations should be grounded in industry norms and your best-case expectation.

    ❑ (*e*) Assign points to the possible outcomes that you identified for each issue.

    ❑ (*f*) Double-check the accuracy of your scoring system.

    ❑ (*g*) Use the scoring system to evaluate any offer that is on the table.

❑ 4. What is your "best alternative to a negotiated agreement" (BATNA)?

❑ 5. What is your resistance point (i.e., the worst agreement you are willing to accept before ending negotiations)? If your BATNA is vague, consider identifying the minimum terms you can possibly accept and beyond which you must recess to gather more information.

B. About the Other Side

❑ 1. How important is each issue to them (plus any new issues they added)?

❑ 2. What is their best alternative to negotiated agreement?

❑ 3. What is their resistance point?

❑ 4. Based on questions B.1, B.2, and B.3, what is your target?

C. The Situation

❑ 1. What deadlines exist? Who is more impatient?

❑ 2. What fairness norms or reference points apply?

❑ 3. What topics or questions do you want to avoid? How will you respond if they ask anyway?

D. The Relationship between the Parties

❑ 1. Will negotiations be repetitive? If so, what are the future consequences of each strategy, tactic, or action you are considering?

❑ 2. ❑ (*a*) Can you trust the other party? What do you know about them?

    ❑ (*b*) Does the other party trust you?

❑ 3. What do you know of the other party's styles and tactics?

❑ 4. What are the limits to the other party's authority?

❑ 5. Consult in advance with the other party about the agenda.

2. What Are The Issues?   What specific issues must be negotiated for the final outcome or agreement to meet your overall goal? For example, if the overall goal is to book a successful convention, what assurances, services, and constraints will be involved? Price may be an obvious component, but it is worthwhile to consider other items, too—items that might make the agreement much more attractive both to yourself and to the other side. Delivery schedules, duration of contract, product or service upgrades, cancellation clauses, contingency plans, transportation services, complimentary room nights, and many other options all have some value to those negotiating a contract. Such side issues may be researched and introduced as part of a food contract, conference booking, or union contract that you are preparing to negotiate.

Consider also whether any of the issues you have considered might be broken down into multiple components or subissues. For the conference-booking negotiation, for example, you might normally consider the room-block guarantee as a single item (i.e., so many rooms reserved until such-and-such a date). In fact, breaking the room reservations down by percentages and multiple deadlines (e.g., 50 percent by one date, 75 percent by another date) might open avenues for mutually beneficial arrangements.

You should anticipate as many issues as possible for the negotiation. By doing so, you will be better informed and thus feel comfortable and confident when negotiating. Also, the more issues you can introduce, the more likely it becomes that creative solutions will arise, as those are often built by packaging or trading off multiple issues. Creative solutions often make it easier to discover an agreement that both parties like.

By adding items to the negotiations agenda, you increase your chance of discovering some issues that you value more than the other party, and discovering other issues that the other party values more than you. Trading off such differently valued issues dramatically increases the value of the agreement to you without costing the other party. Moreover, if you know what issues the other party highly values that you value less, you can use those issues to get concessions on issues that are important to you.

Imagine that you are a food and beverage director of a hotel seeking a dry-goods supplier and that you have written a request for bids from potential vendors. You have considered your storage capacity and specified every-other-week delivery in your request for bids. Now suppose you receive a bid from Alpha Dry Goods, which has another customer in town to whom they deliver once every three weeks. Alpha's quote for biweekly delivery might be mediocre, but it turns out that they could save you substantial money on triweekly delivery. They could save you so much money, in fact, that you consider changing your storage arrangement to accommodate their every-three-weeks delivery schedule. If you had been unwilling to negotiate the delivery schedule, you might never have discovered that opportunity. By adding delivery schedule to the agenda, you were able to discover an issue that improved the business potential for both parties. In this example, you are able to secure a lower overall price in return for a concession on delivery schedule.

In general, the more issues you can put on the table (within reason), the better off you are.[1]

Another reason to consider and discuss many issues in a negotiation is that it minimizes the chance of misunderstandings in the final contract. For any issue that is not discussed, the parties risk the possibility of making different assumptions. For example, the "standard frills" that accompany a banquet may not be known by the person purchasing the banquet.

Once you agree that it's a good idea to discuss many issues, how should you determine how many and which ones? For starters, check with your executive committee or association members. Draw also on outside resources. For example, call some friends and colleagues who have conducted similar negotiations and ask them about what issues they put on the table. Library research and obtaining experts' opinions may be helpful, too. Lawyers can be a marvelous source of ideas about which issues to place on the table, especially for a labor negotiation. Be prepared to include all reasonable and relevant issues that are important to you, even if they are not important to the other party.

You can also call the people with whom you plan to negotiate to ask them what issues they expect to discuss and to share your plans. This kind of conversation will begin the negotiation as a cooperative process and should minimize any delays caused by either negotiator's needing to collect additional information, to get authority, or to figure out the value of issues they had not previously considered. As we discuss later, surprise is usually not conducive to effective negotiations.

3. *How Important Is Each Issue To You?* Now that you have listed all the different issues that might be negotiated, you need to develop as precise a picture as possible of their relative importance. Which issues are most important to you and which are not particularly important? Knowing the answer to that question will help you answer the next: On which issues should you stand firm and on which issues can you afford to concede? In other words, what issues might you be willing to trade away?

Setting such priorities can be a complex task. To deal with the complexity of rating the importance of individual issues, we suggest you develop a system to keep track of all the issues without losing sight of the big picture. Many different kinds of systems are possible. The key requirement is that you list and prioritize issues so that no issue is left out when you structure and compare potential agreements. The system you use must allow you to readily determine how well each possible agreement addresses every issue. We offer one such scoring system for your use, as described next.[2]

We suggest developing a table that lists every issue in the negotiation. For each issue the table should list the possible range of settlements.[3] You will then assign points to each issue to reflect its relative priority and to every possible settlement of each issue to reflect the relative desirability of resolving the issue in that way. Such a table allows you to assess the value of any proposed agreement by adding up the points it generates. You can then accurately and quickly determine which of several complex agreements you prefer. Moreover, it can help you keep the big picture in mind as you discuss the details of your agreement. We describe additional benefits in the next few pages.

The first part of Exhibit 1 shows an example of a scoring system that a conference organizer might use to negotiate with a hotel representative. In that example, the issues on the negotiation table are the duration of the room-block reservation, the room rate to be charged, the number of complimentary rooms to be provided, and the late-cancellation policy.[4] The maximum number of points possible here is 100. (If the conference organizer gets 100 percent of what she wants, then she gets 100 points; if she gets none of the issues that are important to her, then she gets 0 points.) The organizer has said that

EXHIBIT 1 | Creating a Scoring System

The example shown is a scoring system such as a conference organizer might use.

Issue 1: *Block Reservation*

Maximum value: *40 points*

Rooms reserved until 7 days before conference	40 pts.
Rooms reserved until 10 days before conference	37 pts.
Rooms reserved until 14 days before conference	35 pts.
Rooms reserved until 21 days before conference	15 pts.
Rooms reserved until 30 days before conference	5 pts.
Rooms reserved until 31 days before conference	0 pts.

Issue 2: *Room Rate*

Maximum value: *25 points*

$95 per person single, $70 per person double	25 pts.
$105 per person single, $80 per person double	20 pts.
$115 per person single, $90 per person double	15 pts.
$125 per person single, $100 per person double	10 pts.
$135 per person single, $100 per person double	5 pts.
$145 per person single, $110 per person double	0 pts.

Issue 3: *Number of Complimentary Room Nights*

Maximum value: *20 points*

3 room nights per 100 booked	20 pts.
2 room nights per 100 booked	15 pts.
1 room night per 75 booked	10 pts.
1 room night per 100 booked	5 pts.
1 room night per 150 booked	0 pts.

Exhibit explanation: *Develop a scoring system for evaluating offers.*

To construct your own scoring system, we recommend that you use the following steps:

(a) List all issues of importance for the negotiation, from step 2 in the checklist.

(b) Rank-order all issues according to their value to you. Which is the most important? Next? Last?

(c) Assign points to the issues. The highest-ranked issue gets the most points and the lowest-ranked issue gets the fewest points. The sum of maximum points across all issues should be 100. The purpose of this step is to improve upon the simple rank ordering in step *b* by reflecting the size of the difference between adjacently ranked issues (i.e., how much more important the first issue is than the second, the second issue than the third, and so forth). At 40 points, room-block reservation is worth almost twice as much as the next most important issue, room rate. The number of complimentary rooms and room-cancellation policy are slightly less important than room rate.

(d) List the range of possible settlements for each issue. Identify these ranges using industry or local norms or your best assessments of realistic, high, and low expectations. It may be the case that the longest block-reservation policy in the industry is 30 days. This figure establishes a realistic low boundary. Since a seven-day-out guarantee for block reservation is possible but rare, it establishes a challenging high boundary to which one can aspire.

Issue 4: *Late Cancellations*

Maximum value: *15 points*

No penalty up to 14 days before conference	15 pts.
No penalty up to 18 days before conference	9 pts.
No penalty up to 22 days before conference	3 pts.
No penalty up to 26 days before conference	0 pts.

(e) Assign points to the possible outcomes that you identified for each issue. Give the maximum number of points to your preferred settlement for that issue, and assign zero points to any settlement that is least acceptable. Now rank and assign points to the possible settlements in between the best and the worst. Consider that the point values might increase dramatically between certain adjacent pairs of settlements in the range, or might just barely increase. The most important thing to remember about assigning points is that the assignment should reflect what is important to you.

(f) Double-check your scoring system. In completing steps *a* through *e* you undoubtedly will make a few capricious choices based on "gut feeling." For example, you may be so focused on the room-block issue that the points assigned to the other issues could be changed by five points either way without affecting your stance. The point is to make sure your scoring system accurately reflects the important issues and highlights the critical plateaus. To check your numbers, compose three to five completely different hypothetical agreements. Each agreement should emphasize different issues. For example, one agreement might offer a cheap room rate but a short no-penalty cancellation period, while another agreement offers high room rates but a long no-penalty cancellation period. Compare the different agreements on the basis of points and intuitive value. The prospective agreement that has the best "gut feel" should also have the most points. If not, you need to tinker with the values you assigned in steps *a* through *e* or reconsider your priorities.

(g) Use the scoring system to assess any offer that is on the table. You should work toward obtaining the highest-scoring agreement that the other party allows.

keeping the specially priced block of rooms available to last-minute registrants up until the week before the conference is very important. Room rate is somewhat less critical, she says, but is still important. Complimentary rooms and the cancellation policy are also valued by her, but are less weighty than are the first two. Note that it is not critical for all the increments within an issue to be valued equally. The jump from a 21-day-out block reservation to a 14-day-out reservation, for example, is worth 20 points to the conference organizer, while the four-day jump from 14 days to 10 days is worth only two points. Such a difference in value carries an important message. The organizer is saying that it is *very* important to have at least a 14-day-out block reservation, and that any improvement over that would be nice but is not critical.

Constructing a detailed and accurate scoring system can mean considerable work (see the second column of Exhibit 1). However, the task can be worth the effort for several reasons. First, it allows you to compare any package of settlements that may make up an agreement. With large numbers of issues, it quickly becomes difficult to compare different packages without some kind of scoring system.

Second, having a scoring system can keep you analytically focused while keeping your emotions in check. If you force yourself to evaluate each proposal using a predetermined scoring system, you are less likely to lose sight of your original interest during the heat of the actual negotiations. Resist the temptation to revise your scoring system in midnegotiation.[5]

Third, a scoring system is a useful communication tool that gives you a format for soliciting detailed information about the priorities and goals of your boss, your company, or your constituency. Building an accurate scoring system can become the topic of prenegotiation meetings that will improve your chances of pleasing the people you represent.

4. What Is Your BATNA?   Before you begin a negotiation, you need to have a backup plan in case you fail to reach an agreement with the other party. Negotiation scholars refer to this backup plan as the Best Alternative to a Negotiated Agreement, or BATNA for short. Are you, for instance, negotiating with the only supplier in town, or do you already have several attractive bids in your pocket? Alternatives make all the difference.

Each side's BATNA is a key factor in determining negotiation power. The better your BATNA, the better an offer the other party must make to interest you in reaching an agreement. Your BATNA—what you get if you leave the table without an agreement—determines your willingness to accept an impasse, which in turn tells you how hard you can press for a favorable agreement. You can negotiate hard for a job if you already have a few offers in your pocket. The better your BATNA, the more you can demand.

Having a clear BATNA helps protect you from accepting a deal that you would be better off not taking. Often people get caught up in the negotiation process and accept a contract they should have rejected. Knowing your BATNA can keep you from accepting an agreement that would make you worse off than you were before you started negotiating.

Having identified your BATNA, calculate its value based on the scoring system you developed for step 3. That is, if the other party were to make an offer that was identical to your BATNA, how many points would that offer achieve under your scoring system? Use that score as a reference point to identify those agreements that are worth less to you than your BATNA.

Even if it is difficult to assign a score to your BATNA because it is qualitatively different from the deal under negotiation or because it involves risk or uncertainty, you should nevertheless assign it a rough score for comparison purposes.

5. *What Is Your Resistance Point?*   Your resistance point is the worst agreement you are willing to accept before ending negotiations and resorting to your BATNA. The resistance point is the point at which you decide to walk away from the table for good, and the BATNA is where you're headed when you take that walk.

You should choose your resistance point based primarily on how good your BATNA is. If your BATNA is great, you shouldn't accept anything less than a great offer; if your BATNA is poor, you may have to be willing to accept a meager final offer. Don't forget to factor into your resistance point the switching cost and the risk of the unknown that you would be taking if your BATNA involves changing suppliers.

To illustrate the effect of switching costs, put yourself in the "buying" position of the conference organizer described in Exhibit 1. Suppose the hotel you used last year has already offered to book your conference for $100 a night single occupancy, with a 10-day-out block-reservation clause. If another hotel wants your business, you need to determine your BATNA and decide the margin by which the new hotel must beat the existing agreement—say, five dollars a night—to justify the risk of switching. Conversely, if you are the hotel sales representative in this deal, you have to determine the risks you accept for this new business—namely, that the association might fail to deliver the promised room-nights and the opportunity cost of displacing any existing business. Your BATNA as a hotel sales representative is the probability of your booking the rooms that the conference would otherwise occupy at a given rate, adjusted by the effort (labor and expenses) it will take to book them.

The resistance point is meant to encompass all the issues at the same time rather than each issue independently. If you set a resistance point for each issue under consideration, you sacrifice your strategic flexibility. Your BATNA might include a room rate of, say, $100 a night. If you set a resistance point for room rate, rather than for the agreement as a whole, then you might walk away from what is, in fact, an attractive offer—for example, a $105 per night rate that includes more amenities and a better booking policy than your BATNA. So there should be just one resistance point and not a collection of them. The resistance point should be set just slightly better than your BATNA. Numerically, it will be the sum of the points from your scoring system that represents your minimum requirements for all the issues being negotiated.

Being aware of the resistance point is useful in negotiations. It converts a good BATNA into a powerful negotiating stance. Unless you have previously decided how far you can be pushed, you are vulnerable to being pushed below your BATNA, and thereby may accept an agreement that is worse for you than no agreement at all. The more precise your resistance point, the better.

It may seem awkward to apply a precise resistance point, particularly if your BATNA is vague or not strong. In such circumstances, you might consider setting a "tripwire" or a temporary resistance point. Set it slightly above your actual resistance point; the tripwire then gives you the chance to suspend negotiations for further consultation with your team. For example, imagine that you are booking the conference as discussed earlier. Your members have expressed a slight preference for exploring new places, and so you are negotiating with a new hotel. You are willing to pay more for a new location, but you are not sure exactly how much more your membership will accept. You know that members will balk at an exorbitant room rate. Your BATNA is to stay at the same hotel as last year and face an uncertain amount of members' disappointment. To deal with the uncertainty, you can set a tripwire. If you are comfortable signing a contract that entails a $10-a-night increase, but if you are unable to secure a rate that low or better, the tripwire tells you that you should check with your membership before you make a commitment. You have, in effect, built a "safety zone" around an uncertain BATNA.

B. About the Other Side

Good negotiators seek to understand the other party's needs and limits almost as well as they know their own. Such negotiators might be able to accomplish this understanding before the negotiations begin, or early in the negotiation process. Obviously, the final agreement will reflect not only your own preferences and BATNA, but the other party's as well. Thus it is useful to ask the same questions about the other party as you ask about yourself.

1. How Important Is Each Issue to Them (Plus Any New Issues They Added)?
Consider and attempt to estimate the other party's priorities. What trade-offs can you offer that enhance the agreement's value for both sides, or that might be neutral for the other side but a boon for you? If your counterpart had a scoring system like yours, what do you think it would look like? Call people who might have information or insight into the other party's priorities. Build a scoring system like your own that estimates their priorities, and use it to design some potential trade-offs.

As the negotiation proceeds, try to test, correct, and complete your picture of the other party's scoring system. Try to fill out your understanding of what that scoring system might look like if one existed. Gather more information during the negotiations by asking direct questions about priorities, and also by judging the other negotiator's responses to your different offers and proposed trade-offs.

You might also want to probe whether there are any issues about which the other side will completely refuse to negotiate. Such a refusal might simply be a ploy, or it might be a genuine constraint on the way it does business.

2. What Is the Other Side's BATNA?   What are your counterpart's alternatives to doing business with you? How much do you think she or he values those alternatives? How badly does this company want to do business with you? Realize that the other party will probably accept an agreement only if it improves on her or his BATNA.

The other side's BATNA contains key information about how far you can push those negotiators before they walk away. If you are selling, the buyers' BATNA should determine the maximum price they would be willing to pay for your services or product. If you are buying, it should determine the lowest price at which they will sell. If you are booking a hotel conference in Hawaii in December, the hotel representative, who has a waiting list of customers, has a much stronger BATNA than the same representative has in July. If you are absolutely certain of the other side's BATNA, and if you propose an agreement that is just a little more attractive than the other side's BATNA, then those negotiators might accept your proposal.

3. What Is the Other Side's Resistance Point, If Any?   Given your assessment of the other party's BATNA, you can estimate the least favorable deal for which the other party might settle. We say "might" because the other party may not have considered his or her resistance point. We have found, though, that it is wise to assume the other party is well prepared. If you know the other party's resistance point, as noted earlier, you can push for an agreement that barely exceeds it. This kind of lowball deal is often better for you than an "equitable" deal, though not always.

If you are the type of negotiator who prefers amiable negotiation tactics over lowballing, then you still may want to know the other side's resistance point for two reasons. First, the other party may try to lowball you. Knowing the party's resistance point will give you the information and confidence to counter a lowball tactic. Second, many negotiators consider a fair deal to be one that falls halfway between the two parties' resistance points. To find the halfway point, you need to know both resistance points. Since experienced negotiators consider their true resistance point to be confidential information, you will most likely have to make a best guess about how far you can push the other party before seriously risking impasse or generating ill will.

Openly asking for the other party's resistance point carries risks. The other party might lie and therefore be forced to take an uncompromising stance to avoid disclosing that misrepresentation. Or if the other party honestly reveals his or her resistance point to you, that negotiator may expect you to reveal your resistance point, too. At this point, you have two choices. One, you reveal your resistance point and open yourself to being lowballed or, at best, to being offered an agreement that reaches no farther than the halfway point between the two resistance points. Two, if you don't reveal your resistance point, you may violate the norm of reciprocity.

4. What Is Your Target?   You set your target based on what you know about the other side. By this point, you should know what is the least favorable agreement that you will accept, and you have estimated the other side's least favorable, acceptable agreement. Now consider the most favorable agreement for you. This is your upper limit—the top of your range. If you focus primarily on your resistance point, which is the bottom of your range, you are unlikely to secure an agreement that is far superior to that resistance point.

To properly set your target, you must consider the bargaining zone, and to do that you have to sum up the other side's situation. The bargaining zone is the range between the two parties' resistance points, comprising the range of mutually acceptable agreements.

C. The Situation

By this point you have drawn up a fairly accurate picture of the issues and the priorities that constitute the negotiations. Here are some additional contextual factors to consider to help you maximize your advantages and minimize your risk of making mistakes.

1. *What Deadlines Exist? Who Is More Impatient?* The negotiator who feels a greater sense of urgency will often make rapid concessions in an effort to secure a deal quickly. Many Western cultures have a quick-paced approach to negotiations. When paired with negotiators from cultures that negotiate deliberately (e.g., Japan, India), quick negotiators risk getting unfavorable agreements. A good way to slow down your pace is to avoid negotiating under a close deadline. Flexibility with regard to time can be a negotiating strength.

2. *What Fairness Norms or Reference Points Apply?* Negotiations often involve a discussion of what might constitute a "fair deal." In fact, some experts recommend the approach of always negotiating over the "principle" or standard that you will use to assess fairness before getting down to details and numbers. The abstract discussion may be less threatening or emotionally charged than the details, and may result in a more cooperative tone and outcome for the negotiation.

Recognize, however, that there are many valid ways to determine fairness, and each negotiator will often choose the fairness norm that most favors his or her position. Both parties know that the other is doing this; just the same, each party expects the other to justify an offer as fair by showing how an offer complies with some fairness norm. Because offers that are unaccompanied by a fairness argument will rarely be accepted, you should consider alternative norms of fairness for each negotiation. Ask yourself, which ones justify your demands and which ones defeat them? Which ones best reflect your conscience?

An associate of one of the authors, for example, faced a salary negotiation upon considering a new job. The potential employer stated an intent to pay "market value" and thought it fair to define market value as the salary that other starting local faculty members were paid. The job seeker, on the other hand, judged that as unfair and argued that market value should be defined as the salary paid to starting management faculty members at comparable nationally ranked universities. The candidate thereby successfully redefined "market value" by describing the salaries drawn by other graduates of his program who took management faculty jobs. Since the employer had already agreed to pay market value, the employer found itself making concessions to do the fair thing of acting consistently with its own stated principles.

That example shows how a negotiation often hinges on a discussion of fairness. Prepare for each negotiation by considering alternative norms of fairness.

3. *What Topics or Questions Do You Want to Avoid? How Will You Respond If the Other Side Asks Anyway?* You might find yourself in a position where there is something that you do not want the other negotiator to know. Your BATNA may be weak, for instance. Good negotiators plan in advance how to respond to questions they do not want to answer. Prepare an answer that is in no way dishonest but does not expose your weaknesses. Preparation means rehearsing your answer until you can deliver it smoothly, just as if you were practicing for a play. If you do not prepare and practice your answers to dreaded questions, then you risk an awkward pause or gesture that will tip off the other negotiator to a potential weakness. Awkward gestures might even cause the other party to believe you are lying when you are not. We suggest preparation so that you avoid looking like a liar when you tell the truth but choose not to reveal confidential information. If there are things you do not want to discuss, prepare your deflections in advance and polish them until they are seamless.

D. The Relationship between the Parties

1. Are the Negotiations Part of a Continuing Series? If So, What Are the Future Consequences of Each Strategy, Tactic, or Action You Are Considering?   Consider whether you expect or want to continue a business relationship with the party across the table. If the answer is yes, then you probably want to be careful about using negotiation tactics that the other side might perceive as bullying, insulting, or manipulative. Extracting those last few additional concessions out of the other party is usually not worth the loss of goodwill.

The fact that you plan to do business with the other party in the future offers a few freedoms as well as restrictions. The trust and goodwill that you develop in the current deal may have a payoff for the next time. Also, if you can safely assume that the other party wants a relationship with you, then you can worry less about them negotiating in bad faith. Trust facilitates successful negotiations much more than does paranoia.

2. Can You Trust the Other Party? What Do You Know About Them?   Call around to inquire how this company conducts negotiation. How much you trust the other party will influence your negotiation style. To find the trade-offs and creative solutions that ensure that everyone gets a fair deal, you have to share information about your needs and priorities. Unfortunately, though, sharing your information makes you vulnerable to an unscrupulous negotiator across the table. Untrustworthy opponents can ascertain your priorities before you know theirs and use this knowledge to gain maximum concessions from you. They might also lie about their own priorities.

The extent to which you trust the other party should determine your approach to sharing and collecting information. A series of small information "trades" is a good way to build mutual trust without opening either side to exploitation. A second approach to gathering data when you do not trust or know the other party well is to offer multiple proposals and see which ones the other side prefers. Be careful in this approach, however, as you must be willing to live with all the proposals you offer. It is considered a breach of faith if you propose an offer (for any reason) but have no intention of carrying through with the deal even if the other party says OK.

If you already know and trust the other party, your task is much easier. In such cases negotiations can involve an extensive exchange of information about interests and priorities.

3. What Do You Know of the Other Party's Styles and Tactics?   Different negotiators have different personal or cultural preferences. You are likely to secure the best deal and have the most positive interaction if you learn about their style in advance and try to accommodate it.

We have observed three types of negotiators. One type prefers to ease into the issue at hand after some personal contact. Once that negotiator is at ease with you as a person, she or he will be comfortable revealing information afterward.

Another type of negotiator prefers a direct approach and eschews disclosure and creative problem solving. Such a negotiator requires a competitive approach to the interaction.

The third type of negotiator enters the process having carefully computed and decided what is the best deal—and makes that offer up front and announces that it is nonnegotiable. Having already made up his or her mind about what the agreement must be, this negotiator will likely become impatient and annoyed at any attempt at give-and-take. If you know that the person you face prefers to do business this way, recognize that it is probably not a ploy. Simply assess the offer to see if it beats your BATNA. If it does, take it. If it does not, then politely refuse.

Some negotiators use either of two common gambits. One is to return from a break with a request for just one more concession that can seal the deal. This tactic, known as "taking a second bite of the apple," is common among car dealers. The appropriate response is to suggest that if the other party would like to reopen negotiations, you are willing to reopen them, too—but on all the issues, not just one.

"Good cop, bad cop" is a tactic whereby the person with whom you negotiate plays the role of "wanting" to meet all your needs, but "demands" are being made by someone who is higher up and usually absent from the actual negotiation (e.g., the sales manager). One response to this approach is to take a break to reassess the other side's stance compared to your tripwire. Another is to insist on speaking directly with the final decision maker.

4. What Are the Limits to the Other Party's Authority?   Establish early the level of authority held by your counterpart. Most negotiators, unless they are the CEOs of their companies, are authorized to negotiate only certain specified issues and within certain ranges. Determine whether you are negotiating with the right person, or whether far more latitude in generating resolutions might be available if you negotiated with someone else.

5. Consult in Advance with the Other Party about the Agenda.   As we stated earlier, consider calling the other party beforehand to share what issues you plan to discuss and to ask what issues the other party might raise. In general, holding back information is counterproductive, and introducing unexpected issues generally delays the proceedings.

Although good negotiators often get creative in their approach to the issues, this creativity must be well grounded in an understanding of the issues and of both parties' priorities. A well-prepared negotiator has considered these factors in depth, and has also considered the past and future context of the business relationship between the parties. It has been said that no plan survives contact with the enemy—but it remains true that the shrewd general will have memorized the terrain and analyzed the strengths and weaknesses of both sides before an engagement. Fortune favors the prepared mind.

Endnotes

1. There is some risk of overwhelming oneself—and one's negotiation partner—with too many issues. We suggest a combination of moderation in adding issues with an effective system of note taking and organization.

2. Any method that serves as a mnemonic device to track and evaluate multiple issues and deals may work. The one we describe is one that has received much attention in negotiation courses and research. See D. A. Lax and J. K. Sebenius, *The Manager as Negotiator* (New York: Free Press, 1986).

3. Several negotiation sessions may take place before you can identify all the issues and the range of possible resolutions for those issues. However, we recommend that you list in advance as many issues as you know about and then update the table between negotiation sessions to include additional issues and settlements.

4. Note that we have simplified the issues of such a negotiation for expository purposes. Additional issues might include cancellation clauses, airport transportation, continental breakfasts, function space, additional events or amenities, and so on.

5. In the interest of maintaining your original goals, do not adjust your scoring system while in the middle of discussion with the other party. During negotiations you may hear things that suggest your original preferences and priorities may be in error. Such new information might be valid, or it might simply be the other negotiator's effort to mislead you. There are a bad way and a good way to deal with the uncertainty such rhetoric may cause you. The bad way is to lose confidence in the accuracy of your scoring system, throw it out, and continue to negotiate. The good way is to take a break and verify the information as both true and relevant to your preferences. If it is, during that break adjust your scoring system to reflect the new information and restart negotiations with the new scoring system.

Reading 1.7

Negotiation Techniques: How to Keep Br'er Rabbit Out of the Brier Patch

Charles B. Craver

Practicing lawyers negotiate constantly—with their partners, associates, legal assistants, and secretaries, with prospective clients and actual clients, and with opposing parties on behalf of clients. Although practitioners tend to use their negotiation skills more often than their other lawyering talents, few have had formal education about the negotiation process.

The process consists of three formal phases:

- The information phase, where each party endeavors to learn as much about the other side's circumstances and objectives as possible.

- The competitive phase, where negotiators try to obtain beneficial terms for their respective clients.

- The cooperative phase, where if multiple-item transactions are involved, parties may often enhance their joint interests.

The Information Phase

The focus of this phase is always on the knowledge and desires of the opposing party. It is initially helpful to employ general, information-seeking questions instead of those that may be answered with a yes or no. Expansive interrogatories are likely to induce the other party to speak. The more that party talks, the more he is likely to divulge.

Where negotiations have effectively used open-ended questions to induce the other party to disclose its opening position and its general legal and factual assumptions, they should not hesitate to resort to specific inquiries to confirm suspected details. They can do this by asking the other side about each element of its perceived position. What exactly does that party hope to obtain, and why? What are the underlying motivational factors influencing that side's articulated demands?

Negotiators must try to learn as much as possible about the opposing side's range of potential and actual choices, its preferences and their intensity, its planned strategy, and its strengths and weaknesses. Bargainers need to be aware that the opponent's perception of a situation may be more favorable to their own than they anticipated. Even the most proficient negotiators tend to overstate their side's weaknesses and overestimate the opposing party's strengths. Only through patient probing of their adversary's circumstances can they hope to obtain an accurate assessment.

The order in which parties present their initial demands can be informative. Some negotiators begin with their most important topics in an effort to produce an expeditious resolution of those issues. They are anxiety-prone, risk-averse advocates who wish to diminish the tension associated with the uncertainty inherent in the negotiation process.

Source: Reprinted with permission of TRIAL (June 1988). Copyright The Association of Trial Lawyers of America.

They believe they can significantly decrease their fear of not being able to settle by achieving expeditious progress on their primary topics. Unfortunately they fail to appreciate that this approach may enhance the possibility of a counterproductive impasse. If their principal objectives correspond to those of their adversary, this presentation sequence is likely to cause an immediate clash of wills.

Other negotiators prefer to begin bargaining with the less significant subjects, hoping to make rapid progress on these items. This approach is likely to develop a cooperative atmosphere that will facilitate compromise when the more disputed subjects are explored.

Negotiators must decide ahead of time what information they are willing to disclose and what information they must disclose if the transaction is going to be fruitful. Critical information should not always be directly provided. If negotiators voluntarily apprise the other side of important circumstances, they may appear self-serving and be accorded little weight. If, however, they slowly disclose such information in response to opponent questions, what they divulge will usually be accorded greater credibility.

Where an adversary asks about sensitive matters, blocking techniques may be used to minimize unnecessary disclosure. Such techniques should be planned in advance and should be varied to keep the opposing party off balance. A participant who does not wish to answer a question might ignore it, and the other side might go on to some other area.

Where a compound question is asked, a negotiator may respond to the beneficial part of it. Skilled negotiators may misconstrue a delicate inquiry and then answer the misconstrued formulation; they may respond to a specific question with general information or to a general inquiry with a narrow response. On occasion, negotiators may handle a difficult question with a question of their own. For example, if one party asks whether the other is authorized to offer a certain sum, that side may ask about the first party's willingness to accept such a figure.

Many negotiators make the mistake of focusing entirely on their opponents' stated positions. They assume that such statements accurately reflect the desires of the other side. Making this assumption may preclude the exploration of options that might prove mutually beneficial. It helps to go behind stated positions to try to ascertain the underlying needs and interests generating these positions. If negotiators understand what the other party really wants to achieve, they can often suggest alternatives that can satisfy both sides sufficiently to produce an accord.

The Competitive Phase

Once the information phase ends, the focus usually changes from what the opposing party hopes to achieve to what each negotiator must get for his client. Negotiators no longer ask questions about each other's circumstances; they articulate their own side's demands.

"Principled" Offers and Concessions

Negotiators should develop a rational basis for each item included in their opening positions. This provides the other party with some understanding of the reasons underlying their demands, and it helps to provide the person making those demands with confidence in the positions. Successful negotiators establish high, but rational, objectives and explain their entitlement to these goals.

When negotiators need to change their position, they should use "principled" concessions. They need to provide opponents with a rational explanation for modifications of their position.

For example, a lawyer demanding $100,000 for an injured plaintiff might indicate willingness to accept $90,000 by saying that there is a 10 percent chance that the plaintiff might lose at trial or a good probability that the jury in a comparative-negligence jurisdiction will find that the plaintiff was 10 percent negligent. This lets the other party know why the change is being made, and it helps to keep the person at the $90,000 level until he is ready to use a "principled" concession to further reduce the demand.

Argument

The power-bargaining tactic lawyers use most often involves legal and nonlegal argument. Factual and legal arguments are advanced. Public policy may be invoked in appropriate situations. Emotional appeals may be effective in some circumstances. If an argument is to be persuasive, it must be presented objectively.

Effective arguments should be presented in a comprehensive, rather than a conclusionary, fashion. Factual and legal information should be disclosed with appropriate detail. Influential statements must be insightful and carefully articulated. They must not be fully comprehended, but they must go beyond what is expected.

Contentions that do not surprise the receiving parties will rarely undermine their confidence in their preconceived position. But assertions that raise issues opponents have not previously considered will likely induce them to recognize the need to reassess their perceptions.

Threats and Promises

Almost all legal negotiations involve use of overt or at least implicit threats. Threats show recalcitrant parties that the cost of disagreeing with offers will transcend the cost of acquiescence. Some negotiators try to avoid use of formal "threats," preferring less challenging "warnings." These negotiators simply caution opponents about the consequences of their unwillingness to accept a mutual resolution.

If threats are to be effective, they must be believable. A credible threat is one that is reasonably proportional to the action it is intended to deter—seemingly insignificant threats tend to be ignored, while large ones tend to be dismissed. Negotiators should never issue threats unless they are prepared to carry them out, since their failure to do so will undermine their credibility.

Instead of using negative threats that indicate what consequences will result if the opposing party does not alter its position, negotiators should consider affirmative promises that indicate their willingness to change their position simultaneously with the other party. The classic affirmative promise—the "split-the-difference" approach—has been used by most negotiators to conclude a transaction. One side promises to move halfway if only the other side will do the same.

Affirmative promises are more effective than negative threats at inducing position changes, since the first indicates that the requested position change will be reciprocated. A negative threat merely suggests dire consequences if the other side does not alter its position. They are more of an affront to an opponent than affirmative promises, and, as a result, are more disruptive of the negotiation process.

Silence and Patience

Many negotiators fear silence, since they are afraid that they will lose control of the transaction if they stop talking. The more they talk, the more information they disclose and the more concessions they make. When their opponents remain silent, such negotiators often become even more talkative.

When negotiators have something important to say, they should say it and then keep quiet. A short comment accentuates the importance of what they are saying and provides the other party with the chance to absorb what was said. This rule is crucial when an offer or concession is being made. Once such information has been disclosed, it is time for the other side to respond.

Patience can be used effectively with silence. Where the other negotiator does not readily reply to critical representations, he should be given sufficient time to respond. If it is his turn to speak, the first party should wait silently for him to comment. If the first party feels awkward, he should look at his notes. This behavior shows the silent party that a response will be required before further discussion.

Limited Authority

Many advocates like to indicate during the preliminary stages that they do not have final authority from their client about the matter in dispute. They use this technique to reserve the right to check with the client before any tentative agreement can bind their side.

The advantage of a limited-authority approach—whether actual or fabricated—is that it permits the party using it to obtain a psychological commitment to settlement from opponents authorized to make binding commitments. The unbound bargainers can then seek beneficial modifications of the negotiated terms based on "unexpected" client demands. Since their opponents do not want to let such seemingly insignificant items negate the success achieved during the prior negotiations, they often accept the alterations.

Bargainers who meet opponents who initially say they lack the authority to bind their clients may find it advantageous to say that they also lack final authority. This will permit them to "check" with their own absent principal before making any final commitment.

A few unscrupulous negotiators will agree to a final accord with what appears to be complete authority. They later approach their opponent with apparent embarrassment and explain that they did not really have this authority. They say that their principal will require one or two modifications before accepting the other terms of the agreement. Since the unsuspecting opponent and his client are now committed to a final settlement, they agree to the concessions.

Negotiators who suspect that an adversary might use this technique may wish to select—at the apparent conclusion of their transaction—the one or two items they would most like to have modified in their favor. When their opponent requests changes, they can indicate how relieved they are about this, because their own client is dissatisfied. Then they can offer to exchange their items for those their adversary seeks. It is fascinating to see how quickly the opponent will now insist on honoring the initial accord.

The limited-authority situation must be distinguished from the one where an opponent begins a negotiation with no authority. This adversary hopes to get several concessions as a prerequisite to negotiations with a negotiator with real authority.

Negotiators should avoid dealing with a no-authority person, since he is trying to induce them to bargain with themselves. When they give their opening position, the no-authority negotiator will say that it is unacceptable. If they are careless, they will alter their stance to placate the no-authority participant. Before they realize what they have done, they will have made concessions before the other side has entered the process.

Anger

If negotiators become angry, they are likely to offend their opponent and may disclose information that they did not wish to divulge. Negotiators who encounter an adversary who has really lost his temper should look for inadvertent disclosures which that person's anger precipitates.

Negotiators often use feigned anger to convince an opponent of the seriousness of their position. This tactic should be used carefully, since it can offend adversaries and induce them to end the interaction.

Some negotiators may respond with their own retaliatory diatribe to convince their adversary that they cannot be intimidated by such tactics. A quid-pro-quo approach involves obvious risks, since a vituperative exchange may have a deleterious impact on the bargaining.

Negotiators may try to counter an angry outburst with the impression that they have been personally offended. They should say that they cannot understand how their reasonable approach has precipitated such an intemperate challenge. If they are successful, they may be able to make the attacking party feel guilty and embarrassed, shaming the person into a concession.

Aggressive Behavior

Such conduct is usually intended to have an impact similar to that associated with anger. It is supposed to convince an opponent of the seriousness of one's position. It can also be used to maintain control over the agenda.

Those who try to counter an aggressive bargainer with a quid-pro-quo response are likely to fail, due to their inability to be convincing in that role. Negotiators who encounter a particularly abrasive adversary can diminish the impact of his techniques through the use of short, carefully controlled interactions. Telephone discussions might be used to limit each exchange. Face-to-face meetings could be held to less than an hour. These short interactions may prevent the opponent from achieving aggressive momentum.

A few aggressive negotiators try to undermine their opponent's presentation through use of interruptions. Such behavior should not be tolerated. When negotiators are deliberately interrupted, they should either keep talking if they think this will discourage their opponent, or they might say that they do not expect their opponent to speak while they are talking.

Uproar

A few negotiators try to obtain an advantage by threatening dire consequences if their opponent does not give them what they want. For example, a school board in negotiations with a teachers' union might say that it will have to lay off one-third of the teachers due to financial constraints. It will then suggest that it could probably retain everyone if the union would accept a salary freeze.

Negotiators confronted with such predictions should ask themselves two crucial questions: What is the likelihood that the consequences will occur? and What would happen to the other party if the consequences actually occurred? In many cases, it will be obvious that the threatened results will not occur. In others, it will be clear that the consequences would be as bad or worse for the other side as for the threatened party.

Bargainers occasionally may have to call an opponent's bluff. If union negotiators were to indicate that they could accept the layoffs if the school board would only raise salaries of the remaining teachers by 30 percent, the board representatives would probably panic. They know the school system could not realistically function with such layoffs. They were merely hoping that the union would not come to the same realization.

Settlement Brochures and Video Presentations

Some lawyers, particularly in the personal injury field, try to enhance their bargaining posture through settlement brochures or video presentations. A brochure states the factual and legal bases for the claim being asserted and describes the full extent of the plaintiff's injuries. Video presentations depict the way in which the defendant's negligent behavior caused the severe injuries the plaintiff has suffered.

Brochures are often accorded greater respect than verbal recitations, due to the aura of legitimacy generally granted to printed documents. Use of brochures may bolster the confidence of the plaintiff's lawyer and may enable him to seize control of the negotiating agenda at the outset. If the plaintiff's lawyer is fortunate, the opponent will begin by suggesting that the plaintiff is seeking too much for pain and suffering. This opening might implicitly concede liability, as well as responsibility for the property damage, medical expenses, and lost earnings requested.

Those presented with settlement brochures or video reenactments should not accord them more respect than they deserve. Lawyers should treat written factual and legal representations just as they would identical verbal assertions.

If lawyers are provided with settlement brochures before the first negotiating session, they should review them and prepare effective counterarguments, which they can state during settlement discussions.

Lawyers should not allow their adversary to use a settlement brochure to seize control of the agenda. Where appropriate, they may wish to prepare their own brochure or video to graphically depict their view of the situation.

Boulwareism

This technique gets its name from Lemuel Boulware, former vice president for labor relations at General Electric. Boulware was not enamored of traditional "auction" bargaining, which involves using extreme initial positions, making time-consuming concessions, and achieving a final agreement like the one the parties knew from the outset they would reach. He decided to determine ahead of time what GE was willing to commit to wage and benefit increases and then formulate a complete "best-offer-first" package. He presented this to union negotiators on a "take-it-or-leave-it" basis unless the union could show that GE had made some miscalculation or that changed circumstances had intervened.

Boulwareism is now associated with best-offer-first or take-it-or-leave-it bargaining. Insurance company adjusters occasionally try to establish reputations as people who will make one firm, fair offer for each case. If the plaintiff does not accept that proposal, they plan to go to trial.

Negotiators should be hesitant to adopt Boulwareism. The offeror effectively tells the other party that he knows what is best for both sides. Few lawyers are willing to accord such respect to the view of opposing counsel.

Boulwareism deprives the opponent of the opportunity to participate meaningfully in the negotiation process. A plaintiff who might have been willing to settle a dispute for $50,000 may not be willing to accept a take-it-or-leave-it offer of $50,000. The plaintiff wants to explore the case through the information phase and to exhibit his negotiating skill during the competitive phase. When the process has been completed, he wants to feel that his ability influenced the final outcome.

Negotiators presented with take-it-or-leave-it offers should not automatically reject them simply because of the paternalistic way in which they have been extended. They must evaluate the amount being proposed. If it is reasonable, they should accept it. Lawyers should not let their own negative reaction to an approach preclude the consummation of a fair arrangement for their clients.

Br'er Rabbit

In *Uncle Remus, His Songs and His Sayings* (1880), Joel Chandler Harris created the unforgettable Br'er Rabbit. When the fox captured Br'er Rabbit, Br'er Rabbit used reverse psychology to escape. He begged the fox to do anything with him so long as he did not throw him in the brier patch. Since the fox wanted to punish the rabbit, he chose the one alternative the rabbit appeared to fear most and flung him in the brier patch. Br'er Rabbit was thus emancipated.

The Br'er Rabbit technique can occasionally be used against win–lose opponents who evaluate their results not by how well they have done but by an assessment of how poorly their adversary has done. They are satisfied only if they think the other side has been forced to accept a terrible argument.

The Br'er Rabbit approach has risks. Although adroit negotiators may induce a careless, vindictive opponent to provide them with what is really desired, they must recognize that such a device will generally not work against a normal adversary. A typical win–win bargainer would probably accept their disingenuous representations and provide them with the unintended result they have professed to prefer over the alternative that has been renounced.

Mutt and Jeff

In the Mutt and Jeff routine, a seemingly reasonable negotiator professes sympathy toward the "generous" concessions made by the other, while his partner rejects each new offer as insufficient, castigating opponents for their parsimonious concessions. The reasonable partner will then suggest that some additional concessions will have to be made if there is to be any hope of satisfying his associate.

Single negotiators may even use this tactic. They can claim that their absent client suffers from delusions of grandeur, which must be satisfied if any agreement is to be consummated. Such bargainers repeatedly praise their opponent for the concessions being made, but insist that greater movement is necessary to satisfy the excessive aspirations of their "unreasonable" client when their client may actually be receptive to any fair resolution. The opponent has no way of knowing about this and usually accepts such representations at their face value.

Negotiators who encounter these tactics should not directly challenge the scheme. It is possible that their opponents are not really engaged in a disingenuous exercise. One adversary may actually disagree with his partner's assessment. Little is to be gained from raising a Mutt and Jeff challenge. Allegations about the tactics being used by such negotiators will probably create an unproductive bargaining atmosphere—particularly in situations where the opponents have not deliberately adopted such a strategy.

Those who interact with Mutt and Jeff negotiators tend to make the mistake of directing their arguments and offers to the unreasonable participant to obtain approval when it is often better to seek the acquiescence of the reasonable adversary before trying to satisfy the irrational one. In some instances, the more conciliatory opponent may actually agree to a proposal characterized as unacceptable by his associate. If the unified position of the opponents can be shattered, it may be possible to whipsaw the reasonable partner against the demanding one.

It is always important when dealing with unreasonable opponents to consider what might occur if no mutual accord is achieved. If the overall cost of surrendering to such an adversary's one-sided demands would clearly be greater than the cost associated with not settling, the interaction should not be continued.

Belly-Up

Some negotiators act like wolves in sheepskin. They initially say they lack negotiating ability and legal perspicuity in a disingenuous effort to evoke sympathy and to lure unsuspecting adversaries into a false sense of security. These negotiators "acknowledge" the superior competence of those with whom they interact and say that they will place themselves in the hands of their fair and proficient opponent.

Negotiators who encounter a belly-up bargainer tend to alter their initial position. Instead of opening with the tough "principled" offer they had planned to use, they modify it in favor of their pathetic adversary, who praises them for their reasonableness, but suggests that his client deserves additional assistance. They then endeavor to demonstrate their ability to satisfy those needs. The belly-up participant says the new offer is a substantial improvement, but suggests the need for further accommodation. By the time the transaction is finished, the belly-up bargainer has obtained everything he wants. Not only are his opponents virtually naked, but they feel gratified at having assisted such an inept bargainer.

Belly-up bargainers are the most difficult to deal with, since they effectively refuse to participate in the process. They ask their opponent to permit them to forgo traditional auction bargaining due to their professed inability to negotiate. They want their reasonable adversary to do all the work.

Negotiators who encounter them must force them to participate and never allow them to alter their planned strategy and concede everything in an effort to form a solution acceptable to such pathetic souls. When belly-up negotiators characterize initial offers as unacceptable, opponents should make them respond with definite offers. True belly-up negotiators often find it very painful to state and defend the positions they espouse.

Passive–Aggressive Behavior

Instead of directly challenging opponents' proposals, passive–aggressive negotiators use oblique, but highly aggressive, forms of passive resistance. They show up late for a scheduled session and forget to bring important documents. When they agree to write up the agreed-upon terms, they fail to do so.

Those who deal with a passive–aggressive opponent must recognize the hostility represented by the behavior and try to seize control. They should get extra copies of important documents just in case their opponent forgets to bring them. They should always prepare a draft of any agreement. Once passive–aggressive negotiators are presented with such a fait accompli, they usually execute the proffered agreement.

The Cooperative Phase

Once the competitive phase has been completed, most parties consider the process complete. Although this conclusion might be warranted where neither party could possibly obtain more favorable results without a corresponding loss being imposed on the other party, this conclusion is not correct for multi-issue, nonconstant-sum controversies.

During the competitive phase, participants rarely completely disclose underlying interests and objectives. Both sides are likely to use power-bargaining techniques aimed at achieving results favorable to their own circumstances.

Because of the anxiety created by such power-bargaining tactics, Pareto optimal arrangements—where neither party may improve its position without worsening the other side's—are usually not generated. The parties are more likely to achieve merely "acceptable" terms rather than Pareto optimal terms due to their lack of negotiation efficiency. If they were to conclude the process at this point, they might well leave a substantial amount of untapped joint satisfaction at the bargaining table.

Once a tentative accord has been achieved, it is generally advantageous for negotiators to explore alternative trade-offs that might simultaneously enhance the interests of both sides. After the competitive phase, one party should suggest transition into the cooperative phase. The parties can initial or even sign their current agreement, and then seek to improve their joint results.

Each should prepare alternative formulations by transferring certain terms from one side to the other while moving other items in the opposite direction. When these options are shown, each negotiator must candidly indicate whether any of the proposals are preferable to the accord already achieved.

Exploring alternatives need not consume much time. Negotiators may substantially increase their clients' satisfaction through this device, and the negotiators lose little if no mutual gains are achieved.

If the cooperative phase is to work effectively, candor is necessary. Each side must be willing to say whether alternatives are more or less beneficial for it.

On the other hand, this phase continues to be somewhat competitive. If one party offers the other an option much more satisfactory than what was agreed upon, he might merely indicate that the proposal is "a little better." Through this technique, he may be able to obtain more during the cooperative phase than would be objectively warranted.

Satisfying Clients

Lawyers who understand these common negotiating techniques can plan their strategies more effectively. They can enhance their skill in the information phase, increase the likelihood that they will achieve acceptable agreements during the competitive phase, and endeavor to maximize the gains obtained for their clients in the cooperative phase.

Secrets of Power Negotiating

Roger Dawson

The Myth of "Win–Win"

You have probably heard that the objective of negotiation is a win–win solution—a creative way that you and the other person can walk away from the table, both having truly won. Two people have one orange. They assume the best they can do will be to split the orange down the middle—but as they discuss their needs, they find that one wants the orange for juice, and the other wants the rind for a cake. There needn't be a winner and a loser. Both of them can win.

Oh, sure!

That *could* happen in the real world—but not often enough to make the concept meaningful. Let's face it: In a negotiation, chances are that the other side is out for the same thing as you. If they're buying, they want the lowest price, and you want the highest. If they're selling, they want the highest price, and you want the lowest. They want to take money out of your pocket and put it right into theirs.

Power Negotiating takes a different position. It teaches you how to win at the negotiating table but leave the other person *feeling* that he won. And feeling that permanently. He'll be thinking what a great time he had negotiating with you and how he can't wait to see you again.

The ability to make others feel that they won is so important that I would almost give you that as a definition of a Power Negotiator. You come away from the negotiating table knowing that you won and knowing that you have improved your relationship with the other person.

You play Power Negotiating just like the game of chess—by a set of rules. In negotiating, your counterpart doesn't have to know the rules. But in general, he will respond predictably to moves you make.

If you play chess, you know the strategic moves are called Gambits (a word that suggests an element of risk). There are Beginning Gambits to get the game started in your direction. There are Middle Gambits to keep the game moving in your direction. And there are Ending Gambits to use when you get ready to checkmate or, in sales parlance, close the sale. As negotiations progress, you'll find that every advance depends on the atmosphere you created in the early stages.

Ask for More Than You Expect to Get

This Gambit embodies one of the cardinal rules of Power Negotiating. Henry Kissinger said, "Effectiveness at the negotiating table depends upon overstating demands."

Asking for more than you expect raises the perceived value of what you are offering. And it prevents deadlocking.

Let me give you a contrary example: Before the Persian Gulf War, President Bush presented Saddam Hussein with a very clear and precise opening position. But it was not a true *negotiating* position, because it was also his bottom line. He left no room for any concession to the Iraqi side, to give them a little victory and make it easier for them to withdraw from Kuwait. The president did not overstate his demands at all—he announced that Iraq had to pull out of Kuwait. Therefore, nothing happened at the conference table, which resulted in a deadlock and a military conflict. This was no accident. Bush's position was meant to create a deadlock—to provide a reason to go in and take care of Iraq militarily, since we didn't want them to pull out voluntarily today, only to reappear later. But in your negotiation, you may *inadvertently* create deadlocks because you don't have the courage to *ask for more than you expect to get.*

Sometimes it may be intimidating for you to ask for that much. You simply don't have the courage to make sufficiently way-out proposals. There are many reasons why you should learn to do so anyway.

First of all, you never know: When you ask for more than you expect, you might just get it. You don't know how the universe is aligned that day. Perhaps your patron saint is looking down at you over a cloud thinking, "Look at that nice person, working so hard . . ." The only way to find out is to ask.

Here's a rule of thumb about asking: The less you know about whomever you're up against, the higher your initial position should be. Why? He may be willing to pay more than you think. If he's selling, he may be willing to take far less than you think. In any case, in a new relationship, you will look more cooperative to the other side if you're in a position to make larger concessions.

So start with your Maximum Plausible Position (MPP)—which is the most you can ask for and still appear credible. Note: Your MPP is probably much higher than you think. We all fear being ridiculed, so you are probably tempted to ask for less than the maximum that the other side would find plausible. You must be on guard against *yourself.*

So stake out your MPP—and imply flexibility. If you're a salesman, you might say to the buyer, "We may be able to modify this position once we know your needs more precisely, but based on what we know so far about the quantities you'd be ordering, our best price would be in the region of $2.25 per widget." You want him to think, "That's outrageous, but there does seem to be some flexibility there, so I'll invest some time negotiating."

Power Negotiators know that first offers seem extreme but are only the beginning; they know that they will work their way toward a solution both sides can accept. When football players or airline pilots go on strike, initial demands from both sides are outlandish. By making the other side move, eventually both sides can tell the press that they won in negotiations, and both can be magnanimous in victory.

An attorney friend of mine in Amarillo, Texas, was representing a buyer of a piece of real estate. Even though he had a good deal, he dreamed up 23 paragraphs of requests to make of the seller. Some of them were absolutely ridiculous. He felt sure half of them would get thrown out right away. To his amazement, the seller took strong objection to only one sentence in one of the paragraphs.

Even then, he didn't give in right away. He held out for a couple of days before he reluctantly agreed to strike the sentence. And although my friend gave away only that one sentence in 23 paragraphs of requests, the seller felt he had won.

How much more should you ask than you expect to get?

Get the other side to state a position first. If there is no pressure on you, be bold enough to say, "You approached me. The way things are satisfies me. If you want to do this, you'll have to make a proposal to me."

The car dealer is asking $15,000 for the car. You want it for $13,000. So put the price you want in a bracket between what he is asking and what you will offer up front: Offer $11,000.

One of your employees wants to spend $400 on a new desk. You think $325 is reasonable. Say that it can't be more than $250.

In other words, your proposal should be as far from what you want in your direction as the other guy's proposal is in the other direction. If you end up in the middle, you make your objective. You won't always end up in the middle, but how often it happens will amaze you.

Never Say Yes to the First Offer

Why not? If you do, it triggers two negative thoughts in your counterpart's mind:

1. I could have done better.
2. Something must be wrong.

Suppose you are a buyer for a maker of aircraft engines meeting with a salesman for a manufacturer of engine bearings. Bearings are a vital component for you, and your regular supplier has let you down. If you can't make an agreement with this company, your assembly line will shut down within 30 days. And if you can't supply the engines on time, it will invalidate your contract with the aircraft manufacturer who gives you 85 percent of your business.

In these circumstances, the price of the bearings you need is not a high priority. But the thought occurs to you: "I'll be a good negotiator. Just to see what happens, I think I'll make him a super-low offer."

He quotes you $250 each, which surprises you because you have been paying $275. You respond, "We've been paying only $175." He responds, "OK, we can match that."

In thousands of seminars over the years, I've posed a situation like this to audiences and can't recall getting anything other than the two negative responses just listed. It isn't the price. It's the immediate response to the proposal without a struggle that sends up a warning flag in most people.

I was president of a real estate company in Southern California that had 28 offices. One day, a magazine salesman came in trying to sell me advertising space. I knew it was an excellent opportunity, and he made me a very reasonable offer that required a modest $2,000 investment. Because I love to negotiate, I used Gambits on him and got him down to an incredible price of $800. That made me wonder if I could do even better, and I used the Gambit called Higher Authority and said, "This looks fine. I just have to run it by my board or directors. They're meeting tonight."

A couple of days later, I called him and said, "I felt I wouldn't have any problem selling the board of directors on that $800, but they're so difficult to deal with right now. The budget is giving everyone headaches. They did make a counteroffer, but it is so low, I am frankly embarrassed to tell you what it is."

"How much did they agree to?"

"$500."

"I'll take it."

And I felt cheated. I still felt I could have done better. In other words, if you're too agreeable, it makes the other side uneasy. There are several ways to avoid the mistrust that can develop in your relationship.

1. Flinch

Always react with shock and surprise at the other side's proposals.

The truth of the matter is that when people make a proposal to you, they are watching for your reaction. A concession often follows a Flinch. If you don't Flinch, it makes the other person a tougher negotiator. He may not have thought for a moment you would go along with his request, but if you don't Flinch at something outrageous, he may decide to see how far he can get you to go.

Flinching is critical because most people believe what they see more than what they hear. It's safe to assume that with at least 70 percent of the people with whom you will negotiate, the visual overrides the auditory. Don't dismiss Flinching as childish or too theatrical until you've tried it.

A woman told me that she Flinched when selecting a bottle of wine in one of Boston's finest restaurants, and the wine steward immediately dropped the price by $5. A man told me a simple Flinch took $2,000 off the price of a Corvette.

If you're not negotiating face-to-face, you can gasp in shock and surprise. Phone Fliches can be very effective.

2. Avoid Confrontation

What you say in the first few moments often sets the climate of a negotiation. That's one problem I have with the way lawyers negotiate. Your first communication from them is likely to be a threat. In one workshop I taught that included some lawyers, most of them would start a negotiation exercise with a vicious threat and become more abusive from there. I had to stop the exercise and tell them never to be confrontational early on if they wanted to settle a case without expensive litigation. (I doubted their motives on that score.)

If the other side takes a position with which you disagree, don't argue. That only intensifies their desire to be proven right. Get in the habit of agreeing initially and turning it around. Use the Feel, Felt, Found Formula:

> I understand exactly how you Feel about that. Many other people have Felt exactly
> the same way. But you know what we have always Found? When we took a closer look,
> we Found . . . (that they changed their minds, of course).

At the very least, this approach gives you time to think. By the time you get around to saying what you found on a closer look, you will have found what you need to say.

Play the Reluctant Buyer or Reluctant Seller

One of my Power Negotiators owns real estate worth probably $50 million, owes $35 million in loans, and therefore has a net worth of about $15 million. Many smaller investors bring him purchase offers, eager to acquire one of his better-known properties. I have seen him make thousands of dollars with the Reluctant Seller Gambit.

He reads the offer quietly and slides it thoughtfully back across the table, scratches above one ear, and says, "I don't know. Of all my properties, I have very special feelings for this one. I was thinking of keeping it and giving it to my daughter for her college graduation present. I really don't think I would part with it for anything less than the full asking price. But it was good of you to make me this offer, and so that you won't have wasted your time, what is the very best price you feel you could give me?"

Many times, I have seen him make thousands of dollars in a few seconds.

Now put yourself on the other side of the desk for a moment and become the Reluctant Buyer. Let's say you're in charge of buying new computer equipment for your company. How can you get the best possible price? My suggestion is to have the supplier come to your offices and go through the whole presentation. Ask all the questions you can possibly think of, then say, "I really appreciate all the time you've taken. You've obviously put a lot of work into this presentation, but unfortunately, it's not the way we want to go; however, I sure wish you the best of luck."

Pause to examine the crestfallen expression on the salesman's face as he slowly puts away his presentation materials. Then, at the very last moment, as his hand reaches for the doorknob on the way out, come out with the following magic expression. It is one of those expressions in negotiating that, used at the right moment, yields amazingly predictable results. Say, "You know, I really do appreciate the time you took here. Just to be fair to you, what is the very lowest price you would take?"

Would you agree that the first price you were quoted was probably not the bottom? It's a good bet. The first price was probably what I call the "wish number." If you'd signed off on that, the salesman would have shoved the contract into his briefcase, burned rubber all the way back to the office, and run in screaming, "You won't believe what just happened to me!"

When you play the Reluctant Buyer, you'll get a second quote, in which the salesman will probably give away half his negotiating range—between the "wish number" and his lowest possible price, which I call the "walk-away" price. He'll typically respond, "Well, I tell you what. I like your company. It's the end of our quarter, and we're in a sales contest. If you'll place the order today, I'll give it to you for the unbelievably low price of $200,000. . . ."

It's a game. When someone plays Reluctant Buyer to *you*, the correct response is "I don't think there's any flexibility in our price, but if you'll tell me what it would take to get your business (getting the other side to commit to a number first), I'll take it to my people (using a Higher Authority as a foil) and see what I can do for you with them (setting up to play Good Guy/Bad Guy)."

The Vise Technique

The Vise is this simple little expression: "You'll have to do better than that."

A veteran negotiator will simply come back at you with "Just how much better do I have to do?" But it's amazing how often an inexperienced one will give away a big chunk of his range, simply because you did that.

Once you've used that phrase, shut up. Don't say another word. One client called me to say that by using this simple phrase, he got a price $14,000 less than he was prepared to pay.

Are you wondering, "Was that a $50,000 proposal that got knocked down by $14,000, or a multimillion-dollar proposal—in which case, $14,000 is no big deal?" It doesn't matter. The point is that he made $14,000 in those two minutes that it took him to scrawl that phrase on a bid. That would be $420,000 per hour. You'll never make money faster than you do when you're negotiating.

The dollars you save or lose in negotiating are bottom-line dollars, not gross income dollars. I've trained executives at retailers and health maintenance organizations (HMOs) whose profit margin is only 2 percent. They do a billion dollars' worth of business a year, but they bring in only 2 percent in bottom-line profits. In a company like that, a $2,000 concession at the negotiating table has the same effect as a $100,000 sale.

You're probably in an industry that does better than that. In this country, the average profit margin is about 5 percent of gross sales. For such a company, a $2,000 concession at the negotiating table is the equivalent of $40,000 in sales. How long would you be willing to work to get a $40,000 sale?

Perhaps when you read these Gambits you're thinking, "Roger, you've never met the guys I deal with in my business. They make Attila the Hun look like Ann Landers. They'll never fall for that kind of thing." Fair enough. But try these techniques. Time and again, students have told me, "I never thought that would work, but it did. It's amazing." The first time you Flinch or use the Vise on the other person and walk out of negotiations with $1,000 in your pocket that you didn't expect to get, you'll become a believer, too. Negotiating is a game that is played by a set of rules. If you learn the rules well, you can play the game well.

Don't Worry about Price

After two decades of sales training, I am convinced that price is a bigger concern to the people selling than it is to those they're selling to. People want to pay more, not less. Customers who may be asking you to cut your price may be secretly wishing they could pay more. Seriously.

I was the merchandising manager at the Montgomery Ward store in Bakersfield, California, which is not a large town. But in a chain of more than 600 stores, ours ranked thirteenth in volume. Why? The head office left us alone and allowed us to sell to the needs of the local population. We did a huge business in home air conditioners, because in Bakersfield, it's not unusual for it to be 100 degrees Fahrenheit at midnight. A blue-collar home in that city then cost around $30,000. The air conditioners we sold them cost $10,000 to $12,000. The customers were willing to pay that price, but it was very hard to break in new salesmen because they couldn't believe anybody would pay $12,000 to put an air conditioner in a $30,000 house.

But if I could get these same salesmen to succeed to the point where they made big money and installed air conditioners in their own homes, suddenly they didn't find the price outrageous and would dismiss price objections from customers as if they didn't exist.

Beginning stockbrokers are the same. It's very hard for them to ask a client to invest $100,000 when they don't know where their own lunch money is going to come from. But once they become affluent, their sales snowball.

One of my clients tells me that if three products are on a store shelf—let's say three toasters—and the features of each are described on the carton, customers will most frequently select the highest-priced item. But if a salesman working for minimum wage comes along to assist them, he can't justify spending money on the best and talks the customer down to the low-end or the middle-of-the-line toaster.

The key is the description on the carton. You must give customers a *reason* to spend more money, but if you can do that, they want to spend more money, not less. I think that spending money is what Americans do best. We spend $6 trillion a year in this country. And that's when we're spending our own hard-earned, after-tax dollars. What if you're asking someone at a corporation to spend the company's money? One thing better than spending your own money is spending someone else's money. And corporate expenditures are tax deductible, so Uncle Sam is going to pick up 40 percent of the bill.

Let's face it, does what you pay for something really matter? If you're going to buy a new automobile, does it matter if you spend $20,000 or $21,000? Not really. You'll soon forget what you paid, and the slight increase in payments is not going to affect your lifestyle. What matters is the feeling that you got the best possible deal.

If you're trying to get someone to spend money, all you have to do is give him a reason and convince him there is no way to get a better deal.

Even when dealing with the federal government, price is far from the most important thing. I asked a Pentagon procurement officer point-blank if the government has to buy from the lowest bidder.

"Heavens no," he said. "We'd really be in trouble if that were true. The rules say we should buy from the lowest bidder whom we feel is capable of meeting specifications. We're far more concerned with a company's experience and its ability to get a job done on time."

In a company that doesn't have legal requirements to put out requests for bids, price probably counts for even less. AT&T keeps my telephone business even though it's more expensive than Sprint or MCI and has never pretended otherwise. I stay because the service has been trouble-free and simple to use for many years, and I have more important things concerning me than switching long-distance companies to save a few pennies per call. So don't exacerbate the price problem by assuming that price is uppermost in the other person's mind. Assume that it isn't.

As negotiations proceed, don't narrow the negotiation down to just one issue. If everything is resolved and the only issue left is price, then clearly, somebody has to win, and clearly, somebody does have to lose. But as long as you keep more than one issue on the table, you can work trade-offs so that the other fellow doesn't mind conceding on price because you are able to offer something in return.

Find other ways to make him feel he's winning.

Higher Authority

Once you're in negotiations, it's always good for you to postpone a decision and plead that you have to run the deal by some outside person with Higher Authority. The other side will make more concessions to people they *don't* see or know than they will to you alone.

But by the same token, you will be frustrated over and over if this Gambit is used on you. When I was a real estate broker, I taught our agents that before they put buyers into their cars to show them properties, they must always say, "Just to be sure I understand, if we find exactly the right home for you today, is there any reason you couldn't make a decision today?"

Here's something you can count on when dealing with another person: Any concession you make will lose its value quickly. A material object may appreciate in value over the years, but the value of services declines rapidly after you have performed them. Consequently, when you make a concession, you must ask for a reciprocal concession right away, because two hours later, what you have done will count for little or nothing.

That's one reason why you always have to settle your fee before you perform a service. When a real estate salesman offers to help someone get rid of a property, a 6 percent fee doesn't sound enormous—but the minute the realtor has found the buyer, that 6 percent suddenly starts to sound like a tremendous amount of money.

Don't Split the Difference

When you are negotiating price, don't offer to split the difference that is keeping you and the person on the other side from agreement. Let him suggest that. You can usually get him to do so if you point out how long you have been negotiating and what a comparatively small sum is keeping you apart.

It makes all the difference psychologically to someone if *he* makes a suggestion and gets you to agree to it, as opposed to unwillingly accepting a proposal from you. It may seem a very subtle thing, but it's a significant factor in determining who feels he has won.

If your counterpart splits the difference with you and moves half the distance toward your price, you can invoke a Higher Authority—maybe it's your partners or your board. After a delay of hours or days, you come back and say that your Higher Authority is not being cooperative and has vetoed the new offer, then point out how it seems too bad that a little difference—between what you're asking and what he just offered—should derail everything. If you keep that up long enough, he will probably offer to split the difference again. So you have that much more bottom-line profit. But even if he won't do it a second time, if you wind up splitting the difference as he first proposed, he will feel he won—because he proposed it.

Set It Aside

In negotiations, you will often find that you are in complete disagreement on one issue. It's easy for an inexperienced negotiator to feel that the whole deal is threatened, but you can handle an impasse on one issue by the Set Aside Gambit: "Let's just set that aside for a moment and talk about some of the other issues, may we?" If you resolve minor issues that you can discuss easily, you'll put momentum into the negotiations again. The other side will be much more flexible after you've reached agreement on the smaller issues.

A stalemate is something different. That's when both sides are still talking but seem unable to make any progress. At this point, you must change the dynamics of the meeting to reestablish momentum.

Change the people in the negotiating team. Remove any member who may have irritated the other side. Change the venue by proposing to continue over lunch or dinner. Ease the tension—tell a funny story, talk about their hobbies or a piece of gossip that's in the news. Explore the possibility of extended credit, a reduced deposit, restructured payments, or a change in specifications, packaging, or delivery method. Remember that the other side may be reluctant to raise these issues for fear of appearing to be in poor financial condition.

Discuss methods of sharing the risk with the other side.

The Art of Concession

In negotiations over price, be sure you don't set up a pattern in the way you make concessions. Don't make equal-size concessions. That will certainly make the other side expect that another concession of just the same size is practically his right. And never make the final concession a big one. It never looks final if it's big. To refuse a further, smaller concession after you have just made a big one makes you seem difficult and only creates needless hostility.

Make Time Your Ally

The longer you can keep the other party involved in negotiations, the more likely he is to move around to your point of view. Think of the tugboats in the Hudson River off Manhattan. A tiny tugboat can move a huge ocean liner if it does it a little bit at a time. If the tugboat captain were to back off, rev up the engines, and try to force the ocean liner around, it wouldn't do any good. If you have enough patience, you can change anybody's mind a little bit at a time.

Unfortunately, this works both ways. The longer you spend in a negotiation, the more likely you are to make concessions.

An 80/20 split surfaces repeatedly in apparently unrelated fields. In the nineteenth century, the economist Vilfredo Pareto, who studied the distribution of wealth in Italy, pointed out that 80 percent of the wealth was concentrated in the hands of 20 percent of the people. Sales managers tell me that 80 percent of the business is done by 20 percent of the salespeople. Schoolteachers tell me that 20 percent of the children cause 80 percent of the trouble.

It also seems true that on account of the incredible pressure that time can put on a negotiation, 80 percent of the concessions in a negotiation will occur in the last 20 percent of the time available. If demands are presented early on, neither side may be willing to yield, and the entire transaction can fall apart. But if additional demands or problems surface in the final 20 percent of the time available for the negotiation, both sides will be more flexible.

Think back to the last time you bought a piece of real estate. Probably it took about 10 weeks from signing the initial contract until you actually became the owner of the property. Now think of the concessions that were made in the last 2 weeks. Weren't both sides more yielding at that point?

One rule that obviously follows from this: If you have a deadline pushing you in a negotiation, never reveal that fact to the other side. He'll be sure to squeeze you for concessions at the last minute.

If you have flown to Dallas to resolve a negotiation with a hotel developer, and you have a return flight at 6:00, of course you want to make that flight—but don't let the other people know. If they do know, be sure they know that you have a backup flight at 9:00—and that if you need to, you can stay over until you work out a mutually satisfactory arrangement.

The power that comes from knowing the other side's time limit was shown when President Lyndon Johnson wanted to negotiate with the Vietnamese in time to do his party some good in the election of November 1968. He sent our negotiator, Averell Harriman, to Paris with very clear instructions: Get something done, fast, right now, Texas style.

Harriman rented a suite at the Ritz Hotel in Paris on a week-to-week basis. Vietnamese negotiator Xuan Thuy rented a villa in the countryside for two and a half years. Then the Vietnamese proceeded to spend week after week after week talking to us about the shape of the table.

Did they really care about the shape of the table? Of course not. They were projecting, successfully, that they were not under any time pressure. They were trying to exploit Johnson's November deadline. On November 1, only five days before the election, Johnson called a halt to the bombing of Vietnam.

The Most Dangerous Moment

You are at your most vulnerable at the point when you think the negotiations are over, just after the other party has agreed to go ahead. Making a huge sale has excited you. You're feeling good. At such times, you tend to give away things you otherwise wouldn't. Watch your emotions.

If the other side chooses this moment to Nibble at the deal for some concession now, you're likely to think, "Oh no, I thought we had resolved everything. I don't want to take a chance on going back to the beginning and renegotiating the whole thing. If I do that, I might lose the whole sale. I'm better off just giving in on this little point."

Don't lay yourself open to last-minute Nibbles—some of which could negate the benefit of the deal for you. Your protection is to say *you don't have the authority* to make any concessions now. If the other side persists and wants extra training, installation, extended warranties, or anything else, show them the hard price in writing. Don't let the euphoria of finishing a negotiation cost you the store.

Your Most Powerful Weapon

If there's one thing that I can impress upon you that will make you 10 times more powerful as a negotiator, it's this: Learn to develop walk-away power. Often, there's a point you pass in the heat of negotiation when you will no longer walk away. You start thinking,

> "I'm going to buy this car. I'm going to get the best price I can, but I'm not leaving until I get it."
>
> "I'm going to hire this person. For the lowest salary and benefits that I can—but I won't let him get away."
>
> "I have to take this job. I'm going to fight for the best pay and benefits, but I have to take this job."
>
> "I have to make this sale. I can't walk out of here without a commitment."

The minute you're no longer willing to say, "I'm prepared to walk away from this," I guarantee you will lose in the negotiations.

So don't pass that point. There's no such thing as a sale you have to make at any price, or the only car or home for you, or a job or employee you can't do without. The minute you think there is, you've lost.

When people tell me they made a mistake in negotiations, this is always a part of the problem. They passed the point where they were willing to walk away.

Many years ago, my daughter bought her first car. She fell in love with the car, and the dealer knew it. Then she came back from the place and wanted me to go down with her to negotiate a better price. I sat her down and said, "Julia, are you prepared to come home without the car?"

She said, "No, I'm not, I want it, I want it." She was in trouble.

"Julia, you might as well get your checkbook out and give them what they're asking, because you've set yourself up to lose. We've got to be prepared to walk away."

We walked out of the showroom twice in the two hours we spent negotiating over the car and bought it for $2,000 less than she would have paid for it. How much money was she making when she was negotiating? She was making $1,000 an hour. We'd all go to work for $1,000 an hour, wouldn't we? You never make money faster than when you're negotiating.

Defusing the Exploding Offer: The Farpoint Gambit
Robert J. Robinson

Situations in which offers are made with an expiration date attached are common in negotiation. In a way, all offers are inherently limited by time: One cannot, for example, leave a car dealership, return several years later, and attempt to accept the last offer made by a dealer who may or may not be employed there any longer. Obviously, the validity of an offer is affected by the passage of time. "Exploding offers," in contrast, are deliberate, calculated strategies. They are typically offered together with an extremely short, artificially imposed time limit. Consider, for instance, the following common manifestations of this phenomenon:

- Mary is looking for an apartment in a new city, and finally finds one that suits all her needs. When she asks about the rent, the landlord says, "The rent is $900 per month, but I tell you what—give me a check for the security deposit today, and I'll make it $850. Otherwise it's $900."

- John needs to buy a car. He haggles for several hours with a dealer, getting the price lower and lower. Finally an impasse is reached: John is still not happy with the price, but the dealer is unable to offer a more attractive deal. As John gets up to leave, the dealer says, "Look, it's the end of the month. If we can do this today, I'll make my quota, and that's worth another $500 off the price to me. But if you come back on Monday, we start all over again."

- Pat is an MBA student looking for a summer job between the first and second years of the program. The school has a recognized recruitment "season" when various companies come on campus, interview students, and, in many instances, offer summer employment. On the first day of the interviews, Pat interviews with Company X. After about 30 minutes, the Company X spokesperson says, "Well, we'd like to offer you the job," (and names a very generous salary) "but you must say yes or no right now."

Each of these examples illustrates what has become known as an *exploding offer*. However, each case probably evokes a different affective response in the reader, and has different implications for the protagonists in the vignettes. Mary has the choice of saving $50 per month rent but can still have the apartment if she delays until the following day; John probably will not purchase the car unless he takes advantage of the temporary $500 concession; and Pat has the chance to get an attractive summer job—which disappears if Pat's next response is anything but acceptance of the offer. In this brief article my goal is to further refine the notion of exploding offers (the problem faced by Mary, John, and Pat) and suggest some ideas on how to deal with them, including a tactic that I call the "Farpoint Gambit."

Source: Robert J. Robinson, "Defusing the Exploding Offer: The Farpoint Gambit," *Negotiation Journal,* July 1995, Kluwer Academic/Plenum Publishers.

Characteristics of Exploding Offers

Many negotiation scholars use the notion of an exploding offer in informal discussion, and the concept is directly related to analyses of the role of threats and time in negotiating. [S]pecifically, what makes an offer "exploding"? In my opinion, five characteristics separate "exploding" offers from offers that have naturally decaying life spans.

Power Asymmetry   Exploding offers generally only exist in situations where there is a considerable asymmetry of power between the offeror and the person receiving the offer. Thus in the cases of Mary and John, one might consider the offers as tactics being used between consenting adults in relatively equal power positions, which might not arouse any sense of discomfort. In Pat's case, the situation is more ambiguous. Faced with a large company offering a choice between a job or possible unemployment for the summer, a student burdened with loans might feel great pressure to accept as a result of the exploding offer. An even more extreme example is provided by the academic job market which is filled with newly minted PhD recipients who are looking for faculty positions. Colleges routinely make exploding offers, which are the equivalent of offering a person dying of thirst a glass of water—if the person accepts right away. This leads to the second condition of concern.

A Pressure-Inducing "Test of Faith"   The exploding offer often places great pressure on the person receiving the offer. This is not in itself unusual or necessarily reprehensible. However, the situation becomes more complex when the pressure is excessive and is built on power imbalances. Thus in the case of the faculty candidate, I have personally witnessed situations where the person receiving the offer is placed under excessive pressure by the argument that "if you're one of us you'll accept now." This not only applies "normal" negotiation pressure but also raises the threat that accepting later risks making the organization angry with you for "holding out." This makes the act of attempting to negotiate further somehow vaguely (or explicitly, depending on the degree of coercion being applied) treasonable, and leaves the person receiving the offer with no options but to accept or withdraw completely. In another situation I witnessed, excessive pressure was applied by means of an interesting variation, which consisted of offering the job to the individual and telling them that they were the person that the company wanted above all others—followed by informing the individual that if they were unable to accept the job *that day,* the offer would be withdrawn, at least until "further candidates have been considered and interviewed for the position."

Restricting Choice   Another characteristic of the exploding offer is its use as a tool that deliberately restricts the choice of the individual. While there is an element of this factor in the case of Mary (the landlord does not want her looking at other apartments) and John (the salesperson does not want him looking at other cars), it is somewhat peripheral in both of these negotiations, which are aimed at closing a deal. In Pat's case, however, the exploding offer as a means to restrict comparative shopping *is the primary tactic,* and rests on not letting Pat get any other offers or even see representatives of other companies. In fact, it might even emerge that Company X is interviewing particularly early in order to prevent the candidates from seeing anyone else.

Lack of Consideration and Respect   Exploding offers involve arbitrary deadlines that are unnecessarily rigid. They can create enormous hardship for the individual involved, who may be called from family duties, may be forced to break leases, or may suffer other financial hardships in order to accept the offer. Appeals for flexibility and consideration are routinely ignored by the offeror, displaying an utter lack of regard for the other negotiator.

Lack of Good Faith   Exploding offers are sometimes made because a negotiator is ambivalent about the person or proposal in question, or is using this strategy as a means of resolving internal strife within the negotiator's organization. This is a somewhat cynical viewpoint, and it is not uncommon for one side to make an exceptionally self-advantageous exploding offer. If the offer is accepted, then a fine bargain has been achieved; and if the offer is rejected, the offeror can move on to other options. The problem is that the offer, as made, was not a serious, good faith attempt to reach a settlement. Thus while Pat might be told that he or she is the candidate that Company X wants, the reality is more likely that Company X wants a warm body with Pat's qualifications, and if Pat won't accept, then an interchangeable individual will be substituted.

Why Are Exploding Offers Made?

It is not difficult to understand the thinking behind the use of exploding offers, in terms of the perceived advantage this affords the offeror. The ability to impose terms and back them up with a tight time limit may force the other side to capitulate or agree before it might otherwise have done so, increasing the value of the deal for the party making the offer. In many ways, the exploding offer is the ultimate hard-bargaining tactic: Party A makes a final offer and then threateningly says, "And that's good until noon tomorrow. After that, you can find another partner." In essence, the tactic defines an end to the negotiation process. An exploding offer is not only an offer in the traditional sense but is also the last offer. Rejection will automatically terminate the negotiation, and in some cases, the relationship as well.

In terms of the vignettes mentioned earlier, it is easy to understand how exploding offers can serve the interest of the offeror. In Mary's case, the landlord wants to tie in the new tenant that very day. Perhaps the landlord is going away and wants to get the apartment filled. Or maybe he just thinks that Mary is the kind of tenant he wants in the building, and is trying to sweeten the deal. Perhaps the rent really is $850, and the landlord is disingenuously offering the $50 discount. Whatever the reason, it is worth $50 per month to the landlord to commit Mary that day, rather than undergoing the opportunity cost of continuing to search for other tenants.

Similarly in John's case, the dealer may in fact be trying to meet the quota for the month, or he may be looking for a way to make a sweeter offer without undercutting the "going" price for that model car. In any event, having John leave the dealership is to be avoided at all costs, and the $500 exploding offer is an incentive for John to stay and make the deal.

In Pat's case, Company X is presumably interviewing several MBA students over the next several days. The company must pay to have the interviewer stay in a hotel until the process is concluded. During that time, the interviewer makes offers and waits for the students to pick among several offers; if rejected, the interviewer might make another offer and so on. How much simpler it is to tie up the first likely-looking individual the interviewer meets, and go home.

There is also another reason why the exploding offer is used. It can be a sign of offeror weakness that might not be at all apparent to the recipient of the offer, but is almost always present.[1] Negotiators who use exploding offers may perceive themselves to be at a disadvantage relative to their competitors in terms of salary, conditions of sale, or the like. Or they may have severe time or budget constraints. Once again, the function of the exploding offer can be either to force a quick acceptance by ending the negotiation (and thus avoiding the necessity of sweetening the deal to an unacceptably high level) *or* to restrict the ability of the recipient to comparison shop, and therefore discover that the market was willing to pay at a significantly higher level.

Dealing with Exploding Offers: Try Being Reasonable First

In the tradition of *Getting to Yes* (Fisher and Ury 1981) and *Getting Past No* (Ury 1991), a number of possibilities exist for the individual faced with an exploding offer. Most of these involve getting away from positional stances in order to explore underlying interests and to look to create value via "principled negotiation" (Lax and Sebenius 1986). It is important to realize that exploding offers can be dealt with using these techniques, especially if there is some degree of goodwill in the interaction. An exploding offer is often made by a party that believes it stands to lose out in the negotiation or is unsure of its power. Building trust and appealing to reason can go a long way toward addressing this underlying concern, resulting in the exploding aspect of the offer being withdrawn.

For example, apartment hunter Mary might say, "I understand you'd like a check today. Let me be honest. I really like this place, and I want to take it for $850 per month. But I have to see a few other places. How about I call you in the morning, first thing?" This might suffice. Or in the automobile dealership case, John the customer could say, "I really appreciate the $500 reduction. But I need to think this over. What if I call you 9 a.m. Monday? Can we make the offer good until then?" The dealer can accept, in which case the deal is still alive, or reject the counteroffer, in which case John is faced with the same decision as he had before he made the suggestion. If the dealer really wants to make a quota, a sales agreement could be drawn up, dated that day, but requiring John's agreement on Monday before it goes forward (John should probably not pony up any money until Monday).

These are relatively easy situations to resolve. However, the classic exploding offer scenario, replete with elements of hard bargaining, cynicism, and coercion, is the job offer case involving Pat, the student. Here there needs to be a real addressing of interests.

My advice to students in Pat's situation is to have them point out to the organization that, since it wants its employees to be happy and productive, it is in the organization's interests to let the students feel that they have freely chosen this position as the most attractive option. The way to achieve this is to make the most attractive offer, not to constrain choice. Also, if the student is really the one that the organization wants, then the employer should be prepared to wait for that individual, rather than treating him or her like an interchangeable part.

The recipients of exploding offers should also be prepared to make sensible counteroffers. They should be able to say when they *would* be in a position to accept, and to explain why this date makes sense (as opposed to choosing an equally arbitrary future time such as a week or 10 days). I usually tell my students about my most enjoyable employment experience, when I was made an offer and told, in effect, "take your time deciding. You're the one we want, and we want you to do the thing that's right for you. We are here to help you make that decision in any way we can." The contrast between this kind of attitude and an exploding offer, both in terms of an individual's feelings and the likelihood of a good future relationship for the parties, should be obvious. I have academic friends who are tortured, years after accepting their jobs, with the question of what would have happened if their employers had allowed them the time to take one more interview, or await the decision of another school.

My first recommendation is, then, to engage in problem solving with respect to uncovering interests, generating and exploring options, moving to creative solutions, and emphasizing relationship issues. However, this can fail if the other party is unsympathetic or locked into a positional or cynical stance. In such an instance, particularly if one feels that the other side is behaving in an ethically questionable fashion, I recommend the "Farpoint Gambit."

Fighting Fire with Fire: The Farpoint Gambit

While I always recommend first attempting a "principled" or "integrative" solution, I believe that when such tactics prove untenable, more assertive steps need to be taken. Doing this successfully depends on understanding where the power of the exploding offer resides. Exploding offers pivot on a credible, inviolable deadline. If the deadline is violated and the negotiation continues, the credibility of the explosion (the removal of the offer) is destroyed. And if the other side has depended on this threat as a central tactic, their entire position may collapse, putting the recipient of the initial offer in a very advantageous position. The technique I recommend, which I call the "Farpoint Gambit," is from the catalog of "hoist-them-by-their-own-petard" tools, which sometimes makes it particularly satisfying to employ.

The Farpoint Gambit derives from an episode of the science fiction television show *Star Trek, The Next Generation,* in which the crew of the *Enterprise* (the spaceship from Earth) is put on trial by a powerful alien "for the crimes of humanity." (The episode is called "Encounter at Farpoint," hence the name of the technique.) The alien creates a kangaroo court with himself as judge, and the captain of the *Enterprise* (Jean-Luc Picard) defends the human race. At a certain point, the alien judge becomes piqued by the captain's spirited defense, and says to the bailiff, "Bailiff, if the next word out of the defendant's mouth is anything but guilty, kill him!" He then turns to Picard and asks, "Defendant, how do you plead?" Picard thinks for a moment as the bailiff menacingly points a weapon at him, them firmly announces, "Guilty." As the courtroom gasps (and after an inevitable television commercial break), he adds, "Provisionally." This is essentially the Farpoint Gambit.

The alien has presented Picard with the ultimate coercive offer: Say you're guilty or I'll kill you. Obviously, Picard doesn't think he's guilty, but he doesn't want to die. The power of the threat depends on getting Picard to admit that he's guilty—he does, but in such a way ("provisionally") that the alien judge is compelled to ask, "And what is the provision?" Picard then proceeds to talk his way out of the jam (as always happens with television heroes), and all is well. The point is that the alien is caught in his own trap: He's still arguing with Picard, who is still not guilty or dead. In the same way, an exploding offer can be defused by *embracing it,* using the Farpoint Gambit.

Consider again Pat's situation. Essentially, Company X is the alien, saying to Pat, "either the next words out of [your] mouth are 'I accept,' or it's no deal." Pat can attempt to reason with the company's representative, and if that does not work either walk away, accept, or use the Farpoint Gambit by saying, "I accept. Provisionally." The provision could be anything that takes the negotiation beyond that day, and might be things like "provided I can meet with the person I would be working for," or "provided my coworkers prove satisfactory," or even "provided I don't get a better offer from the companies I'm still waiting to hear from."

The key is to make requests that are completely reasonable, but which will eventually result in the deadline being violated, due to the need for further clarification, or the lack of authority of the negotiator making the offer. Once the deadline passes, the credibility of the threat is destroyed, and successive attempts to set arbitrary deadlines can be dealt with in exactly the same way. The recipient of the offer can accept at his or her leisure, or reject the offer based on an unsatisfactory resolution of the provisions of the original acceptance.

The Farpoint Gambit also works by leveraging off fractures in the other side or the imperfections in their informational strategies. Thus in Pat's case, the company's negotiator may not be authorized to offer moving and relocation expenses, or know what the policy is on day care for children. In such situations it is extremely easy to accept "pending satisfactory resolution of these issues" and then to continue to negotiate those and other issues.

The success of the Farpoint Gambit ultimately rests on the notion that the person receiving the exploding offer can eventually withdraw from the situation if no satisfactory resolution is forthcoming, without the offeror being able (or inclined) to sanction them for doing so. While this technique is about helping people get what they want from a coercive negotiating partner, it is *not* about helping people find a way to wriggle out of commitments given in good faith when they change their minds or get a better offer.

Inevitably, some negotiations, even those resuscitated by the Farpoint Gambit, are bound to fail. However, if conditions are attached to the acceptance—and these are not, by a reasonable assessment, met—then there really is not anything the company can do when the student withdraws, or the faculty candidate accepts an offer elsewhere, although possible reputational damage should still not be overlooked. It may be that each side has as much at stake as the other, which will help to keep both reasonable—no organization wants to get the reputation for strong-arming prospective employees with techniques of dubious morality. In other cases, there may be actual legal provisions that allow the individual to withdraw within a specified time limit after accepting, such as in the case of signing an agreement to purchase a car.

The Farpoint Gambit has a further advantage: It is nonescalative (Pruitt and Rubin 1986) and non-zero-sum in nature. Like the crew of the *Enterprise* in their endless quest for new frontiers, the Farpoint Gambit may force negotiators toward improved solutions at the "Pareto frontier" (see, e.g., Raiffa 1982). It moves the parties in the "right" direction—that is, toward one another rather than apart. In this sense, the Farpoint Gambit is not as dangerous as techniques that require one side to call the other's bluff, or see who can hold out the longest. In these latter cases, someone frequently wins, and someone loses. The Farpoint Gambit is about both sides being able to take care of underlying interests, and thus able both to "win" and get what they want, with the offeror paying a fair price.

In Conclusion: When to Use—Or Not Use—The Gambit

I would strongly caution against using the Farpoint Gambit as a routine technique to gain advantage. Nothing is more frustrating and unacceptable than someone who makes a habit of taking a deal, and who then continues to impose conditions or introduce new issues. Indeed, this is the flip side of the reprehensible lowballing technique employed by shady salespersons. In pondering this, I have come up with some guidelines for situations in which I believe it is legitimate to employ the Farpoint Gambit.

Ideally, I would make sure that all three of these conditions were present before I would feel completely comfortable in using this tactic.

- The other side is perceived by the recipient of the exploding offer to be behaving unethically, and does not respond to appeals to reason.
- The recipient is truly interested in making a deal but needs more time to make a decision.
- There genuinely are issues that need clarification, which would make the difference between accepting or rejecting the deal.

The Farpoint Gambit is a technique that should not be used lightly, in a spirit of deception, or with a lack of good faith. However, in situations where the individual is trapped by the hardball tactics of an offeror who relies on an exploding offer, the Farpoint Gambit offers a means whereby the pressure applied by the other side can be turned against them, much as a judo expert can use a foe's momentum to provide the energy that leads to the latter's own undoing. To be sure, this is itself a hardball tactic (Schelling 1960; Deutsch 1973), and many might not feel comfortable using it. I offer the Farpoint Gambit as someone who has seen many friends, loved ones, and students put under enormous pressure, forced to make critical life decisions under unnecessarily difficult circumstances due to the callous use of power by people and institutions not operating in good faith.

Notes

The author would like to acknowledge the useful criticism he received on earlier drafts of this work from Professors Roy J. Lewicki of the Ohio State University; the late Jeffrey Z. Rubin of Tufts University; and Michael Wheeler of the Harvard Business School. Also significantly contributing to this work were members of the Program on Negotiation/Fletcher School of Law and Diplomacy "Tuesday Evening Reading Group."

1. Only in the case of a true monopolist, making an offer with many potential buyers, can one argue that the exploding offer is truly an act of self-serving arrogance and convenience on the part of the offeror.

References

Deutsch, M. 1973. *The resolution of conflict.* New Haven: Yale University Press.

Fisher, R., and W. L. Ury. 1981. *Getting to yes: Negotiating agreement without giving in.* Boston: Houghton Mifflin.

Lax, D. A., and J. K. Sebenius. 1986. *The manager as negotiator.* New York: Free Press.

Pruitt, D. G., and J. Z. Rubin. 1986. *Social conflict: Escalation, stalemate, and settlement.* New York: Random House.

Raiffa, H. 1982. *The art and science of negotiation.* Cambridge, MA: Harvard University Press.

Schelling, T. 1960. *The strategy of conflict.* Cambridge, MA: Harvard University Press.

Shell, G. R. 1991. When is it legal to lie in negotiations? *Sloan Management Review* 32, pp. 93–101.

Ury, W. 1991. *Getting past no: Negotiating your way from confrontation to cooperation.* New York: Bantam Books.

Implementing a Collaborative Strategy
Roy J. Lewicki
Alex. Hiam
Karen W. Olander

This chapter shows how to use the collaborative strategy. The word *collaboration* may sound strange to people who are used to viewing negotiation as competitive. But bargaining does not have to be a win–lose proposition—the pie does not have to be fixed. In many cases, conflict and competitiveness between the parties lead them to *believe* that there are only limited resources to be divided between the parties. It is often possible to find solutions to problems that will satisfy all parties by changing or growing the pie instead of fighting over it. The pie analogy, however, leads us to the principal challenge of a collaborative strategy: the parties must somehow learn how to work together. Collaboration, which is an open, sharing, creative process, does not come naturally when you are in a conflict situation or do not trust the other party. Collaboration is therefore difficult for many negotiators to master.

Some negotiators think they are collaborating when in fact all they have done is wrap their competitive strategy in a friendly package. Thus they put on the "image" of collaboration, only to move in for a competitive "grab" near the end of the negotiation. This is not collaboration—it is competitiveness in a collaborative disguise. True collaboration requires the parties to move beyond their initial concerns and positions and go on a joint quest for new, creative ways to maximize their individual and joint outcomes. Before we examine how the collaboration strategy works, let's see how our demonstration case can be adapted to this strategy. Here are Felice and Sara again, this time taking a cooperative, win–win approach to setting up a partnership to develop their interior decorating business:

> "The bottom line is, we need $50,000 in cash, right now, if we want to do this right. I know you have the money—why are you hesitating to use it when we obviously need it?"
>
> "But Sara," Felice objected, "what's the rush? This is a big decision for me. What if things don't work out? I'd be taking all the financial risks and suffering most of the losses. Whatever happened to getting a bank loan?"
>
> "Well, I tried a few banks, but I didn't have any luck—my credit history isn't so great." Sara paused to offer some homemade cookies to Felice. "I'm sorry I'm being so pushy, I know this is something that you need to think through, and I'm not helping. It's just that I've already made some important contacts, and found promising offices for rent; I'm afraid if we don't get started soon, we'll never get going."
>
> Felice thought for a minute as she ate the cookie. "I understand your impatience, I'm impatient, too. I'm excited about working together and I don't want to waste more time. Maybe we're going about this in the wrong way. Let's just take a few minutes to go over our situation. We want to start an interior decorating business together. You have a lot of

Source: From Roy J. Lewicki, A. Hiam, and K. W. Olander, *Think before You Speak* (New York: John Wiley, 1996), pp. 99–119. Used with permission.

experience, but no money to invest, and I have no experience but possibly a lot of money to invest. However, I'm reluctant to sink all my savings into something that may not work out, partly because I'd lose everything I have, but mostly because I'm afraid of ruining our friendship if it doesn't work out. I could probably get a bank loan, but then I'd still be responsible for all the finances, so it seems to me that we should consider bringing in a third party in some capacity."

"Hey—that's not a bad idea. But we would need someone who'd only help us financially—we still need to have control of the business," Sara absently picked crumbs off her sweater. "You know, that reminds me—an old friend of my dad is an architect in a very respected firm. I wonder if we could hook up with them somehow, maybe exchange the rent for an office in their building with a percentage of our business. They could refer customers to us, and eventually we could do the same for them. It's a beautiful old business—you'll love it. It would be a terrific showplace for our work. Do you think I should call him?"

"Well, let's think for a minute," said Felice, "What percentage would we offer them? How about 20 percent? That gives them enough to feel it's worthwhile without taking away our control. Then I could invest $20,000 in the business to get us started and we'll each keep 40 percent of the ownership."

"That sounds great! Let me try it—I'll call my dad right now and get the architect's phone number."

When Sara and Felice proposed the deal to the architect, he was very enthusiastic about their work and the potential for the fit with his business. He offered them office space in his building, and they moved into an office the following week. Within a month, they had landed several jobs that generated a cash flow and helped to establish their reputation as creative, reliable decorators. Over time, the business flourished. They eventually bought the 20 percent back from the architect (with a handsome profit), and their friendship remains strong.

Characteristics of the Collaborative Strategy

In the collaborative strategy both the relationship *and* the outcome are important to both parties. The two parties usually have long-term goals that they are willing to work for together. Both parties are committed to working toward a mutually acceptable agreement that preserves or strengthens the relationship. Because each party values the relationship, they will attempt to find a mutually satisfying solution for both parties. Working together effectively in a collaborative negotiation process can itself enhance the quality of the relationship. This approach is very different from the competitive strategy, where both sides want to win so badly that they pursue their goal at all costs and ignore all the factors that might allow a collaborative process.

In addition, in the collaborative model, intangibles are important and accounted for. These include such items as each party's reputation, pride, principles, and sense of fairness. Because these concerns are important, the negotiations must stay on a rational, reasonable, and fair level. If the parties get angry at each other, the collaborative atmosphere will degenerate into a competitive one. Allow for plenty of venting time if you or the other party begins to get irritated, and be sure to listen to complaints about your behavior with an open mind to avoid conflicts that can derail collaboration. There must be a great deal of trust, cooperation, openness, and communication between the parties to engage in effective problem solving.

Finally, the parties must be willing to make *concessions* to accomplish their goals. These concessions should be repaid with creative win–win solutions, but they represent a risk for each party that the other party must be careful not to abuse.

In the collaborative strategy, the constituency (if there is one) plays a very different role from that which it plays in competitive negotiations. Generally, the members of the constituency are supportive and will promote the relationship between the two parties.

The collaborative strategy relies on deadlines that are mutually determined and observed. They are not used for manipulation, as we found in the competitive strategy. Information flows freely and is not used to control the situation or guarded to maintain power. The objective is to find the best solution *for both sides.* Similarities between the two parties, not differences, are emphasized.

There are four major steps in carrying out a collaborative strategy: (1) identify the problem; (2) understand the problem; (3) generate alternative solutions; (4) select a solution. We will examine each in detail.

Steps in the Collaborative Strategy

Identify the Problem

This may sound like a simple step, but in the collaborative model both sides are involved equally in the process, and both need to agree on what the problem is. When you were gathering information you focused on *your* point of view, but for the collaborative strategy to work, you will need to work closely with the other party to find a common view of the problem.[1]

When defining the problem, try to use neutral language and to keep it impersonal. For example, you might say "We are not able to get our work out on time" rather than "You are preventing us from doing our work and getting it out on time." It is important to define the obstacles to your goals without attacking other people.

Try to define the problem as a common goal. For example, in the Sara and Felice situation, they might say, "Our goal is to find a way to start our business without Felice having to assume too much financial risk." Keep the goal definition as simple as possible. Try not to load the situation with peripheral issues that are not really related to the central concern. Stick with the primary issues.

Each party needs to be assertive, but cooperative at the same time: You need to be clear about what you want to achieve, yet not at the expense of dominating the other side. Because the relationship is important, you need to see the problem from the other party's perspective—"to walk a mile in the other person's shoes" as much as possible. Understanding and empathy[2] go a long way to finding the common issues.

Watch out for a tendency to define solutions before you have fully defined the problem. In fact, you should avoid discussing solutions until you have thoroughly defined and understood the problem(s). And remember, the more creative the problem definition, the more likely you are to discover a new, beneficial win–win solution. Throw caution to the wind, brainstorm wildly, and hope for a creative insight that will make it fun and easy to solve the problem.

Understand the Problem

In this step, you try to get behind the issues to the underlying needs and interests.[3] As noted earlier, an *interest* is a broader perspective that each side has, which is usually "behind" their position. In our example, Felice's position is that she does not want to provide full financial backing for the new business; her interest is to minimize her financial risk while also helping to get the business started and into a profitable mode. You need to learn not only about the needs and interests of each party, but also about their fears and concerns. Felice's fear is that she will lose a large amount of her investment (and her savings) if the business goes bad. The reason for getting behind the positions is that they tend to be fixed and rigid; modifying them requires the parties to make concessions either toward or away from the target point. In contrast, interests define what the parties care about more broadly, and there are often multiple "roads to Rome," or several ways to resolve the conflict between these competing interests. In addition, a focus on interests tends to take some of the personal dimension[4] out of the negotiation and shifts it to the underlying concerns. Since there is bound to be a difference in thinking styles, people will approach even similar issues in different ways. Positions offer only one way to think about an issue; interests offer multiple ways to think about it. Thus you can find out "where they are coming from" more effectively by discussing interests than by stating positions.

Interests may reflect current or longer-term concerns. And parties are likely to have multiple interests. It is also important to realize that each party may have different interests. By using "why" questions, you can dig deeper into the reasons for each party's position. An interest is the why of a position.

Interests[5] may be substantive, as with concerns for prices, rates, and availability of resources. Interests may have to do with the process, as in how we will conduct the actual negotiation. This concern may, in turn, be based on how the process has been completed in the past, or on how we want to change and improve it for the future. Concerns may also center around sustaining and enjoying the relationship. Or a party may have a strong interest in principles. They may be concerned about what is fair or ethical, right or acceptable. For example, Felice and Sara have a number of interests at stake in addition to the substantive interest of their specific solution to funding their new business. Because they are starting a business in which they will work together actively, they are trying to get off on the right foot in the way they solve and deal with joint problems. Thus they want to establish a good problem-solving process, they want to preserve—and even enhance—their relationship with one another, and they probably care a great deal about principles, such as the precedent created by both the outcome and the process of this negotiation or the perceived fairness of their agreement. Felice and Sara have a lot riding on this deliberation, and it is most important that they work it out in a way that creates a good outcome and strengthens their working relationship.

Remember that even if you define interests carefully, they can change. Since the negotiation process is an evolving one, you may need to stop from time to time to reconsider interests. If the conversation begins to change in tone or the focus seems to shift, this may be a signal that interests have changed. Since the collaborative strategy is one of openness, the parties with changing interests should be encouraged to share their shifts in needs. The other party may facilitate this by being willing to expand resources,[6] extend the time frame, or change the details of the negotiation to accommodate the changed interests (we say more about some of these tactics in the next section). As Sara and Felice's business took off and prospered, their interests changed. As the business was successful, Felice was less worried that her financial investment would be seriously at risk. As the new decorating contracts were assured, she became more confident and trusted Sara more, and the two were eventually able to buy the 20 percent investment back from the architect. Both the changed nature of the business and the trust level between Sara and Felice had a lot to do with changing the interests of these two negotiators.

Generate Alternative Solutions

Once you have defined the issues to the satisfaction of both parties, you can begin to look for solutions. Notice that this is plural: *solutions.* You want to find a group of possible solutions, then select from among them the best solution for both parties.

There are two major ways to go about finding solutions. One is to redefine the problem so you can find win–win alternatives for what at first may have seemed to be a win–lose problem. The second is to take the problem at hand and generate a long list of options for solving it.

Redefining the Problem   To illustrate the different approaches, we will use an example suggested by Dean Pruitt, about a husband and wife who are trying to decide where to spend a two-week vacation.[7] He wants to go to the mountains for hiking, fishing, and some rest; she wants to go to the beach for sun, swimming, and night life. They have decided that spending one week in each place will not really be adequate for either person, because too much time is spent in packing, unpacking, and traveling between the two locations.

- *Expand the pie:* If the problem is based on scarce resources, the object would be to find a way to expand or reallocate the resources so that each party could obtain their desired end. Knowing the underlying interests can help in this endeavor. For example, the parties could take a four-week vacation and spend two weeks in each place. While this would require more time and money, each person would get a two-week vacation in the chosen spot.

- *Logroll:* If there are two issues in a negotiation and each party has a different priority for them, then one may be able to be traded off for the other. For example, if Problems A and B are common to both parties, but Party 1 cares most about Problem A and Party 2 cares most about Problem B, then a solution that solves both problems can provide each party with a happy resolution. "You get this and I get that." If there are multiple issues, it may take some trial and error to find what packages will satisfy each party. In our example, if the husband really wants to stay in an informal rustic mountain cabin, and the wife really wants to stay in a fancy hotel, then another resolution is for them to go to the mountains but stay in a fancy hotel (or an informal beach house at the shore).

- *Offer nonspecific compensation:* Another method is for one party to "payoff" the other for giving in on an issue. The "payoff" may not be monetary, and it may not even be related to the negotiation. The party paying off needs to know what it will take to keep the other party so happy that they won't care about the outcome of this negotiation. In a house sale negotiation, for example, the seller might include all window coverings (curtains, drapes, blinds) as part of the deal. The buyer may be so delighted that he decides not to ask for any other price break. In our vacation example, the wife might buy the husband a set of golf clubs, which will make him so happy that he will go anywhere she wants to go (since there are golf courses everywhere).

- *Cut costs:* In this method, one party accomplishes specific objectives and the other's costs are minimized by going along with the agreement. This differs from nonspecific compensation because in this method the other party can minimize costs and "suffering," whereas in the other method, the costs and suffering do not go away, but the party is somehow compensated for them. This method requires a clear understanding of the other party's needs and preferences, along with their costs. In our vacation example, the wife says to the husband, "What can I do to make going to the beach as painless as possible for you?" He tells her that he wants to stay in a beach house away from the big hotels, get some rest, and be near a golf course and near several places where he can go fishing. They both go down to their favorite travel agent and find a location that offers all these things.

- *Bridge:* In bridging, the parties invent new options that meet each other's needs. Again, both parties must be very familiar with the other party's interests and needs. When two business partners (Sara and Felice) bring in a third partner who can offer resources neither of them wanted to contribute, this is an effective example of bridging. In our vacation example, the husband and wife go to a travel agent and find a place that offers hiking, fishing, beaches, swimming, golf, privacy, and night life. They book a two-week vacation for Hawaii and have a wonderful time!

Generating a List of Solutions   The second approach to inventing solutions is to take the problem as defined and try to generate a list of possible solutions. The key to finding answers in this approach is to generate as many solutions as possible without evaluating them. The solutions should be general rather than party-specific—they should not favor one party over the other. At a later stage, each solution can then be evaluated to determine whether it adequately meets the needs and interests of both parties.

What is interesting in this process is that both parties engage in trying to solve the other party's problem as much as they do their own.[8] It is a cooperative endeavor. And, as you have probably heard many times before, two heads are better than one.

If you get to this stage, but the issues still seem murky, you may need to go back to the problem definition and rework that step. It should be easy to generate solutions if the problem is clearly stated in a way that does not bias solutions toward one party or the other. Otherwise, if you are comfortable with the definition of the problem, forge ahead.

There are a number of ways to generate ideas for solutions. Remember that you are only *generating* solutions in this step, not evaluating them or deciding whether to use them—yet. That will happen in the next step.

- *Brainstorming:* This common method for generating ideas usually works best in several small groups rather than one large one, depending on the number of people involved. Write down as many ideas as possible, without judging them. It is best to write or post the ideas on a flip chart, chalkboard, or similar display device, so that everyone can see them and keep track of what has been done. The key ground rule is that *ideas must not be evaluated as they are suggested.* Don't let anyone say, "Oh, that's a dumb idea!" or "That won't work!" Keep ideas flowing, keep focused on the problem and how to solve it, without associating people with the problem or the solutions.

  It often happens that people quickly think of a few possibilities, and then run out of ideas. At this point, it is easy to think you are done because you have a few solutions. Don't stop here—stick at it for a while longer. Otherwise you may miss some really good ideas, particularly creative ones that no one has considered before. Ask outsiders for ideas, too. Sometimes they bring a fresh approach to the problem.

- *Piggybacking*[9] can be used in conjunction with brainstorming. This technique is simply to build on someone else's idea to produce yet another idea. It's often done by working in a sequence order; one person starts with a brainstormed idea, then the next person has to "piggyback" until possible variations on the idea are exhausted.

- *Nominal groups:* In this method, each negotiator works with a small group—perhaps his or her constituency—and makes a list of possible solutions. These are discussed within the group, then considered, one at a time, by the group as a whole. They can be ranked in terms of preferences or likely effectiveness. The drawback of this method is that anyone not present at the session will miss offering input or helping to shape the solution.

- *Surveys:* Another useful method is to distribute a questionnaire stating the problem and asking respondents to list possible solutions. In this case, each person works alone on the survey, so people miss out on the synergy of working together. However, the advantage is that a number of people who have good ideas, but are normally reticent about getting into a group's conversation, can offer their thoughts and ideas without being attacked or critiqued. Another advantage is that this draws in the ideas of people who may not be able to attend the negotiation or formally participate in it.

Prioritize the Options and Reduce the List   Once you have a list of possible solutions, you can reduce it by rating the ideas. In communicating your priorities and preferences to the other party, it's important to maintain an attitude of "firm flexibility."[10] Be firm about achieving your interests, while remaining flexible about how those interests might be achieved. There are a number of tactics to keep the discussion collaborative while being clear and consistent about your preferences:

- Remember that you are only *prioritizing* the list, not yet deciding on the actual solution.

- Be assertive in defending and establishing your basic interests, but do not demand a particular solution.

- Signal to the other party your flexibility and willingness to hear the other party's interests by practicing your listening skills.

- Indicate your willingness to modify a position or have your interests met in an alternative way. Perhaps you will be able to trade one point for another. This will demonstrate your openness to suggestions and willingness to work together.

- Show ability and willingness to problem-solve. Skill in problem solving is valuable here, especially if you get stuck on a particular point and need to find some way to resolve it to everyone's satisfaction. If you can settle this issue, it will help when you get to the next step and are actually deciding on the solution. You will have set the stage for collaboration.

- Keep lines of communication open. If tempers flare, take a break, and talk about it if need be. Also talk with the other party about how you can continue to work on the problem without getting angry or losing control. Make sure both parties feel that they are being heard. Steer discussion away from personalities, and concentrate on the issues: "Separate the people from the problem."[11]

- Underscore what is most important to you by saying, "This is what I need to accomplish," or "As long as I can accomplish _____, I'll be very happy." Resist the temptation to give in just to get a resolution. Giving in is an accommodating strategy that will not result in the best outcome for both parties.

- Reevaluate any points on which you disagree. Be sure that both sides agree on the adjusted prioritized list so that you will both feel comfortable as you move to the final step.

- Eliminate competitive tactics by identifying them and either confronting them or renegotiating the process. If the discussion becomes competitive, point out that this is happening. Then try to resolve the problem *before* the entire negotiation becomes competitive.

Select a Solution[12]

Using your prioritized list of potential solutions from the previous step, narrow the range of possibilities by focusing on the positive suggestions that people seemed to favor most. For example, one way to prioritize is to logroll (package each person's first choice together). If parties have the same first choice, but very different preferences for it, try to invent a way for both sides to "win" on this issue.

Try to change any negative ideas into positive ones,[13] or else eliminate them from the list. Stating alternatives as positives keeps the negotiation upbeat and on a positive note. Avoid attributing negative ideas to any particular person or side.

Evaluate the solutions on the basis of quality and acceptability. Consider the opinions of both parties. Do not require people to justify their preferences. People often do not know why they have a preference; they just do.

When you are preparing to select a solution, if you foresee any potential problems with this process, you may want to establish objective criteria for evaluation before you start the selection process.[14] In other words, before you move toward picking among prioritized options, work against a set of objective facts, figures, data, and criteria that were developed independently of the options. There are numerous examples. In our example between Felice and Sara, they might go to a small business assistance agency, such as a local bank or small business development group, to find out how other business partnerships have dealt with this situation. If a car owner and a garage mechanic are having a dispute about how much it should cost to repair a starter motor, there are books available that indicate the "standard" cost for parts and labor for this repair. Finally, if a group of people is trying to pick a job candidate from among a group who applied for the job, their work will be considerably facilitated if they spend time developing criteria by which to evaluate the applicants before they actually look at résumés and interview people. If you can't find objective criteria, another technique is to have a third party help you.

If necessary, use subgroups. These are helpful if the problem is complex or if the outcome will affect a large group. It may be more efficient to use several small groups than to use one large one. Be sure the subgroups contain representatives from each party.

Fairness and Other Intangibles   Intangibles are often operating in the decisions. For example, gaining recognition or looking strong to a constituency may be important factors in the selection of solutions. Acknowledge the importance of intangibles by building them into the decisions. For example, if the other party needs to maintain esteem with a constituency, they may be willing to settle on a lesser point that still allows them to appear in a favorable light. In fact, it will help them greatly if you work with them to determine how to make them look strong and capable to the constituency.

Fairness is usually one of the most important intangibles. In a win–win negotiation, both parties want to achieve a fair outcome, rather than maximize their outcome—which they might push for in a competitive negotiation. There are a number of ways to decide what is fair, but three common criteria often apply:[15]

- An outcome that gives each side *equal* outcomes. Thus it is not surprising that one of the most common ways to solve negotiation problems—particularly win–lose, competitive ones—is for the parties to agree to "divide it down the middle."

- An outcome that gives each side more or less based on *equity* (what it has earned or deserves, based on the time or energy committed). In this case, the side that puts in more should get out more. Equity is usually based on the ratio of outcome to input, so that the person who works harder, suffers more, and so on deserves a proportionally larger share of the results.

- An outcome that gives each side more or less, depending on what it *needs*. In this case, if one side can create a legitimate claim that it needs or deserves a better outcome, there may be a good case to be made for dividing up the resources so that those with greater needs actually gain more.

We can see how the equity versus equality arguments can easily come into play in the discussions between Felice and Sara. Sara—having no money but great creative skills—could argue that they should split all profits from the business equally. In essence, she is arguing that creative contribution and financial contribution to the business should be weighted equally. In contrast, Felice—having few creative skills but a lot of money to put toward the venture—could argue that they should split profits in proportion to the amount of money contributed during the start-up. If the two of them stuck to these positions strongly, they could have an intractable dispute over how to value financial and creative contributions, which would be a major block in their discussions.

Emotional Escalation   If emotions surface, or if people get angry, take a break. Give people an opportunity to discuss the reasons for their dissatisfaction. Be sure everyone has cooled off before you start again, and try to keep personalities out of the deliberations. If taking a break does not work, seek out a third party to help you.

Other Suggestions for Keeping the Decision-Making Process on Track   You can use logrolling to make combination options. You can also take advantage of risk preferences, differences in expectations, and differences in time preferences. For example, one party may prefer an option with low risk, while the other party is willing to accept an option with a much higher risk; you may be able to combine these so that each party gets its preferred outcome. Likewise, some options may satisfy only short-term concerns, but may be more important to one party than longer-term issues. These, too, can be traded off.

It is very important not to rush the process of selecting solutions, appealing as it may be to do so. If you get to the bottom line too quickly, you may miss some good potential options, and you may fail to ensure that both sides participate equally.[16] Collaborative efforts require the participation of both sides; they may also require time to mull over alternatives and think through all the consequences. Good collaborative negotiation requires time and cannot be rushed.

Remember that *everything is tentative until the very end*. During the solution-generating phase, some people may even object to writing anything down, as this may make them nervous. They may feel they are being railroaded into commitments they have not agreed to. Other than the "working documents" that you may create as you define the problem and invent options, you may want to begin to record decisions only when the group is close to consensus. That way, nothing is set in stone until the very end. This open, fluid approach makes it possible to share creative ideas and suggestions. The minute one party says, "But you said yesterday you'd be willing to . . . ," the collaboration starts to unravel as participants begin to worry about being held accountable for "positions." This difficult and critical rule is violated too often as people revert instinctively to a competitive style without realizing the impact on idea generation and sharing.

Once the parties have agreed on solutions and prepared a document to outline the agreement, it should be passed around for everyone to read. Some people have suggested that this may even be an excellent way to manage the entire prioritization and decision-making process. Start with a tentative draft of what people agree to, then continue to pass it around, sharpening language, clarifying words, and writing out agreements so that all agree with it and pledge to live by it. You may want to make a plan for implementing the agreement, and to set up a time frame in which the parties can try out the solution.[17] This again allows for all to fully participate and to become committed to the plan.

How to Be Successful with Collaborative Negotiation

Researchers have identified several keys to successful collaboration.[18] They are useful as a checklist for the strategic negotiator in planning and implementing a collaborative strategy.

Create Common Goals or Objectives

There may be three different ways the goals will be played out: All parties will share in the results equally; the parties will share a common end but receive different benefits; or the parties will have different goals, but share in a collective effort to accomplish them. In any of these cases, both parties believe that they can benefit by working together as opposed to working separately, and that the results will be better than they would be if each party worked separately.

Maintain Confidence in Your Own Ability to Solve Problems

This is more or less a matter of "If you think you can, you can." As we mentioned earlier, it helps to have a strong knowledge of the problem area, but lack of knowledge can be overcome if the desire is there. Probably the most important element is to develop skills in negotiating collaboratively, since it is a less common form of negotiation. The more you do it, the better you will become at doing it.

Value the Other Party's Opinion

Valuing the other party's point of view is difficult if you have been accustomed in the past to focusing only on your own position and maintaining it. In the collaborative strategy, you value the other party's position equally with your own.[19] You need good listening skills and openness to hear the other party's point of view.

Share the Motivation and Commitment to Working Together

In the collaborative strategy, you are not only committed to the idea of working together with the other party, you take actions to do so. You pursue both your own needs and those of the other party. This means each party must be explicit about their needs.

In collaborative negotiation, the parties strive to identify their similarities to each other and to downplay their differences. The differences are not ignored, they are simply recognized and accepted for what they are.

The parties are aware that they share a common fate, particularly if they expect to work together after this negotiation has been completed. They know they can gain more if they work jointly than if they work separately. To do this, they focus on outputs and results.[20]

Motivated, committed parties will control their behavior in a number of ways. Individuals will avoid being competitive, combative, evasive, defensive, or stubborn. They will work at being open and trusting, flexible, and willing to share information and not hoard it for their own use.

A Cautionary Note   Believe it or not, there is such a thing as too much collaboration! The two parties must not be so committed to each other that they do not look out for their own needs. If they begin to subordinate their needs to the other party, they will be moving toward the accommodating or lose–win strategies and will lose out on the benefits that the collaborative strategy can offer.

Trust

Because trust creates more trust—which is necessary to begin and sustain cooperation—it is important to make the opening moves in collaborative negotiation in a way that engenders trust.[21] Opening conversations may occur even before the formal negotiations begin, when the parties are just becoming acquainted. If one party finds a reason to mistrust the other party at this time, this may stifle any future efforts at collaboration.

If the parties are new to each other, or if they have been combative or competitive in the past, they will have to build trust. Each party will approach the negotiation with expectations based on the research they did on each other or on past history. Generally, we trust others if they appear to be similar to us, if they have a positive attitude toward us, or if they appear cooperative and trusting. We also tend to trust them if they are dependent on us. Likewise, making concessions appears to be a trusting gesture, so we are likely to respond in kind.

In contrast, it is easy to engender mistrust. This often begins either with a competitive, hostile action, or with an indication that one does not trust the other. Once mistrust gets started, it is very easy to build and escalate, and very difficult to change over to collaboration. Trust escalation and deescalation have often been compared with the children's game "Chutes and Ladders." In this analogy, it is easy to move down the "chute" of mistrust, rapidly sliding to the bottom, but much more difficult to climb back up the "ladder" that will restore and sustain good trust between parties.[22]

Clear, Accurate Communication

Communicating effectively is the bedrock of negotiation, no matter what form the bargaining strategy takes. In the collaborative strategy, precise and accurate communication is of the utmost importance. It is crucial to listen well so that you know what the other party wants and why they want it. This requires more than just superficial listening.

It is through communication that one party shares information[23] with the other party. This communication must be delivered in the most concrete terms so there is no confusion or misinterpretation. Feedback and frequent questions can clarify the message if necessary.

Some of the communication in negotiation may be formal, based on procedural or other rules such as rules of order. Sometimes communication will be informal, as during breaks and after sessions. Or perhaps the entire undertaking will be informal, depending on the personal characteristics and styles of the participants.

Obstacles to Achieving Good Collaboration

Collaborative negotiation is a lot of work. But the rewards can be great. Sometimes, however, no matter how much you want to succeed, obstacles may prevent you from moving ahead with a collaborative strategy. One (or both) of the parties

- May not be able to do the required work.
- May have a win–lose attitude.
- May not be able to see the potential for collaboration.
- May be motivated to only achieve their own goals.
- May not be capable of establishing or maintaining productive working relationships.
- May be inhibited by biases.
- May have a constituency that is pressing for competitive behavior or quick outcomes.

Further, the situation may contain elements that require a mix of strategies. Then you need to separate the issues into the component parts and deal with each separately.

Sometimes you may feel that you do not have the time or energy to push forward with a collaborative strategy, especially if you encounter one or more of the preceding situations.

What If There Is a Breakdown?

If there is a conflict, try to move the discussion to a neutral point, and summarize where you are.[24] If there is a total breakdown in communication, and you just cannot get the negotiation back on track, you may need to resort to conflict resolution strategies or to third-party intervention. And also note that you and the other party can, at any point, reach a mutual agreement to abandon your collaboration and adopt another negotiating style. For instance, you might try collaborating, decide you don't like working together, and decide that you will "agree to disagree" and revert to a conventional competitive strategy—or toward a more expedient and simple outcome through compromising. Remember, however, that you will give up the relationship benefits, so do not advocate the competitive strategy unless you decide your initial estimation of relationship importance was too high. Also, since you will have shared much information through your collaboration attempt, it can now be used against you in a competitive negotiation. Therefore, the slide from collaboration to competition is not generally a happy or profitable one because some of the actions you undertook under the assumption that you could trust the other and work with them may now be used against you as weapons.

A Case Study: Negotiating Strategic Alliances

A business example of the use of negotiation is in the area of strategic alliances, which are gaining in importance worldwide, particularly in Europe. Global competition has intensified the scramble for access to markets, products, and technologies. Strategic alliances are one strategy that companies are using to survive or to keep up with the new developments in industry.

Negotiating a strategic alliance presents a challenge. "A bad negotiation tactic may do lasting damage; good negotiation tactics must be repeated a number of times before the partner accepts this as a pattern."[25] In a strategic alliance, the relationship concerns will be very important.

In 1985 Corning and Ciba-Geigy formed Ciba Corning Diagnostics, an alliance based in the United States, designed to enhance Corning's medical diagnostics business. Ciba-Geigy is a global pharmaceutical and chemical company based in Switzerland. Corning, based in New York, is a world leader in glass and ceramics technology. The alliance would combine the strengths of the two partners to develop innovative medical diagnostic tests.

There was synergy in what each partner could offer to the alliance. Negotiation went smoothly, as Ciba was willing to have Corning manage more extensively in the beginning. Corning's managers were willing to concede on points of strong interest to Ciba, and thus they were able to agree on a time line for their work. Each partner appointed its director of research and development to the board of the new alliance, which signaled to the other party a willingness to share technology, while garnering internal support for the alliance as well.

Each side had representatives to build consensus, improve communication, and obtain support for the parent organization, Ciba and Corning actively looked into ways for each partner to gain by opening up possibilities for broadening the product line, marketing, technology, and growth. They were able to negotiate any issues that arose because, as mutual trust grew, they were willing to discuss such problems clearly and openly.

A strategic alliance will not succeed if the two potential partners have conflicting underlying motives. If they are both leaders in their field, it may be difficult for them to collaborate. Likewise, if they have strongly differing views of which activities should take priority or what the time lines should be, the success of such an alliance would be questionable.

To create a successful alliance, each organization must be willing to support the efforts to create an alliance agreement. This means that political support must be generated within the organizations of the potential partners. Building support may take time. For example, the Japanese take a long time to complete this process (at least from the American point of view). Conversely, the Japanese see American firms as too pushy.

Negotiating with Your Boss

Since everyone has had some sort of experience dealing with a boss at one time or another, we will take a moment here to look at ways to negotiate collaboratively with a manager.[26] Although performance review, salary, and benefits are usually the major areas for discussion and possible conflict with one's manager, there are others that arise more often. For example, what if you are asked by your boss to do a project that you realize you cannot possibly complete without working overtime? If you do not mind staying late, go ahead. But if you find yourself doing this frequently and resenting it, maybe you need to consider negotiating about it the next time.

Negotiating with the boss is often viewed as a competitive, win–lose, or fixed-pie situation. It can also be viewed as a lose–win situation, in which it is better to accommodate and let the boss win all the time, rather than try to argue for a preferred outcome and have the boss be angry at your "assertiveness." But if you think about it, both parties might be able to gain something from collaborative negotiation.

Think about the steps in the collaborative strategy we covered earlier in the chapter. Look at your own needs, as well as those of your boss. Remember that the key to collaborative bargaining is to find a way to solve the other person's problem.

So in our hypothetical situation, your boss may have been asked by her boss to drop everything and get this project out, at any cost. (Your boss may have some bargaining of her own to do.) At any rate, your boss has to have this project done, and there is no way for you to complete it during normal hours, given the other work you have to do and the deadlines for those projects. Your boss could ask someone else to do it, but perhaps she knows you can do the job better and more quickly.

First, clarify the situation. Find out the circumstances from your boss. Be sure you understand the details of the project. Gather information you may need about what you are working on at the present time.

When it is time to discuss the project again, you will be prepared. Be sure your boss knows and understands the situation from your side. List what you are currently working on, and make sure she is willing for you to put those things aside to work on this rush project. Or does she prefer to have you give it only part of your attention? We knew one person who, when her boss piled new work on her desk, made a list of all the projects she was currently managing. Then she handed the list to her boss, and asked him to number the list in the order that he wanted things done. It made him decide what his priorities were.

You can make a number of suggestions for how to complete the project given the circumstances. (This means you will have brainstormed for ideas before you meet with her.) One option might be for the boss (perhaps with your help) to find more resources. Two people could perhaps help with the project, thus halving the time it will take to complete.

Another option would be for your boss to get an extension of the time allotted for the project. To do this, she would have to negotiate with her boss.

A third option might be to change the "specs" of the project (e.g., make it less detailed or more streamlined), which would allow you to complete it in less time.

You also could suggest, "If I stay late several nights to do this project, I would like to take compensating time off," or "If I do this project, then I need help to complete my other projects on time, or else an extension." These are compromising strategies.

This example illustrates that even an apparently simple negotiation can be more complex than we realize. In this case, it involves not just you and your boss, but her boss as well (and who knows who else?). In any situation, it helps to break down a problem into its component parts and try to get at the underlying needs.

Summary

In this chapter, we have outlined the collaborative strategy. When using this strategy, your objective is to both maximize your outcome on the substantive issues and sustain or enhance the quality of the relationship between you and the other side. To do so, you need to meet your outcome needs as well as the needs of the other party in a manner that strengthens the trust, mutuality, and productive problem-solving in the relationship.

Good collaboration is a wonderful thing to be able to create and sustain. But it is not an all-purpose panacea, and making it work well often requires a large commitment of time and energy. There are times when the parties might be just as well off to compromise, accommodate, or even avoid negotiations.

Endnotes

1. A. C. Filley, *Interpersonal Conflict Resolution* (Glenview, IL: Scott, Foresman, 1975); G. F. Shea, *Creative Negotiating* (Boston: CBI Publishing, 1983).

2. A. Williams, "Managing Employee Conflict," *Hotels,* July 1992, p. 23.

3. R. Fisher and W. Ury, *Getting to Yes* (Boston: Houghton Mifflin, 1981); R. Fisher, W. Ury, and B, Patton, *Getting to Yes: Negotiating Agreement without Giving In,* 2nd ed. (New York: Penguin Books, 1991).

4. M. Freedman, "Dealing Effectively with Difficult People," *Nursing 93* (September 1993), pp. 97–102.

5. D. Lax and J. Sebenius, *The Manager as Negotiator: Bargaining for Cooperation and Competitive Gain* (New York: Free Press, 1986).

6. T. Gosselin, "Negotiating with Your Boss," *Training and Development,* May 1993, pp. 37–41.

7. D. G. Pruitt, "Achieving Integrative Agreements," in M. Bazerman and R. Lewicki (Eds.), *Negotiating in Organizations* (Beverly Hills, CA: Sage, 1983); R. J. Lewicki, J. Litterer, J. Minton, and D. A. Saunders, *Negotiation,* 2nd ed. (Burr Ridge, IL: Richard D. Irwin, 1994).

8. M. B. Grover, "Letting Both Sides Win," *Forbes,* September 30, 1991, p. 178.

9. G. F. Shea, "Learn How to Treasure Differences," *HR Magazine,* December 1992, pp. 34–37.

10. D. G. Pruitt, "Strategic Choice in Negotiation," *American Behavioral Scientist 27* (1983), pp. 167–194; Fisher, Ury, and Patton, *Getting to Yes: Negotiating Agreement without Giving In.*

11. Fisher and Ury, *Getting to Yes.*

12. Filley, *Interpersonal Conflict Resolution;* D. G. Pruitt and P. J. D. Carnevale, *Negotiation in Social Conflict* (Pacific Grove, CA: Brooks-Cole, 1993); Shea, *Creative Negotiating;* R. Walton and R. McKersie, *A Behavioral Theory of Labor Negotiations* (New York: McGraw-Hill, 1965).

13. Shea, "Learn How to Treasure Differences."

14. Fisher and Ury, *Getting to Yes.*

15. B. H. Sheppard, R. J. Lewicki, and J. Minton, *Organizational Justice* (New York: Free Press, 1992).

16. R. H. Mouritsen, "Client Involvement through Negotiation: A Key to Success," *The American Salesman,* August 1993, pp. 24–27.

17. A. Williams, "Managing Employee Conflict," *Hotels,* July 1992, p. 23.

18. Pruitt, "Strategic Choice in Negotiation"; D. G. Pruitt, *Negotiation Behavior* (New York: Academic Press, 1981); Filley, *Interpersonal Conflict Resolution.*

19. Fisher, Ury, and Patton, *Getting to Yes: Negotiating Agreement without Giving In.*

20. Freedman, "Dealing Effectively with Difficult People."

21. C. M. Crumbaugh and G. W. Evans, "Presentation Format, Other Persons' Strategies and Cooperative Behavior in the Prisoner's Dilemma," *Psychological Reports 20* (1967), pp. 895–902; R, L. Michelini, "Effects of Prior Interaction, Contact, Strategy, and Expectation of Meeting on Gain Behavior and Sentiment," *Journal of Conflict Resolution 15* (1971), pp. 97–103; S. Oksamp, "Effects of Programmed Initial Strategies in a Prisoner's Dilemma Game," *Psychometrics 19* (1970), pp. 195–196; V. Sermat and R. P. Gregovich, "The Effect of Experimental Manipulation on Cooperative Behavior in a Checkers Game," *Psychometric Science 4* (1966), pp. 435–436.

22. R. J. Lewicki and B. B. Bunker, "Trust in Relationships: A Model of Trust Development and Decline," in J. Z. Rubin and B. B. Bunker (Eds.), *Conflict, Cooperation and Justice* (San Francisco: Jossey-Bass, 1995).

23. M. Neale and M. H. Bazerman, *Cognition and Rationality in Negotiation* (New York: Free Press, 1991).

24. R. H. Mouritsen, "Client Involvement through Negotiation: A Key to Success," *The American Salesman,* August 1993, pp. 24–27.

25. Stephen Gates, "Alliance Management Guidelines," *Strategic Alliances: Guidelines for Successful Management* (New York: Conference Board, Report Number 1028, 1993).

26. T. Gosselin, "Negotiating with Your Boss," *Training and Development,* May 1993, pp. 37–41; M. B. Grover, "Letting Both Sides Win," *Forbes,* September 30, 1991. p. 178.

Reading 1.11

Interest-Based Negotiation: An Engine-Driving Change

John R. Stepp
Kevin M. Sweeney
Robert L. Johnson

Every year, 25,000 to 30,000 managers and union representatives negotiate collective bargaining agreements. These events are the most strategic opportunities they have to produce change, yet they often remain the last bastion of the status quo and old-style labor relations. Most negotiators still engage in old rituals that often result in leaving problems unsolved and potential solutions "on the table."

The inadequacies of traditional negotiations first surface in the preparation phase, which resembles a mobilization for war. Differences are accentuated, villains identified, weapons honed, war paint generously applied. The parties then arrive at the bargaining table in full battle dress. The focus tends to be on separate or what are assumed to be competing interests. The negotiation process resembles a strategic retreat from exaggerated positions. Collective bargaining, arguably the parties' most valuable tool, is reduced to an instrument of conflict.

In fairness to traditional bargaining, it works well when the parties control their markets, when they face little competition, when change is proceeding at a digestible pace, and when bargaining structures are centralized, thereby permitting coordinated or pattern bargaining to remove labor costs from the competitive equation.

A New Bargaining Tool

Interest-based negotiation, on the other hand, has demonstrated its capacity to enhance bargaining outcomes without impairing the parties' relationship. Its essence is information-sharing, creative exploration, and working toward mutually beneficial solutions. There are six basic steps to the process.

1. *The bargainers describe and define the issue,* such as the topic to be discussed and/or the problem to be resolved.

2. *An opportunity for each party is provided to identify its interests in regard to the issue—and to explore the interests of the other party.* An interest is a reason why the issue is important to one or both of the parties.

3. *With a shared understanding of all the interests, the parties create options or potential solutions* to satisfy as many of the interests as possible.

4. *The parties agree on the criteria they will use to evaluate the options.* Criteria are the characteristics of an acceptable solution.

Source: Reprinted with permission of The American Society for Quality from the Sep/Oct 1998 issue of *The Journal for Quality and Participation,* Cincinnati, Ohio. © 1998. All rights reserved. For more information contact ASQ at 414-272-8575 or visit www.asq.org.

5. *The parties select the options that best meet the agreed-upon criteria.*

6. *The parties integrate or craft these options into a comprehensive solution,* concluding the process.

Preparation

A decade of experience in assisting managers and union representatives in conducting interest-based negotiations has convinced us that applying certain approaches and techniques to both the preparation and execution phases of the negotiation can make all the difference between success and failure.

Preparation, an essential key, should begin four to six months in advance of bargaining. An early start allows the bargaining committees sufficient time to be trained in the interest-based negotiation process. Interest-based negotiation training is comprised of three key parts:

1. *An introduction to the interest-based negotiation model.*

2. *Skill(s) building.*

3. *Practice through simulations.*

Familiarization with the theoretical constructs of interest-based negotiation is the starting point. Just as traditional bargaining requires a discernible set of skills, so does interest-based negotiation. Active listening, brainstorming, and consensus decision making lead the list. After initial skill-building practice, participants deepen their understanding and hone their skills during a series of increasingly complex and challenging simulations, accompanied by critical feedback from a skilled practitioner.

Following the training, both parties can make an informed decision whether or not to utilize the interest-based negotiation process. If yes, then preparatory work must begin immediately with the constituents of each party. All constituents should be given an explanation of the process to include how it works, why the bargaining committees have elected to utilize it, and how both the preparation and conduct of bargaining will differ from the old rituals witnessed in previous negotiations.

In our experience, the traditional approach thrives on the perception of fervent advocacy. The only means of counteracting this perception is to inform one's constituents of the shortcomings of the traditional bargaining process in today's environment and to explain how interest-based negotiation is less likely to leave problems and potential solutions on the table.

In the end, it is results that matter. Interest-based negotiation yields superior outcomes and undamaged relationships.

How to Start Off

Before formal negotiations begin, the parties should identify the key issues and determine data needs. For complex issues, brainstorming during bargaining may not be an adequate tool. Imagine brainstorming wages, pensions, or a new work system. For these kinds of issues, joint task forces or subcommittees should be specifically chartered—well in advance of bargaining—to gather data, explore options, and/or benchmark best practices.

One large pharmaceutical firm and its union jointly studied a variety of pay-for-performance systems well before bargaining. Their recommendations were then presented to the bargaining committees for consideration and ultimately adopted. Likewise, a Great Lakes utility and one of its largest unions met jointly for nearly a year before bargaining, in an effort to gather information, benchmark best practices, and select the best pension plan for their particular age mix of employees. Their efforts paid off with a newly negotiated, defined contribution pension plan that better met their needs.

If having the right data is important to expedite negotiations, having the right people present is equally important. The decision to utilize interest-based negotiation requires that careful attention be paid to the composition of the bargaining committees. This is particularly true for management participants in large organizations. In traditional bargaining—utilizing the procedure of proposal, caucus, counterproposal, caucus, and so on—all proposals can be carefully reviewed up and down the organizational hierarchy.

In contrast, interest-based negotiation is a more free-flowing, dynamic, and spontaneous process. Where traditional bargaining emphasizes control, interest-based negotiation accents creativity. Through the synergy resulting from the problem-solving process, unimaginable options are often generated. If every fledgling idea has to be first run up and down the hierarchical flagpole to see who salutes, this synergy and creativity would be stymied.

There are at least three solutions to this dilemma:

1. *Make certain that the key players or decision makers are on the bargaining committee.* In one large (50,000 person) organization, the chief spokesperson for management was five layers down in the organization.

2. *"Empower fully" those at the table to make most, if not all, of the decisions that must be made to reach an agreement.* While most senior managers are not personally inclined to devote the time and attention required to be direct participants in the negotiations, neither are they prepared to delegate such critical issues to subordinates.

3. *Establish wide, but clearly defined, parameters or boundaries around each issue.* So long as the bargainers remain within this predetermined "field of play," they are licensed to do whatever they deem appropriate. Whenever negotiations take them near or perhaps beyond these boundaries, they must be permitted to pursue further guidance from their constituents.

A new set of norms is required for the successful utilization of interest-based negotiation. Reverting to traditional norms and behaviors is commonplace when interest-based negotiation is being attempted for the first time. Only by utilizing an experienced facilitator can this be avoided.

Setting the Ground Rules

Both procedural and behavioral ground rules are critically important to the successful conduct of interest-based negotiation. A mutual understanding should develop around the timetable for bargaining. This timetable would include commencement of bargaining, frequency of meetings, dovetailing local negotiations with master negotiations, discussing any parameters around the field of play, and reviewing the ratification procedure.

A ground rule on information sharing is needed to encourage free disclosure of information. Ground rules defining the role of spokespersons should be discussed. Participation should not be limited to or funneled through spokespersons. Another key to a successful negotiation is a clear understanding or a ground rule defining consensus decision making. What are the individual's obligations when he or she provides consent?

In addition, parties should adopt a ground rule that holds the solution to any one issue to be a tentative agreement pending the solution of all issues. Solutions reached on issues important to one party have no permanent standing unless all issues are resolved to the satisfaction of both parties.

Ground rules addressing the issue of notes and official records are necessary. Bargaining in the interest-based negotiation format requires engaged participants, not passive stenographers. Flip charts and summary minutes should suffice as a "history" between meetings. There should be a clear understanding (ground rule) that nothing said or done during the interest-based negotiation process can or will be used later, by either party, in an adversarial setting.

The parties should also agree on how communications will be handled. At a minimum, there should be a ground rule prohibiting any revelation of the internal discussions, play-by-play attributions, and options developed during the interest-based negotiation process. It is vital that all participants be confident that they can speak freely and exchange creative, "out-of-the-box" ideas without political or personal risk.

Caucuses should not be discouraged. A ground rule should permit either side to caucus whenever either side feels a need or experiences discomfort.

Finally, a day of negotiations should not exceed eight hours. Interest-based negotiation is very demanding; therefore, marathon sessions should never be attempted.

Getting Started

We recommend that the first session begin with statements of commitment to the values supporting the interest-based negotiation process. The parties should next examine the issues and determine the relative importance of each to establish a "time budget" for the negotiations.

Knowing which issue to tackle first can have a strong bearing on the success of the negotiations and set the tone. Parties do well to pick an easy, yet meaningful, issue first. It is important that the parties see that the time and energy they have applied to their first issue resulted in a satisfactory solution, one that has brought about meaningful gains for both parties.

Both parties should be encouraged to take risks and to let go of the desire to control the outcome. Exhibiting behaviors aimed at helping the other benefit goes a long way toward creating the positive climate that encourages both parties to find creative solutions.

Finally, alternating between each party's issues may minimize the perception that all of the focus and attention (and possibly the gain) is being given to one party.

Tackling the Issues

The negotiators must take each issue and work through the six-step interest-based negotiation process.

1. Describe and Define the Issue.   Properly framing the issue is critically important. Issues can be defined too narrowly or too broadly. If defined too narrowly, the issue may allow little opportunity to develop an adequate option pool. Defining too broadly—ballooning an issue, or making a mountain out of a molehill—invariably leads to frustration or exasperation. The rule of thumb is to be as specific as possible in defining the issue, without becoming so specific that only part of the described problem can be resolved.

2. Identify and Explore Interests.   This step must be done well. Interest-based negotiation, as the name implies, is an interest-driven process, and well-developed and clearly articulated interests are essential.

The parties must exhibit a genuine desire to understand the other's point of view. Interests, by their very nature, must be accepted as legitimate and not-to-be-debated. To ask clarifying questions and confirm understanding of the interests is desirable.

Next, it is useful to determine which of the interests are mutual. This is not a "matching" process requiring each interest to appear on both lists. It is simply a means of quickly surfacing common or shared interests, which in turn, reveals fertile opportunities for developing viable options. Interests not shared by both parties are referred to as separate interests and remain because they may be required to be satisfied in the final solution.

3. Create Options.   The key to success in this step is to go for quantity. A technique to encourage brainstorming is to focus on the list of interests. Multiple options should be generated to cover every interest.

4. Agree on Criteria.   This is a difficult step. Criteria are the gauges by which we measure, compare, and judge options. There are few "objective criteria." One of the best gauges for evaluating options is the respective interests of the parties. Generally, there are a few interests that must be satisfied for the solution to be viable or acceptable. In effect, these are criteria and should be treated as such. Coming to agreement on these and any other appropriate criteria determines the outcome of this step.

5. Test the Options against the Criteria.   Evaluating each option in light of the agreed-upon criteria can inhibit dialogue and become overly mechanical and cumbersome, especially when there is a long list of options and a number of criteria. We have discovered several techniques that enable the parties to avoid getting bogged down.

- Review the list of options and focus on those that present broad approaches to solving the problem. Each broad approach is thoroughly discussed and evaluated for its ability to satisfy the interests of the parties.

- Give each participant a marker and ask him or her to place a checkmark next to the five or six options that he or she believes best meet the criteria. One must make clear that this is not a voting process, but a way of testing for initial preferences. The heavily favored options then become the primary focal points. The remaining options are examined to see if they meet the criteria and can be incorporated into the favored options to enhance their utility. Frequently, many ideas are woven together, in ways that meet as many interests as possible.

- In the case of large committees, utilize a "fishbowl." The fishbowl is a table placed within the larger U-shaped table. Chief spokespersons are each asked to designate two or three people who are particularly knowledgeable about the issue being bargained. The designees are seated at the small table (fishbowl) and are tasked with weaving together the promising options identified by the full committees. Two empty chairs are placed at the small table. At any time, other participants observing the deliberations may occupy the empty chairs to offer suggestions or make comments. Then they must return to the outer table, thus making the seats available for others to do likewise.

Process difficulties are not the only obstacles that can arise at this stage. Substantive concerns can also surface. Groups frequently discover that the ultimate solution to the issue being worked on is dependent upon what is being done on some closely related issue. When this situation is encountered, "parking" the unfinished solution and working on the related issues is the best course of action. Once the solutions to these related issues are more clearly focused, the parties can resume work on the parked issue.

Interest-based negotiation, however, does not utilize a "tit-for-tat" procedure. No one must give up something on one issue to realize a gain on another. "Horse trading" is discouraged. Each issue must be viewed as a joint problem to be solved.

6. *Write the Contract Language.*   The final step can be done by a drafting committee, union–management pair, or an individual. In drafting, confusion or gaps may appear requiring clarification from the full committee. The final written solution comes back to the group to ensure the group's consensus approval.

Common Concerns

One concern we have experienced regarding interest-based negotiation is the amount of time required. Arriving at the table with problems clearly identified, interests articulated, and a time line developed expedites the flow of negotiations. As the parties become more experienced with interest-based negotiation, process efficiencies are realized. Some complex issues may be broken into several separate subissues to expedite resolution. An abbreviated process may also be used to resolve an issue where little is in dispute. Jointly developed data will focus the discussion.

Finally, by using subcommittees to explore complex issues well in advance of the beginning of negotiations, it is possible to have agreements in principle or jointly supported recommendations for the bargaining committee's consideration. In dozens of interest-based negotiations—and many more traditional negotiations—the time required for each is essentially the same.

Another concern frequently expressed by traditional negotiators is whether they should reveal their bottom line. Interest-based negotiation neither requires nor encourages disclosing one's bottom line. The process is designed to yield the most elegant or comprehensive solution possible.

There is, on the other hand, a requirement to reveal one's interests. The articulation of interests on a particular issue is an expression of the issue's importance. Interests must be articulated and data shared, but neither party should be expected to reveal the minimum level for satisfying its interests on an issue.

A third and closely related concern is the applicability of interest-based negotiation to economic issues, particularly wages. Applying interest-based negotiation to these issues may be difficult, but helpful. With an agreement on appropriate data, the parties can frequently create a salary or benefit range. Interest-based negotiation is helpful in focusing the parties away from extreme staked-out positions toward substantive discussion on the value associated with job elements, the interest of employees, the needs of the employer in attracting and retaining talent, and competitive requirements or market forces.

Cooperation Is the Best Policy

On many an occasion, the fledgling efforts of union and management representatives working together have been thwarted by the dynamics of traditional bargaining. Interest-based negotiation, on the other hand, employs the same behaviors, norms, and problem-solving methodologies that are utilized when the parties cooperate during the terms of the agreement. Jekyll and Hyde personae are no longer required.

Interest-based negotiation's subtlety encourages the parties to expand the scope of bargaining. In one automotive parts plant, the negotiators devoted half of their bargaining time to the issue of how to improve throughput in the operations. Interest-based negotiation fosters problem solving and encourages frank discussions of complex issues. Since strategic issues frequently are not mandatory subjects for bargaining under current labor law, management's willingness to negotiate policy issues is very limited when traditional bargaining prevails.

In arriving at the decision to adopt an interest-based approach to negotiations, the parties need to recognize that interest-based negotiation is an art, not a science, and that flexibility is a must.

Many issues lend themselves to an interest-based approach, but in particular circumstances, the use of a rigid step-by-step interest-based negotiation may not be appropriate. Openness, sharing of information, working to meet each other's interests, exploring new or creative ideas, and employing mutually agreed-upon criteria, rather than power, will be the ingredients of successful negotiations.

Interest-based negotiation is not a magic potion, nor a religion or panacea. It is a tool that can help negotiators be more effective in achieving their aims.

Finally, interest-based negotiation need not be relegated to contract negotiations. Its methods are equally appropriate in resolving day-to-day conflicts in the workplace. Its reliance on a clinical analysis of the underlying interests is more likely to yield lasting solutions than the symptoms-focused, rights-based, litigious techniques employed in traditional grievance handling. The values embedded in interest-based negotiations are consistent with those needed for a high-performance workplace.

Reading 1.12
_____

Negotiating Lessons from the Browser Wars
James K. Sebenius

In 1996 the browser wars became headline news. The conflict involved three of the most important companies of the early Internet era: Netscape, Microsoft, and America Online. At stake was AOL's choice of a browser for its online service, either Netscape's Navigator or Microsoft's Internet Explorer. Microsoft's apparent victory in this battle has inspired important books on antitrust, legal, and business strategy issues, but the war seems endless. As recently as January 2002, AOL and Netscape filed suit yet again against Microsoft.[1]

For all the analysis that this triangular struggle has generated, one area has gone mostly unnoticed: the negotiation among the players. All negotiations can be examined in terms of a core of common elements—parties, interests, no-deal options, the possibilities for creating and claiming value, perceptions, and psychological dynamics—but a select few shed special light on the process itself.[2] The negotiation over Web browsers offers one such case. Drawing only on the copious public record, I will provide thumbnail sketches of the players and a brief description of the dramatic process dynamics—characterized by *The Wall Street Journal* as akin to TV's *Melrose Place,* "where no bed goes unslept and no back unstabbed." Then I will draw a series of broader negotiation lessons suggested by these process dynamics.

The Background

By the beginning of 1996, Netscape Communications was on a roll. Founded in April 1994 with a management team led by Jim Clark (former chairman of Silicon Graphics), Marc Andreessen (the programmer behind Mosaic, an early Web browser), and Jim Barksdale (former CEO of McCaw Cellular), Netscape owned the dominant Web browser on the market. The Navigator browser had been released in 1994, and by January 1996 consumers and businesses had downloaded 10 million to 12 million copies. Netscape's product was technically superior and far easier to use than that of competitors, and as a result Navigator enjoyed a daunting 70 percent to 85 percent share of the browser market.

The company was also booming financially. Shares of its stock had climbed from $28 per share at the opening of its IPO in August 1995 to $174 that December, which translated to a $3.6 billion market cap on revenues of $346 million. In order to validate that high price, investors were putting pressure on management to rapidly increase earnings. Netscape's response was to reorient its strategy: It would now move away from the consumer market and focus on selling servers and applications to the corporate market.

The dominance of Netscape's Navigator, combined with the overall explosive growth in use of the Web, threatened one very large competitor in particular: Microsoft.

Source: From *MIT Sloan Management Review,* Summer, 2002, pp. 43–50.

Because Navigator worked across multiple platforms and with networks, it opened the possibility that software developers could create a vast library of applications using Java or other programming languages that were neutral regarding operating systems. In other words, the applications wouldn't be dependent on Windows, Microsoft's core asset. As a senior Microsoft executive put it at the time, "If there were ever a bullet with Microsoft's name on it, Navigator is it." (Sources for quotations and facts that are not footnoted can be found in my two Harvard Business School cases on the browser wars, which are cited in the acknowledgments at the end of this article.)

Microsoft's response to Netscape came in the form of Internet Explorer. Released in August 1995, the new browser was a dud. Although it was free to consumers and was bundled with Windows, it was also technically buggy and had only a 3 percent to 4 percent share of the market in January 1996.

While trying to establish Internet Explorer in the browser market, Microsoft was also investing hundreds of millions of dollars in its own online service, Microsoft Network. MSN was designed to compete directly with AOL and other online services such as CompuServe and Prodigy. Microsoft's service was also bundled with Windows: Its icon appeared on the desktops of 50 million new computers each year. This sort of (near) zero-cost distribution led many businesspeople to regard the Windows desktop as the most valuable virtual real estate in the world.

AOL viewed Microsoft's bundling of MSN with Windows with great concern. By now, the animosity between AOL and Microsoft was legendary; indeed, Microsoft's market dominance and frequent hardball tactics had led to broad-based, deep-seated ill will toward the company in much of the computer industry. Paul Allen, Microsoft's co-founder and the owner of 29 percent of AOL in the early 1990s, had wanted to take over AOL at one point but was blocked by AOL's CEO, Steve Case. At a later meeting between Case and Microsoft CEO Bill Gates, the latter reportedly said, "I can buy 20 percent of you. I can buy all of you. Or I can go into this business myself and bury you." In response, AOL held large rallies at its headquarters in suburban Washington, D.C., asking its employees to pledge to "destroy the beast from Redmond." Gates himself was routinely demonized at AOL, which filed a formal complaint against Microsoft with the U.S. Department of Justice.

Like Netscape, AOL had exploded in size and value by the mid-1990s. It had 5 million subscribers and a market cap of $3.9 billion, and 250,000 new subscribers were signing up each month, largely thanks to AOL's strategy of "carpet bombing" consumers with free AOL disks. But also like Netscape, AOL was under pressure to change. Many industry observers confidently predicted that fee-based online services would fade away altogether as the "free Web" became the norm, but the company had more immediate concerns. Its successful distribution strategy, for example, was costing an unsustainable $40 to $80 per new customer. And despite its commercial success, AOL had an image as the "Internet for dummies." Top management was concerned that this perception would spread, damage its franchise, and blunt future growth prospects. In short, AOL had a pressing need for a cutting-edge browser to improve its image and to allow its customers easy access to the Web that lay beyond AOL's proprietary confines. Netscape's Navigator was management's first choice. As Jean Villanueva, a senior AOL executive, later observed, "The deal was Netscape's to lose. They were dominant. We needed to get what the market wanted. Most importantly, we saw ourselves as smaller companies fighting the same foe—Microsoft."[3]

The Negotiations

Although Navigator had the inside track to AOL, Microsoft wasn't about to give up without a fight. In November 1995, Bill Gates pitched Explorer to Steve Case in a meeting at Microsoft's headquarters, but Case rebuffed him. Not long thereafter, Gates chose the potent symbolism of Pearl Harbor Day to declare that Microsoft was "hard-core about the Internet." Microsoft had been slow to recognize the Internet "tidal wave," said Gates, but now it became a top priority. In particular, Gates and his top team now saw winning the browser war with Netscape as crucial, since Navigator put Microsoft's "core assets at risk." He also articulated what seemed like a puzzlingly (and uncharacteristically) modest aspiration: for Explorer to capture at least 30 percent of the browser market. But the implications weren't really so modest. If Explorer could reach that target, software developers would not be able to ignore it. They would feel compelled to write code for Web sites and related products that would be compatible with Explorer as well as Navigator. Microsoft would then buy the vital time it needed to pour resources into improving Explorer and deny Navigator a winner-take-all knockout punch. Recognizing Microsoft's new orientation, the stock market pummeled Netscape's share price—it dropped 28 percent in five days.

In January, Steve Case flew out to California to have dinner at Jim Barksdale's home while discussing potential AOL links to Netscape. Case proposed that Netscape produce a special Navigator version for AOL that would serve as the principal browser for AOL's subscribers. He also proposed that AOL run Netscape's extremely popular but woefully underexploited Web site, which was receiving millions of hits daily. AOL certainly had the capacity to leverage the commercial potential of such massive traffic (it may also have wanted to control a potential competitor to its own site). Finally, Case suggested that Netscape and AOL actively cross-promote each other and that Netscape include an AOL seat on its board in order to cement the partnership.

Barksdale discussed this proposal with managers and engineers at Netscape. They opposed the move, citing the effort that would be required to create an AOL-specific Navigator, one that would be "componentized" to fit with AOL's look and feel. And Netscape wanted to focus strategically on servers and the corporate market; it was less concerned about the consumer market served by AOL at this point. Barksdale ended up telling Case that the partnership proposal was a nonstarter. He countered by saying that AOL would be a "good distribution channel for Navigator" at a cost to AOL of $10 per downloaded copy.

The AOL executive newly in charge of closing a browser deal was David Colburn. He initially felt that Navigator's brand name, market dominance, and best-of-breed functionality made it the "obvious choice for AOL licensing." As someone fairly new to AOL—he joined the company in September 1995 as vice president for corporate development—and perhaps less imbued with the prevailing corporate view, he now reacted to these new developments with relative detachment: "I didn't care what the hell Silicon Valley thought or that Microsoft was the antichrist or that Netscape was so cool, I only thought, Who's got what we need?" Microsoft responded to this new expression of pragmatism and open-mindedness by promising to create, on a tight schedule, a browser that would be integrated into AOL's client software and have AOL's look and feel.

These were the essential positions of the three companies leading up to the stunning events of March. First, on March 11, Netscape and AOL announced a deal in which Netscape appeared to have triumphed over Microsoft. According to the terms of the deal, Navigator would become the "preferred" AOL browser on a nonexclusive basis; AOL would pay a fee for every downloaded browser. Until Navigator was integrated into AOL's client software, its presence (and thus visibility) on the site would be limited to a small AOL subsidiary, but Netscape's executives seemed to view that limitation as only a temporary problem. The market applauded the deal, as both AOL's and Netscape's stock rose between 10 percent and 15 percent that day.

Yet on March 12, the very next day, AOL and Microsoft announced a stunning deal that supplanted the Netscape–AOL agreement. Now Microsoft's Explorer would become the "default" browser for AOL's subscribers. Further, Explorer would effectively enjoy exclusive distribution and marketing by AOL. Navigator was for all intents and purposes confined to a small AOL subsidiary, and Microsoft was seeking to enforce Explorer's de facto exclusivity. Further, unlike the fee-based Navigator arrangement, Microsoft's Explorer would be provided to AOL for free. Explorer would be seamlessly integrated into AOL's software as rapidly as possible in the context of a multiyear deal.

Most remarkable to outside observers, Microsoft agreed that AOL client software would be bundled with the new Windows operating system; the AOL icon would be positioned on the Windows desktop right next to the MSN icon. This positioning on "the most valuable desktop real estate in the world" would permit AOL to reach an additional 50 million people per year at effectively zero cost. The value to AOL of having its icon on the Windows desktop was immense for marketing, distribution, and competitive reasons, blunting the threat from MSN. In effect, Bill Gates was sacrificing the near-and medium-term position of the Microsoft Network to the larger goal of winning the browser wars. (Microsoft also hoped to score points with the Department of Justice by favoring an MSN competitor in this way.)

After the deal was announced, Microsoft's and AOL's stock prices jumped while Netscape's plunged. The head of MSN resigned. And Netscape's management was stunned and disgusted at what it saw as an unbelievable double-cross on the part of AOL's leaders. Explorer's superior status as AOL's "default" browser had trumped Navigator's apparent victory and "preferred" status.

The Lessons

To explore the implications of the negotiations that led to this abrupt reversal of fortune, I will look first at the four basic negotiation elements: the parties, their interests, their no-deal alternatives, and the opportunities for what I call "dealcrafting" (structuring agreements to create value). Examined in isolation, each yields insight; taken together, these factors constitute a fundamental analysis that yields lessons concerning Netscape's approach and for effective negotiation in general.

Parties

Naturally, Netscape focused attention mainly on AOL, its direct negotiating counterpart. But while the company's executives were certainly aware of Microsoft's efforts, they largely neglected and dismissed Netscape's principal competitor as technically inept and irrelevant to the deal. Marc Andreessen, for example, infamously caricatured the Windows operating system as little more than a "poorly debugged set of device drivers." Such dismissive attitudes of other potential parties are almost always risky and short-sighted. Another mistake is to view negotiating partners as monolithic: Organizations do not negotiate and make decisions, individuals do. In this case, internal factions and participants played critical roles: Netscape's engineers had decisive influence, and AOL's David Colburn, a relatively new arrival to the negotiations, brought a view to the table that differed from others at the company.

Lesson #1: Look beyond your immediate negotiation counterpart and make a full analysis of your competitors as well. Don't treat players as monolithic; map internal factions that could block or enable a deal.

Interests

Netscape apparently saw its own interest mainly as adding incremental browser revenue in the consumer segment, an area it already dominated to the point where it was no longer a strategic focus. The company seemingly failed to appreciate that its real strategic interest was in preventing Explorer from breaking out of its tiny niche.

Meanwhile, Microsoft saw AOL's base of subscribers dangling like an arcade prize; if it could lay claim to that audience, it would be able to avoid the painful attempt to win market share for Explorer little by little. Instead, it would take a major step toward Gates's goal of 30 percent market share, and software developers would have to start writing code for Explorer as well as Navigator. Microsoft would gain precious time to convert a winner-take-all standards war that Netscape was on the verge of winning into a war of attrition, a battleground on which Microsoft's size, resources, and staying power would likely give it a decisive edge over time.

Microsoft also was clearer than Netscape about the full set of AOL's interests. Netscape acted as if AOL primarily wanted to get a good browser for a low price. Microsoft, which pushed to understand AOL better, appreciated the importance to AOL of a browser that would be integrated into AOL's software and have the proper look and feel. Microsoft understood AOL's sense of urgency and was willing to adapt Explorer extremely rapidly. Microsoft also found a way—by putting the AOL icon on every copy of Windows—not only to solve AOL's problem of extremely high customer acquisition costs but also to allay its competitive fear of MSN. In short, Microsoft reconceptualized the negotiation from a browser-for-dollars deal into one that aligned with a larger set of AOL's interests.

Like Microsoft, AOL saw the negotiation as being about more than the sale of a browser. In fact, AOL's executives seemed to have a better sense of the full set of Netscape's potential interests in the deal than Netscape's own management did. Steve Case, after all, had explicitly proposed the equivalent of a partnership in which AOL would take a seat on the Netscape board, the two companies would run cross-promotions on each other's Web sites, AOL would help leverage Netscape's underexploited Web site, and they would join forces to oppose Microsoft, their putative common enemy.

Lesson #2: Don't just consider your own interests and those of your counterpart across the table in terms of the immediate issue under negotiation. Instead, think broadly, deeply, and strategically about the full set of actual and potential interests at stake.

No-Deal Options

Netscape's narrow field of vision about its own and others' interests was mirrored in its view of each side's no-deal options, or BATNAs ("best alternative to negotiated agreement"). Netscape effectively assumed that AOL had no meaningful BATNA to a deal for Navigator; to start with, Explorer was technically inferior, but even if it had been on a par with Navigator, Microsoft was the enemy. A Microsoft–AOL deal was unthinkable. But Netscape failed to recognize how catastrophically Microsoft viewed its own BATNA to an AOL deal: The view from Redmond was that failure to strike an agreement with AOL would threaten the Windows empire. Netscape also saw its own no-deal option as a minor problem: a bit of forgone incremental revenue.

AOL, on the other hand, exploited the power of its no-deal option with Netscape. By keeping another serious player "warm" in the process, AOL effectively created a potent bidding war in which a loss for one of the bidders (Microsoft) meant losing the business to a strategically lethal competitor (Netscape). As an AOL executive later said, commenting in general on the company's strategy in negotiations with Internet companies, "You could be guaranteed that we were talking to two or three companies in the exact same space at the same time. You would never do a deal without talking to anyone else. Never."[4]

Lesson #3: Explicitly assess your own BATNA as well as those of your counterparts and competitors. Consider ways to enhance your own no-deal option while worsening those of other parties.

This analysis of parties, interests, and BATNAs suggests two powerful implications that, arguably, should have been apparent to Netscape by January 1996, if not earlier. First, Microsoft would do everything in its power to win this deal; paranoia and extreme urgency on the part of Netscape's executives would have been the *rational* responses. Second, Netscape's overwhelming imperative and, indeed, likely its sole chance for success, was to make a deal with AOL as fast as possible, being as flexible as necessary on the financial terms. And most critically, Netscape should have pressed for a legally ironclad exclusive deal of the kind AOL was almost certainly willing to give earlier in the process. Such an agreement could have effectively blocked Microsoft for a period of time that, in the context of Internet competition, would have been a near-eternity. It could have added billions of dollars to Netscape's market capitalization.

Dealcrafting

Netscape seemed to think of the AOL deal as a short-term customer-supplier transaction; the barrier to closure was mainly an impasse over the browser price. As Marc Andreessen bluntly put it, "If you have an economic relationship, then you're a customer." Steve Case later said as much, having proposed a more comprehensive deal to Barksdale: "Netscape had no desire to treat us as a partner; they only wanted to treat us like a customer."[5] Netscape acted according to the standard script in such value-claiming situations. As Barksdale's team saw things, AOL urgently needed a cutting-edge browser and had no alternative; Netscape could wait. Conventional haggling wisdom offered clear advice: Take advantage of your situation, start high with a firm position, concede slowly if at all, and count on time to be on your side.

By contrast, Microsoft seemed to conceptualize the deal as a longer-term partnership with AOL. By probing hard for a greater set of AOL's interests and devising a value-creating deal that operated on more than one dimension, Microsoft was able to triumph. Ironically, giant Microsoft played the role of the hungry upstart in this drama while Netscape acted like the complacent incumbent. (Skeptics offer a less benign view. According to one, "A partnership with Microsoft is like the Nazi nonaggression pact—it just means you're next."[6])

Lesson #4: Think in terms of creating sustainable value rather than claiming short-term value. Think long-term partnership rather than short-term transaction. And consider crafting a broader business relationship as well as closing a clean technical sale.

Unwarranted Assumptions, Psychological Biases, and Arrogance

An overarching theme links Netscape's mistakes: The company's executives and engineers confidently held a series of plausible—but false—assumptions about the negotiation and the underlying competitive strategy. At the risk of hindsight-induced smugness on my part, here is my view of some of the more glaring examples:

- The issues in the negotiation are price and whose browser is technically superior.
- The relevant parties are Netscape and AOL.
- All that is at stake for us is a few incremental browser dollars.
- AOL has no meaningful BATNA since we have superior technology, Explorer is junk, and we enjoy market dominance.
- AOL will never do a deal with Microsoft because Microsoft represents the devil incarnate to AOL and to all right-thinking people in the industry.
- Microsoft will never do a desktop real estate deal with AOL because it would harm MSN.
- A "preferred" browser deal clinches it; we won!

In making these assumptions and misjudgments, Netscape arguably fell prey to a series of common biases in perception that cognitive and social psychologists have extensively documented in negotiating situations.

Overconfidence   When faced with the need to choose among a series of possibilities, negotiators frequently make a judgment, rapidly become attached to that view, and dismiss other alternatives as being far less likely than they may be. In their assessments and actions, overconfident negotiators unconsciously and unjustifiably restrict the full range of genuinely uncertain countervailing factors.[7] As Alex Edelstein, an assistant to Jim Barksdale, later put it, "I think we were too arrogant. The bottom line is that Netscape thought its stuff was so good it was enough just to put it out there."[8]

Biased Assimilation of Information   Cognitive psychologists have long understood how people unconsciously interpret information in self-serving ways.[9] For example, disputants frequently overestimate their chances of prevailing in a court battle; the sum of the probability estimates for victory on two sides will often far exceed 100 percent. Likewise, sellers of companies consistently overestimate the value of the business in comparison with the way neutral observers and potential buyers see things. Netscape was strongly convinced that it was both right and in the catbird seat.

Partisan Perceptions   Especially in situations of conflict, there is a tendency to demonize the other side or sides.[10] Netscape treated the negotiation as good (itself) versus evil (Microsoft). The company would have been better served if it had followed this advice from *The Godfather, Part III:* "Never hate your enemies. It affects your judgment."

False Consensus   An unspoken conviction that others must see the world just as you do exacerbates the problems of self-serving biases and partisan perceptions.[11] In the heat of conflict, it becomes nearly irresistible to assume that what you see is what everyone else sees, and hence a false consensus is assumed. AOL's David Colburn commented once that "Netscape thought we had nowhere else to go. It was like, 'AOL *has* to do a deal with us, because we're the leading browser, and Microsoft is its arch-enemy.'"[12] But everyone at AOL did not, in fact, share this view. There was no consensus.

In tandem with these biases went a remarkable culture of arrogance. AOL's Steve Case: "They were very aggressive about selling a browser, but they wanted a very high per-copy fee. The attitude was we're so hot we'll license to everyone so you'd better take it."[13] That attitude was not confined to AOL. For example, Michael Dell, CEO of Dell Computer, commented, "Netscape was surprisingly arrogant for a company of their size and age and did not seem to aggressively pursue our business."[14] And Charles Ferguson, founding CEO of Vermeer Technologies, claimed, "Until recently, Netscape was one of the most arrogant companies in Silicon Valley history, which is saying quite a lot."[15]

These observations apply to a particular company in a particularly hot industry at a particular time. It was a company that, by many measures, had every reason to be arrogant. And yet this attitude, whether in retail, services, manufacturing, or technology, can be a real deal killer.

Lesson #5: Be aware of these psychological biases and take steps to fight them. Try to lay bare all of your key assumptions going into a negotiation. Don't automatically trust your instincts in tough negotiations involving considerable conflict. Explicitly ask what evidence supports your views and, more important, what evidence would change them. Appoint an internal devil's advocate. Check out your perceptions with uninvolved parties whom you can trust to tell you what you don't want to hear. Overall, avoid arrogance!

Changing the Game

If the main problem at Netscape was an arrogance that stemmed from false assumptions, the main reason for success by AOL and Microsoft was an ability to change the game.

Many people, including most academics who formally study the subject, analyze negotiation primarily as a process that takes place "at the table" with a fixed set of parties, interests, issues, and no-agreement alternatives. Within that specified configuration, or game, negotiating skill can be deployed. The most effective negotiators, however, think beyond this limited view; they try to change the game to their advantage by focusing on substantive issues and potential actions away from the table.[16]

In a tactical sense, AOL changed the bilateral AOL–Netscape game to its advantage by engaging Microsoft as a serious, if seemingly unlikely, negotiation party—improving its BATNA and worsening that of Netscape. In the long term, AOL may have preferred a world with competing browsers to facing a Netscape monopoly.

More interesting than such common BATNA-improving moves are actions to change the issues at stake. Microsoft successfully took such action at the beginning of 1996. Its technically inferior browser meant that it could not win on that battleground regardless of its negotiating skills "at the table." While Netscape was confidently playing a waiting game to bring AOL around, Microsoft was using this precious reprieve to shift the negotiating ground to encompass a far broader range of business issues of keen interest to AOL. In addition, rather than focus its attention on the pure technologists at AOL (who would have been the natural players in a negotiation over the technical merits of the competing browsers), Microsoft concentrated on engaging many of the business-oriented people at AOL.

Lesson #6: Don't limit your negotiation to playing the game skillfully at the table; take actions away from the table to change the game advantageously.

It's tempting, with the benefit of hindsight, to see Microsoft's victory as foreordained— another garden-variety case of the monster squashing the upstart. But such an interpretation won't really stand up to scrutiny. Microsoft's leaders had to change the game in order to win it. And they also needed Netscape's people to say no when they should have said yes.

Take Yes for an Answer

In January 1996, Netscape arguably could have blocked Microsoft for what might have been a long time, if not permanently, in the standards game simply by saying yes to an eager AOL in return for an airtight exclusive deal.[17] It failed to do so—not once, but twice. Four months after the Microsoft–AOL deal, a technicality apparently reopened the door to an AOL–Netscape deal. Ram Shriram, a vice president of Netscape, recounted what happened next: "AOL came to us again. AOL's stock was tanking and it was getting sued by the attorneys general of various states. They were keen to come back to the table and forge a relationship with us."[18] Barksdale and Shriram met with Steve Case, but Netscape's engineering team rejected the proposed deal, saying, as Shriram put it, "'Look, we're all busy. We're not really interested. Our focus is not consumers.' We lost out on another opportunity to take charge of another 10 to 12 million browsers."[19] Thus Netscape lost another opportunity to retain control of the browser market. Given these facts, it's hard to see Microsoft's victory as a foregone conclusion.

Foregone or not, by mid-1999 Explorer had taken almost three-quarters of the browser market while Navigator's share had shrunk to less than 25 percent.[20] Ironically, AOL acquired Netscape in March 1999 for $4.2 billion, and Jim Barksdale joined the AOL board. AOL made this move partly to boost Navigator and forestall the dominance of Explorer and partly to gain commercial access to the 20 million monthly visitors to Netscape's Netcenter. In the end, then, Netscape was not a total business failure, but the unsuccessful negotiation of 1996 was one among many actions that sharply limited the company's potential.

Netscape's fall from dominance involved far more than faulty negotiation.[21] But the negotiations that were part of the browser wars offer important lessons—about the need to assess the full set of parties, issues, and BATNAs; about the benefits of crafting sustainable value-creating deals rather than value-claiming ones; about the risks of arrogance and biases; and about changing the game away from the table, not just playing it well at the table. There's no guarantee, of course, that a broader view of the negotiating process would have changed Netscape's ultimate fate. But executives who find themselves in similarly thorny situations may be able to do themselves, and their companies, a great deal of good by looking beyond the mythical table that too often limits the possibilities inherent in any negotiation.

Acknowledgments

I would like to thank David Metcalfe for his extensive research assistance on the two Harvard Business School cases on which this article is heavily based, "Double Dealmaking in the Browser Wars (A) and (B),"case numbers 800-050 and 800-051, 1999, available from www.hbsp.hbs.edu. Unless otherwise noted, Metcalfe's research in these two extensively footnoted cases is the source of all facts and quotations in this article.

References

1. See J. Heilemann, *Pride before the Fall: The Trials of Bill Gates and the End of the Microsoft Era* (New York. HarperCollins. 2001). More extensive analysis is in K. Auletta, *World War 3.0: Microsoft and Its Enemies* (New York: Random House, 2001). On the latest lawsuit, see "Netscape Sues Microsoft," *CNN/Money* online, January 22, 2002: http://money.cnn.com/2002/01/22/technology/netscape/. For business strategy implications, see M. Cusumano and D. Yoffie, *Competing on Internet Time: Lessons from Netscape and Its Battle with Microsoft* (New York: Free Press, 1998).

2. For example, see J. Sebenius, "Six Habits of Merely Effective Negotiators," *Harvard Business Review,* April 2001, pp. 87–95. More complete approaches can be found in many sources, including D. Lax and J. Sebenius, *The Manager as Negotiator: Bargaining for Cooperation and Competitive Gain* (New York: Free Press, 1986); and J. Sebenius, *Dealmaking Essentials: Creating and Claiming Value for the Long Term,* item no. 2-800-443 (Boston: Harvard Business School Publishing, 2000). More technical treatment is contained in H. Raiffa, *The Art and Science of Negotiation* (Cambridge. MA: Harvard University Press, 1982).

3. K. Swisher, *aol.com: How Steve Case Beat Bill Gates, Nailed the Netheads, and Made Millions in the War for the Web* (New York: Times Business, 1998), p. 135.

4. G. Rivlin, "AOL's Rough Riders," *The Standard,* October 20, 2000: http://www.thestandard.com/article/display/0.1151.19461.00. htm.

5. Swisher, "aol.com," p. 136.

6. C. Ferguson. *High St@kes, No Prisoners* (New York: Times Business, 2001), p. 288.

7. See, for example, M. Neale and M. Bazerman, *Cognition and Rationality in Negotiation* (New York: Free Press, 1991); M. Bazerman and M. Neale, *Negotiating Rationally* (New York: Free Press, 1991).

8. Cusumano and Yoffie, "Competing on Internet Time," p. 83.

9. See R. Robinson, *Errors in Social Judgment: Implications for Negotiation and Conflict Resolution. Part I: Biased Assimilation of Information,* item no. 9-897-103 (Boston: Harvard Business School Publishing, 1997).

10. See R. Robinson, *Errors in Social Judgment: Implications for Negotiation and Conflict Resolution. Part II: Partisan Perceptions,* item no. 9-897-104 (Boston: Harvard Business School Publishing, 1997).

11. Ibid.

12. Ibid, p. 137.

13. Swisher, "aol.com," p. 114.

14. Cusumano and Yoffie, "Competing on Internet Time," p. 87.

15. Ferguson, "High St@kes," p. 289.

16. See A, Brandenburger and B. Nalebuff, *Coopetition* (New York: Currency Doubleday, 1996). For development of these Ideas in a negotiation context, see D. Lax and J. Sebenius, *The Manager as Negotiator.*

17. There is no direct evidence that AOL would have granted such an exclusive deal if asked, but the strong preference of AOL for a Navigator deal cited above (from Colburn and Villanueva), combined with AOL's antipathy toward Microsoft, suggest that an exclusive could easily have been in the cards, especially if Netscape had been more forthcoming both financially and with respect to AOL's "partnership" proposal.

18. Cusumano and Yoffie, "Competing on Internet Time," p. 116.

19. Ibid., pp. 117–118.

20. D. Toft, IDG News Service, Boston Bureau, August 9, 1999: http://www.idg.net/idgns/1999/08/09/NetscapeBrowserMarketShareDropsTo.shtml. Such market share figures are notoriously tricky, but the qualitative point is beyond argument.

21. See especially Cusumano and Yoffie as well as Ferguson for more complete assessments of Netscape's strategic and operational errors.

Negotiation Subprocesses

Reading 2.1

Negotiating Rationally: The Power and Impact of the Negotiator's Frame

Margaret A. Neale
Max H. Bazerman

Everyone negotiates. In its various forms, negotiation is a common mechanism for resolving differences and allocating resources. While many people perceive negotiation to be a specific interaction between a buyer and a seller, this process occurs with a wide variety of exchange partners, such as superiors, colleagues, spouses, children, neighbors, strangers, or even corporate entities and nations. Negotiation is a decision-making process among interdependent parties who do not share identical preferences. It is through negotiation that the parties decide what each will give and take in their relationship.

The aspect of negotiation that is most directly controllable by the negotiator is how he or she makes decisions. The parties, the issues, and the negotiation environment are often predetermined. Rather than trying to change the environment surrounding the negotiation or the parties or issues in the dispute, we believe that the greatest opportunity to improve negotiator performance lies in the negotiator's ability to make effective use of the information available about the issues in dispute as well as the likely behavior of an opponent to reach more rational agreements and make more rational decisions within the context of negotiation.

To this end, we offer advice on how a negotiator should make decisions. However, to follow this advice for analyzing negotiations rationally, a negotiator must understand the psychological forces that limit a negotiator's effectiveness. In addition, rational decisions require that we have an optimal way of evaluating behavior of the opponent. This requires a psychological perspective for anticipating the likely decisions and subsequent behavior of the other party. Information such as this not only can create a framework that predicts how a negotiator structures problems, processes information, frames the situation, and evaluates alternatives but also can identify the limitations of his or her ability to follow rational advice.

Rationality refers to making the decision that maximizes the negotiator's interests. Since negotiation is a decision-making process that involves other people that do not

Source: Reprinted from *Academy of Management Executive* 6, no. 3 (1992), pp. 42–51. Used with permission of the authors and publisher.

have the same desires or preferences, the goal of a negotiation is not simply reaching an agreement. The goal of negotiations is to reach a *good* agreement. In some cases, no agreement is better than reaching an agreement that is not in the negotiator's best interests. When negotiated agreements are based on biased decisions, the chances of getting the best possible outcome are significantly reduced, and the probabilities of reaching an agreement when an impasse would have left the negotiator relatively better off are significantly enhanced.

A central theme of our work is that our natural decision and negotiation processes contain biases that prevent us from acting rationally and getting as much as we can out of a negotiation. These biases are pervasive, destroying the opportunities available in competitive contexts, and preventing us from negotiating rationally. During the last 10 or so years, the work that we and our colleagues have done suggests that negotiators make the following common cognitive mistakes: (1) negotiators tend to be overly affected by the frame, or form of presentation, of information in a negotiation; (2) negotiators tend to nonrationally escalate commitment to a previously selected course of action when it is no longer the most reasonable alternative; (3) negotiators tend to assume that their gain must come at the expense of the other party and thereby miss opportunities for mutually beneficial trade-offs between the parties; (4) negotiator judgments tend to be anchored upon irrelevant information—such as an initial offer; (5) negotiators tend to rely on readily available information; (6) negotiators tend to fail to consider information that is available by focusing on the opponent's perspective; and (7) negotiators tend to be overconfident concerning the likelihood of attaining outcomes that favor the individual(s) involved.

Describing the impact of each of these biases on negotiator behavior is obviously beyond the scope of this article. What we will attempt to do, however, is to focus on one particular and important cognitive bias, *framing,* and consider the impact of this bias on the process and outcome of negotiation. The manner in which negotiators frame the options available in a dispute can have a significant impact on their willingness to reach an agreement as well as the value of that agreement. In this article, we will identify factors that influence the choice of frame in a negotiation.

The Framing of Negotiations

Consider the following situation adapted from Russo and Schoemaker:[1]

> You are in a store about to buy a new watch which costs $70. As you wait for the sales clerk, a friend of yours comes by and remarks that she has seen an identical watch on sale in another store two blocks away for $40. You know that the service and reliability of the other store are just as good as this one. Will you travel two blocks to save $30?

Now consider this similar situation:

> You are in a store about to buy a new video camera that costs $800. As you wait for the sales clerk, a friend of yours comes by and remarks that she has seen an identical camera on sale in another store two blocks away for $770. You know that the service and reliability of the other store are just as good as this one. Will you travel two blocks to save the $30?

In the first scenario, Russo and Shoemaker report that about 90 percent of the managers presented this problem reported that they would travel the two blocks. However, in the second scenario, only about 50 percent of the managers would make the trip. What is the difference between the two situations that makes the $30 so attractive in the first scenario and considerably less attractive in the second scenario? One difference is that a $30 discount on a $70 watch represents a very good deal; the $30 discount on an $800 video camera is not such a good deal. In evaluating our willingness to walk two blocks, we frame the options in terms of the percentage discount. However, the correct comparison is not whether a percentage discount is sufficiently motivating, but whether the savings obtained is greater than the expected value of the additional time we would have to invest to realize those savings. So if a $30 savings were sufficient to justify walking two blocks for the watch, an opportunity to save $30 on the video camera should also be worth an equivalent investment of time.

Richard Thaler illustrated the influence of frames when he presented the following two versions of another problem to participants of an executive development program.[2]

> You are lying on the beach on a hot day. All you have to drink is ice water. For the last hour you have been thinking about how much you would enjoy a nice cold bottle of your favorite brand of beer. A companion gets up to make a phone call and offers to bring back a beer from the only nearby place where beer is sold: a fancy resort hotel. She says that the beer might be expensive and asks how much you are willing to pay for the beer. She will buy the beer if it costs as much as or less than the price you state. But if it costs more than the price you state, she will not buy it. You trust your friend and there is no possibility of bargaining with the bartender. What price do you tell your friend you are willing to pay?

Now consider this version of the same story:

> You are lying on the beach on a hot day. All you have to drink is ice water. For the last hour you have been thinking about how much you would enjoy a nice cold bottle of your favorite brand of beer. A companion gets up to make a phone call and offers to bring back a beer from the only nearby place where beer is sold: a small, run-down grocery store. She says that the beer might be expensive and asks how much you are willing to pay for the beer. She will buy the beer if it costs as much as or less than the price you state. But if it costs more than the price you state, she will not buy it. You trust your friend and there is no possibility of bargaining with the store owner. What price do you tell your friend you are willing to pay?

In both versions of the story, the results are the same: you get the same beer and there is no negotiating with the seller. Also you will not be enjoying the resort's amenities since you will be drinking the beer on the beach. Recent responses of executives at a Kellogg executive training program indicated that they were willing to pay significantly more if the beer were purchased at a "fancy resort hotel" ($7.83) than if the beer were purchased at the "small, run-down grocery store" ($4.10). The difference in price the executives were willing to pay for the same beer was based upon the frame they imposed on this transaction. Paying over $5 for a beer is an expected annoyance at a fancy resort hotel; however, paying over $5 for a beer at a run-down grocery store is an obvious "rip-off." So even though the same beer is purchased and we enjoy none of the benefits of the fancy resort hotel, we are willing to pay almost a dollar more because of the way in which we frame the purchase. The converse of this situation is probably familiar to many of us. Have you ever purchased an item because "it was too good of a deal to pass up," even though you had no use for it? We seem to assign a greater value to the quality of the transaction over and above the issue of what we get for what we pay.

Both of these examples emphasize the importance of the particular frames we place on problems we have to solve or decisions we have to make. Managers are constantly being exposed to many different frames, some naturally occurring and others that are purposefully proposed. An important task of managers is to identify the appropriate frame by which employees and the organization, in general, should evaluate its performance and direct its effort.

The Framing of Risky Negotiations

The way in which information is framed (in terms of either potential gains or potential losses) to the negotiator can have a significant impact on his or her preference for risk, particularly when uncertainty about future events or outcomes is involved. For example, when offered the choice between gains of equal expected value—one for certain and the other a lottery—we strongly prefer to take the *certain* gain. However, when we are offered the choice between potential losses of equal expected value, we clearly and consistently eschew the loss for certain and prefer the risk inherent in the *lottery.*

There is substantial evidence to suggest that we are not indifferent toward risky situations and we should not necessarily trust our intuitions about risk. Negotiators routinely deviate from rationality because they do not typically appreciate the transient nature of their preference for risk; nor do they take into consideration the ability of a particular decision frame to influence that preference. Influencing our attitudes toward risk through the positive or negative frames associated with the problem is the result of evaluating an alternative from a particular referent point or base line. A referent point is the basis by which we evaluate whether what we are considering is viewed as a gain or a loss. The referent point that we choose determines the frame we impose on our options and, subsequently, our willingness to accept or reject those options.

Consider the high-performing employee who is expecting a significant increase in salary this year. He frames his expectations on the past behavior of the company. As such, he is expecting a raise of approximately $5,000. Because of the recession, he receives a $3,500 salary increase. He immediately confronts his manager, complaining that he has been unfairly treated. He is extremely disappointed in what his surprised manager saw as an exceptional raise because the employee's referent point is $1,500 higher. Had he known that the average salary increase was only $2,000 (and used that as a more realistic referent point), he would have perceived the same raise quite differently, and it may have had the motivating force that his manager had hoped to create.

The selection of which relevant frame influences our behavior is a function of our selection of a base line by which we evaluate potential outcomes. The choice of one referent point over another may be the result of a visible anchor, the "status quo," or our expectations. Probably one of the most common referent points is what we perceive to be in our current inventory (our status quo)—what is ours already. We then evaluate offers or options in terms of whether they make us better off (a gain) or worse off (a loss) from what (we perceive to be) our current resource state.

Interestingly, what we include in our current resource state is surprisingly easy to modify. Consider the executive vice president of a large automobile manufacturing concern that has been hit by a number of economic difficulties because of the recession in the United States. It appears as if she will have to close down three plants, and the employee rolls will be trimmed by 6,000 individuals. In exploring ways to avoid this alternative, she has identified two plans that might ameliorate the situation. If she selects the first plan, she will be able to save 2,000 jobs and one of the three plants. If she implements the second plan, there is a one-third probability that she can save all three plants and all 6,000 jobs, but there is a two-thirds probability that this plan will end up saving none of the plants and none of the jobs. If you were this vice president, which plan would you select (#1 or #2)?

Now consider the same options (Plan 1 or Plan 2) framed as losses: If the vice president implements Plan 1, two of the three plants will be shut down and 4,000 jobs will be lost. If she implements Plan 2, then there is a two-thirds probability of losing all three plants and all 6,000 jobs, but there is a one-third probability of losing no plants and no jobs. If you were presented with these two plans, which would be more attractive? Plan 1 or Plan 2?

It is obvious that from a purely economic perspective, there is no difference between the two choices. Yet managers offered the plans framed in terms of gains select the first plan about 76 percent of the time. However, managers offered the choice between the plans framed in terms of losses select the first plan only about 22 percent of the time. When confronted with potential losses, the lottery represented by Plan 2 becomes relatively much more attractive.

An important point for managers to consider is that the way in which the problem is framed, or presented, can dramatically alter the perceived value or acceptability of alternative courses of action. In negotiation, for example, the more risk-averse course of action is to accept an offered settlement; the more risk-seeking course of action is to hold out for future, potential concessions. In translating the influence of the framing bias to negotiation, we must realize that the selection of a particular referent point or base line determines whether a negotiator will frame his or her decision as positive or negative.

Specifically, consider any recurring contract negotiation. As the representative of Company A, the offer from Company B can be viewed in two ways, depending on the referent point I use. If my referent point were the current contract, Company B's offer can be evaluated in terms of the "gains" Company A can expect relative to the previous contract. However, if the referent point for Company A is an initial offer on the issues under current consideration, then Company A is more likely to evaluate Company B's offers as losses to be incurred if the contract as proposed is accepted. Viewing options as losses or as gains will have considerable impact on the negotiator's willingness to accept side B's position—even though the same options may be offered in both cases.

Likewise, the referent points available to an individual negotiating his salary for a new position in the company include (1) his current salary; (2) the company's initial offer; (3) the least he is willing to accept; (4) his estimate of the most the company is willing to pay; or (5) his initial salary request. As his referent moves from 1 to 5, he progresses from a positive to a negative frame in the negotiation. What is a modest *gain* compared to his current wage is perceived as a loss when compared to what he would like to receive. Along these same lines, employees currently making $15/hour and demanding an increase of $4/hour can view a proposed increase of $2/hour as a $2/hour gain in comparison to last year's wage (Referent 1) or as a $2/hour loss in comparison to their stated or initial proposal of $19/hour (Referent 5). Consequently, the location of the referent point is critical to whether the decision is positively or negatively framed and affects the resulting risk preference of the decision maker.

In a study of the impact of framing on collective bargaining outcomes, we used a five-issue negotiation with participants playing the roles of management or labor negotiators.[3] Each negotiator's frame was manipulated by adjusting his or her referent point. Half of the negotiators were told that any concessions they make from their initial offers represented losses to their constituencies (i.e., a negative frame). The other half were told that any agreements they were able to reach that were better than the current contract were gains to their constituencies (i.e., the positive frame). In analyzing the results of their negotiations, we found that negatively framed negotiators were less concessionary and reached fewer agreements than positively framed negotiators. In addition, negotiators who had positive frames perceived the negotiated outcomes as more fair than those who had negative frames.

In another study, we posed the following problem to negotiators:

> You are a wholesaler of refrigerators. Corporate policy does not allow any flexibility in pricing. However, flexibility does exist in terms of expenses that you can incur (shipping, financing terms, etc.), which have a direct effect on the profitability of the transaction. These expenses can all be viewed in dollar value terms. You are negotiating an $8,000 sale. The buyer wants you to pay $2,000 in expenses. You want to pay less expenses. When you negotiate the exchange, do you try to minimize your expenses (reduce them from $2,000) or maximize net profit, i.e., price less expenses (increase the net profit from $6,000)?

From an objective standpoint, the choice you make to reduce expenses or maximize profit should be irrelevant. Because the choice objectively is between two identical options, selecting one or the other should have no impact on the outcome of the negotiation. What we did find, in contrast, is that the frame that buyers and sellers take into the negotiation can systematically affect their behavior.[4]

In one study, negotiators were led to view transactions in terms of either (1) net profit or (2) total expenses deducted from gross profits. These two situations were objectively identical. Managers can think about maximizing their profits (i.e., gains) or minimizing their expenses (i.e., losses). These choices are linked: If one starts from the same set of revenues, then one way to maximize profits is to minimize expenses; and if one is successful at minimizing expenses, the outcome is that profit may be maximized. That is, there is an obvious relationship between profits and expenses. So objectively, there is no reason to believe that an individual should behave differently if given the instructions to minimize expenses or to maximize profits. However, those negotiators told to maximize profit (i.e., a positive frame) were more concessionary. In addition, positively framed negotiators completed significantly more transactions than their negatively framed (those told to minimize expenses) counterparts. Because they completed more transactions, their overall profitability in the market was higher, although negatively framed negotiators completed transactions of greater mean profit.[5]

The Endowment Effect

The ease with which we can alter our referent points was illustrated in a series of studies conducted by Daniel Kahneman, Jack Knetsch, and Richard Thaler.[6] In any exchange between a buyer and a seller, the buyer must be willing to pay at least the minimum amount the seller is willing to accept for a trade to take place. In determining the worth of an object, its value to the seller may, on occasion, be determined by some objective third party such as an economic market. However, in a large number of transactions, the seller places a value on the item—a value that may include not only the market value of the item but also a component for an emotional attachment to or unique appreciation of the item. What impact might such an attachment have on the framing of the transaction?

Let's imagine that you have just received a coffee mug.[7] (In the actual demonstration, coffee mugs were placed before one-third of the participants, the "sellers," in the study.) After receiving the mug, you are told that in fact you "own the object (coffee mug) in your possession. You have the option of selling it if a price, to be determined later, is acceptable to you." Next you are given a list (see Exhibit 1) of possible selling prices, ranging from $.50 to $9.50, and are told for each of the possible prices, you should indicate whether you would (*a*) sell the mug and receive that amount in return, or (*b*) keep the object and take it home with you. What is your selling price for the mug?

Another third of the group (the "buyers") were told that they would be receiving a sum of money and they could choose to keep the money or use it to buy a mug. They

EXHIBIT 1 | The Coffee Mug Questionnaire

For each price listed below, indicate whether you would be willing to sell the coffee mug for that price or keep the mug.

If the price is $0.50, I will sell _____ ; I will keep the mug _____.
If the price is $1.00, I will sell _____ ; I will keep the mug _____.
If the price is $1.50, I will sell _____ ; I will keep the mug _____.
If the price is $2.00, I will sell _____ ; I will keep the mug _____.
If the price is $2.50, I will sell _____ ; I will keep the mug _____.
If the price is $3.00, I will sell _____ ; I will keep the mug _____.
If the price is $3.50, I will sell _____ ; I will keep the mug _____.
If the price is $4.00, I will sell _____ ; I will keep the mug _____.
If the price is $4.50, I will sell _____ ; I will keep the mug _____.
If the price is $5.00, I will sell _____ ; I will keep the mug _____.
If the price is $5.50, I will sell _____ ; I will keep the mug _____.
If the price is $6.00, I will sell _____ ; I will keep the mug _____.
If the price is $6.50, I will sell _____ ; I will keep the mug _____.
If the price is $7.00, I will sell _____ ; I will keep the mug _____.
If the price is $7.50, I will sell _____ ; I will keep the mug _____.
If the price is $8.00, I will sell _____ ; I will keep the mug _____.
If the price is $8.50, I will sell _____ ; I will keep the mug _____.
If the price is $9.00, I will sell _____ ; I will keep the mug _____.
If the price is $9.50, I will sell _____ ; I will keep the mug _____.

were also asked to indicate their preferences between a mug and sums of money ranging from $.50 to $9.50. Finally, the last third of the participants (the "choosers") were given a questionnaire indicating that they would later be given an option of receiving either a mug or a sum of money to be determined later. They indicated their preferences between the mug and sums of money between $.50 and $9.50. All of the participants were told that their answers would not influence either the predetermined price of the mug or the amount of money to be received in lieu of the mug.

The sellers reported a median value of $7.12 for the mug; the buyers valued the mug at $2.88; and the choosers valued the mug at $3.12. It is interesting that in this exercise, being a buyer or a chooser resulted in very similar evaluations of worth of the mug. However, owning the mug (the sellers) created a much greater sense of the mug's worth. In this case, it was approximately 40 percent greater than the market (or retail) value of the mug.

The explanation for this disparity lies in the fact that different roles (buyer, seller, or chooser) created different referent points. In fact, what seems to happen in such situations is that owning something changes the nature of the owner's relationship to the commodity. Giving up that item is now perceived as loss, and in valuing the item, the owner may include a dollar value to offset his or her perceived loss. If we consider this discrepancy in the value of an item common, then the simple act of "owning" an item, however briefly, can increase one's personal attachment to an item—and typically, its perceived value. After such an attachment is formed, the cost of breaking that attachment is greater and is reflected in the higher price the sellers demand to part with their mugs as compared to the value the buyers or the choosers place on the exact same commodity. In addition, we would expect that the endowment effect intensifies to the extent that the value of the commodity of interest is ambiguous or subjective, or the commodity itself is unique or not easily substitutable in the marketplace.

Framing, Negotiator Bias, and Strategic Behavior

In the previous discussion, we described the negotiator behaviors that may arise from positive and negative frames within the context of the interaction. In this section, we identify some of the techniques for strategically manipulating framing to direct negotiator performance.

Framing has important implications for negotiator tactics. Using the framing effect to induce a negotiating opponent to concede requires that the negotiator create referents that lead the opposition to a positive frame by couching the proposal in terms of their potential gain. In addition, the negotiator should emphasize the inherent risk in the negotiation situation and the opportunity for a sure gain. As our research suggests, simply posing problems as choices among potential gains rather than choices among potential losses can significantly influence the negotiator's preferences for specific outcomes.

Framing can also have important implications for how managers choose to intervene in dispute among their peers or subordinates. Managers, of course, have a wide range of options to implement when deciding to intervene in disputes in which they are not active principals. If the manager's goal is to get the parties to reach an agreement rather than having the manager decide what the solution to the dispute will be, he or she may wish to facilitate both parties' viewing the negotiation from a positive frame. This is tricky, however, since the same referent that will lead to a positive frame for one negotiator is likely to lead to a negative frame for the other negotiator if presented simultaneously to the parties. Making use of the effects of framing may be most appropriate when a manager can meet with each side separately. He or she may present different perspectives to each party to create a positive frame (and the subsequent risk-averse behavior associated with such a frame) for parties on both sides of the dispute. Again, if the manager is to affect the frame of the problem in such a way to encourage agreement, he or she may also emphasize the possible losses inherent in continuing the dispute. Combining these two strategies may facilitate both sides' preference for the certainty of a settlement.

Being in the role of buyer or seller can be a naturally occurring frame that can influence negotiator behavior in systematic ways. Consider the curious, consistent, and robust finding in a number of studies that buyers tend to outperform sellers in market settings in which the balance of power is equal.[8] Given the artificial context of the laboratory settings and the symmetry of the design of these field and laboratory markets, there is no logical reason why buyers should do better than sellers. One explanation for this observed difference may be that when the commodity is anonymous (or completely substitutable in a market sense), sellers may think about the transaction in terms of the dollars exchanged. That is, sellers may conceptualize the process of selling as gaining resources (e.g., how many dollars do I gain by selling the commodity); whereas buyers may view the transaction in terms of loss of dollars (e.g., how many dollars do I have to give up). If the dollars are the primary focus of the participants' attention, then buyers would tend to be risk seeking and sellers risk averse in the exchange.

When a risk-averse party (i.e., the seller, in this example) negotiates with a risk-seeking party (i.e., the buyer), the buyer is more willing to risk the potential agreement by demanding more or being less concessionary. To reach agreement, the seller must make additional concessions to induce the buyer, because of his or her risk-seeking propensity, to accept the agreement. Thus in situations where the relative achievements of buyers and seller can be directly compared, buyers would benefit from their negative frame (and subsequent risk-averse behavior). The critical issue is that these naturally occurring frames such as the role demands of being a "buyer" or "seller" can easily influence the way in which the disputed issues are framed—even without the conscious intervention of one or more of the parties.

It is easy to see that the frames of negotiators can result in the difference between impasse and reaching an important agreement. Both sides in negotiations typically talk in terms of a certain wage, price, or outcome that they must get—setting a high referent point against which gains and losses are measured. If this occurs, any compromise below (or above) that point represents a loss. This perceived loss may lead negotiators to adopt a negative frame to all proposals, exhibit risk-seeking behaviors, and be less likely to reach settlement. Thus negotiators, similar to the early example involving the beach and the beer, may end up with no beer (or no agreement) because of the frame (the amount of money I will pay for a beer from a run-down grocery store) that is placed on the choices rather than an objective assessment of what the beer is worth to the individual.

In addition, framing has important implications for the tactics that negotiators use. The framing effect suggests that to induce concessionary behavior from an opponent, a negotiator should always create anchors or emphasize referents that lead the opposition to a positive frame and couch the negotiation in terms of what the other side has to gain.

In addition, the negotiator should make the inherent risk salient to the opposition while the opponent is in a risky situation. If the sure gain that is being proposed is rejected, there is no certainty about the quality of the next offer. Simultaneously, the negotiator should also not be persuaded by similar arguments from opponents. Maintaining a risk-neutral or risk-seeking perspective in evaluating an opponent's proposals may, in the worst case, reduce the probability of reaching an agreement; however, if agreements are reached, the outcomes are more likely to be of greater value to the negotiator.

An important component in creating good negotiated agreements is to avoid the pitfalls of being framed while, simultaneously, understanding the impact of positively and negatively framing your negotiating opponent. However, framing is just one of a series of cognitive biases that can have a significant negative impact on the performance of negotiators. The purpose of this article was to describe the impact of one of these cognitive biases on negotiator behavior by considering the available research on the topic and to explore ways to reduce the problems associated with framing. By increasing our understanding of the subtle ways in which these cognitive biases can reduce the effectiveness of our negotiations, managers can begin to not only improve the quality of agreements for themselves but also fashion agreements that more efficiently allocate the available resources—leaving both parties and the communities of which they are a part better off.

Endnotes

This article is based on the book by M. H. Bazerman, and M. A. Neale, *Negotiating Rationally* (New York: Free Press, 1992).

1. Adapted from J. E. Russo and P. J. Schoemaker, *Decision Traps* (New York: Doubleday, 1989).

2. R. Thaler, "Using Mental Accounting in a Theory of Purchasing Behavior," *Marketing Science* 4 (1985), pp. 12–13.

3. M. A. Neale and M. H. Bazerman, "The Effects of Framing and Negotiator Overconfidence," *Academy of Management Journal* 28 (1985), pp. 34–49.

4. M. H. Bazerman, T. Magliozzi, and M. A. Neale, "The Acquisition of an Integrative Response in a Competitive Market Simulation," *Organizational Behavior and Human Performance* 34 (1985), pp. 294–313.

5. See, for example, Bazerman, Magliozzi, and Neale (1985), op. cit.; Neale and Bazerman, (1985), op. cit.; or M. A. Neale and G. B. Northcraft, "Experts, Amateurs, and Refrigerators: Comparing Expert and Amateur Decision Making on a Novel Task," *Organizational Behavior and Human Decision Processes* 38 (1986), pp. 305–17; M. A. Neale, V. L. Huber, and G. B. Northcraft, "The Framing of Negotiations: Context versus Task Frames," *Organizational Behavior and Human Decision Processes* 39 (1987), pp. 228–41.

6. D. Kahneman, J. L. Knetsch, and R. Thaler, "Experimental Tests of the Endowment Effect and Coarse Theorem," *Journal of Political Economy,* 1990.

7. The coffee mugs were valued at approximately $5.00.

8. Bazerman et al., (1985), op. cit.; M. A. Neale, V. L. Huber, and G. B. Northcraft, (1987), op. cit.

Psychological Traps

Jeffrey Z. Rubin

You place a phone call and are put on hold. You wait. And then you wait some more. Should you hang up? Perhaps. After all, why waste another second of your valuable time? On the other hand, if you hang up you'll only have to call again to accomplish whatever business put you on the phone in the first place. Anyway, you've already spent all this time on hold, so why give up now? So you wait some more. At some point you finally resign yourself to the likelihood that you've been left on hold forever. Even as you hang up, though, your ear remains glued to the receiver, hoping to the bitter end that all the time spent waiting was not in vain.

Almost all of us have spent too much time caught in little traps like that. Even when it no longer makes sense, we continue to spend money on a failing automobile or washing machine, on an aging and decrepit house, a risky stock investment, or a doubtful poker hand. We simply do not know when to cut our losses and get out. And the same goes for more serious situations. Some of us remain longer than we should in a marriage or love relationship, a job or career, a therapy that is yielding diminishing returns. On a grander scale, entrapment is part of the dynamic in political controversies—Abscam, Watergate, the war in Vietnam.

A common set of psychological issues and motivations underlies all such situations, a process of entrapment that shares many of the characteristics of animal traps and con games and has been studied in a variety of laboratory and natural settings. As researchers, we are attempting to describe the properties of psychological traps: what they have in common, where they lurk, whom they tend to snare, and how they can be avoided.

When I was growing up in New York City there was a cunning little device that we called the Chinese Finger Trap—a woven straw cylinder about three or four inches long, with an opening at each end just large enough for a child's finger to be inserted. Once you put a finger into each end, the trap was sprung. The harder you tugged in opposite directions in an effort to get free, the more the woven cylinder stretched and pulled tight around each finger. Only by pushing inward, by moving *counter* to the direction in which escape appeared to lie, could you get free. So it is with entrapping situations. The tighter one pulls, the greater the conflict between the lure of the goal and the increasing cost of remaining in pursuit of it. And the tighter one pulls, the greater the trap's bite. Only by letting go at some point can we escape the trap. Or as the Chinese philosopher Lao-tzu put it, "Those who would conquer must yield; and those who conquer do so because they yield."

To understand psychological entrapment, we must first understand the simplest traps of all—physical traps for animals. Sometime rather early in the evolution of our species, human beings came to understand that the active pursuit of quarry by hunting was often impractical or undesirable. Thus trapping was invented. A trap allows hunters to outwit their quarry, to offset any advantage that the quarry may have by virtue of its greater power or speed or the limited destructive capacity of the hunters' weapons. An animal trap accomplishes these ends in a strikingly simple and clever way: it brings the quarry to the hunter rather than the other way around. Instead of continuing to hunt for quarry, often in vain and at considerable cost, trappers get the quarry to catch itself. Once set, the animal trap takes on a life of its own, a surrogate hunter waiting with infinite patience for the quarry to make the unwise choice. The consequence of having this surrogate is that hunters' limited resources can now be devoted to other pursuits, including the construction of additional traps.

Ingenious devices, these animal traps, devilishly clever and efficient—and utterly sinister in their effect on the victims who fall prey to them. What properties, then, make them work?

First of all, an effective trap must be able to lure or distract the quarry into behaving in ways that risk its self-preservation. Often this important first step is accomplished with some form of bait that is so tantalizingly attractive, so well suited to the quarry's particular needs, that the animal is induced to pursue it, oblivious to the trap's jaws.

Second, an effective animal trap permits traffic in one direction only. It is far easier for a lobster to push its way through the cone-shaped net into the lobster trap than, once in, to claw its way out. The bait that motivated the quarry to enter the trap in the first place obscures the irreversibility of that move. Doors that yield easily, inviting the quarry's entry, slam shut with a vengeance.

Third, an effective trap is often engineered so that the quarry's very efforts to escape entrap it all the more. The bear's considerable strength, applied in an effort to pull its paw from a trap, only sinks the trap's teeth deeper into its flesh. A fish's tendency to swim away from anything that constrains its free movement only deepens the bite of the hook. An effective trap thus invites the quarry to become the source of its own entrapment or possible destruction.

Finally, an effective animal trap must be suited to the particular attributes of the quarry it is designed to capture. One cannot catch a guppy with a lobster trap or a mosquito with a butterfly net. Consider the awful and awesomely effective nineteenth-century American wolf trap. The simplicity and frightening elegance of this trap is that it depends on the wolf's appetite for the taste of blood. A bloodied knife blade was left to freeze in the winter ice. While licking the knife, the wolf would cut its tongue and begin to bleed. It would then start to lick at the knife all the more, which in turn led to a greater flow of blood—and the wolf's ultimate undoing. The animal's blood attracted other wolves, who then attacked the victim and, eventually, one another. Thus a whole pack of wolves could be destroyed with just one trap.

Confidence games are psychological traps for capturing people and are remarkably similar to self-entrapment. Like animal traps, they rely for their effectiveness on the trapper's (con artist's) ability to lure the quarry (mark) into a course of action that becomes entrapping. The lure is typically based on the mark's cupidity; the fat, wriggling worm is the tempting possibility of getting something for nothing, a big killing that appears to happen at the expense of someone else.

The effective con also depends on the mark's willingness to cheat another person in order to reap large and easy profits. As a result, the mark's progressive pursuit of the lure tends to obscure the fact that the path taken is not easily reversible. With the con artist's kind assistance, the mark is increasingly rendered a coconspirator in a crime against another, a bit like Macbeth: "I am in blood/stepp'd so far that, should I wade no more,/ Returning were as tedious as go o'er."

In addition, the mark's very efforts to escape—by making a quick, glorious, and final big killing before quitting once and for all—only lead to deeper entrapment. The more money the mark is persuaded to put up in this effort, the more carefully he or she is apt to guard the investment—and to justify it through the commitment of additional resources.

Finally, just as an animal trap is tailored to its quarry, so must a con be geared to the brand of avarice and dishonesty of the mark. "Different traps for different saps" is the rule.

There are two kinds of cons: so-called short cons, such as Three-Card Monte or the Shell Game, in which the mark is fleeced for a few dollars on the spot; and big cons, in which the mark is directed to a "big store"—a place where the con is played out. Big cons reached their heyday around the turn of the nineteenth century in this country and lined the pockets of skilled con artists with hundreds of thousands of dollars. Big cons included the Rag, the Pay-Off, and the Wire, the last of these made famous by Paul Newman and Robert Redford in *The Sting*. In that con, a mark was persuaded that horse-race results had been delayed long enough for him to place a bet *after* the race had been run, thereby betting on a sure thing. The con took place in a large ground-floor room, rented for a week as the big store. All the roles in the drama, save that of the mark, were played by confederates creating an elaborate and complex ruse.

These steps or stages involved in most big cons are remarkably consistent:

1. "Putting the mark up"—finding the right person to fleece.
2. "Playing the con"—befriending the mark and gaining the mark's confidence.
3. "Roping the mark"—steering the victim to the "inside man," the person who is in charge of running the big store.
4. "Telling the tale"—giving the inside man an opportunity to show the mark how a large sum of money can be made dishonestly.
5. "Giving the convincer"—allowing the mark to make a substantial profit in a test run of the swindle.
6. "Giving the breakdown"—setting the mark up to invest a large sum of money for the final killing.
7. "Putting the mark on the send"—sending the mark home for that amount of money.
8. "The sting"—fleecing the mark in the big store.
9. "Blowing the mark off"—getting the mark out of the way as quickly and quietly as possible.

In psychological entrapment, one person may simultaneously play the role of roper, inside man, and mark. In so doing, we manage to ensnare ourselves. As with physical and psychological devices for capturing others, these traps only work when people are, first and foremost, interested in—and distracted by—the lure of some goal. Final victory in

Vietnam, a happy marriage, a big killing at the gambling table, or simply the return of the person who pushed the hold button: all may be viewed as worthy goals—or as bait that conceals a dangerous hook. In entrapping situations, marks initially look in one direction only—forward—as they pursue the mirage of a goal that lies just beyond their grasp.

In their single-minded rush toward the objective, marks neglect the possibility that they are being sucked into a funnel from which escape may prove remarkably difficult. The first stage of entrapment—eager, forward-looking pursuit of one's goal—is thus followed by attention to the costs that have been unwittingly incurred along the way. The compulsive gambler's drive for a killing is inevitably followed by attention to the mounting costs of the pursuit, costs that in turn need to be justified by greater commitment. Similarly, when our personal or professional lives are disappointing—and our efforts to achieve a turnaround do not pay off quickly enough—we may decide to justify the high cost by renewing our commitment and remaining on the treadmill.

But notice that the more resources committed to attaining the goal, the greater the trap's bite. Each additional step toward a rewarding but unattained goal creates new and greater costs, requiring greater justification of the course of action than ever before. With each additional year that a person remains in a dissatisfying job, hoping it will take a turn for the better, he or she feels more compelled to rationalize the time invested by remaining in the job even longer.

In certain entrapping situations, those in which several people are competing with one another, reward pursuit and cost justification are followed by a third stage, in which people try to make sure that their competitors end up losing at least as much—if not more—than they. Like two children in a breath-holding contest or two nations in an arms race, many entrapping situations evolve to the point where each side's focus is no longer on winning or even on minimizing losses, but on getting even with the adversary who engineered the mess.

In the last major stage of entrapment, marks must finally let go, either because their resources are gone, because they are rescued by another person, or because they recognize the desperation of the pursuit. Just as the Chinese Finger Trap can be escaped only by pushing inward, entrapment can be avoided only by letting go.

One devilishly simple and effective example of entrapment is a game known as the Dollar Auction, invented about 10 years ago by Martin Shubik, an economist at Yale. As his proving ground, Shubik allegedly used the Yale University cocktail party circuit. Anyone can make some money—but perhaps lose some friends—by trying it out at a party.

Take a dollar bill from your pocket and announce that you will auction it off to the highest bidder. People will be invited to call out bids in multiples of five cents until no further bidding occurs, at which point the highest bidder will pay the amount bid and win the dollar. The only feature that distinguishes this auction from traditional auctions, you point out, is the rule that the *second-highest* bidder will also be asked to pay the amount bid, although he or she will obviously not win the dollar. For example, Susan has bid 30 cents and Bill has bid 25 cents; if the bidding stops at this point, you will pay Susan 70 cents ($1 minus the amount she bid), and Bill, the second-highest bidder, will have to pay you 25 cents. The auction ends when one minute has elapsed without any additional bidding.

If my own experience is any indication, the game is likely to follow a general pattern. One person bids a nickel, another bids a dime, someone else jumps the bidding to a quarter or so, and the bidding proceeds at a fast and furious pace until about 50 or 60 cents is reached. At around that point, the number of people calling out bids begins to decrease, and soon there are only three or four people still taking part. The bidding continues, at a somewhat slower pace, until the two highest bids are at about $1 and 95 cents. There is a break in the action at this point, as the two remaining bidders seem to consider what has happened and whether they should continue. Suddenly the person who bid 95 cents calls out $1.05, and the bidding resumes. Soon the two remaining bidders have escalated matters so far that both bids are over $4. Then one of the guests suddenly escalates the bidding by offering $5, the other (who has already bid $4.25 or so) refuses to go any higher, and the game ends. You proceed to collect $4.25 from the loser and $4 from the "winner."

Several researchers have had people play the Dollar Auction game under controlled laboratory conditions and have found that the participants typically end up bidding far in excess of the $1 prize at stake, sometimes paying as much as $5 or $6 for a dollar bill. The interesting question is, of course, why? What motivates people to bid initially and to persist in a self-defeating course of action?

Thanks primarily to the extensive research of Allan Teger, a social psychologist at Boston University, the question has been answered. Teger found that when Dollar Auction participants were asked to give reasons for their bidding, their responses fell into one of two major motivational categories: economic and interpersonal. Economic motives include a desire to win the dollar, a desire to regain losses, and a desire to avoid losing more money. Interpersonal motives include a desire to save face, a desire to prove one is the best player, and a desire to punish the other person.

Economic motives appear to predominate in the early stages of the Dollar Auction. People begin bidding with the hope of winning the dollar bill easily and inexpensively. Their bids increase a little bit at a time, in the expectation that their latest bid will prove to be the winning one. If the other participants reason the same way, however, the bidding escalates. At some subsequent point in the Dollar Auction, the bidders begin to realize that they have been drawn into an increasingly treacherous situation. Acknowledging that they have already invested a portion of their own resources in the auction, they begin to pay particular attention to the amount they stand to lose if they come in second. As the bidding approaches $1—or when the amount invested equals the objective worth of the prize—the tension rises. At this stage, Teger has found, the participants experience intense inner conflict, as measured by physiological measures of anxiety and nervousness; about half of them then quit the game.

People who remain in the auction past the $1 bid, however, typically stick with it to the bitter end—until they have exhausted their resources or their adversary has quit. Interpersonal motives come to the fore when the bid exceeds the objective value of the prize. Even though both players know they are sure to lose, each may go out of his or her way to punish the other, making sure that the other person loses even more, and each may become increasingly concerned about looking foolish by yielding to the adversary's aggression. Teger found that this mutual concern occasionally leads bidders to a cooperative solution to the problem of how to quit without losing face: a bid of $1 by one player, if followed by a quick final raise to $2 by the second, allows the first person to quit in the knowledge that both have lost equally.

If entrapping situations are as ubiquitous and powerful as I have suggested, how do people ever avoid getting into them? What, if anything, can people do to keep from getting in deeper? Over the past six years or so, I have been working with a research group at Tufts University to find some answers to these questions. We have conducted most of our research in the laboratory, using the Dollar Auction and several other procedures. We have begun to study entrapment in naturalistic settings, by holding contests in which residents of the Boston area, chosen at random, are invited to solve a series of increasingly difficult problems that require more and more of their time.

In one experimental model, people were invited to pay for the ticks of a numerical counter in the hope that they would obtain a jackpot—either by reaching the number that had been randomly generated by computer or by outlasting an adversary. A second laboratory paradigm challenged people to solve a jigsaw puzzle correctly within a limited period; if they succeeded, they received a cash jackpot, but if they failed, they had to pay for the number of pieces they had requested. Finally, in a third type of experiment, undergraduates were instructed to wait for an experimenter or another participant to arrive at the laboratory so that they could receive a research credit; naturally, the experimenter was always late, and the subjects had to continually decide how much longer they would wait.

In one such experiment, Tufts undergraduates were seated in individual rooms, given $2.50 in cash for agreeing to come to our laboratory, and invited to win an additional $10 jackpot by solving a crossword puzzle. The puzzle consisted of 10 words of varying difficulty, 8 or more of which had to be correctly solved in order to win the jackpot. Each student was given three "free" minutes to work on the puzzle; after that, 25 cents was deducted from the initial $2.50 stake for each additional minute. People could quit the experiment at any point and leave with their initial stake—minus 25 cents for each minute they remained in the study past the first three. If they remained in the study after 13 minutes had passed, they had to begin paying out of their own pockets, since their initial stake was exhausted at that point. The study was stopped after 15 minutes.

Almost everyone found the puzzle too difficult to solve without the aid of a crossword puzzle dictionary, which they were told was available on request. Participants were also told that because there were two people working on the puzzle and only one dictionary, it would be available on a first-come, first-served basis. (No such dictionary was actually available.) When students requested the dictionary, they had to turn their puzzles face down, so they were not able to wait for the dictionary and work on the puzzle at the same time. Surprisingly, nearly 20 percent of the students stayed in the experiment the full 15 minutes.

We investigated several important influences on the entrapment process here. First, we created either a competitive or noncompetitive relationship between the participants by telling the students either that the $10 jackpot would be awarded to the first person who solved the puzzle or that it would go to anyone who was able to do so. We found that students who believed they were in a competition became more entrapped—they played the game far longer and spent more of their money—than those not in competition.

We also studied the nature of the investment process by giving participants different instructions about quitting the experiment. Some were told that they could quit at any time. Others were advised that the experimenter would ask them every three minutes if they wished to continue. We expected that the experimenter's intervention would serve as an indirect reminder of the cost of continued participation and that those students who were spoken to would become less entrapped than the others. That is exactly what happened. Students who were not asked if they wished to continue remained in the experiment far longer and, as a group, lost more than twice as much money.

In all of our experiments, as in the one just described, we encourage subjects to move toward some rewarding goal, while we increase the time or money they must invest in it and give them the option to quit at any time. Both our research and Teger's reveal certain repeating themes in the behavior of the participants, which I can summarize in the form of some advice on how to avoid entrapment.

- *Set limits on your involvement and commitment in advance.* We find that people who are not asked to indicate the limits of their participation become more entrapped than those who do indicate a limit, especially publicly. Depending on the entrapping situation you are in, you may wish to set a limit based on your past experience (for example, the average time you've spent waiting on hold); your available resources (the amount of time or money you have left to spend); the importance of reaching your goal on this occasion (you may be able to call later to make a plane reservation); and the possibility of reaching your goal in some other way (using a travel agent to make the reservation).

- *Once you set a limit, stick to it.* We all play little games with ourselves—we flip a coin to make a decision and then when we don't like the result, decide to make the contest two out of three flips. We set limits that are subsequently modified, shaded, and shifted as we get close to the finish. Each new investment, like the addition of an AM/FM radio to a new car that has already been decked out with extras, tends to be evaluated not in relation to zero (the total cost of the investment) but in relation to that inconsequential, minuscule increment above and beyond the amount we've already agreed to spend. If you're the sort of person who has trouble adhering to limits, get some help. Find a friend, tell him or her the limit you wish to set, and have your friend rope you in when you get to the end of your self-appointed tether. Ulysses used that method to resist the deadly temptation of the Sirens' wail.

- *Avoid looking to other people to see what you should do.* It's one thing to use a friend to rope you in, and it's another matter entirely to deal with your uncertainty about what to do by sheepishly following others. Given the uncertainty in entrapping situations, it is tempting to look to others for clues about the appropriateness of one's own behavior. Our research indicates that the presence and continued involvement of another person in an entrapping situation increases one's own entrapment, and that this occurs even when the behavior of each person has no effect on the other's fate. Proprietors of Las Vegas gambling casinos know what they're doing when they use shills to "prime the pump" and get the gambler's competitive juices flowing. Similarly, one is far more likely to continue waiting for a bus that has not yet arrived—and even wait for an outrageous, irrationally long time—if other people are also waiting.

- *Beware of your need to impress others.* Other people are not only a source of information about what to do in entrapping situations; they are also a critically important source of praise or disapproval for our behavior. We all want to be liked, loved, and respected by people whose opinions matter to us. This motive is perfectly healthy and often appropriate, but not in entrapping situations. Our research shows that people become more entrapped when they believe their effectiveness is being judged and scrutinized by others. This is particularly powerful when the perceived evaluation occurs early in the game, and diminishes in importance if evaluative observers are introduced later on. We also find that people who are especially anxious about their appearance in the eyes of others and who feel that they have something to prove by toughing things out get more entrapped than their less anxious counterparts.

- *Remind yourself of the costs involved.* Our research indicates that people are less likely to become entrapped when they are made aware early on of the costs associated with continued participation. Even the availability of a chart that depicts investment costs is sufficient to reduce entrapment. The new effect of such information about costs is to offset the distracting, shimmering lure of the goal ahead—especially if the cost information is introduced right away. If you don't start paying attention to the cost of your involvement until fairly late in the game, you may feel compelled to justify those costs by investing even more of your resources.

- *Remain vigilant.* Entrapping situations seem to sneak up on us. People who understand and avoid one brand of trap often manage to get caught in others with surprising frequency and ease. Just because you knew when to bail out of that lousy stock investment doesn't mean that you will have the good sense to give up on an unsatisfactory relationship or a profession in which you feel you have too much invested to quit. Obviously, people who are told about entrapment and its dangers are less likely to become entrapped. Our studies also show that being forewarned about one kind of trap, moreover, can put people on guard against other kinds of traps.

Although very little is known at this point about the kinds of people who tend to get entrapped, we have recently begun to study this issue and can therefore engage in a bit of informed speculation. First, people who go for bait are also likely to end up hooked. Those who are exceptionally ambitious or greedy or unusually self-confident and self-assured about their ability to reach a goal must tread warily. There may be icebergs lurking in those calm and glassy seas ahead. Second, the sort of person who believes that he should—indeed must—profit according to his efforts may also be ripe for the plucking. Those who tend to trust excessively in a just world, who think that people get what they deserve and deserve what they get, may end up caught in a version of the Chinese Finger Trap. They use their belief in justice to rationalize continued investments—and so tighten the noose all the more. Finally, the man or woman who tends to get swept up in macho ideology, who feels that nothing else applies, is also especially vulnerable to entrapment. Such people may be willing to invest more and more in order to avoid some small embarrassment—only to suffer greater humiliation in the final reckoning.

Despite cautionary advice, we all still manage to get ourselves entrapped. When the inevitable happens, when you find yourself asking "What have I done?" remember there are times when the wisest course may be to quit, not fight. There may just not be a way of salvaging the time, effort, money, even the human lives that have gone into a particular sinking ship. Know when to give it up, when to push rather than pull those fingers, and when to yield and wait for victory another day. For there is almost always another day, despite our proclivity for ignoring that fact.

Reading 2.3

The Behavior of Successful Negotiators

Neil Rackham

Background

Almost all publications about negotiating behavior fall into one of three classes:

1. Anecdotal "here's how I do it" accounts by successful negotiators. These have the advantage of being based on real life but the disadvantage that they frequently describe highly personal modes of behavior, which are a risky guide for would-be negotiators to follow.

2. Theoretical models of negotiating, which are idealized, complex, and seldom translatable into practical action.

3. Laboratory studies, which tend to be short term and contain a degree of artificiality.

Very few studies have investigated what actually goes on face-to-face during a negotiation. Two reasons account for this lack of published research. First, real negotiators are understandably reluctant to let a researcher watch them at work. Such research requires the consent of both negotiating parties and constitutes a constraint on a delicate situation. The second reason for the poverty of research in this area is lack of methodology. Until recently there were few techniques available that allowed an observer to collect data on the behavior of negotiators without the use of cumbersome and unacceptable methods such as questionnaires.

Since 1968 a number of studies have been carried out by Neil Rackham of Huthwaite Research Group, using behavior analysis methods. These have allowed direct observation during real negotiations, so that an objective and quantified record can be collected to show how the skilled negotiator behaves.

The Successful Negotiator

The basic methodology for studying negotiating behavior is simple—find some successful negotiators and watch them to discover how they do it. But what is the criterion for a successful negotiator? The Rackham studies used three success criteria:

1. *He should be rated as effective by both sides.* This criterion enabled the researchers to identify likely candidates for further study. The condition that both sides should agree on a negotiator's effectiveness was a precaution to prevent picking a sample from a single frame of reference.

2. *He should have a track record of significant success.* The central criterion for choosing effective negotiators was track record over a time period. In such a complex field the researchers were anxious for evidence of consistency. They

also wished to avoid the common trap of laboratory studies—looking only at the short-term consequences of a negotiator's behavior and therefore favoring those using tricks or deceptions.

3. *He should have a low incidence of implementation failures.* The researchers judged that the purpose of a negotiation was not just to reach an agreement but to reach an agreement that would be viable. Therefore, in addition to a track record of agreements, the record of implementation was also studied to ensure that any agreements reached were successfully implemented.

A total of 48 negotiators were picked who met all of these three success criteria. The breakdown of the sample was

Industrial (Labor) Relations Negotiators	
Union representatives	17
Management representatives	12
Contract negotiators	10
Others	9

Altogether the 48 successful negotiators were studied over a total of 102 separate negotiating sessions. For the remainder of this document these people are called the "skilled" group. In comparison, a group of negotiators who either failed to meet the criteria or about whom no criterion data were available were also studied. These were called the "average" group. By comparing the behavior of the two groups, it was possible to isolate the crucial behaviors that made the skilled negotiators different.

The Research Method

The researchers met the negotiator before the negotiation and encouraged her/him to talk about his/her planning and his/her objectives. For 56 sessions with the skilled negotiators and 37 sessions with the average negotiators, either this planning session was tape-recorded or extensive notes were taken.

The negotiator then introduced the researcher into the actual negotiation. The delicacy of this process can be judged from the fact that although most cases had been carefully prehandled, the researchers were not accepted in upward of 20 instances and were asked to withdraw.

During the negotiation the researcher counted the frequency with which certain key behaviors were used by the negotiators, using behavior analysis methods. In all of the 102 sessions interaction data were collected, while in 66 sessions content analysis was also obtained.

How the Skilled Negotiator Plans

Negotiation training emphasizes the importance of planning. How does the skilled negotiator plan?

Amount of Planning Time

No significant difference was found between the total planning time that skilled and average negotiators claimed they spent prior to actual negotiation. This finding must be viewed cautiously because, unlike the other conclusions in this document, it is derived from the negotiator's impressions of themselves, not from their actual observed behavior. Nevertheless, it suggests the conclusion that it is not the amount of planning time that makes for success, but how that time is used.

Exploration of Options

The skilled negotiator considers a wider range of outcomes or options for action than the average negotiator.

Outcomes/Options Considered during Planning (per Negotiable Issue)	
Skilled negotiator	5.1
Average negotiator	2.6

The skilled negotiator is concerned with the whole spectrum of possibilities, both those that s/he could introduce himself and those that might be introduced by the people s/he negotiates with. In contrast, the average negotiator considers few options. An impression of the researchers, for which, unfortunately, no systematic data were collected, is that the average negotiator is especially less likely to consider options that might be raised by the other party.

Common Ground

Does the skilled negotiator concentrate during his/her planning on the areas that hold most potential for conflict, or does s/he give his/her attention to possible areas of common ground? The research showed that although both groups of negotiators tended to concentrate on the conflict areas, the skilled negotiators gave over three times as much attention to common ground areas as did average negotiators:

Skilled negotiators—38 percent of comments about areas of anticipated agreement or common ground.

Average negotiators—11 percent of comments about areas of anticipated agreement or common ground.

This significant finding can be interpreted in a variety of ways. It may be, for example, that the skilled negotiator has already built a climate of agreement so that undue concentration on conflict is unnecessary. Equally, concentration on the common-ground areas may be the key to building a satisfactory climate in the first place. A relatively high concentration on common-ground areas is known to be an effective strategy from other Huthwaite Research Group studies of persuasion, notably with "pull" styles of persuasion in selling.

In any event, a potential negotiator wishing to model himself on successful performers would do well to pay special attention to areas of anticipated common ground and not just to areas of conflict.

Long-Term or Short-Term?

It is often suggested that skilled negotiators spend much of their planning time considering the long-term implications of the issues, while unskilled negotiators concentrate on the short term. Is this true in practice? The studies found that both groups showed an alarming concentration on the short-term aspects of issues.

Percentage of Planning Comments about Long-Term Considerations of Anticipated Issues	
Skilled negotiators	8.5
Average negotiators	4.0

With the average negotiator, approximately 1 comment in 25 during his/her planning met our criterion of a long-term consideration, namely a comment that involved any factor extending beyond the immediate implementation of the issue under negotiation. The skilled negotiator, while showing twice as many long-term comments, still averages only 8.5 percent of his/her total recorded planning comments. These figures must necessarily be approximate, partly because of the research methods (which may have inadvertently encouraged verbalization of short-term issues) and partly because our ignorance of individual circumstances made some comments hard to classify. Even so, they demonstrate how little thought is given by most negotiators to the long-term implications of what they negotiate.

Setting Limits

The researchers asked negotiators about their objectives and recorded whether their replies referred to single-point objectives (e.g., "we aim to settle at 83p") or to a defined range (e.g., "we hope to get 37p but we would settle for a minimum of 34p"). Skilled negotiators were significantly more likely to set upper and lower limits—to plan in terms of a range. Average negotiators, in contrast, were more likely to plan their objectives around a fixed point. Although one possible explanation is that the skilled negotiator has more freedom, which gives him/her the discretion of upper and lower limits, this seems unlikely from the research. Even where the average negotiator had considerable capacity to vary the terms of an agreement, s/he usually approached the negotiation with a fixed-point objective in mind. The conclusion, for would-be negotiators, is that it seems to be preferable to approach a negotiation with objectives specifying a clearly defined range rather than to base planning on an inflexible single-point objective.

Sequence and Issue Planning

The term *planning* frequently refers to a process of sequencing—putting a number of events, points, or potential occurrences into a time sequence. Critical path analysis and other forms of network planning are examples. This concept of planning, called *sequence planning,* works efficiently with inanimate objects, or in circumstances where the planner has real control that allows him/her to determine the sequence in which events will occur. The researchers found that average negotiators place very heavy reliance on sequence planning. So, for example, they would frequently verbalize a potential negotiation in terms like "First I'll bring up A, then lead to B, and after that I'll cover C, and finally go on to D." In order to succeed, sequence planning always requires the consent and cooperation of the other negotiating party. In many negotiations this cooperation is not forthcoming. The negotiator would begin at point A and the other party would only be interested in point D. This could put the negotiator in difficulty, requiring him/her to either mentally change gear and approach the negotiation in a sequence s/he had not planned for, or to carry through his/her original sequence, risking disinterest from the other party. In many negotiations, sequences were in themselves negotiable, and it was ill-advised for the negotiator to plan on a sequence basis.

Typical Sequence Plan Used by Average Negotiators

A   then   B   then   C   then   D
in which issues are linked

Typical Issue Plan Used by Skilled Negotiators

A

B

D

C

in which issues are independent and
not linked by a sequence

They would consider issue C, for example, as if issues A, B, and D didn't exist. Compared with the average negotiators, they were careful not to draw sequence links between a series of issues. This was demonstrated by observing the number of occasions during the planning process that each negotiator mentioned sequence of issues.

Number of Mentions Implying Sequence in Planning	
Skilled negotiators	2.1 per session
Average negotiators	4.9 per session

The clear advantage of issue planning over sequence planning is flexibility. In planning a negotiation it is important to remember that the sequence of issues itself (unless a preset agenda is agreed) may be subject to negotiation. Even where an agenda exists, within a particular item, sequence planning may involve some loss of flexibility. So it seems useful for negotiators to plan their face-to-face strategy using issue planning and avoiding sequence planning.

Face-to-Face Behavior

Skilled negotiators show marked differences in their face-to-face behavior, compared with average negotiators. They use certain types of behavior significantly more frequently while they tend to avoid other types.

Irritators

Certain words and phrases that are commonly used during negotiation have negligible value in persuading the other party but do cause irritation. Probably the most frequent example of these is the term *generous offer* used by a negotiator to describe his/her own proposal. Similarly, words such as *fair* or *reasonable,* and other terms with a high positive value loading, have no persuasive power when used as self-praise, while serving to irritate the other party because of the implication that they are unfair, unreasonable, and so on. Most negotiators avoid the gratuitous use of direct insults or unfavorable value judgments. They know that there is little to gain from saying unfavorable things about the other party during face-to-face exchanges. However, the other side of the coin—saying gratuitously favorable things about themselves—seems harder for them to avoid. The researchers called such words *irritators* and found that although the average negotiator used them fairly regularly, the skilled negotiator tended to avoid them.

Use of Irritators per Hour of Face-to-Face Speaking Time	
Skilled negotiators	2.3
Average negotiators	10.8

It is hardly surprising that skilled negotiators use fewer irritators. Any type of verbal behavior that antagonizes without a persuasive effect is unlikely to be productive. More surprising is the heavy use of irritators by average negotiators. The conclusion must be that most people fail to recognize the counterproductive effect of using positive value judgments about themselves and, in doing so, implying negative judgments of the other party.

Counterproposals

During negotiation it frequently happens that one party puts forward a proposal and the other party immediately responds with a counterproposal. The researchers found that skilled negotiators made immediate counterproposals much less frequently than average negotiators.

Frequency of Counterproposals per Hour of Face-to-Face Speaking Time	
Skilled negotiators	1.7
Average negotiators	3.1

This difference suggests that the common strategy of meeting a proposal with a counterproposal may not be particularly effective. The disadvantages of counterproposals are

- They introduce an additional option, sometimes a whole new issue, which complicates and clouds the clarity of the negotiation.
- They are put forward at a point where the other party has least receptiveness, being concerned with his/her own proposal.

- They are perceived as blocking or disagreeing by the other party, not as proposals. A study of 87 controlled-pace negotiation exercises by the researchers showed that when one side in a negotiation put forth a proposal there was an 87 percent chance that the other side would perceive it as a proposal. However, if the proposal immediately followed a proposal made by the other side (if in other words it was a counterproposal) the chance of being perceived as a proposal dropped to 61 percent, with a proportionate increase in the chances of being perceived as either disagreeing or blocking.

These reasons probably explain why the skilled negotiator is less likely to use counterproposing as a tactic than is the average negotiator.

Defend/Attack Spirals

Because negotiation frequently involves conflict, negotiators may become heated and use emotional or value-loaded behaviors. When such behavior was used to attack the other party or to make an emotional defense, the researchers termed it *defending/ attacking*. Once initiated, this behavior tended to form a spiral of increasing intensity: One negotiator would attack, and the other would defend himself, usually in a manner which the first negotiator perceived as an attack. In consequence, the first negotiator attacked more vigorously, and the spiral commenced. Defending and attacking were often difficult to distinguish from each other. What one negotiator perceived as a legitimate defense, the other party might see as an unwarranted attack. This was the root cause of most defending/attacking spirals observed during the studies. Average negotiators, in particular, were likely to react defensively, using comments such as "You can't blame us for that" or "It's not our fault that the present difficulty has arisen." Such comments frequently provoked a sharp defensive reaction from the other side of the table.

Percentage of Negotiators' Comments Classified as Defending/Attacking	
Skilled negotiators	1.9
Average negotiators	6.3

The researchers found that average negotiators used more than three times as much defending/attacking behavior as skilled negotiators. Although no quantitative measure exists, the researchers observed that skilled negotiators, if they did decide to attack, gave no warning and attacked hard. Average negotiators, in contrast, usually began their attacking gently, working their way up to more intense attacks slowly and, in doing so, causing the other party to build up its defensive behavior in the characteristic defending/ attacking spiral.

Behavior Labeling

The researchers found that skilled negotiators tended to give an advance indication of the class of behavior they were about to use. So, for example, instead of just asking "How many units are there?" they would say, "Can I ask you a question—how many units are there?" giving warning that a question was coming. Instead of just making a proposal they would say, "If I could make a suggestion . . . " and then follow this advance label with their proposal. With one exception, average negotiators were significantly less likely to label their behavior in this way. The only behavior that the average negotiator was more likely to label in advance was disagreeing.

Percentage of All Negotiators' Behavior Immediately Preceded by a Behavior Label		
	Disagreeing	**All Behavior Except Disagreeing**
Skilled negotiator	0.4	6.4
Average negotiator	1.5	1.2

This is a slightly unusual finding, and it may not be immediately evident why these differences should exist. The researcher's interpretation was that, in general, labeling of behavior gives the negotiator the following advantages:

- It draws the attention of the listeners to the behavior that follows. In this way social pressure can be brought to force a response.

- It slows the negotiation down, giving time for the negotiator using labeling to gather his/her thoughts and for the other party to clear his/her mind from the previous statements.

- It introduces a formality that takes away a little of the cut-and-thrust and therefore keeps the negotiation on a rational level.

- It reduces ambiguity and leads to clearer communication.

The skilled negotiator does, however, avoid labeling his or her disagreement. While the average negotiator will characteristically say "I disagree with that because of . . . ," thus labeling that s/he is about to disagree, the skilled negotiator is more likely to begin with the reasons and lead up to the disagreement.

Skilled Negotiators		
Reason/ explanation	Leading to	Statement of disagreement

Average Negotiators		
Statement of disagreement	Leading to	Reason/ explanation

If one of the functions of behavior labeling is to make a negotiator's intentions clear, then it is hardly surprising that the skilled negotiator avoids making it clear that s/he intends to disagree. S/he would normally prefer his/her reasons to be considered more neutrally so that acceptance involved minimal loss of face for the other party. But if labeling disagreement is likely to be counterproductive, why does the average negotiator label disagreeing behavior more than all the other types of behavior put together? Most probably this tendency reflects the order in which we think. We decide that an argument we hear is unacceptable and only then do we assemble reasons to show why. The average negotiator speaks his/her disagreement in the same order as s/he thinks it—disagreement first, reasons afterward.

Testing Understanding and Summarizing

The researchers found that two behaviors with a similar function, testing understanding and summarizing, were used significantly more by the skilled negotiator. Testing understanding is a behavior that checks to establish whether a previous contribution or statement in the negotiation has been understood. Summarizing is a compact restatement of previous points in the discussion. Both behaviors sort out misunderstandings and reduce misconceptions.

	Percentage of All Behavior by Negotiator		
	Testing Understanding	Summarizing	Testing Understanding and Summarizing
Skilled negotiators	9.7	7.5	17.2
Average negotiators	4.1	4.2	8.3

The higher level of these behaviors by the skilled negotiator reflects his/her concern with clarity and the prevention of misunderstanding. It may also relate to two less obvious factors.

1. *Reflecting:* Some skilled negotiators tended to use testing understanding as a form of reflecting behavior—turning the other party's words back in order to obtain further responses. An example would be "So do I understand that you are saying you don't see any merit in this proposal at all?"

2. *Implementation concern:* The average negotiator, in his/her anxiety to obtain an agreement, would often quite deliberately fail to test understanding or to summarize. S/he would prefer to leave ambiguous points to be cleared later. S/he would fear that making things explicit might cause the other party to disagree. In short, his/her predominant objective was to obtain an agreement, and s/he would not probe too deeply into any area of potential misunderstanding that might prejudice immediate agreement, even if it was likely to give rise to difficulties at the implementation stage. The skilled negotiator, on the other hand, tended to have a greater concern with the successful implementation (as would be predicted from the success criteria earlier in this document). S/he would therefore test and summarize in order to check out any ambiguities at the negotiating stage rather than leave them as potential hazards for implementation.

Asking Questions

The skilled negotiator asked significantly more questions during negotiation than did the average negotiator.

Questions as a Percentage of All Negotiators' Behavior	
Skilled negotiator	21.3
Average negotiator	9.6

This is a very significant difference in behavior. Many negotiators and researchers have suggested that questioning techniques are important to negotiating success. Among the reasons frequently given are

1. Questions provide data about the other party's thinking and position.
2. Questions give control over the discussion.
3. Questions are more acceptable alternatives to direct disagreement.
4. Questions keep the other party active and reduce his/her thinking time.
5. Questions can give the negotiator a breathing space to allow him/her to marshal his/her own thoughts.

Feelings Commentary

The skilled negotiator is often thought of as a person who plays his/her cards close to the chest and who keeps his/her feelings to her/himself. The research studies were unable to measure this directly because feelings are, in themselves, unobservable. However, an indirect measure was possible. The researchers counted the number of times that the negotiator made statements about what was going on inside his/her mind. The behavior category of "giving internal information" was used to record any reference by the negotiator to his/her internal considerations such as feelings and motives.

Giving Internal Information as a Percentage of All Negotiators' Behavior	
Skilled negotiator	12.1
Average negotiator	7.8

The skilled negotiator is more likely to give information about his/her internal events than the average negotiator. This contrasts sharply with the amount of information given about external events, such as facts, clarifications, general expressions of opinion, and so forth. Here the average negotiator gives almost twice as much.

The effect of giving internal information is that the negotiator appears to reveal what is going on in his/her mind. This revelation may or may not be genuine, but it gives the other party a feeling of security because such things as motives appear to be explicit and aboveboard. The most characteristic and noticeable form of giving internal information is a feelings commentary, where the skilled negotiator talks about his/her feelings and the impression the other party has of him/her. For example, the average negotiator, hearing a point from the other party that s/he would like to accept but doubts whether it is true, is likely to receive the point in uncomfortable silence. The skilled negotiator is more likely to comment on his/her own feelings, saying something like "I'm uncertain how to react to what you've just said. If the information you've given me is true, then I would like to accept it; yet I feel some doubts inside me about its accuracy. So part of me feels happy and part feels suspicious. Can you help me resolve this?"

The work of psychologists such as Carl Rogers has shown that the expression of feelings is directly linked to establishing trust in counseling situations. It is probable that the same is true for negotiating.

Argument Dilution

Most people have a model of arguing that looks rather like a balance of a pair of scales. In fact, many of the terms we use about winning arguments reflect this balance model. We speak of "tipping the argument in our favor" of "the weight of the arguments" or how an issue "hangs in the balance." This way of thinking predisposes us to believe that there is some special merit in quantity. If we can find five reasons for doing something, then that should be more persuasive than being able to think of only a single reason. We feel that the more we can put on our scale pan, the more likely we are to tip the balance of an argument in our favor. If this model has any validity, then the skilled negotiator would be likely to use more reasons to back up his/her argument than the average negotiator.

Average Number of Reasons Given by Negotiator to Back Each Argument/Case S/he Advanced	
Skilled negotiator	1.8
Average negotiator	3.0

The researchers found that the opposite was true. The skilled negotiator used fewer reasons to back up each of his/her arguments. Although the balance-pan model may be very commonly believed, the studies suggest that it is a disadvantage to advance a whole series of reasons to back an argument or case. In doing so, the negotiator exposes a flank and gives the other party a choice of which reason to dispute. It seems self-evident that if a negotiator gives five reasons to back his/her case and the third reason is weak, the other party will exploit this third reason in their response. The most appropriate model seems to be one of dilution. The more reasons advanced, the more a case is potentially diluted. The poorest reason is a lowest common denominator: a weak argument generally dilutes a strong.

Unfortunately, many negotiators who had the disadvantage of higher education put a value on being able to ingeniously devise reasons to back their case. They frequently suffered from this dilution effect and had their point rejected, not on the strength of their principal argument, but on the weakness of the incidental supporting points they introduced. The skilled negotiator tended to advance single reasons insistently, moving to subsidiary reasons only if his/her main reason was clearly losing ground. It is probably no coincidence that an unexpectedly high proportion of the skilled negotiators studied, both in labor relations and in contract negotiation, had relatively little formal education. As a consequence, they had not been trained to value the balance-pan model and more easily avoided the trap of advancing a whole flank of reasons to back their cases.

Reviewing the Negotiation

The researchers asked negotiators how likely they were to spend time reviewing the negotiation afterward. Over two-thirds of the skilled negotiators claimed that they always set aside some time after a negotiation to review it and consider what they had learned. Just under half of average negotiators, in contrast, made the same claim. Because the data are self-reported, they may be inaccurate. Even so, it seems that the old principle that more can be learned after a negotiation than during it may be true. An interesting difference between management and union representatives was observed. Management representatives, with other responsibilities and time pressures, were less likely to review a negotiation than were union representatives. This may, in part, account for the observation made by many writers on labor relations that union negotiators seem to learn negotiating skills from taking part in actual negotiations more quickly than management negotiators.

Summary of the Successful Negotiator's Behavior

The successful negotiator

- Is rated as effective by both sides.
- Has a track record of significant success.
- Has a low incidence of implementation failure.

   Forty-eight negotiators meeting these criteria were studied during 102 negotiations.

Planning		
	Negotiators	
	Skilled	**Average**
Overall amount of time spent	No significant difference	
Number of outcomes/options considered per issue	5.1	2.6
Percentage of comments about areas of anticipated common ground	38%	11%
Percentage of comments about long-term considerations of issues	8.5%	4%
Use of sequence during planning (per session)	2.1	4.9
Face-to-Face (Skilled Negotiators)		
Avoid	**Use**	
Irritators	Behavior labeling (except disagreeing)	
Counterproposals	Testing understanding and summarizing	
Defend/attack spirals	Lots of questions	
Argument dilution	Feelings commentary	

Staying with No

Holly Weeks

It's hard to say no. It's harder still to stay with the no in the face of your counterpart's disappointment or anger. Here is how to be heard and respected without damaging relationships.

Roger Fisher, negotiation expert and coauthor of the widely influential book *Getting to Yes,* used to tell his law students that sometimes he wished he had written a book about getting to no. He didn't have trouble saying no, he said, but he had trouble staying with the no: when family members were disappointed or associates pressed him, he would give up, and give in—even to things he didn't want to do.

Like Fisher, most of us want to be agreeable; we want to accommodate people. For one thing, people generally like us better when we say yes to them than when we say no. For another, saying no can be unpleasant—sometimes very much so. Particularly when we are saying no—to someone senior—we feel considerable tension between our desire to stay with no and our desire to stay out of trouble.

The people to whom we say no rarely like hearing it, and it's no wonder. Our saying no signals rejection—of their ideas, of their wishes, of their priorities. Consequently, most people will try to get us to change the no to a yes. That means we have to work to defuse emotion on both sides: our discomfort at staying with an unpopular no and our counterpart's irritation, disappointment, or anger at hearing it.

We could, of course, cut the Gordian knot by giving in. But in the end, the consequences of not staying with no can cause much more damage—to our self-confidence, to our relationship with the other person, and to our credibility and effectiveness as a professional.

If we want to reduce the tension around staying with no, we will do better to think not about *whether* to stay with no, but *how.*

Many Reasons for the Other's Resistance

First, however, it helps to recognize why your counterparts want to "yes the no" and readjust your own emotional response to their efforts.

Business Culture

It isn't inherently insulting to you that the other person wants you to back off your no—it's part of our business climate to try to yes the no. If you want to keep the emotional temperature cool, don't read her challenging your no as an affront to your dignity or credibility.

Source: From *Harvard Management Communication Letter,* vol. 1, no. 4 (Fall 2004).

Personal Experience and Expectations

Your counterpart's personal experience and expectations rather than the interpersonal relations between you may be the strongest determinant of how he responds to your no. He may be argumentative, wheedling, stunned, or angry because that's how he always handles hearing no.

I was staying with no in a conversation with a lawyer until I was eventually persuaded to his view. After I agreed, however, he kept right on hammering me to change my mind. Finally I laughed and said, "But Peter, I'm agreeing with you."

He paused and said, "Mostly people don't."

Context

There may be something about your staying with no—maybe something interpersonal, maybe not—that makes your no particularly difficult to accept. It's not unusual, for example, for someone who might be able to hear a no privately to be embarrassed to consent to it publicly. She may want you to back down so she can save face.

Not all of the friction between the effort to stay with no and the effort to yes the no is bad, but some of it is. Bad friction turns into a contest of wills, with one side winning and the other caving in or backing down. That's hard on relationships and often leads to payback.

Your Own Resistance

While your counterpart's resistance to your no can be hard to take, part of the problem may lie on your side, even if it doesn't feel that way. Far more people are coached to yes the no than to stay with no. Anyone who simply picks up a general interest magazine is instructed never to take no for an answer; in contrast, those of us who are trying to stay with no get very little guidance. So without practiced techniques to fall back on, we respond emotionally.

Staying with no puts us in two different predicaments. On the one hand, we don't like to be negative. On the other, we don't like to be pushed. If you especially don't like to be negative, you probably tend to soften your no. It feels natural to you to try to stay with no gently. But this may result in your no not getting heard.

If you especially don't like to be pushed, you likely tend to become combative as you stay with no. For you, the natural thing is to get the conversation over with, not stretch it out. The problem with this strategy is that it may require you to spend a lot of time on after-the-fact damage control.

The solution in both cases is to change how you say no—that's the piece you can control. You need to acquire the skill of saying and staying with no neutrally—to say no simply, clearly, and directly, using arguments that are not easily weakened by your counterpart.

The Neutral No

A neutral no is steady, uninflected, and clear. It's mostly illustrated by what it's not. It's not harsh, it's not pugnacious or apologetic, it's not reluctant or heavily buffered, and it's not overly nice. Neutral and nice are not the same. Even if you're nice, use neutral to stay with no.

By sticking with neutral, you're concentrating on the business end of no, not the personal. If your first no is tentative, your second is brusque, and your third is caustic, I don't necessarily hear your intentions, whatever they may be. It's not my job to read intentions. I hear that first you give me hope and then you lose your temper. That's hard on relationships and on your reputation.

You want a referee's manner. A ref just says what he says—good news for some, bad news for others—regardless of the strong feelings on both sides that his message may inspire. His job is to give his message neutrally and stay with it neutrally if challenged.

A neutral manner doesn't prevent you from speaking directly about the friction between staying with no and trying to yes the no. "It's hard for me to tell you no; it must be hard for you to hear" is consistent with neutral. Use your own language here, but check that what you say is neutrally spoken:

- If you know or suspect why your counterpart is resisting your no, acknowledge his concern honestly but without giving hope. "You have a lot invested in what you're asking, and it looks like I'm personally blocking you." Give a reason or justification for your no. "I see my job as balancing valid, but competing, needs. I'm focusing on that." Aren't you just creating an opening for an argument there? Sometimes, yes. But the objective of staying with no is not necessarily to terminate this conversation with a monosyllable.

- If your reason is well chosen and neutrally spoken, stay with it. Don't volley different arguments with your counterpart. Changing an argument is not necessarily an improvement over repetition.

- In some cases, you may want to tell your counterpart what you could say yes to. That's not a foundation of staying with no, it's an option and the beginning of a negotiation. If you're open to that, you don't have to wait for the counterpart to ask.

Do's and Don'ts

Keep Your Eye on the Issue, Not the Personal

You see your job as staying with no; I see my job as yessing that no. No one is doing anything wrong—we just don't want the same outcome here. It helps to think of the push–pull between us as an honest disagreement about how the tension should be resolved. It does not help to think of my resistance to your no as disrespect for you.

Know Your Triggers

Your counterpart may be trying out different tactics to get you to yes your no. The tactic the counterpart uses matters only if you're vulnerable to it. Which arguments are you most susceptible to? Which tactics? Does an ominous suggestion that the union will hear about this roll off or rattle you? Do tears move you to offer a tissue or to fold? Most of us know where we're vulnerable. If, for example, you are undermined by a counterpart who says she is disappointed in you and personally let down because you stay with no, you have probably been vulnerable to that sense of falling short of expectations before.

Don't Give Them Too Much to Read

It is very hard to pick out what part of a message to read if, first, the message is mixed and, second, there's an emotional flare in it. A harsh no that offends or angers people makes them stick to their guns, even if all you wanted to do was get the conversation over with. On the other hand, people who are uncomfortable staying with no often overdo the apologetic nature of their no—they say no, express their regret for it, and ask to be forgiven for staying with no, all at the same time. The message surrounding the no seems to be, "I want to stay with no and yet have you like me." That's hard to read, but more important, if I don't want to hear the no, it's very easy for me to overlook it.

Don't Weaken Your No

Curiously, many people do this backward. They start saying no using lightweight reasons, holding back the real, heavyweight reason. And the counterpart swats away the little reasons because they aren't very persuasive. To limit the frustration on both sides, give reasons with good weight up front.

An executive assistant had been helping out a colleague by taking on work that was not his responsibility. Now he needed to curtail his tendency to say yes all the time because he was swamped. The next time his colleague asked for his customary help with photocopying, he said, "I have to say no, and it's really my fault because I don't seem to be managing my time very well." His colleague disagreed that he wasn't managing his time well—in fact, she praised how well he managed his time. And, not accepting that the executive assistant had a time-management fault, the colleague also didn't accept his no.

He had offered a self-criticism with his no because he wanted to head off the potential criticism that he wasn't being very helpful. But he weakened his no by doing so.

Beware Misguided Empathy

Most of us genuinely regret it if our counterpart is disappointed when we stay with no. But be careful and clear about what you can legitimately claim to share.

A newly married couple was surprised and upset to have their mortgage application declined by their new bank. The mortgage officer agreed that it was disappointing. She listened to their protests and arguments, making suggestions while staying with no. But as the couple was leaving her office, she said, "Believe me, I feel as bad about this as you do." The young wife turned to her, stiff with new indignation, and said, "No. You don't."

The mortgage officer undermined her good no by claiming that her pain was as great as theirs. That will almost never feel right to those who must accept the no.

Avoid a Battlefront Attitude: "I Won't Give In; You Lose"

Not everyone tries to soften her no. Some of us say no combatively, and treat staying with no as escalating warfare. This could be you if you find a battle of wills stimulating. When staying with no feels like a triumph of the will, good outcomes—and good judgment—are in jeopardy.

Don't Give False Hope

Staying with no tentatively, or with a show of reluctance, makes it easy for your counterpart to hope you will change your no—and hard for him to accept the no. It sounds like your no is on the edge of tipping over into yes, so your counterpart is encouraged to keep pushing. Try the positive approaches suggested here to break a pattern of giving in, instead of falling back on a manner of saying no that suggests you are about to give in.

Practice Staying With No; Don't Avoid It

If you want to get better at staying with no in the face of the arguments and tactics that trigger you, it makes sense to practice with someone who will play the part of your worst nightmare in a protected setting. That's better than waiting until a real situation arises, when a lot is on the line.

You want to practice for four reasons: (1) so you'll stay with your message, (2) so you won't edit it on your feet, (3) so you'll know what it's going to feel like to say it, and (4) so you can see whether you really want to stay with this no—or whether you should yes it.

Where Does Power Come From?

Jeffrey Pfeffer

Long-term studies of companies in numerous industries ranging from glass and cement manufacturing to the minicomputer industry "show that the most successful firms maintain a workable equilibrium for several years . . . but are also able to initiate and carry out sharp, widespread changes . . . when their environments shift."[1] These so-called discontinuous or frame-breaking changes always alter the distribution of power. Consequently, organizational innovation often if not inevitably involves obtaining the power and influence necessary to overcome resistance.

To be successful in this process, we need to understand where power comes from. It is critical to be able to diagnose the power of other players, including potential allies and possible opponents. We need to know what we are up against. Knowing where power comes from also helps us to build our own power and thereby increase our capacity to take action. It is useful to know that getting a new product introduced may involve power and politics, and to understand the pattern of interdependence and the points of view of various participants. But to be effective, we also need to know how to develop sources of power and how to employ that power strategically and tactically.

We all have implicit theories of where power comes from, and we occasionally act on these theories. For instance, we may read and follow the advice of books on "power dressing," pondering issues such as whether yellow ties are in or out and whether suspenders are a signal of power. The cosmetic surgery business is booming, in part, at least, because some executives are worried that the signs of aging may make them appear to be less powerful and dynamic. People attend courses in assertiveness training, go through psychotherapy, and take programs in public speaking for numerous reasons, but among them is the desire to be more powerful, dynamic, and effective.

Many of our theories about the origins of power emphasize the importance of personal attributes and characteristics—which are very difficult to alter, at least without herculean efforts. We sometimes overlook the importance of situational factors over which we may have more direct influence. If we are going to be effective in organizations, we need to be skillful in evaluating our theories of the sources of power, as well as sensitive to various cognitive biases. This chapter briefly outlines some issues to think about as we observe the world and try to diagnose the sources of power. It also sets the stage for the consideration of personal characteristics and situational factors as sources of power.

Personal Attributes as Sources of Power

When we walk into an organization, we see people first, not situations. People are talking, moving around, and doing things. People have personalities, idiosyncrasies, and mannerisms that engage our attention and hold our interest. Our preoccupation with the

Source: Reprinted by permission of Harvard Business School Press. From *Managing with Power: Politics and Influence in Organizations* by Jeffrey Pfeffer (Boston, MA: 1992), pp. 71–81. Copyright © 1992 by Harvard Business School Publishing Corporation, all rights reserved.

vividness of the people we meet leads to what some psychologists have called "the fundamental attribution error"—our tendency to overemphasize the causal importance of people and their characteristics, and underemphasize the importance of situational factors.[2] The phenomenon is pervasive, and there are many examples. One striking manifestation of the tendency to ignore situational factors in evaluating people is provided in an experimental study done by a colleague.[3] The study entailed assessing the performance of a speaker—a situation not dissimilar to assessing the power of someone we encounter in an organization. In the study, evaluators asked questions that were either positively or negatively biased—and moreover, they were aware of the bias when asked about it later. Nevertheless, evaluators were themselves affected by the answers they elicited through their biased questions. They "underestimated the potential effect of their own behavior (the situation) in drawing conclusions based on potentially constrained answers."[4] Instead of discounting the diagnostic value of the behavior they had affected, evaluators used that information in making assessments both of the performance and (in other studies) of the attitudes of others. In other words, even when we know that the behavior we observe is strongly affected by situational factors, we readily make attributions and evaluations about others based on that behavior.

Not only do we overattribute power to personal characteristics, but often the characteristics we believe to be sources of power are almost as plausibly the consequence of power instead. Interviews with 87 managerial personnel (including 30 chief executive officers, 28 high-level staff managers, and 29 supervisors) in 30 Southern California electronics firms assessed beliefs about the personal characteristics of people thought to be most effective in the use of organizational politics and in wielding power.[5] The percentages of all respondents mentioning various characteristics are displayed in Table 1.

Without, for the moment, denying that these characteristics are associated with being powerful and politically effective, consider the possibility that at least some of them result from the experience of being in power. Are we likely to be more articulate and

TABLE 1 | Personal Traits Characterizing Effective Political Actors

Personal Characteristic	Percentage Mentioning
Articulate	29.9
Sensitive	29.9
Socially adept	19.5
Competent	17.2
Popular	17.2
Extroverted	16.1
Self-confident	16.1
Aggressive	16.1
Ambitious	16.1

Source: Allen et al., p. 80. Copyright 1979 by The Regents of the University of California. Reprinted from the *California Management Review* 22, no. 1. By permission of The Regents.

poised when we are more powerful? Are we likely to be more popular? Isn't it plausible that power causes us to be extroverted, as much as extroversion makes us powerful? Aren't more powerful and politically effective people likely to be perceived as more competent? Certainly power and political skill can produce more self-confident and even aggressive behavior. And considering that people usually adjust their ambitions to what is feasible, people who are more powerful are probably going to be more ambitious, and to be viewed as such.

Why is the causal ordering of more than academic interest? The answer is that we may try to develop attributes to help us attain power, and if those attributes are ineffective or dysfunctional, we can get into trouble. Most of us can recall people who "acted out the role" and behaved as if they were more powerful and important than they were. This behavior typically only erodes support and makes one ineffective, even if the same behavior, exhibited by someone holding power, is accepted and enhances that person's effectiveness.

A third problem in drawing inferences from personal attributes lies in the fact that people are seldom randomly assigned to their situations. External factors often have a direct bearing on the success or failure of an individual, and yet many studies of power fail to take account of such factors. Consider David Winter's study of the effect of three individual dispositions—the power motive, the need for achievement, and the affiliation–intimacy motive—on various indicators of leader effectiveness, including one measure closely related to a common definition of power: the ability to get one's way in terms of appointments or initiatives.[6]

Winter's sample is the U.S. presidents, a nonrandom sample if ever there was one. Each president's personality traits were assessed by scoring the first inaugural address for imagery that represents the underlying motive. Winter's results are correlations between presidential scores on the three traits and several outcome measures such as being re-elected, having court and cabinet appointments approved, and avoiding or entering war.[7] The analysis does not consider the possibility that the type of person elected to office is not independent of the times and conditions that bracket the election, and that perhaps these factors, not just motive profiles, help explain outcomes such as avoiding or entering war.

Errors of this type are made routinely. For instance, in evaluating own-recognizance bail programs, studies often don't account for the fact that the people are not randomly released on their own recognizance; only the less dangerous prisoners are likely to be released.[8] Thus the tendency of those released without bail not to commit crimes does not necessarily mean that if the program were extended to all prisoners the same results would hold. The wider point here is that we need to understand and account for how people wind up in various situations, and to use this information in evaluating their power and their effectiveness. In general, we need to be thoughtful when we analyze personal characteristics as sources of power, particularly if we intend to take action based on those insights.

Structural Sources of Power

Structural perspectives on power argue that power is derived from where each person stands in the division of labor and the communication system of the organization. The division of labor in an organization creates subunits and differentiated roles, and each subunit and position develops specialized interests and responsibilities. Further, each subunit or position makes claims on the organization's resources.[9] In the contest for resources, those who do well succeed on the basis of the resources they possess or control as well as the ties they can form with people who influence allocations.[10] Control over resources, and the importance of the unit in the organization, are derived from the division of labor, which gives some positions or groups more control over critical tasks and more access to resources than others.[11] Power, then, comes from the control over resources, from the ties one has to powerful others, and from the formal authority one obtains because of one's position in the hierarchy.

For instance, in a study of 33 purchase decisions, the most frequently mentioned characteristic of those perceived to have influence over the decision was that the choice would affect them:

> . . . in a company which makes musical instruments, the choice of a tractor truck was said by one informant to have been influenced most by the traffic supervisor. "He lives with the situation, so he must have the choice," he said.[12]

Who is affected by a decision is determined, obviously, by the division of labor. According to those interviewed in the study, people with formal responsibility for the unit where the product was to be used, or with responsibility for the performance or output of the product, were also viewed as influential. Although interviewees were asked to judge who had the most influence "regardless of who had the final authority," authority and responsibility were often-mentioned sources of influence in these purchase situations.[13] Authority and responsibility, too, are conveyed by one's position in the formal structure of the organization.

Or consider the power sometimes possessed by purchasing agents.[14] They stand between engineering, production scheduling, and marketing on the one hand, and outside vendors on the other. Some purchasing agents were able to use this intermediary position to obtain substantial influence over other departments that, in many instances, possessed more formal status and authority than they did. By relying on purchasing rules and procedures (which they often had developed themselves), the agents made it necessary for other departments to accede to their power—as is evidenced by the willingness of other departments to provide favors to those in purchasing in exchange for preferential treatment.

The point about situational sources of power is that one possesses power simply by being in the right place—by being in a position of authority, in a place to resolve uncertainty, in a position to broker among various subunits and external vendors—almost regardless of one's individual characteristics. Authority and responsibility are vested in positions, and one's ability to broker is affected significantly by where one sits in the structure of interaction. Of course, not all people in the same situations are able to do equally well. Some purchasing agents, for instance, were much more successful than others in raising the power and status of their departments, in spite of the fact that virtually all wanted to do so, and some of this difference resulted from variations in political skill among the purchasing agents in the various companies. This suggests that while situations are important, one's ability to capitalize on the situation also has decisive implications.

The Fit between Situational
Requirements and Personal Traits

An important source of power is the match between style, skill, and capacities and what is required by the situation. For instance, in a study of influence at a research and development laboratory of 304 professionals, the participants were questioned about influence in their organization. Was influence primarily related to being (1) an internal communication star, someone who had extensive contacts within the laboratory but who was not linked to external sources of information; (2) an external communication star, someone linked primarily to external information and not well connected in his own unit; or (3) a boundary spanner, someone linked both to others within his own unit and to external sources of information?[15] Influence was measured with respect to technical, budgetary, and personnel decisions. The principal finding was that the type of person who was influential depended on the nature of the project: in technical service projects, with less task uncertainty, internal communication stars were most influential, while in applied research units, boundary spanners carried the most weight.

Another illustration of the contingency between situations and the characteristics that provide influence comes from a study of 17 organizations that had recently purchased a piece of offset printing equipment.[16] For some organizations, the purchase was new and therefore totally unfamiliar; for others, it involved the replacement of an existing piece of equipment; and for still others, it involved adding a piece of equipment. Clearly, the amount of uncertainty differed, it being greatest for those buying offset printing equipment for the first time, and posing the smallest problem for those firms that were merely acquiring another piece of the same equipment they already had. Individual experience was most highly related to influence in the case of purchasing an additional piece of equipment. Internal communication and the number of different sources of information consulted were most strongly related to influence in the case of new purchase decisions. Those who were able to affect perceptions of need were most influential in adding a piece of equipment, while those who gathered external information were more influential in the situation in which new equipment was being purchased. These two studies, as well as other research, strongly suggest that

> The influence of a subunit or individual on a decision is a function of (1) the kind of uncertainty faced by an organization, (2) the particular characteristic or capability which enables reducing organizational uncertainty, and (3) the degree to which a particular subunit [or individual] possesses this characteristic. As decision-making contexts vary, so do the sources of organizational uncertainty, and consequently, the bases for influence in organizational decision making.[17]

The necessity of matching personal characteristics to the situation can be seen in politics as well as in business. Ronald Reagan, the former movie actor and U.S. president, came to office at a time in which mass communication, through the medium of television, was essential. Reagan had no skill in dealing with details, but was a "great communicator." Lyndon Johnson rose to power at a time when television was less important and party organizations were stronger. The ability to pay attention to small details and the willingness to do favors for colleagues and constituents were critical. Had Reagan and Johnson been able to exchange decades, it is likely that neither one would have been elected president. Johnson's difficulty in responding to the rise of the media in his administration shows his inability to flourish in an era of mass communication. And Reagan would have been unsuited for the continual attention to detail that was required of old-style party politicians. Not only are particular kinds of knowledge and skill differentially critical across time and settings, but personal attributes also become more or less important, depending on the setting.

Can Charisma Be Transferred?

Charisma is perhaps the best illustration of the fit between situations and personal attributes. The concept of charisma came into social science from theology, where it means "endowment with the gift of divine grace."[18] Charismatic leaders often emerge in times of stress or crisis. They create an emotional (rather than purely instrumental) bond with others; they take on heroic proportions and appeal to the ideological values of followers.[19] President John Kennedy, Martin Luther King, and Gandhi were all charismatic figures.

Some have asserted that charisma is a characteristic of the individual, based on the person's need for power, achievement, and affiliation, as well as on his inhibitions in using power.[20] Moreover, charisma and personality are said to explain the effectiveness of leaders—for instance, that of U.S. presidents.[21] A careful longitudinal study of a school superintendent in Minnesota provides some interesting evidence on the interaction between charismatic properties and situational constraints.[22]

While serving in a large, suburban school district in Minnesota, the superintendent exhibited both charisma and effectiveness. Her work drew attention in the media and the legislature. She "gained wide acclaim for her massive grassroots program to cut $2.4 million from the budget while at the same time successfully avoiding the 'bloodletting' of retrenchment."[23] School personnel described her in interviews as "a mover, a shaker, a visionary . . . who had made a dramatic, unprecedented impact on the district. People believed that she had extraordinary talents."[24] She developed an extremely loyal following, unlike the superintendents who had preceded her. She involved many people in the process of change in the district, forming task forces to investigate district policy and budget problems, hiring consultants to conduct workshops to develop a vision of the future, and redesigning jobs and the administrative structure of the district office. Her effect on the district was striking:

> Budget reductions were scheduled without acrimonious debate. The school board unanimously approved the superintendent's budget reductions after only a brief discussion. Teachers awarded her a standing ovation, despite her recommendations to cut support jobs and program funding. Innovative ideas poured in from district personnel. . . . At the end of her two years as superintendent, the district had cataloged over 300 suggestions for innovative ventures.[25]

Then she was appointed by the governor of Minnesota to be the head of the state Department of Education. She brought to this new position the same modus operandi she had used as district superintendent: "Begin with a mission and a vision that outline where one wants to go; generate enthusiasm and support for the vision at the grassroots level; . . . create a structure for change at the Department of Education that will serve to channel the interest and energy into innovative programs."[26] During her first year in her new job, she personally visited almost every one of the 435 school districts in the state. She initiated town meetings held in 388 public school districts, which drew about 15,000 citizens. She sponsored public opinion polls. She replaced the top five assistant commissioners with her own team of nine people, all formerly outsiders to the Department of Education.[27] And what were the results of all of these efforts?

As one might imagine, efforts to restaff and restructure the Department of Education were immediately opposed by those already well served by the existing structure. Five of the new assistants were either fired or resigned from office within the first year.[28] The press soon heard of morale problems, departures of key middle managers, and confusion over routine tasks and job assignments. Instead of being able to focus on long-term change, she now found herself "embroiled in the day-to-day details of established bureaucratic order."[29] Charisma, so evident at the school district level, clearly did not transfer to her new position at the state level, nor could it be created at will.

The administrator had more success in her role as superintendent because it gave her more control and more autonomy over educational matters. She was also able to have closer, more personal relationships with those she wanted to influence when she operated at the local level. As the governor's political appointee, she had to worry about what her actions would mean for him. As head of a large state department, she "was embedded in a much more complex web of relations among the legislature, state executive departments, constituents, interest groups and networks, and state and national educational communities."[30] Her freedom of action was constrained, and her personal contacts were worth much less; in short, she needed to rely more on bureaucratic politics and less on emotional appeal than she had been accustomed to.

As situational factors change, the attributes required to be influential and effective change as well. That is why it is important not only to find positions with the political demands that match our skills and interests, but also to tailor our actions to the circumstances we confront. In any event, we can probably best understand the sources of power as deriving from individual characteristics, from advantages the situation provides, and from the match between ourselves and our settings.

Endnotes

1. Michael L. Tushman, William H. Newman, and Elaine Romanelli, "Convergence and Upheaval: Managing the Unsteady Pace of Organizational Evolution," *California Management Review* 29 (1986), pp. 29–44.

2. R. E. Nisbett and L. Ross, *Human Inferences: Strategies and Shortcomings of Social Judgment* (Englewood Cliffs, NJ: Prentice Hall, 1980).

3. Linda E. Ginzel, "The Impact of Biased Feedback Strategies on Performance Judgments," Research Paper #1102 (Palo Alto, CA: Graduate School of Business, Stanford University, 1990).

4. Ibid., p. 26.

5. Robert W. Allen et al., "Organizational Politics: Tactics and Characteristics of Its Actors," *California Management Review* 22 (1979), pp. 77–83.

6. David G. Winter, "Leader Appeal, Leader Performance, and the Motive Profiles of Leaders and Followers: A Study of American Presidents and Elections," *Journal of Personality and Social Psychology* 52 (1987), pp. 196–202.

7. Ibid., p. 200.

8. Christopher H. Achen, *The Statistical Analysis of Quasi-Experiments* (Berkeley: University of California Press, 1986).

9. Andrew M. Pettigrew, *Politics of Organizational Decision-Making* (London: Tavistock, 1973), p. 17.

10. Ibid., p. 31.

11. D. J. Hickson et al., "A Strategic Contingencies' Theory of Intraorganizational Power," *Administrative Science Quarterly* 16 (1971), pp. 216–29.

12. Martin Patchen, "The Locus and Basis of Influence in Organizational Decisions," *Organizational Behavior and Human Performance* 11 (1974), p. 209.

13. Ibid. p. 213.

14. George Strauss, "Tactics of Lateral Relationship: The Purchasing Agent," *Administrative Science Quarterly* 7 (1962), pp. 161–86.

15. Michael L. Tushman and Elaine Romanelli, "Uncertainty, Social Location and Influence in Decision Making: A Sociometric Analysis," *Management Science* 29 (1983), pp. 12–23.

16. Gerald R. Salancik, Jeffrey Pfeffer, and J. Patrick Kelly, "A Contingency Model of Influence in Organizational Decision Making," *Pacific Sociological Review* 21 (1978), pp. 239–56.

17. Ibid., p. 253.

18. Bernard M. Bass, "Evolving Perspectives on Charismatic Leadership," *Charismatic Leadership,* eds. Jay A. Conger, Rabindra N. Kanungo, and Associates (San Francisco: Jossey-Bass, 1988), pp. 40–77.

19. Robert J. House, William D. Spangler, and James Woycke, "Personality and Charisma in the U.S. Presidency: A Psychological Theory of Leadership Effectiveness," unpublished, Wharton School, University of Pennsylvania, 1989.

20. Ibid.; Robert J. House, "A 1976 Theory of Charismatic Leadership," *Leadership: The Cutting Edge,* eds. J. G. Hunt and L. L. Larson (Carbondale: Southern Illinois University Press, 1977).

21. House, Spangler, and Woycke, "Personality and Charisma."

22. Nancy C. Roberts and Raymond Trevor Bradley, "Limits of Charisma," *Charismatic Leadership,* eds. Jay A. Conger, Rabindra N. Kanungo and Associates (San Francisco: Jossey-Bass, 1988), pp. 253–75.

23. Ibid., p. 254.

24. Ibid., p. 260.

25. Ibid., p. 263.

26. Ibid.

27. Ibid., p. 264.

28. Ibid., p. 269.

29. Ibid.

30. Ibid., p. 268.

Reading 2.6

Harnessing the Science of Persuasion
Robert B. Cialdini

A lucky few have it; most of us do not. A handful of gifted "naturals" simply know how to capture an audience, sway the undecided, and convert the opposition. Watching these masters of persuasion work their magic is at once impressive and frustrating. What's impressive is not just the easy way they use charisma and eloquence to convince others to do as they ask. It's also how eager those others are to do what's requested of them, as if the persuasion itself were a favor they couldn't wait to repay.

The frustrating part of the experience is that these born persuaders are often unable to account for their remarkable skill or pass it on to others. Their way with people is an art, and artists as a rule are far better at doing than at explaining. Most of them can't offer much help to those of us who possess no more than the ordinary quotient of charisma and eloquence but who still have to wrestle with leadership's fundamental challenge: getting things done through others. That challenge is painfully familiar to corporate executives, who every day have to figure out how to motivate and direct a highly individualistic workforce. Playing the "Because I'm the boss" card is out. Even if it weren't demeaning and demoralizing for all concerned, it would be out of place in a world where cross-functional teams, joint ventures, and intercompany partnerships have blurred the lines of authority. In such an environment, persuasion skills exert far greater influence over others' behavior than formal power structures do.

Which brings us back to where we started. Persuasion skills may be more necessary than ever, but how can executives acquire them if the most talented practitioners can't pass them along? By looking to science. For the past five decades, behavioral scientists have conducted experiments that shed considerable light on the way certain interactions lead people to concede, comply, or change. This research shows that persuasion works by appealing to a limited set of deeply rooted human drives and needs, and it does so in predictable ways. Persuasion, in other words, is governed by basic principles that can be taught, learned, and applied. By mastering these principles, executives can bring scientific rigor to the business of securing consensus, cutting deals, and winning concessions. In the pages that follow, I describe six fundamental principles of persuasion and suggest a few ways that executives can apply them in their own organizations.

The Principle of Liking: People Like Those Who Like Them
The Application: Uncover Real Similarities and Offer Genuine Praise

The retailing phenomenon known as the Tupperware party is a vivid illustration of this principle in action. The demonstration party for Tupperware products is hosted by an individual, almost always a woman, who invites to her home an array of friends, neighbors, and relatives. The guests' affection for their hostess predisposes them to buy from

Source: From *Harvard Business Review,* October 2001, pp. 72–79.

her, a dynamic that was confirmed by a 1990 study of purchase decisions made at demonstration parties. The researchers, Jonathan Frenzen and Harry Davis, writing in the *Journal of Consumer Research,* found that the guests' fondness for their hostess weighed twice as heavily in their purchase decisions as their regard for the products they bought. So when guests at a Tupperware party buy something, they aren't just buying to please themselves. They're buying to please their hostess as well.

What's true at Tupperware parties is true for business in general: If you want to influence people, win friends. How? Controlled research has identified several factors that reliably increase liking, but two stand out as especially compelling—similarity and praise. Similarity literally draws people together. In one experiment, reported in a 1968 article in the *Journal of Personality,* participants stood physically closer to one another after learning that they shared political beliefs and social values. And in a 1963 article in *American Behavioral Scientists,* researcher F. B. Evans used demographic data from insurance company records to demonstrate that prospects were more willing to purchase a policy from a salesperson who was akin to them in age, religion, politics, or even cigarette-smoking habits.

Managers can use similarities to create bonds with a recent hire, the head of another department, or even a new boss. Informal conversations during the workday create an ideal opportunity to discover at least one common area of enjoyment, be it a hobby, a college basketball team, or reruns of *Seinfeld.* The important thing is to establish the bond early because it creates a presumption of goodwill and trustworthiness in every subsequent encounter. It's much easier to build support for a new project when the people you're trying to persuade are already inclined in your favor.

Praise, the other reliable generator of affection, both charms and disarms. Sometimes the praise doesn't even have to be merited. Researchers at the University of North Carolina writing in the *Journal of Experimental Social Psychology* found that men felt the greatest regard for an individual who flattered them unstintingly even if the comments were untrue. And in their book *Interpersonal Attraction* (Addison-Wesley, 1978), Ellen Berscheid and Elaine Hatfield Walster presented experimental data showing that positive remarks about another person's traits, attitude, or performance reliably generate liking in return, as well as willing compliance with the wishes of the person offering the praise.

Along with cultivating a fruitful relationship, adroit managers can also use praise to repair one that's damaged or unproductive. Imagine you're the manager of a good-sized unit within your organization. Your work frequently brings you into contact with another manager—call him Dan—whom you have come to dislike. No matter how much you do for him, it's not enough. Worse, he never seems to believe that you're doing the best you can for him. Resenting his attitude and his obvious lack of trust in your abilities and in your good faith, you don't spend as much time with him as you know you should; in consequence, the performance of both his unit and yours is deteriorating.

The research on praise points toward a strategy for fixing the relationship. It may be hard to find, but there has to be something about Dan you can sincerely admire, whether it's his concern for the people in his department, his devotion to his family, or simply his work ethic. In your next encounter with him, make an appreciative comment about that trait. Make it clear that in this case at least, you value what he values. I predict that Dan will relax his relentless negativity and give you an opening to convince him of your competence and good intentions.

The Principle of Reciprocity: People Repay in Kind
The Application: Give What You Want to Receive

Praise is likely to have a warming and softening effect on Dan because, ornery as he is, he is still human and subject to the universal human tendency to treat people the way they treat him. If you have ever caught yourself smiling at a coworker just because he or she smiled first, you know how this principle works.

Charities rely on reciprocity to help them raise funds. For years, for instance, the Disabled American Veterans organization, using only a well-crafted fund-raising letter, garnered a very respectable 18 percent rate of response to its appeals. But when the group started enclosing a small gift in the envelope, the response rate nearly doubled to 35 percent. The gift—personalized address labels—was extremely modest, but it wasn't what prospective donors received that made the difference. It was that they had gotten anything at all.

What works in that letter works at the office, too. It's more than an effusion of seasonal spirit, of course, that impels suppliers to shower gifts on purchasing departments at holiday time. In 1996, purchasing managers admitted to an interviewer from *Inc.* magazine that after having accepted a gift from a supplier, they were willing to purchase products and services they would have otherwise declined. Gifts also have a startling effect on retention. I have encouraged readers of my book to send me examples of the principles of influence at work in their own lives. One reader, an employee of the state of Oregon, sent a letter in which she offered these reasons for her commitment to her supervisor:

> He gives me and my son gifts for Christmas and gives me presents on my birthday. There is no promotion for the type of job I have, and my only choice for one is to move to another department. But I find myself resisting trying to move. My boss is reaching retirement age, and I am thinking I will be able to move out after he retires. . . . [F]or now, I feel obligated to stay since he has been so nice to me.

Ultimately, though, gift giving is one of the cruder applications of the rule of reciprocity. In its more sophisticated uses, it confers a genuine first-mover advantage on any manager who is trying to foster positive attitudes and productive personal relationships in the office: Managers can elicit the desired behavior from coworkers and employees by displaying it first. Whether it's a sense of trust, a spirit of cooperation, or a pleasant demeanor, leaders should model the behavior they want to see from others.

The same holds true for managers faced with issues of information delivery and resource allocation. If you lend a member of your staff to a colleague who is shorthanded and staring at a fast-approaching deadline, you will significantly increase your chances of getting help when you need it. Your odds will improve even more if you say, when your colleague thanks you for the assistance, something like, "Sure, glad to help. I know how important it is for me to count on your help when I need it."

The Principle of Social Proof: People Follow the Lead of Similar Others

The Application: Use Peer Power Whenever It's Available

Social creatures that they are, human beings rely heavily on the people around them for cues on how to think, feel, and act. We know this intuitively, but intuition has also been confirmed by experiments, such as the one first described in 1982 in the *Journal of Applied Psychology*. A group of researchers went door-to-door in Columbia, South Carolina, soliciting donations for a charity campaign and displaying a list of neighborhood residents who had already donated to the cause. The researchers found that the longer the donor list was, the more likely those solicited would be to donate as well.

To the people being solicited, the friends' and neighbors' names on the list were a form of social evidence about how they should respond. But the evidence would not have been nearly as compelling had the names been those of random strangers. In an experiment from the 1960s, first described in the *Journal of Personality and Social Psychology,* residents of New York City were asked to return a lost wallet to its owner. They were highly likely to attempt to return the wallet when they learned that another New Yorker had previously attempted to do so. But learning that someone from a foreign country had tried to return the wallet didn't sway their decision one way or the other.

The lesson for executives from these two experiments is that persuasion can be extremely effective when it comes from peers. The science supports what most sales professionals already know: Testimonials from satisfied customers work best when the satisfied customer and the prospective customer share similar circumstances. That lesson can help a manager faced with the task of selling a new corporate initiative. Imagine that you're trying to streamline your department's work processes. A group of veteran employees is resisting. Rather than try to convince the employees of the move's merits yourself, ask an old-timer who supports the initiative to speak up for it at a team meeting. The compatriot's testimony stands a much better chance of convincing the group than yet another speech from the boss. Stated simply, influence is often best exerted horizontally rather than vertically.

The Principle of Consistency: People Align with Their Clear Commitments

The Application: Make Their Commitments Active, Public, and Voluntary

Liking is a powerful force, but the work of persuasion involves more than simply making people feel warmly toward you, your idea, or your product. People need not only to like you but to feel committed to what you want them to do. Good turns are one reliable way to make people feel obligated to you. Another is to win a public commitment from them.

My own research has demonstrated that most people, once they take a stand or go on record in favor of a position, prefer to stick to it. Other studies reinforce that finding and go on to show how even a small, seemingly trivial commitment can have a powerful effect on future actions. Israeli researchers writing in 1983 in the *Personality and Social*

Psychology Bulletin recounted how they asked half the residents of a large apartment complex to sign a petition favoring the establishment of a recreation center for the handicapped. The cause was good and the request was small, so almost everyone who was asked agreed to sign. Two weeks later, on National Collection Day for the Handicapped, all residents of the complex were approached at home and asked to give to the cause. A little more than half of those who were not asked to sign the petition made a contribution. But an astounding 92 percent of those who did sign donated money. The residents of the apartment complex felt obligated to live up to their commitments because those commitments were active, public, and voluntary. These three features are worth considering separately.

There's strong empirical evidence to show that a choice made actively—one that's spoken out loud or written down or otherwise made explicit—is considerably more likely to direct someone's future conduct than the same choice left unspoken. Writing in 1996 in the *Personality and Social Psychology Bulletin,* Delia Cioffi and Randy Garner described an experiment in which college students in one group were asked to fill out a printed form saying they wished to volunteer for an AIDS education project in the public schools. Students in another group volunteered for the same project by leaving blank a form stating that they didn't want to participate. A few days later, when the volunteers reported for duty, 74 percent of those who showed up were students from the group that signaled their commitment by filling out the form.

The implications are clear for a manager who wants to persuade a subordinate to follow some particular course of action: Get it in writing. Let's suppose you want your employee to submit reports in a more timely fashion. Once you believe you've won agreement, ask him to summarize the decision in a memo and send it to you. By doing so, you'll have greatly increased the odds that he'll fulfill the commitment because, as a rule, people live up to what they have written down.

Research into the social dimensions of commitment suggests that written statements become even more powerful when they're made public. In a classic experiment, described in 1955 in the *Journal of Abnormal and Social Psychology,* college students were asked to estimate the length of lines projected on a screen. Some students were asked to write down their choices on a piece of paper, sign it, and hand the paper to the experimenter. Others wrote their choices on an erasable slate, then erased the slate immediately. Still others were instructed to keep their decisions to themselves.

The experimenters then presented all three groups with evidence that their initial choices may have been wrong. Those who had merely kept their decisions in their heads were the most likely to reconsider their original estimates. More loyal to their first guesses were the students in the group that had written them down and immediately erased them. But by a wide margin, the ones most reluctant to shift from their original choices were those who had signed and handed them to the researcher.

This experiment highlights how much most people wish to appear consistent to others. Consider again the matter of the employee who has been submitting late reports. Recognizing the power of this desire, you should, once you've successfully convinced him of the need to be more timely, reinforce the commitment by making sure it gets a public airing. One way to do that would be to send the employee an e-mail that reads, "I think your plan is just what we need. I showed it to Diane in manufacturing and Phil in shipping, and they thought it was right on target, too." Whatever way such commitments are formalized, they should never be like the New Year's resolutions people privately make and then abandon with no one the wiser. They should be publicly made and visibly posted.

More than 300 years ago, Samuel Butler wrote a couplet that explains succinctly why commitments must be voluntary to be lasting and effective: "He that complies against his will/Is of his own opinion still." If an undertaking is forced, coerced, or imposed from the outside, it's not a commitment; it's an unwelcome burden. Think how you would react if your boss pressured you to donate to the campaign of a political candidate. Would that make you more apt to opt for that candidate in the privacy of a voting booth? Not likely. In fact, in their 1981 book *Psychological Reactance* (Academic Press), Sharon S. Brehm and Jack W. Brehm present data that suggest you'd vote the opposite way just to express your resentment of the boss's coercion.

This kind of backlash can occur in the office, too. Let's return again to that tardy employee. If you want to produce an enduring change in his behavior, you should avoid using threats or pressure tactics to gain his compliance. He'd likely view any change in his behavior as the result of intimidation rather than a personal commitment to change. A better approach would be to identify something that the employee genuinely values in the workplace—high-quality workmanship, perhaps, or team spirit—and then describe how timely reports are consistent with those values. That gives the employee reasons for improvement that he can own. And because he owns them, they'll continue to guide his behavior even when you're not watching.

The Principle of Authority: People Defer to Experts

The Application: Expose Your Expertise; Don't Assume It's Self-Evident

Two thousand years ago, the Roman poet Virgil offered this simple counsel to those seeking to choose correctly: "Believe an expert." That may or may not be good advice, but as a description of what people actually do, it can't be beaten. For instance, when the news media present an acknowledged expert's views on a topic, the effect on public opinion is dramatic. A single expert-opinion news story in *The New York Times* is associated with a 2 percent shift in public opinion nationwide, according to a 1993 study described in the *Public Opinion Quarterly*. And researchers writing in the *American Political Science Review* in 1987 found that when the expert's view was aired on national television, public opinion shifted as much as 4 percent. A cynic might argue that these findings only illustrate the docile submissiveness of the public. But a fairer explanation is that, amid the teeming complexity of contemporary life, a well-selected expert offers a valuable and efficient shortcut to good decisions. Indeed, some questions, be they legal, financial, medical, or technological, require so much specialized knowledge to answer, we have no choice but to rely on experts.

Since there's good reason to defer to experts, executives should take pains to ensure that they establish their own expertise before they attempt to exert influence. Surprisingly often, people mistakenly assume that others recognize and appreciate their experience. That's what happened at a hospital where some colleagues and I were consulting. The physical therapy staffers were frustrated because so many of their stroke patients abandoned their exercise routines as soon as they left the hospital. No matter how often the staff emphasized the importance of regular home exercise—it is, in fact, crucial to the process of regaining independent function—the message just didn't sink in.

Interviews with some of the patients helped us pinpoint the problem. They were familiar with the background and training of their physicians, but the patients knew little about the credentials of the physical therapists who were urging them to exercise. It was a simple matter to remedy that lack of information: We merely asked the therapy director to display all the awards, diplomas, and certifications of her staff on the walls of the therapy rooms. The result was startling: Exercise compliance jumped 34 percent and has never dropped since.

What we found immensely gratifying was not just how much we increased compliance, but how. We didn't fool or browbeat any of the patients. We *informed* them into compliance. Nothing had to be invented; no time or resources had to be spent in the process. The staff's expertise was real—all we had to do was make it more visible.

The task for managers who want to establish their claims to expertise is somewhat more difficult. They can't simply nail their diplomas to the wall and wait for everyone to notice. A little subtlety is called for. Outside the United States, it is customary for people to spend time interacting socially before getting down to business for the first time. Frequently they gather for dinner the night before their meeting or negotiation. These get-togethers can make discussions easier and help blunt disagreements—remember the findings about liking and similarity—and they can also provide an opportunity to establish expertise. Perhaps it's a matter of telling an anecdote about successfully solving a problem similar to the one that's on the agenda at the next day's meeting. Or perhaps dinner is the time to describe years spent mastering a complex discipline—not in a boastful way but as part of the ordinary give-and-take of conversation.

Granted, there's not always time for lengthy introductory sessions. But even in the course of the preliminary conversation that precedes most meetings, there is almost always an opportunity to touch lightly on your relevant background and experience as a natural part of a sociable exchange. This initial disclosure of personal information gives you a chance to establish expertise early in the game, so that when the discussion turns to the business at hand, what you have to say will be accorded the respect it deserves.

The Principle of Scarcity: People Want More of What They Can Have Less of

The Application: Highlight Unique Benefits and Exclusive Information

Study after study shows that items and opportunities are seen to be more valuable as they become less available. That's a tremendously useful piece of information for managers. They can harness the scarcity principle with the organizational equivalents of limited-time, limited-supply, and one-of-a-kind offers. Honestly informing a coworker of a closing window of opportunity—the chance to get the boss's ear before she leaves for an extended vacation, perhaps—can mobilize action dramatically.

Managers can learn from retailers how to frame their offers not in terms of what people stand to gain but in terms of what they stand to lose if they don't act on the information. The power of "loss language" was demonstrated in a 1988 study of California home owners written up in the *Journal of Applied Psychology.* Half were told that if they fully insulated their homes, they would save a certain amount of money each day. The other half were told that if they failed to insulate, they would lose that amount each day. Significantly more people insulated their homes when exposed to the loss language. The same phenomenon occurs in business. According to a 1994 study in the journal *Organizational Behavior and Human Decision Processes,* potential losses figure far more heavily in managers' decision making than potential gains.

In framing their offers, executives should also remember that exclusive information is more persuasive than widely available data. A doctoral student of mine, Amram Knishinsky, wrote his 1982 dissertation on the purchase decisions of wholesale beef buyers. He observed that they more than doubled their orders when they were told that, because of certain weather conditions overseas, there was likely to be a scarcity of foreign beef in the near future. But their orders increased 600 percent when they were informed that no one else had that information yet.

The persuasive power of exclusivity can be harnessed by any manager who comes into possession of information that's not broadly available and that supports an idea or initiative he or she would like the organization to adopt. The next time that kind of information crosses your desk, round up your organization's key players. The information itself may seem dull, but exclusivity will give it a special sheen. Push it across your desk and say, "I just got this report today. It won't be distributed until next week, but I want to give you an early look at what it shows." Then watch your listeners lean forward.

Allow me to stress here a point that should be obvious. No offer of exclusive information, no exhortation to act now or miss this opportunity forever should be made unless it is genuine. Deceiving colleagues into compliance is not only ethically objectionable, it's foolhardy. If the deception is detected—and it certainly will be—it will snuff out any enthusiasm the offer originally kindled. It will also invite dishonesty toward the deceiver. Remember the rule of reciprocity.

Putting It All Together

There's nothing abstruse or obscure about these six principles of persuasion. Indeed, they neatly codify our intuitive understanding of the ways people evaluate information and form decisions. As a result, the principles are easy for most people to grasp, even those with no formal education in psychology. But in the seminars and workshops I conduct, I have learned that two points bear repeated emphasis.

First, although the six principles and their applications can be discussed separately for the sake of clarity, they should be applied in combination to compound their impact. For instance, in discussing the importance of expertise, I suggested that managers use informal, social conversations to establish their credentials. But that conversation affords an opportunity to gain information as well as convey it. While you're showing your dinner companion that you have the skills and experience your business problem demands, you can also learn about your companion's background, likes, and dislikes—information that will help you locate genuine similarities and give sincere compliments. By letting your expertise surface and also establishing rapport, you double your persuasive power.

And if you succeed in bringing your dinner partner on board, you may encourage other people to sign on as well, thanks to the persuasive power of social evidence.

The other point I wish to emphasize is that the rules of ethics apply to the science of social influence just as they do to any other technology. Not only is it ethically wrong to trick or trap others into assent, it's ill-advised in practical terms. Dishonest or high-pressure tactics work only in the short run, if at all. Their long-term effects are malignant, especially within an organization, which can't function properly without a bedrock level of trust and cooperation.

That point is made vividly in the following account, which a department head for a large textile manufacturer related at a training workshop I conducted. She described a vice president in her company who wrung public commitments from department heads in a highly manipulative manner. Instead of giving his subordinates time to talk or think through his proposals carefully, he would approach them individually at the busiest moment of their workday and describe the benefits of his plan in exhaustive, patience-straining detail. Then he would move in for the kill. "It's very important for me to see you as being on my team on this," he would say. "Can I count on your support?" Intimidated, frazzled, eager to chase the man from their offices so they could get back to work, the department heads would invariably go along with his request. But because the commitments never felt voluntary, the department heads never followed through, and as a result the vice president's initiatives all blew up or petered out.

This story had a deep impact on the other participants in the workshop. Some gulped in shock as they recognized their own manipulative behavior. But what stopped everyone cold was the expression on the department head's face as she recounted the damaging collapse of her superior's proposals. She was smiling.

Nothing I could say would more effectively make the point that the deceptive or coercive use of the principles of social influence is ethically wrong and pragmatically wrongheaded. Yet the same principles, if applied appropriately, can steer decisions correctly. Legitimate expertise, genuine obligations, authentic similarities, real social proof, exclusive news, and freely made commitments can produce choices that are likely to benefit both parties. And any approach that works to everyone's mutual benefit is good business, don't you think? Of course, I don't want to press you into it, but, if you agree, I would love it if you could just jot me a memo to that effect.

Reading 2.7

Breakthrough Bargaining
Deborah M. Kolb
Judith Williams

Negotiation was once considered an art practiced by the naturally gifted. To some extent it still is, but increasingly we in the business world have come to regard negotiation as a science—built on creative approaches to deal making that allow everyone to walk away winners of sorts. Executives have become experts in "getting to yes," as the now familiar terminology goes.

Nevertheless, some negotiations stall or, worse, never get off the ground. Why? Our recent research suggests that the answers lie in a dynamic we have come to call the *shadow negotiation*—the complex and subtle game people play before they get to the table and continue to play after they arrive. The shadow negotiation doesn't determine the "what" of the discussion, but the "how." Which interests will hold sway? Will the conversation's tone be adversarial or cooperative? Whose opinions will be heard? In short, how will bargainers deal with each other?

The shadow negotiation is most obvious when the participants hold unequal power—say, subordinates asking bosses for more resources or new employees engaging with veterans about well-established company policies. Similarly, managers who, because of their race, age, or gender, are in the minority in their companies may be at a disadvantage in the shadow negotiation. Excluded from important networks, they may not have the personal clout, experience, or organizational standing to influence other parties. Even when the bargainers are peers, a negotiation can be blocked or stalled—undermined by hidden assumptions, unrealistic expectations, or personal histories. An unexamined shadow negotiation can lead to silence, not satisfaction.

It doesn't have to be that way. Our research identified strategic levers—we call them power moves, process moves, and *appreciative moves*—that executives can use to guide the shadow negotiation. In situations in which the other person sees no compelling need to negotiate, *power moves* can help bring him or her to the table. When the dynamics of decision making threaten to overpower a negotiator's voice, *process moves* can reshape the negotiation's structure. And when talks stall because the other party feels pushed or misunderstandings cloud the real issues, *appreciative moves* can alter the tone or atmosphere so that a more collaborative exchange is possible. These strategic moves don't guarantee that bargainers will walk away winners, but they help to get stalled negotiations out of the dark of unspoken power plays and into the light of true dialogue.

Power Moves

In the informal negotiations common in the workplace, one of the parties can be operating from a one-down position. The other bargainer, seeing no apparent advantage in negotiating, stalls. Phone calls go unanswered. The meeting keeps being postponed, or if it does take place, a two-way conversation never gets going. Ideas are ignored or overruled, demands dismissed. Such resistance is a natural part of the informal negotiation process. A concern will generally be accorded a fair hearing only when someone believes two things: the other party has something desirable, and one's own objectives will not be met without giving something in return. Willingness to negotiate is, therefore, a confession of mutual need. As a result, a primary objective in the shadow negotiation is fostering the perception of mutual need.

Power moves can bring reluctant bargainers to the realization that they must negotiate: they will be better off if they do and worse off if they don't. Bargainers can use three kinds of power moves. *Incentives* emphasize the proposed value to the other person and the advantage to be gained from negotiating. *Pressure levers* underscore the consequences to the other side if stalling continues. And the third power move, *enlisting allies,* turns up the volume of the incentives or of the pressure. Here's how these strategies work.

Offer Incentives

In any negotiation, the other party controls something the bargainer needs: money, time, cooperation, communication, and so on. But the bargainer's needs alone aren't enough to bring anyone else to the table. The other side must recognize that benefits will accrue from the negotiation. These benefits must not only be visible—that is, right there on the table—but they must also resonate with the other side's needs. High-tech executive Fiona Sweeney quickly recognized this dynamic when she tried to initiate informal talks about a mission-critical organizational change.

Shortly after being promoted to head operations at an international systems company, Sweeney realized that the organization's decision-making processes required a fundamental revamping. The company operated through a collection of fiefdoms, with little coordination even on major accounts. Sales managers, whose bonuses were tied to gross sales, pursued any opportunity with minimal regard for the company's ability to deliver. Production scrambled to meet unrealistic schedules; budgets and quality suffered. Sweeney had neither the authority nor the inclination to order sales and production to cooperate. And as a newcomer to corporate headquarters, her visibility and credibility were low.

Sweeney needed a sweetener to bring sales and production together. First, she made adjustments to the billing process, reducing errors from 7.1 percent to 2.4 percent over a three-month period, thereby cutting back on customer complaints. Almost immediately, her stock shot up with both of the divisions. Second, realizing that sales would be more reluctant than production to negotiate any changes in the organization's decision-making processes, she worked with billing to speed up processing the expense account checks so that salespeople were reimbursed more quickly, a move that immediately got the attention of everyone in sales. By demonstrating her value to sales and production, Sweeney encouraged the two division managers to work with her on improving their joint decision-making process.

Creating value and making it visible are key power moves in the shadow negotiation. A bargainer can't leave it up to the other party to puzzle through the possibilities. The benefits must be made explicit if they are to have any impact on the shadow negotiation. When value disappears, so do influence and bargaining power.

Put a Price on the Status Quo

Abba Eban, Israel's former foreign minister, once observed that diplomats have "a passionate love affair with the status quo" that blocks any forward movement. The same love affair carries over into ordinary negotiations in the workplace. When people believe that a negotiation has the potential to produce bad results for them, they are naturally reluctant to engage on the issues. Until the costs of *not* negotiating are made explicit, ducking the problem will be the easier or safer course.

To unlock the situation, the status quo must be perceived as less attractive. By exerting pressure, the bargainer can raise the cost of business-as-usual until the other side begins to see that things will get worse unless both sides get down to talking.

That is exactly what Karen Hartig, one of the women in our study, did when her boss dragged his heels about giving her a raise. Not only had she been promoted without additional pay, but she was now doing two jobs because the first position had never been filled. Although her boss continued to assure her of his support, nothing changed. Finally, Hartig was so exasperated that she returned a headhunter's call. The resulting job offer provided her with enough leverage to unfreeze the talks with her boss. No longer could he afford to maintain the status quo. By demonstrating that she had another alternative, she gave him a push—and the justification—he needed to argue forcefully on her behalf with his boss and with human resources.

Enlist Support

Solo power moves won't always do the job. Another party may not see sufficient benefits to negotiating, or the potential costs may not be high enough to compel a change of mind. When incentives and pressure levers fail to move the negotiation forward, a bargainer can enlist the help of allies.

Allies are important resources in shadow negotiations. They can be crucial in establishing credibility, and they lend tangible support to incentives already proposed. By providing guidance or running interference, they can favorably position a bargainer's proposals before talks even begin. At a minimum, their confidence primes the other party to listen and raises the cost of not negotiating seriously.

When a member of Dan Riley's squadron faced a prolonged family emergency, the air force captain needed to renegotiate his squadron's flight rotation orders. The matter was particularly sensitive, however, because it required the consent of the wing commander, two levels up the chain of command. If Riley approached the commander directly, he risked making his immediate superior look bad since his responsibilities covered readiness planning. To bridge that difficulty, Riley presented a draft proposal to his immediate supervisor. Once aware of the problem, Riley and his superior anticipated some of the objections the commander might raise and then alerted the wing commander to the general difficulties posed by such situations. When Riley finally presented his proposal to the commander, it carried his immediate superior's blessing, and so his credibility was never questioned; only the merits of his solution were discussed.

Process Moves

Rather than attempt to influence the shadow negotiation directly through power moves, a bargainer can exercise another kind of strategic move, the process move. Designed to influence the negotiation process itself, such moves can be particularly effective when bargainers are caught in a dynamic of silencing—when decisions are being made without their input or when colleagues interrupt them during meetings, dismiss their comments, or appropriate their ideas.

While process moves do not address the substantive issues in a negotiation, they directly affect the hearing those issues receive. The agenda, the prenegotiation groundwork, and the sequence in which ideas and people are heard—all these structural elements influence others' receptivity to opinions and demands. Working behind the scenes, a bargainer can plant the seeds of ideas or can marshal support before a position becomes fixed in anyone's mind. Consensus can even be engineered so that the bargainer's agenda frames the subsequent discussion.

Seed Ideas Early

Sometimes parties to a negotiation simply shut down and don't listen; for whatever reason, they screen out particular comments or people. Being ignored in a negotiation doesn't necessarily result from saying too little or saying it too hesitantly. When ideas catch people off guard, they can produce negative, defensive reactions, as can ideas presented too forcefully. Negotiators also screen out the familiar: if they've already heard the speech, or a close variant, they stop paying attention.

Joe Lopez faced this dilemma. Lopez, a fast-track engineer who tended to promote his ideas vigorously in planning meetings, began to notice that his peers were tuning him out—a serious problem since departmental resources were allocated in these sessions. To remedy the situation, Lopez scheduled one-on-one lunch meetings with his colleagues. On each occasion, he mentioned how a particular project would benefit the other manager's department and how they could work together to ensure its completion. As a result of this informal lobbying, Lopez found he no longer needed to oversell his case in the meetings. He could make his ideas heard with fewer words and at a lower decibel level.

Preliminary work like this allows a bargainer to build receptivity where a direct or aggressive approach might encounter resistance. Once the seeds of an idea have been planted, they will influence how others view a situation, regardless of how firmly attached they are to their own beliefs and ideas.

Reframe the Process

Negotiators are not equally adept in all settings. Highly competitive approaches to problem solving favor participants who can bluff and play the game, talk the loudest, hold out the longest, and think fastest on their feet. Bargainers who are uncomfortable with this kind of gamesmanship can reframe the process, shifting the dynamic away from personal competition. That's what Marcia Philbin decided to do about the way in which space was allocated in her company. Extra room and equipment typically went to those who pushed the hardest, and Philbin never fared well in the negotiations. She also believed that significant organizational costs always accompanied the process since group leaders routinely presented the building administrator with inflated figures, making it impossible to assess the company's actual requirements.

Positioning herself as an advocate not only for her department but also for the company, Philbin proposed changing the process. Rather than allocating space in a series of discrete negotiations with the space administrator, she suggested, why not collaborate as a group in developing objective criteria for assessing need? Management agreed, and Philbin soon found herself chairing the committee created to produce the new guidelines. Heated arguments took place over the criteria, but Philbin was now positioned to direct the discussions away from vested and parochial interests toward a greater focus on organizational needs.

Within organizations or groups, negotiations can fall into patterns. If a bargainer's voice is consistently shut out of discussions, something about the way negotiations are structured is working against his or her active participation. A process move may provide a remedy because it will influence how the discussion unfolds and how issues emerge.

Build Consensus

Regardless of how high a bargainer is on the organizational ladder, it is not always possible—or wise—to impose change on a group by fiat. By lobbying behind the scenes, a bargainer can start to build consensus before formal decision making begins. Unlike the first process move, which aims at gaining a hearing for ideas, building consensus creates momentum behind an agenda by bringing others on board. The growing support isolates the blockers, making continued opposition harder and harder. Moreover, once agreement has been secured privately, it becomes difficult (although never impossible) for a supporter to defect publicly.

As CEO of a rapidly growing biotechnology company, Mark Chapin gradually built consensus for his ideas on integrating a newly acquired research boutique into the existing company. Chapin had two goals: to retain the acquired firm's scientific talent and to rationalize the research funding process. The second goal was at odds with the first and threatened to alienate the new scientists. To mitigate this potential conflict, Chapin focused his attention on the shadow negotiation. First, he met one-on-one with key leaders of the board and the research staffs of both companies. These private talks provided him with a strategic map that showed where he would find support and where he was likely to meet challenges. Second, in another round of talks, Chapin paid particular attention to the order in which he approached people. Beginning with the most supportive person, he got the key players to commit, one by one, to his agenda before opposing factions could coalesce. These preliminary meetings positioned him as a collaborator—and, equally important, as a source of expanding research budgets. Having privately built commitment, Chapin found that he didn't need to use his position to dictate terms when the principal players finally sat down to negotiate the integration plan.

Appreciative Moves

Power moves exert influence on the other party so that talks get off the ground. Process moves seek to change the ground rules under which negotiations play out. But still, talks may stall. Two strong advocates may have backed themselves into respective corners. Or one side, put on the defensive, even inadvertently, may continue to resist or raise obstacles. Communication may deteriorate, turn acrimonious, or simply stop as participants focus solely on their own demands. Wariness stifles any candid exchange. And without candor, the two sides cannot address the issues together or uncover the real conflict.

Appreciative moves break these cycles. They explicitly build trust and encourage the other side to participate in a dialogue. Not only do appreciative moves shift the dynamics of the shadow negotiation away from the adversarial, but they also hold out a hidden promise. When bargainers demonstrate appreciation for another's concerns, situation, or "face," they open the negotiation to the different perspectives held by that person and to the opinions, ideas, and feelings shaping those perspectives. Appreciative moves foster open communication so that differences in needs and views can come to the surface without personal discord. Frequently the participants then discover that the problem they were worrying about is not the root conflict, but a symptom of it. And at times, before a negotiation can move toward a common solution, the participants must first experience mutuality, recognizing where their interests and needs intersect. A shared problem can then become the basis for creative problem solving.

Help Others Save Face

Image is a concern for everyone. How negotiators look to themselves and to others who matter to them often counts as much as the particulars of an agreement. In fact, these are seldom separate. "Face" captures what people value in themselves and the qualities they want others to see in them. Negotiators go to great lengths to preserve face. They stick to their guns against poor odds simply to avoid losing face with those who are counting on them. If a bargainer treads on another's self-image—in front of a boss or colleague, or even privately—his or her demands are likely to be rejected.

Sensitivity to the other side's face does more than head off resistance: it lays the groundwork for trust. It conveys that the bargainer respects what the other is trying to accomplish and will not do anything to embarrass or undermine that person. This appreciation concedes nothing, yet as Sam Newton discovered, it can turn out to be the only way to break a stalemate.

Newton's new boss, transferred from finance, lacked experience on the operations side of the business. During department meetings to negotiate project schedules and funding, he always rejected Newton's ideas. Soon it was routine: Newton would make a suggestion and before he got the last sentence out, his boss was issuing a categorical veto.

Frustrated, Newton pushed harder, only to meet increased resistance. Finally, he took a step back and looked at the situation from his boss's perspective. Rubberstamping Newton's proposals could have appeared as a sign of weakness at a time when his boss was still establishing his credentials. From then on, Newton took a different tack. Rather than present a single idea, he offered an array of options and acknowledged that the final decision rested with his boss. Gradually, his boss felt less need to assert his authority and could respond positively in their dealings.

Bosses aren't the only ones who need to save face; colleagues and subordinates do, too. Team members avoid peers who bump a problem upstairs at the first sign of trouble, making everyone appear incapable of producing a solution. Subordinates muzzle their real opinions once they have been belittled or treated dismissively by superiors. In the workplace, attention to face is a show of respect for another person, whatever one's corporate role. That respect carries over to the shadow negotiation.

Keep the Dialogue Going

Sometimes talks don't get off the ground because the timing is not right for a participant to make a decision; information may be insufficient, or he or she is simply not ready. People have good reasons—at least, reasons that make sense to them—for thinking it's not yet time to negotiate. Appreciating this disposition doesn't mean abandoning or postponing a negotiation. Instead, it requires that a bargainer keep the dialogue going without pushing for immediate agreement. This appreciative move allows an opportunity for additional information to come to the surface and affords the other side more time to rethink ideas and adjust initial predilections.

Francesca Rossi knew instinctively that unless she kept the communication lines open, discussions would derail about the best way for her software firm to grow. The company had recently decided to expand by acquiring promising applications rather than developing them in-house from scratch. As head of strategic development, Rossi targeted a small start-up that designed state-of-the-art software for office computers to control home appliances. The director of research, however, was less than enthusiastic about acquiring the firm. He questioned the product's commercial viability and argued that its market would never justify the acquisition cost.

Needing his cooperation, Rossi pulled back. Instead of actively promoting the acquisition, she began to work behind the scenes with the start-up's software designers and industry analysts. As Rossi gathered more data in support of the application's potential, she gradually drew the director of research back into the discussions. He dropped his opposition once the analysis convinced him that the acquisition, far from shrinking his department's authority, would actually enlarge it. Rossi's appreciative move had given him the additional information and time he needed to reevaluate his original position.

Not everyone makes decisions quickly. Sometimes people can't see beyond their initial ideas or biases. Given time to mull over the issues, they may eventually reverse course and be more amenable to negotiating. As long as the issue isn't forced or brought to a preemptive conclusion—as long as the participants keep talking—there's a chance that the resistance will fade. What seems unreasonable at one point in a negotiation can become more acceptable at another. Appreciative moves that keep the dialogue going allow the other side to progress at a comfortable speed.

Solicit New Perspectives

One of the biggest barriers to effective negotiation and a major cause of stalemate is the tendency for bargainers to get trapped in their own perspectives. It's simply too easy for people to become overly enamored of their opinions. Operating in a closed world of their making, they tell themselves they are right and the other person is wrong. They consider the merits of their own positions but neglect the other party's valid objections. They push their agendas, merely reiterating the same argument, and may not pick up on cues that their words aren't being heard.

It's safe to assume that the other party is just as convinced that his or her own demands are justified. Moreover, bargainers can only speculate what another's agenda might be—hidden or otherwise. Appreciative moves to draw out another's perspectives help negotiators understand why the other party feels a certain way. But these moves serve more than an instrumental purpose, doing more than add information to a bargainer's arsenal. They signal to the other side that differing opinions and perspectives are important. By creating opportunities to discover something new and unexpected, appreciative moves can break a stalemate. As understanding deepens on both sides of the table, reaching a mutual resolution becomes increasingly possible.

Everyone agreed that a joint venture negotiated by HMO executive Donna Hitchcock between her organization and an insurance company dovetailed with corporate objectives on both sides. The HMO could expand its patient base and the insurance carrier its enrollment.

Although the deal looked good on paper, implementation stalled. Hitchcock couldn't understand where the resistance was coming from or why. In an attempt to unfreeze the situation, she arranged a meeting with her counterpart from the insurance company. After a brief update, Hitchcock asked about any unexpected effects the joint venture was exerting on the insurance carrier's organization and on her counterpart's work life. That appreciative move ultimately broke the logjam. From the carrier's perspective, she learned, the new arrangement stretched already overworked departments and had not yet produced additional revenues to hire more staff. Even more important, her counterpart was personally bearing the burden of the increased work.

Hitchcock was genuinely sympathetic to these concerns. The extra work was a legitimate obstacle to the joint venture's successful implementation. Once she understood the reason behind her counterpart's resistance, the two were able to strategize on ways to alleviate the overload until the additional revenues kicked in.

Through these appreciative moves—actively soliciting the other side's ideas and perspectives, acknowledging their importance, and demonstrating that they are taken seriously—negotiators can encourage the other person to work with them rather than against them.

There's more to negotiation than haggling over issues and working out solutions. The shadow negotiation, though often overlooked, is a critical component. Whether a bargainer uses power, process, or appreciative moves in the shadow negotiation depends on the demands of the situation. Power moves encourage another party to recognize the need to negotiate in the first place. They help bring a reluctant bargainer to the table. Process moves create a context in which a bargainer can shape the negotiation's agenda and dynamic so that he or she can be a more effective advocate. Appreciative moves engage the other party in a collaborative exchange by fostering trust and candor in the shadow negotiation. While power and process moves can ensure that a negotiation gets started on the right foot, appreciative moves can break a stalemate once a negotiation is under way. By broadening the discourse, appreciative moves can also lead to creative solutions. Used alone or in combination, strategic moves in the shadow negotiation can determine the outcome of the negotiation on the issues.

Reading 2.8

Ethics in Negotiation: Oil and Water or Good Lubrication?

H. Joseph Reitz
James A. Wall, Jr.
Mary Sue Love

In his 1996 year-end column for *Forbes,* merchant banker and economist John Rutledge describes two weeks of negotiations over an acquisition for a private equity fund. The hours of bargaining were tense, long, hard, and far more complicated than he had envisioned. Nevertheless, he reports,

> Despite all the haggling, we ended on a friendly note. All of us—buyer, seller, lender—shook hands and clinked champagne glasses. As we were leaving, the seller said he would like to discuss teaming up with us in a joint venture. I beamed. Some buyers wouldn't have liked this. They think if the seller doesn't hate them at the end of the deal, they haven't squeezed out every last drop of money. I disagree. We believe that when someone wants to do repeat business with us, it is the highest form of praise. Allowing your opponent in a transaction to walk away with his dignity, his humor, and his bearing intact, and with a pretty good deal in his pocket, is the right way to do business.

Rutledge then lists a set of principles learned from his first business partner and admonishes his readers to

> walk away from a deal, any deal, rather than violate your principles to win it. . . . The twist, of course, is that business organizations organized around principles are often more successful and make more money that those organized around the idea that greed is good. Nice guys often finish first.

Rutledge's thesis that ethical negotiating is not only the right thing to do but frequently is also more profitable represents an argument more common today than in the so-called decade of greed in the 1980s—and one that finds more receptive audiences.

Should businesspeople take this as an article of faith? Or can reason bring us to similar conclusions? In probing that question, we shall list a number of questionable negotiation tactics or behaviors and evaluate them according to four commonly used ethical criteria. This will help us assess the costs and benefits of ethical versus unethical negotiation tactics.

Questionable Negotiation Tactics and Ethical Criteria

We all have a general idea of what negotiation is: two parties attempting to work out a trade of items or services that is acceptable to both sides. Each side has an array of

Source: Reprinted with permission from *Business Horizons,* May–June 1998. Copyright 1998 by the Board of Trustees at Indiana University, Kelley School of Business with permission from Elsevier.

215

tactics to employ in achieving this trade. Below are 10 popular tactics, the ethics of which have been challenged over the years:

1. *Lies:* Statements made in contradiction to the negotiator's knowledge or belief about something material to the negotiation.

2. *Puffery:* Exaggerating the value of something in the negotiation.

3. *Deception:* An act or statement intended to mislead the opponent about the negotiator's own intent or future actions relevant to the negotiations.

4. *Weakening the opponent:* Actions or statements designed to improve the negotiator's own relative strength by directly undermining that of the opponent.

5. *Strengthening one's own position:* Actions or statements designed to improve the negotiator's own position without directly weakening that of the opponent.

6. *Nondisclosure:* Keeping to oneself knowledge that would benefit the opponent.

7. *Information exploitation:* Using information provided by the opponent to weaken him, either in the direct exchange or by sharing it with others.

8. *Change of mind:* Engaging in behaviors contrary to previous statements or positions.

9. *Distraction:* Acts or statements that lure the opponent into ignoring information or alternatives that might benefit him.

10. *Maximization:* The negotiator's single-minded pursuit of payoffs at the cost of the opponent's payoffs.

How do negotiators decide if such tactics—laid out in greater detail in Figure 1—are ethical? Our interviews with businesspeople have yielded such comments as

- A lie is not a lie when a lie is expected.
- When someone tells the truth, that's good: when someone lies, that's wrong. It's that simple.
- What's right or wrong really depends on the situation.

The variety in comments vis-à-vis the first tactic indicates that opinions can vary as to what is ethical. Fortunately, moral reasoning can help negotiators assess the ethical nature of lies and other tactics. Summarized in Figure 2, the four criteria most widely used in business ethics today are the *Golden Rule, utilitarianism, universalism,* and *distributive justice.*

The Golden Rule

Most managers tend to explain ethical behavior as a function of personal values. One of the most frequently cited values is the Golden Rule: Do unto others as you would have them do unto you. A relatively popular principle, perhaps its most famous and vocal advocate in the industry was J. C. Penney, who used it in building and running his business from his youth until his nineties. In practice, it requires decision makers to apply the same standards of fairness and equity to their own actions that they would demand of others.

FIGURE 1 | Questionable Tactics

Tactic	Description / Clarification / Range
Lies	Subject matter for lies can include limits, alternatives, the negotiator's intent, authority to bargain, other commitments, acceptability of the opponent's offer, time pressures, and available resources.
Puffery	Among the items that can be puffed up are the value of one's payoffs to the opponent, the negotiator's own alternatives, the cost of what one is giving up or is prepared to yield, importance of issues, and attributes of the products or services.
Deception	Acts and statements may include promises or threats, excessive initial demands, careless misstatements of facts, or asking for concessions not wanted.
Weakening the opponent	The negotiator here may cut off or eliminate some of the opponent's alternatives, blame the opponent for his own actions, use personally abrasive statements to or about the opponent, or undermine the opponent's alliances.
Strengthening one's own position	This tactic includes building one's own resources, including expertise, finances, and alliances. It also includes presentations of persuasive rationales to the opponent or third parties (e.g., the public, the media) or getting mandates for one's position.
Nondisclosure	Includes partial disclosure of facts, failure to disclose a hidden fact, failure to correct the opponents' misperceptions or ignorance, and concealment of the negotiator's own position or circumstances.
Information exploitation	Information provided by the opponent can be used to exploit his weaknesses, close off his alternatives, generate demands against him, or weaken his alliances.
Change of mind	Includes accepting offers one had claimed one would not accept, changing demands, withdrawing promised offers, and making threats one promised would not be made. Also includes the failure to behave as predicted.
Distraction	These acts or statements can be as simple as providing excessive information to the opponent, asking many questions, evading questions, or burying the issue. Or they can be more complex, such as feigning weakness in one area so that the opponent concentrates on it and ignores another.
Maximization	Includes demanding the opponent make concessions that result in the negotiator's gain and the opponent's equal or greater loss. Also entails converting a win–win situation to win–lose.

FIGURE 2 | Ethical Criteria

Criteria	Explanation / Interpretation
Golden Rule	Do unto others as you would have them do unto you.
Universalism	People are not to be used as a means to an end.
Utilitarianism	Do the greatest good for the greatest number of people.
Distributive justice	Everyone is better off because of this act.

Universalism

A more complex ethical base is universalism, which argues that the rightness or wrongness of actions can be determined a priori, or before the actual outcomes of those actions can be realized. Based on a system of individual rights and obligations founded by philosopher Immanuel Kant, it argues that human beings are incapable of foreseeing all the outcomes of their decisions and actions, and thus should be held morally accountable for the *way* they made them.

For an act or decision to be moral, it must meet several criteria:

1. It must respect the inherent worth and dignity of those involved or affected; people must never be used primarily as a means to an end.

2. It must be universally applicable to all human beings facing similar situations—there are no special treatments.

3. It must be consistent with all other universal moral principles.

Consider the dilemma of downsizing. Universalism would permit downsizing for sound economic reasons, but it would require informing all those being laid off of that decision when it is made. Withholding such information from employees to keep them working with the same level of dedication and effort would be unethical because it would be using them primarily as a means to an end. Unaware of their impending doom, they might make family, career, or financial decisions they would not have made with valid information about their employer's plans.

Utilitarianism

In contrast to universalism, utilitarianism judges the rightness or wrongness of actions and decisions by their consequences. It argues that human beings ought to seek those alternatives that produce the greatest amount of good for the greatest number of people, or to maximize the total good produced. When seeking the greatest net good, one must consider all people likely to be affected by a set of alternatives and the array of outcomes (both good and bad) each alternative might generate for each person.

Distributive Justice

John Rawls's ethical concept of justice implies that individuals have an obligation to exercise their own rights in a way that permits others to enjoy theirs. Justice occurs when all individuals get what they deserve; injustice, when people are deprived of that to which they have a right. In brief, this ethical norm asks, Is everyone (the group) better off because of this act? And for each person, it asks, Would you be willing to trade places with any of the other parties after this act takes place?

Rawls's concept of justice, like universalism, focuses on the *process* by which outcomes are distributed rather than on the outcomes themselves. Like Kant's universalist perspective, Rawls's attempts to derive a set of principles that would be acceptable to all rational people.

In considering the justice of any process, we are asked to assume a *veil of ignorance*. That is, we act as if we are ignorant of our *own* roles in the situation, and assume we could be assigned *any* role. Would we be willing to abide by our decision if we might be any of the players affected by it? According to Rawls, the veil of ignorance leads us to construct processes in which

1. All members of the process could agree to be part of it, regardless of the position they might happen to occupy in the process.
2. Each person would have an equal right to the most extensive liberty that can accommodate similar liberties for others.
3. Inequalities work to the benefit of all.
4. These inequalities are attached to positions that are accessible to all.

Using Multiple Criteria

Evaluating bargaining tactics raises the question of which of these four criteria takes precedence. If a tactic is condoned by one criterion and condemned by another, what is a negotiator to do?

In the first place, if applied correctly, these criteria ought to yield similar results. They are not designed to bring about different answers; rather they are different ways of looking for the same answer. Which criterion one uses can be a matter of personal preference or may be dictated by the nature of the dilemma. Utilitarianism is useful when the number of affected parties is relatively small and known and the outcomes are relatively predictable. However, when the number of affected parties is large, knowledge of their preferences is unreliable, or outcomes are unpredictable, then other criteria are more useful. When dealing with unfamiliar situations (new technology), unfamiliar parties (new markets), or complex issues (mergers and acquisitions), principle-based criteria such as universalism are going to be more reliable than those, such as utilitarianism, that require predictions about very uncertain future events.

Ethical Negotiations

Having delineated these four standards, we shall now apply them to the 10 questionable negotiation tactics, from lying to maximizing.

Lies

A lie is a statement made by a negotiator that contradicts his knowledge or beliefs about something material to the negotiations. In negotiating, lies are intended to deceive the opponent about values, intents, objectives, alternatives, constraints, and beliefs. Examples include

- "Why should I buy it from you for $10,000 when I've got another seller willing to let me have one just as good for $8,500"—when the buyer has no such alternative.
- "I can't possibly pay $10,000. I have only $8,500 to spend"; or "My client has directed me to pay no more than $9,000"—when the negotiator has no such constraints.

Lying and the Golden Rule   Most religions, including Christianity, Judaism, and Islam, contain strict injunctions against lying. Some religions, however, permit lying when it is the only possible way to prevent a greater harm. For example, you may lie to someone in a murderous rage in order to prevent a homicide, or to a drunken, abusive person in search of his usual victims. These exceptions are really not inconsistent with the Golden Rule. The question would be, Would you prefer to be lied to if that were the only way to keep you from committing a terrible deed? The rational answer is yes.

The examples of lying in negotiations, however, do not prevent a greater harm. They are simply examples of immediate self-interest, of doing harm by deceit to further your own interest. The question would be, Would you prefer that others deceive you to enrich themselves at your expense? The rational answer is no.

Lying and Universalism   In his late years, Kant argued that honesty was so important to the concept of intrinsic human worth and dignity that *no* lie could be justified. The argument is that human beings rely on information to make decisions for themselves. And to make the best decisions, they must have the truth. When others deprive them of the truth through lies, the victims of those lies may be led to make faulty decisions.

Some will propose that lying is permissible when you believe your opponent is lying. They argue, in fact, that lying is the only defense against an opponent who lies. But this argument is flawed. First, there are other options, one of which is to terminate the negotiation. Second, you can try to discover the truth that will expose the lie, thus turning a disadvantage into an advantage. If you cannot possibly ascertain the truth, then you must admit that you only believe your opponent to be lying; you don't know it as fact. Such a belief is not sufficient to justify a lie.

Lying and Utilitarianism   At first blush, it might seem that utilitarianism could make a case for lying under certain circumstances. A negotiator might think, This lie helps my company a lot and doesn't harm my opponent very much. However, utilitarianism requires us to consider all the possible consequences to all the people potentially affected by the action—and to consider all the people so affected as equals. We cannot weight the interests of some, such as ourselves, as greater than the interests of others.

A further problem with attempting to justify lying through utilitarianism is that one must consider the effects of the lying itself. Beyond the direct effects of a lie are the indirect effects of harm done to society in general by increasing cynicism and decreasing trust. The liar also suffers some loss of self-esteem by admitting that his success, however noteworthy, was achieved by dishonorable means. Cynicism and lack of trust entail significant costs for any society, which requires more laws, surveillance, and sanctions—none of which add value to a transaction—to be in place before enacting agreements.

Lying and Distributive Justice   Distributive justice requires us to be willing to take the role of either party in the situation. Would we willingly trade places with the party being lied to? No, because being lied to increases our chances of making a decision that is not in our best interests.

Second, does a lie decrease the freedom to act of any of the parties? Yes; consistent with the maxim that the truth frees us to make the best decisions, a lie reduces that freedom. One can also argue that a lie decreases the freedom of the liar, whose subsequent statements and actions are now constrained to be (or appear to be) consistent with the lie. Suppose a buyer lies about her reservation price, claiming she could never pay more than $8,000 for an object for which she is willing to pay $9,000, and for which the seller is asking $11,000. If the seller reduced his price to $10,000, the buyer cannot reinforce that concession by raising her offer above $8,000, lest her lie be exposed. Lies constrain the freedom of both the victim and the liar.

None of the four ethical models can justify lying in negotiations. Lying is seen to be what it is—an act of self-interest usually taken as a convenient alternative to (*a*) the hard work of preparing for negotiations, including improving one's knowledge about an opponent, or (*b*) walking away from a negotiation when one comes to believe the opponent is lying. Only when a lie is the only possible means of preventing a greater harm to another could it possibly be justified. Such an exceptional circumstance is extremely rare in most negotiations, and those circumstances, such as hostage negotiation, would be dramatic enough to be relatively obvious.

Puffery

Puffery is exaggerating the value of something, such as its cost, condition, or worth. Negotiators will often exaggerate the value of alternatives, what they are giving up or are prepared to give up, the importance of issues, product or service attributes, or the value of their case. Examples:

- "I have a six-figure offer from another company"—when no such offer has actually been made, or the offer is less than six figures.

- "This union will never give up the right to strike"—when job security is actually more important.

- "I consistently get up to 33 miles per gallon"—when in fact that happened only once in the car's lifetime.

- "We have enough evidence right now to put your client away for 20 years"— when the real evidence at hand is less than convincing.

Clearly, puffery is simply a euphemism for lying. Every one of these statements contradicts the negotiator's knowledge or beliefs. Exaggeration may be considered by some as a milder form of lying in that there is a shred of truth in it; nevertheless, a statement that contradicts the truth is a lie. Like lies, exaggerations are intended to deceive and gain advantage at another's expense.

Deception

A deception is an act or statement intended to mislead another about one's own intent or future actions relevant to the negotiations. These include false promises or empty threats, excessive initial demands, careless statements of fact, and asking for things not wanted. Examples include

- "If you give us the contract, we'll begin shipments in 30 days"—when such a delivery date is known to be impossible (false promise).
- "If we don't settle this right now, the whole deal is off and we'll just find somebody else"—when the negotiator has no intention of losing this deal (empty threat).
- "In order to accept a position on your board, I would expect to receive 20,000 shares of stock, luxury class travel and lodging, and to be named chair of the personnel committee"—when what the negotiator really wants is 10,000 shares and a seat on the personnel committee (excessive demands, asking for things not wanted).
- "We need at least a $50,000 contribution from loyal supporters like you because our people tell us that the opposition plans to eliminate Medicare for people like you if they are elected"—when the negotiator knows that the opponents will only seek to halt increases in Medicare spending (careless statement of facts).

Some of these deceptive tactics clearly fall into the first category of lies. False promises and empty threats are statements made in contradiction to the negotiator's knowledge or beliefs. We have already determined that lies are unethical. But what about excessive demands, careless statements of fact, asking for things not wanted, or distracting statements?

Deception as a category of acts is clearly designed to profit at others' expense—to lead others into acts that are not in their self-interest, or away from an act that is. In this light, deceptive acts can be seen to be unethical.

None of us wants to be deceived, so deception fails the Golden Rule. It does not treat the deceived parties with respect, but takes advantage of their trust or vulnerability, so it fails the test of universalism. It does not create the greatest good for the greatest number of people, but only allows the deceiver to profit at the expense of the deceived, violating the standards of utilitarianism. And it limits the deceived person's choices, failing the test of distributive justice. In the end, then, deception fails all four tests of ethical behavior.

Weakening the Opponent

A tactic for improving your relative position is to weaken that of your opponent, either psychologically or economically. Direct attacks are generally aimed at lowering another's self-esteem, often through guilt or embarrassment. Indirect attacks include closing off another's alternatives or undermining his support or alliances.

Frequently, the means for weakening one's opponent involve lying, deception, or exaggeration. You could blame your opponent for damage caused by others of unknown origin, or create the impression that he was the author of harm done to you or others when no real harm had been done. We have already demonstrated that such tactics are unethical.

But what about those cases in which the negotiator can weaken an opponent by telling the truth? The morality of the tactic depends on a number of factors. Information about your own position ("Our company will be bankrupt if we increase wages by that much") would meet ethical criteria. Such admissions are usually painful, and you should be permitted to make personal sacrifices under any of the frameworks we have studied. They typically involve uncertainty and risk for the discloser; the opponent may ignore or even exploit such knowledge.

However, when the information concerns the opponent, the situation becomes murkier. Can you ethically publicize personal information about an opponent that would undermine his support or embarrass him in some way? If you obtained that information in confidence during the negotiations, you may not use it to do your opponent harm for your benefit. It would be permissible only if revealing the information would prevent a greater harm to others, such as disclosing evidence of criminal activity. If you did not obtain the information in confidence, the moral question would shift to one of intent: Would you be morally required to reveal the information if you and your opponent were not negotiating? In other words, your benefit in the revelation should not influence your decision.

The difference between taking risks for oneself and doing direct harm to another is best understood in the context of distributive justice. A key maxim is whether an action would increase or decrease the other's freedom. Risk taking and self-disclosure increase an opponent's options, so they are permissible. Harming him reduces his options, and thus requires other justification.

Strengthening One's Own Position

A host of tactics are designed to improve one's own position without doing direct harm to the opponent. Instead of involving lying, deception, or exaggeration, they entail ability, effort, and intelligence. Moreover, conceptually at least, they are available to all parties in a negotiation.

Again, distributive justice tells us inequalities are permitted as long as all parties have the opportunity to pursue them. If you work harder, train better, prepare more effectively, or create and follow a more successful strategy than your opponents, you have done them no direct harm. You are willing to permit them to do their best in preparation and execution. We are all permitted to improve ourselves; none of the four ethical frameworks deny self-improvement.

Under the Golden Rule, we are willing to permit others to strengthen themselves. According to utilitarianism, the net benefits of strengthening go to those who have done the best job—a "survival of the fittest" outcome. Under universalism, one can argue that preparation and discipline in execution actually enhance the dignity of one's opponent. To be well prepared is to show respect for the other; shoddy preparation is actually demeaning to the opponent.

Nondisclosure

We have determined that negotiators are ethically required to tell the truth—lying, deception, and exaggeration are wrong. But are they required to tell the *whole* truth? May a negotiator withhold factual information that could be of use to an opponent? The answer depends on the nature of the hidden truth.

If failure to disclose the truth would harm one's opponent, it would be unethical. Hiding a product or service defect or flaw that would mislead the other about the value of the item being bargained for would be wrong. If, to induce a potential buyer into paying a higher price, you fail to disclose a lien on property or a mechanical problem with an automobile you are attempting to sell, you are wrong. Just so, potential buyers who fail to disclose information revealing that they are, in fact, unlikely to be able to make payments on a purchase are acting unethically.

However, you are not required to disclose personal information that could be harmful to your case. You need not reveal that you are able and/or willing to pay far more for an item than the asking price. And you are not required to disclose your reservation price, although you are not permitted to lie about it.

Likewise, if you—as a buyer—suspect that the value of an offered item is greater than the asking price, you are not required to disclose that fact to the seller, presuming the seller has the competence to assess the value of the object. It would be wrong to take advantage of someone incapable of evaluating the worth of an object.

From a different perspective, are you permitted to disclose the true value of an object to a misinformed seller? Yes; there is nothing wrong with being more generous in a negotiation than you are morally required to be, as long as you are negotiating for yourself. However, if you are acting as an agent for another, you are required to obtain the best deal that is legally and ethically permissible, so you cannot disclose the true value.

Exploiting Information

Effective negotiators uncover information about themselves, their opponents, and the object of a negotiation during both the preparation phase and the negotiation itself. If that information is gained by legal and ethical means, no ethical proscription forbids a negotiator from using it. If you learn that your opponent *really* wants what you have to offer—in fact, values it more than he is disclosing—you are permitted to raise your asking price. If you learn that your opponent has fewer options than he suggests, thereby raising his valuation of what you have to offer, you may do likewise. As long as that information is legally and ethically accessible to both parties, you are permitted to use it to strengthen your position.

Are you permitted to use information obtained by illegal or unethical means? Certainly not if you had a hand in the unethical or illegal act—committed it yourself or induced someone else to commit it. But what if information so gained became public knowledge, and you had nothing to do with either the discovery or the publication of that information? Then you would be permitted to exploit it. Earlier, we concluded that one is not permitted to do direct harm to an opponent; however, if the harm has already been done by another, one may take advantage of it. If a police report of a burglary reveals that your opponent has a greater need or ability to pay for an item over which you are negotiating, you are permitted to use the information to your advantage. May you use it to defame your opponent, thereby decreasing his options or weakening his alliances? No, because that would be doing direct harm to him that would not be done without your action.

Change of Mind

Sometimes in the course of negotiations, something happens to alter the attraction of the object for one of the parties. The need is diminished or increased; an attractive alternative appears or vanishes; one's ability to pay is changed. May you abruptly change your negotiating position in light of these new circumstances? As long as you are not breaking a commitment or agreement, you are permitted to change your mind. You may decide to accept an offer you said you would never accept, or to pay a higher price than your original reservation price. If you intentionally lied about your reservation price, the act of lying was wrong. However, paying more than you said you would pay or accepting less than you said you would accept is not wrong—your act is doing no harm to your opponent; in fact, it benefits him.

May you withdraw an offer you have made? Yes, providing your withdrawal meets the legal requirements and the opponent has not accepted the offer. However, once the opponent has *accepted* an offer or commitment in any way, you may not ethically withdraw it even if it is legal to do so. Reneging on agreements is wrong from all standpoints. You would not wish others to do so to you. It does more harm than good, not only to your opponent but to the general level of trust among negotiators. And you certainly would not be willing to trade places with the person who accepted your offer.

Of course, you are permitted to ask an opponent to withdraw his acceptance of your offer or release you from your commitment because of changed circumstances. However, if he refuses to do so, then you are morally bound to your agreement.

Distraction

Negotiators are sometimes tempted to protect a weakness or conceal their interest in a particular issue by distracting their opponents. As long as the distractive tactic did not involve lying, puffery, or outright deception, is one ethically permitted to distract an opponent?

We concluded earlier that you need not disclose harmful information about yourself if the nondisclosure would do no harm to another. We can assume that the other is entitled to a fair outcome in the negotiation; however, he is not *entitled* to maximize his outcomes at your expense. He may attain them through his skill, your ineptitude, or other factors; you are not depriving him of his rights by limiting his outcomes to something between fair and maximization.

Distraction as a tactic does not reduce an opponent's options, according to distributive justice. It also provides him with information—if he is skilled enough to uncover it—about your perceptions of what *you* believe to be important and what you believe *he* considers to be important. If you evade answering certain questions, your opponent may learn that you do so to protect a weakness. Burying issues that you see as important or surrounding critical questions with questions you consider trivial reflect your own judgments. They may not be correct; they do not limit the opponent's options; they provide an opponent with opportunities to learn from them; they certainly involve risk on your part. Neither the Gold Rule nor universalism would prohibit distraction.

Maximization

Is it ethical to pursue your own payoffs at another's expense? Yes, but it depends on the manner in which the gain is pursued. Keep in mind that a negotiation has two facets. First, one side usually does not have the same goals as the other, yet both share a goal in that they want to have an exchange with the other side. A machine shop operator buying bolts from a manufacturer has a goal that differs from the manufacturer's. The operator wants a low price and the manufacturer seeks a high one. Yet they both want an exchange, because the machine shop operator needs bolts to produce machines and the manufacturer prefers money to an inventory of bolts.

In the negotiation exchange, the two sides usually bargain over a number of items. And the value of each item differs for each side. In the bolt negotiation, there might be four issues: antirust coating, bolt strength, delivery schedule, and method of payment. For the machine shop operator, the first two items would be very important. He needs antirust coating so that the bolts don't rust in inventory, and he must have strong bolts in order to produce high-quality machines. Because these two characteristics are important, he is willing to pay handsomely for them.

By contrast, the bolt manufacturer knows he can put an antirust coating on the bolts rather inexpensively, and, with some minor modifications of his production process, produce very strong bolts. Consequently, the bolts are of low cost to him. However, the delivery schedule is important to the manufacturer, as is the method of payment. Specifically, he would prefer to make deliveries when he is sending bolts to other customers in the city, and he wants the shop owner to use a standard invoicing system that cuts the amount of paperwork.

In this setting, it would be unethical for the manufacturer to maximize his own goals—at the machine shop owner's expense—on every item. To do so would violate the Golden Rule; he probably would not want the operator to behave in this manner. It violates the universalism criterion because it exploits the opponent; that is, it uses the opponent for the benefit of the negotiator rather than permitting the opponent, as well as the negotiator, to share adequately in the negotiation benefits. It also violates the utilitarianism criterion because this approach does not provide the greatest good to the greatest number. Rather, it forces the negotiation into a win–lose result and does not allow the two sides to improve their total joint benefit. Likewise, it violates the distributive justice criterion because everyone is not better off from this act.

How, then, should the negotiator bargain if all items are fixed sum ("My loss is your gain") and of equal value to the negotiator and opponent? The utilitarian criterion offers no guidance here because there is no variation in the total value; rather, all points have equal total value. Moreover, distributive justice provides modest instruction because everyone will not be better off in the various agreement points.

However, the universalism and Golden Rule criteria do assist us. The former dictates that the negotiator must consider the well-being of the opponent. Therefore, it posits that the negotiator can press his own interests up to the point at which the well-being of the opponent is endangered. The Golden Rule's dictate is consistent with this idea; the negotiator should pursue his own interests only as far as he would want the opponent to do so.

Applying Ethics to Negotiations: Oil on Water?

A cynic's retort to these evaluations might be "Ethics are fine in theory. I can negotiate ethically and sleep well at night, but I'll be hungry tomorrow, and next week." In other words, some might expect that ethical bargaining would lead to low payoffs, or no agreement, or one that costs them their job. How do we respond to that?

True, ethical bargaining does entail risks and sometimes seems to place a negotiator in a vulnerable position. Yet the ethical route, for operational as well as moral reasons, is the preferable one, because unethical negotiation has four major costs that are often overlooked:

- Rigidity in future negotiations.
- A damaged relationship with the opponent.
- A sullied reputation.
- Lost opportunities.

Rigid Negotiating

Even when it is successful, unethical behavior has a personal cost for negotiators. If their lies, deceptions, and puffery yield high-outcome agreements, they will repeat those behaviors in subsequent negotiations, because such actions have paid off. In addition, they will tend to attribute their success to such acts. Consequently, unethical negotiators will sacrifice some of their flexibility, creativity, and openness to others' ideas, thereby trapping themselves into a rigid bargaining approach that will eventually be matched by their opponents.

Keep in mind that unethical negotiating is not as advantageous as it may seem. One may lie about an alternative; but doesn't silence about an alternative prove as valuable as the lie? Wouldn't the comment "I'd better find another buyer" be just as potent as the statement "I've got another buyer"? Moreover, it is a wiser strategy to interrupt the negotiation, find another buyer, and let the original opponent know about it than to lie about already having another buyer.

Damaged Relationships

Unethical negotiation also mars the relationship between the two sides, causing emotional fallout (such as anger) as well as higher operational costs. When the negotiation is a single event—such as the sale of building materials—a negotiator who has been the victim of unethical behavior is less likely to implement the deal fully, perhaps not delivering all the materials. Or he will be less than cooperative when postagreement problems arise, such as if some of the building materials are defective or do not meet construction specifications.

When negotiations are of a repeated nature, the costs of unethical behavior mount. Today's bargainer becomes an embittered enemy rather than tomorrow's customer. Such an enemy might refuse to bargain with an unethical opponent, could return to the table with some open Machiavellian tactics of his own, or, more devastatingly, could voice no complaints but secretly seek revenge in the next round.

Sullied Reputation

Seldom do victims of unethical behavior hold their tongue, in public or across the bargaining table. At times, they are even apt to embellish. Thus an unethical reputation often permeates the business environment and precedes or accompanies its owner to the bargaining arena. Consequently, the opposing negotiator expects unethical behavior. A building contractor once commented about a subcontractor, "He'll lie to you, cheat you, steal from you, and then brag about it, if you give him a chance."

Once an opponent has experienced unethical behavior, he will prepare to counteract your unethical tactics in the future. Moreover, he will suspect that they are present, even if they are not. And often he will use them as excuses for his own obstinate behavior.

Lost Opportunities

The most detrimental effect of unethical behavior comes in the negotiation itself. The explanation for this is somewhat complex, but with assistance from a simple example it can be quickly understood: The essence of a productive negotiation is trading a *package* of issues in which each party concedes heavily on issues that are of low cost (or value) to it in return for major concessions on issues that are of high cost (or value) to it.

A company supplying tractor seats to John Deere probably finds that the cost of painting them green and packing them 10 to a carton for shipment is not very difficult. If Deere places high value on green seats packed 10 to a carton, it would be wise for the supplier to agree (or concede) on these issues. In turn, the firm could have John Deere—with its large storage facilities—accept the supplier's entire production run and store it until used. This concession would cost Deere quite little and would be a major benefit to a small company with limited storage facilities.

Most negotiations have manifold issues like these—namely, they are of low cost to one side and high value to the other. For the negotiators, the key is to find as many of these issues as possible and arrange trades among packages of them. In such trades, the first step is to determine which issues—of those currently under negotiation—have differential value to the two sides. To locate these, the parties must exchange valid information. If either side lies, deceives, or engages in puffery or distracts the other, it is very difficult, if not impossible, to determine the win–win trades, because the opponent does not receive accurate information. Moreover, the unethical behavior, if detected, motivates the opponent to withhold information (that he feels will be used against him) about the cost and values of the issues.

Not only does unethical behavior undermine the first step toward package trading, it also precludes the second: discovery of new issues. Productive negotiations are those that grow beyond the issues on the table. A simple expansion is one in which both sides agree on a two-year contract, even though the negotiation began with a one-year frame. A more complex expansion, taken from our earlier example, might be that Deere and its seat supplier jointly discover that Deere has vibration reduction expertise that the supplier could use in its production machines. And the supplier has discovered a method for mixing and applying paint that makes it highly chip-resistant—which Deere would no doubt find useful. With an open, trusting negotiation, the two sides probably would be able to ferret out the two new issues and, through some creative discussions, arrange a trade on these or explore the prices for each technology transfer.

Here the impact of unethical bargaining is clear. Not only does it undermine the negotiators' capabilities to reach win–win agreements on the current issues, it also interferes with discussions that would bring new, mutually profitable issues to the table.

Coming full circle, then, we agree with John Rutledge that ethical negotiation is not only morally right, it is frequently more profitable. Business men and women often feel they move into a different environment when they negotiate—one in which anything goes and the rules are understood by all players.

Yet negotiations today are not a separate function; they are an integral part of all business environments. Joint ventures, purchasing options, labor contracts, leasing agreements, salaries and benefits, day-to-day disputes, mergers, and spinoffs are all negotiated. And in such bargaining, ethical rules must apply. The four we have touched on—the Golden Rule, universalism, utilitarianism, and distributive justice—rule out several negotiation tactics, guide the use of some, and permit the use of others.

This guidance does not make negotiating easy. With their high stakes, complexity, deadlines, uncertainty, emotions, and stress, negotiations will always remain tough going. But those who take care to negotiate ethically should find the process better for them—personally, interpersonally, and economically.

References

Richard T. DeGeorge, *Business Ethics,* 4th ed. (New York: Prentice Hall, 1994).

Larue Tone Hosmer, *Moral Leadership in Business* (Burr Ridge, IL; Richard D. Irwin, 1994), Ch. 4.

J. C. Penney, *View from the Ninth Decade* (New York: Thomas Nelson & Sons, 1985).

John Rawls, *A Theory of Justice* (Cambridge, MA: Harvard University Press, 1971).

John Rutledge, "The Portrait on My Office Wall," *Forbes,* December 30, 1996, p. 78.

Reading 2.9
_____

Three Schools of Bargaining Ethics

G. Richard Shell

The three schools of bargaining ethics I want to introduce for your consideration are (1) the "It's a game" Poker School, (2) the "Do the right thing even if it hurts" Idealist School, and (3) the "What goes around, comes around" Pragmatist School.

Let's look at each one in turn. As I describe these schools, try to decide which aspects of them best reflect your own attitudes. After you figure out where you stand today, take a moment and see if that is where you ought to be. My advice is to aim as high as you can, consistent with your genuinely held beliefs about bargaining. In the pressured world of practice, people tend to slide down rather than climb up when it comes to ethical standards.

The "It's a Game" Poker School

The Poker School of ethics sees negotiation as a "game" with certain rules. The rules are defined by the law. Conduct within the rules is ethical. Conduct outside the rules is unethical.

The modern founder of the Poker School was Albert Z. Carr, a former special consultant to President Harry Truman. Carr wrote a book in the 1960s called, appropriately enough, *Business as a Game*. In a related article that appeared in the *Harvard Business Review,* Carr argued that bluffing and other misleading but lawful negotiating tactics are "an integral part of the [bargaining] game, and the executive who does not master [these] techniques is not likely to accumulate much money or power."

People who adhere to the Poker School readily admit that bargaining and poker are not exactly the same. But they point out that deception is essential to effective play in both arenas. Moreover, skilled players in both poker and bargaining exhibit a robust and realistic distrust of the other fellow. Carr argues that good players should ignore the "claims of friendship" and engage in "cunning deception and concealment" in fair, hard-bargaining encounters. When the game is over, members of the Poker School do not think less of a fellow player just because that person successfully deceived them. In fact, assuming the tactic was legal, they may admire the deceiver and vow to be better prepared (and less trusting) next time.

We know how to play poker, but how exactly does one play the bargaining "game"? Stripped to its core, it looks like this: Someone opens, and then people take turns proposing terms to each other. Arguments supporting your preferred terms are allowed. You can play or pass in each round. The goal is to get the other side to agree to terms that are as close as possible to your last proposal.

In the bargaining game, it is understood that both sides might be bluffing. Bluffs disguise a weak bargaining hand—that is, the limited or unattractive alternatives you

Source: From *Bargaining for Advantage: Negotiating Strategies for Reasonable People* by G. Richard Shell (New York: Penguin Books, 1999), pp. 215–22. Used by permission of Viking Penguin, a division of Penguin Group (USA) Inc.

have away from the table, your inability to affect the other side's alternatives, and the arguments you have to support your demands. Unlike poker players, negotiators always attempt to disclose a good hand if they have one in the bargaining game. So the most effective bluffs are realistic, attractive, difficult-to-check (but false) alternatives or authoritative (but false) supporting standards. Experienced players know this, so one of the key skills in the bargaining game is judging when the other party's alternatives or arguments are really as good as he or she says. If the other side calls you on your bargaining bluff by walking away or giving you a credible ultimatum, you lose. Either there will be no deal when there should have been one, or the final price will be nearer to their last offer than to yours.

As mentioned, the Poker School believes in the rule of law. In poker, you are not allowed to hide cards, collude with other players, or renege on your bets. But you are expected to deceive others about your hand. The best plays come when you win the pot with a weak hand or fool the other players into betting heavily when your hand is strong. In bargaining, you must not commit outright, actionable fraud, but negotiators must be on guard for anything short of fraud.

The Poker School has three main problems as I see it. First, the Poker School presumes that everyone treats bargaining as a game. Unfortunately, it is an empirical fact that people disagree on this. For a start, neither the idealists nor the pragmatists (more on these next) think bargaining is a game. This problem does not deter the Poker School, which holds that the rules permit its members to play even when the other party disagrees about this premise.

Second, everyone is supposed to know the rules cold. But this is impossible, given that legal rules are applied differently in different industries and regions of the world.

Finally, the law is far from certain even within a single jurisdiction. So you often need a sharp lawyer to help you decide what to do.

The "Do the Right Thing Even If It Hurts" Idealist School

The Idealist School says that bargaining is an aspect of social life, not a special activity with its own unique set of rules. The same ethics that apply in the home should carry over directly into the realm of negotiation. If it is wrong to lie or mislead in normal social encounters, it is wrong to do so in negotiations. If it is OK to lie in special situations (such as to protect another person's feelings), it is also OK to lie in negotiations when those special conditions apply.

Idealists do not entirely rule out deception in negotiation. For example, if the other party assumes you have a lot of leverage and never asks you directly about the situation as you see it, you do not necessarily have to volunteer information weakening your position. And the idealist can decline to answer questions. But such exceptions are uncomfortable moments. Members of the Idealist School prefer to be candid and honest at the bargaining table even if it means giving up a certain amount of strategic advantage.

The Idealist School draws its strength from philosophy and religion. For example, Immanuel Kant said that we should all follow the ethical rules that we would wish others to follow. Kant argued that if everyone lied all the time, social life would be chaos.

Hence you should not lie. Kant also disapproved of treating other people merely as the means to achieve your own personal ends. Lies in negotiation are selfish acts designed to achieve personal gain. This form of conduct is therefore unethical—period. Many religions also teach adherents not to lie for personal advantage.

Idealists admit that deception in negotiation rarely arouses moral indignation unless the lies breach a trust between friends, violate a fiduciary responsibility, or exploit people such as the sick or elderly, who lack the ability to protect themselves. And if the only way you can prevent some terrible harm like a murder is by lying, go ahead and lie. But the lack of moral outrage and the fact that sometimes lying can be defended do not make deception in negotiations right.

Idealists strongly reject the idea that negotiations should be viewed as "games." Negotiations, they feel, are serious, consequential communication acts. People negotiate to resolve their differences so social life will work for the benefit of all. People must be held responsible for all their actions, including the way they negotiate, under universal standards.

Idealists think that the members of the Poker School are predatory and selfish. For its part, the Poker School thinks that idealists are naive and even a little silly. When members of the two schools meet at the bargaining table, tempers can flare.

Some members of the Idealist School have recently been trying to find a philosophical justification for bluffs about bottom lines. There is no agreement yet on whether these efforts have succeeded in ethical terms. But it is clear that outright lies such as fictitious other offers and better prices are unethical practices under idealist principles.

The big problem for the idealists is obvious: Their standards sometimes make it difficult to proceed in a realistic way at the bargaining table. Also, unless adherence to the Idealist School is coupled with a healthy skepticism about the way other people will negotiate, idealism leaves its members open to exploitation by people with standards other than their own. These limitations are especially troublesome when idealists must represent others' interests at the bargaining table.

Despite its limitations, I like the Idealist School. Perhaps because I am an academic, I genuinely believe that the different parts of my life are, in fact, a whole. I aspire to ethical standards that I can apply consistently. I will admit that I sometimes fall short of idealism's strict code, but by aiming high I hope I am leaving myself somewhere to fall that maintains my basic sense of personal integrity.

I confess my preference for the Idealist School so you will know where I am coming from in this discussion. But I realize that your experience and work environment may preclude idealism as an ethical option. That's OK. As I hope I am making clear, idealism is not the only way to think about negotiation in ethical terms.

The "What Goes Around Comes Around" Pragmatist School

The final school of bargaining ethics, the Pragmatist School, includes some original elements as well as some attributes of the previous two. In common with the Poker School, this approach views deception as a necessary part of the negotiation process. Unlike the Poker School, however, it prefers not to use misleading statements and overt lies if there is a serviceable, practical alternative. Uniquely, the Pragmatist School displays concern for the potential negative effects of deceptive conduct on present and future relationships. Thus lying and other questionable tactics are bad not so much because they are "wrong" as because they cost the user more in the long run than they gain in the short run.

As my last comment suggests, people adhere to this school more for prudential than idealistic reasons. Lies and misleading conduct can cause serious injury to one's credibility. And credibility is an important asset for effective negotiators both to preserve working relationships and to protect one's reputation in a market or community. This latter concern is summed up in what I would call the pragmatist's credo: What goes around comes around. The Poker School is less mindful of reputation and more focused on winning each bargaining encounter within the rules of the "game."

What separates the Pragmatist School from the Idealist School? To put it bluntly, a pragmatist will lie a bit more often than will an idealist. For example, pragmatists sometimes draw fine distinctions between lies about hard-core facts of a transaction, which are always imprudent (and often illegal), and misleading statements about such things as the rationales used to justify a position. A pragmatic car salesman considers it highly unethical to lie about anything large or small relating to the mechanical condition of a used car he is selling. But this same salesman might not have a problem saying "My manager won't let me sell this car for less than $10,000" even though he knows the manager would sell the car for $9,500. False justification and rationales are marginally acceptable because they are usually less important to the transaction and much harder to detect as falsehoods than are core facts about the object being bought and sold.

Pragmatists are also somewhat looser within the truth when using so-called blocking techniques—tactics to avoid answering questions that threaten to expose a weak bargaining position. For example, can you ethically answer "I don't know" when asked about something you *do* know that hurts your position? An idealist would refuse to answer the question or try to change the subject, not lie by saying "I don't know." A pragmatist would go ahead and say "I don't know" if his actual state of knowledge is hard to trace and the lie poses little risk to his relationships.

The Ethical Schools in Action

As a test of ethical thinking, let's take a simple example. Assume you are negotiating to sell a commercial building and the other party asks you whether you have another offer. In fact, you do not have any such offers. What would the three schools recommend you do?

A Poker School adherent might suggest a lie. Both parties are sophisticated businesspeople in this deal, so a lie about alternatives is probably legally "immaterial." But a member of the Poker School would want to know the answers to two questions before making his move.

First, could the lie be easily found out? If so, it would be a bad play because it wouldn't work and might put the other side on guard with respect to other lies he might want to tell. Second, is a lie about alternatives the best way to leverage the buyer into making a bid? Perhaps a lie about something else—a deadline, for example—might be a better choice.

Assuming the lie is undetectable and will work, how might the conversation sound?

BUYER: Do you have another offer?

POKER SCHOOL SELLER: Yes. A Saudi Arabian firm presented us with an offer for $_____ this morning, and we have only 48 hours to get back to it with an answer. Confidentiality forbids us from showing you the Saudi offer, but rest assured that it is real. What would you like to do?

How would an idealist handle this situation? There are several idealist responses, but none would involve a lie. One response would be the following:

BUYER: Do you have another offer?

IDEALIST SELLER 1: An interesting question—and one I refuse to answer.

Of course, that refusal speaks volumes to the buyer. Another approach would be to adopt a policy on "other buyer" questions:

BUYER: Do you have another offer?

IDEALIST SELLER 2: An interesting question, and one I receive quite often. Let me answer you this way. The property's value to you is something for you to decide based on your needs and your own sense of the market. However, I treat all offers with the greatest confidence. I will not discuss an offer you make to me with another buyer, and I would not discuss any offer I received from someone else with you. Will you be bidding?

Of course, this will work for an idealist only if he or she really and truly has such a policy—a costly one when there is another attractive offer he or she would like to reveal.

A final idealist approach would be to offer an honest, straightforward answer. An idealist cannot lie or deliberately mislead, but he is allowed to put the best face he can on the situation that is consistent with the plain truth:

BUYER: Do you have another offer?

IDEALIST SELLER 3: To be honest, we have no offers at this time. However, we are hopeful that we will receive other offers soon. It might be in your interest to bid now and take the property before competition drives the price up.

How about the pragmatists? They would suggest using somewhat more sophisticated, perhaps even deceptive, blocking techniques. These techniques would protect their leverage in ways that were consistent with maintaining working relationships. Once again, assume that the buyer has asked the "other offer" question and there are no other offers. Here are five ways a pragmatist might suggest you block this question to avoid an out-and-out factual lie about other offers while minimizing the damage to your leverage. Some of these blocking techniques would work for idealists, too:

- *Declare the question out of bounds:* "Company policy forbids any discussion of other offers in situations like this"—note that, if untrue, this is a lie, but it is one that carries less risk to your reputation because it is hard to confirm. If there really is such a company policy, an idealist could also use this move to block the question.

- *Answer a different question:* "We will not be keeping the property on the market much longer because the market is moving and our plans are changing." Again, if untrue, this statement is a mere lie about a "rationale" that troubles pragmatists less than idealists.

- *Dodge the question:* "The more important question is whether we are going to get an offer from you—and when."

- *Ask a question of your own:* "What alternatives are you examining at this time?"

- *Change the subject:* "We are late for our next meeting already. Are you bidding today or not?"

Blocking techniques of this sort serve a utilitarian purpose. They preserve some leverage (though not as much as the Poker School) while reducing the risk of acquiring a reputation for deception. Relationships and reputations matter. If there is even a remote chance of a lie coming back to haunt you in a future negotiation with either the person you lie to or someone he may interact with, the pragmatists argue that you should not do it.

So—which school do you belong to? Or do you belong to a school of your own such as "pragmatic idealism"? To repeat: My advice is to aim high. The pressure of real bargaining often makes ethical compromisers of us all. When you fall below the standard of the Poker School, you are at serious risk of legal and even criminal liability.

Reading 2.10

Deception and Mutual Gains Bargaining: Are They Mutually Exclusive?

Raymond A. Friedman
Debra L. Shapiro

In the interest of being fair, a prospective car buyer goes to a car dealership with price-related information obtained from objectively valid sources, such as the American Automobile Association, *Consumer Reports,* and the "book" value (which reflects the car's model, year, and mileage). The car salesperson expresses an interest in reducing inventory *today* and the prospective buyer indicates that is possible, if they can agree on a price that is fair. The two parties share information regarding price-related criteria and their respective priorities with regard to car features, payment terms, and service-related concerns. In so doing, they learn that they have complementary needs, and only the issue of price seems competing (since the seller and buyer want a higher and lower price, respectively). Differences regarding price, however, seem resolvable when the parties focus their conversation on their mutual interests, these being a fair price and a long-term, car service–based relationship. Two hours later, the parties have reached an agreement—at a price both deem fair.

The above scenario describes two parties engaged in problem-solving behaviors, such as focusing on being fair, basing proposals on objective (neutral) criteria, sharing information regarding priorities, discussing more than one issue as a means for determining possible concessionary trade-offs, and focusing on their shared interests, which results in a mutually satisfying agreement. This is a description of what has become commonly known as "integrative," "win–win," or "mutual gains" bargaining, or MGB (see, e.g., Walton and McKersie 1965; Fisher and Ury 1981; Susskind and Cruikshank 1987)

How would we characterize this scenario if the buyer was deceptive during the exchange—for example, by referring to a lower price obtainable from another, phantom dealership? Would such a tactic be considered distributive (win–lose) negotiation? No, because even in light of the deception created by referring to a nonexistent alternative, the car buyer and the salesperson have engaged in an exchange that is predominantly mutual gains bargaining. The modifier "predominantly" highlights the fact that the bargaining situation is *not* purely integrative. Indeed, many theorists have argued that no bargaining situation is purely integrative or purely distributive, and thus all are "mixed-motive" (Lax and Sebenius 1986; Stevens 1963; Raiffa 1982; Walton and McKersie 1965).

Because of this duality, we believe negotiators can practice integrative bargaining effectively, even when this strategy includes deception (for example, the car buyer's phantom dealership). Yet negotiation scholars and trainers may leave the impression instead that anyone who wishes to be deceptive cannot engage in integrative bargaining,

Source: Raymond A. Friedman and Debra L. Shapiro, "Deception and Mutual Gains Bargaining: Are They Mutually Exclusive?" *Negotiation Journal,* July 1995, Blackwell Publishers, Ltd.

or MGB—that is, MGB and deception are presented as mutually exclusive. We arrived at this conclusion after a discussion among negotiation scholars at a recent national academic conference regarding what is ethical and unethical behavior in negotiations and what we should be teaching students in our courses on negotiations. About an hour into the discussion, someone suggested that, in pursuit of being ethical teachers and promoting ethical behavior on the part of students, we should teach students integrative bargaining tactics only, and not traditional distributive bargaining tactics. This proposal created quite a debate among those attending, and an ensuing vote among the scholars showed that an overwhelming majority favored the proposal.

The turn of events was, for us, a great cause for concern. Should integrative bargaining really be promoted based on ethical arguments? Should we automatically label distributive bargaining as unethical? We were concerned because this equating of ethics and integrative, or mutual gains, bargaining had a familiar ring to it. In both training sessions and classrooms, it is not uncommon for MGB to be confused with being good, ethical, or nice. Moreover, confounding ethics and MGB can have negative effects—on our ability to understand ethical conventions in traditional negotiations, and on our ability to teach and implement MGB.

In this article, our goal is to clarify the *distinction* between ethics and MGB. In particular, our focus is on the one bargaining strategy—deception—that triggers many ethical discussions (Blodgett 1968; Lewicki 1983). We believe that negotiation teachers and trainers should be careful to keep ethics and integrative bargaining separate. It is obviously important to teach about ethics in bargaining, including the issue of deception, and to teach about integrative bargaining, but these are separate issues—both in theory and practice.

Ethically Ambiguous Tactics

Many commonly used or taught negotiation tactics are fraught with ethical concerns. The types of tactics that are most often cited as being ethically ambiguous are ones involving deception (Dees and Cramton 1993; Carr 1968; Lewicki 1983; Shapiro and Bies 1994). For example, when a manufacturer is negotiating the price of a part, and no other supplier is available at the time, she or he would refrain from sharing that fact during negotiations. In addition to hiding this information, the manufacturer would probably try to lead the other side to believe that there were many suppliers to choose from, either by saying so explicitly or making statements that imply this. Negotiators commonly hide their true level of dependency, and commonly exaggerate the value of their options in the event of no agreement, their willingness and ability to choose other options, and the likelihood that their constituents (whose supposed demands may even be fabricated) will disapprove of concessions under discussion.

In such situations, the negotiator's goal is to shift the opponent's perception of the zone of possible agreement in one's favor. When this is done well, the opponent is left to decide whether s/he would rather risk having no agreement, or give in to the demands that have been made. Since the opponent has the same goal, if one listens to what is said early in the negotiations one might believe that there is no zone of possible agreement at all when in fact there may be. The process of negotiating is at its core a process of shaping perceptions of reality (Berger and Luckman 1967). Deceptive tactics like hiding or exaggerating information often shape the perception of negotiators' power, which some have identified to be the most critical perception of all (Bacharach and Lawler 1988).[1]

Whether these behaviors are ethical is a great source of debate. People with absolutist moral positions might argue that misleading others is unethical in general and therefore should not be used in the context of bargaining. A more tolerant approach is to say that we should not do things that are acknowledged to be socially unacceptable. Using the test of whether people would want their actions told to their mother (Murnighan 1993) or described in a newspaper (Lax and Sebenius 1986), many would find it embarrassing for others to know that they acted deceptively. Others might counter that whether deception is considered ethical or not depends on the context, not the act of deceiving. For example, if one is negotiating with terrorists for the release of hostages and lives could be saved through deception, many would say the use of deception was ethical. Or if one is acting as a negotiator for a relatively powerless community group trying to block the construction of a toxic waste dump, deception may be one of the few ways to create a balance of power in the negotiations, especially if the dump's owner has a history of misrepresenting data about the effects of toxins on drinking water. The ethically good "end" thus justifies the use of deception in some negotiation situations.

These are complex issues that are difficult to resolve on a philosophical level. It is not our goal in this article to make a definitive statement about the ethics of deceptive negotiating tactics. Rather, we shall examine the relationship between ethically ambiguous behaviors in negotiations and the use of MGB in negotiations. Our contention is that it is easy to confuse MGB with behaviors that are ethically pure, and that doing so may actually make it harder to teach MGB or get people to use it.

Mutual Gains Bargaining and Ethical Claims

MGB is an approach that helps negotiators produce the greatest joint gains possible. As noted earlier, it is also called "integrative bargaining" or "win–win" or "principled" negotiation, and is often contrasted with "distributive" bargaining—that is, bargaining that is zero-sum or focused on getting more for oneself by forcing the opponent to take less. As explained by Fisher and Ury (1981), MGB is based on four principles: separating the people from the problem; focusing on interests, not positions; inventing options for mutual gain; and insisting on objective criteria.

There is nothing in these principles that directly addresses the issue of ethical behavior or deceptive tactics. However, there are several ways in which these principles can be inadvertently related to ethical behavior and trainees may come to believe that the primary reason for MGB is that it is more "honest" than traditional negotiations. It is possible that some trainers do frame MGB as the more ethical way to bargain, or that the "principled" and "mutual gains" labels themselves convey that message to trainees. More importantly, the connection between MGB and ethics may come from more deep-seated and fundamental misunderstandings of the ideas of MGB, especially the difference between interests and positions.

MGB suggests that negotiators explain to their opponent what their *interests* are, so that the opponent can propose actions that meet one's real needs at least cost. It does not, however, say anything about revealing one's alternatives to a negotiated agreement, what one's true reservation price is, or how much money is in the bargaining budget—all of which influence what final *position* will be acceptable. The problem is that the distinction is difficult for many negotiators to understand; even for trainers, the line between the two is frequently not completely clear. In fact, the distinction represents more of a continuum than an absolute difference. For example, a "5 percent pay raise" is a position in that it is one way to achieve the interest of "a better quality of life." From another perspective, it is an interest that may be achieved in various ways (such as 3 percent base wage increase and a 2 percent lump sum or via other "positions"). Therefore, some will tend to hear the MGB prescriptions as saying "reveal everything about oneself." MGB says only that you should not deceive the other party about your core, underlying interests. And—this is worth emphasizing—the reason for this prescription is not that being honest about interests is inherently ethical. Rather, it is that being honest about your interests can help you get more. If others do not know what really matters to you, they cannot help search for ways to meet your needs that are feasible for them.

Confusion is also likely to the degree that MGB is framed as an alternative to distributive bargaining. For pedagogical reasons it may be necessary at some stage of training to present MGB as a completely different model for negotiations, but few scholars would presume that many negotiations are wholly integrative. Rather, most negotiations are "mixed motive" (Stevens 1963); they include both opportunities for joint gain, and opportunities for grabbing more from the other side. Walton and McKersie (1965) call this the integrative and distributive dimensions of negotiation, while Lax and Sebenius (1986) write of the distinction between creating and claiming value in negotiation. There is indeed a tension between the two: strategies that are wise for creating are often opposite from those that are wise for claiming (e.g., deception about positions and power is necessary for claiming, while deception about interests is disruptive for creating). But all negotiations include both elements, and few negotiations occur where a wise negotiator would not employ at least some of each set of behaviors. Indeed, one of the more interesting challenges faced by negotiators is how to balance both of these elements.

Pruitt and Lewis (1977) have argued that the two approaches appear in the same negotiation by means of separating creating and claiming into distinct phases of the process, or by having different individuals on bargaining teams engage in creating or claiming. More recently, Friedman (1994) has argued that the two approaches coexist by having separate "stages" for each. While distributive tactics and deception occur front stage, integrative tactics and honest communication about interests occur backstage. In public, labor negotiators engage in a great deal of bravado, exaggeration, hiding, and, in general, attempts to deceive the other about what they want, what they are willing to accept, and what they are willing to fight over. But out of public view, negotiators engage in a well-understood process of signaling to opponents, discounting information, and engaging in private sidebar meetings to clarify interests.

In sum, MGB does teach negotiators not to deceive the opponent—about their interests. But it makes this suggestion based on effectiveness, not ethics. And it does not presume that all parts of negotiations are integrative—there is a domain for distributive bargaining in most negotiations. This distinction can be easily lost if the interest–position distinction is not made clear, or if teachers express a preference for MGB because of its higher ethical status.

If, in these ways, ethics and MGB become conflated, several problems can occur. First, negotiators may miss the distinctions between ethical and unethical behavior that exist in traditional negotiation. Second, they may misunderstand the true benefits that MGB provides. And third, they may perceive MGB as naive and therefore avoid using it.

Ethical Conventions in Labor Negotiations

Equating MGB with ethics overlooks the fact that there are ethical constraints on deception in traditional negotiations. We can see this by looking at the example of labor negotiations. During a study of labor negotiations (Friedman 1994), the first author studied 13 negotiations, including direct observations of eight cases and over 150 interviews, and in addition interviewed 19 experienced labor negotiators. The negotiators in that study talked extensively about their relationships with opponents and the kinds of tactics that they used and expected others to use. From these interviews and observations, it became clear that professional labor negotiators have a definite sense, in practice, of what is appropriate and inappropriate behavior. Experienced labor negotiators expect that opponents will hide information and try to build up false perceptions about their limits and determination. Negotiators on both sides expect their opponents to have "laundry lists" of demands, put exaggerated financial offers on the table, declare that constituents will not accept less, say that they and their constituents could and would weather a strike, and even put on displays of anger and resolve to show how tough they will be in defense of these demands.

Nonetheless, some types of deception are beyond the pale. The same negotiators who expressed tolerance for some levels of deception also reported that there was a limit to what was acceptable. Overtly inaccurate statements are considered unethical (and unprofessional) by lead bargainers. It is acceptable and expected for the company to say "we cannot pay a penny more for health care," while it is unacceptable to say "adding physical therapy to the benefit package will cost us an additional $100 a year per employee" when it is known that it would only add $20 a year. The first statement is a general claim that can be readily interpreted as a bargaining stance; the latter is a factual claim that is either true or false. The first type of statement would be considered "bargaining" by experienced labor negotiators, and those who do it with cleverness and gusto are respected as savvy and skilled. The latter type of statement would be considered a lie, and the bargainer who was caught in such a lie would be deemed unprofessional and untrustworthy. In addition, for these negotiators it makes a difference if either statement is made in private between lead bargainers or in public across the main table. What is said across the table is expected to be exaggerated and not fully accurate; what is said in private is expected to be accurate. To claim inaccurately that the company cannot spend one penny more on health care across the table is expected and not deemed unethical; to make that same false claim in private would produce outrage if the lie was discovered.

Underlying this distinction is an understanding that some statements are *expected* to be untrue, while others are not. When negotiators make statements that are expected to be untrue, the other negotiators are able to make appropriate adjustments, calculations, and predictions. These statements are interpreted, discounted, and treated with caution (Friedman 1994). Negotiators anticipate that these statements are made as bargaining stances, open to change, or that they are positions that need to be stated to look good to constituents and teammates. By contrast, when one negotiator makes statements that are expected to be true, the other party proceeds to act on them; this information is often represented to constituents as true, and major decisions are made based on it. The consequences of deception in those situations can be great: there might be an unnecessary strike, the negotiators could be hurt professionally if constituents find out that they were duped, and negotiators' ability to count on some truthful communication between the two sides is eliminated and their ability to manage the negotiations wisely is greatly diminished.

The ethical conventions that are common among labor negotiators ensure that both deception and honesty can occur, and that there is a common understanding of when and how deception is limited. These conventions are based not on some abstract moralism, but a very practical concern for enabling the negotiators to do their jobs, negotiate well for their side, and avoid an unnecessary strike. Negotiators still try to indicate that their side will stand tough against the opponent, and they still try to deceive (as one labor lawyer put it, even in sidebar meetings "I don't put all my cards on the table"). But there is also much trust and communication between opponents, particularly the lead bargainers. This lessens the personal nature of the conflict and makes the integrative bargaining possible. While these negotiators would never want to be completely honest with their opponents, they do place limits on deception and will withdraw cooperation from those who cross the line.

The example from labor relations shows that there are ethical constraints on negotiations, regardless of whether one mentions mutual gains bargaining. And it shows that these ethical constraints operate despite the acknowledged presence of deception during much of negotiations. What might appear logically as mutually exclusive behaviors—being honest and deceiving—are not so in practice.

Thus there are reasons to engage in both deception *and* honesty in negotiations, and there are enormous risks associated with either a purely honest or purely deceptive strategy. And negotiators have developed mechanisms to engage in both strategies. This mixture of tactics works exactly because negotiators recognize the need for both tactics, because the divide between them is well understood, and because an ethical system exists that ensures that negotiators act honestly when expected to and that keeps deception within some practical limit.

Putting the MGB Message in Context

If the message of mutual gains bargaining is not that integrative tactics alone should be used or that deception should be completely precluded, and if integrative tactics (including prohibitions against deception during integrative phases of negotiations) already exist in most negotiations, why have MGB training? We can identify three primary benefits to teaching MGB that do not depend on the "do-not-ever-be-deceptive" message. First, MGB training can help inexperienced trainees to discover that there is an integrative—and not only a distributive—side to bargaining. This discovery is especially likely among negotiators who may have been exposed only to the more public, high-conflict aspects of bargaining.

Second, MGB can help negotiators anticipate times when their emotions make them forget what they know about integrative bargaining, and focus only on distributive bargaining. In this way, emotionally triggered escalation traps are made less likely (Pruitt and Rubin 1986). Although professional bargainers usually know how to keep their emotions under control and "focus on the problem not the person," less experienced bargainers may not be as well prepared for the pressures of bargaining. And there may be times when relations between the two sides have become so difficult that even experienced bargainers have a difficult time sustaining the integrative side to bargaining that they know should exist. Third, MGB can encourage negotiators to be integrative bargainers somewhat more than they traditionally are. More specifically, MGB training may help negotiators to lengthen the phase of negotiations that is more integrative, or to include more people in the backstage arena where integrative bargaining is done. While not eliminating hard bargaining or telling negotiators to give up the deceptive tactics that are central to hard bargaining, MGB training may be able to shift the balance somewhat toward integrative bargaining.

The Dangers of Naive MGB Training

Not only is the "do-not-ever-deceive" message unnecessary in MGB training, it may also reduce the effectiveness of the training. The message "do-not-ever-deceive" does not recognize the fact that, even when integrative bargaining works well, there is still a need to engage in distributive tactics, nor the fact that being completely honest about one's fall-back positions can diminish one's power. For these distributive elements of negotiations, tactics such as hiding information and shaping impressions are often necessary and do work. To teach that negotiators should abandon all impression management tactics would be unwise from an analytic perspective, would make the teacher appear naive, and would ensure that the MGB approach would be seen as damaging to one's negotiating goals.

Moreover, these costs are not necessary; practicing mutual gains bargaining does not require that negotiators make themselves vulnerable through comprehensive revelations about their situation. It says only that it makes no sense to deceive the opponent about one's *interests*. Finally, to the degree that trainers signal an ethical priority (or allow trainees to read that into the training), trainees have a more difficult time seeing that MGB helps people to negotiate *smarter* and get better results. While some may believe that MGB helps make negotiations more ethical, that is unlikely to generate among trainees a true commitment to understand and use the MGB lessons.

That is not to say, however, that there are no ethical constraints. MGB does not free negotiators to be deceptive in ways that are traditionally unacceptable. If one is found to have lied, that would be a source of distrust during negotiations, it would engender uncooperative behavior by the opponent, and it would make him or her less likely to engage in integrative bargaining—with or without MGB training. To the degree that we might encourage people to use MGB techniques, or at least not to do less of it, negotiators should stay within commonly understood norms of acceptable behavior.

Misrepresentations that cross the line have been found to interfere with negotiators' willingness to use MGB (Friedman 1993), just as those that cross the line make backstage interactions more difficult in traditional negotiations.

Recommendations for Teaching MGB

From this analysis we suggest that those who teach mutual gains bargaining make clear that the benefits of MGB are practical, not ethical. Operationally, this means that MGB trainers may wish to consider the following three suggestions:

1. Given the degree to which it is easy for students to read into MGB training the message that they should "do MBG because it seems 'nicer' or more 'ethical,'" special care must be taken to highlight the practical benefits of MGB and to avoid moralistic statements that enhance this misreading.

2. Since MGB does encourage disclosure of one's interests, special care must be taken to clarify the distinction between interests and positions. Only then will it be possible for students to see that revealing one aspect of what a bargainer knows (i.e., his or her interests) does not imply that all information about one's strategies and fall-back positions must be revealed.

3. MGB teachers and trainers should also teach their students about tough bargaining tactics, including deception, and acknowledge that there are benefits to hard bargaining. Moreover, students need to understand the "mixed motives" of negotiations and the need to be prepared for both integrative and distributive aspects of bargaining.

This advice does not mean that teachers should not teach ethics in bargaining. It is extremely valuable for students to evaluate both the ethical and practical costs of crossing the line. They need to understand what actions constitute fraud from a legal point of view (see, e.g., Shell 1991) and what actions are considered among negotiators to be excessive misrepresentation or lying. They also need to consider the effects that unethical behaviors can have on trust, and the effects that lack of trust can have on one's ability to negotiate effectively and one's ability to maintain a relationship with the opponent after negotiations are over. Teaching the effects of unethical behavior in negotiation does not require negotiation trainers to confuse MGB (and an understanding of the techniques and logic of integrative bargaining) with ethical concerns, nor does it require efforts to preclude all types of deception in negotiations. Indeed, we believe confusing ethics and MGB threatens a teacher's ability to teach effectively and to obtain a commitment to using MGB principles in practice. Such confusion diminishes the positive impact that MGB can otherwise have.

Conclusion

We have made great strides in recent years teaching more people—in classrooms, corporate training sessions, and actual negotiations—about negotiations, including how to be more ethical and how to ensure that integrative joint gains are not left on the table.

The fact that we even need to write an article like this is an indication of the advances that have been made.

Yet exactly because of these advances, more care needs to be taken to ensure that the subtle distinction between what is ethical and what is integrative is maintained. Being ethical in negotiations is more complicated than producing greater joint utility, and the techniques that are helpful for producing greater joint utility should not be made more complicated by the addition of ethical concerns. Each issue—ethics and mutual gains bargaining—can stand on its own, and benefits by being considered on its own. By maintaining this distinction, we believe each will have greater clarity and greater impact, and our teaching and training will be both better received and more valuable to those we teach.

Notes

1. Negotiators can actually reshape reality itself, not just perceptions of it. This is done by taking actions that really do tie one's hands so that compromise is impossible. Such commitment tactics are discussed by Schelling (1960) and Raiffa (1982). These tactics are not considered in this article since they are not instances of deception.

References

Bacharach, S. B., and E. J. Lawler. 1988. *Bargaining: Power, tactics, and outcomes.* San Francisco: Jossey-Bass.

Berger, P. I., and T. Luckman. 1967. *The social construction of reality.* Garden City, NY: Anchor Books.

Carr, A. Z. 1968. Is business bluffing ethical? *Harvard Business Review,* January–February, pp. 143–50.

Dees, J. Gregory, and P. Cramton. 1993. Promoting honesty in negotiations: An exercise in practical ethics. *Business Ethics Quarterly* 3(4), pp. 44–61.

Fisher, R., and W. L. Ury. 1981. *Getting to yes. Negotiating agreement without giving in.* Boston: Houghton Mifflin.

Friedman, R. A. 1994. *Front stage, backstage: The dramatic structure of labor negotiations.* Cambridge, MA: MIT Press.

_____. 1993. Bringing mutual gains bargaining to labor negotiations: The role of trust, understanding, and control. *Human Resource Management Journal* 32(4), pp. 435–59.

Lax, D. A., and J. K. Sebenius. 1986. *The manager as negotiator.* New York: Free Press.

Lewicki, R. 1993. Comments presented as part of the symposium "Ethical dilemmas in negotiating and getting people to 'yes.'" Conflict Management Division, National Academy of Management meeting, Atlanta.

_____. 1983. Lying and deception. In *Negotiating in organizations,* edited by M. H. Bazerman and R. J. Lewicki. Beverly Hills, CA: Sage.

Murninghan, K. 1993. Comments presented as part of the preconference workshop "Ethical dilemmas in negotiating and getting people to 'yes.'" Conflict Management Division, National Academy of Management meeting, Atlanta.

Pruitt, D. G., and S. A. Lewis. 1977. The psychology of integrative bargaining. In *Negotiations: Social psychological perspectives,* edited by D. Druckman. London: Sage.

Pruitt, D. G., and J. Z. Rubin. 1986. *Social conflict: Escalation, stalemate, and settlement.* New York: Random House.

Raiffa, H., 1982. *The art and science of negotiation.* Cambridge, MA: Harvard University Press.

Shapiro, D. I., and R. J. Bies. 1994. Threats, bluffs, and disclaimers in negotiation. *Organization Behavior and Human Decision Processes* 60, pp. 14–35.

Shell, R. 1991. When is it legal to lie in negotiations? *Sloan Management Review* 32(3), pp. 78–94.

Schelling, T. C. 1960. *The strategy of conflict.* Cambridge, MA: Harvard University Press.

Stevens, C. 1963. *Strategy and collective bargaining negotiations.* New York: McGraw Hill.

Susskind, I., and J. Cruikshank. 1987. *Breaking the impasse.* New York: Basic Books.

Walton, R. E., and R. B. McKersie. 1965. *A behavioral theory of labor negotiations: An analysis of a social interaction system.* New York: McGraw Hill.

Negotiation Contexts

Reading 3.1

Can We Negotiate and Still Be Friends?

Terri Kurtzberg
Victoria Husted Medvec

You have finally decided to indulge your midlife fantasy and buy yourself a sports car. Knowing that this car is not all that practical, you're considering buying a secondhand one. You have been scouting the car lots and scouring the want ads when you hear that one of your colleagues from work is selling a cherry-red, five-year-old sports car. Red isn't your top choice for color (it seems a little splashy) but you could live with it, and other than the color, this could be perfect: You know that your colleague is the type of person who would have taken care of the car. Before discussing the idea of buying this car, however, you hesitate; somehow, it seems like it might be uncomfortable to negotiate the price of the car with your friend. You don't exactly know why, but your instincts are telling you to call the used car salesman. Why would you rather negotiate with a used car salesman—whom you don't trust—than negotiate with someone with whom you share a trusting relationship?

In this essay we want to explore why people may prefer to negotiate with a stranger rather than risk harming a relationship by negotiating with a friend. Do people want to separate their negotiations from their social relationships? This paper summarizes a discussion of these topics at the January 1999 Hewlett Conference, held at Northwestern University's Kellogg Graduate School of Management. We propose a two-pronged approach to analyzing the interplay between negotiations and relationships: namely, that relationships can be affected by the negotiation process, and that the negotiation process itself (i.e., the fundamental dynamics and assumption in a negotiation) can be altered by the relationship between the parties involved.

Relationships Affect Negotiations

Social relationships are an integral part of every human interaction. When the parties know each other outside of the negotiation context, the negotiation takes on an emotional overtone that can, depending on how it is dealt with, either help or hurt the process. Previous research has looked at the cost of having a bad relationship on the negotiation

Source: Terri Kurtzberg and Victoria Medvec, "Can We Negotiate and Still be Friends?" *Negotiation Journal,* October 1999, Kluwer Academic/Plenum Publishers.

process by examining what happens when trust is broken and conflict spirals out of control (Ross and LaCroix 1996; Bies and Tripp 1996; Lewicki and Bunker 1995 and 1996; Pruitt 1981). While discussion at this conference generally focused on the positive effects of relationships on negotiation, we in our session focused on the limits of these benefits and asked the question, When is it a problem to negotiate with a friend?

Negotiators may pay more attention to their behaviors and may monitor their words and actions for standards of trust and fairness when negotiating with a friend rather than a stranger. Even unconsciously, speech, gesture, and tone can all signal relationship cues that can affect the negotiation process. Generally, as described in the scenario that opens this brief report, our intuition often warns us to steer clear of these situations, since the potential risk to the friendship seems to far outweigh the potential gain to be had through negotiating in a trusting manner.

People in any society carry around "scripts" for every context as to what constitutes appropriate behavior. When we go to a restaurant, we know to wait to be seated, to look at a menu, to select a meal. Similarly, we know how to act with friends, including which behaviors are acceptable and which are not. We have yet another script for how to act in a negotiation situation: don't tell the other side too much about your other offers, but do look for ways to trade off issues to the benefit of both sides. Try to grow the pie, while also trying to claim as much of the pie as possible for oneself.

Negotiating within a preexisting relationship can cause these scripts to clash; friendship dictates that we should be concerned with fairness and the other person's welfare, while negotiations dictate that we should get a good deal for ourselves. For example, when you're selling a car to a friend, are you really "selling a car *to a friend*" or are you "*selling a car* to a friend"? Which script takes priority? These conflicting scripts point us to a key issue: It can be difficult to assess appropriate behavior when negotiating with a friend.

Friendship scripts may lead to a new set of "appropriate" negotiation behaviors. For example, people who feel like they received too good a deal from a friend may insist on giving gifts in return to "even the score." Here the conflicting priority is between friendship and money. In the "friendship world," money is only important in that it can help promote caring. Thus, when we do sell a car to a friend, we sell it at a lower price and assume a contract of responsibility instead of creating the highest-value deal. Relationship norms and scripts may limit the amount of surplus we can create in a negotiated agreement.

One way around this potential pitfall is for negotiators to change the dialogue and labels associated with negotiation when in a friendship context. For example, it is not uncommon in a negotiation context to hear someone say that what they are doing and asking for is "just business," meaning that nobody should interpret the behaviors in a personal way, or one which relates to the relationship of the parties involved. Yet successful people constantly remind us that good business sense is rooted in good relationship sense, and that the best businesspeople always return their phone calls first, signaling their priority on maintaining positive relationships.

Relationships are not always on equal footing, however. Some types of relationships, such as mentoring and parenting, are designed around teaching and caring, instead of reciprocity. This may create an entirely new dynamic when it comes to negotiations, because the scripts for appropriate behavior are unique to this context. For example, the teaching assistant strikes that occurred recently at some U.S. universities came with a lot of very bad feelings because the mentoring relationship does not include an easy forum for the student to make demands on the mentor. This, like a discussion of sacred values, establishes the bonds of a relationship and demonstrates how negotiations in these situations can sometimes create discord and break down.

Clearly, relationships play many important psychological roles in the minds of negotiators. Even when focusing on the larger-scale relationships between and among countries, organizations, or other large groups of the population, the dynamics that motivate us to consider and maintain a relationship as an important goal in a negotiation process will alter how we approach and proceed with a negotiation.

Measuring the Effects of Friendship on the Negotiation

How can we even tell what the outcome effects are in these friendship–negotiation instances? In terms of newly formed relationships, there are many approaches to measuring these effects on negotiated outcomes. For example, one way to assess the success and quality of a newly formed relationship on the negotiation outcomes is by examining the salesperson–customer interaction. Future sales from a particular salesperson to a particular customer can be an indication of the quality of the relationship that has been established initially in this dyad. Another example involves the judgments made by people in terms of discounting future events for the sake of current events. This could be a measure of relationship strength by showing that the more connected a negotiator feels with someone who has a future stake in the deal on the table, the more they might take that future stake into account in their own actions, decisions, and concessions. In this way, researchers can measure the value that a negotiator places on the future based on present relationships.

In the case of longer-term relationships that exist prior to negotiations, there are both benefits and risks associated with negotiating with a friend to the value of the negotiated agreement. It is possible that the trust associated with a preexisting relationship will promote more sharing of information and more cooperation and therefore increase the likelihood of creating good deals. Friendship may, in this way, eliminate the asymmetries of information and value typically associated with negotiation situations. Relationships may also cloud the negotiation process, though, by providing expectations of overconcessionary behavior or too much sharing of information.

What Happens When Things Go Wrong?

Things can go wrong for the relationship and for the negotiation when scripts are broken. The effects of negotiation on any relationship depend, of course, on the power of the negotiation and the strength of the relationship. Sometimes, negotiators will bow to the relationship and forgo their negotiating position. In this case, a friend might say, "I paid too much for this lamp because fighting with my friend wasn't worth the extra $30." Sometimes, though, the relationship is severed by the necessities of the negotiation process. A vivid example of this is when students face a professor after they get their midterm grades with a disappointed expression that reads, "I thought we were friends." In this case, the hard negotiating power of the professor based on exam scores overrides the good feelings that the professor and students have toward each other in class.

An interesting repercussion of script breaking is in the attributions that people expect and make toward one another. For example, when negotiating with a friend, one party might take a hard line in an effort to be a "good" negotiator, not realizing that the other party may well take this behavior as a personal affront, resulting in a damaged friendship. In addition, we know from previous research that when faced with someone else's behavior, people tend to perceive actions as characteristics of the individual person, while when faced with their own behavior, people tend to attribute actions to situational influences. Clearly, this difference leaves room for some misinterpretations of actions among friends engaged in negotiations with each other. So, in summary, though negotiators may not actually behave any differently when facing a friend than they would have otherwise, the perception of behavior can be entirely changed when it is coming from a friend. Though negotiation behaviors may not have been intended on a personal level, the presence of a relationship encourages us to make attributions that we would not normally develop.

Measuring the Impact of a Negotiation on Friendship

Professional athletes refuse to engage in negotiations directly with their team owners, so that the hard stances and bargaining tactics used will not affect the future of the relationship, and instead employ an agent to take the heat off of the principal negotiators. Clearly, people understand that negotiations require elements that may not be conducive to positive relationships. The task is left to researchers to isolate and analyze the critical elements of this interplay and be able to quantify in some way the potential benefits and damage that can be done to the relationship.

For starters, it is crucial that researchers be able to define and measure both the relationship and the negotiation occurring. In some cases, this is an easy task: If people are all asked to participate in the same negotiation exercise, the parameters of the negotiation are fixed. But in more natural settings, it can be more difficult to define what constitutes a negotiation, the issues, and the time frame. For instance, a married couple may regularly trade off on issues across time without clearly defining that a "negotiation" has taken place. Inefficiency on a one-term deal may actually be an indication of intertemporal logrolling. Similarly, in terms of relationships, it can be difficult to define exactly what a relationship consists of and how it changes over time.

It is important to distinguish what types of relationships are being discussed. Again, one major criterion for distinction is the amount of time that the relationship has existed. Clearly, the longer the relationship, the more that is at stake when engaging in a potentially damaging negotiation. Short-term relationships (or newly formed relationships) may be easier to observe and measure than preexisting long-term relationships. One approach to look at newly formed relationships is to pair strangers together in a negotiation task, and then ask them afterward how likely each party would be to acknowledge the other in a chance meeting (Morris and Drolet 1997) or to ask them how likely they would be to want to negotiate with each other again (Moore, Kurtzberg, Thompson, and Morris 1999).

Another mechanism might be to have people negotiate together, then report the outcomes to a researcher, and then measure how far apart the pair stands from each other after the negotiation (e.g., see Byrne and Griffith 1973; Byrne, Baskett, and Hodges 1971). These types of behaviors might reflect the degree of relationship established between the negotiators. Furthermore, for researchers to study more clearly the dynamics of a negotiation's effect on relationships, people most likely need to engage in real-world negotiations, as opposed to being assigned into a role-play exercise. There is an argument to be made as well that the most effective way to assess people's feelings about a relationship is to ask them—have people rate their degree of liking and trust both before and after a negotiation has occurred. Since relationships are subjective by nature, this might be a worthwhile tool for researchers.

Yet these kinds of tools, used primarily to assess the effects of negotiations on *developing* relationships, often miss the "romance" of interpersonal relationships that have a longer-term past and future to them. Also, the more that each person cares about the other, the stronger the concern will be about potentially damaging the relationship through negotiation. It is possible to become friends with someone with whom you are negotiating, as a salesperson–customer interaction would demonstrate. Other real-world examples of this situation include people who become friends while maintaining ongoing negotiations, such as labor–management negotiators who continually work out deals over the years and create a warm relationship with each other. Yet this is distinctly different from negotiating with someone with whom you have a preexisting relationship.

In order for a negotiation situation to affect an ongoing relationship, the negotiation clearly has to be one of some importance to the negotiators. This can be either because the negotiation takes place over a long period of time or because the issues involved are ones that are meaningful to the participants. The risks are great, though. While newly formed couples are still engaged in pushing the boundaries of their relationship, couples already settled in long-term relationships have their own mechanisms for dealing with each other to keep negotiations from damaging their relationship. This can be viewed by observing the differences between the arguments and negotiation strategies of young married couples and older couples ("There goes Harry being Harry again!") who have much more experience with their partner.

Generally speaking, it seems that many elements of a relationship can be impacted by a negotiation, such as the affect between the parties, the parties' communication, and their level of trust. Negotiators must remain aware of the potential effects that their interchange can have on their relationship.

Conclusion

In summary, we have addressed why it is that people may not feel comfortable negotiating with friends. We have hypothesized what the effects of friendship could be on the negotiation process and outcome, and have proposed also how a negotiation could impact a friendship. Finally, we have suggested means for measuring this impact. The discussion at the conference did not provide the answers, but instead proposed the questions, with the hope that these questions will provoke future research into these areas.

References

Bies, R. J., and T. M. Tripp. 1996. Beyond revenge: "Getting even" and the need for revenge. In *Trust in organizations: Frontiers of theory and research,* ed. R. M. Kramer, T. R. Tyler, et al. Thousand Oaks, CA: Sage.

Byrne, D., G. D. Baskett, and L. Hodges. 1971. Behavioral indicators of interpersonal attraction. *Journal of Applied Social Psychology* 1, pp. 137–49.

Byrne, D., and W. Griffith. 1973. Interpersonal attraction. *Annual Review of Psychology 1973,* pp. 317–36.

Lewicki, R. J., and B. B. Bunker. 1995. Trust in relationships: A model of trust development and decline. In *Conflict, cooperation, and justice,* ed. B. B. Bunker and J. Z. Rubin. San Francisco: Jossey-Bass.

_____. 1996. Developing and maintaining trust in work relationships. *Trust in organizations: Frontiers of theory and research,* ed. R. M. Kramer, T. R. Tyler, et al. Thousand Oaks, CA: Sage.

Moore, D. A., T. R. Kurtzberg, L. L. Thompson, and M. W. Morris. 1999. Long and short routes to success in electronically mediated negotiations: Group affiliations and good vibrations. *Organizational Behavior and Human Decision Processes* 77, pp. 22–43.

Morris, M. W., and A. Drolet. 1997. *Rapport and dominance: Nonverbally mediated dyadic dynamics that affect value creation and value claiming in negotiation.* Unpublished manuscript. Graduate School of Business, Stanford University.

Pruitt, D. G. 1981. *Negotiation behavior.* Orlando, FL: Academic Press.

Ross, W., and J. LaCroix. 1996. Multiple meanings of trust in negotiation theory and research: A literature review and integrative model. *The International Journal of Conflict Management* 7, pp. 314–60.

Reading 3.2

Staying in the Game or Changing It: An Analysis of *Moves* and *Turns* in Negotiation
Deborah M. Kolb

As parties bargain over the terms of an agreement, they are concurrently negotiating their relationship. In this parallel negotiation, parties seek to position themselves to advantage by using a variety of strategic moves. In so doing the other party can be put into a defensive position making it difficult to advocate effectively. Turns, such as interrupting, correcting, questioning, naming, and diverting, challenge these moves. Turns can be used restoratively to move out of a defensive position or participatively, to engage the other in collaboration. Anticipating strategic moves and having turns in mind is part of preparing to negotiate.

Negotiation strategy and tactics typically cover how negotiators deal with the substantive dimensions of the issues in dispute. And it is convention to distinguish strategies and tactics that apply in distributive from those in integrative and mutual gains. In distributive negotiations, strategic thinking covers such matters as opening offers, the pattern of concessions, and the use of threats and commitments. Integrative negotiating strategy centers on learning about interests and needs, looking for opportunities for trades, and developing creative options (Fisher, Ury, and Patton 1991; Pruitt and Carnevale 1993).

In a field where the lure of prescription is strong, the strategic advice on how to manage the process vis-à-vis the substantive issues can be very useful. However, our research with women suggests that it is an incomplete picture of the strategic repertoire a negotiator needs—incomplete because it ignores the issues of power and position so central to most negotiated interactions. Consider the following examples:

A self-employed consultant negotiates a contract renewal with a valued client, who claims that the consultant's rates are out of line with what he delivers and threatens to hire a different provider.

The vice president of global ventures is in negotiation with the vice president of European operations to close down a nonperforming subsidiary. They agree that the VP operations will take care of it, but nothing happens. When the VP global ventures questions him about the status, he tells her that she is overreacting and to calm down.

A director of marketing schedules a meeting to negotiate salary and bonus with her boss based on a profitable year and the extra work she has picked up in the face of increased turnover. Her boss reminds her that times are tight and that, in fact, she is lucky to still have a job. He asks her not to raise salary issues at this time and says he knows that she can be counted on to do this favor.

In each of these examples, one party is seeking to control the negotiation by challenging the other's claims to legitimacy and credibility. In a defensive position, it is difficult

Source: Deborah M. Kolb, "Staying in the Game or Changing It: An analysis of *Moves* and *Turns* in Negotiation" from *Negotiation Journal* 20, no. 2 (April 2004), pp. 253–68, Blackwell Publishing, Ltd. Reprinted with permission.

for the challenged party to advocate for his or her own interests and concerns. Contrary to best practice assumptions, mutual gain solutions are unlikely to be achieved in these situations. These are examples of strategic moves, actions taken by a negotiator to position him or herself in an advantageous light. These moves can have the effect, even though not necessarily intentionally, of putting the other party in a defensive or down position. Turns are the ways that negotiators can challenge a move.

The notion of moves and turns began with our interest in gender (Kolb and Williams 2003). As we were doing the research for the book *Everyday Negotiation: Navigating the Hidden Agendas of Bargaining,* women told us about some rather horrific experiences in negotiation. A travel agent had to keep her cool in a negotiation with a corporate travel planner who yelled at her when she refused to give him a rebate. "Look bitch," he shouted, "either you give me a rebate or the deal is off!" A labor negotiator had her proposal rejected when her counterpart said, "You think this is all a Zen experience; you can't really speak for the management group." A consultant, in negotiation with a client, was told to "take the deal back to your boss."

These women were being diminished and demeaned in their negotiations in ways that made it almost impossible for them to use the prescriptive advice about strategies and tactics no matter what type of negotiation it was. What these examples suggested was that positioning in the negotiation was critically related to how competent and credible the negotiator was perceived. For a host of structural and cultural reasons having to do with race, class, status, and hierarchical position, negotiators can find themselves in a down position. Indeed, even people who hold power and influence in some contexts can find themselves challenged in others. It is important to emphasize, therefore, that these incidents are not just experienced by women.

Positioning is central to the idea of moves and turns, and indeed, to the notion of the shadow negotiation. In the first section of this essay, I will discuss the idea of positioning and root it in a number of different intellectual traditions. In the next section, I will concentrate on the concept of the shadow negotiation and how moves and turns fit within that framework. I want to suggest that moves and turns constitute critical moments in negotiation. They can be critical in a number of different respects. The next section proposes a typology of moves and turns and how each type can function as a critical moment. In putting forth these ideas, I will draw from a variety of case examples, my own and those of others.

Positioning in Negotiation

In the recent past, the negotiation field has been dominated by several perspectives: economic decision analysis (Raiffa 1982; Lax and Sebenius 1986); social psychology (Rubin, Pruitt, and Kim 1994; Thompson 2001); and cognitive psychology (Neale and Bazerman 1994). These perspectives focus on individual actors (as either principals or agents) engaged in transactional deal making. The best outcomes are achieved through the rational analysis of the game and the required strategy. In so doing, these rather technical negotiation models ignore the very social and political processes that make the kind of deal making they espouse possible. To focus, for example, on cognition and analytic prowess as major barriers to agreement minimizes the connection between how a negotiator is positioned (and continually positioning) in the process and his or her ability to engage the substantive issues in the ways the models suggest. For they presume a party has agency in the process, in the sense that she is positioned to advocate for herself, and that that agency is credited (Kolb and Putnam 1997). I suggest that agency is more problematic and is an ongoing accomplishment in the process.

The notion of social positioning is not a new one in the field, but it has not been central to either theorizing or prescriptive work in negotiation. For the most part, the perspective has been most developed in mediation and disputing scholarship (Mather and Yngvesson 1980–81; Silbey and Merry 1986; Cobb 1993) that draws on theories of social construction (Berger and Luckman 1966; Blumer 1969). This work views people as engaged in constructing their roles and identities in social interaction subject to expectations and the constraints of the social structure they find there. This focus on the interaction as the nexus of analysis encourages us to see roles and the display of identity as quite fluid. Indeed, *role negotiation* is often a term that is used to describe these processes (Gerson and Preiss 1985).

In my work on mediation, I have argued that the roles mediators play shape how they see the process and its demands. The roles they play are very much negotiated and created in the context of the relationships they have with significant others—namely the professionals in labor relations with whom they work. Through the actions the mediators take, they seek to control and frame the process in such a way that they can effectively act within it (Kolb 1983). Managing impressions of their role is part of this process as well.

Translating these ideas to the negotiation context suggests that agency, a concept so central to the dominant paradigms in the field, is not a given, but rather is socially constructed in an interactive context. By focusing on these interactions, we must attend to the ways parties present themselves and their positions in ways that make them feel (and appear) competent and in control. This is the *face* they present in negotiations. To have these presentations challenged can, to a greater or lesser degree, undermine a negotiator's face, sense of herself (Wilson 1992), and ultimately the agency that she claims in advocating for her interests.

Discourse analysis nests these ideas in conversation. Rather than see a negotiator's strategy and tactics as a manifestation of a self-interested individual negotiator, a discourse perspective locates these ideas in an interactive conversation. The notion of position is central to this perspective (Davies and Harre 1990). Gherardi (1995) describes position as "what is created in and through a conversation as speakers and hearers construct themselves as persons: it creates a location through which social relations and actions are mediated."

Negotiators are concerned with constructing legitimate social positions for themselves (and others) in order for them to both create and claim value. From a delegitimated or defensive position, it is difficult to do either (Cobb 1993). Therefore, one way to look at *moves* and *turns* in negotiation is to see them as the cocreation of structure or moral order in which the process can play out.[1]

A discourse perspective underlies one way that feminist scholars look at gender. Although it is still pretty common to conceptualize gender in terms of binary categories—that is, to compare men and women and how they act—this essentialist and static conception is increasingly being challenged (Flax 1990; Gherardi 1995; Calas and

Smircich 1996; Fletcher 1999). In the negotiation field, for example, studies of the differences between women and men have only two outcomes—women are either different from or the same as men. What this work does is generally highlight women's deficiencies. It fails to take into account how social structures and the very knowledge base of negotiation may create these deficiencies. More recent work seeks to understand the conditions under which gender differences would occur, but they still take a rather static view of differences between men and women (Riley 2001; Gelfand et al. 2002; Babcock and Laschever 2003).

Feminists, who work from a postmodern perspective, highlight the fluid and contextual character of gender relations. By embracing discourse, these scholars shift from a focus on the rational, self-interested subject to looking at how subjective and objective positions are produced in language and conversations (Weedon 1987). Part of that project focuses on disciplinary knowledge and how it shapes power relations (Weedon 1987; Calas and Smircich 1996). Others, however, focus more on interactive settings where meanings about gender are produced. So when feminist scholars talk about positioning, they are interested in how women define themselves and are defined within a particular context.

Lorber (1994) describes the various ways that women in workplace interactions can have their positions undercut through, among other means, condescending chivalry, supportive discouragement, radiant devaluation, considerate domination, and collegial exclusion. While it is expected in such interactions that women will passively accept these positions, that men will do dominance and women deference, these choices are not inevitable. When Alcoff (1988) defines the concept of *positionality,* she highlights how women can actively utilize their location to construct new meanings about gender roles and relations rather than simply take up ones that are assigned. This perspective highlights two things: that women have choices in the positions they take up in discourse and that predetermined positions can be resisted. While expectations might suggest that women take up a one-down position, a position that is consistent with gender identity, these expectations can be disrupted and destabilized (Gherardi 1995). And from such destabilization, new meanings about role and position can be constructed.

Another perspective that helps inform this work concerns different ways of looking at power. In negotiation, the dominant model of power has been Emerson's: the power of A to get B to do something that B would rather not do. Determinants of power in negotiation typically focus on degrees of dependence and independence (Bacharach and Lawler 1981). Thus negotiators with good BATNAs are presumably in more powerful positions in negotiation. Obviously, other dimensions of power are also relevant—access to resources, hierarchical position, and access to influential others. However, as Lax and Sebenius (1986) note, positional power achieved in any of these manners is not determining—witness weaker parties who come out ahead. Scott (1987) calls these successful—and often low-profile actions—the *weapons of the weak.*

Power is exerted in more nuanced ways in social interactions. Following the work of Michel Foucault, scholars observe how knowledge and accepted truths, which appear natural and neutral, serve to discipline action. Certain discourses become dominant and hold sway in ways actors do not necessarily recognize as exercises of power. Elsewhere we have argued that in the negotiation field, the discourse of individual psychology and economic decision making privileges certain ways of being and marginalizes others, and this contributes to gender inequities (Kolb and Putnam 1997; Putnam and Kolb 2000; Kolb 2003). Feminist scholars have embraced this perspective with some important caveats.

The focus on the dispersion of power and its multiple modes of functioning has helped scholars focus on the microprocesses that construct gender in the workplace (Martin and Meyerson 1998; Fletcher 1999). It also serves to empower people in workplace interactions to resist these exercises of power (Meyerson 2001). By recognizing the ways social structures operate through microprocesses of power in commonplace interactions, individuals can act individually and collectively to change narratives that position them to disadvantage (Ewick and Silbey 1995).

In sum, this work on positioning suggests an alternative, yet complementary, perspective on how to describe what is occurring in a negotiated interaction. Although parties are focused on the issues, they are engaged in an interactive process. Elements of that process have been theorized and studied—the use of threats and bluffs for example or the challenges of dealing with difficult situations (Schelling 1960; Ury 1990; Stone, Patton, and Heen 1999; McGinn and Keros 2002). The concept of positioning in the negotiation gives coherence to these disparate approaches. It is that concept that the notion of the *shadow negotiation* attempts to capture.

Moves and Turns in the Shadow Negotiation

The *shadow negotiation* refers to the complementary and parallel dynamic that occurs as parties work on the issues that separate them. Our identities as negotiators, the legitimacy of our positions, the power and authority we claim, the import of gender and race, are always part of what is being negotiated while we are negotiating over the substantive issues. Of course, they are intimately connected. Establishing and maintaining visible presence and credibility are intended to influence how the other responds to our demands. The distinctions are not neat: At the same time as parties are focused on their issues—learning about them, putting out proposals and arguments, and making concessions—they are engaged in a shadow negotiation that is about relative positioning.

It is not that these two processes are separable, but rather that we can look at what is occurring from these two perspectives. We can focus on how parties are dealing with their issues and working (or not) toward agreement and at the same time, pay attention to how what they say and do also represents a process of positioning (or challenges/ acceptance of it). To look at negotiations from the perspective of the shadow negotiation is to attend to how parties manage impressions of themselves, how they claim and maintain legitimacy and credibility, how they assert what power and influence they have, and how they shape perceptions of what is possible (Kolb and Williams 2003). Central to the shadow negotiation is the idea of moves and turns.

Moves

Goffman (1969) developed the idea of a move in his application of game theory to social interaction: "A move, analytically speaking, is not a thought or decision or expression, or anything else that goes on in the mind of a player; it is a course of action which involves real consequences."

Goffman specifically does not define a *move* too precisely (1981). Rather, he uses it as a vehicle to capture streams of interaction and how they play out in various expression games. As Pentland (1992) observes, "Moves have the desirable properties of being meaningful to the interactants, related to structural properties of the situation, and yet under the willful control of the interactants." In other words, moves need to be looked at in terms of the action itself, how others respond ("ratifying" is how Goffman puts it), and their role in the overall game.

How do we look at moves in the negotiation game? Strategic moves are actions negotiators take to position themselves (and others) in the negotiation process. In making these moves, negotiators want to position themselves as competent and legitimate in order to be credible advocates for themselves and their interests. In making their moves, negotiators try to project an image of themselves and what they want in the best possible light.

As part of the normal byplay of negotiations, negotiators use *strategic moves* to enhance their position.[2] These moves can have the effect of undermining or delegitimizing the other party (Kolb and Williams 2003). Negotiators are most credible when they are positioned to advocate for their interests. When a party is challenged in ways that put them in a one-down (sometimes a gendered) position, they have a more difficult time pressing for what they need.

Moves that challenge a party's positioning potentially cover a wide spectrum of action. One type discussed widely in the literature are the so-called "dirty tricks" where negotiators employ some familiar tactics, such as good cop–bad cop, in order to throw the other negotiator off (Fisher, Ury, and Patton 1991). There are other forms of action that are so demeaning of a person that they verge on harassment (Kolb and Williams 2003). Undoubtedly these moves do occur; however, we are more interested in more routine, normal moves that stem from one party's efforts to advocate for him or herself.

In moving to put oneself into a good position, the effect of this type of advocacy is to challenge some aspect of the position the other negotiator is claiming. These are part of the normal interactive byplay of negotiation. The moves that are of interest are ones that challenge a negotiator's own presentation of self and/or put him/her on the defensive so that s/he finds it hard to advocate credibly. Several of the most common moves are listed below:

> *Challenging competence or expertise:* With these moves, claims of experience and expertise are called into question. In the contract negotiation mentioned earlier, the move—"your fees are way out of line with what you deliver"— calls into question the value of the product/service. The implication is that asking for higher fees is not possible.

> *Demeaning ideas:* With these moves, the ideas themselves are attacked in ways that give the proponent little room to respond. Saying something like "you can't be serious about this proposal" makes the idea and the proponent sound ridiculous. Obviously, these moves make it difficult to argue for what might otherwise be a reasonable idea.

Criticizing style: Using phrases like "don't get so upset," the person—who s/he is, and how s/he acts—becomes the subject of the move. To be challenged as overreacting or inconsiderate positions a negotiator as an irrational person who cannot be reasoned with, or who is selfish or not nice. This move can call forth unfortunate stereotypes such as the hysterical female (Gherardi 1995). These moves can be unsettling as few of us think of ourselves as unreasonable or difficult.

Making threats: Threats are used to try to force a choice on a negotiator: "Cut your rates or there is no deal." As assertions of power, these moves can back a negotiator into a corner, making it risky to propose some other solution.

Appealing for sympathy or flattery: The moves described thus far have been critical of the person and his/her ideas. But in everyday negotiation in the workplace, appeals for sympathy and flattery also can be quite powerful. When people say, "I know you won't let me down" or "I really need your help on this," they are counting on the move to silence you, to make it difficult for you to advocate and press for what you want.

Strategic moves like these five (and there are likely variants) can be seen as situated exercises of power meant to put a person in his or her place. In the interactive byplay, these moves are intended to position the negotiator in a one-down, defensive position. To have one's competence, motives, ideas, legitimacy, and style challenged as the other party presses for advantage not only challenges the potential argument or claim a negotiator wants to make, it can also undermine the negotiator's sense of self-competence and confidence. In a one-down position, the other negotiator can have the advantage. Strategic moves present the recipient with a choice. She can make a defensive countermove or she can *turn* it.

Moves can be responded to with *reactive countermoves,* which are comebacks in kind. For example, when somebody says, "Don't get so upset" a reactive countermove would be to respond, "I am not upset." Although such a reactive countermove is quite common, it is clear that it tends to reinforce the previous move. That is, the recipient of the move stays in the original, defensive position. One of the reasons that reactive countermoves are so common is because negotiators do not recognize that a move is being used as a tactic and so they respond emotionally and defensively.

Strategic moves can also be ignored. In a sales negotiation, for example, when the buyer of advertising from a TV station mentions the poor ratings of a show under discussion, the seller can just ignore the aspersion. Of course the move has been made and it sits there. It is not clear whether the seller agrees or not. When seriously demeaning moves are made about sex or race, to ignore them is potentially to collude in that positioning (Gherardi 1995; Kolb and Williams 2003). Remaining silent implicitly reinforces racist or sexist aspersions.

Moves can be resisted through the use of *turns.* Again we draw on Goffman who introduced the idea of a turn (1969). But his use of *turn* refers to the idea of *turn taking;* in other words, when it is your turn in the game, you can choose to make a move. We extend Goffman's idea of *turn* in a number of different ways.

First, turns are responses to moves. They are the moments of potential resistance, where the recipient of the move refuses to take up the defensive position in which she is placed (Gherardi 1995). Second, turns change meaning and so reposition the person. Turns shift the meaning of the move: They resist the positioning and reframe it. When meanings are unstable, as they are in an unfolding negotiation where two or more interpretations exist at any given moment, these indirect methods or turns can reframe how parties are viewed (Ferguson 1991; Gherardi 1995). A repertoire of turns, such as interrupting the action, naming a challenge, questioning the move, correcting impressions, and diverting to the problem, are means a negotiator can use to resist the positioning.[3]

Turns

Turns are actions negotiators take in response to strategic moves, moves that put them in a one-down or defensive position. The argument is that to accept that definition of oneself hampers the negotiator's credibility and sense of agency, giving some advantage to the mover. Turns are an effort to restore some parity to positioning. In my work, I have identified five turns:

- *Interruption:* Interrupting the action disrupts the move. Even the shortest break means that people are not in precisely the same position after it.

- *Naming:* To name a move signals recognition of what is occurring. It suggests that the negotiator is not taken in. The turner, in other words, rejects the positioning.

- *Questioning:* Questioning suggests something puzzling about a move. Rather than directly naming a move, to question it is to throw it back to the mover—implying one is not sure what prompted it.

- *Correcting:* A correcting turn substitutes a different version or motivation to the one the move implied. Rather than just rejecting the positioning, a correcting turn constructs a different positioning for the turner that can neutralize the move.

- *Diverting:* A diverting turn shifts the focus to the problem itself. It is a way of ignoring the implication of the move but also has the negotiator take control of the process.

There are some important points to make about turns before we analyze them in terms of critical moments. With the exception of interruption, I have emphasized the verbal. However, nonverbal actions, such as laughing off a comment or turning away, can also have the effect of turning a situation.

In a turn, tone of voice is as important as what is said. The use of humor, sarcasm, and irony can be most effective in naming or correcting a move. Gherardi (1995) uses a wonderful example to make this point in a kind of everyday negotiation. After returning from a conference, one of her senior male colleagues went to open the door for her: "Do you want me to open the door for you or will you react as if I'd grabbed your arse?"

Gherardi observes that she was put in a position of either a hysterical feminist or a sweet and docile lady who knew her place in academia as well as society. "I decided on sarcasm and told him emphatically that I formally authorized him to open that door and all the other doors and obstacles that might stand in my way."

Gherardi's turn points up another dimension of moves and turns, the degree to which they are accomplished in the moment or occur over time. The challenge of thinking on one's feet to be prepared for a move can be daunting. We have argued that it often possible to anticipate moves as one plays out several scenarios in preparing for a negotiation (Kolb and Williams 2003). However, such preparation can never be complete, and one can always be caught unawares. It is here that interruption can be useful.

But moves can also be turned over time. Meyerson (2001) describes how people in everyday negotiation in the workplace pick their time to turn moves that previously happened. When a move is made in a public space, like a meeting, the target may judge that it is risky to raise the issue in the moment. Under those circumstances, it is more likely that the other will hear the turn and learn from it later in a more private setting.

Finally, it is important to note, that recognizing a move as such and acting to turn it is not always clear-cut. I have observed how overtures intended to uncover interests and learn more about a party's situation can often be read as a move. For example, in a buyer–seller negotiation, one can ask about the success of the seller's product or service or what her aspirations are for how it will do in the future. This kind of inquiry can lead to the creation of contingent agreements (Bazerman and Gillespie 1999). However, it can also be read as a move to discredit the seller's service. Rather than being forthcoming about aspirations (a good thing), the seller gets into a defensive mode or tries to turn what they misread as a move (a bad thing).

How Turns Can Work: Implications for Critical Shifts

The concept of *moves* and *turns* gives us a lens into the political dimensions of the negotiation process. As such, moves and turns are critical moments in negotiation. But they can function differently. In this section, I want to take a preliminary look at how moves and turns might function as restorative and participative moments in negotiation.

Restorative Turns

Up to this point, I have used *moves* and *turns* in one particular way, as a means to create or restore some kind of equity in the process. For some time, I have been concerned with how negotiators (particularly women) who find themselves in a one-down or defensive position can turn moves to get themselves into a more proactive, agentic position. From that proactive position, they can more credibly advocate for themselves. All the examples I have used so far exemplify this restorative dimension of turns. Thus, when competence, ideas, or style are challenged, the negotiator turns the move in order to try to level the playing field.

Restorative[4] *turns* are important from two perspectives. Restoring one's position to be in a more credible role is important to the progress of the negotiation. Without a negotiator who is equally able to advocate for her own self, there is little incentive for the other party to engage in the work of mutual gains negotiation or to claim value in distributive bargaining (Rubin et al. 1994). That is, the other party needs a credible advocate, not a defensive wimp, in order to engage.

Restorative turns are a means to promote mutual interdependence in negotiation. Moves that serve to disempower or put a party on the defensive can be seen as an action by the mover to assert power and control in the process. These moves signal that the mover sees herself in a one-up position and hence less dependent on the outcome of the negotiation. What follows is that the target of the move is seen in a one-down position and more dependent. By turning such moves, the target resists this definition. By turning the move, the turner encourages the mover to reconsider; they are more interdependent than the mover might want to acknowledge. In this way, restorative turns are about how parties negotiate their relative power in the process. Returning to our earlier scenarios,

> The self-employed consultant *turned* the move that challenged his competence. The client claimed that his rates were out of line with what was delivered. The consultant *corrected* the move by bringing in the fee schedules of other like firms. In response to the threat of using another provider, the consultant *named* the move, "You and I both know that will mean more work for you," implying that the threat was not taken seriously.
>
> The VP of global ventures likewise *corrected* the move that positioned her as overreacting by saying, "This is serious. You know Jim (CEO) is looking very carefully at this. We are both under the gun." In turning this move, the VP of global operations reframed the position she was put in—not out of control, but responding to legitimate pressure from the CEO.

Restorative turns are important because negotiators cannot effectively advocate if their legitimacy or credibility is being challenged. Restorative turns also disrupt the assertion of control by one party over the range of possible agreements. If the consultant stays anchored by the statement "your fees are out of line," it will be difficult for him to advocate for a fee schedule more to his liking. Restorative turns are most likely to occur in the early phases of a negotiation when parties are posturing for each other and testing the range of what is possible. As such they tend to restore the balance of power that existed; naming and correcting turns are most likely to accomplish this.

Participative Turns

Participative turns are intended to engage the other party. Whereas restorative turns can put the other party on the defensive, *participative turns* position the other party more as a partner. Turns are participative when they are phrased in such a way that they leave space for the other person to talk from her own legitimate, not defensive, position. Looking back at an earlier scenario, for example,

> In her negotiation over salary, the director can turn the *appeal for sympathy* move, a move that could silence her, with a *correcting* turn: "I know you are in a difficult position and I'd like to do what I can" or with a *questioning* turn: "I wonder how you could respond in my situation?" Or she could *divert* the move: "I know things are tight, but I want to explore some other ideas with you."

These turns acknowledge the problem but open up the possibility that both can talk about the situation. They can shift the negotiation from blaming and defending to an exploration of what may be possible in the circumstances. Notice that the turns in this example work differently from the earlier restorative examples. In the fee negotiation, the correcting turn shows that the other person is mistaken. Although it restores the credibility of the consultant, it could result in a defensive response from the client. Likewise in the subsidiary example, the VP global ventures invokes the CEO to correct the move, which could invite backlash. In the salary example, the director talks about intentions and invites the boss to work with her. Participative turns not only resist the move, but do so in a way that has the potential to open up the dialogue in ways that restorative turns are not likely to do.

In an interesting example from the world stage, in trade negotiations between U.S. Trade Representative Charlene Barshefsky and her Chinese counterpart over intellectual property, Barshefsky used interruption and diverting turns participatively in response to a threat.

> Menacingly, he (Chinese negotiator) leaned forward across the table toward Barshefsky and said flatly, "It's take it or leave it." Barshefsky, taken aback by the harsh tone, surprised, her counterpart by sitting quietly. She waited 30–40 seconds—an eternity given the intensity of the negotiation—and came back with a measured reply: "If the choice is take or leave it, of course I'll leave it. But I can't imagine that's what you meant. I think what you mean is that you'd like me to think over your last offer and that we can continue tomorrow."[5]

Barshefsky's participative turns of the threat disrupted it and resulted in a major compromise the next morning. The interruption (her silence) was important; it enabled her to reassert control. Further, her diverting turn signaled her intention to revise the Chinese negotiator's offer, but did it in a way that gave him space to back down. In this case, her turning a threat signaled that this tactic would not work and pushed the mover to reconsider.

Both restorative and participative turns have the potential to be critical in shifting a negotiation. Restorative turns can involve each party testing the other's mettle. Such posturing can move the negotiations along. Of course, it is also possible that this kind of posturing can result in backlash and impasse. Participative turns seem to be more likely to lead to positive transitions and even the possibility that some forms of transformation might occur.

Meyerson (2001) has used the concept of moves and turns in her work on tempered radicals. These are people who are successful in existing systems, but negotiate change, especially around identity group issues. Meyerson argues that turns can be moments of learning and transformation. Responding to a move, a negotiator can make a turn that does more than restore a balance or shift the discussion: It actually causes the mover to reflect on his or her action. And in so doing, the turn has potential as a moment of learning for the individual mover and to advance the relationship between the mover and turner and may lead the negotiation in directions that could not be predicted (Putnam 2004).

Conclusion

This essay attempts to lay out some new ways of thinking about the negotiation process. Based on a number of different literatures in the social sciences—especially feminist postmodern work—I have suggested that negotiators are negotiating about their positions in the process while they are engaging their issues. *Moves* and *turns* is a framework

I propose that can begin to unpack what is occurring in the positional byplay of the process. Finally, I suggest that moves and turns can function as different types of critical moments.

This essay raises more questions than it answers. First, the repertoire of moves and turns comes from our research on women (primarily) in the workplace and generally from their descriptions of what occurred. This limitation suggests several directions for future work, including looking at moves and turns in other domains and having access to actual scripts of the process. Second, moves and turns as separable actions is a fairly rudimentary approach to the process. Indeed, Goffman (1981) proposes that moves describe a course of action. Thus a promising approach would be to try to identify various streams of moves and turns. Looking at restorative and participative turns might be an interesting beginning.

Finally, there is the issue of prescription. If moves and turns happen in the moment, how can we help negotiators become more adept at the "mindfulness" (Wheeler 2002) it takes to manage this complexity? I know from my students and from executive workshops I have given that having confidence in one's ability to both make moves and to turn them is a skill many want to enhance.

Endnotes

1. Kathleen McGinn's work focuses, in part, on how a conjoint or shared moral order is constructed in negotiations.

2. There are also situations where negotiators use appreciative moves that position the other party as legitimate and credible. From such mutual positioning, collaboration is more likely.

3. These are examples of what Sylvia Gherardi calls the *postmodern tools of resistance.* "This is a paradoxical form of communication, but it is quite normal in handling interaction situations comprising a double-bind and requiring, simultaneously, a ritualistic form of communication which is 'supportive' of the symbolic order of gender, one that is 'restitutive' of the violation of that order, and one that is 'resistant' to the domination it expresses." (Gherardi 1995: 139).

4. I recognize that *restorative* may be a problematic term because it implies that there was some preexisting situation. I use the term just to indicate that negotiators want to restore a face in the interaction that might be challenged.

5. *Charlene Barshefsky (B),* Harvard Business School Case, 9-801-422 (Sebenius and Hulse 2001).

References

Alcoff, L. 1988. Cultural feminism versus post-structuralism: The identity crisis in feminist theory. *Signs* 13(3), pp. 405–436.

Babcock, L., and S. Laschever. 2003. *Women don't ask: Negotiation and the gender divide.* Princeton, NJ: Princeton University Press.

Bacharach, S., and E. Lawler. 1981. *Bargaining*. San Francisco, CA: Jossey-Bass.

Bazerman, M.H., and J.J. Gillespie. 1999. Betting on the future: The virtues of contingent contracts. *Harvard Business Review,* September–October, pp. 155–60.

Berger, P., and T. Luckman. 1966. *The social construction of reality: A treatise in the sociology of knowledge*. New York: Doubleday.

Blumer, H. 1969. *Symbolic interaction*. Englewood Cliffs, NJ: Prentice-Hall.

Calas, M., and L. Smircich. 1996. From a woman's point of view: Feminist approaches to organization studies. In *Handbook of organization studies,* ed. S. Clegg, C. Hardy, and W. Nord. Newbury Park, CA: Sage.

Cobb, S. 1993. Empowerment and mediation: A narrative perspective. *Negotiation Journal* 9(3), pp. 245–59.

———. 1994. A narrative perspective on mediation: Toward the materialization of the "story-telling" metaphor. In *New directions in mediation,* ed. J.P. Folger and T.S. Jones. Thousand Oaks, CA: Sage.

Davies, B., and R. Harre. 1990. Positioning: The discursive production of selves. *Journal of the Theory of Social Behavior* 1, pp. 43–63.

Ewick, P., and S.S. Silbey. 1995. Subversive stories and hegemonic tales: Toward a sociology of narrative. *Law and Society Review* 29, pp. 197–226.

Ferguson, K. 1991. Interpretation and genealogy in feminism. *Signs* 16, pp. 322–39.

Fisher, R., W. Ury, and B. Patton. 1991. *Getting to YES: Negotiating agreement without giving in,* 1st ed., 2d ed. Boston: Houghton Mifflin.

Flax, J. 1990. *Thinking fragments: Psychoanalysis, feminism, and postmodernism in the contemporary west*. Berkeley, CA: University of California Press.

Fletcher, J. 1999. *Disappearing acts: Gender, power, and relational practice at work*. Cambridge, MA: MIT Press.

Gelfand, M., V. Smith Major, J.L. Raver, L.H. Hishi, and K. O'Brien. 2002. *Dynamic theory of gender and negotiation*. Unpublished paper, University of Maryland.

Gerson, J.M., and K. Preiss. 1985. Boundaries, negotiation, consciousness: Reconceptualizing gender relations. *Social Problems* 32(4), pp. 317–31.

Gherardi, S. 1995. *Gender, symbolism, and organizational culture*. Newbury Park, CA: Sage.

Goffman, E. 1969. *Strategic interaction*. Philadelphia: University of Pennsylvania Press.

———. 1981. *Forms of talk*. Philadelphia: University of Pennsylvania Press.

Kolb, D. 1983. *The mediators*. Cambridge, MA: MIT Press.

Kolb, D.M. 2003. Gender and negotiation. In *Gender, work, and organizations,* ed. R. Ely, E. Foldy, and M. Scully. London: Blackwell Publishers.

Kolb, D.M., and L.L. Putnam. 1997. Through the looking glass: Negotiation theory refracted through the lens of gender. In *Frontiers in dispute resolution in industrial relations and human resources,* ed. S. Gleason. Ann Arbor, MI: Michigan State University Press.

Kolb, D.M., and J. Williams. 2003. *Everyday negotiation: Navigating the hidden agendas of bargaining*. San Francisco, CA: Jossey-Bass/John Wiley.

Lax, D., and J. Sebenius. 1986. *The manager as negotiator.* New York: The Free Press.

Lorber, J. 1994. *The paradoxes of gender.* New Haven: Yale University Press.

Martin, J., and D. Meyerson. 1998. Women and power. In *Power and influence in organizations,* ed. R. Kramer and M. Neale. Thousand Oaks, CA: Sage.

Mather, L., and B. Yngvesson. 1980–1981. Language, audience, and the transformation of disputes. *Law and Society Review* 15, pp. 775–821.

McGinn, K.L., and A. Keros. 2002. Improvisation and the logic of exchange in embedded negotiations. *Administrative Science Quarterly* 47(3), pp. 442–73.

Meyerson, D. 2001. *Tempered radicals.* Cambridge, MA: Harvard University Press.

Neale, M., and M. Bazerman. 1994. *Cognition and rationality in negotiation.* New York: The Free Press.

Pentland, B.T. 1992. Organizing moves in software support hot lines. *Administrative Science Quarterly* 37, pp. 527–48.

Pruitt, D.G., and P.J. Carnevale. 1993. *Negotiation in social conflict.* Buckingham, England: Open University Press.

Putnam, L.L. 2004. Transformations and critical moments in Negotiations. *Negotiation Journal* 20 (2), pp. 275–95.

Putnam, L.L., and D.M. Kolb. 2000. Rethinking negotiation: Feminist views of communication and exchange. In *Rethinking organizational communication from feminist perspectives,* ed. P. Buzannell. Newburg Park, CA: Sage Publications.

Raiffa, H. 1982. *The art and science of negotiation.* Cambridge, MA: Harvard University Press.

Riley, H. 2001. *When does gender matter in negotiations? The case of distributive bargaining.* Unpublished dissertation, Harvard University.

Rubin, J., D.G. Pruitt, and S.H. Kim. 1994. *Social conflict: Escalation, stalemate and settlement.* New York: McGraw Hill.

Schelling, T. 1960. *The strategy of conflict.* Cambridge, MA: Harvard University Press.

Scott, J. 1987. *Weapons of the weak.* New Haven: Yale University Press.

Sebenius, J. and R. Hulse. 2001, *Charlene Barshefsky (B).* Cambridge, MA: Harvard Business School Case.

Silbey, S.S., and S. Merry. 1986. Mediator settlement strategies. *Law and Policy* 8, pp. 7–32.

Stone, D., B. Patton, and S. Heen. 1999. *Difficult conversations.* New York: Viking.

Thompson, L. 2001. *The mind and heart of the negotiator.* Englewood Cliffs, NJ: Prentice-Hall.

Ury, W. 1990. *Getting past no.* New York: Bantam.

Weedon, C. 1987. *Feminist practice and poststructuralist theory.* Oxford: Blackwell.

Wheeler, M. 2002. *Presence of mind.* Harvard Business School Note, 9-903-009.

Wilson, S.R. 1992. Face and face work in negotiation. In *Communication and negotiation,* ed. L. Putnam and M.E. Roloff. Newbury Park, CA: Sage.

Reading 3.3

The High Cost of Low Trust
Keith G. Allred

Counteracting misperception and mistrust at the beginning of a negotiation can help negotiators avoid vicious cycles and sustain virtuous ones.

For decades, Hormel Foods and its employees enjoyed one of the most cooperative and productive labor–management relationships in the processed foods industry. But beginning in the late 1970s, when Hormel pushed for wage concessions, the company's relationship with its workforce began to deteriorate, especially at the plant in Austin, Minnesota, the quiet "company town" where Hormel was founded.

By the time the labor contract with the local union was up for renegotiation in 1985, each side in the Austin dispute had decided to take an aggressive approach, convinced of the other side's hostility and unreasonableness. Contract negotiations concluded in 1986 only after a bitter nine-month employee strike and after the vast majority of unionized employees had been fired, forced to take early retirement, or placed on recall lists. In the process, neighbors in Austin turned against one another, and the fabric of the community was torn to shreds.

Such stories of relationships gone bad are unfortunately common in the business world. In negotiation, as in the business world at large, relationships are key. Those that become contentious and suspicious are liable to result in frustrating and costly outcomes. By contrast, relationships that are cooperative and trusting tend to foster negotiation success.

How do suspicion and retaliation—or, by contrast, trust and cooperation—become embedded in a relationship? Decades of social science research confirm the strength of the *norm of reciprocity*—the human tendency to respond to the actions of others with similar actions. If we're treated with respect and cooperation, we tend to respond with respect and cooperation. What's more, a single round of action followed by a reciprocal response can work itself into an ongoing cycle. A cooperative interaction often initiates a virtuous cycle in which cooperation sustains itself, while a hostile interaction tends to perpetuate a vicious cycle of contention and suspicion.

Building on others' research into the particular triggers of such vicious and virtuous cycles, I've identified the triggers most likely to help managers avoid vicious cycles and sustain virtuous ones. In my studies, hundreds of executives were each rated by between 4 and 10 of their colleagues on a range of items. Here I'll show how my findings and those of other social scientists can help you replace vicious cycles with the virtuous cycles you need to improve your negotiations and your ongoing business relationships.

Source: From *Negotiation,* a newsletter published by Harvard Business School Publishing and the Program on Negotiation at Harvard Law School. Vol. 7, no. 7 (June 2004), pp. 1–4.

Vicious Cycle Triggers

Vicious cycles frequently grow out of the widespread human tendency to take an exaggerated view of others' perceived hostility or unreasonable behavior. This exaggeration leads us to reciprocate with negative behavior of our own. Although based on an initial misperception, our own hostility creates a self-fulfilling prophecy—the other side is likely to respond negatively in return. Taking this genuinely hostile response as confirmation of our earlier perceptions, we fail to recognize that our own actions created exactly what we feared. Here are some particularly potent triggers of this vicious cycle:

Naive Realism

Most people tend to assume that their view of the world reflects reality. Researchers Rob Robinson, Dacher Keltner, Andrew Ward, and Lee Ross describe three aspects of this phenomenon, known as *naive realism*. First, when confronting a problem, we typically think that we're reasonable and objective. Second, we assume that anyone looking at the same evidence would draw the same conclusions we do. Third, when others reach different conclusions, we suspect they're unreasonable or driven by dubious motives. This last inference triggers vicious cycles: differences of opinion firm up our belief that, given the other side's unreasonableness, extreme measures are our only option. Often these perceptions are painfully symmetric, with each side convinced of the other's obstinacy and unaware of the other's view. As each side escalates accordingly, costs mount and relationships are destroyed.

The Confirmatory Bias

In negotiation, we're also likely to fall victim to the *confirmatory bias*—the tendency to seek out information that verifies our preexisting beliefs and to ignore or find flaws with disconfirming information. Although it's counterintuitive, providing the same information to two opposing parties can further polarize their beliefs. Charles Lord, Lee Ross, and Mark Lepper studied this effect by examining the views of activists on both sides of the capital punishment debate. After giving their views on the issue, the activists read two articles from law journals, one in favor of capital punishment and one opposed. The researchers then measured changes in the activists' views.

The Sincerity Gap

I've seen organizations try to manipulate fairness perceptions with disastrous results. An aerospace company implemented a "quality circle" program aimed at generating employee feedback. When the company failed to respond to any of the employees' concerns, workers were infuriated. "It was fine that the company didn't care what I thought," one employee told me, "but it was truly insulting to ask for my views and then ignore them." There's a simple rule of thumb here. If you're not genuinely interested in the other side's perspective, don't ask for it.

Despite the fact that they had all read the same articles, pro–capital punishment activists felt even more strongly about their position, and anti–capital punishment activists were also more convinced that they were right. When reading the articles, each side sought out evidence to support their opinions and found fault with the disconfirming information. Because both sides thought they were being reasonable and objective, they were baffled by the other side's inability to see the "facts." The result? A vicious cycle of polarization.

Accuser and Excuser Biases

How we assign responsibility for harmful behavior also triggers vicious cycles. In our research, my colleagues and I found an *accuser bias:* when someone does something that causes us harm, we tend to hold him or her excessively responsible. Suppose that Lisa, a development director for a nonprofit agency, needs a report from Ron, the agency's marketing director, for a grant application she's writing. If Ron fails to deliver the report on time, Lisa is likely to blame the hardship caused by the missed deadline on factors within Ron's control, perhaps condemning him as irresponsible. She's also likely to underestimate the extent to which factors beyond Ron's control, such as another urgent task handed to him at the last minute by their boss, explain the harmful behavior. The accuser bias fosters anger and hostility, which foster the impulse to retaliate.

While we're liable to blame others for harmful behaviors, our studies show that people are likely to let themselves off the hook for the harm that they cause. The *excuser bias* describes the tendency to focus on factors beyond our control to explain away our behavior, while turning a blind eye toward factors within our control. Ron is likely to claim to Lisa that their boss's urgent request is responsible for his tardiness, while overlooking the fact that he was already far behind schedule and probably would have missed the deadline anyway.

Winning Traits

In my studies, the managers and executives who were most successful in avoiding contentious relationships were rated by their colleagues as (1) above average in their ability to recognize that reasonable people could come to different conclusions and (2) slow to blame others and willing to accept personal responsibility for problems. Similarly, professionals rated effective at listening to, understanding, and respecting others' perspectives were best able to sustain cooperative and trusting relations.

Whether colleagues, departments, organizations, or countries are negotiating, the pernicious interplay of the accuser and excuser biases can snowball into a vicious cycle. Suppose Lisa blows up at Ron for the missed deadline. He's likely to fall victim to the accuser bias himself, attributing Lisa's "unjustified" attack to her hostile personality. The stage is set for a relationship fraught with bitterness and retaliation.

Virtuous Cycle Triggers

We've seen how vicious cycles get started, but what about their opposite, virtuous cycles? My research found that a particularly powerful trigger of virtuous relationships is *fairness perceptions.* Researchers have long understood the importance of people's perceptions of the fairness of a negotiation outcome. More recently, it's been discovered that we also attend closely to whether the negotiation *process* was itself fair. We tend to judge a negotiation to have been fair when we ourselves had ample opportunity to voice our point of view. Our sense of fairness increases the more we sense that the other side has genuinely considered our perspective.

Fairness perceptions have strong implications for those seeking to build strong relationships. First, the more fairly we feel we've been treated, the greater our satisfaction with the outcome, even if it isn't what we wanted. Second, we're more willing to abide by agreements reached through a process that felt fair than we are to comply with agreements reached through a process that didn't feel fair. Third, the more fairly we feel we've been treated, the more likely we are to trust the other side and cooperate with them. Studies indicate that the sense of being carefully listened to is more likely to inspire cooperation and trust in negotiation than are substantive concessions.

Avoiding Vicious Cycles, Promoting Virtuous Cycles

It would be far easier to overcome vicious cycles if they were always rooted in misperception. But while most people reciprocate cooperative moves, others will try to take advantage. How can you distinguish your misperceptions of hostility from genuine ill will? The first thing to do is to test your assumptions. Before mounting an aggressive response to the other side's perceived unreasonable behavior, check your perspective with others who don't have a stake in the issue. If others are more understanding of a view that strikes you as wholly unreasonable, it may be that you and your negotiating partner have honest and reasonable differences of opinion. Before assuming ill intent, look for extenuating circumstances that might provide an alternative explanation. Better yet, ask the other party to explain her behavior.

As you're working to promote a virtuous cycle, keep in mind that having a close and positive relationship with the other party is no guarantee that a negotiation will result in a mutually beneficial outcome. As Harvard Business School professor Kathleen McGinn has found in her research, negotiating partners who share a high regard don't necessarily succeed in finding mutually beneficial solutions. Sometimes negotiators can become so concerned about each other's outcomes that they overlook their own best interests. Good will should always be combined with the active pursuit of joint gains.

When Should We Use Agents? Direct versus Representative Negotiation

Jeffrey Z. Rubin
Frank E. A. Sander

Although we typically conceive of negotiations occurring directly between two or more principals, often neglected in a thoughtful analysis are the many situations where negotiations take place indirectly, through the use of representatives or surrogates of the principals. A father who speaks to his child's teacher (at the child's request), two lawyers meeting on behalf of their respective clients, the foreign service officers of different nations meeting to negotiate the settlement of a border dispute, a real estate agent informing would-be buyers of the seller's latest offer—each is an instance of negotiation through representatives.

In this brief essay, we wish to build on previous analyses of representative negotiation[1] to consider several key distinctions between direct and representative negotiations, and to indicate the circumstances under which we believe negotiators should go out of their way either to choose *or* to avoid negotiation through agents.

The most obvious effect of using agents—an effect that must be kept in mind in any analysis of representative negotiation—is complication of the transaction. As indicated in Figure 1, if we begin with a straightforward negotiation between two individuals, then the addition of two agents transforms this simple one-on-one deal into a complex matrix involving at least four primary negotiators, as well as two subsidiary ones (represented by the dotted lines in Figure 1). In addition, either of the agents may readily serve as a mediator between the client and the other agent or principal. Or the two agents might act as comediators between the principals. At a minimum, such a complex structure necessitates effective coordination. Beyond that, this structural complexity has implications—both positive and negative—for representative negotiation in general. Let us now review these respective benefits and liabilities.

Expertise

One of the primary reasons that principals choose to negotiate through agents is that the latter possess expertise that makes agreement—particularly favorable agreement—more likely. This expertise is likely to be of three different types:

Substantive knowledge: A tax attorney or accountant knows things about the current tax code that make it more likely that negotiations with an IRS auditor will benefit the client as much as possible. Similarly, a divorce lawyer, an engineering consultant, and a real estate agent may have substantive knowledge in a rather narrow domain of expertise, and this expertise may redound to the client's benefit.

Source: Jeffrey Z. Rubin and Frank E. A. Sander, "When Should We Use Agents? Direct vs. Representative Negotiation" from *Negotiation Journal,* October 1988, Copyright Kluwer Academic/Plenum Publishers.

FIGURE 1 | Possible Relations among Two Principals (P1 and P2) and Their Respective Agents (A1 and A2). (A solid line denotes an actual relation, a dotted line a potential one.)

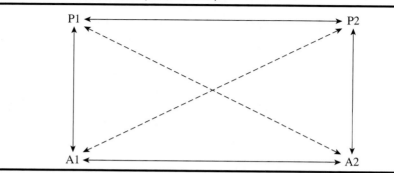

Process expertise: Quite apart from the specific expertise they may have in particular content areas, agents may have skill at the negotiation *process,* per se, thereby enhancing the prospects of a favorable agreement. A skillful negotiator— someone who understands how to obtain and reveal information about preferences, who is inventive, resourceful, firm on goals but flexible on means, and so on—is a valuable resource. Wise principals would do well to utilize the services of such skilled negotiators, unless they can find ways of developing such process skills themselves.

Special influence: A Washington lobbyist is paid to know the "right" people, to have access to the "corridors of power" that the principals themselves are unlikely to possess. Such "pull" can certainly help immensely, and is yet another form of expertise that agents may possess, although the lure of this "access" often outweighs in promise the special benefits that are confirmed in reality.

Note that the line separating these three forms of expertise is often a thin one, as in the case of a supplier who wishes to negotiate a sales contract with a prospective purchaser, and employs a former employee of the purchaser to handle the transaction; the former employee, as agent, may be a source of both substantive expertise *and* influence.

Note also that principals may not always know what expertise they need. Thus a person who has a dispute that seems headed for the courts may automatically seek out a litigator, not realizing that the vast preponderance of cases are settled by negotiation, requiring very different skills that the litigator may not possess. So although agents do indeed possess different forms of expertise that may enhance the prospects of a favorable settlement, clients do not necessarily know what they need; it's a bit like the problem of looking up the proper spelling of a word in the dictionary when you haven't got a clue about how to spell the word in question.

Detachment

Another important reason for using an agent to do the actual negotiation is that the principals may be too emotionally entangled in the subject of the dispute. A classic example is divorce. A husband and wife, caught in the throes of a bitter fight over the end of their marriage, may benefit from the "buffering" that agents can provide. Rather than confront each other with the depth of their anger and bitterness, the principals (P1 and P2 in Figure 1) may do far better by communicating only *indirectly,* via their respective representatives, A1 and A2. Stated most generally, when the negotiating climate is adversarial—when the disputants are confrontational rather than collaborative— it may be wiser to manage the conflict through intermediaries than run the risk of an impasse or explosion resulting from direct exchange.

Sometimes, however, it is the *agents* who are too intensely entangled. What is needed then is the detachment and rationality that only the principals can bring to the exchange. For example, lawyers may get too caught up in the adversary game and lose sight of the underlying problem that is dividing the principals (e.g., how to resolve a dispute about the quality of goods delivered as part of a long-term supply contract). The lawyers may be more concerned about who would win in court, while the clients simply want to get their derailed relationship back on track. Hence the thrust of some modern dispute resolution mechanisms (such as the minitrial) is precisely to take the dispute *out* of the hands of the technicians and give it back to the primary parties.[2]

Note, however, that the very "detachment" we are touting as a virtue of negotiation through agents can also be a liability. For example, in some interpersonal negotiations, apology and reconciliation may be an important ingredient of any resolution (see, e.g., Goldberg, Green, and Sander, 1987). Surrogates who are primarily technicians may not be able to bring to bear these empathic qualities.

Tactical Flexibility

The use of agents allows various gambits to be played out by the principals, in an effort to ratchet as much as possible from the other side. For example, if a seller asserts that the bottom line is $100,000, the buyer can try to haggle, albeit at the risk of losing the deal. If the buyer employs an agent, however, the agent can profess willingness to pay that sum but plead lack of authority, thereby gaining valuable time and opportunity for fuller consideration of the situation together with the principal. Or an agent for the seller who senses that the buyer may be especially eager to buy the property can claim that it is necessary to go back to the seller for ratification of the deal, only to return and up the price, profusely apologizing all the while for the behavior of an "unreasonable" client. The client and agent can thus together play the hard-hearted partner game.

Conversely, an agent may be used in order to push the other side in tough, even obnoxious, fashion, making it possible—in the best tradition of the "good cop–bad cop" ploy—for the client to intercede at last, and seem the essence of sweet reason in comparison with the agent. Or the agent may be used as a "stalking horse" to gather as much information about the adversary as possible, opening the way to proposals by the client that exploit the intelligence gathered.

Note that the tactical flexibility conferred by representative negotiations presupposes a competitive negotiating climate, a zero-sum contest in which each negotiator wishes to outsmart the other. It is the stuff of traditional statecraft, and the interested reader can do no better than study the writings of Schelling (1960) and Potter (1948), as well as Lax and Sebenius (1986). To repeat, the assumption behind this line of analysis is that effective negotiation requires some measure of artifice and duplicity, and that this is often best accomplished through the use of some sort of foil or alter ego—in the form of the agent. But the converse is not necessarily true: Where the negotiation is conducted in a problem-solving manner (cf. Fisher and Ury, 1981), agents may still be helpful, not because they resort to strategic ruses, but because they can help articulate interests, options, and alternatives. Four heads are clearly better than two, for example, when it comes to brainstorming about possible ways of reconciling the parties' interests.

Offsetting—indeed, typically *more* than offsetting—the three apparent virtues of representative negotiation are several sources of difficulty. Each is sufficiently important and potentially problematic that we believe caution is necessary before entering into negotiation through agents.

Extra "Moving Parts"

As indicated in Figure 1, representative negotiations entail greater structural complexity, additional moving parts in the negotiation machinery that—given a need for expertise, detachment, or tactical flexibility—can help move parties toward a favorable agreement. Additional moving parts, however, can also mean additional expense, in the form of the time required in the finding, evaluating, and engaging of agents, as well as the financial cost of retaining their services. And it can mean additional problems, more things that can go wrong. For instance, a message intended by a client may not be the message transmitted by that client's agent to the other party. Or the message received by that agent from the other party may be very different from the one that that agent (either deliberately or inadvertently) manages to convey to his or her client.

At one level, then, the introduction of additional links in the communication system increases the risk of distortion in the information conveyed back and forth between the principals. Beyond that lies a second difficulty: the possibility that eventually the principals will come to rely so extensively on their respective agents that they no longer communicate directly—even though they could, and even though they might well benefit from doing so. In effect (see Figure 1), P1, in order to reach P2, now invariably goes through the A1–A2 chain, even though such maneuvering is no longer warranted. Consider, for example, the case of a divorcing couple who, in explicit compliance with the advice of their adversary lawyers, have avoided any direct contact with each other during the divorce proceedings. Once the divorce has been obtained, will the parties' ability to communicate effectively with each other (e.g., over support and custody issues) be adversely affected by their excessive prior reliance on their attorneys?

Yet another potentially problematic implication of this increasingly complex social machinery is that unwanted conditions may arise that apply undue pressure on individual negotiators. Thus A2, in performing a mediatory function between P2 and the other side (P1 and A1), may be prone to become allied with the opposing team—or at least to be so viewed by P2. Greater number does not necessarily mean greater wisdom, however, and the pressures toward uniformity of opinion that result from coalition formation may adversely affect the quality of the decisions reached.

In sum, the introduction of agents increases the complexity of the social apparatus of negotiation, and in so doing increases the chances of unwanted side effects. A related problem should be briefly noted here: the difficulty of asymmetry, as when an agent negotiates not with another agent but directly with the other principal. In effect, this was the case in 1978 when Egypt's Sadat negotiated with Israel's Begin at Camp David. Sadat considered himself empowered to make binding decisions for Egypt, while—at least partly for tactical purposes—Begin represented himself as ultimately accountable to his cabinet and to the Israeli parliament. While this "mismatched" negotiation between a principal (Sadat) and an agent (Begin) *did* result in agreement (thanks in good measure to President Carter's intercession as a mediator), it was not easy. The asymmetry of role meant that the two sides differed in their readiness to move forward toward an agreement, their ability to be shielded by a representative, and their willingness/ability to guarantee that any agreement reached would "stick."[3]

Different dynamics will characterize the negotiation depending on whether it is between clients, between lawyers, or with both present. If just the clients are there, the dealings will be more direct and forthright, and issues of authority and ratification disappear. With just the lawyers present, there may be less direct factual information but concomitantly more candor about delicate topics. Suppose, for example, that an aging soprano seeks to persuade an opera company to sign her for the lead role in an upcoming opera. If she is not present, the opera's agent may try to lower the price, contending that the singer is past her prime. Such candor is not recommended if the singer is present at the negotiation!

Problems of "Ownership" and Conflicting Interests

In theory, it is clear that the principal calls the shots. Imagine, however, an agent who is intent on applying the *Getting to Yes* (Fisher and Ury, 1981) approach by searching for objective criteria and a fair outcome. Suppose the client simply wants the best possible outcome, perhaps because it is a one-shot deal not involving a future relationship with the other party. What if the agent (a lawyer, perhaps) *does* care about his future relationship with the other *agent,* and wants to be remembered as a fair and scrupulous bargainer? How *should* this conflict get resolved and how, in the absence of explicit discussion, *will* it be resolved, if at all? Conversely, the client, because of a valuable long-term relationship, may want to maintain good relations with the other side. But if the client simply looks for an agent who is renowned for an ability to pull out all the stops, the client's overall objectives may suffer as the result of an overzealous advocate.

This issue may arise in a number of contexts. Suppose that, in the course of a dispute settlement negotiation,[4] a lawyer who is intent on getting the best possible deal for a client turns down an offer that was within the client's acceptable range. Is this proper behavior by the agent? The Model Rules of Professional Conduct for attorneys explicitly require (see Rules 1.2(a), 1.4) that every offer must be communicated to the principal, and perhaps a failure to do so might lead to a successful malpractice action against the attorney if the deal finally fell through.

Another illustration involves the situation where the agent and principal have divergent ethical norms. Suppose that a seller of a house has just learned that the dwelling is infested with termites, but instructs the agent not to reveal this fact, even in response to specific inquiry from the buyer. How should these tensions be fairly resolved, keeping in mind the fact that the agent may be subject to a professional code of conduct that gives directions that may conflict with the ethical values of the client?[5] There may, of course, be artful ways of dealing with such dilemmas, as, for example, slyly deflecting any relevant inquiry by the buyer. But preferably these problems should be explicitly addressed in the course of the initial discussion between agent and principal. To some extent, the problem may be resolved by the principal's tendency to pick an agent who is congenial and compatible. But as we pointed out before, principals are not always aware of and knowledgeable about the relevant considerations that go into the choice of an agent. Hence if these issues are not addressed explicitly at the outset, termination of the relationship midstream in egregious cases may be the only alternative.

Differing goals and standards of agent and principal may create conflicting pulls. For example, the buyer's agent may be compensated as a percentage of the purchase price, thus creating an incentive to have the price as high as possible. The buyer, of course, wants the lowest possible price. Similarly, where a lawyer is paid by the hour, there may be an incentive to draw out the negotiation, whereas the client prefers an expeditious negotiation at the lowest possible cost.

While these are not insoluble problems, to be sure, they do constitute yet another example of the difficulties that may arise as one moves to representative negotiations. Although in theory the principals are in command, once agents have been introduced the chemistry changes, and new actors—with agenda, incentives, and constraints of their own—are part of the picture. Short of an abrupt firing of the agents, principals may find themselves less in control of the situation once agents have come on the scene.

Encouragement of Artifice and Duplicity

Finally, as already noted, the introduction of agents often seems to invite clients to devise stratagems (with or without these agents) to outwit the other side. Admittedly, there is nothing intrinsic to the presence of representatives that dictates a move in this direction; still, perhaps because of the additional expense incurred, the seductive lure of a "killing" with the help of one's "hired gun," or the introduction of new, sometimes perverse incentives, representative negotiations often seem to instill (or reflect) a more adversarial climate.

Conclusion

It follows from the preceding analysis that, ordinarily, negotiations conducted directly between the principals are preferable to negotiation through representatives. When the principals' relationship is fundamentally cooperative or informed by enlightened self-interest, agents may often be unnecessary; since there is little or no antagonism in the relationship, there is no need for the buffering detachment afforded by agents. Moreover, by negotiating directly, there is reduced risk of miscoordination, misrepresentation, and miscommunication.

On the other hand, representative negotiation *does* have an important and necessary place. When special expertise is required, when tactical flexibility is deemed important and—most important—when direct contact is likely to produce confrontation rather than collaboration, agents *can* render an important service.

Above all, the choice of whether to negotiate directly or through surrogates is an important one, with significant ramifications. It therefore should be addressed explicitly by weighing some of the considerations advanced here. And if an agent *is* selected, careful advance canvassing of issues such as those discussed here (e.g., authority and ethical standards) is essential.

Notes

We thank Michael Wheeler for the many constructive comments, suggestions, and conversations that preceded this article; and we gratefully acknowledge the helpful comments of Stephen B. Goldberg on an earlier draft of this manuscript.

1. See, in particular, the concise and insightful discussion by Lax and Sebenius (1986) in Chapter 15 of their *The Manager as Negotiator.*

2. Compare in this connection the unfortunate recent decision of the United States Court of Appeals for the Seventh Circuit to the effect that a federal district court judge has no power to compel principals with settlement authority to attend a settlement conference. *G. Heileman Brewing Co. v. Joseph Oat Corp.,* 848 F. 2d 1415 (7th Circuit 1988).

3. Compare in this connection Rule 4.2 of the American Bar Association's Model Rules of Professional Conduct, which prohibits a lawyer from dealing directly with the opposing principal, if that principal is represented by an attorney.

4. See Sander and Rubin (1988) for a discussion of the differences between dealmaking and dispute settlement negotiation.

5. See, for example, Rule 4.1 of the ABA's Model Rules of Professional Conduct, prohibiting attorneys from making materially false statements.

References

Fisher, R., and W. L. Ury. (1981). *Getting to yes: Negotiating agreement without giving in.* Boston: Houghton Mifflin.

Goldberg, S., E. Green, and F. E. A. Sander. (1987). "Saying you're sorry." *Negotiation Journal* 3, pp. 221–24.

Lax, D. A., and J. K. Sebenius. (1986). *The manager as negotiator.* New York: Free Press.

Potter, S. (1948). *The theory and practice of gamesmanship: The art of winning games without actually cheating.* New York: Holt.

Sander, F. E. A., and J. Z. Rubin. (1988). "The Janus quality of negotiation: Dealmaking and dispute settlement." *Negotiation Journal* 4, pp. 109–13.

Schelling, T. (1960). *The strategy of conflict.* Cambridge, MA: Harvard University Press.

When a Contract Isn't Enough: How to Be Sure Your Agent Gets You the Best Deal

James K. Sebenius

Negotiation is often handled by an agent or representative. Here's some advice on managing this potentially double-edged relationship.

When selling your house or company, working out terms with your publisher, or handling a lawsuit, you often engage an agent. Lawyers, investment bankers, literary agents, and others who negotiate on your behalf may help you in many ways: They may have greater specialized expertise than you do, they may be better bargainers, they may have superior access to the other side, they may serve as a useful buffer, and they may save your time. (In "When You Shouldn't Go It Alone," an article in the March issue of *Negotiation,* my colleague Lawrence Susskind delves into some of the advantages of relying on agents and offers good advice on how to use them effectively.)

With the benefits of employing an agent, however, come certain risks. A faulty contract, for instance, can set the stage for disaster by failing to properly align her incentives and provide for appropriate monitoring of her work. (See the sidebar "The Pitfalls of Faulty Contracts.") Even experienced negotiators who take great care in constructing agent contracts may unexpectedly find themselves facing agent incentive and monitoring problems. These issues, which often arise from factors that fall heavily *outside* the structure of the contract, can lead to three kinds of problem agents.

In this article, I describe the telltale signs of *faulty agents, free agents,* and *double agents.* If you fail to look out for these problem agents, your interests may suffer in negotiation.

1. Faulty Agents

A *Wall Street Journal* article tells the story of top executive pay attorney Joseph Bachelder, who was representing a client who'd just been chosen as a company's next CEO. After a first session with the board's representative to hammer out a compensation package, Bachelder took his client aside and informed him that he would get everything he wanted from the negotiation.

Why was Bachelder so confident of total victory? Because, he explained, the board had put the firm's well-regarded general counsel in charge of the negotiations. Why was this a mistake? "When this is over, you're going to be that guy's boss," Bachelder happily informed his client. "He knows that. He can't fight you too hard on anything."

Source: From *Negotiation,* a newsletter published by Harvard Business School Publishing and the Program on Negotiation at Harvard Law School. July 2004, pp. 3–5.

The board picked a *faulty agent* for this negotiation—one whose underlying incentives conflicted with the board's best interests. The general counsel's dominant interest was to lay the groundwork for a good relationship with the future CEO. As its representative in these critical talks, the board should have instead hired an outside specialist with properly aligned interests.

The faulty agent problem often shows up in Pentagon contracting. Procurement officers are charged with representing the public interest when negotiating with defense contractors. Yet some of these officers quietly make plans to leave the civil service and join one of these defense contractors—at a far higher salary. While still representing the Pentagon, such agents are likely to go much easier on the other side than they should.

While an overriding self-interest in a future relationship with a negotiation counterpart may create a faulty agent, so may the *lack* of any meaningful future concern. Consider a company that is negotiating an alliance or acquisition through a heavily price-driven process with a strong legalistic component. In such instances, it's common for one internal team, such as the business development unit, to act as the company's agent. When the team's job is done—often after a nasty, adversarial process—the company's operational management unit inherits the unenviable job of making the arrangement work.

Jerry Kaplan, founder of GO Corporation, an early pen computing firm, criticized the process by which IBM invested in his firm. In his book *Startup* (reprint ed., Penguin, 1996), Kaplan writes, "Rather than empowering the responsible party to make the deal, IBM assigns a professional negotiator, who usually knows or cares little for the substance of the agreement but has absolute authority. . . . The negotiator begins by assembling a list of interested internal constituents, all of whom are free to add new requirements . . . or block some minor concession."

When a faulty agent leads a negotiation, it's unlikely the right minds will converge on a productive arrangement. Similarly, while the top management of two companies in a supply chain may speak glowingly of the strength and quality of their partnership, the buyer's procurement agent may be motivated by monthly targets and penny-pinching while overlooking broader concerns. A fanatical focus on getting the best price may be due in part to how the agent is evaluated by her superior, but also may derive from the organization's culture.

When suppliers seek advice on dealing with faulty agents, they might be told to listen actively, to improve their body language, and to decide who should make the first offer. Another strategy is to nurture an internal champion on the other side who truly benefits from your added quality and service—and who will pressure the agent on your behalf.

2. Free Agents

Supposedly a negotiator who works faithfully on behalf of his principal's real interests, a free agent has incentives and control over the process that effectively lead him to act independently. Investment bankers or other deal makers with a powerful interest in closing a deal can function as free agents. For example, when Matsushita Electric Industrial

Co. paid $6.59 billion in 1990 for MCA, the owner of Universal Pictures and several record companies and theme parks, its rationale was to ensure a steady flow of "creative software" for its global hardware businesses. Senior MCA management agreed to the acquisition largely with the expectation that its new, cash-rich Japanese parent could provide capital for entertainment businesses needed to make MCA competitive with rivals such as Disney and Cap Cities/ABC.

Matsushita chose Mike Ovitz, a former Hollywood talent agent with a burning ambition to become a corporate matchmaker, to represent it at the bargaining table. Ovitz masterminded an intricate set of maneuvers that kept the two parties mostly *apart* during the process, managing the information flow and both sides' expectations until the deal was virtually closed.

Both Matsushita and MCA developed a distorted perception of the other's real intentions, leading to postdeal friction and the sale of MCA five years later to Seagram, at a substantial loss to Matsushita both in terms of face and money— ¥165 billion, or about $1.6 billion. In part due to the cultural chasms dividing old-line industrial Japan, creative Hollywood, and the New York financial community, neither side truly probed the other's underlying expectations until it was too late. But even more than culture, a free agent with a dominant interest in forging a deal— almost any deal—was a key factor, as was the substantial freedom he was given to act on that interest.

The Pitfalls of Faulty Contracts

Some of the trickier aspects of designing the right contract with your agent include properly aligning her incentives and monitoring her work. Supervising your agent can be especially hard when she knows more than you do about the area of work. For example, hiring an agent who's a lawyer and paying her on an hourly basis may induce her to spend more time than you think necessary—at your expense. She might become a literary perfectionist, spending hours crafting and polishing an offer letter to the other side when, as far as you're concerned, the second draft would have done just fine. To prevent her from running up needless hours, you might opt instead for a fixed-fee engagement. Then, however, she may cut corners, doing just enough to reach her fee.

Contingent contracts that grant higher agent fees as your outcome improves may superficially align both your interests. Yet here, too, conflicts may lurk. For example, as a negotiation unfolds, if your agent believes that the odds that the deal will close are falling, he may reduce his effort, and the no-deal outcome may become self-fulfilling. By contrast, once a profitable agreement seems very likely, your agent, unbeknownst to you, may take excessive negotiating risks on your behalf, hoping for a much better outcome or even a "trophy deal" to burnish his reputation. In short, even when both you and your agent have incentives to reach a strong deal, your appetites for risk may radically differ.

These pitfalls suggest the need for awareness and clarity when drawing up a contract with an agent. Specifically, you should work to design the financial arrangement most suited to your situation, align incentives and monitor the agent's work as well as possible, and engage either someone you've worked with successfully or someone who has a solid reputation for efficiency, effectiveness, and faithful representation.

For more on this topic, see *Beyond Winning: Negotiating to Create Value in Deals and Disputes* by Robert H. Mnookin et al. (Harvard University Press, 2000) and *Negotiating on Behalf of Others,* ed. by Robert H. Mnookin and Lawrence E. Susskind (Sage, 1999).

---

3. Double Agents

When their incentives are wrong enough and their control over the negotiation process is high, merely faulty agents can morph into *double agents.* Many buyers of real estate and of companies can wryly testify how standard financial arrangements can unwittingly produce this result. Consider the common practice of compensating the real estate agents or investment bankers on both sides with a percentage of the sale price. What tacit alignments do such arrangements create? Just like the seller and his agent, the buyer's agent now benefits from a high-priced deal. Pity the hapless buyer, the sole player looking for a bargain.

Beyond faulty contracts, other factors can produce double agents. After a small business suffered a fire, for example, its owner hired an experienced consultant to negotiate damage claims with his insurance company. The consultant was promised a fixed fee for success, plus a sliding bonus based on the settlement amount. The consultant very quickly negotiated an adequate settlement, but the owner soon became disenchanted with the outcome. Why? Because he learned that his agent, after dealing for years with the same small set of insurance companies, had fallen into a pattern of rapid but relatively modest claims settlements. If he had bargained harder for his client, the consultant might have gained an incremental incentive fee but would have risked retaliation from the insurance company. In effect, the business owner was a one-time bit player in a long-term game that powerfully aligned the interests of the insurance company with those of the consultant.

Here's a more unusual instance of a double agent. *New York Times* columnist Nicholas Kristof was reporting from Iraq when he was summoned to a government ministry to account for an "outrageous" article he'd written detailing the Saddam Hussein regime's brutal torture of a Muslim leader. Included in the meeting was Kristof's official Iraqi government minder. In a 2003 column, Kristof describes the experience of being "menacingly denounced by two of Saddam's henchmen":

> Neither man could speak English and they hadn't actually read the offending column . . . my government minder took my column and translated it for them. I saw my life flash before my eyes. But my minder's job was to spy on me, and he worried that my tough column would reflect badly on his spying. Plus, he was charging me $100 a day, and he would lose a fortune if I was expelled, or worse. So he translated my column very selectively. There was no mention of burning beards or nails in heads. He left out whole paragraphs. When he finished, the two senior officials shrugged and let me off scot-free.

Kristof was fortunate indeed that the incentives of this Iraqi government representative—just like those of double agents in more benign settings—were dramatically misaligned from those of his superiors. Contrary interests plus the capacity to control and shape the information that he passes along is a common trait of a double agent.

How can you avoid becoming the next victim of a faulty agent (wrong interests), a free agent (wrong interests plus control of the process and information), or a double agent (an extreme version of faulty and free)? When evaluating and engaging a potential agent, you need to focus on more than just designing a contract that aligns your financial incentives. To keep a problem agent at bay, fix a penetrating eye on her present and future relationships, her full set of interests, and the extent to which she will be able to filter information and control the negotiating process.

The Closer

Erin Strout

Sports agent Leigh Steinberg likes to win—but not at all costs. Here's what sales executives can learn from his surprising negotiation tactics.

Leigh Steinberg prefers Levi's and sneakers to a suit and tie. His hair? Not a hint of gel or mousse to be found. He doesn't talk fast. He isn't brash. On first glance he looks more like a high school history teacher than the high-powered sports agent that he is. Get Steinberg talking, though, and there's no mistaking why he's among the best in his business, negotiating more than a billion dollars in professional sports contracts in 27 years.

Just an hour off of a flight from Milwaukee, where he spent most of the previous night hobnobbing at Major League Baseball's All Star Game festivities, Steinberg is back in California, battling exhaustion. The home-run derby ran late, he says, and the parties didn't begin until after 10 p.m., keeping him up into the wee hours of the morning. That's the least of the problems in Milwaukee, though, where there's talk of a players' strike and the game ended in a disappointing tie. Media savvy to the extreme, Steinberg knows the circumstances are leading to more than a few disgruntled fans. "Labor versus management is a process that needs to be rationally and sensibly resolved," he says, now relaxing in a pair of jeans and a casual button-down shirt, his white sneakers propped up on a glass coffee table, strewn with sports trade magazines and newspapers. "If the median income of a fan is $40,000, there's no sympathy there—it seems absurd to people."

But just because players' salaries may come off as obscene to the general public doesn't mean Steinberg can't justify every one that he's negotiated. He built his business on wooing some of the best NFL quarterbacks as clients, cinching the largest contracts in football history during their time. His Newport Beach, California, office, overlooking the Pacific Ocean, is a shrine to his success. The walls and bookshelves are crammed with framed newspaper clippings; photos of himself with scores of movie stars, politicians, and athletes; autographed posters, helmets, and footballs; and original paintings of the biggest names in sports, like Troy Aikman, Drew Bledsoe, Warren Moon, Steve Young, and dozens of others—all current or former clients. It's a setting that befits a man who claims to be the real-life inspiration for the title character of the movie Jerry Maguire. Show me the money? Steinberg has shown boatloads of greenbacks to his clients.

But before his life revolved around salary caps and signing bonuses, Steinberg had to learn the finer points of negotiation. He's mastered those skills through trial and error, discovering that success only comes with hefty research, absolute knowledge of the other side's position, an ability to prioritize goals, and using a spirit of compromise instead of conflict.

Source: From *Sales & Marketing Management* 154, no. 9 (Sept. 2002). © 2002 VNU Business Media, Inc. Published with permission.

Steinberg believes some of the most meaningful lessons came during his time as an undergraduate at the University of California at Berkeley. It was 1969, he was student body president, and each day brought another student demonstration against the Vietnam War. Talks among the university administration, the community, and the students broke down over the use of the People's Park—where the protests took place—and the police became involved. Tear gas was sprayed from helicopters, shots were fired, students retaliated by throwing bottles and rocks. Ultimately a student was killed and the National Guard arrived. "The results of unsuccessful negotiation became clear," Steinberg says. "When both sides have an absolute sense of righteousness, self-destruction ensues. Nothing can be more illustrative of that than police shooting tear gas at a group of students."

The experience at Berkeley illustrated the human side of negotiating for Steinberg, who 33 years later still regards that lesson as one of the greatest he's learned. He's based his career on the notion that he can get the job done—and done well—without compromising his integrity. But it's not an easy charge to stick to ideals fostered in the 1960s, when the sports world was a distinctly different place. "Now there's a heightened level of coverage of the business side of sports," Steinberg says. "That makes each negotiation a public event subject to controversy and talk everywhere."

That's why Steinberg isn't afraid to take his time, using his soft-spoken, analytical candor as a weapon. He invites long silences as a chance to think and uses them as an outward expression of his patience. Fidgeting in his tan leather chair, playing with his glasses, and fiddling with a water bottle, only taking a sip every now and then, he ponders every sentence in his head before he speaks in sound bites.

Steinberg knows the key to his own success lies in resilience and endurance, because inevitably every negotiation will run into barriers—even the one that in hindsight is among his best didn't start out so well. It was 1995 and quarterback Drew Bledsoe's contract with the New England Patriots was about to expire. In a hotel lobby in Arizona, Steinberg and Patriots' owner Bob Kraft tucked themselves away in a corner for initial talks, agreeing to give each other their best offers. Kraft considered $4 million a year for six years and a signing bonus of $5 million a fair deal. Steinberg, on the other hand, countered with $6.5 million per year for six years, and a $12 million signing bonus. "Our offers weren't even close," Steinberg says.

Discussion ceased and months passed with absolutely no talks. By July, when training camps began, there was still no word. Finally Steinberg, who was about to travel east to finalize contracts for his rookie clients, called Kraft and asked for a meeting. At an Italian restaurant in Boston, Kraft and Steinberg discussed the future of the Patriots and the reason why so much time had passed without revisiting Bledsoe's contract. Kraft was disappointed in the initial meeting, which he entered presuming a deal would result. When it didn't, he thought Steinberg wanted to wait for Bledsoe to reach free-agent status and shop him elsewhere. "The questioning of motives without communication is the genesis of unsuccessful negotiation," Steinberg says. "But we reopened the lines of communication and started all over again. Kraft had to understand that Bledsoe wanted to be a Patriot and I had to understand the pressure he felt to build a competitive franchise. Ultimately that team got what they bargained for—a Pro Bowl quarterback that went on to take them to the Super Bowl."

The next morning Kraft and Steinberg met again to come up with final figures. The compromise? An increased bonus and a bit less salary to free up immediate money for the Patriots to sign other key players. It was a historic, seven-year, $42 million package that included an $11.5 million signing bonus. That July week was a lucrative one all around for Steinberg, who signed quarterback Kerry Collins to a $23 million deal with the Carolina Panthers, wrapped up Kordell Stewart's contract with the Pittsburgh Steelers, and closed a $19 million deal with the Cincinnati Bengals for running back Ki-Jana Carter. "Your level of stamina is important," Steinberg says. "You have to be able to think under sleep deprivation, when you're bored, hungry, and uncomfortable."

Understanding the other side's motives and perspective, as Steinberg eventually did with Kraft and the Patriots, is a priority in successful negotiations. Steinberg invests heavily in exhaustive research, figuring out how valuable his client is compared with similarly situated players in the league, and clearly determining the revenue picture of the franchise. He also considers the negotiation style of the other side, determining if they are sincere, bombastic, or employ a high–low tactic (bargaining with unrealistically high or low numbers).

But the research doesn't stop there: Steinberg knows exactly what he wants and what he's willing to compromise, a component most people neglect. "The pitfall of negotiations is people fail to prioritize. The human psyche can withstand only so much stress, so when you swing back and forth between situations, eventually someone will make a decision to stop the stress, and perhaps lose out on something important to them," Steinberg says. "For me, I have to ask my clients a series of probing questions. Do they want short-term gain or long-term security? Is geographic location important? Or are profile, exposure, and endorsements a priority? If a client is desperate to return home, he might be willing to take less money to do so. You have to prioritize ahead of time."

Helping clients realize what's important on and off the field has earned Steinberg an enviable reputation among NFL players. "He has a reputation as the least sleazy of all the agents," claims one former NFL kicker.

Warren Moon, former Pro Bowl quarterback for the Houston Oilers, Minnesota Vikings, Seattle Seahawks, and Kansas City Chiefs, says his decision to hire Steinberg was an easy one. "He has built relationships with so many people in the NFL, because they know he's fair and ethical," says Moon, who retired two years ago and now works with Steinberg, helping his NFL clients with their charitable causes and other off-field needs. "At first a lot of players don't think he's for real, because he dresses in jeans and a golf shirt—he's not some slick attorney. Then they talk to him and find out that he's an intelligent guy whose interests go beyond the scope of professional sports."

Steinberg holds his athletes to a high standard, Moon says, requesting that they immediately begin thinking of postfootball careers and create charities or scholarships that benefit the communities they came from. It's a brilliant PR move for Steinberg and the players, but in the end the tactic also gives the agent peace of mind. "I had a revelation early on in my career that football players serve as role models, that they have the power to trigger imitative behavior," Steinberg says. "It's important to me to have a compelling rationale to justify what I do—that these players deserve and earn all the money that they have coming to them."

Cultivating that good-guy image for himself and his clients no doubt only helps Steinberg at the negotiating table, where his objective, he says, is always a win–win outcome. Creating unquestionable leverage—whether it's an MVP's free-agent status or a rookie player's upstanding character—doesn't hurt either. Such strategies, he says, help all parties stay on track, as his biggest pet peeve is a discussion that ends in hurt feelings or raised voices. "Allowing personal competitiveness and a desire to win at all costs can outweigh the benefits of a healthy compromise," he says. "When people use intemperate, antagonistic language, it obscures communication. To me, that's just covering up for a lack of preparation, and it destroys future relations."

It's not that Steinberg hasn't had his share of soured discussions. "There's been a lot of them," he says, with a laugh. For instance, while fans may blame Cincinnati Bengals' owner Mike Brown for a poor choice in the 1992 draft, Steinberg actually blames himself for quarterback David Klingler's paltry NFL career—only 33 games played over six seasons. Steinberg says that Brown had proven over time to be as tough a negotiator as they come, and although in the end Klingler was a well-paid player, it came at a far greater price than either party anticipated. "Discussions degenerated into a hold-out," Steinberg says. "Klingler ended up out of training camp most of the summer of his rookie year—for a quarterback the time spent as a rookie in camp is critical. Now he's not playing in the NFL because I couldn't get the Bengals to sign in time for Klingler to have a good rookie year."

Did Steinberg glean any redeeming lesson from the experience? "Don't get drafted by the Bengals," he deadpans.

Sometimes the best strategy is to walk away, Steinberg surmises. "I've learned not to push a losing argument to the end because it allows the other person to become even more locked into his position," he says. "If you find yourself unable to persuade the other party, it's time to back off for a while and design another approach. At the end of the process you want to be able to describe the outcome as mutually satisfying—that both parties used give and take."

With that, Steinberg gets up from the chair he was comfortably reclining on and meanders over to his desk, where he grabs three pieces of chewing gum from a crystal candy dish and proceeds to pop them into his mouth one at a time. While it seems like he could reminisce about each player, deal, and contract endlessly, he's growing weary as rush hour sets in on the freeways eight floors below. "Really, every human being can justify why his or her own position is the only truth," he summarizes, taking his glasses off and running his hand through his rumpled hair. "But you only win when your reality prevails."

Negotiating Tip

Problem: A potential customer is about to sign a huge deal, when a competitor suddenly makes a tempting last-minute offer with lower prices. There's no way you can cut your prices further, but also no way you can return to the company empty-handed. How can you seal the deal?

Solution: Salespeople should always be prepared for just such a competitive ambush, warns Bill Brooks, CEO of The Brooks Group, a sales management training firm in

Greensboro, North Carolina. "Don't make your best offer your last offer," he says. "You always have to have a trump card." Brooks suggests asking to compare offerings, and then finding value-added areas where your competitor's deal lacks. If price isn't the factor that improves your contract then it could be a service, like additional training, adjusted ordering levels, extension of payment terms, or volume allowances, Brooks says. You should assure your client that you are willing to make concessions in areas that will add just as much, if not more, value to their bottom line than would a mere price break. And when revising the contract, "differentiate it so your offering can never be compared apple-to-apple," Brooks says.

—Julia Chang

Negotiating Tip

Problem: Your best channel partner is hesitant about renewing his contract. If the partner leaves, your company will be missing a lucrative revenue stream. How do you maintain the relationship without compromising profitability?

Solution: It's likely the partner perceives he's getting a low ratio of value to the investment involved, says T.K. Kieran, principal with Nashville-based sales consultancy NewLeaf Partners. "So find nontraditional ways of bringing value to the partnership," Kieran says.

She suggests asking the client to have a half-day powwow to brainstorm what his business goals are, and how you can help meet them. For example, if the client seeks more sales lead generation, offer to introduce him to new customers. Or if he seeks more technical support, offer to lend some of your engineers for a period of time. Placing an estimated cost to these types of value-added elements—which likely won't encroach on your own profits—also proves to the partner the additional worth you are bringing to the table. Kieran also suggests that companies include high-level executives in these sessions to prove how much your firm values the partnership.

—J.C.

Negotiating Tip

Problem: Your company just raised prices, and one of your top customers is about to bolt to the competition. How can you keep him on board?

Solution: First make clear the interests of both parties. Explain to the customer why you need to raise prices—maybe your costs have risen. When you negotiate, speak to someone who has the influence within the company and who can clarify the client's interests; then criteria on both sides can be established. "At that point, they'll either say, 'I understand,' or they'll say, 'I'm ready to walk,'" says David Pearson, director of sales distribution for Reno, Nevada–based Miller Heiman, a sales consulting firm.

If the customer is ready to walk, don't let him do it yet—brainstorm solutions. Maybe there are financing or payment options. Maybe something can be offered in trade: Pearson had a client who simply couldn't stretch his budget any further, but offered Pearson's company free use of a 10,000-square-foot training facility in exchange for the difference in price. "We could have easily walked away," Pearson says. "But this was an option the client came up with, and it was an agreeable option for me."

—Michael Weinreb

Negotiating Tip

Problem: You've had a huge year, surpassed your quota, and assumed new management responsibilities. How do you negotiate a raise?

Solution: Start by evaluating yourself. Determine your value to the company—be able to document your success. Know what others are getting paid, inside and outside of the company, by checking Web sites like Salary.com and even by asking colleagues. Understand where the company stands financially. "Money's not a dirty topic," says Deborah Kolb, a professor of management at Simmons Graduate School of Management, in Boston. "If your boss tells you that you're out of line, you want to be able to tell her that this is consistent with the information you've gathered."

Also try to see the situation from your boss's perspective. Understand her style and what you know about dealing with her previously. Will she require a formal proposal or be comfortable with an informal conversation? Come up with five reasons why she shouldn't honor your request. "It may mean changing what you ask for," Kolb says. Ask yourself how flexible you're willing to be—perhaps you'd accept an increase in your commission or a bonus.

—M.W.

Negotiating Tip

Problem: You've been offered two identical sales positions with separate companies. How do you negotiate between the two offers?

Solution: Once again, look inward. Ask yourself, What are my priorities? Is it freedom to work from home? Is it money? When you figure out what you want, gather information about each company's priorities by using the Web and talking to colleagues. Ask questions during interviews. "Be clear on what the companies' interests are," says Irma Tyler-Wood, principal of Cambridge, Massachusetts–based ThoughtBridge, a negotiation training firm. "Asking about the company gives you leverage."

Try to get one job offer while negotiating. If one company offers what you want, and you still find yourself interested in the other job, raise the issue in a manner that's in keeping with the company's management style. Explain your motivations, especially if you're asking what may be intrusive questions. If you want more than what they're willing to offer, explain why you're worth it. "Companies look for their salespeople to be aggressive," Tyler Wood says. "But they also expect you to have people skills."

—M.W.

A 12-Step Program

Sports agent Leigh Steinberg reveals his winning style in his best seller, *Winning with Integrity: Getting What You Want without Selling Your Soul* (Three Rivers Press, 1998). Here are his 12 rules for negotiation success:

1. Align yourself with people who share your values.
2. Learn all you can about the other party.
3. Convince the other party that you have an option.
4. Set your liners before the negotiation begins.
5. Establish a climate of cooperation, not conflict.
6. In the face of intimidation, show no fear.
7. Learn to listen.
8. Be comfortable with silence.
9. Avoid playing split-the-difference.
10. Emphasize your concessions; minimize the other party's.
11. Never push a losing argument to the end.
12. Develop relationships, not conquests.

Reading 3.7

The New Boss
Matt Bai

Andy Stern, who leads the largest and fastest-growing union in the country, is determined to save the American worker.
*   And he's willing to tear apart the labor movement—and perhaps the Democratic Party as well—in order to do it.*

Purple is the color of Andrew Stern's life. He wears, almost exclusively, purple shirts, purple jackets, and purple caps. He carries a purple duffel bag and drinks bottled water with a purple label, emblazoned with the purple logo of the Service Employees International Union, of which Stern is president. There are union halls in America where a man could get himself hurt wearing a lilac shirt, but the SEIU is a different kind of union, rooted in the new service economy. Its members aren't truck drivers or assembly-line workers but janitors and nurses and home health care aides, roughly a third of whom are black, Asian, or Latino. While the old-line industrial unions have been shrinking every year, Stern's union has been organizing low-wage workers, many of whom have never belonged to a union, at a torrid pace, to the point where the SEIU is now the largest and fastest-growing trade union in North America. Once a movement of rust brown and steel gray, Big Labor is increasingly represented, at rallies and political conventions, by a rising sea of purple.

All of this makes Andy Stern—a charismatic 54-year-old former social service worker—a very powerful man in labor, and also in Democratic politics. The job of running a union in America, even the biggest union around, isn't what it once was. The age of automation and globalization, with its "race to the bottom" among companies searching for lower wages overseas, has savaged organized labor. Fifty years ago, a third of workers in the United States carried union cards in their wallets; now it's barely 1 in 10. An estimated 21 million service industry workers have never belonged to a union, and between most employers' antipathy to unions and federal laws that discourage workers from demanding one, chances are that the vast majority of them never will.

Over the years, union bosses have grown comfortable blaming everyone else—timid politicians, corrupt CEOs, greedy shareholders—for their inexorable decline. But last year, Andy Stern did something heretical: He started pointing the finger back at his fellow union leaders. Of course workers had been punished by forces outside their control, Stern said. But what had big labor done to adapt? Union bosses, Stern scolded, had been too busy flying around with senators and riding around in chauffeur-driven cars to figure out how to counter the effects of globalization, which have cost millions of Americans their jobs and their pensions. Faced with declining union rolls, the bosses made things worse by raiding one another's industries, which only diluted the power of

Source: From *The New York Times Magazine*, January 30, 2005, pp. 38–45, 62, 68, 71.

their workers. The nation's flight attendants, for instance, are now divided among several different unions, making it difficult, if not impossible, for them to wield any leverage over an entire industry.

Stern put the union movement's eroding stature in business terms: if any other $6.5 billion corporation had insisted on clinging to the same decades-old business plan despite losing customers every year, its executives would have been fired long ago.

"Our movement is going out of existence, and yet too many labor leaders go and shake their heads and say they'll do something, and then they go back and do the same thing the next day," Stern told me recently. He is a lean, compact man with thinning white hair, and when he reclines in the purple chair in his Washington office and crosses one leg over the other, he could easily pass for a psychiatrist or a math professor. He added, "I don't have a lot of time to mince words, because I don't think workers in our country have a lot of time left if we don't change."

A week after the election in November, Stern delivered a proposal to the AFL–CIO that sounded more like an ultimatum. He demanded that the federation, the umbrella organization of the labor movement, embrace a top-to-bottom reform, beginning with a plan to merge its 58 unions into 20, for the purpose of consolidating power. If the other bosses wouldn't budge, Stern threatened to take his 1.8 million members and bolt the federation—effectively blowing up the AFL–CIO on the eve of its 50th anniversary. Stern's critics say all of this is simply an excuse to grab power. "What Andy's doing now with his compadres is what Vladimir Putin is trying to do to the former Communist bloc countries," says Tom Buffenbarger, president of the union that represents machinists and aerospace workers. "He's trying to implement dictatorial rule."

Stern says he is done caring what the other bosses think. "If I don't have the courage to do what my members put me here to do, then how do I ask a janitor or a child care worker to go in and see a private-sector employer and say, 'We want to have a union in this place'?" Stern asks. "What's my risk? That some people won't like me? *Their* risk is that they lose their jobs."

The implications of Stern's crusade stretch well beyond the narrow world of organized labor and into the heart of the nation's politics. The stale and paralyzed political dialogue in Washington right now is a direct result of the deterioration of industrial America, followed by the rise of the Wal-Mart economy. Lacking any real solutions to the growing anxiety of working-class families, the two parties have instead become entrenched in a cynical battle over who or what is at fault. Republicans have made an art form of blaming the declining fortunes of the middle class on taxes and social programs; if government would simply get out of the way, they suggest, businesses would magically provide all the well-paying jobs we need. Democrats, meanwhile, cling to the mythology of the factory age, blaming Republican greed and "Benedict Arnold CEOs"—to use John Kerry's phrase—for the historical shift toward globalization; if only Washington would close a few tax loopholes, they seem to be saying, the American worker could again live happily in 1950.

About the last place you might expect to find a more thoughtful and compelling vision for the global age is in the fossilized, dogmatic leadership of organized labor. But Andy Stern is a different kind of labor chief. He intends to create a new, more dynamic kind of movement around the workers of the 21st century. And if some old friends in labor and the Democratic Party get their feelings hurt in the process, that's all right with him.

The Old Boss

Earlier this month, Tom Buffenbarger invited me down to the machinists' union's training facility on the Patuxent River in southern Maryland, about a 90-minute drive from Washington. The little campus features 87 hotel rooms, a library, a theater, and a dockside dining room. There was no training going on that week, and as I wandered the empty halls, I peered into glass cases containing some of the products made by the heavy machine operators and plant workers who make up much of the union's rank and file: a parking meter, aluminum soda cans, a Winchester rifle, a box of animal crackers. There were black-and-white photos of the union's past presidents with Harry Truman, Hubert Humphrey, and Ted Kennedy. I glimpsed an exhibit meant to celebrate what the machinists apparently considered a triumphant moment: the Eastern Airlines strike that began in 1989 and ended, two years later, with the destruction of the company. It was as if I had wandered into the industrial economy's version of Jurassic Park: "Welcome to Laborland, U.S.A., and please be careful—there are actual union leaders wandering around."

At its zenith, in 1969, the machinists' union was about a million strong, but that was before robots supplanted assembly-line workers and Chinese factories began replacing a lot of American plants. The union now has some 380,000 active, dues-paying members. Buffenbarger told me that the union had lost more than 100,000 members in the last four years alone—members whose jobs were eliminated or moved overseas—for which he placed the blame squarely on free-trade deals and the Bush administration. Buffenbarger looks like what you would probably imagine a union boss to look like. He is a big, fleshy man with a bald crown and ursine hands. He began his career, decades ago, as a tool-and-dye apprentice. Now he flies around in the union's very own Lear jet. "We couldn't do what we do without it," he explained unapologetically.

Buffenbarger said that Andy Stern is wrong in his central point about the labor movement; in fact, unions have as much power as ever. The problem, as Buffenbarger sees it, is one of public relations and messaging. All the unions need to do to reverse their fortunes, Buffenbarger said, is to speak up louder. To that end, Buffenbarger has proposed that the AFL–CIO spend $188 million to create, among other things, a Labor News Network on cable TV. "There is no bigger organization than the collective labor movement," he told me. "Even the NRA doesn't have 13 million members. But they act like they do, and I think that's where we fall down. We need to act like we do."

In a speech earlier that morning, Buffenbarger took on Stern, portraying him as an arrogant usurper and comparing him to "a rather small peacock." Buffenbarger, of course, stands to lose clout if the AFL–CIO meets Stern's demands, since the machinists might well be forced to merge with other unions, some of whom might not see the need for a private jet. But I sensed a reason for his resentment that went beyond simple self-interest; underneath his rhetoric, you could detect the fault line between an industrial economy and a service economy, between old labor and new. Buffenbarger sneered at Stern's Ivy League education—Stern got his degree from the University of Pennsylvania, where he spent his freshman year studying business—and mocked him for setting up a blog. What Buffenbarger didn't like about Stern is that he looked and sounded so much like management.

"He's trying to corporatize the labor movement," Buffenbarger said. "When you listen to him talk, it's all about market share. It's about loss and gain. It's about *producers* and *consumers*." He wrinkled his face when he said this, as if the words themselves tasted sour in his mouth. "I think he's enamored of all the glitz and hype of the Wall Street types. He must be a fan of Donald Trump. I think he wants his own TV show."

Reengineering the Union

Stern, it's true, is about as far from a tool-and-dye man as you can get. His father built a profitable legal practice in northern New Jersey by catering to small Jewish businesses, helping their owners make the jump from corner store to full-service retailer. After college, where, by his own account, he mostly avoided thinking about classes or the future, an aimless Stern took a job with the Pennsylvania welfare department, compiling case histories for aid recipients. The department's social service workers had just won the right to collective bargaining, and a group of young idealists, Stern included, seized control of the local union.

Nothing in Stern's prototypically suburban background made him a natural candidate for organized labor—for many affluent college kids of his generation, the notion of unions brought to mind images of dank social halls and cigar-chewing thugs—but this was the early 1970s, and when you had a genuine chance to scream truth to power, you took it. Soon he went to work full-time for the union. Stern and his cadre got the pay increases and better benefits they demanded—and went on strike anyway. "Most of us were just playing union," he says now, laughing. "We'd watched enough movies so we could figure it out."

Unlike most union bosses, who rise up through the administrative ranks, ploddingly building alliances and dispatching their enemies, Stern spent most of his career as an organizer in the field, taking on recalcitrant employers and bargaining contracts. In 1984 John Sweeney, then the president of the SEIU, summoned Stern to Washington to coordinate a national organizing drive. When Sweeney ran for president of the entire AFL–CIO in 1995, Stern helped run his campaign; after Sweeney won, the brash and ambitious Stern maneuvered to replace him as head of the SEIU. The ensuing drama was a classic of labor politics. Before an election could be held, Sweeney left the union in the hands of a top lieutenant, who wasted no time in firing Stern and having him escorted from the building. As Stern tells the story, he vowed that he wouldn't set foot back in the L Street headquarters unless he was moving into the president's fifth-floor office. Six weeks later, his reform-minded allies in the locals helped get him elected, and he became, at 45, the youngest president in the union's history.

Having grown up around his father's small business clients, and having spent much of his adult life at bargaining tables, Stern had learned a few things about the way business works. He came to embrace a philosophy that ran counter to the most basic assumptions of the besieged labor movement: the popular image of greedy corporations that want to treat their workers like slaves, Stern believed, was in most cases just wrong. The truth was that companies in the global age, under intense pressure to lower costs, were simply doing what they thought they had to do to survive, and if you wanted them to behave better, you had to make good behavior viable for them.

Stern's favorite example concerns the more than 10,000 janitors who clean the office buildings in the cities and suburbs of northern New Jersey. Five years ago, only a fraction of them were unionized, and they were making $10 less per hour than their counterparts across the river in Manhattan. Stern and his team say they were convinced from talking to employers in the fast-growing area that the employers didn't like the low wages and poor benefits much more than the union did. Cleaning companies complained that they had trouble retaining workers, and the workers they did keep were less productive. The problem was that for any one company to offer better wages would have been tantamount to an army unilaterally disarming in the middle of a war, cheaper competitors would immediately overrun its business.

The traditional way for a union to attack this problem would be to pick the most vulnerable employer in the market, pressure it to accept a union, and then try to expand from there. Instead, Stern set out to organize the entire market at once, which he did by promising employers that the union contract wouldn't kick in unless more than half of them signed it. (Getting the first companies to enter into the agreement took some old-fashioned organizing tactics, including picket lines.) The SEIU ended up representing close to 70 percent of the janitors in the area, doubling their pay in many cases; from minimum wage to more than $11 an hour. Stern found that by bringing all of the main employers in an industry to the table at one time, rather than one after the other, he was able to effectively regulate an entire market.

Stern talks about giving "added value" to employers, some of whom have come to view him, warily, as a partner. At about the time Stern took over the union, his locals in several states were at war with Beverly Health and Rehabilitation Services, an Arkansas-based nursing home chain. The company complained that cuts in state aid were making it all but impossible to pay workers more while operating their facilities at a profit. Stern and his team proposed an unusual alliance: If Beverly would allow its workers to organize, the SEIU's members would use their political clout in state legislatures to deliver more money. It worked. "I do believe Andy's a stand-up guy," says Beverly Health's COO Dave Devereaux.

At the same time Stern was employing inventive labor tactics to work with business, he was also using new-age business theory to remake the culture of his union. When Stern came into power, the SEIU represented a disparate coalition of local unions that identified themselves by different names and maintained separate identities. This was the way it had always been, which was fine in an era when employers and unions were confined to individual markets. To Stern, however, this was now a problem. If his members were going to go up against national and global companies, they were going to have to convey the size and stature of a national union. "You know your employer is powerful, so you want to believe you're part of something powerful as well" is the way he explained it to me.

Stern hired a corporate consulting firm versed in the jargon of the new economy and undertook a campaign to "rebrand" the union. He used financial incentives to get all the local branches of the union to begin using the SEIU name, its new logo and, of course, its new color. In some respects, the SEIU now feels very much like a *Fortune* 500 company.

In the lobby of its headquarters, a flat-screen TV plays an endless video of smiling members along with inspirational quotes from Stern, as if he were Jack Welch or Bill Gates. The union sold more than $1 million worth of purple merchandise through its gift catalog last year, including watches, sports bras, temporary tattoos, and its very own line of jeans. (The catalog itself features poetry from members and their children paying tribute to the union, along with recipes like Andy Stern's Chocolate Cake with Peanut-Butter Frosting.)

In all of this, Stern's critics in other unions see a strange little cult of personality. Another way to look at it, though, is that Stern understands the psychology of a movement; workers in the union want to feel as if someone is looking out for them. When he and I walked into the SEIU campaign office in Miami shortly before the presidential election, the union's activists greeted him with hugs or shy smiles. Stern took a moment to chat with each member. "I got to have my picture taken with you once before, you know," one man told him proudly. "You mean *I* got to have my picture taken with *you*," Stern replied with the timing of a politician.

As the SEIU was soaring in membership and strength during the late 1990s, much of big labor was seeing its influence further erode. And there were those who thought the SEIU wasn't doing enough for the movement as a whole. Cecil Roberts, president of the mineworkers, personally challenged Stern to follow the example of the mineworkers' legendary leader John L. Lewis, who helped build up the entire labor movement in the 1930s. But Stern demurred. Just running the union was taking all of his time, and what was left he wanted to spend with his son, Matt, and his daughter, Cassie. There would be time later, when his children were older, to think about reshaping the future of American labor.

Then, all at once, Stern's personal world collapsed. A little more than two years ago, Cassie, 14, who was born unusually small and with poor muscle tone, became ill after returning home from a routine operation, stopped breathing in her father's arms, and died. In the aftermath, Stern's 23-year marriage to Jane Perkins, a liberal advocate, unraveled. He rented an apartment in northwest Washington and shed most of his furniture, hurling himself into his work at the union. He is very close to his 18-year-old son, but his son splits his time between his parents' homes. On weeks when Stern is alone, he told me, he looks forward to stopping by the Dancing Crab, a local bar, to eat dinner alone and read the paper. "I'm in a very transitional moment of life," he says.

Often, when Stern talks about his daughter, he wanders off, without really meaning to, into a story about a union member he has met somewhere who reminds him of Cassie, or whose own daughter—"someone else's Cassie"—is stuck in a failing school. The recollections bring him to the brink of tears. It is as if he can't help conflating the fate of workers with the fate of his daughter. Time has become a paradox for him; on one hand, he has more of it than ever before, and yet he can't escape the panicky feeling that time is running out.

"When Cassie died," Stern said, "it was like: 'I'm 52 years old. How many more years am I really going to do this? Why am I so scared to say what I really think?'" If he were a religious man, Stern told me, he might think that it was not a coincidence that he was given, through his loss, so much free time and clarity at the very moment when organized labor was in crisis. He says it would be comforting to believe he has been chosen for a mission. It is clear, from the way he says this, that part of him believes it anyway.

Big Labor's Big Brawl

Stern's plan to rescue the American worker begins with restructuring the AFL–CIO. Since the 1960s, a lot of struggling unions have chosen to merge rather than perish, to the point where there are half as many unions in the federation today as there were at its height. Stern argues that this Darwinian process, so lamented by labor leaders, is in fact healthy and hasn't gone far enough. Unions, he says, work best when they're large enough to organize new workers at the same time as they fight battles on behalf of old ones, and when they represent a large concentration of the workers in any one industry. Smaller unions lack the muscle to organize entire markets the way that the SEIU has been able to do with janitors and home health care workers. At the same time, some unions have desperately scrambled to maintain or increase their memberships—and thus their revenue—by signing up workers well outside their core areas. So the United Auto Workers ends up representing graduate students, and the machinists represent park rangers. This is self-defeating, Stern argues; all it does is divide labor's strength.

Stern's 10-point plan would essentially tear down the industrial-age framework of the House of Labor and rebuild it. The AFI–CIO, he says, would consist of 20 large unions, and each union would be devoted to a single sector of the 21st-century economy, like health care or airlines. Ever the apostle of field organizing, Stern wants these restructured unions to put more time and resources into recruiting new members in fast-growing exurban areas—in the South and the West especially—where a new generation of workers has never belonged to a union. His plan would slash the amount that each union pays in dues to the AFL–CIO by half, provided that those unions put some of the money back into local organizing. This is not a small idea; it would, essentially, take resources away from the federation's headquarters, which uses it for policy studies and training programs, and give it back to the guys who set up picket lines and rallies.

The basic strategy is to take the same principles Stern demonstrated organizing New Jersey's janitors and make them the model for the entire American labor movement. If only two or three large unions represented all the nation's health care workers, they could go into a growing market—Reno, say, or Albuquerque—and bargain with all the hospitals at the same time. Labor would be able to focus on setting standards for entire industries, as opposed to battling one employer at a time.

Stern's plan has incited fury within a lot of smaller unions, whose members don't seem to think the movement needs a self-appointed savior. The proposed reorganization would sweep away a lot of small unions as if they were debris on the factory floor. "Andy is impatient, and he sprang this on his peers without any discussion," says John Sweeney, Stern's former mentor. "I think he needs to stand still for a minute and listen to what other people think, and learn from other experiences as well."

You would imagine, given how often Stern's critics have called him arrogant, that he'd be used to it by now, but clearly the word still stings him. He is a man who prides himself on his emotional connection with janitors and nursing aides, and he almost cannot bear the suggestion that he thinks he's smarter than everyone else. Stern prefers to see himself as a man who gets along with all kinds of people, whether they drive the limousine or ride in the back. ("I actually was the most popular person in my high school class," he once told me.)

During an airport layover, I saw him open his laptop and peruse the Unite to Win blog. (Stern actually contributes from time to time to three separate blogs, including Purpleocean.org, an SEIU site designed for like-minded people who aren't even in a union.) Stern established the online forum so that everyone in the labor movement—whether supportive of his plan or opposed to it—could tell him exactly what they thought of his ideas. They haven't held back. "Sometimes I really hate this," he said in the airport lounge, wincing slightly. "I don't like seeing my name there and people calling me an arrogant idiot."

Even Stern's allies admit that his ultimatum to big labor is a little high-handed. John Wilhelm, copresident of the union that represents hotel, restaurant, and garment workers, is supportive of Stern, and Wilhelm is said to be considering a challenge to Sweeney when he runs for another term as AFI–CIO president this year. But he said he disagrees with Stern's idea of merging unions against their will. Because Stern's union is so powerful, Wilhelm told me, Stern doesn't always feel the need to tread as softly as he might. "Frankly, he doesn't have to be as diplomatic as others do," Wilhelm said. "There's a thin and perhaps indiscernible line between a person who comes across as arrogant and a person who tries to tell the truth even when it's unpleasant. And the truth about our labor movement is unpleasant."

When I first started talking to Stern about his controversial plan last summer, he seemed to regard it more as a provocation to big labor than as a proposal that might actually be adopted. He talked as if he were resigned to the idea that the SEIU would ultimately break from the federation. But as the next meeting of the AFL–CIO executive board in March draws near, there seems to be in union headquarters around the nation the faintest stirrings of a revolt. Stern's ideas have become the basis for an entirely new debate about the future of labor, and now several unions have offered their own, more modest versions of a reform plan in response. The biggest surprise came in December, when James P. Hoffa, president of the famously old-school Teamsters, weighed in with a set of recommendations quite similar to Stern's.

Increasingly the question for Stern is not whether he is prepared to leave the AFL–CIO, but how much of his plan has to be enacted in order for the SEIU to stay. It is a question he evades. "What I won't do," he said, "is pretend we made change. It's not worth having this fight or discussion if, in the end, you can't look people in the eye and say we really have taken a big step forward."

Workers of the World, Globalize?

Even if big labor eventually does come to be made up of bigger unions, Stern sees a larger challenge: can you build a multinational labor movement to counter the leverage of multinational giants whose tentacles reach across oceans and continents? The emblem of this new kind of behemoth, of course, is Wal-Mart, the nation's largest employer. Wal-Mart has, in a sense, turned the American retail model inside out. It used to be that a manufacturer made, say, a clock radio, determined its price and the wages of the employees who made it, and then sold the radio to a retail outlet at a profit. Wal-Mart's power is such that the process now works in reverse: In practice, Wal-Mart sets the price for that clock radio, and the manufacturer, very likely located overseas, figures out how low wages will have to be in order to make it profitable to produce it. In this way, Wal-Mart not only resists unions in its stores with unwavering ferocity but also drives down the wages of its manufacturers—all in the service of bringing consumers the lowest possible price.

"What was good for G.M. ended up being good for the country," Stern says. "What's good for Wal-Mart ends up being good for five families"—the heirs to the Walton fortune. Stern's reform plan for the AFL–CIO includes a $25 million fund to organize Wal-Mart's workers. But as a retail outlet, Wal-Mart doesn't really fall within the SEIU's purview. What Stern says he is deeply worried about is what he sees as the next generation of Wal-Marts, which *are* on his turf: French, British, and Scandinavian companies whose entry into the American market threatens to drive down wages in service industries, which are often less visible than retail. "While we were invading Iraq, the Europeans invaded us," Stern says. Most of these companies have no objection to unionizing in Europe, where organized labor is the norm. But when they come to the United States, they immediately follow the Wal-Mart model, undercutting their competitors by shutting out unions and squeezing paychecks.

Take, for instance, the case of Sodexho, a French company that provides all the services necessary to operate corporate buildings, from catering the food to guarding the lobby. In Europe, Sodexho is considered a responsible employer that works with unions and compensates its employees fairly. In the United States and Canada, where the company employs more than 100,000 workers, Sodexho's policy is to discourage its employees from joining unions. As a maneuver to get Sodexho to the bargaining table, last year the SEIU resorted to taking out ads in French newspapers, shaming the company's executives in their own country, where the idea of scorning unions is considerably less chic. Stern says Sodexho has started negotiating.

Stern's big idea for coping with this new kind of multinational nemesis is to build a federation of unions, similar to the AFL–CIO except that its member unions would come from all over the world. As Stern explained it, a French company might not be so brazen about bullying American workers if it had to worry about a French union protesting back home. The point, he said, is to force companies like Sodexho to adhere to the same business standards in New York and Chicago as it does in Paris, by building a labor alliance that is every bit as global as modern capital.

At first, this global vision sounded a little dreamy to me, as if Stern might have been watching too many *Superfriends* reruns. Then he invited me, just before Christmas, on a one-day trip to Birmingham, England. The occasion was a meeting of Britain's reform-minded transportation union. Tony Woodley, the union's general secretary, flashed a broad smile and threw his arm around Stern when Stern arrived, after flying all night, to give the keynote address. Two SEIU employees were already on hand; it turned out that Stern had dispatched them to London temporarily to help Woodley set up an organizing program.

As we drank coffee backstage, Stern and Woodley told me about the case of First Student, a company that in the last few years had become the largest, most aggressive private school bus company in the United States. The company had become a target of SEIU locals in several cities because it wouldn't let its drivers unionize. "We keep seeing these things about them in the union newsletter," Stern said. "And it starts nibbling at your brain. I said, 'Who are these people, First Student? What's going on here?' And then we do a little research, and we find out what idiots we are. This is a major multinational company. They're 80 percent unionized in the United Kingdom. So we write a letter to the union here, and we say, 'Can you help us?'"

Woodley sent British bus drivers to Chicago to meet with their American counterparts. Then the American bus drivers went to London, and lobbyists for the British union took them to see members of Parliament. They also held a joint demonstration outside the company's annual meeting. Woodley told me that First Student—known as First Group in Britain—was now making a bid for rail contracts there, and his union intended to lobby against it unless the company sat down with its American counterparts in Florida and Illinois.

I asked Woodley, who looks like Rudy Giuliani with more hair, why he would use his own union's political capital to help the SEIU. He nodded quickly, in a way that suggested that there were a lot of people who didn't yet understand this. He explained that it worked both ways; his union was suffering at the hands of multinationals, too, and Stern would be able to return the favor by pressuring American companies doing business in Britain. Moreover, Woodley went on to say, if European companies get used to operating without unions in America, it might be only a matter of time before they tried to export that same mentality back to Europe. "I don't expect miracles," Woodley said. "I don't expect international solidarity to bring huge companies to their knees overnight. But we've got to do a damn sight more than we're doing."

Stern invited the top executives of about a dozen unions from Europe and Australia to a meeting in London this April, which will be the maiden gathering of what he says he hopes will become a formalized global federation. He recently met with union leaders in Beijing too. Most labor experts assume that the Chinese unions are tools of the business-friendly government, but Stern says he came away believing that they are as jolted by the global economy as workers in America. "You have to understand, they're just seeing something new," he says. "These are public unions that are used to health benefits and real discussions, and suddenly they're meeting these huge corporations— like Wal-Mart—that, because the executives can make a phone call to someone in the local government, won't even talk to them. It's all new."

There are, however, painful questions inherent in globalizing the labor movement. At a recent meeting with his executive board, Stern mused out loud about the possibility of conducting a fact-finding mission to India, along with executives from one of the companies outsourcing its jobs there. Perhaps that could be a first step, he thought, toward raising the pay of Indian workers who have inherited American jobs.

Then Stern stopped himself and considered a problem. Sure, there was an obvious logic to unionizing foreign phone operators or machinists: American workers won't be able to compete fairly for jobs until companies have to pay higher wages in countries like China and India. But how would it look to workers in America? How would you avoid the appearance that you were more worried about the guy answering the phone in Bangalore than you were about the guy he replaced in Iowa? John Kerry and other

Democrats had been railing against the CEOs who outsourced American jobs—and here was Andy Stern, considering joining forces with those very same CEOs to make sure their Indian workers were making enough money.

"The truth is that as the living standard in China goes up, the living standard in Ohio goes down," Stern said. "What do you do about that? Are we a global union or an American union? This is a hard question for me to answer. Because I'm not comfortable with the living standard here going down. This is a question I think we need to think about going forward, but I don't think that means we should be scared."

The idea of a global union isn't entirely new. But the concept has never been translated into a formal alliance, and experts who study labor think Stern may be onto something important. I realized during our brief time in Birmingham why Stern seemed ambivalent about whether the AFL–CIO approved his reform plan, or whether his union even stayed in the federation. In a sense, no matter how the conversation is resolved, it is bound to lag a full generation behind the reality of the problem; it is as if the unions are arguing against upgrading from LPs to compact discs while the rest of the world has moved on to digital downloads. Even if the leaders of big labor do kill off half their unions and reorganize the rest, all they will have done, at long last, is create a truly national labor movement—at exactly the moment that capital has become a more sprawling and more obstinate force than any one nation could hope to contain.

Reengineering the Party

The more Andy Stern looks at organized labor and the Democratic Party, the more he sees the parallels between them. Like big labor, the modern Democratic Party was brought into being by imaginative liberal thinkers in the 1930s and reached its apex during the prosperity of the postwar industrial boom. Like the union bosses, Democratic leaders grew complacent in their success; they failed to keep pace with changing circumstances in American life and didn't notice that their numbers were steadily eroding. Now, Stern says, Democrats and the unions both find themselves mired in the mind-set of a bygone moment, lacking the will or perhaps the capacity to innovate or adapt. What you see in both cases, Stern told me borrowing from the new-age language of business theory, is "the change pattern of a dying institution."

The big conversation going on in Democratic Washington at the moment, at dinner parties and luncheons and think-tank symposia, revolves around how to save the party. The participants generally fall into two camps of unequal size. On one side, there is the majority of Democrats, who believe that the party's failure has primarily been one of communication and tactics. By this thinking, the Democratic agenda itself (no to tax cuts and school vouchers and Social Security privatization; yes to national health care and affirmative action) remains as relevant as ever to modern workers. The real problem, goes this line of thinking, is that the party has allowed ruthless Republicans to control the debate and has failed to sufficiently mobilize its voters. A much smaller group of prominent Democrats argues that the party's problems run deeper—that it suffers, in fact, from a lack of imagination, and that its core ideas are more an echo of government as it was than government as it ought to be.

Virtually everyone in the upper echelons of organized labor belongs solidly to the first camp. Stern has his feet firmly planted in the second. The economic policy of the Democratic Party, he says, "is basically being opposed to Republicans and protecting the New Deal. It makes me realize how vibrant the Republicans are in creating 21st-century ideas, and how sad it is that we're defending 60-year-old ideas." Like big labor, Stern says, the party needs to challenge its orthodoxy—and its interest groups—if it wants to put forward a program that makes sense for new-economy workers. Could it be that the Social Security system devised in the 1930s isn't, in fact, the only good national retirement program for today's wage earner? Is it possible that competition is the best way to rescue an imperiled public school system?

"I'm not convinced that you can do this from the inside," Stern told me at one point. Just as he is willing to strike out from the AFL–CIO, he doesn't rule out a split from the Democratic Party. "I feel like we have to do everything we can within our power to get both the labor movement and the parties in this country to represent workers the way they should," he said. "And if we can't, then we have to decide what our strategy is. Do we spend all our money running ballot initiatives and forget about candidates? Do we look for people to create an independent worker party? I don't know."

Stern isn't the only Democrat in Washington making this case—but he may be the most powerful and connected. Among his friends and allies he counts at least two billionaires: the financier George Soros and the philanthropist Eli Broad, who is talking with Stern about ideas to reform Los Angeles schools. Stern was one of the founding members of America Coming Together, the largest private get-out-the-vote effort ever assembled. His top political aide, Anna Burger, who is the SEIU's secretary treasurer, recently took a seat on the board of the Democracy Alliance, a network of wealthy liberal donors. How Stern wields this influence—and his union's money—can have a real impact on the direction of the party.

Other union leaders can spend their money on Buffenbarger's news network if they want, but Stern seems bent on leveraging his money against the party establishment. Last year, while he campaigned as many as six days a week for Kerry and other Democrats, Stern nevertheless undertook a series of actions that infuriated party leaders. First, with his encouragement, the SEIU's locals voted to endorse Howard Dean before the primaries. Then Stern gave more than $500,000 to the Republican Governors Association because, he said, some of the GOP's gubernatorial candidates had better positions for workers. As if that wasn't provocative enough a signal, Stern chose the moment of the Democratic convention in Boston to remark publicly, in an interview with *The Washington Post,* that it might be better for the party and the unions if John Kerry lost the election.

Stern told me he had been partly inspired, oddly enough, by the example of Stephen Moore, the arch-conservative ideologue who, until recently, ran the Club for Growth. The club, which is anathema to both Democrats and moderate Republicans in Washington, raises millions from corporate antitax crusaders, then spends it not only against Democrats (Tom Daschle was a prime target) but also against Republican incumbents who aren't deemed sufficiently conservative. Moore has infuriated some Republican leaders, who say he divides the party, but the Club for Growth has helped push the party to the right, putting moderates on the defensive and making Republicans think twice before they cast a vote against a tax cut.

Stern invited Moore to speak at an SEIU meeting in Chicago a few years ago—which is roughly the equivalent of Michael Moore being asked over to the National Rifle Association for lunch. Now Stern has begun to emulate the club's model; last year, the SEIU ran its own candidate, a union ally, against the Democratic House speaker in Washington State, because the speaker voted against a health benefits package for home health care workers. The union's challenger lost—but only by about 500 votes. "I think we need to spend more time running candidates against Democrats," Stern says matter-of-factly.

This approach holds some risk for a union boss. Most of Stern's members, after all, are lifelong Democrats. Will they be OK with a leader who's willing to entertain an overhaul of Social Security? Would they support Stern if he crossed the teachers' unions and came out for school vouchers? Stern seems convinced that his members want new solutions to these problems, not dogmatic answers, and he is betting that they're more loyal to him and the union than they are to the party. He seems poised to fill a space—between the world of organized labor and the world of social and economic policy—that hasn't been filled since Walter Reuther, the head of the United Auto Workers, advised the Kennedys and Lyndon Johnson on civil rights. "There's been no analog to Andy in the last 30 or 40 years in America," says Simon Rosenberg, who heads the New Democrat Network and is running for Democratic Party chairman. "There's been no labor leader who has emerged as a thought leader as well."

This spring, Stern plans to convene an eclectic group of Democrats to begin outlining a new economic agenda. "We don't want it to be the same old people," Stern told me. "We want people who might say, for example, 'Maybe privatization isn't such a terrible thing for people,' even if that's not what the Democratic Party thinks. Or, for example, 'Wal-Mart isn't the worst thing for the economy after all.'" He laughed heartily at that one. "We need to shock people out of their comfort zone and make them think."

The Big Questions

Stern is not the first giant of the labor movement to talk about breaking up big labor or the Democratic Party. Reuther and the United Auto Workers stormed out of the AFL–CIO in 1968 and formed a new alliance with the Teamsters. A few labor leaders, furious at Harry Truman's treatment of workers, followed Henry Wallace out of the Democratic Party in 1948. Neither venture lasted long enough for anyone to remember much about it. Reuther died suddenly in 1970, and the new alliance barely outlived him; Wallace's Progressive Party finished fourth in the 1948 election, behind the Dixiecrats, and faded away. Arguably, the lesson of these and other rebellions is that the threat of building new workers' institutions usually proves more potent than the reality.

The question that Stern's detractors ask is this: What is Andy Stern really after? Does he long to be the Reuther of his day, phoning presidents and holding forth to rooms full of reporters?

"I don't like politics," Stern said more than once. "After the last election, a lot of people called me and said everything from 'You should run for president' to 'You should be chairman of the DNC.' And neither of them had the slightest bit of reality or held any interest for me." That Stern can mention this casually—that someone suggested he not merely phone a president, but run for president—would indicate that he is as susceptible to self-glorification as the next guy, and maybe more so. But if what Stern really wanted was to run the world, he could surely spend his nights in more powerful company than that of the bartender at the Dancing Crab. When I asked what he envisioned himself doing in his 60s, Stern said, "I hope I find someone to fall in love with and travel with and watch my son have grandkids."

His adversaries will say this is disingenuous, but, as so often happens in public life, they may be misunderstanding the human factor that compels Andy Stern. Everyone who knows him well will tell you that he is driven by an authentic passion for workers. And yet, at the same time, it doesn't take a psychology degree to see that he lives these days in a state of suspended agony. Stern gives the impression of having been shaken loose from conformity by the death of his daughter and the end of his marriage; nothing can hurt him more than he has already been hurt, which breeds in him the kind of abandon that can be dangerous to the status quo.

This is how history often changes; it's the people who are running from something worse who are willing to hurl themselves into walls that others won't scale. The facts of our time are clear enough: A ruthless kind of globalized economy is upon us, and it is not going away. Many American industries are bound to be surpassed by leaner competitors, and the workers left behind by this tectonic shift have little power to influence the decisions of corporate barons whose interests know no national boundaries. More Americans now hold stock—often in a 401k—than are members of a union. And the institutions that have, for the last century, protected the ideal of the American worker—organized labor and the Democratic Party—are clinging mightily to structures and programs born in the era of coal and steel, perhaps out of fear that innovation would somehow discredit the things they have worked for all these years, or perhaps for the simple reason that no one knows what to do next.

The visionary men who built big labor and the modern Democratic Party met the challenges specific to their moment. What Andy Stern is doing, in his own way, is provoking an argument more relevant to our moment. Can American workers ever be secure in a global market? Can a service economy sustain the nation's middle class? And are we brave enough to have the conversation?

Get Things Done through Coalitions
Margo Vanover

What do the American Paper Institute, National Coffee Association, Milk Industry Foundation, and American Council on Education have in common?

It may seem unlikely, but the answer is "an interest in sewer user charges."

These 4 associations and 11 others formed the Coalition for ICR Repeal to protect their members' interests in sewer user charges. Coalition members term industrial cost recovery (ICR) as "an unfair, unnecessary, and costly provision of the 1972 Federal Water Pollution Control Act."

This particular example of a coalition illustrates two very important points that you, a leader of your association, should be aware of. First of all, the coalition was successful. The industrial cost recovery provision was repealed on October 1, 1980, and coalition members frankly admit that they could never have done it alone. It took the efforts and—even more important—the clout of all 15 members to accomplish their goal.

The second point is this: Coalition members seemed like unlikely allies. Who would have thought they had anything in common?

"It's an interesting conglomeration of business groups with one similar interest," acknowledges Sheldon E. Steinbach, general counsel for the American Council on Education, Washington. "We all had one common problem—a proposed increase in sewer user charges."

"I remember the stunned look on the faces of the people at the first coalition meeting," he says with a chuckle. "They found out quickly that my association had the exact concern theirs did."

Who Are Your Allies?

Right now, your association is probably a member of a coalition. But do you know what the coalition's purpose is? If you don't, ask your association's chief paid officer. He or she usually represents an association's interests in a coalition effort.

And while you are talking to your chief paid officer, ask what other associations comprise the coalition. You could be surprised. Like the Coalition for ICR Repeal, their names might not suggest a tie-in with your association's cause. In fact, they may be the names of associations that have been adversaries or competitors in the past.

It's not all that unusual, says Steinbach. "We look for common cause with other groups. We may be allies on one cause and enemies on another. It's happened time after time."

It's important to overlook past differences and concentrate on the present goal of the coalition, agrees Dr. Paul A. Kerschner, associate director for legislation, research, and programs at the National Retired Teachers Association/American Association of Retired

Persons, Washington. "Two organizations can be in deep dissent on some issues," he says. "On those issues, we know we disagree. But on the issues where we do agree, it's much more powerful to speak in a unified voice."

Of course, sometimes your association's allies are obvious. Such was the case when the Distributive Services Committee was formed 17 years ago. Eighteen Ohio associations whose members were involved in distributing formed the coalition to reduce property tax on retail inventory. At the time, the tax was 70 percent of the value of the inventory. The coalition has successfully obtained several reductions since its formation, and the coalition's goal of a 35 percent inventory tax will go into effect in two years.

In this case, both the allies and the enemy were obvious. The allies: trade associations with retail merchant members. The enemy: the state legislature.

So Many Success Stories

Case after case of association coalitions that have been successful in their pursuits can be cited. William T. Robinson, CAE, senior vice president of the American Hospital Association, Chicago, relates one coalition success story.

Several years ago, he says, the annual rate of increase in the level of expenditures for health care was out of control. Predictions were that if health care costs continued at the same rate it would be necessary to spend the entire gross national product on health care alone by the year 2010. In fact, the government's outlay for health care—Medicare and Medicaid—was beginning to compete with the defense budget.

Government officials, concerned, issued a challenge to the health care field to voluntarily control the rate of increase. A coalition called Voluntary Effort was created. It represented the interests of trade associations, commercial insurance companies, and others. Now, three years after the start of the coalition, "the rate of increase has been sufficiently retarded," Robinson says.

Edie Fraser, president of Fraser/Associates, Washington, has been involved in enough similar success stories to become a firm believer in their power. "Coalitions are the new trend in business relations on policy issues," she says. "I believe they are the most effective means of achieving results."

What's Their Purpose?

She explains that the basic purpose of a coalition is "to join forces together behind a mutual interest—generally a policy issue—and work together for common effectiveness and results."

"More and more associations are recognizing the power of coalitions," Fraser continues, "because they can achieve far more by integrating their resources and dividing the effort behind a common cause."

Paul Korody, director of public affairs for the National Meat Association, Washington, says coalitions are growing in numbers in response to a changing Congress. "Within the past 10 years, we have seen a decentralization of power on Capitol Hill. Today, every congressman is almost as important as another. They all have to be talked to."

That means, he says, that only the really large associations with members in every congressional district can tackle an issue alone.

The rest of us have to pool our memberships to be effective in Congress. Whereas we have a lot of meatpackers in the Northwest and Southwest, there are many congressional districts where we have no members at all. We would be less effective in those states [without a coalition]. By combining resources with a number of associations with different memberships but the same goals, you can cover the country.

He adds that, in most cases, congressional staffs appreciate a coalition's efforts. Why? Because it makes their jobs that much easier. They can get one document or have one conversation with a coalition leader and know who and how many are for or against an issue. That's in lieu of speaking with 50,000—a number that five association executives involved in a coalition can easily represent.

Choosing a Leader

In order for any coalition to be successful, it has to have a leader or coordinator with a commitment to the cause and time to devote to it, says Sheldon Steinbach, American Council on Education.

The effectiveness of the ICR repeal was solely due to the continuous scrutiny and daily monitoring of one person.
A coalition functions only when one person is given responsibility to make that issue move. Someone must call the shots. A leader must have ample time to spend on the issue, almost to the point of making it his or her primary preoccupation.

Because of the considerable time requirement, choosing a coalition coordinator is often simply a process of elimination. Who has the time to spend on it? Who was the expertise on the issue?
When these questions are answered, only a few eligibles are likely to remain. Usually it's the executive of the association which the outcome of the issue most affects.
Or as Fraser puts it, "The leader usually represents the one association that has the most to gain . . . or lose."

Guidelines for Effectiveness

Obviously, the selection of the leader can either make or break a coalition. But other factors also enter into the outcome of your association's coalition.
Here are just a few elements common to successful coalition efforts:

- A commitment by members to work, not in their own self-interest, but in the interest of the group.
- Expertise on the part of all members on the subject matter and its ramifications.
- Knowledge of how the legislature—either state or federal—works.
- Ability to plan a strategy and allow enough lead time to develop it detail by detail so nothing slips through the cracks and is left undone.

- Communication with members of the coalition—whether it's through meetings, newsletters, memos, or telephone calls.

- Keeping on the offensive, rather than the defensive. "Use facts, data, and public opinion to build on your important points," Fraser says. "It's not necessary to attack your opposition." She ticks off campaign after campaign that was lost because one side began to react defensively to the opposition.

- Member involvement. "If the issue is important to your members—and it should be or you shouldn't be part of the coalition—get them involved," Fraser urges. "The grassroots campaign is important. The work should really come from members; your association should serve as the catalyst."

- Latitude from you and your board of directors. "Our board sets broad policy," says John C. Mahaney, Jr., president of the Ohio Council of Retail Merchants in Columbus. "After that, my board leaves me alone. It doesn't tie the staff's hands."

A Commitment to Go

The last point, the latitude you give to your chief paid executive, can be a crucial item to your association's contribution to the coalition. "The board gives us a broad delegation of authority," Sheldon Steinbach says. "We are paid to exercise good judgment and proceed. If you are hamstrung, it will slow you down, if not completely cripple your coalition."

He explains that if he had to go back to his board of directors every time a decision was made in a coalition, he would lose valuable time—not to mention the confidence of other coalition members.

Survey of Membership

To make sure his board of directors will agree with his decisions, Steinbach surveys his membership on major issues that concern the association. "If they think it is important, they tell us to go," he says. "But they don't tell us how to go."

Kerschner explains that the only time he goes back to his board for a coalition decision is when the issue is controversial and the association's stance involves a change in previous policy.

"What do you do with dissent among coalition members?" asks Kerschner. "How do you handle it? Do you avoid the issue? Do you go with the majority?"

He explains that chief paid officers must answer these questions, and answer them adequately, for a coalition to work. He has found one possible answer for the coalitions he has been involved with: If there is a disagreement on one particular point of an issue, the dissenting party removes his or her name and endorsement from that specific letter but continues to endorse the remainder of the issue.

"Trade-offs are important because one small issue can divide the coalition," he says. "Before you say 'I will not sign that,' look at all sides. You might have to make a compromise. Internal negotiations are necessary to present a united front to those you are dealing with."

Goodwill a Key Ingredient

William Robinson advises associations to go into a coalition with the idea that there might have to be a trade-off. "Your pet ideas are going to be examined by others," he says.

> You might have to accept the fact that the publicity will be given to the coalition and not to your association. A coalition takes goodwill by the participants. Sometimes the goodwill is there in the beginning; sometimes it takes time for it to grow.

Speaking realistically, Edie Fraser says it almost never happens that members of a coalition agree on every item, every detail of a coalition.

> That's where the art of negotiation is important. The common end of the allies is more important than the priority of any one association.

Sharing in the Glory

You may wonder why your association's past efforts in coalitions have not been more heavily publicized . . . why your association didn't take more credit for the outcome.

"A coalition, to be effective, is without limelight or glory for the association involved," says Paul Korody.

> The purpose is to get a particular job done. We're there to serve our members, and coalitions are the more effective means of doing that. Any glory is in the fact that we satisfactorily served our members.

Sheldon Steinbach admits that sharing the spotlight is a problem for some associations. Sometimes they are so greedy for the recognition that they won't participate in a coalition—and risk losing the fight. Other times they might participate in a coalition, but afterward they will attempt to garner all of the credit for their association alone.

When William Robinson was working on Voluntary Effort, he says that the businesses and associations involved had no qualms about giving complete credit to the coalition, not to themselves. "It would have been counterproductive to publish under any one member's name," Robinson says. "We wanted the coalition to become a familiar name . . . to have its own identity."

Potential Problems

Powerful though they may be, coalitions are not perfect. Problems arise, and they have to be alleviated before the cause can be won. Here are some snags that can occur. With negotiation, respect, and planning, all can be overcome.

1. *One member dominates:* Sometimes, when a coalition is composed of one or two large, domineering associations and a variety of small ones, representatives from the smaller associations are not given the chance to express their opinions. Or if they are given the opportunity, they are not given priority. All members must listen to one another.

2. *Jealousy between members:* This usually occurs at the outset, Fraser points out, until coalition members realize that "they can achieve far more by integrating their resources and dividing the effort behind a common cause."

3. *Conflicting goals:* "You've got to go for the greatest good for the greatest number," Steinbach says.

4. *Conflicting strategy:* This occurs most often when two or more coalition members have considerable legislative experience. Because of their backgrounds, each thinks his own plan of attack is best.

5. *Minor disagreements:* Even though the association executives agree on the major issue, they sometimes bicker about a minor part of it. "You can't let a specific point divide and conquer the group," Kerschner says.

6. *Too formal:* Kerschner differentiates between organization, which you can never have enough of, and formalization, which you can. He says it's important to remember that each member of the coalition has an association to which he is responsible and that the coalition should not become a substitute for it.

7. *Too many meetings:* Some coalitions are permanent. Others are temporary—disbanded as soon as their cause is settled. Kerschner warns that members of permanent coalitions have to be careful not to call a meeting just to be calling a meeting. Unless a crisis has occurred or a new development has come up, he recommends meeting about once a month. Between meetings, he uses the phone for exchanges of information.

8. *Lack of follow-through:* Sometimes a coalition member will slip up, and the work assigned to him or her will not get done. If that happens, and it is not caught in time, all of the coalition efforts will be wasted.

Everyone's Doing It

Coalitions are not limited to associations. Business groups, consumer groups—just about any group you can think of is involved in some type of coalition. "On any side of any issue, you can find a coalition that has formed, is being formed, or will be formed," Korody says.

Whatever type of coalition your association may now be involved in, your chances of victory are better through unity. Mahaney firmly believes Ohio merchants would not have received inventory tax relief without the Distributive Service Committee. "We could not have done it alone," he states. "It took everyone in the coalition to do it."

"Sometimes a coalition is the only way to do something," he continues. "Especially now, as the problems become more complex. It seems like they are too big for any one—or even two—associations to handle."

Paul Korody couldn't agree more. "A smart association executive seeks his peers and works through a coalition. The days of trying to do it all yourself are long gone."

Twenty Tips for Making a Coalition Work

If you aren't convinced of the value of coalitions, talk to Edie Fraser, president of Fraser/Associates, Washington, D.C. She's a firm believer in the effectiveness of coalitions and presents a persuasive argument on their behalf.

She asserts that coalitions are the wave of the future. "On most policy issues, a coalition is the only way to go—if you have a common interest," she says.

In her opinion, more and more association executives are recognizing the potential—and power—of coalitions, but they aren't sure how to proceed. "Carrying out the program is where they often fall down."

Here are her 20 rules for participating in an effective coalition:

1. Clearly define issues and strategy.
2. Determine a timetable and needs.
3. Identify both allies and opposition.
4. Build constituency and recruit allies.
5. Select leadership from within allies.
6. Devise a clear plan of action.
7. Determine resources and budget, and meet those needs.
8. Divide up tasks within the coalition.
9. Establish a working task force or executive committee.
10. Keep coalition members informed and involved.
11. Establish a communication program plan; clearly distribute tasks.
12. Build supportive case materials.
13. Develop an internal communication program with each association involving its members.
14. Enlist experts to support the coalition's case.
15. Explain the issue in economic impact terms when possible; use appropriate public opinion.
16. Utilize all pertinent media for greatest impact.
17. Remember to keep all coalition constituents informed and involved.
18. If it's a legislative issue, review the congressional strategy on a regular basis.
19. Determine if the coalition leadership is serving as a catalyst for communication.
20. Prove the results and communicate them to the member constituencies.

When Interests Collide: Managing Many Parties at the Table

Susan Hackley

As director of the Massachusetts Institute of Technology's Technology Licensing Office (TLO), Lita Nelsen routinely negotiates complex, high-stakes deals that marry innovative technology with venture capital to create profitable new companies. An MIT-educated chemical engineer who spent 20 years working for companies such as Amicon, Millipore, and Applied Biotechnology, Nelsen joined MIT's Technology Licensing Office in 1986 and has served as director since 1993. In 2003 alone, the TLO managed 484 new inventions from MIT scientists, was granted 152 patents, and collected royalties of nearly $27 million. In an interview with Negotiation contributor Susan Hackley, Nelsen describes her experiences as a professional negotiator in the fast-paced environment where business and new technology merge.

HACKLEY: Your role in negotiating deals among inventors, investors, and the university helps protect and commercialize the inventions that come from MIT's research. How do you represent the university in complex negotiations that include so many different stakeholders?

NELSEN: The university typically has a variety of objectives in these negotiations: developing new technology, motivating faculty, and, sometimes, attracting industrial sponsorship of laboratory work. At the same time, we need to manage conflicts of interest and uphold the traditional academic freedom to publish and pursue future research directions. We're always balancing the needs of faculty, the university, the developer, and industry. The university's biggest negotiating card is its credibility and good name. I have to get the best deal I can, while leaving enough goodwill on the table to preserve relationships.

HACKLEY: While you are representing the university, you're also negotiating in effect as an agent for a faculty member who has developed marketable intellectual property.

NELSEN: Yes, and the faculty member's interests may diverge from those of the university. He or she may want to start a company based on the technology, and we'll end up negotiating with that company for equity, royalties, licensing fees, and milestones. It's our policy not to allow faculty in the room when we are negotiating with their company because of their conflict of interest as founders and MIT professors.

Until the deal is signed, we're on opposite sides of the negotiating table with the company, which may be represented by venture capitalists or others who want to commercialize the new technology. We've got the innovative idea—and the

Source: From *Negotiation,* a newsletter published by Harvard Business School Publishing and the Program on Negotiation at Harvard Law School. September 2004, pp. 7–9.

intellectual property protection—but the technology may not pay off for many years, if ever. Meanwhile, we're asking investors to take the financial risks of development and to compensate us for intellectual property. So it's somewhat adversarial at that point. Once the deal has been made, we all work together to maximize the success of the new business venture.

HACKLEY: What are some of the special challenges for managers engaging in multiparty negotiations, as opposed to two-party negotiations?

NELSEN: Things become more complicated, of course. When two or more universities jointly own a patent, one of us will negotiate on behalf of the others with a private company. Because universities may have varying objectives and standards, the university taking the lead must balance its own goals with those of its partners when making compromises with the company.

HACKLEY: What is your general philosophy of negotiation at TLO?

NELSEN: We strive for "wise" agreements—ones that benefit all sides so that the deal will last. Without sacrificing its own goals, each side must be willing to make concessions that will benefit the other sides.

In our field of intellectual property, written agreements must be completely unambiguous so that others can interpret them 10 years from now. You can't put off hard points for later on; such vagueness will later become an invitation for litigation. This isn't always easy, as the other side often won't realize the value of establishing a strong, ongoing relationship. Someone might ask, "Don't you trust me?" Even if I do trust him, that doesn't mean I'll trust his replacement a decade from now.

Most people are reasonable, and even those who aren't find it difficult to withstand a well-articulated, calmly presented explanation. Consistency and honesty are even harder to withstand.

HACKLEY: Tell me about an important deal you've negotiated.

NELSEN: Three years ago, one of our professors, a Nobel laureate, came to us with a radically new concept for "turning off" genes in mammals. The process has two major applications: as a biological research tool for determining the function of genes and as a therapeutic molecule to shut off harmful, disease-causing genes.

The professor told us that this would be one of the most important biological research developments of the decade. Hearing that, we wanted to make sure that we didn't grant a license for the research tool to just one company, even if that path would bring us the most profits. The implications for fighting disease were too important.

However, if we made licenses widely available too early, companies might sell subquality materials, and the new method might be discredited. And in the therapeutic field, enormous investments would be required to develop a process to deliver the method effectively to the body. Thus an exclusive license was probably necessary.

Adding to the complexity was the fact that inventors from four different public and private universities were involved. One school delayed its approval for our negotiations with the therapeutic company again and again. I told them to take over the talks but warned them that if they didn't wrap up the deal in 120 days, we would leave with our piece of the patent. They came up with an acceptable deal on the 119th day.

HACKLEY: What kind of agreement did you negotiate?

NELSEN: In the therapeutic field, we granted one exclusive license to a company that has raised a large amount of venture capital. In the research tool field, we granted four licenses to four competing companies, dependent on high-quality work.

Though we expected the method to be wildly successful, we didn't expect it to be accepted so quickly. Limiting research licenses to four for the life of the patent was a mistake. We're looking for ways to create more licenses.

In our entrepreneurial culture, we regard such mistakes as a learning experience. MIT won't tolerate ethical mistakes, but TLO tolerates smart mistakes rather well. We learned from this incident that we should have spent more time brainstorming possible future scenarios—and perhaps have gotten more people involved in doing so. When the future is uncertain, the more time you spend examining possible paths, the wiser your decision will be.

HACKLEY: What lessons can you offer others negotiating from a position of prestige or competitive advantage?

NELSEN: Prestige is both a strength and a responsibility. The benefits are obvious: potential negotiating partners seek us out. But those in a position of prestige need to avoid taking undue advantage of their position, because a reputation for [making] unrealistic demands can get around fast. We can't afford to skate close to the ethical line just to make a little more money on a particular deal. In the long run, the extra money would never compensate for a loss of reputation.

HACKLEY: How would you describe your negotiating style?

NELSEN: I started out as a typical nerdy engineer. I was smart, but I didn't have good people skills, and politically I was inept. While working in industry, I quickly learned that being smart wasn't enough. When I came to TLO, I didn't have negotiation training, but I learned fast, both from experience and by reading.

Men sometimes come into a negotiation and say to me, "I hear that you're tough." My impression is that this is a putdown to me as a woman—that they wouldn't say this to a man. I ask them, "Have you heard that I'm fair?" They almost always answer yes. Then I ask, "Have you heard that I can get the deal done?" They answer yes again, and I say, "Being tough is my job. What's important is that we end up in the right place."

People often think that being tough means getting the hardest deal, whereas, to me, it means being resilient and willing to stand up to pressure.

HACKLEY: You have found opportunities to use your deal-making skills in the non-profit sector as well.

NELSEN: I serve pro bono as an adviser to the International AIDS Vaccine Initiative (IAVI), a nonprofit organization working to develop an AIDS vaccine for developing countries. Given the rate of infection by HIV in developing countries, if my negotiating skills move this project ahead just 24 hours, I figure I will have saved 8,000 lives.

I worked as part of a negotiation "SWAT team" handling critical issues of intellectual property. For example, Oxford University and the University of Nairobi were set to begin trials of the AIDS vaccine in Kenya when a dispute arose over the filing of the patent. Mix academic egos with 300 years of colonial history, and there are bound to be issues. We found a solution that recognized many different types of contributions, aside from the formal activities that would lead to a name on a patent—tissue samples, funds, clinical insights, and so on. We agreed that any financial benefit from the patent would be shared equally by all of the parties.

HACKLEY: The public benefit from your work in developing countries is obvious. There is a public benefit from your work at MIT as well.

NELSEN: The Bayh-Dole Act, which allows universities to own the patents that arise out of federally sponsored research, has led to the creation of hundreds of thousands of jobs. At MIT alone, each year we help create about 20 new start-up companies. University technology transfer brings people together from many different sectors for the benefit of everyone involved, including the public.

Reading 3.10

Negotiating Teams: A Levels of Analysis Approach

Susan Brodt

Leigh Thompson

In light of the increasing presence of teams and work groups in organizations and their role in negotiations, the authors outline a framework for understanding the dynamics of negotiating teams. The traditional context of dyadic negotiations (i.e., one-on-one) is used as a point of departure for the analysis. The authors bring together research on negotiation, small group dynamics, and individual social cognition into a coherent framework to analyze negotiating teams. At the heart of the framework are three categories of psychological processes, corresponding to different levels of analysis, which highlight the contributions of individual, intragroup, and intergroup processes. These processes are discussed in terms of traditional negotiation concepts, such as integrative and distributive bargaining. Finally, guidance for future research is provided.

Much research on cognitive and social processes of negotiation has been conducted in the context of dyadic (i.e., one-on-one) negotiation.[1] Our observations of business practices, however, challenge this research tradition. Consider the example of a manager in a U.S. software firm who describes one of his first negotiation encounters:

> Because I had done the analysis, I was asked to fly to Tokyo to conduct the negotiation. It was an extraordinary opportunity, and I was ready for the challenge. I had negotiated other software distribution deals before, but this would be my first international negotiation—and this deal could impact the company's viability and financial health.
>
> Without hesitation, I accepted the assignment. The VP then asked me if I wanted anyone to accompany me. I quickly declined. I did not need anyone to hold my hand.
>
> My first day in Tokyo was spent sightseeing and getting acquainted with a group of company executives. Later, I returned to my hotel and reviewed my materials. A few hours later, I was shown into the meeting room and was surprised to be greeted by a team of five negotiators. My careful preparation never led me to imagine that I might face a negotiating team rather than a "solo" negotiator like myself. Questions raced through my mind: Why did they bring a team? Should I have brought a team of associates? Is the situation more complex than I thought? What tactics should I use? How will I fare as a solo negotiator facing a team?[2]

Negotiating teams often appear at the bargaining table, and not just in international negotiations. With the expanding role of teams and work groups in organizations,[3]

Source: Reprinted by permission of Susan Brodt, Fuqua School of Business, Duke University; Leigh Thompson, Kellogg Graduate School of Management, Northwestern University. This article was supported in part by a Global Scholars Award grant from Citibank and by Grants SBR-90221192 and SES-9210298 from the National Science Foundation. The authors gratefully acknowledge the thoughtful comments and suggestions of Jeff Polzer and participants in faculty seminars at Harvard and Duke Universities.

Previously published in *Group Dynamics: Theory, Research and Practice* 5, no. 3, (2001), pp. 208–219.

groups of people negotiate agreements and resolve conflicts with other groups in the same organization and with individuals or groups in other organizations. As well, the globalization of business and the increased business relations with people from collectivist cultures[4] mean that negotiators may find a group on the other side of the bargaining table. Moreover, the complexity of international negotiations may also extend beyond the scope of a single individual's capabilities, requiring a negotiating team's expanded knowledge base. Finally, organizations are evolving into complex entities that involve multiple constituencies, relationships, communities, and cultures.[5] United by a common interest, such groups often join together to negotiate as a single party across the table from another individual or group.

A few negotiation researchers have begun to study team negotiations.[6] In this article, we bring together their work along with diverse research streams, such as traditional one-on-one (dyadic) negotiation, small group dynamics, and individual social cognition literatures, into a coherent framework. Our goal is to provide a framework for the analysis of negotiating teams. To achieve this, we selectively draw on social psychological research. Most theories of teams—for example, social impact theory,[7] social categorization theory,[8] and social identity theory[9]—do not focus exclusively on negotiating teams, however, and thus there is no direct theoretical precedent in this area.

The traditional context of dyadic negotiations is used as a point of departure for our analysis. We identify distinguishing features of negotiating teams and describe their underlying cognitive, social, and motivational processes. In the end, we seek to answer the following question: Under what conditions might a negotiating team enhance or hinder negotiation effectiveness?

What Is a Negotiating Team?

A negotiating team is a group of two or more interdependent persons who join together as a single negotiating party because of their similar interests and objectives related to the negotiation and who are all present at the bargaining table.[10] (We use the words *team* and *group* interchangeably.) The team is considered monolithic regarding any settlement; that is, in negotiation, individual team members may not impose or accept an offer without the consent of other team members. However, teams are monolithic only in that members are presumed to have similar underlying interests related to the negotiation at hand; the manifestation of interests and members' strategic behavior may differ significantly. For example, individual team members may act in ways that do not necessarily meet with the approval of their fellow team members.

Team members may also differ regarding interests unrelated to the negotiation. For example, environmental groups may join forces in a negotiation involving offshore oil exploration even though they may vehemently disagree about the appropriateness of strikes, boycotts, protests, and other forms of civil disobedience. Differences in these extranegotiation interests may pose significant problems for teams if, for example, during negotiation, discussion deviates from issues related to shared interests and focuses instead on those issues for which members are sharply divided.

Finally, negotiating teams may be involved in either bilateral or multiparty negotiations. A team may find itself sitting across the bargaining table from another team, several other teams, a solo negotiator, several solo negotiators, and so forth. For the purpose of our analysis, we focus specifically on two-party (i.e., bilateral) negotiations in which one or both parties are a team.*

Comparing Dyadic and Intergroup Negotiations

Negotiations between two individuals (dyadic negotiations) and those that involve teams on either side of the table differ in terms of three psychological processes, corresponding to different levels of analysis: individual, intragroup, and intergroup. *Individual psychological processes* refer to negotiator cognition and social perception and in particular how they are affected by teams. *Intragroup processes* are the internal dynamics of teams, particularly role specialization, shared memory systems, coordination among team members, and also within team relationships and cohesiveness. *Intergroup processes* refer to relations across the bargaining table, such as competitiveness and social influence (e.g., the ability to alter the other party's expectations).

These factors provide a conceptual framework for analyzing differences between dyadic and intergroup negotiations and for understanding negotiating teams. Table 1 summarizes the framework, highlighting the complexity of the negotiating team context relative to that of the solo negotiator. We do not imply that our framework represents an exhaustive consideration of the many social psychological processes that may operate within and between negotiation teams. Rather, it represents processes that have clear implications for negotiation teamwork in terms of empirical findings.

Individual Processes

Cognitive–Informational Processes   Negotiation is a cognitively challenging task. Negotiators must think creatively, process incoming information, and remember that information while keeping in mind one's own preferences, priorities, and goals. Indeed, the more ideas a negotiator generates and considers, the more likely the parties will reach a mutually agreeable solution.[11] One way of increasing the number and diversity of ideas as well as cognitive capacity is to increase the number of persons involved.[12] From the cognitive perspective, two heads should be better than one at generating ideas and synthesizing information, particularly if the task is beyond the scope of a single individual's expertise and if group interaction is structured so as to identify such expertise.[13] Hence negotiating teams may be at a cognitive–informational advantage in integrative bargaining stemming from their enhanced capacity to (a) attend to and analyze information learned during negotiations and (b) generate ideas about possible solutions and effective tactics for reaching favorable agreements.

However, negotiating teams, like groups, may suffer from some potential disadvantages, such as diffusion of responsibility, incoordination, social loafing, social inhibituation, collective information sampling bias, problems with brainstorming, and the like.[14] On balance, we expect that small teams might perform better than solo negotiators.

---

*Our definition of a *negotiating team* comes from the literature, which distinguishes between negotiating teams and group negotiations. *Group negotiations,* also called *multiparty negotiations,* consist of a number of different parties that typically have different interests, priorities, and goals. These parties negotiate among themselves to reach an agreement. In contrast, *negotiating teams* come to the bargaining table as a single party and negotiate with the other party (or parties) at the table to reach an agreement.

TABLE 1 | Psychological Processes in Solo and Team Negotiation

	Psychological Processes			
	Individual Processes			
Context	**Cognitive–Informational**	**Social–Cognitive**	**Intragroup Processes (within-party)**	**Intergroup Processes (between-party)**
Solo negotiators	Judge other's interests Generate acceptable proposals Biases (framing, anchoring, overconfidence)	Confirmatory information processing Primacy effects Egocentrism	Does not apply to solo negotiators	Norm development and maintenance (between the two solo negotiators)
Negotiating team members	Judge interests (own and other party) Generate acceptable solutions Polarization of individual judgment Increased task complexity	Develop high aspirations Confirmatory information processing Primacy effects Egocentrism Conformity	Develop and enact strategy Role differentiation Transactive memory system Cohesion Coalition formation Communication Accountability pressure	Norm development and maintenance Group Identity Group categorization Social influence Group boundaries

There are three key justifications for this argument. First, whereas the comparison of groups to individuals in small group research is based on nominal groups,[15] the comparison in the negotiation literature is based on individuals. There is no logical equivalent of a nominal group in a negotiation context. Second, the small body of empirical evidence to date favors teams over individual negotiators.[16] Finally, the factors that are often the culprit of poor group performance, such as lack of identifiability, accountability, engagement, and performance goals,[17] are not present in most negotiation situations.

A particular challenge in negotiation is making accurate judgments about the other party. Individual negotiators often have biased perceptions about the other party's interests;[18] to the extent that members of a negotiating team are able to correct each other's faulty perceptions and biases,[19] negotiating teams will enhance integrative bargaining. Research is mixed, however, as to whether or not group discussion reduces judgment and decision biases and increases accuracy.[20] Some studies show self-censorship and pressures toward consensus[21] as well as group polarization effects;[22] that is, groups make decisions or hold attitudes that are more extreme than, but in the same direction as, the initial tendencies of a population.[23]

On the other hand, in a review of logical problem solving by groups and individuals, Hastie (1986) reported that groups are generally more accurate than individuals in terms of judgments of quantities, logical problems, and general knowledge.[24] This finding is also consistent with research on minority influence, which shows that it takes only one or two people espousing the correct solution to persuade a misguided majority.[25] Group accuracy depends on whether the solution, once achieved, is demonstrable; whether individual judgment accuracy is perturbed by unsystematic or haphazard errors;

and whether individuals possess different pieces of information that must be combined to solve the problem. If so, then groups tend to be more accurate than individuals.

Research on negotiating teams has demonstrated their potential for enhancing mutual gain attributable to enhanced judgment accuracy. Thompson et al. (1996) compared three negotiation configurations—solo–solo (i.e., dyadic), team–solo, and team–team negotiations—and found that dyadic negotiators were the *least* likely to reach integrative agreements. Underlying this result was a team's ability to make accurate judgments about the other party's preferences, develop mutually beneficial trade-offs, and discover compatible issues.

Social–Cognitive Processes   This term refers to general social and interpersonal processes that affect individual cognition and behavior. Examples include conformity pressures, aspirations, and perceptions of advantage and control. Several theoretical principles support our proposition that teams should express greater goal commitment and conviction than solo negotiators, who are not influenced by members of a group. According to the group polarization literature,[26] teammembers mutually reinforce one another's beliefs, engendering opinion conformity and extremity, especially if normative standards are set and certain opinions are "right" to espouse. This situation is attributable to individuals' desire for belongingness and approval from their teammembers and their wish to live up to fellow group members' expectations.[27] On the other hand, a shared understanding may underlie this effect.[28] According to Tindale et al., "If all the members of a group share a knowledge or belief system that lends credence to a particular alternative, that alternative becomes easier to defend in a group discussion" (p. 86).

More directly, according to the discontinuity effect,[29] groups are more competitive than individuals. Whereas this heightened competitiveness can lead to suboptimal behavior in a Prisoner's Dilemma game (Insko et al.), higher goals and lack of concessions can lead to improved performance in some negotiation situations.[30] Most notably, higher aspirations and greater commitment are directly associated with more effective distributive bargaining.[31] Negotiators who represent constituencies and are accountable to them also set high aspirations and behave competitively. Because of accountability pressures and contact with a constituency, these negotiators make high demands and are slow to make concessions, which leads to long and often contentious negotiations.[32] Evidence on the effectiveness of these negotiations is mixed and seems to depend on the nature of the negotiation.[33]

Our claim that teams express greater goal commitment than solos is also contingent on culture. Research in the United States consistently demonstrates that accountability produces heightened competitiveness, but this result is not universal.[34] Individualism–collectivism theory explains this finding: Accountability leads people to behave in ways that are acceptable to their constituents, and the definition of what is acceptable differs between individualists and collectivists. Norms for individualists tend to be competitive, and hence accountability heightens competitiveness; for collectivists, accountability enforces cooperative norms and heightens cooperativeness.

Intragroup Processes

We consider three intragroup (within-party) processes that affect the performance of negotiating teams: role differentiation, conflict, and relationships. In terms of role differentiation, teams offer the possibility of highly coordinated, almost choreographed actions in which team members adopt particular roles. The familiar good cop–bad cop negotiating team tactic is one example of roles individual team members can adopt.[35] Another possibility (related to teams' cognitive–informational processes) is specialization according to knowledge or expertise. A highly coordinated team, with roles suited to members' expertise, may therefore enhance the quality of negotiated agreements. The effectiveness of within-party coordination will depend in large part on the relative abilities of team members, their common understanding of the negotiation situation,[36] their previous interaction, and situational factors, such as the option to caucus privately.[37]

A theoretical perspective on role differentiation and the shared cognitive understanding of those roles among team members is offered by transactive memory.[38] *Transactive memory systems* are group-level information-processing systems that represent shared systems for attending to, encoding, storing, processing, and retrieving information. Moreland et al. examined the conditions under which teams are likely to develop a transactive memory system and then compared those teams with teams who presumably did not have an opportunity to develop a transactive memory system. Teams who had an opportunity to train and practice together as a group overwhelmingly outperformed all other teams in terms of accuracy, shared understanding, and efficiency.

The key to developing an effective transactive memory system is training together[39] and the absence of imposed structures, particularly those that interfere with existing memory systems.[40] Research on negotiating teams has supported transactive memory systems as facilitators of performance.[41]

Intragroup conflict can occur even among parties who share a common goal, such as a negotiating team. Power struggles, coalition formation, and task demands can jeopardize team effectiveness. For example, teams that are preoccupied with electing a leader[42] are unlikely to negotiate effectively.

Another key factor within teams is the development of interpersonal relationships. Teams might form because of attraction among group members; in a similar manner, working as a team may lead group members to feel attracted to one another. The evidence on how interpersonal relationships affect performance is particularly mixed, with close relationships *across* the negotiating table often resulting in worse dyadic performance[43] but close relationships *within teams* resulting in improved decision making and motor task performance.[44] Thompson et al. (1996) found, for example, that cohesion improved overall negotiation performance and that teams of friends were more cohesive than teams of acquaintances. However, acquaintance teams outperformed friend teams when controlling for team cohesion. Teams of friends made less accurate judgments and reached fewer integrative agreements compared with teams of acquaintances. Interpersonal relationships may extend beyond the boundaries of the team in terms of a networking analysis. For example, Friedman and Podolny (1992) found that groups enhance information exchange and problem solving in organizations because of the roles played by boundary spanners communicating between groups. *Boundary spanners* manage task-oriented as well as socioemotional (trust) relationships and the flow of information toward ("representatives") and from ("gatekeepers") the other party. These roles are managed by different people, which minimizes role conflict and encourages information exchange.

Intergroup Processes

Intergroup processes refer to the interaction between competing negotiating teams. Our analysis considered three key factors: conformity effects in group interaction, social categorization, and social comparison processes. A number of research programs have produced converging evidence that the presence of unanimous others increases conformity.[45] Investigations of behavior in a competitive context revealed that groups increase self-interested behavior.[46] For example, as noted earlier, negotiators bargaining on behalf of a larger constituency are less likely to use cooperative, integrative strategies and are more likely to use distributive bargaining strategies.[47] The effect of a group, whether an audience, team, or constituency, is to increase goal motivation and attention to self-presentational concerns. For example, doing well is construed by negotiators to mean beating the other party.[48]

Social categorization processes also heighten self-interest and competitive behaviors.[49] In-group biases have been observed in negotiation contexts.[50] Moreover, the salience of social categories enhances intergroup competition.[51] Polzer found that the presence of teams significantly increased perceived competitiveness and distrust between negotiating parties and did not lead to greater joint outcomes. Wilder and Shapiro's work on the effects of the perceptions of groups as collections of individuals or as units helps us understand this phenomenon. When acting in the presence of an in-group audience (i.e., other team members), an encounter with an individual member of an out-group, for example, will be perceived as an intergroup interaction, which heightens competitiveness.[52] (This may also heighten misunderstandings or inaccuracies in people's perceptions of out-groups.) Competitive intergroup behavior may be linked to several underlying motives, including self-interest, as mentioned but also self-enhancement[53] and uncertainty reduction,[54] all of which are associated with social categorization processes.

We analyze social comparison processes in terms of perceptions of fairness related to the allocation of resources. Fairness perceptions in negotiation contexts are highly egocentrically tainted, meaning that people typically believe they are entitled to more than what the other party, or even a neutral third party, may be willing to grant them.[55] Because of the convergence of several social processes, such as conformity and group polarization, we suspect that teams may feel a greater sense of entitlement as compared with solo negotiators. We further expect that teams will experience a greater sense of injustice on learning of the other party's outcomes than would a solo negotiator. There are several factors that may fuel these perceptions, including social loafing[56] and the concerns that teams may have about allocating resources within the team.

At the same time, teams may very well experience an advantage when it comes to allocating resources as compared with solos. By sheer numbers alone, negotiating teams present a perceptibly formidable front, which may give them increased social influence—that is, greater ability than an individual to alter the expectations of opponents.[57] According to Walton and McKersie (1965), a key aspect of negotiator effectiveness is in altering the expectations—specifically, decreasing the aspirations—of one's counterpart. Teams may be perceived as more powerful, influential, and correct in their views than a solo negotiator who articulates the same view.[58] Their public commitment to a course of action or position may appear impenetrable because of the credibility and power attributed to a united group of persons. Thompson et al. found that this process results solely from a group's size and solidarity, independent of any informational value. Thus, even though (rational) negotiators may expect an opposing negotiating team to express a singular view, they may nonetheless fail to account for this role-conferred advantage[59] in their assessment of the other party and of the negotiation situation. Hence the psychological impact of confronting a united opposition may lead a solo negotiator to lower his or her aspirations and to concede more than if he or she faced a similarly situated solo negotiator.

Conclusion

We used the traditional context of dyadic negotiation as a point of departure for our analysis of negotiating teams. At the heart of our framework are three types of psychological processes, corresponding to different levels of analysis: individual, intragroup, and intergroup. For each process, we discussed theory and research that bear on the critical measures of negotiation behavior—namely, process (e.g., strategies and judgments), the creation of joint gain, and the allocation of resources. We pointed out that negotiation is best conceptualized as a mixed-motive endeavor, involving elements of both cooperation and competition.

Table 2 outlines the two key economic measures of negotiation performance, integrative and distributive measures, and identifies the psychological processes that affect those performance measures. According to Table 2, the integrative aspect of negotiation refers to the creation and discovery of joint gain, usually accomplished by means of value-added trade-offs on differentially valued issues. The achievement of integrative agreements involves cognitive–informational, social–cognitive, and intragroup (within-party) processes in terms of accurately representing and prioritizing issues, soliciting accurate information about the other party's interests, establishing trust, and exploring a variety of alternatives among parties' interests. In contrast, the distributive component of negotiation is strictly competitive and refers to the division of resources among parties. According to Table 2, the distributive aspect of negotiation involves social–cognitive, intragroup (within-party), and intergroup (between party) processing in terms of goal identification and argumentation, uniformity of team conviction, and power and persuasion.

TABLE 2 | Relationship between Negotiating Teams' Psychological Processes and the Components of Mixed-Motive Negotiations

Negotiation Component	Definition	Facilitating Factors	Primary Psychological Processes
Integrative	Creation and discovery of joint gain via common interests and trade-offs on differentially valued issues	Information exchange Accurate judgments about other party's interests Creative problem solving Trust	Cognitive–informational Social–cognitive Intragroup (cohesiveness, transactive memory)
Distributive	Division of resources measured in terms of individual gain	High aspirations Competitive argumentation Persuasion and social influence	Social–cognitive Intragroup (role differentiation) Intergroup

*Additional resources for this reading are found on p. 703.

Individual Differences

Reading 4.1

The Power of Talk: Who Gets Heard and Why
Deborah Tannen

The head of a large division of a multinational corporation was running a meeting devoted to performance assessment. Each senior manager stood up, reviewed the individuals in his group, and evaluated them for promotion. Although there were women in every group, not one of them made the cut. One after another, each manager declared, in effect, that every woman in his group didn't have the self-confidence needed to be promoted. The division head began to doubt his ears. How could it be that all the talented women in the division suffered from a lack of self-confidence?

In all likelihood, they didn't. Consider the many women who have left large corporations to start their own businesses, obviously exhibiting enough confidence to succeed on their own. Judgments about confidence can be inferred only from the way people present themselves, and much of that presentation is in the form of talk.

The CEO of a major corporation told me that he often has to make decisions in five minutes about matters on which others may have worked five months. He said he uses this rule: If the person making the proposal seems confident, the CEO approves it. If not, he says no. This might seem like a reasonable approach. But my field of research, sociolinguistics, suggests otherwise. The CEO obviously thinks he knows what a confident person sounds like. But his judgment, which may be dead right for some people, may be dead wrong for others.

Communication isn't as simple as saying what you mean. How you say what you mean is crucial, and differs from one person to the next, because using language is learned social behavior: How we talk and listen are deeply influenced by cultural experience. Although we might think that our ways of saying what we mean are natural, we can run into trouble if we interpret and evaluate others as if they necessarily felt the same way we'd feel if we spoke the way they did.

Since 1974, I have been researching the influence of linguistic style on conversations and human relationships. In the past four years, I have extended that research to the workplace, where I have observed how ways of speaking learned in childhood affect judgments of competence and confidence, as well as who gets heard, who gets credit, and what gets done.

The division head who was dumbfounded to hear that all the talented women in his organization lacked confidence was probably right to be skeptical. The senior managers were judging the women in their groups by their own linguistic norms, but women—like people who have grown up in a different culture—have often learned different styles of speaking than men, which can make them seem less competent and self-assured than they are.

What Is Linguistic Style?

Everything that is said must be said in a certain way—in a certain tone of voice, at a certain rate of speed, and with a certain degree of loudness. Whereas often we consciously consider what to say before speaking, we rarely think about how to say it, unless the situation is obviously loaded—for example, a job interview or a tricky performance review. Linguistic style refers to a person's characteristic speaking pattern. It includes such features as directness or indirectness, pacing and pausing, word choice, and the use of such elements as jokes, figures of speech, stories, questions, and apologies. In other words, linguistic style is a set of culturally learned signals by which we not only communicate what we mean but also interpret others' meaning and evaluate one another as people.

Consider turn taking, one element of linguistic style. Conversation is an enterprise in which people take turns: One person speaks, then the other responds. However, this apparently simple exchange requires a subtle negotiation of signals so that you know when the other person is finished and it's your turn to begin. Cultural factors such as country or region of origin and ethnic background influence how long a pause seems natural. When Bob, who is from Detroit, has a conversation with his colleague Joe, from New York City, it's hard for him to get a word in edgewise because he expects a slightly longer pause between turns than Joe does. A pause of that length never comes because, before it has a chance to, Joe senses an uncomfortable silence, which he fills with more talk of his own.

Both men fail to realize that differences in conversational style are getting in their way. Bob thinks that Joe is pushy and uninterested in what he has to say, and Joe thinks that Bob doesn't have much to contribute. Similarly, when Sally relocated from Texas to Washington, D.C., she kept searching for the right time to break in during staff meetings—and never found it. Although in Texas she was considered outgoing and confident, in Washington she was perceived as shy and retiring. Her boss even suggested she take an assertiveness training course. Thus slight differences in conversational style—in these cases, a few seconds of pause—can have a surprising impact on who gets heard and on the judgments, including psychological ones, that are made about people and their abilities.

Every utterance functions on two levels. We're all familiar with the first one: Language communicates ideas. The second level is mostly invisible to us, but it plays a powerful role in communication. As a form of social behavior, language also negotiates relationships. Through ways of speaking, we signal—and create—the relative status of speakers and their level of rapport. If you say, "Sit down!" you are signaling that you have higher status than the person you are addressing, that you are so close to each other that you can drop all pleasantries, or that you are angry. If you say, "I would be honored if you would sit down," you are signaling great respect—or great sarcasm, depending on your tone of voice, the situation, and what you both know about how close you really are. If you say, "You must be so tired—why don't you sit down," you are communicating either closeness and concern or condescension. Each of these ways of saying "the same thing"—telling someone to sit down—can have a vastly different meaning.

In every community known to linguists, the patterns that constitute linguistic style are relatively different for men and women. What's "natural" for most men speaking a given language is, in some cases, different from what's "natural" for most women. That is because we learn ways of speaking as children growing up, especially from peers, and children tend to play with other children of the same sex. The research of sociologists, anthropologists, and psychologists observing American children at play has shown that, although both girls and boys find ways of creating rapport and negotiating status, girls tend to learn conversational rituals that focus on the rapport dimension of relationships whereas boys tend to learn rituals that focus on the status dimension.

Girls tend to play with a single best friend or in small groups, and they spend a lot of time talking. They use language to negotiate how close they are; for example, the girl you tell your secrets to becomes your best friend. Girls learn to downplay ways in which one is better than the others and to emphasize ways in which they are all the same. From childhood, most girls learn that sounding too sure of themselves will make them unpopular with their peers—although nobody really takes such modesty literally. A group of girls will ostracize a girl who calls attention to her own superiority and criticize her by saying, "She thinks she's something"; and a girl who tells others what to do is called "bossy." Thus girls learn to talk in ways that balance their own needs with those of others—to save face for one another in the broadest sense of the term.

Boys tend to play very differently. They usually play in larger groups in which more boys can be included, but not everyone is treated as an equal. Boys with high status in their group are expected to emphasize rather than downplay their status, and usually one or several boys will be seen as the leader or leaders. Boys generally don't accuse one another of being bossy because the leader is expected to tell lower-status boys what to do. Boys learn to use language to negotiate their status in the group by displaying their abilities and knowledge and by challenging others and resisting challenges. Giving orders is one way of getting and keeping the high-status role. Another is taking center stage by telling stories or jokes.

This is not to say that all boys and girls grow up this way or feel comfortable in these groups or are equally successful at negotiating within these norms. But, for the most part, these childhood play groups are where boys and girls learn their conversational styles. In this sense, they grow up in different worlds. The result is that women and men tend to have different habitual ways of saying what they mean, and conversations between them can be like cross-cultural communication: You can't assume that the other person means what you would mean if you said the same thing in the same way.

My research in companies across the United States shows that the lessons learned in childhood carry over into the workplace. Consider the following example: A focus group was organized at a major multinational company to evaluate a recently implemented flextime policy. The participants sat in a circle and discussed the new system.

The group concluded that it was excellent, but they also agreed on ways to improve it. The meeting went well and was deemed a success by all, according to my own observations and everyone's comments to me. But the next day, I was in for a surprise.

I had left the meeting with the impression that Phil had been responsible for most of the suggestions adopted by the group. But as I typed up my notes, I noticed that Cheryl had made almost all those suggestions. I had thought that the key ideas came from Phil because he had picked up Cheryl's points and supported them, speaking at greater length in doing so than she had in raising them.

It would be easy to regard Phil as having stolen Cheryl's ideas—and her thunder. But that would be inaccurate. Phil never claimed Cheryl's ideas as his own. Cheryl herself told me later that she left the meeting confident that she had contributed significantly, and that she appreciated Phil's support. She volunteered, with a laugh, "It was not one of those times when a woman says something and it's ignored, then a man says it and it's picked up." In other words, Cheryl and Phil worked well as a team, the group fulfilled its charge, and the company got what it needed. So what was the problem?

I went back and asked all the participants who they thought had been the most influential group member, the one most responsible for the ideas that had been adopted. The pattern of answers was revealing. The two other women in the group named Cheryl. Two of the three men named Phil. Of the men, only Phil named Cheryl. In other words, in this instance, the women evaluated the contribution of another woman more accurately than the men did.

Meetings like this take place daily in companies around the country. Unless managers are unusually good at listening closely to how people say what they mean, the talents of someone like Cheryl may well be undervalued and underutilized.

One Up, One Down

Individual speakers vary in how sensitive they are to the social dynamics of language—in other words, to the subtle nuances of what others say to them. Men tend to be sensitive to the power dynamics of interaction, speaking in ways that position themselves as one up and resisting being put in a one-down position by others. Women tend to react more strongly to the rapport dynamic, speaking in ways that save face for others and buffering statements that could be seen as putting others in a one-down position. These linguistic patterns are pervasive; you can hear them in hundreds of exchanges in the workplace every day. And, as in the case of Cheryl and Phil, they affect who gets heard and who gets credit.

Getting Credit

Even so small a linguistic strategy as the choice of pronoun can affect who gets credit. In my research in the workplace, I heard men say "I" in situations where I heard women say "we." For example, one publishing company executive said, "I'm hiring a new manager. I'm going to put him in charge of my marketing division," as if he owned the corporation. In stark contrast, I recorded women saying "we" when referring to work they alone had done. One woman explained that it would sound too self-promoting to claim credit in an obvious way by saying "I did this." Yet she expected—sometimes vainly—that others would know it was her work and would give her the credit she did not claim for herself.

Managers might leap to the conclusion that women who do not take credit for what they've done should be taught to do so. But that solution is problematic because we associate ways of speaking with moral qualities: The way we speak is who we are and who we want to be.

Veronica, a senior researcher in a high-tech company, had an observant boss. He noticed that many of the ideas coming out of the group were hers but that often someone else trumpeted them around the office and got credit for them. He advised her to "own" her ideas and make sure she got the credit. But Veronica found she simply didn't enjoy her work if she had to approach it as what seemed to her an unattractive and unappealing "grabbing game." It was her dislike of such behavior that had led her to avoid it in the first place.

Whatever the motivation, women are less likely than men to have learned to blow their own horn. And they are more likely than men to believe that if they do so, they won't be liked.

Many have argued that the growing trend of assigning work to teams may be especially congenial to women, but it may also create complications for performance evaluation. When ideas are generated and work is accomplished in the privacy of the team, the outcome of the team's effort may become associated with the person most vocal about reporting results. There are many women and men—but probably relatively more women—who are reluctant to put themselves forward in this way and who consequently risk not getting credit for their contributions.

Confidence and Boasting

The CEO who based his decisions on the confidence level of speakers was articulating a value that is widely shared in U.S. businesses: One way to judge confidence is by an individual's behavior, especially verbal behavior. Here again, many women are at a disadvantage.

Studies show that women are more likely to downplay their certainty and men are most likely to minimize their doubts. Psychologist Laurie Heatherington and her colleagues devised an ingenious experiment, which they reported in the journal *Sex Roles* (Volume 29, 1993). They asked hundreds of incoming college students to predict what grades they would get in their first year. Some subjects were asked to make their predictions privately by writing them down and placing them in an envelope; others were asked to make their predictions publicly, in the presence of a researcher. The results showed that more women than men predicted lower grades for themselves if they made their predictions publicly. If they made their predictions privately, the predictions were the same as those of the men—and the same as their actual grades. This study provides evidence that what comes across as lack of confidence—predicting lower grades for oneself—may reflect not one's actual level of confidence but the desire not to seem boastful.

These habits with regard to appearing humble or confident result from the socialization of boys and girls by their peers in childhood play. As adults, both women and men find these behaviors reinforced by the positive response they get from friends and relatives who share the same norms. But the norms of behavior in the U.S. business world are based on the style of interaction that is more common among men—at least, among American men.

Asking Questions

Although asking the right questions is one of the hallmarks of a good manager, how and when questions are asked can send unintended signals about competence and power. In a group, if only one person asks questions, he or she risks being seen as the only ignorant one. Furthermore, we judge others not only by how they speak but also by how they are spoken to. The person who asks questions may end up being lectured to and looking like a novice under a schoolmaster's tutelage. The way boys are socialized makes them more likely to be aware of the underlying power dynamic by which a question asker can be seen in a one-down position.

One practicing physician learned the hard way that any exchange of information can become the basis for judgments—or misjudgments—about competence. During her training, she received a negative evaluation that she thought was unfair, so she asked her supervising physician for an explanation. He said that she knew less than her peers. Amazed at his answer, she asked how he had reached that conclusion. He said, "You ask more questions."

Along with cultural influences and individual personality, gender seems to play a role in whether and when people ask questions. For example, of all the observations I've made in lectures and books, the one that sparks the most enthusiastic flash of recognition is that men are less likely than women to stop and ask for directions when they are lost. I explain that men often resist asking for directions because they are aware that it puts them in a one-down position and because they value the independence that comes with finding their way by themselves. Asking for directions while driving is only one instance—along with many others that researchers have examined—in which men seem less likely than women to ask questions. I believe this is because they are more attuned than women to the potential face-losing aspect of asking questions. And men who believe that asking questions might reflect negatively on them may, in turn, be likely to form a negative opinion of others who ask questions in situations where they would not.

Conversational Rituals

Conversation is fundamentally ritual in the sense that we speak in ways our culture has conventionalized and expect certain types of responses. Take greetings, for example. I have heard visitors to the United States complain that Americans are hypocritical because they ask how you are but aren't interested in the answer. To Americans, How are you? is obviously a ritualized way to start a conversation rather than a literal request for information. In other parts of the world, including the Philippines, people ask each other, "Where are you going?" when they meet. The question seems intrusive to Americans, who do not realize that it, too, is a ritual query to which the only expected reply is a vague "Over there."

It's easy and entertaining to observe different rituals in foreign countries. But we don't expect differences, and are far less likely to recognize the ritualized nature of our conversations, when we are with our compatriots at work. Our differing rituals can be even more problematic when we think we're all speaking the same language.

Apologies

Consider the simple phrase *I'm sorry*.

> CATHERINE: How did that big presentation go?
>
> BOB: Oh, not very well, I got a lot of flak from the VP for finance, and I didn't have the numbers at my fingertips.
>
> CATHERINE: Oh, I'm sorry. I know how hard you worked on that.

In this case, *I'm sorry* probably means "I'm sorry that happened," not "I apologize," unless it was Catherine's responsibility to supply Bob with the numbers for the presentation. Women tend to say *I'm sorry* more frequently than men, and often they intend it in this way—as a ritualized means of expressing concern. It's one of many learned elements of conversational style that girls often use to establish rapport. Ritual apologies—like other conversational rituals—work well when both parties share the same assumptions about their use. But people who utter frequent ritual apologies may end up appearing weaker, less confident, and literally more blameworthy than people who don't.

Apologies tend to be regarded differently by men, who are more likely to focus on the status implications of exchanges. Many men avoid apologies because they see them as putting the speaker in a one-down position. I observed with some amazement an encounter among several lawyers engaged in a negotiation over a speakerphone. At one point, the lawyer in whose office I was sitting accidentally elbowed the telephone and cut off the call. When his secretary got the parties back on again, I expected him to say what I would have said: "Sorry about that. I knocked the phone with my elbow." Instead, he said, "Hey, what happened? One minute you were there; the next minute you were gone!" This lawyer seemed to have an automatic impulse not to admit fault if he didn't have to. For me, it was one of those pivotal moments when you realize that the world you live in is not the one everyone lives in and that the way you assume is the way to talk is really only one of many.

Those who caution managers not to undermine their authority by apologizing are approaching interaction from the perspective of the power dynamic. In many cases, this strategy is effective. On the other hand, when I asked people what frustrated them in their jobs, one frequently voiced complaint was working with or for someone who refuses to apologize or admit fault. In other words, accepting responsibility for errors and admitting mistakes may be an equally effective or superior strategy in some settings.

Feedback

Styles of giving feedback contain a ritual element that often is the cause for misunderstanding. Consider the following exchange: A manager had to tell her marketing director to rewrite a report. She began this potentially awkward task by citing the report's strengths and then moved to the main point: the weaknesses that needed to be remedied. The marketing director seemed to understand and accept his supervisor's comments, but his revision contained only minor changes and failed to address the major weaknesses. When the manager told him of her dissatisfaction, he accused her of misleading him: "You told me it was fine."

The impasse resulted from different linguistic styles. To the manager, it was natural to buffer the criticism by beginning with praise. Telling her subordinate that this report is inadequate and has to be rewritten puts him in a one-down position. Praising him for the parts that are good is a ritualized way of saving face for him. But the marketing director did not share his supervisor's assumption about how feedback should be given. Instead, he assumed that what she mentioned first was the main point and that what she brought up later was an afterthought.

Those who expect feedback to come in the way the manager presented it would appreciate her tact and would regard a more blunt approach as unnecessarily callous. But those who share the marketing director's assumptions would regard the blunt approach as honest and no-nonsense, and the manager's as obfuscating. Because each one's assumptions seemed self-evident, each blamed the other: The manager thought the marketing director was not listening, and he thought she had not communicated clearly or had changed her mind. This is significant because it illustrates that incidents labeled vaguely as "poor communication" may be the result of differing linguistic styles.

Compliments

Exchanging compliments is a common ritual, especially among women. A mismatch in expectations about this ritual left Susan, a manager in the human resources field, in a one-down position. She and her colleague Bill had both given presentations at a national conference. On the airplane home, Susan told Bill, "That was a great talk!" "Thank you," he said. Then she asked, "What did you think of mine?" He responded with a lengthy and detailed critique, as she listened uncomfortably. An unpleasant feeling of having been put down came over her. Somehow she had been positioned as the novice in need of his expert advice. Even worse, she had only herself to blame, since she had, after all, asked Bill what he thought of her talk.

But had Susan asked for the response she received? When she asked Bill what he thought about her talk, she expected to hear not a critique but a compliment. In fact, her question had been an attempt to repair a ritual gone awry. Susan's initial compliment to Bill was the kind of automatic recognition she felt was more or less required after a colleague gives a presentation, and she expected Bill to respond with a matching compliment. She was just talking automatically, but he either sincerely misunderstood the ritual or simply took the opportunity to bask in the one-up position of critic. Whatever his motivation, it was Susan's attempt to spark an exchange of compliments that gave him the opening.

Although this exchange could have occurred between two men, it does not seem coincidental that it happened between a man and a woman. Linguist Janet Holmes discovered that women pay more compliments than men (*Anthropological Linguistics,*

Volume 28, 1986). And, as I have observed, fewer men are likely to ask, "What did you think of my talk?" precisely because the question might invite an unwanted critique.

In the social structure of the peer groups in which they grow up, boys are indeed looking for opportunities to put others down and take the one-up position for themselves. In contrast, one of the rituals girls learn is taking the one-down position but assuming that the other person will recognize the ritual nature of the self-denigration and pull them back up.

The exchange between Susan and Bill also suggests how women's and men's characteristic styles may put women at a disadvantage in the workplace. If one person is trying to minimize status differences, maintain an appearance that everyone is equal, and save face for the other, while another person is trying to maintain the one-up position and avoid being positioned as one down, the person seeking the one-up position is likely to get it. At the same time, the person who has not been expending any effort to avoid the one-down position is likely to end up in it. Because women are more likely to take (or accept) the role of advice seeker, men are more inclined to interpret a ritual question from a woman as a request for advice.

Ritual Opposition

Apologizing, mitigating criticism with praise, and exchanging compliments are rituals common among women that men often take literally. A ritual common among men that women often take literally is ritual opposition.

A woman in communications told me she watched with distaste and distress as her office mate argued heatedly with another colleague about whose division should suffer budget cuts. She was even more surprised, however, that a short time later they were as friendly as ever. "How can you pretend that fight never happened?" she asked. "Who's pretending it never happened?" he responded, as puzzled by her question as she had been by his behavior. "It happened," he said, "and it's over." What she took as literal fighting to him was a routine part of daily negotiation: a ritual fight.

Many Americans expect the discussion of ideas to be a ritual fight—that is, an exploration through verbal opposition. They present their own ideas in the most certain and absolute form they can, and wait to see if they are challenged. Being forced to defend an idea provides an opportunity to test it. In the same spirit, they may play devil's advocate in challenging their colleagues' ideas—trying to poke holes and find weaknesses—as a way of helping them explore and test their ideas.

This style can work well if everyone shares it, but those unaccustomed to it are likely to miss its ritual nature. They may give up an idea that is challenged, taking the objections as an indication that the idea was a poor one. Worse, they may take the opposition as a personal attack and may find it impossible to do their best in a contentious environment. People unaccustomed to this style may hedge when stating their ideas in order to fend off potential attacks. Ironically, this posture makes their arguments appear weak and is more likely to invite attack from pugnacious colleagues than to fend it off.

Ritual opposition can even play a role in who gets hired. Some consulting firms that recruit graduates from the top business schools use a confrontational interviewing technique. They challenge the candidate to "crack a case" in real time. A partner at one firm told me,

> Women tend to do less well in this kind of interaction, and it certainly affects who gets hired. But, in fact, many women who don't "test well" turn out to be good consultants. They're often smarter than some of the men who looked like analytic powerhouses under pressure.

The level of verbal opposition varies from one company's culture to the next, but I saw instances of it in all the organizations I studied. Anyone who is uncomfortable with this linguistic style—and that includes some men as well as many women—risks appearing insecure about his or her ideas.

Negotiating Authority

In organizations, formal authority comes from the position one holds. But actual authority has to be negotiated day to day. The effectiveness of individual managers depends in part on their skill in negotiating authority and on whether others reinforce or undercut their efforts. The way linguistic style reflects status plays a subtle role in placing individuals within a hierarchy.

Managing Up and Down

In all the companies I researched, I heard from women who knew they were doing a superior job and knew that their coworkers (and sometimes their immediate bosses) knew it as well, but believed that the higher-ups did not. They frequently told me that something outside themselves was holding them back and found it frustrating because they thought that all that should be necessary for success was to do a great job, that superior performance should be recognized and rewarded. In contrast, men often told me that if women weren't promoted, it was because they simply weren't up to snuff. Looking around, however, I saw evidence that men more often than women behaved in ways likely to get them recognized by those with the power to determine their advancement.

In all the companies I visited, I observed what happened at lunchtime. I saw young men who regularly ate lunch with their boss, and senior men who ate with the big boss. I noticed far fewer women who sought out the highest-level person they could eat with. But one is more likely to get recognition for work done if one talks about it to those higher up, and it is easier to do so if the lines of communication are already open. Furthermore, given the opportunity for a conversation with superiors, men and women are likely to have different ways of talking about their accomplishments because of the different ways in which they were socialized as children. Boys are rewarded by their peers if they talk up their achievements, whereas girls are rewarded if they play theirs down. Linguistic styles common among men may tend to give them some advantages when it comes to managing up.

All speakers are aware of the status of the person they are talking to and adjust accordingly. Everyone speaks differently when talking to a boss than when talking to a subordinate. But, surprisingly, the ways in which they adjust their talk may be different and thus may project different images of themselves.

Communications researchers Karen Tracy and Eric Eisenberg studied how relative status affects the way people give criticism. They devised a business letter that contained some errors and asked 13 male and 11 female college students to role-play delivering criticism under two scenarios. In the first, the speaker was a boss talking to a subordinate; in the second, the speaker was a subordinate talking to his or her boss. The researchers measured how hard the speakers tried to avoid hurting the feelings of the person they were criticizing.

One might expect people to be more careful about how they deliver criticism when they are in a subordinate position. Tracy and Eisenberg found that hypothesis to be true for the men in their study but not for the women. As they reported in *Research on Language and Social Interaction* (Volume 24, 1990/1991), the women showed more concern about the other person's feelings when they were playing the role of superior. In other words, the women were more careful to save face for the other person when they were managing down than when they were managing up. This pattern recalls the way girls are socialized: Those who are in some way superior are expected to downplay rather than flaunt their superiority.

In my own recordings of workplace communication, I observed women talking in similar ways. For example, when a manager had to correct a mistake made by her secretary, she did so by acknowledging that there were mitigating circumstances. She said, laughing, "You know, it's hard to do things around here, isn't it, with all these people coming in!" The manager was saving face for her subordinate, just like the female students role-playing in the Tracy and Eisenberg study.

Is this an effective way to communicate? One must ask, effective for what? The manager in question established a positive environment in her group, and the work was done effectively. On the other hand, numerous women in many different fields told me that their bosses say they don't project the proper authority.

Indirectness

Another linguistic signal that varies with power and status is indirectness—the tendency to say what we mean without spelling it out in so many words. Despite the widespread belief in the United States that it's always best to say exactly what we mean, indirectness is a fundamental and pervasive element in human communication. It also is one of the elements that vary most from one culture to another, and it can cause enormous misunderstanding when speakers have different habits and expectations about how it is used. It's often said that American women are more indirect than American men, but in fact everyone tends to be indirect in some situations and in different ways. Allowing for cultural, ethnic, regional, and individual differences, women are especially likely to be indirect when it comes to telling others what to do, which is not surprising, considering girls' readiness to brand other girls as bossy. On the other hand, men are especially likely to be indirect when it comes to admitting fault or weakness, which also is not surprising considering boys' readiness to push around boys who assume the one-down position.

At first glance, it would seem that only the powerful can get away with bold commands such as "Have that report on my desk by noon." But power in an organization also can lead to requests so indirect that they don't sound like requests at all. A boss who says, "Do we have the sales data by product line for each region?" would be surprised and frustrated if a subordinate responded, "We probably do" rather than "I'll get them for you."

Examples such as these notwithstanding, many researchers have claimed that those in subordinate positions are more likely to speak indirectly, and that is surely accurate in some situations. For example, linguist Charlotte Linde, in a study published in *Language in Society* (Volume 17, 1988), examined the black-box conversations that took place between pilots and copilots before airplane crashes. In one particularly tragic instance, an Air Florida plane crashed into the Potomac River immediately after attempting takeoff from National Airport in Washington, D.C., killing all but 5 of the 74 people on board. The pilot, it turned out, had little experience flying in icy weather. The copilot had a bit more, and it became heartbreakingly clear on analysis that he had tried to warn the pilot but had done so indirectly. Alerted by Linde's observation, I examined the transcript of the conversations and found evidence of her hypothesis. The copilot repeatedly called attention to the bad weather and to ice buildup on other planes:

> COPILOT: Look how the ice is just hanging on his, ah, back, back there, see that? See all those icicles on the back there and everything?
>
> PILOT: Yeah.
>
> (The copilot also expressed concern about the long waiting time since deicing.)
>
> COPILOT: Boy, this is a, this is a losing battle here on trying to deice those things; it [gives] you a false feeling of security, that's all that does.
>
> (Just before they took off, the copilot expressed another concern—about abnormal instrument readings—but again he didn't press the matter when it wasn't picked up by the pilot.)
>
> COPILOT: That don't seem right, does it? (3-second pause). Ah, that's not right. Well—
>
> PILOT: Yes it is, there's 80.
>
> COPILOT: Naw, I don't think that's right (7-second pause). Ah, maybe it is.

Shortly thereafter, the plane took off, with tragic results. In other instances as well as this one, Linde observed that copilots, who are second in command, are more likely to express themselves indirectly or otherwise mitigate, or soften, their communication when they are suggesting courses of action to the pilot. In an effort to avert similar disasters, some airlines now offer training for copilots to express themselves in more assertive ways.

This solution seems self-evidently appropriate to most Americans. But when I assigned Linde's article in a graduate seminar I taught, a Japanese student pointed out that it would be just as effective to train pilots to pick up on hints. This approach reflects assumptions about communication that typify Japanese culture, which places great value on the ability of people to understand one another without putting everything into words. Either directness or indirectness can be a successful means of communication as long as the linguistic style is understood by the participants.

In the world of work, however, there is more at stake than whether the communication is understood. People in powerful positions are likely to reward styles similar to their own, because we all tend to take as self-evident the logic of our own styles. Accordingly, there is evidence that in the U.S. workplace, where instructions from a superior are expected to be voiced in a relatively direct manner, those who tend to be indirect when telling subordinates what to do may be perceived as lacking in confidence.

Consider the case of the manager at a national magazine who was responsible for giving assignments to reporters. She tended to phrase her assignments as questions. For example, she asked, "How would you like to do the X project with Y?" or said, "I was thinking of putting you on the X project. Is that OK?" This worked extremely well with her staff; they liked working for her, and the work got done in an efficient and orderly manner. But when she had her midyear evaluation with her own boss, he criticized her for not assuming the proper demeanor with her staff.

In any work environment, the higher-ranking person has the power to enforce his or her view of appropriate demeanor, created in part by linguistic style. In most U.S. contexts, that view is likely to assume that the person in authority has the right to be relatively direct rather than to mitigate orders. There also are cases, however, in which the higher-ranking person assumes a more indirect style. The owner of a retail operation told her subordinate, a store manager, to do something. He said he would do it, but a week later he still hadn't. They were able to trace the difficulty to the following conversation: She had said, "The bookkeeper needs help with the billing. How would you feel about helping her out?" He had said, "Fine." This conversation had seemed to be clear and flawless at the time, but it turned out that they had interpreted this simple exchange in very different ways. She thought he meant, "Fine, I'll help the bookkeeper out." He thought he meant, "Fine, I'll think about how I would feel about helping the bookkeeper out." He did think about it and came to the conclusion that he had more important things to do and couldn't spare the time.

To the owner, "How would you feel about helping the bookkeeper out?" was an obviously appropriate way to give the order "Help the bookkeeper out with the billing." Those who expect orders to be given as bold imperatives may find such locutions annoying or even misleading. But those for whom this style is natural do not think they are being indirect. They believe they are being clear in a polite or respectful way.

What is atypical in this example is that the person with the more indirect style was the boss, so the store manager was motivated to adapt to her style. She still gives orders the same way, but the store manager now understands how she means what she says. It's more common in U.S. business contexts for the highest-ranking people to take a more direct style, with the result that many women in authority risk being judged by their superiors as lacking the appropriate demeanor—and, consequently, lacking confidence.

What to Do?

I am often asked, What is the best way to give criticism? or What is the best way to give orders?—in other words, What is the best way to communicate? The answer is that there is no one best way. The results of a given way of speaking will vary depending on the situation, the culture of the company, the relative rank of speakers, their linguistic styles, and how those styles interact with one another. Because of all those influences, any way of speaking could be perfect for communicating with one person in one situation and disastrous with someone else in another. The critical skill for managers is to become aware of the workings and power of linguistic style, to make sure that people with something valuable to contribute get heard.

It may seem, for example, that running a meeting in an unstructured way gives equal opportunity to all. But awareness of the differences in conversational style makes it easy to see the potential for unequal access. Those who are comfortable speaking up in groups, who need little or no silence before raising their hands, or who speak out easily without waiting to be recognized are far more likely to get heard at meetings. Those who refrain from talking until it's clear that the previous speaker is finished, who wait to be recognized, and who are inclined to link their comments to those of others will do fine at a meeting where everyone else is following the same rules but will have a hard time getting heard in a meeting with people whose styles are more like the first pattern. Given the socialization typical of boys and girls, men are more likely to have learned the first style and women the second, making meetings more congenial for men than for women. It's common to observe women who participate actively in one-on-one discussions or in all-female groups but who are seldom heard in meetings with a large proportion of men. On the other hand, there are women who share the style more common among men, and they run a different risk of being seen as too aggressive.

A manager aware of those dynamics might devise any number of ways of ensuring that everyone's ideas are heard and credited. Although no single solution will fit all contexts, managers who understand the dynamics of linguistic style can develop more adaptive and flexible approaches to running or participating in meetings, mentoring or advancing the careers of others, evaluating performance, and so on. Talk is the lifeblood of managerial work, and understanding that different people have different ways of saying what they mean will make it possible to take advantage of the talents of people with a broad range of linguistic styles. As the workplace becomes more culturally diverse and business becomes more global, managers will need to become even better at reading interactions and more flexible in adjusting their own styles to the people with whom they interact.

Reading 4.2

Women Don't Ask

Linda Babcock
Sara Laschever

A few years ago, when Linda (one of the authors of this piece) was serving as the director of the PhD program at her school, a delegation of women graduate students came to her office. Many of the male graduate students were teaching courses of their own, the women explained, while most of the female graduate students had been assigned to work as teaching assistants to regular faculty. Linda agreed that this didn't sound fair, and that afternoon she asked the associate dean who handled teaching assignments about the women's complaint. She received a simple answer: "I try to find teaching opportunities for any student who approaches me with a good idea for a course, the ability to teach, and a reasonable offer about what it will cost," he explained. "More men ask. The women just don't ask."

The women just don't ask. This incident and the associate dean's explanation suggested to Linda the existence of a more pervasive problem. Could it be that women don't get more of the things they want in life in part because they don't think to ask for them? Are there external pressures that discourage women from asking as much as men do—and even keep them from realizing that they can ask? Are women really less likely than men to ask for what they want?

To explore this question, Linda conducted a study that looked at the starting salaries of students graduating from Carnegie Mellon University with their master's degrees.[1] When Linda looked exclusively at gender, the difference was fairly large: The starting salaries of the men were 7.6 percent or almost $4,000 higher on average than those of the women. Trying to explain this difference, Linda looked next at who had negotiated his or her salary (who had asked for more money) and who had simply accepted the initial offer he or she had received. It turned out that only 7 percent of the female students had negotiated but 57 percent (eight times as many) of the men had asked for more money. Linda was particularly surprised to find such a dramatic difference between men and women at Carnegie Mellon because graduating students are strongly advised by the school's Career Services department to negotiate their job offers. Nonetheless, hardly any of the women had done so. The most striking finding, however, was that the students who had negotiated (most of them men) were able to increase their starting salaries by 7.4 percent on average, or $4,053—almost exactly the difference between men's and women's average starting pay. This suggests that the salary differences between the men and the women might have been eliminated if the women had negotiated their offers.

Spurred on by this finding, Linda and two colleagues, Deborah Small and Michele Gelfand, designed another study to look at the propensity of men and women to ask for more than they are offered.[2] They recruited students at Carnegie Mellon for an experiment

Source: From *Women Don't Ask: Negotiation and the Gender Divide* by Linda Babcock and Sara Laschever, pp. 1–20. Copyright © 2003 by Princeton University Press, Princeton, NJ.

and told them that they would be paid between $3 and $10 for playing *Boggle*™, a game by Milton Bradley. In *Boggle,* players shake a cube of tile letters until all the letters fall into a grid at the bottom of the cube. They must then identify words that can be formed from the letters vertically, horizontally, or diagonally. Each research subject was asked to play four rounds of the game, and then an experimenter handed him or her $3 and said, "Here's $3. Is $3 okay?" If a subject asked for more money, the experimenters would pay that participant $10, but they would not give anyone more money if he or she just complained about the compensation (an indirect method of asking). The results were striking—almost *nine times* as many male as female subjects asked for more money.[3] Both male and female subjects rated how well they'd played the game about equally, meaning that women didn't feel they should be paid less or should accept less because they'd played poorly. There were also no gender differences in how much men and women complained about the compensation (there was plenty of complaining all around). The significant factor seemed to be that for men, unhappiness with what they were offered was more likely to make them try to fix their unhappiness—by asking for more.

In a much larger study, Linda, Michele Gelfand, Deborah Small, and another colleague, Heidi Stayn, conducted a survey of several hundred people with access to the Internet (subjects were paid $10 to log on to a Web site and answer a series of questions).[4] The survey asked respondents about the most recent negotiations they'd attempted or initiated (as opposed to negotiations they'd participated in that had been prompted or initiated by others). For the men, the most recent negotiation they'd initiated themselves had occurred two weeks earlier on average, while for the women the most recent negotiation they'd initiated had occurred a full month before. Averages for the second most recent negotiations attempted or initiated were about 7 weeks earlier for men and 24 weeks earlier for women.

These results suggest that men are asking for things they want and initiating negotiations much more often than women—two to three times as often.[5] Linda and her colleagues wanted to be sure that this discrepancy was not produced simply by memory lapses, however, so the survey also asked people about the *next* negotiation they planned to initiate. In keeping with the earlier findings, the negotiations planned by the women were much further in the future than those being planned by the men—one month ahead for the women but only one week ahead for the men. This means that men may be initiating *four* times as many negotiations as women. The sheer magnitude of this difference is dramatic, especially since respondents to the survey included people of all ages, from a wide range of professions, and with varied levels of education. It confirms that men really do take a more active approach than women to getting what they want by asking for it.

The more than 100 interviews we conducted—with men and women from a range of professions (including full-time mothers) and from Britain and Europe as well as the United States—supported these findings.[6] When asked to identify the last negotiation in which they had participated, the majority of the women we talked to named an event several months in the past and described a recognized type of structured negotiation, such as buying a car. (The exceptions were women with small children, who uniformly said, "I negotiate with my kids all the time.") The majority of the men described an event that had occurred within the preceding week, and frequently identified more informal transactions, such as negotiating with a spouse over who would take the kids to soccer practice, with a boss to pay for a larger-size rental car because of a strained back, or with a colleague about which parts of a joint project each team member would undertake. Men were also more likely to mention more ambiguous situations—situations that could be construed as negotiations but might not be by many people. For the most part, the men we talked to saw negotiation as a bigger part of their lives and a more common event than the women did.

One particularly striking aspect of our findings was how they broke down by age. The changes brought about by the women's movement over the last 40 years had led us to expect greater differences between older men and women than between their younger counterparts. And indeed when we discussed the ideas with younger women they often suggested that the problems we were studying were "boomer" problems, afflicting older women but not themselves. To our surprise, however, when we looked exclusively at respondents to the Web survey who were in their twenties and early thirties, the gender differences in how often they initiated negotiations were similar to or slightly *larger* than the differences in older cohorts (with men attempting many more negotiations than women).[7] In addition, both the starting salary study and the *Boggle* study used subjects who were in their twenties. This persuaded us that the tendency among women to accept what they're offered and not ask for more is far from just a "boomer" problem.

The Asking Advantage

But just because women don't ask for things as often as men do, is that necessarily a problem? Perhaps directly negotiating for advantage—asking for what you want—is a male strategy, and women simply employ other equally effective strategies to get what they want. This is an important point, but only partly accurate. Women often worry more than men about the impact their actions will have on their relationships. This can prompt them to change their behavior to protect personal connections, sometimes by asking for things indirectly, sometimes by asking for less than they really want, and sometimes simply by trying to be more deserving of what they want (say, by working harder) so they'll be given what they want without asking. Women also frequently take a more collaborative approach to problem solving than men take, trying to find solutions that benefit both parties or trying to align their own requests with shared goals. In many situations, women's methods can be superior to those typically employed by men. Unfortunately, however, in our largely male-defined work culture, women's strategies can often be misinterpreted and can leave them operating from a position of weakness. And in many cases, the only way to get something is to ask for it directly.

So let's look at the importance of asking.

First, consider the situation of the graduating students at Carnegie Mellon, in which eight times as many men as women negotiated their starting salaries. The women who did not negotiate started out not just behind their male peers, but behind where they could and should have been. With every future raise predicated on this starting point, they could be paying for this error for a long time—perhaps for the rest of their careers.

Liliane, now 46, is an electrical engineer and a successful software designer in New England's competitive high-tech industry. Although she earned excellent grades in college, she was so insecure when she started out in her field that she felt she didn't even deserve to be interviewed for an engineering job—she was only "faking it." Despite her doubts, she quickly received an offer from a highly regarded company. When the company's personnel manager asked her what kind of salary she was looking for, she said, "I don't care what you pay me as long as you give me a job." A big smile spread across the personnel manager's face, she remembers. She later learned that he gave her the absolute bottom of the range for her position, which was 10 to 20 percent less than her peers were earning. It took her 10 years to fix this inequity, and she only did so, finally, by changing jobs.

Quantifying—in terms of dollars and cents—the loss to Liliane and women like her from not negotiating their salaries produces sobering results. Take the following example. Suppose that at age 22 an equally qualified man and woman receive job offers for $25,000 a year. The man negotiates and gets his offer raised to $30,000. The woman does not negotiate and accepts the job for $25,000. Even if each of them receives identical 3 percent raises every year throughout their careers (which is unlikely, given their different propensity to negotiate and other research showing that women's achievements tend to be under-valued), by the time they reach age 60 the gap between their salaries will have widened to more than $15,000 a year, with the man earning $92,243 and the woman only $76,870. While that may not seem like an enormous spread, remember that the man will have been making more all along, with his extra earnings over the 38 years totaling $361,171. If the man had simply banked the difference every year in a savings account earning 3 percent interest, by age 60 he would have $568,834 more than the woman—enough to underwrite a comfortable retirement nest egg, purchase a second home, or pay for the college education of a few children. This is an enormous "return on investment" for a *one-time* negotiation. It can mean a higher standard of living throughout one's working years, financial security in old age, or a top-flight education for one's kids.

The impact of neglecting to negotiate in this one instance—when starting a new job—is so substantial and difficult to overcome that some researchers who study the persistence of the wage gap between men and women speculate that much of the disparity can be traced to differences in entering salaries rather than differences in raises.[8]

Another estimate of a woman's potential lost earnings from not negotiating appears in the book *Get Paid What You're Worth* by two professors of management, Robin L. Pinkley and Gregory B. Northcraft. They estimate that a woman who routinely negotiates her salary increases will earn over $1 million more by the time she retires than a woman who accepts what she's offered every time without asking for more. And that figure doesn't include the interest on the extra amount earned.[9] Even in such a small matter as the *Boggle* experiment, the gains to asking were great. Everyone who asked for more money received $10, more than three times as much as those who didn't ask and received only $3.

We all know that few employers will pay us any more than they need to. They're prepared to spend extra to get an applicant they want, but happy to pay less if they can. Assuming applicants will negotiate, they routinely offer less than they're able to pay.[10] But if we fail to ask for more, it's a rare employer who will insist that we're not being paid enough. A recent study shows that this is true even at institutions with a committed policy against discriminating between men and women. This study describes a man and a woman with equivalent credentials who were offered assistant professorships by the same large university. Shortly after the two were hired, a male administrator noticed that the man's salary was significantly higher than the woman's. Looking into it, he learned that both were offered the same starting salary. The man negotiated for more, but the woman accepted what she was offered. Satisfied, the administrator let the matter drop. He didn't try to adjust the discrepancy or alert the female professor to her mistake. The university was saving money and enjoying the benefits of a talented woman's hard work and expertise. He didn't see the long-term damage to his institution and to society from not correcting such inequities, and she didn't know how much she had sacrificed by not negotiating the offer she'd received.[11]

More than Money

The penalties for not negotiating extend far beyond the merely monetary, too. As Pinkley and Northcraft demonstrate,

> Applicants with identical experience and performance records but different salary histories are rated differently by employers. If your compensation record is better than others, employers will assume that your performance is better too . . . . Accepting less will imply that you have less value than other new hires.[12]

In many cases, employers actually respect candidates more for pushing to get paid what they're worth. This means that women don't merely sacrifice additional income when they don't push to be paid more, they may sacrifice some of their employers' regard too. The experience of Hope, a business school professor, tells this story clearly. When she completed graduate school, Hope was offered a job at a prestigious management consulting firm. Not wanting to "start off on the wrong foot," she accepted the firm's initial salary offer without asking for more. Although she feared that negotiating her salary would damage her new bosses' impression of her, the opposite occurred: She later learned that her failure to negotiate almost convinced the senior management team that they'd made a mistake in hiring her.

Similarly, Ellen, 44, a senior partner at a large law firm, was checking the references of an experienced paralegal named Lucy whom she wanted to hire. One of Lucy's former supervisors described a long list of Lucy's strengths and recommended her highly. But when Ellen asked about Lucy's weaknesses, the supervisor said that Lucy could be more assertive. Ellen asked if she meant Lucy needed to be more assertive on behalf of the firm's clients. The supervisor said no, Lucy was terrific at tracking down any information that could benefit a client's case. What she meant, the supervisor explained, was that Lucy needed to be more assertive on her own behalf. "She could be a lot more assertive when it comes to her own professional needs and rewards," the woman explained. This supervisor felt that not asking for more on her own behalf was a professional weakness in Lucy—and a serious enough weakness that she mentioned it when providing an otherwise glowing reference.

Women also make sacrifices in their personal lives by not asking for what they need more of the time. Miriam, 46, an architect, is also married to an architect. But whereas her husband works for an internationally known firm and travels regularly for his job, Miriam works for herself. And because they have two children, she restricts herself to residential projects in her home state. When her children were small, her husband was out of town two to five days a week, and she was taking care of the children pretty much by herself. Although she enjoyed a lot of artistic freedom in her work and built up a successful practice constructing $2–3 million houses (houses that won awards and were featured in design magazines), the demands of her family life felt crushing. "I just felt like this is the way that life is for me and there is not anything that I can do about this." Now she wonders "if there would have been ways of asking for more help" instead of "working and working until I fell apart." The problem was that "asking didn't really seem like a possibility, but I'm sure that it was."

Missing the Chance

Besides not realizing that asking is possible, many women avoid negotiating even in situations in which they know that negotiation is appropriate and expected (like the female students in the starting salary study). In another one of Linda's studies, 20 percent of the women polled said that they never negotiate at all.[13] Although this seems unlikely (perhaps these women think of their negotiations as something else, such as "problem-solving" or "compromising" or even "going along to get along"), their statement conveys a strong antipathy toward negotiating among a huge number of women. (In the United States alone, 20 percent of the female adult population equals 22 million people.)

That many women feel uncomfortable using negotiation to advance their interests— and feel more uncomfortable on average than men—was confirmed by a section of Linda's Internet survey. This part of the survey asked respondents to consider various scenarios and indicate whether they thought negotiation would be appropriate in the situations described. In situations in which they thought negotiation was appropriate, respondents were also asked to report how likely they would be to negotiate in that situation. Particularly around work scenarios, such as thinking they were due for a promotion or a salary increase, women as a group were less likely to try to negotiate than men—even though they recognized that negotiation was appropriate and probably even necessary.[14]

These findings are momentous because until now research on negotiation has mostly ignored the issue of when and why people attempt to negotiate, focusing instead on tactics that are successful once a negotiation is under way—what kinds of offers to make, when to concede, and which strategies are most effective in different types of negotiations.[15] With few exceptions, researchers have ignored the crucial fact that the most important step in any negotiation process must be deciding to negotiate in the first place.[16] Asking for what you want is the essential first step that "kicks off" a negotiation. If you miss your chance to negotiate, the best negotiation advice in the world isn't going to help you much. And women simply aren't "asking" at the same rate as men.

Endnotes

1. Babcock 2002.

2. Small, Babcock, and Gelfand 2003.

3. Only 2.5 percent of the female subjects but 23 percent of the male subjects asked for more.

4. Babcock, Gelfand, Small, and Stayn 2002. The survey was hosted by Jonathan Baron's Web site at the University of Pennsylvania.

5. Another interpretation is possible, however. Men may not really be doing more negotiating than women; men and women may behave in the same ways but label or describe their behavior differently. That is, what a man calls a negotiation, a woman calls something else. This interpretation seems less plausible because it suggests that men and women define a common word in our language differently. But even if it is true, it still has implications for behavior. If women aren't calling their interactions negotiations and men are, women may not be viewing those encounters as strategically and instrumentally as men do and may therefore gain less from them in significant ways.

6. Although we strove to make our sample as representative as possible of the full diversity of women in Western culture, we use the interviews only to illustrate the ideas in the book and did not try to ensure that our sample exactly matched current demographic patterns in the population. We also interviewed far more women than men.

7. Babcock, Gelfand, Small, and Stayn 2002.

8. Gerhart 1990.

9. Pinkley and Northcraft 2000. Example is from page 6.

10. Ibid.

11. Janoff-Bulman and Wade 1996.

12. Pinkley and Northcraft 2000. Quotation is from page 6.

13. Babcock, Gelfand, Small, and Stayn 2002.

14. Ibid.

15. For good texts that summarize negotiation research, see Thompson 1998; Raiffa 1982; Lewicki, Saunders, and Minton 1997; Neale and Bazerman 1991.

16. Janoff-Bulman and Wade 1996; Gerhart and Rynes 1991; Kaman and Hartel 1994.

References

Babcock, L. 2002. Do graduate students negotiate their job offers? Carnegie Mellon University. Unpublished report.

Babcock, L., M. Gelfand, D. Small, and H. Stayn. 2002. Propensity to initiate negotiations: A new look at gender variation in negotiation behavior. Carnegie Mellon University. Unpublished manuscript.

Gerhart, B. 1990. Gender differences in current and starting salaries: The role of performance, college major, and job title. *Industrial and Labor Relations Review* 43(4):418–433.

Gerhart, B., and S. Rynes. 1991. Determinants and consequences of salary negotiations by male and female MBA graduates. *Journal of Applied Psychology* 76:256–262.

Janoff-Bulman, R., and M. B. Wade. 1996. The dilemma of self-advocacy for women: Another case of blaming the victim? *Journal of Social and Clinical Psychology* 15(2):143–152.

Kaman, V. S., and C. E. Hartel. 1994. Gender differences in anticipated pay negotiation strategies and outcomes. *Journal of Business and Psychology* 9(2):183–197.

Lewicki, R., D. Saunders, and J. Minton. 1997. *Essentials of negotiation*. Boston, Mass.: Irwin/McGraw-Hill.

Neale, M. A., and M. H. Bazerman. 1991. *Cognition and rationality in negotiation*. New York: Free Press.

Pinkley, R. L., and G. B. Northcraft. 2000. *Get paid what you're worth*. New York: St. Martin's Press.

Raiffa, H. 1982. *The art and science of negotiation*. Cambridge, Mass.: Harvard University Press.

Small, D., L. Babcock, and M. Gelfand. 2003. Why don't women ask? Carnegie Mellon University. Unpublished manuscript.

Thompson, L. 1998. *The mind and heart of the negotiator*. Upper Saddle River, N.J.: Prentice Hall.

Reading 4.3

Should You Be a Negotiator?
Ray Friedman
Bruce Barry

For decades, researchers have tried to find if there were any connections between individual characteristics and bargaining outcomes. These researchers studied an array of personality measures—including "Machiavellianism," "authoritarianism," and "interpersonal orientation"—but the results were contradictory and inconclusive. We decided to conduct a more comprehensive and careful study of individual differences and negotiations. The results were surprising.

We began by building upon recent advances in the study of personality. Instead of hundreds of idiosyncratic personality types, psychologists have identified five overarching elements of personality and developed better ways to measure these elements. Three of them, we thought, might relate to negotiations. A person who is "extroverted" is sociable, talkative, and excitable. An "agreeable" person tends to be generous, cooperative and flexible. And a "conscientious" person is organized, persevering, and planful. In addition to these three personality factors or traits, we examined how general intelligence affects the outcome of negotiating situations.

For win–lose negotiations, such as haggling over a used car, we thought those who were agreeable would tend to be more easily influenced by their opponent and more uncomfortable with the conflict. They would be less aggressive in opening offers, more easily anchored by their opponent's opening offer, and more likely to give in to the other side. We thought those who were extroverted would be more likely to reveal secret information and more influenced by opponent opening offers, since they were more socially engaged with the opponent. Those who were conscientious would plan better for negotiations, we thought, and be better able to counter opponent tactics. Similarly, we assumed general intelligence helps negotiators, making it easier to understand what tactics make sense.

To test these predictions, we put hundreds of students through a simulated business negotiation involving a simple win–lose premise: a supplier and a manufacturer negotiating over the price of a single component. We had these same students fill out personality tests, and we consulted their standardized academic test scores as a measure of intelligence. (Tests like the SAT and the GMAT are well accepted as pretty good measures of what psychologists call "general cognitive ability," or general intelligence.)

To our surprise, conscientiousness and intelligence had no effects. (In other studies of employee accomplishments these were usually the most important factors predicting success.) Agreeableness and extroversion, however, did impact bargaining outcomes and in the ways we predicted.

Those who were extroverted tended more than others to raise their opening offers when their opponent started high. In other words, extroverts were likely to be swayed by an opponent's extreme first offer (for example, thinking "hmm, she's asking a very high

Source: Reprinted from *Owen Manager* (Summer 1999), pp. 8–9. Used with permission.

price—perhaps those widgets are worth more than I thought"). Those who were agreeable had the same problem and in the end came away with lower results for themselves.

Thus, for this type of win–lose negotiation, how you tend to engage socially with the opponent makes a difference, but intelligence and planning do not. The implication: If you are extroverted or agreeable, be aware that your personality may undermine your ability to do well in this kind of bargaining encounter. You may be easily influenced by an opponent's tactics in win–lose bargaining. Perhaps you should not be the one to negotiate these types of deals.

We did, however, find one silver lining that may help people high in extroversion or agreeableness overcome these risks. The effects of these traits were less pronounced among those who entered our simulated negotiations with high expectations for themselves. A robust principle, confirmed by many research studies, is that negotiators who come to the bargaining table with high aspirations generally do better for themselves. People with high aspirations seem to pay more attention to the dynamics of the situation and bargain more aggressively.

So if you are high in these traits of extroversion or agreeableness, and have to or want to be at the bargaining table, make sure you set high aspirations for yourself. Although this may seem like good commonsense advice, the fact is many negotiators, especially inexperienced ones, don't take the time to think seriously in advance about what they hope to gain from an encounter. And those who do may have relatively little confidence in their ability to do well, and as a result carry into the encounter rather modest expectations. The research tells us that high expectations often translate into better outcomes, and this may be particularly true for individuals whose personalities otherwise work against them.

We also studied a very different type of negotiation—one that allows for the creation of mutual gain through creative problem solving. There are many situations like the previous one in this article, where negotiating is just a pure haggle over a single issue, like the price of an object for sale. But other situations are far more complex, with negotiators trying to sort their way through several issues—some of which involve shared interests and some of which involve divergent interests. The challenge in these situations is to figure out where agreements can benefit both parties and where compromises have to be made—all while juggling a variety of concerns and issues. These types of encounters, sometimes called "mixed motive" situations, are more likely to be found in complex business negotiations, political disputes, and the like. To the extent that bargainers can successfully find common ground and produce a settlement that pleases both parties, these situations are also sometimes referred to as "win–win" bargaining encounters.

For these negotiations we had different predictions. We expected those who were agreeable and extroverted to do better, since information sharing and cooperation help problem solving. We also expected intelligence to be a plus, since cognitive ability helps negotiators develop creative solutions to complex problems. We tested these predictions by, again, having students participate in a bargaining simulation. But this time, the simulation was more complex—a negotiation between a shopping mall developer and a potential retail tenant. Price was not the issue; rather, bargainers had to hammer out a contractual agreement regarding several issues related to the use, potential subletting, and assignment of the leased property. We evaluated and coded these agreements in order to test our predictions about how personality and intelligence would affect who does well and whether both parties can benefit from the individual characteristics of bargainers.

To our surprise, agreeableness and extroversion had no effects. How one interacts socially with the other side did not affect the results of this type of "win–win" negotiation. Intelligence, however, did yield the results we expected. The smarter negotiators were, the more they were able to produce creative, well-structured solutions to difficult bargaining problems. The smarter the negotiators were, the bigger the pie that was split between the two sides.

In one twist to this story, we examined whether one side or the other captured for themselves a bigger share of the increased value from joint gains. In other words, if bargaining pairs featuring at least one "smarter" person were able to generate a bigger pie to split, who got how much of the pie? You might assume that the smarter of the two individuals would grab the bigger share of whatever is at stake. But surprisingly, it turned out that those who bargained with a smarter opponent did better for themselves. The moral of the story: In negotiations where there is a need for creative problem solving, try to negotiate with the smartest opponent you can. In these kinds of complex situations, the real gains come not necessarily from crushing the other person with aggressiveness, but from finding creative ways to solve problems that add value for both parties. Our study suggests that more smarts at the bargaining table—whether yours or the other person's—increases the chances that creative solutions benefiting both parties can be discovered.

Stepping back to look at both of our studies, the results were intriguing. For win–lose negotiations, personality matters but intelligence does not matter. For win–win negotiations, personality does not matter, but intelligence does matter. There is no one overall best person to do all negotiations; rather, who is best for negotiation depends on the type of negotiation. Whether you are the right person to negotiate depends on the situation.

The challenge is to know yourself and what type of negotiation you are facing. Many people assume that success in bargaining is a simple matter of nerve and tactical aggressiveness. Our research tells a different and more complicated story. Different types of bargaining situations call for different types of tactics and quite possibly different types of negotiators. Personality traits that help you in one kind of situation may undermine your success in another. Much of our teaching covers exactly these points—what are your tendencies when you negotiate, and how can you tell if a negotiation has the potential for mutual gains? Effective negotiators are apt to have a thoughtful response to both of these questions.

Negotiation across Cultures

Reading 5.1

Negotiation and Culture: A Framework
Jeanne M. Brett

At the height of foreign investment in Russia, BP PLC spent $484 million to buy 10 percent of Sidanko, one of the five largest Russian oil companies. Eighteen months later, BP was enmeshed in a bankruptcy proceeding and takeover fight that resulted in the loss of BP's investment. What went wrong with this deal? In the race to have a foothold in an emerging market, BP apparently overlooked negotiating fundamentals and cultural issues. A young pro-Western banker with excellent political connections ran Sidanko. He had taken the company private for $470 million, only slightly less than what BP paid for 10 percent ownership, 20 percent voting rights, and a few senior management positions. BP clearly wanted access to Sidanko's oil fields but unfortunately did not negotiate enough leverage to take over the direction of the company and make it profitable. According to one commentator who follows foreign investment in Russia, the BP executives' instructions were not carried out either because Russian management culturally would not do so or because Russian management was getting orders from somewhere else.[1] BP ended up facing off with a recalcitrant creditor who owned part of Sidanko's $450 million in outstanding debt and wanted the oil fields itself.

Culture is often the culprit when deals that cross national borders, like the one between BP and Sidanko, lead to disputes and unanticipated costs. This chapter lays the groundwork for understanding how culture affects negotiation. It begins by describing negotiation fundamentals, those elements of negotiation that are the same across cultures. It then describes culture and explains how culture affects negotiations.

Negotiation Fundamentals

When you ask people all over the world what comes to mind when you say *negotiation,* most describe some sort of a market in which two people exchange a series of offers. Implicit in their answer is the assumption that a deal is in the making, that the two are speaking directly (though the medium may be electronic), and that they are bargaining to divide a fixed pie of resources. Yet negotiations are not limited to direct deal making over fixed resources. In all cultures, people negotiate to resolve disputes and to make decisions in teams. When negotiators reach agreement, resources are always distributed,

Source: Jeanne M. Brett, *Negotiating Globally* (San Francisco: Jossey-Bass, 2001).

but the amount of resources available for distribution is not necessarily fixed. Fundamental to negotiation are the circumstances in which people negotiate and the types of agreements they reach.

Types of Negotiations

All types of negotiations occur because people perceive that their goals are incompatible. When people see themselves as interdependent (or potentially so) but in *conflict,* they naturally negotiate to try to deal with the conflict. Negotiators from BP trying to buy Sidanko wanted to pay as little as possible. Negotiators from Sidanko trying to raise capital by selling a stake to a foreign oil company wanted to gain as much as possible. Their *deal-making negotiations* sought terms that were better than either party could negotiate elsewhere despite their conflicting goals. Conflict is frequently the subtext when groups or teams are trying to make decisions. BP placed managers in top executive positions at Sidanko, but these managers did not have sufficient leverage to influence *decision-making negotiations* at the top. When BP realized that its goals were not being met, it made a series *of claims* for more management control. When its claims were rejected, *dispute resolution negotiations* ensued. Deal-making, decision-making, and dispute resolution negotiations occur in all cultures. However, because culture affects how negotiators reach deals, resolve disputes, and make decisions, it also affects their agreements.

Distributive and Integrative Agreements

Negotiation is about claiming *value:* how much of a set of resources you are going to get and how much the other party gets. Successful *value-claiming negotiation* leads to a *distributive* outcome that divides a fixed set of resources such that your interests or the needs underlying your positions are met. But negotiation can also be about creating value: how you and the other party can increase the resources available to divide. Successful *value-creating negotiation* leads to an agreement that is both integrative and distributive, one that divides an enhanced set of resources.

The concept of *integrative agreements,* much less how to reach them, is not intuitive. To create value takes transforming what appears to be a fixed set of resources into a set of resources that are differentially valued by the negotiators and then distributing resources to the negotiators who value them the most.

There may be opportunities to create value in even the simplest of negotiations. While living in a small village in France, my husband and I offered to organize a traditional Halloween party for the 30 children in the local grade school. Our children had told their French friends about making jack-o'-lanterns (pumpkins are hollowed out, a face is carved, and a lighted candle is placed inside). My job was to purchase enough pumpkins for 30 children to carve. I had difficulty locating any pumpkins but finally found a roadside stand outside a small house with some for sale. I counted; there were exactly 30. I knocked on the door, and a woman came out. I told her I wanted to buy the pumpkins and asked the price. She named a reasonable figure, and I said, "Fine, I'll take all of them." "Oh, no," she replied, "I cannot sell you all of them." I immediately had visions of making jack-o'-lanterns with pumpkin halves, holding a lottery to determine which children got to carve and which got to take home a jack-o'-lantern, carving melons instead . . . But then I thought, wait a minute, you're supposed to know something about negotiation. So I asked, "Why won't you sell me all the pumpkins?" She answered, "If I sell all of them to you, I won't have any seeds to plant next year." I asked her if having the seeds by November 1 would allow sufficient time for planting. She said it would and sold me all the pumpkins on the condition that I return the seeds on November 1, which I did.

Madame Petit and I negotiated an integrative agreement. We created value by my asking and her answering truthfully a series of questions that led us to separate the pumpkins and the seeds. There are two sources of integrative potential in negotiations: differences in negotiators' *preferences* and compatibility of preferences. Madame Petit had a stronger preference for the seeds and I for the rind of the pumpkins. Madame Petit did not need the seeds immediately and I did not want to give them to her right away. Our interests on the timing issue were compatible. Our integrative negotiation took advantage of our different uses for the pumpkins and our compatible time frame.

Had I accepted Madame Petit's refusal to sell me all the pumpkins, our agreement would have been distributive. I would have bought as many pumpkins as she would sell, and she would have kept as many as she needed for seeds. Neither of our interests would have been as fully satisfied as they were with the integrative agreement. With the integrative agreement, Madame Petit gained more money by selling me all the pumpkins, and she gained all the seeds. I gained all the pumpkins I needed so that every child could make a jack-o'-lantern.

Had I stood on principle, refusing to buy any pumpkins if I could not buy all of them, we would have reached an *impasse*. I thought my best alternative, if I could not buy pumpkins, was to have the children carve melons, a messier prospect at best. Madame Petit's alternative was to interrupt her housework repeatedly to get rid of her stock of pumpkins.

Note that our integrative agreement over the pumpkins was also distributive. Madame Petit got all of the seeds *and* her full asking price; I got all of the pumpkins. In fact, all integrative agreements also distribute value.

This is one important reason to integrate: Negotiators who integrate have more value available to distribute and are therefore more likely to claim what they want. A second important reason to integrate is that negotiators who integrate are sometimes able to structure an agreement when otherwise there would be none. Impasses normally occur when a seller asks more than a buyer can pay. However, if the seller learns why the buyer cannot pay the asking price or the buyer learns why the asking price is so high, the negotiators may be able to structure the deal—for example, with creative financing or with nonfinancial compensation that corresponds to both parties' interests.

The term *integrative* is frequently used with a great deal of imprecision to mean an agreement that is mutually satisfactory. Mutual satisfaction, however, is an evaluation of an agreement, not a type of agreement. Negotiators who have failed to look for or find an integrative agreement may be quite satisfied with a distributive agreement. For example, if I were only able to buy 26 pumpkins and evaluated that outcome against the alternative of carving melons, I might have been satisfied. Madame Petit, who had no intention of selling all her pumpkins anyway, would also have been satisfied. Distribution and integration have to do with the *amount* of resources, not with the evaluation of them.

When I tell the pumpkin story in class, someone invariably suggests that I did not get such a great deal because I did not negotiate a discount for buying all the pumpkins. It is possible that had I pushed for a better price, I might have gotten one. Yet I did not for several reasons. First, I knew that haggling over price is not common in the open-air food markets in that part of France. Second, I was concerned that if I did haggle, Madame Petit might refuse to sell me any pumpkins, and my melon alternative was not particularly attractive. Third, I thought it possible that the school might want to continue the Halloween tradition and I might have future interactions with Madame Petit. My poor alternative and my concern for the relationship affected my distributive outcome. In the negotiation literature, especially the cross-cultural literature, the relationship is sometimes represented as an outcome. Yet as the example illustrates, relationship is an issue in negotiation and can be one element of a distributive or an integrative agreement.

Negotiation Fundamentals Affected by Culture: Interests, Priorities, and Strategies

All negotiators have interests and priorities, and all negotiators have strategies. *Interests* are the needs or reasons underlying the negotiator's positions. *Priorities* reflect the relative importance of various interests or positions. My interest in the negotiation with Madame Petit was having a pumpkin for each child. As we negotiated, we realized that we had different priorities: hers was for seeds and mine for the rind. A negotiation *strategy* is an integrated set of behaviors chosen because they are thought to be the means of accomplishing the goal of negotiating. My strategy negotiating with Madame Petit included confronting her directly and asking for information. I could have sent a third party, but I did not. I also refrained from using *influence* because my alternative was so poor.

Negotiators' interests, priorities, and use of strategies are affected by culture. So it is useful to have an understanding of culture before considering how and why culture affects interests, priorities, and strategies.

Culture and Negotiation

Culture is the unique character of a social group.[2] Cultures consist of psychological elements, the values and norms shared by members of a group, as well as social structural elements: the economic, social, political, and religious institutions that are the context for social interaction.[3] Cultural *values* direct attention to what issues are more and less important and influence negotiators' interests and priorities. Cultural *norms* define what behaviors are appropriate and inappropriate in negotiation and influence negotiators' strategies. Cultural *institutions* preserve and promote values and norms. Cultural values, norms, and *ideologies* serve as shared standards for interpreting situations (this is a negotiation, therefore I ought to . . .) and the behavior of others (she threatened me, therefore I should . . .).[4]

When two parties negotiate, both bring culture to the table with their interests and priorities and their negotiation strategies. Exhibit 1 illustrates how culture affects negotiation. It shows culture affecting the interests and priorities that underlie negotiators' positions on the issues. That is, culture may affect why the negotiators have taken the

EXHIBIT 1 | How Culture Affects Negotiation

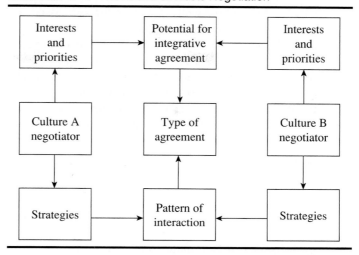

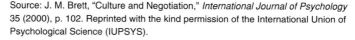

Source: J. M. Brett, "Culture and Negotiation," *International Journal of Psychology* 35 (2000), p. 102. Reprinted with the kind permission of the International Union of Psychological Science (IUPSYS).

position they have or why one issue is of higher priority than another is. The fit between negotiators' priorities and interests is what generates the potential for an integrative agreement.

Culture may also affect the strategies that the negotiators bring to the table—for example, the way they go about negotiating, whether they confront directly or indirectly, their motivations, and the way they use information and influence. Exhibit 1 shows that negotiators' strategies cause patterns of interaction in negotiation. Those interaction patterns can be functional and facilitate integrative agreements, or they may be dysfunctional and lead to suboptimal agreements in which integrative potential is left on the table.

Effects of Culture on Interests and Priorities

Cultural values may reveal the interests underlying negotiators' positions. Negotiators from cultures that value tradition over change, for example, may be less enthusiastic about economic development that threatens valued ways of life than negotiators from cultures that value change and development. This was the situation in which Disney found itself after purchasing a large tract of land south of Paris to construct EuroDisney. Although EuroDisney promised jobs and economic development to an area that had high unemployment and few nonfarm jobs for youth, the local populace valued its traditional agricultural lifestyle. EuroDisney management, with its American values for economic development, had difficulty reconciling the local population's preferences for tradition over development.

The example also points out that the same values that generate cultural differences in preferences may also act as cultural blinders. Negotiators from one culture, expecting preferences to be compatible, cannot understand the rationality of negotiators from another culture whose views on the same issue are at odds with their own.[5] It is generally unwise in negotiation to label the other party as irrational. Such labeling encourages persuasion to get the other party to adopt your view of the situation and distributive outcomes, rather than the search for differences and the *trade-offs* that are the foundation of integrative agreements. There is opportunity for integration in differences. Instead of trying to persuade local French farmers that they should want to give up their traditional way of life, Disney had the opportunity to seek ways to preserve the traditions in the agrarian community in return for the community's support of the new park.

How Culture Affects Negotiation Strategies

When people negotiate, their behaviors are strategic and their strategies may be culturally based. This means that negotiators in one culture are more likely to enact a strategy with one set of behaviors and negotiators from another culture are more likely to enact that same strategy with another set of behaviors. Not only are there differences in strategic behavior between cultures, but there are also differences within cultures and overlap between cultures, with the result that some members of a culture may negotiate less like their own cultural *prototype* and more like the prototype of another culture.

Exhibit 2 shows the distribution of a negotiation strategy in two different cultures. The horizontal axis shows the level of strategic behaviors, ranging from low to high. The vertical axis shows frequency in terms of proportions of cultural members who exhibit different strategic behaviors. The normal curves drawn for cultures A and B indicate that the two cultures' prototypes are quite different but there is variability within each culture. Some members' behaviors are more and some less similar to the cultural prototype. There is also some overlap between the two cultures such that Smith from culture A behaves more like the prototype for culture B than the prototype for his own culture and vice versa for Chen from culture B.

Negotiation strategies are linked with culture because cultures evolve norms to facilitate social interaction. Norms are functional because they reduce the number of

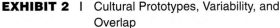

EXHIBIT 2 I Cultural Prototypes, Variability, and Overlap

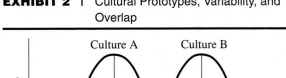
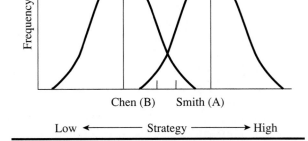

choices a person has to make about how to behave and because they provide expectations about how others in the culture will behave. Functional norms become institutionalized, meaning that most people use them and new members of the culture learn them because they make social interaction efficient. Our research indicates that there is a range of behaviors available for negotiators to use when enacting confrontation, information, influence, and motivation strategies and that culture has an impact on what behaviors negotiators use. Exhibit 3 summarizes these strategies and the alternative behaviors that negotiators can use to enact them.

Confrontation   Negotiations are not always direct verbal interactions between principals. Sometimes the verbal message is indirect. A U.S. company had a contract from a German buyer to sell bicycles produced in China. When the first shipment was ready, there was a problem. The bikes rattled. The U.S. buyer did not want to accept the shipment, knowing that with the rattle, they would not be acceptable to the German customer, whose high-end market niche was dominated by bikes that were whisper-quiet. What to do? In the U.S. culture, the normal approach would be to tell the manufacturer that the rattling bikes were unacceptable and that the problem had to be fixed. In China, such a direct *confrontation* would be extremely rude and cause much loss of *face*. Knowing this, the U.S. manager went to the Chinese plant, inspected the bicycles, rode a few, and asked about the rattle. "Is this rattle normal? Do all the bikes rattle? Do you think the German buyer will think there is something wrong with the bike if it rattles?" Then he left. The next shipment of bikes had no rattles.

Sometimes nonverbal behavior sends the message. An Asian woman, a new member of a multicultural team I was observing, was participating in discussion at a low level until an issue arose that involved her part of the organization and on which she had clearly been briefed. She spoke clearly and forcefully about the problems the team's plans would cause in her area. The rest of the team listened politely, asked no questions, and went ahead with the plan. Her response was to withdraw and stop participating altogether. Unfortunately, the rest of the team was not attuned to her nonverbal behavior.

EXHIBIT 3 | Negotiation Strategies and Behaviors

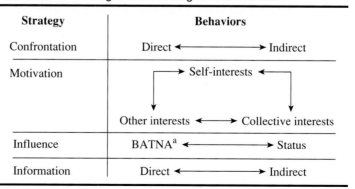

Strategy	Behaviors
Confrontation	Direct ←——————→ Indirect
Motivation	Self-interests / Other interests ←——→ Collective interests
Influence	BATNA[a] ←——————→ Status
Information	Direct ←——————→ Indirect

[a]Best alternative to a negotiated agreement.

At other times, instead of direct confrontation, a third party gets involved. When a U.S. manager in a U.S.–Chinese joint venture did not receive the information he was expecting in a report, he asked the Chinese woman responsible for the report for a meeting to discuss his needs. She politely put him off. A day later, he was called into her manager's office and told that there was no problem with the report, the report had the information it always had, and the report could not be changed.

People from different cultures vary in their preferences for direct verbal confrontation in negotiation. Some who are comfortable negotiating deals face-to-face are not comfortable engaging in face-to-face confrontation over a dispute or in a team meeting. Global negotiators need to understand how to confront directly and indirectly.

Motivation   *Motivation* is all about negotiators' interests. Negotiators may be concerned about *self-interests,* about the interests of the other party at the table, or about *collective interests* that extend beyond the immediate negotiation table. My negotiation with Madame Petit was motivated by self-interests and *other interests*—mine with the pumpkins, hers with the seeds. Collective interests did not really enter into the negotiation. The children might have been just as happy carving melons! However, in some negotiations, collective interests are very important. For example, when the French automaker Renault bought a large stake in Nissan in 1999, business commentators predicted that the measures required to make Nissan profitable—plant closings, lay offs, winnowing of suppliers—would be extremely difficult to accomplish. Japanese companies traditionally feel responsible for their employees and to the communities in which their plants are located. Laying off employees, closing plants, and generating competition among suppliers is not a normative business practice in Japan, where collective interests dominate.

The relative importance of negotiators' self-interests, other interests, and collective interests vary by culture. Negotiators from some cultures are much more concerned with self-interests; negotiators from other cultures pay as much attention to the interests of others as to their own; and negotiators from still other cultures take the interests of the collective into account when setting priorities and deciding whether to accept a proposal or continue negotiating. Global negotiators need to be sensitive to cultural differences in negotiators' goals and motivation and in negotiators' interests.

Influence   *Power* is the ability to influence the other party to accede to your wishes.[6] There are many different bases of power in social interaction,[7] but two, BATNAs and fairness standards, seem to be particularly important for negotiation and to be relied on differently in different cultures.

BATNA stands for the *best alternative to a negotiated agreement.*[8] The worse a negotiator's BATNA, the more dependent the negotiator is on reaching an agreement and the less powerful in terms of extracting concessions. My BATNA in negotiating with Madame Petit was buying melons—not very good. I could hardly have influenced her to sell me all her pumpkins by threatening to go elsewhere and buy melons!

Fairness standards are decision rules, wrapped in a veneer of justice. The rule might be precedent, it might be contract or law, or it might be social status (for example, age or experience) or social ideology (for example, equity, equality, or need). I could have proposed need as a fair standard to try to convince Madame Petit to sell me all her pumpkins. However, she had needs too, and this illustrates the problem with fair standards as influence strategies: There are almost always competing standards, even within a culture.

Across cultures, differences in ideology are likely to make it difficult to agree on a fairness standard. For example, ideology is at the heart of the long-standing "banana wars" between the United States and the European Union (EU). The fair standard that applies is the open markets standard that both parties have agreed to as members of the World Trade Organization (WTO). Yet France, an EU and WTO member, effectively blocked the importation of bananas from U.S. companies by imposing tariffs, making U.S. bananas more expensive than bananas from former French colonies whose economies in the near term depend on bananas. French ideology has a social welfare slant that extends to its former colonies. U.S. ideology is more capitalistic.[9]

The relative importance of BATNAs versus fairness standards, especially standards based on social status, as a basis of power in negotiations varies by culture. The relative frequency of use of influence tactics also varies by culture.

Information   *Information* is the currency of negotiation. Information about BATNAs, status, and other fair standards affects distributive agreements. Information about interests and priorities affects integrative agreements. When negotiators do not understand the information conveyed by the other party, integrative potential is almost always left on the table, and sometimes negotiations end in impasse.

Consider the inauspicious opening in the following negotiation. A U.S. negotiator on his first trip to Japan was confused by the formal opening meeting, which his Japanese hosts filled with a recitation of the history of their company, a story about the founder, and a litany about their product. After the meeting, the U.S. negotiator turned to his local representative and said, "What was that all about? Do they think I would arrive so unprepared as not to know about their company and their product? I want to buy their product. Why are they treating me as though I've never heard of it or their company? All the information they conveyed this afternoon is readily available in the marketplace, and I already know it." The local representative explained that the Japanese negotiators were attempting to convey information, albeit indirectly, about the status of their company and the product. The U.S. negotiator, fully aware of the Japanese company's status, was eager to get down to direct negotiations.

Culture affects whether information is conveyed directly, with meaning on the surface of the communication, or indirectly, with meaning conveyed within the context of the message. Culture also affects whether information is conveyed at all.

Why Culture Affects Negotiation Strategy

The behaviors that negotiators from a culture characteristically use to enact a negotiation strategy are related to other features of that culture, including its values, norms for social interaction other than negotiation, and ideologies. Three widely studied features of culture seem to be related to the variability in negotiation strategy across cultures: the cultural values of individualism versus collectivism and egalitarianism versus hierarchy, and the low- versus high-context norm for communication.

Individualism versus Collectivism   The most widely studied cultural value, *individualism* versus *collectivism,* distinguishes between cultures that place individuals' needs above collective needs and cultures that place the needs of the collective above the needs of individuals.[10] In individualist cultures, norms promote the autonomy of the individual. Social and economic institutions reward individual accomplishments. Legal institutions protect individual rights. In collectivist cultures, norms promote the interdependence of individuals by emphasizing social obligation. Social and economic institutions reward classes of people rather than individuals. Legal institutions support collective interests above individual rights.

The way a society treats people affects how they construe themselves and how they interact. People in all cultures distinguish between *in-groups,* of which they are members, and *out-groups,* of which they are not.[11] In individualist cultures, self-identity is likely to consist of attributes that are independent of in-group membership.[12] A negotiator from an individualist culture might say, "I am tall; I am intelligent; I have a sense of humor." In collectivist cultures, self-identity is likely to be interdependent with in-group membership. A negotiator from a collectivist culture might say, "I am a wife, mother, and daughter; I am a Kellogg faculty member."

Two researchers, Geert Hofstede and Shalom Schwartz, have measured social values in many cultures.[13] They used questionnaires and classified cultures by differences in average scores. Exhibit 4 summarizes Hofstede's classification of individualist and collectivist cultures, ranked in each category in decreasing order of individualism.

EXHIBIT 4 | Individualist and Collectivist Cultures

Individualist Cultures	Intermediate Cultures	Collectivist Cultures
United States	Austria	Brazil
Australia	Israel	Turkey
Great Britain	Spain	Greece
Canada	India	Philippines
Netherlands	Japan	Mexico
New Zealand	Argentina	Portugal
Italy	Iran	Hong Kong
Belgium		Chile
Denmark		Singapore
Sweden		Thailand
France		Taiwan
Ireland		Peru
Norway		Pakistan
Switzerland		Colombia
Germany		Venezuela
Finland		

Source: G. Hofstede, *Culture's Consequences: International Differences in Work-Related Values* (Thousand Oaks, CA: Sage, 1980), p. 158, copyright © 1980 by Sage. Reprinted by permission of Sage Publications, Inc.

EXHIBIT 5 | Individualism–Collectivism and Negotiation Strategy

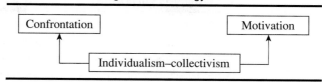

Members of individualist and collectivist cultures differ in many ways. Exhibit 5 suggests that both confrontational and motivational behaviors may stem from this cultural value.

Reluctance to confront directly in a negotiation may stem from the emphasis on cooperation in collectivist cultures.[14] Confronting—for example, telling the bicycle maker that the rattles indicated unacceptable quality—signals a lack of respect for an individual with whom you have a relationship.[15] An indirect approach is thought to be relationship-preserving.[16]

Negotiators' motivational orientations may also stem from their culture's values for individualism versus collectivism. This cultural value reflects a society's goal orientation.[17] Individualist cultures emphasize self-interests. Collectivist cultures emphasize collective interests.

Egalitarianism versus Hierarchy   The second most widely studied cultural value distinguishes *hierarchical cultures,* which emphasize differentiated social status, from *egalitarian cultures,* which do not. In hierarchical cultures, social status implies social power. Social inferiors are expected to defer to social superiors, who in return for the power and privilege conferred on them by right of their status have an obligation to look out for the well-being of low-status people.[18]

Hofstede and Schwartz have also classified cultures on this dimension, which Hofstede calls "power distance." High-power-distance cultures are hierarchical ones where social status is differentiated into ranks. Exhibit 6 summarizes Schwartz's classification of egalitarian and hierarchical cultures, ranked in descending order of egalitarian and hierarchical commitment.

Members of egalitarian and hierarchical cultures may have rather distinct confrontational styles. They may also use influence differently. Exhibit 7 suggests that both confrontational and influence behaviors may be related to this cultural value.

People in hierarchical cultures may be reluctant to confront directly in negotiation because confrontation implies a lack of respect for social status and may threaten social structures. The norm in such a culture is not to challenge higher-status members. When conflict does occur, it is more likely to be handled by a social superior than by direct confrontation.[19] When a higher-status third party gets involved in a dispute, that party's decision reinforces his authority without necessarily conferring differential status on the contestants, as a negotiation that one party lost and the other won would do. In an egalitarian culture, differentiated status due to success in direct negotiations is not likely to translate into permanent changes in social status because there are few avenues for setting precedents in egalitarian cultures.

EXHIBIT 6 | Egalitarian and Hierarchical Cultures

Egalitarian Cultures	Hierarchical Cultures
Portugal	Thailand
Italy	China
Spain	Turkey
Denmark	Zimbabwe
France	Japan
Netherlands	Taiwan
Germany	Hong Kong
Greece	Singapore
Finland	Brazil
Switzerland	Poland
New Zealand	Malaysia
Turkey	Hungary
United States	United States
Mexico	New Zealand
Australia	Australia
Brazil	Mexico
Israel	Germany
Hong Kong	Netherlands
Poland	Switzerland
Singapore	France
Japan	Portugal
Taiwan	Spain
Malaysia	Finland
China	Greece
Zimbabwe	Denmark
Slovenia	Slovenia
Thailand	Italy

Source: S. Schwartz, "Beyond Individualism/Collectivism: New Cultural Dimensions of Values," in H. C. Triandis, U. Kim, and G. Yoon (eds.), *Individualism and Collectivism* (London: Sage, 1994), pp. 113–14, copyright © 1994 by Sage. Reprinted by permission of Sage Publications, Inc.

Negotiators from hierarchical and egalitarian cultures may use influence rather differently if their views of power in negotiation reflect the way power is construed in their cultures. In egalitarian cultures, power is transitory and situational; in hierarchical cultures, power is long-term and general. The concept of BATNA fits well with the conceptualization of power in egalitarian cultures. BATNAs are situational and flexible. If a negotiator is unhappy with his BATNA, he may be able to improve it. Power as status fits well with the conceptualization of power in hierarchical cultures. Status-based power should endure over time and across situations.[20]

The reliance on a status-based interpretation of power can be seen in Japanese commercial relationships in the 1960s and the 1980s. Japan is a hierarchical culture. In the

EXHIBIT 7 | Egalitarianism–Hierarchy and Negotiation
Strategy

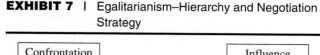
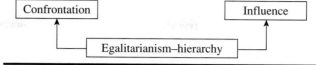

1960s, when Japanese automobile companies were trying to break into the U.S. market, they sold their cars at a very low margin. Presumably, they viewed themselves as having lower status than the American carmakers, and that status dictated that they could not charge the same high prices for their cars as the higher-status Americans. When the Japanese economy was booming in the 1980s, Japan's self-image of its economic status improved, and Japanese companies paid top dollar, bidding and winning against American companies for commercial real estate and private companies.

These events can be interpreted, as indeed they were in the U.S. press, from an in-group versus out-group perspective. Japan is a collectivist culture. Negotiators from collectivist cultures are said to deal with in-group members cooperatively and out-group members competitively. Japanese commercial behavior in both the 1960s and the 1980s was motivated by competition. This explanation based on competitiveness due to collectivism may be correct, but it is simplistic. Selling at or below margin, as the Japanese automakers did in the 1960s, does not make a lot of competitive sense because it does not build market share when competitors drop their prices too. (Japanese market share for automobiles in the United States was ultimately built on quality, not on price.) Paying significant premiums when you are the powerful buyer in the market and presumably have many options for investment also does not make competitive sense. An explanation based on hierarchy and the status of the Japanese in the marketplace in the 1960s and the 1980s provides additional insight into the behavior of Japanese negotiators.

Low-Context versus High-Context Communications   People in low-context cultures prefer to communicate directly. Meaning is on the surface of the message. Information is explicit, without nuance, and relatively context-free. People in high-context cultures prefer to communicate indirectly. Meaning is embedded in the context of the message and must be inferred to be understood.

Exhibit 8 identifies national cultures according to whether high- or low-context communication is normative.[21] In general, high-context cultures are those in which people have extensive information networks among family, friends, colleagues, and clients and are involved in close personal relationships.

Negotiators from low- and high-context cultures may have rather distinct confrontational styles. They may also use information differently. Exhibit 9 suggests that both confrontational and information-sharing behaviors may be influenced by this cultural value.

The Western manager in the rattling bicycles story was using high-context communication. He expected his Chinese counter-part to infer from his calling attention to the rattle that the bicycles needed to be repaired. He was neither confronting directly nor communicating directly. The Asian manager on the multicultural team was showing her

EXHIBIT 8 | Low- and High-Context Cultures

Low-Context Cultures	High-Context Cultures
Germany	Arab cultures
Scandinavian cultures	France
Switzerland	Japan
United States	Mediterranean cultures
	Russia

Source: E. T. Hall and M. R. Hall, *Understanding Cultural Differences*
(Yarmouth, ME: Intercultural Press, 1990), pp. 7–8, 23.

displeasure at being ignored by in turn ignoring the team for the rest of the meeting. Her behavior was a form of indirect confrontation and communication. The Chinese manager in the joint venture confronted and communicated indirectly by having a third party, who just happened to be the boss, communicate the refusal.

Culture and Negotiation Strategy: A Complex Link

It would be helpful if the relationships between negotiation strategies and other features of a culture were strong and straightforward. The research to date indicates quite clearly that this is not the case. The link between cultural values and cultural ideology and negotiation strategies is complex.

A look back at Exhibit 2 reveals two reasons why this link between features of a culture and negotiators' strategy is not straightforward: Not all members of a culture behave like the cultural prototype, and cultural profiles overlap.

Another reason for the complex relationship between culture and negotiation strategy is that cultures are not composed of single features. Cultures have profiles of features. Single cultural features may be more or less important, depending on the profile in which they are embedded. Given the state of the research, we can make at most general statements about single cultural features and negotiation strategy.

Yet another reason why negotiation strategy is not perfectly related to other features of a culture is that cultural norms for negotiation may be cued more strongly in some situations than others.[22] For example, members of a multicultural team may act more in accordance with their national cultural norms when they report to local superiors. When they report to a senior manager at corporate headquarters, they may act more in accordance with corporate norms.

EXHIBIT 9 | Low- and High-Context Communication
and Negotiation Strategy

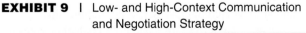
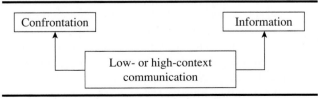

Finally, there is the influence of the strategies of the other negotiators at the table. Negotiators are quite likely to reciprocate each other's strategies.[23] When all negotiators are from the same culture, reciprocity reinforces culturally normative negotiation behaviors. When negotiators are from different cultures, reciprocity may help negotiators adjust their strategies to each other.[24]

Given all of these caveats, it is not unreasonable to wonder why we should study culture and negotiation strategy at all. The answer is that there are cultural differences in the behaviors negotiators use to enact a strategy. Anticipating these differences helps negotiators make sense of them and adjust their own behaviors to reinforce or to block the other party's strategy. However, the global negotiator needs to be aware of several important points:

- Research is only beginning to profile the characteristic negotiation strategies of different cultures. There may be important strategic differences between cultures in addition to the motivational, influence, information, and confrontational strategies discussed here. Many cultures have not yet been thoroughly studied.

- Individual cultural members may not act like the cultural prototype, especially in particular situations. The cultural typologies based on individualism–collectivism, egalitarianism–hierarchy, and low- or high-context communication may not characterize the negotiators you are dealing with.

- A negotiator's strategy is not immutable; negotiators adjust their strategies to accommodate one another.

There is a risk in knowing too much about the other party's culture and assuming that he will act according to the cultural prototype. Excellent cross-cultural negotiators proceed slowly, testing their assumptions about what strategy will be effective with the other party. They are willing to adjust their use of negotiation strategy to achieve their goals but not compromise on their goals.

Endnotes

1. N. Banerjee, "BP's Losses in Russia Seen as a Warning for Investors," *International Herald Tribune,* Aug. 13–14, 1999, pp. 9, 13.

2. Individuals are members of many different cultural groups in addition to their nation–state. Furthermore, cultural subgroups are embedded within nation–state cultural groups. This all gets rather confusing. So when doing cultural research, it is imperative to identify the type of group you are studying. In our studies, negotiators bring their individual differences to the table; they bring their employer's culture to the table, the culture of their ethnic group, and their national culture. We are interested only in the cultures of nation–states, and those cultures are relevant only if there are systematic differences between them. This requirement is a reasonably high hurdle for the research. If there are no differences between national cultural groups, then there is no basis for drawing cultural inferences.

3. A. L. Lytle, J. M. Brett, Z. I. Barsness, C. H. Tinsley, and M. Janssens, "A Paradigm for Confirmatory Cross-Cultural Research in Organizational Behavior," in L. L. Cummings and B. M. Staw (eds.), *Research in Organizational Behavior* (Greenwich, CT: JAI Press, 1995).

4. S. T. Fiske and S. E. Taylor, *Social Cognition* (New York: McGraw-Hill, 1991).

5. U.S. companies apparently do not learn well from each other's experiences. Mondavi Vineyards announced in May 2000 that it was planning to lease a forested hillside above Aniane, near Montpellier, to produce France's first foreign-owned *vin de terroir*. Mondavi expected Aniane's 2,120 inhabitants to be pleased that this fine American company would be pumping $8 million into the local economy over the next 10 years. Instead, villagers protested the destruction of the communal forest where they hunt wild boar: V. Walt, "French Village Unwilling to Welcome Mondavi," *International Herald Tribune,* July 20, 2000, p. 11.

6. Ury, Brett, and Goldberg, *Getting Disputes Resolved.*

7. J. French and B. Raven, "The Bases of Social Power," in D. Cartwright (ed.), *Studies in Social Power* (Ann Arbor, MI: Institute for Social Research, 1959).

8. R. Fisher, W. Ury, B. Patton, *Getting to Yes* (New York: Penguin, 1991).

9. Office of the U.S. Trade Representative, "USTR Kantor Makes Preliminary Decision That EU Banana Regime Harms U.S. Interests" (press release), Jan. 9, 1999.

10. G. Hofstede, *Culture's Consequences: International Differences in Work-Related Values* (Thousand Oaks, CA: Sage, 1980); S. Schwartz, "Beyond Individualism/Collectivism: New Cultural Dimensions of Values," in H. C. Triandis, U. Kim, and G. Yoon (eds.), *Individualism and Collectivism* (London: Sage, 1994); H. C. Triandis, *Individualism and Collectivism* (Boulder, CO: Westview Press, 1995).

11. J. C. Turner, *Rediscovering the Social Group: A Self-Categorization Theory* (Cambridge: Blackwell, 1987).

12. Triandis, *Individualism and Collectivism.*

13. Hofstede, *Culture's Consequences;* Schwartz, "Beyond Individualism/Collectivism."

14. W. B. Gudykunst, G. Gao, K. L. Schmidt, T. Nishida, M. H. Bond, K. Leung, G. Wang, and R. A. Barraclough, "The Influence of Individualism–Collectivism, Self-Monitoring, and Predicted Outcome Value on Communication in Ingroup and Outgroup Relationships," *Journal of Cross-Cultural Psychology,* 23 (1992), pp. 196–213.

15. A more technical and psychologically insightful explanation for why negotiators from collectivist cultures are reluctant to use confrontation focuses on the importance of in-groups in these cultures. In-groups provide social identity to their members. In a collectivist culture, group-based social identity is very important because individual needs and values are subordinate to collective needs and values. People do not want to risk ostracism from in-groups that confer identity and social benefits. For this reason, cooperation and harmony with in-group members is emphasized. Confronting a member of an in-group signals a lack of respect for that person, and for yourself, since you are both members of the same social identity group: Turner, *Rediscovering the Social Group.*

16. As a member of a Western culture, I admit that I find it difficult to understand how being told no indirectly by the boss is going to preserve my relationship with my peer, whom I originally asked for something and who did not respond to that request. Some things about culture you just have to accept, and one of them seems to be that in some cultures, involving the boss (indirect confrontation) is seen as a way of preserving the peer relationship and in others it is not. Recognizing the difference does not mean that you have to accept it as your own way of interpreting the situation, just that there is another way to frame the same situation that is legitimate in other cultures.

17. Schwartz, "Beyond Individualism/Collectivism."

18. K. Leung, "Negotiation and Reward Allocations across Cultures," in P. C. Earley, M. Erez, and Associates, *New Perspectives on International/Industrial Organizational Psychology* (San Francisco: Jossey-Bass, 1997).

19. Leung, "Negotiation and Reward Allocations across Cultures."

20. J. M. Brett and T. Okumura, "Inter- and Intra-Cultural Negotiation: U.S. and Japanese Negotiators," *Academy of Management Journal* 41 (1998), pp. 495–510.

21. E. T. Hall and M. R. Hall, *Understanding Cultural Differences* (Yarmouth, ME: Intercultural Press, 1990). See also M. Rajan and J. Graham, "Nobody's Grandfather Was a Merchant: Understanding the Soviet Commercial Negotiation Process and Style," *California Management Review,* Spring 1991, pp. 40–57.

22. Leung, "Negotiation and Reward Allocations across Cultures"; M. W. Morris, K. Leung, D. Ames, and B. Lickel, "Views from the Inside and Outside: Integrating Emic and Etic Insights about Culture and Justice Judgments," *Academy of Management Review* 24 (1999), pp. 781–96.

23. J. M. Brett, D. L. Shapiro, and A. L. Lytle, "Breaking the Bonds of Reciprocity in Negotiations," *Academy of Management Journal* 41 (1998), pp. 410–24; W. L. Adair, "Reciprocity in the Global Market," unpublished doctoral dissertation, Department of Management and Organizations, Northwestern University, 2000.

24. Adair, "Reciprocity in the Global Market."

Reading 5.2

Intercultural Negotiation in International Business
Jeswald W. Salacuse

Introduction

Although negotiating a purely domestic business deal and negotiating an international transaction have much in common, the factor that is almost always present in an international negotiation and generally absent from a domestic negotiation is a difference in culture among the parties. In international business, transactions not only cross borders, they also cross cultures. Culture profoundly influences how people think, communicate, and behave, and it also affects the kinds of deals they make and the way they make them. Differences in culture among business executives (for example, between a Chinese public-sector plant manager in Shanghai and an American division head of a family company in Cleveland) can therefore create barriers that impede or completely stymie the negotiating process. The purpose of this article is to examine the effect of differences in culture on international business negotiations and to suggest ways to overcome problems encountered in intercultural dealings.

The Nature of Culture

Definitions of culture are as numerous and often as vague as definitions of negotiation itself (Moran and Stripp 1991, pp. 43–56; Zartman 1993, p. 19). Some scholars would confine the concept of culture to the realm of ideas, feeling, and thoughts. For example, one working definition offered by two negotiation experts is that "Culture is a set of shared and enduring meanings, values, and beliefs that characterize national, ethnic, and other groups and orient their behavior" (Faure and Sjostedt 1993, p. 3). Others would have culture also encompass behavior patterns and institutions common to a given group or community. E. Adamson Hoebel, a noted anthropologist, defined culture as "the integrated system of learned behavior patterns which are characteristic of the members of a society and which are not the result of biological inheritance" (Hoebel 1972, p. 7). While the essence of culture may reside in the mind, it must be pointed out that persons gain their understanding of their and others' cultures primarily, if not exclusively, from observing the behavior and institutions of a particular group.

For purposes of this paper, culture is defined as the socially transmitted behavior patterns, norms, beliefs, and values of a given community (Salacuse 1991, p. 45). Persons from that community use the elements of their culture to interpret their surroundings and guide their interactions with other persons. So when an executive from a corporation in Dallas, Texas, sits down to negotiate a business deal with a manager from a Houston company, the two negotiators rely on their common culture to interpret each other's statements and actions. But when persons from two different cultures—for

Source: Reprinted from Jeswald W. Salacuse, "Intercultural Negotiation in International Business," *Group Decision and Negotiation,* vol. 8, pp. 217–36, © 1999 Kluwer Academic/Plenum Publishers.

example an executive from Texas and a manager from Japan—meet for the first time, they usually do not share a common pool of information and assumptions to interpret each others' statements, actions, and intentions. Culture can therefore be seen as a language, a "silent language" which the parties need in addition to the language they are speaking if they are truly to communicate and arrive at a genuine understanding (Hall 1959). Like any language, the elements of culture form a system, which has been variously characterized as a "system for creating, sending, storing, and processing information" (Hall and Hall 1990, p. 179) and a "group problem-solving tool that enables individuals to survive in a particular environment" (Moran and Stripp 1991, p. 43). Culture serves as a kind of glue—a social adhesive—that binds a group of people together and gives them a distinct identity as a community. It may also give them a sense that they are a community different and separate from other communities.

This article is concerned primarily with national cultures, cultures identified with a particular country. But culture and nationality are not always the same thing. Within Nigeria, for example, the culture of the Ibos of the largely Christian southeastern part of the country and the Hausas of the mainly Muslim north are different and distinct. Similarly, individual corporations and professions may have their own distinct organizational or professional cultures whose norms and behavior patterns may predominate in certain respects over the ethnic or national cultures of their professions' members. For example, a continuing concern in the current wave of mergers and acquisitions in the United States is the problem of blending the cultures of two organizations, such as Morgan Stanley and Dean Witter, after the deal has been signed (Lublin and O'Brian, 1997). But while cultural values, attitudes, and behavior patterns may appear permanently embedded in a group, particularly in the context of an encounter between two different cultures, in fact culture is dynamic. It is constantly changing (Bohannan 1995).

And finally, in considering the role of culture in international business negotiation and relationships, it is important to remember that the world has a staggering diversity of cultures. For example, while certain observers speak of "Asian culture" as if it were a homogeneous set of values, beliefs, and behavior patterns followed by all Asians (Mahbubani 1995), in reality Asia has many different and distinct cultures from India to Laos, from Korea to Indonesia. Each has its own values and practices that may differ markedly from those prevailing in another country—or indeed in another part of the same country. The negotiating style of Koreans, for example, is not the same as that of the Lao. And even within countries that from outward appearances seem to have a fairly uniform cultural identity, like the French and the Germans, significant differences may nonetheless exist between regions—such as the difference between the business community in Paris and that of the *midi* in southern France.

The Elements of Culture

One may conceive of the four cultural elements mentioned in the previous definition—behavior, attitudes, norms, and values—as forming a series of concentric circles, like the layers of an onion, illustrated by Figure 1.

FIGURE 1 | Culture as an Onion

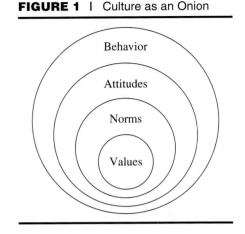

The process of understanding the culture of a counterpart in a negotiation is similar to peeling an onion. The outermost layer of the onion is behavior, the words and actions of one's counterpart. It is this layer which a negotiator first perceives in an intercultural negotiation. A second inner layer consists of attitudes of persons from that culture toward specific events and phenomena—for example, attitudes about beginning meetings punctually or the appropriate format of presentations. Attitudes may become evident to a counterpart in an intercultural negotiation only after protracted discussions. Next are norms, the rules to be followed in specific situations. Here, for example, a negotiator may come to realize that his or her counterpart's seemly rigid insistence on punctuality is not merely a personal idiosyncrasy but is based on a firm rule derived from his or her culture.

The innermost layer—the core—consists of values. Norms about the way meetings are conducted, representatives chosen, or persons rewarded are usually based on certain values that are important to that culture. Such differences in values are often the most difficult for negotiators to detect and understand. Indeed, the parties to an international negotiation may discover their value differences only after they have signed the contract and begun to work together. Such differences in cultural values between partners in an international joint venture, for example, may lead to severe conflict and ultimately the failure of their enterprise, a factor that may explain why many international ventures have a short life.

In their valuable book *The Seven Cultures of Capitalism,* based on extensive survey research among thousands of executives from throughout the world, Hampden-Turner and Trompenaars (1993) found sharp differences that could be explained only by different cultural values to such basic management tasks as group decision making, hiring, rewarding employees, and making and applying rules. For example, with respect to group decision making, wide variations among cultural groups existed in answering the following question:

What is the better way to choose a person to represent a group?

A. All members of the group should meet and discuss candidates until almost everybody agrees on the same person; or

B.   The group members should meet, nominate persons, vote, and choose the person with a majority of the votes even if several people are against the person.

In this question, according to the authors, the values of adversarial democracy and consensual democracy were in tension. While 84.4 percent of the Japanese opted for Answer A (consensual democracy), only 37.7 percent of the Americans did so. It is interesting to note that there were differences among Asians on this question. For example, unlike the Japanese, only 39.4 percent of the Singaporeans chose Answer A, exhibiting an aversion to consensual democracy that is perhaps reflected in Singapore's authoritarian political system. One can imagine that this difference in cultural values about decision making between Japanese and American executives in a joint venture might lead to serious conflict between the joint venture partners. Other kinds of value conflicts may arise, for example, between individualism prized by Americans and communitarianism embodied in many Asian cultures; about whether in hiring an employee it is more important to consider individual talent or the ability to fit into the organization; or about whether to reward persons on the basis of group performance or by individual achievement only.

Differences in cultural values can present themselves in international business transactions and relationships time after time and day after day, and they may ultimately turn what appeared to be a harmonious negotiation or business relationship into a continuing source of conflict between the parties. Once the conflict surfaces, it may be exacerbated by the way the parties try to cope with it. One unfortunate tendency is for each of the parties to extol their own cultural values but to denigrate those of their business or negotiating partner. For example, Americans, with their high store on individualism, will tend to see their value system positively: as for individual rights and human freedom, as putting the individual above the tyranny of the group, as knowing that a group prospers only when individuals prosper, and as efficient. Persons coming from cultures where communitarian values are prized will see themselves as unselfish, humane, for group interests and rights, and knowing that individuals prosper only when the group prospers. Yet Americans, when confronted with a communitarian culture, may tend to ascribe to it only negative characteristics. So Americans, reacting to Japanese values in a decision to retain a 15-year employee whose performance has declined, might consider their Japanese counterparts as tolerant of freeloaders, giving in to the tyranny of the group, weak, and inefficient. On the other hand, the Japanese would probably characterize the Americans as ignoring the contributions and needs of the group, lacking in loyalty, inhumane, and selfish.

It is important therefore for business executives in a negotiation to understand the values inherent in the culture of their counterparts and not to characterize those values in a negative way.

The Effect of Cultural Differences on Negotiation

Differences in culture between deal makers can obstruct negotiations in many ways. First, they can create misunderstandings in communication. If one American executive responds to another American's proposal by saying, "That's difficult," the response, interpreted against American culture and business practice, probably means that the door is still open for further discussion, that perhaps the other side should sweeten its offer. In some other cultures, for example in Asia, persons may be reluctant to say a direct and emphatic no, even when that is their intent. So when a Japanese negotiator, in response to a proposal, says, "That is difficult," he is clearly indicating that the proposal is unacceptable. "It is difficult" means "no" to the Japanese, but to the American it means "maybe."

Second, cultural differences create difficulties not only in understanding words, but also in interpreting actions. For example, most Westerners expect a prompt answer when they make a statement or ask a question. Japanese, on the other hand, tend to take longer to respond. As a result, negotiations with Japanese are sometimes punctuated with periods of silence that seem excruciating to an American. For the Japanese, the period of silence is normal, an appropriate time to reflect on what has been said. The fact that they may not be speaking in their native language lengthens even more the time needed to respond.

From their own cultural perspective, Americans may interpret Japanese silence as rudeness, lack of understanding, or a cunning tactic to get the Americans to reveal themselves. Rather than wait for a response, the American tendency is to fill the void with words by asking questions, offering further explanations, or merely repeating what they have already said. This response to silence may confuse the Japanese, who are made to feel that they are being bombarded by questions and proposals without being given adequate time to respond to any of them.

On the other hand, Latin Americans, who place a high value on verbal agility, have a tendency to respond quickly. Indeed, they may answer a point once they have understood it even though the other side has not finished speaking. While inexperienced American negotiators are sometimes confused by Japanese delays in responding, they can become equally agitated in negotiations with Brazilians by what Americans consider constant interruptions.

Third, cultural considerations also influence the form and substance of the deal you are trying to make. For example, in many parts of the Muslim world, where Islamic law prohibits the taking of interest on loans, one may need to restructure or relabel finance charges in a deal as "administrative fees" in order to gain acceptance at the negotiating table. More substantively, differences in culture will invariably require changes in products, management systems, and personnel practices. For example, in Thailand, the relationship between manager and employee is more hierarchical than it is in the United States. Workers are motivated by a desire to please the manager, but they in turn expect and want their managers to sense their personal problems and be ready to help with them. In other cultures, such as in Australia, employees neither expect nor want managers to become involved with employees' personal problems. Thus an Australian project in Thailand would need to change its concept of employee relations because of the local culture (Hughes and Sheehan 1993).

And finally, culture can influence "negotiating style," the way persons from different cultures conduct themselves in negotiating sessions. Research indicates fairly clearly that negotiation practices differ from culture to culture (Weiss 1994, p. 51). Indeed, culture may influence how persons conceive of the very nature and function of negotiation itself. Studies of negotiating styles are abundant (e.g., Binnendijk 1987; Fisher 1980; Graham et al. 1988; Campbell et al. 1988). Some seek to focus on describing and analyzing the negotiating styles of particular groups. Indeed, the practitioner's fascination with cultural negotiating styles seems to have spawned a distinct literary genre: the "Negotiating with . . ." literature. Numerous books and articles bearing such titles as "Negotiating with the Japanese," "Negotiating with the Arabs," and "Negotiating with the Chinese" seek to lead the novice through the intricacies of negotiating in specific cultures (for a bibliography of such literature, see Salacuse 1991, pp. 174–83). Another approach to studying negotiating style is cross-cultural and comparative. It seeks to identify certain basic elements in negotiating style and to determine how they are reflected in various cultures. It is this approach which the next part of this article will adopt.

Culture and Negotiating Styles: Ten Factors in Deal Making

The great diversity of the world's cultures makes it impossible for any negotiator, no matter how skilled and experienced, to understand fully all the cultures that he or she may encounter. How then should an executive prepare to cope with culture in making deals in Singapore this week and Seoul the next? One approach is to identify important areas where cultural differences may arise during the negotiation process. A knowledge of those factors may help an international business negotiator to understand a counterpart and to anticipate possible misunderstandings. Toward this end, scholars have developed a variety of frameworks and checklists that may be applied cross-culturally (e.g., Weiss 1985; Moran and Stripp 1991; Salacuse 1991). Based on a review of the literature as well as interviews with practitioners, the author, in an earlier work (Salacuse 1991), identified 10 factors that seemed to be the most problematic. These 10 factors, each of which consisted of two poles, were (1) negotiating goals (contract or relationship?); (2) attitudes to the negotiating process (win–win or win–lose?); (3) personal styles (formal or informal?); (4) styles of communication (direct or indirect?); (5) time sensitivity (high or low?); (6) emotionalism (high or low?); (7) agreement form (specific or general?); (8) agreement-building process (bottom up or top down?); (9) negotiating team organization (one leader or consensus?); and (10) risk taking (high or low?). Negotiating styles, like personalities, display a wide range of variation. The 10 negotiating traits listed here can be placed on a spectrum or continuum as illustrated in Figure 2.

FIGURE 2 | The Impact of Culture on Negotiation

Trait			
Goal	Contract	↔	Relationship
Attitudes	Win–lose	↔	Win–win
Personal styles	Informal	↔	Formal
Communications	Direct	↔	Indirect
Time sensitivity	High	↔	Low
Emotionalism	High	↔	Low
Agreement form	Specific	↔	General
Agreement building	Bottom up	↔	Top down
Team organization	One leader	↔	Consensus
Risk taking	High	↔	Low

The purpose of the matrix in Figure 2 is to identify specific negotiating traits affected by culture and to show the possible variation that each trait or factor may take. With this knowledge, an international business negotiator may be able to understand better the negotiating styles and approaches of his counterparts from other cultures. Equally important, it may help negotiators determine how their own styles appear to those same counterparts on the other side of the bargaining table.

In order to test this approach to understanding negotiating style, the matrix was translated into a survey questionnaire and administered to 310 business executives, lawyers, and graduate business students (many of whom had substantial work experience) from all continents at various sites in North America, Latin America, and Europe. The respondents came from 12 countries: the United States, the United Kingdom, France, Germany, Spain, Mexico, Argentina, Brazil, Nigeria, India, China, and Japan. After receiving an explanation of the matrix and questionnaire, respondents were asked to rate their own attitudes anonymously toward each of these negotiating traits on a five-point scale. In general, as will be seen, the survey revealed significant correlations between the respondents' assessment of certain traits of their negotiating styles and the national cultures from which they came.

The results of the survey must be read with several caveats. First, the answers that the respondents gave reflected only how they saw themselves (or would like others to see them) rather than their negotiating styles and behavior in actual negotiations. The results can be read only as indicating a certain predisposition of individual cultures toward certain factors affecting the negotiation process. Second, negotiating style in a given negotiation may be influenced by numerous factors besides culture, including personality, bureaucracy, business experience, and the nature of the transactions under negotiation. For example, an executive who is predisposed to approach a business negotiation as a problem-solving, integrative process (win–win) may behave in a distributive, confrontational way (win–lose) when confronted by a hostile counterpart at the negotiating table. Third, all the respondents spoke English, completed the survey in English, had substantial international experience, and were participating in graduate university education or advanced executive seminars, also conducted in the English language. As a result, they may not be representative of most business executives in their cultures. On the other hand, they are fairly representative of the kinds of persons who conduct international negotiations on behalf of companies. Fourth, the meaning of key terms in the survey, such as *direct, indirect, risk, general,* and *specific,* were not strictly defined but instead were interpreted by each respondent according to his or her own subjective interpretation, a factor obviously influenced by culture. Fifth, both the size of the sample and the number of cultures surveyed were limited.

Negotiating Goal: Contract or Relationship?

Different cultures may view the very purpose of a business negotiation differently. For many American executives, the goal of a business negotiation, first and foremost, is often to arrive at a signed contract between the parties. Americans consider a signed contract as a definitive set of rights and duties that strictly binds the two sides, an attitude succinctly summed up in the statement "a deal is a deal."

Japanese, Chinese, and other cultural groups in Asia, it is said, often consider that the goal of a negotiation is not a signed contract, but the creation of a relationship between the two sides (e.g., Pye 1982). Although the written contract describes the relationship, the essence of the deal is the relationship itself. For Americans, signing a contract is closing a deal; for many Asians, signing a contract might more appropriately be called opening a relationship. This difference in view may explain why Asians tend to give more time and effort to prenegotiation, while Americans want to rush through this first phase in deal making. The activities of prenegotiation, whereby the parties seek to get to know one another thoroughly, are a crucial foundation for a good business relationship. They may seem less important when the goal is merely a contract.

The results of the survey showed significant differences among the cultures surveyed with respect to the negotiating goals of contract and relationship. Thus only 26 percent of the Spanish respondents claimed that their primary goal in a negotiation was a relationship compared to 66 percent of the Indians. On the other hand, the preference for a relationship was not as pronounced among the Chinese (54.5 percent) as one might have expected from the literature, and the Japanese appeared almost evenly divided on the question, with a slight preference for a contract as a negotiating goal. Table 1 summarizes the survey results on this issue.

Negotiating Attitude: Win–Lose or Win–Win?

Because of differences in culture or personality, or both, businesspersons appear to approach deal making with one of two basic attitudes: that a negotiation is either a process in which both can gain (win–win) or a struggle in which of necessity, one side wins and the other side loses (win–lose). Win–win negotiators see deal making as a collaborative and problem-solving process; win–lose negotiators see it as confrontational. In a reflection of this dichotomy, negotiation scholars have concluded that these approaches represented two basic paradigms of the negotiation process: (1) distributive bargaining (i.e., win–lose) and (2) integrative bargaining or problem solving (i.e., win–win) (e.g., Hoppman 1995; Lewicki et al. 1993). In the former situation, the parties see their goals as incompatible, while in the latter they consider themselves to have compatible goals.

For example, developing country officials often view negotiations with multinational corporations as win–lose competitions. In negotiating investment contracts, they often consider profits earned by the investor as automatic losses to the host country. As a result, they may focus their efforts in the negotiation fixedly on limiting investor profit in contrast to discovering how to maximize benefits from the project for both the investor and the country. It is interesting to note that those same officials might approach negotiations in their home villages with members of their ethnic group or clans on a win–win basis.

TABLE 1 | Goal: Contract or Relationship?

Contract:	Spn.	Fr.	Braz.	Jpn.	USA	Ger.	UK	Nig.	Arg.	Chi.	Mex.	Ind.
Percentage:	73.7	70	66.7	54.5	53.7	54.5	47.1	46.7	46.2	45.5	41.7	33.3

TABLE 2 | Negotiating Attitude: Win–Win or Win–Lose?

Win–Win:	Jpn.	Chi.	Arg.	Fr.	Ind.	USA	UK	Mex.	Ger.	Nig.	Braz.	Sp.
Percentage:	100	81.8	80.8	80	77.8	70.7	58.8	50	54.5	46.7	44.4	36.8

The survey conducted by the author found wide differences among the cultures represented in the survey on this question. Whereas 100 percent of the Japanese viewed business negotiation as a win–win process, only 36.8 percent of the Spanish were so inclined. The Chinese and Indians, the other two Asian cultures represented in the survey, also claimed that negotiation was for them win–win, and the French, alone among Europeans, took a similarly pronounced position on the question. Table 2 summarizes the results of all groups surveyed with respect to this attitude toward negotiation.

Personal Style: Informal or Formal?

Personal style concerns the way a negotiator talks to others, uses titles, dresses, speaks, and interacts with other persons. Culture strongly influences the personal style of negotiators. It has been observed, for example, that Germans have a more formal style than Americans (Hall and Hall 1990, p. 48). A negotiator with a formal style insists on addressing counterparts by their titles, avoids personal anecdotes, and refrains from questions touching on the private or family life of members of the other negotiating team. An informal-style negotiator tries to start the discussion on a first-name basis, quickly seeks to develop a personal, friendly relationship with the other team, and may take off his jacket and roll up his sleeves when deal making begins in earnest. Each culture has its own formalities, which have special meaning within that culture. They are another means of communication among the persons sharing that culture, another form of adhesive that binds them together as a community. Negotiators in foreign cultures must respect appropriate formalities. As a general rule, it is always safer to adopt a formal posture and move to an informal stance, if the situation warrants it, than to assume an informal style too quickly.

On the other hand, an encounter between negotiators having different personal styles can sometimes lead to conflict that impedes a negotiation. For an American or an Australian, calling someone by his or her first name is an act of friendship and therefore a good thing. For a Japanese or an Egyptian, the use of the first name at a first meeting is an act of disrespect and therefore a bad thing.

Except for the Nigerians, a majority of the respondents within each of the 12 groups surveyed claimed to have an informal negotiating style; however, the strength of this view varied considerably. While nearly 83 percent of the Americans considered themselves to have an informal negotiating style, only 54 percent of the Chinese, 52 percent of the Spanish, and 58 percent of the Mexicans were similarly inclined. Among the four European national cultures surveyed, the French were the strongest in claiming an informal style. Although both the Germans and Japanese have a reputation for formality, only slightly more than one-quarter of the respondents in these two groups believed they had a formal negotiating style. Differences in cultures with respect to the meaning of the terms *formal* and *informal* may have influenced this result. The survey's findings on this negotiating trait are summarized in Table 3.

TABLE 3 | Personal Style: Formal or Informal?

Formal:	Nig.	Spn.	Chi.	Mex.	UK	Arg.	Ger.	Jpn.	Ind.	Braz.	Fr.	USA
Percentage:	53	47.4	45.5	41.7	35.3	34.6	27.3	27.3	22.2	22.2	20	17.1

Communication: Direct or Indirect?

Methods of communication vary among cultures. Some place emphasis on direct and simple methods of communication; others rely heavily on indirect and complex methods. It has been observed, for example, that whereas Germans and Americans are direct, the French and the Japanese are indirect (Hall and Hall 1990, p. 102). Persons with an indirect style of communication often make assumptions about the level of knowledge possessed by their counterparts and to a significant extent communicate with oblique references, circumlocutions, vague allusions, figurative forms of speech, facial expressions, gestures, and other kinds of body language. In a culture that values directness such as the American or the Israeli, one can expect to receive a clear and definite response to proposals and questions. In cultures that rely on indirect communication, such as the Japanese, reaction to proposals may be gained by interpreting seemingly indefinite comments, gestures, and other signs.

The confrontation of these styles of communication in the same negotiation can lead to friction. For example, the indirect ways Japanese negotiators express disapproval have often led foreign business executives to believe that their proposals were still under consideration when they had in fact been rejected by the Japanese side. In the Camp David negotiations, the Israeli preference for direct forms of communication and the Egyptian tendency to favor indirect forms sometimes exacerbated relations between the two sides. The Egyptians interpreted Israeli directness as aggressiveness and, therefore, an insult. The Israelis viewed Egyptian indirectness with impatience and suspected them of insincerity, of not saying what they meant.

In the survey, respondents in all cultural groups by a high margin claimed to have a direct form of communication. Here too the organizational culture of the participants and their international experience may have strongly influenced their responses to the questionnaire. It is worth noting, however, that the two cultural groups with the largest percentage of persons claiming an indirect style were the Japanese and the French. Table 4 summarizes the results on this issue.

Sensitivity to Time: High or Low?

Discussions of national negotiating styles invariably treat a particular culture's attitudes toward time. So it is said that Germans are always punctual, Latins are habitually late,

TABLE 4 | Communication: Direct or Indirect?

Indirect:	Jpn.	Fr.	Chi.	UK	Braz.	Ind.	Ger.	USA	Arg.	Spn.	Mex.	Nig.
Percentage:	27.3	20	18.2	11.8	11.1	11.1	9.1	4.9	3.8	0	0	0

Japanese negotiate slowly, and Americans are quick to make a deal. Commentators sometimes claim that some cultures "value" time more than others, but this may not be an accurate characterization of the situation. Rather they may value differently the amount of time devoted to and measured against the goal pursued. For Americans, the deal is a signed contract and "time is money," so they want to make a deal quickly. Americans therefore try to reduce formalities to a minimum and get down to business quickly. Japanese and other Asians, whose goal is to create a relationship rather than simply sign a contract, will need to invest time in the negotiating process so that the parties can get to know one another well and determine whether they wish to embark on a long-term relationship. They may view aggressive attempts to shorten the negotiating time with suspicion as efforts to hide something.

As a general rule, Asians tend to devote more time and attention to the prenegotiation phase of deal making than do Americans. Whereas American executives and lawyers generally want to "dispense with the preliminaries" and "to get down to cases," most Asians view prenegotiation as an essential foundation to any business relationship; consequently, they recognize the need to conduct prenegotiation with care before actually making a decision to undertake substantive negotiations of a deal. One of the consequences of this difference in approach is that Americans sometimes assume that discussions with Asian counterparts have passed from prenegotiation to a subsequent stage when in fact they have not because the Asians have not yet decided to undertake substantive negotiations. This type of misunderstanding can lead to suspicions of bad faith, resulting ultimately in total failure of the talks. Negotiators need to be sure that they and their counterparts are always in the same phase of the deal-making process. One way of making sure is by using written agendas, memoranda, and letters of intent to mark the various phases.

The survey did not reveal significant divergences with respect to time. A majority of the respondents from all cultural groups surveyed claimed to have a high sensitivity to time; however, the strength of the minority view on this question varied considerably among the groups. The Indians, French, and Germans included a substantial percentage of respondents asserting a low sensitivity to time. Table 5 summarizes the results.

These survey results on this question could have been affected by the organizational cultures of the respondents, as well as by variations in the way that respondents interpreted the term *time sensitivity*. Cultural discussions about time in negotiations often refer to two elements: promptness is meeting deadlines and the amount of time devoted to a negotiation. Thus Germans, it has been observed, are highly time sensitive with regard to promptness but less so with respect to their willingness to devote large amounts of time to a negotiation (Hall and Hall 1990, p. 37). Thus they are punctual (high time sensitivity) but slow to negotiate and make decisions (low time sensitivity).

TABLE 5 | Sensitivity to Time: High or Low?

Low:	Ind.	Fr.	Ger.	Mex.	Spn.	Arg.	US	Jpn.	Chi.	Nig.	UK	Braz.
Percentage:	44.4	40	36.4	33.3	21.1	15.4	14.6	9.1	9.1	6.7	5.9	0

Emotionalism: High or Low?

Accounts of negotiating behavior in other cultures almost always point to a particular group's tendency or lack thereof to act emotionally. According to the stereotype, Latin Americans show their emotions at the negotiating table, while Japanese and many other Asians hide their feelings. Obviously, individual personality plays a role here. There are passive Latins and hotheaded Japanese. Nonetheless, various cultures have different rules as to the appropriateness and form of displaying emotions, and these rules are brought to the negotiating table as well.

In the survey conducted by the author, Latin Americans and the Spanish were the cultural groups that ranked themselves highest with respect to emotionalism in a clearly statistically significant fashion. Among Europeans, the Germans and English ranked as least emotional, while among Asians the Japanese held that position, but to a lesser degree than the two European groups. Table 6 summarizes the results with regard to emotionalism.

Form of Agreement: General or Specific?

Cultural factors also influence the form of the written agreement that parties try to make. Generally, Americans prefer very detailed contracts that attempt to anticipate all possible circumstances and eventualities, no matter how unlikely. Why? Because the "deal" is the contract itself, and one must refer to the contract to handle new situations that may arise in the future. Other cultures, such as the Chinese, prefer a contract in the form of general principles rather than detailed rules. Why? Because it is claimed that the essence of the deal is the relationship between the parties. If unexpected circumstances arise, the parties should look to their relationship, not the contract, to solve the problem. So in some cases, a Chinese may interpret the American drive to stipulate all contingencies as evidence of lack of confidence in the stability of the underlying relationship.

Some practitioners argue that differences over the form of an agreement are caused more by unequal bargaining power than by culture. In a situation of unequal bargaining power, the stronger party usually seeks a detailed agreement to "lock up the deal" in all its possible dimensions, while the weaker party prefers a general agreement to give it room to "wiggle out" of adverse circumstances that are bound to occur. So a Chinese commune as the weaker party in a negotiation with a multinational corporation will seek a general agreement as a way of protecting itself against an uncertain future. According to this view, it is context, not culture, that determines this negotiating trait.

The survey showed that a majority of respondents in each cultural group preferred specific agreements over general agreements. This result may be attributed in part to the relatively large number of lawyers among the respondents, as well as to the fact that multinational corporate practice favors specific agreements and many of the respondents,

TABLE 6 | Emotionalism: High or Low?

Low:	Ger.	UK	Jpn.	Ind.	Fr.	Nig.	USA	Chi.	Spn.	Mex.	Arg.	Braz.
Percentage:	63.6	52.9	45.5	44.4	40	40	36.6	27.3	21.1	16.7	15.4	11.1

TABLE 7 | Agreement Form: General or Specific?

General:	Jpn.	Ger.	Ind.	Fr.	Chi.	Arg.	Braz.	USA	Nig.	Mex.	Spn	UK
Percentage:	45.5	45.4	44.4	30	27.3	26.9	22.2	22	20	16.7	15.8	11.8

regardless of nationality, had experience with such firms. The survey responses on this point may have been a case where professional or organizational culture dominated over national cultural traits. On the other hand, the degree of intensity of responses on the question varied considerably among cultural groups. While only 11 percent of the British favored general agreements, 45.5 percent of the Japanese and of the Germans claimed to do so. Table 7 sets out the survey results with respect to agreement form.

Building an Agreement: Bottom Up or Top Down?

Related to the form of the agreement is the question of whether negotiating a business deal is an inductive or a deductive process. Does it start from agreement on general principles and proceed to specific items, or does it begin with agreement on specifics, such as price, delivery date, and product quality, the sum total of which becomes the contract? Different cultures tend to emphasize one approach over the other.

Some observers believe that the French prefer to begin with agreement on general principles, while Americans tend to seek agreement first on specifics. For Americans, negotiating a deal is basically making a series of compromises and trade-offs on a long list of particulars. For the French, the essence is to agree on basic principles that will guide and indeed determine the negotiation process afterward. The agreed-upon general principles become the framework, the skeleton, upon which the contract is built.

A further difference in negotiating style is seen in the dichotomy between "the building-down approach" and the "building-up approach." In the building-down approach, the negotiator begins by presenting the maximum deal if the other side accepts all the stated conditions. In the building-up approach, one side begins by proposing a minimum deal that can be broadened and increased as the other party accepts additional conditions. According to many observers, Americans tend to favor the building-down approach, while the Japanese tend to prefer the building-up style of negotiating a contract.

The survey did not reveal significant cultural trends on this issue among Americans, Germans, and Nigerians, since the respondents from these three groups were relatively evenly divided on the question. On the other hand, the French, Argentineans, and Indians tended to view deal making as a top-down (deductive) process, while Japanese, Mexicans, and Brazilians tended to see it as a bottom-up (inductive) process. Table 8 summarizes the results on the question.

TABLE 8 | Building an Agreement: Bottom Up or Top Down?

Top down:	Ind.	Arg.	Fr.	UK	Chi.	Ger.	USA	Nig.	Spn.	Jpn.	Braz.	Mex.
Percentage:	66.7	61.5	60	58.8	54.5	54.5	53.7	53.3	52.6	36.4	33.3	33.3

Team Organization: One Leader or Group Consensus?

In any international business negotiation, it is important to know how the other side is organized, who has the authority to make commitments, and how decisions are made. Culture is one important factor that affects how executives and lawyers organize themselves to negotiate a deal. Some cultures emphasize the individual while others stress the group. These values may influence the organization of each side to a negotiation. One extreme is the negotiating team with a supreme leader who has complete authority to decide all matters. Many American teams tend to follow this approach, which has been labeled the "John Wayne style of negotiations" (Graham and Herberger 1983, p. 160). Other cultures, notably the Japanese, stress team negotiation and consensus decision making. When you negotiate with such a team, it may not be apparent who is the leader and who has authority to commit the side. In the first type, the negotiating team is usually small; in the second it is often large. For example, in negotiations in China on a major deal, it would not be uncommon for the Americans to arrive at the table with 3 persons and for the Chinese to show up with 10. Similarly, the one-leader team is usually prepared to make commitments and decisions more quickly than a negotiating team organized on the basis of consensus. As a result, the consensus type of organization usually takes more time to negotiate a deal.

The survey on negotiating styles revealed differences in preference among respondents, depending on culture. The group with the strongest preference for a consensus organization were the French. French individualism has been noted in many studies (Hall and Hall 1990), and perhaps a consensus arrangement in French eyes is the best way to protect that individualism. Despite the Japanese reputation for consensus arrangements, only 45 percent of the Japanese respondents claimed to prefer a negotiating team based on consensus. The Brazilians, the Chinese, and Mexicans, to a far greater degree than any other groups, preferred one-person leadership, a reflection perhaps of the political traditions in those countries. The results of the survey on this point are summarized in Table 9.

Risk Taking: High or Low?

Research supports the conclusion that certain cultures are more risk averse than others (Hofstede 1980). In deal making, the culture of the negotiators can affect the willingness of one side to take "risks" in the negotiation—to divulge information, try new approaches, or tolerate uncertainties in a proposed course of action. A negotiator who senses that the other side is risk averse needs to focus efforts on proposing rules and mechanisms that will reduce the apparent risks in the deal for them.

The Japanese, with their emphasis on requiring large amounts of information and their intricate group decision-making process, tend to be risk averse, a fact affirmed by the author's survey, which found Japanese respondents to be the most risk averse of all

TABLE 9 | Team Organization: One Leader or Consensus?

One Leader:	Braz.	Chi.	Mex.	UK	USA	Spn.	Arg.	Ger.	Jpn.	Ind.	Nig.	Fr.
Percentage:	100	90.9	90.9	64.7	63.4	57.7	57.7	54.5	54.5	44.4	40	40

TABLE 10 | Risk Taking: High or Low?

Low:	Fr.	Ind.	UK	Chi.	USA	Nig.	Arg.	Ger.	Braz.	Mex.	Spn.	Jpn.
Percentage:	90	88.9	88.2	81.8	78	73.3	73.1	72	55.6	50	47.4	18.2

countries covered in the survey. Americans in the survey, by comparison, considered themselves to be risk takers, but an even higher percentage of French, British, and Indians claimed to be risk takers. Table 10 summarizes the survey results with respect to risk.

Coping with Culture

In view of the importance of cultural differences in international business negotiations, how should negotiators seek to cope with them? The following are a few simple rules.

Rule 1: Learn the Other Side's Culture

In any international business dealing, it is important for a negotiator to learn something about the other side's culture. The degree to which such learning takes place depends on a number of factors, including the nature and importance of the transaction, the experience of the negotiators, the time available for learning, and the similarities or lack thereof between the cultures represented in the negotiation. For example, the negotiation of a simple, one-time export sale may demand less cultural knowledge than the negotiation of a long-term strategic alliance, which may require the parties to audit each other's culture as well as their financial assets.

Ideally, learning another's culture can require several years of study, mastery of a foreign language, and prolonged residence in the country of that culture. An American faced with the task of negotiating a strategic alliance with a Thai company in Bangkok in two weeks' time cannot, of course, master Thai culture that fast. At best, he or she can learn enough to cope with some of the principal effects that Thai culture may have on making the deal. Important sources of information on Thai culture would include histories of the country, consultation with persons having business experience in the country, local lawyers and consultants, anthropological and ethnographic studies, reports on the current political situation, and accounts, if any, on negotiating with the Thais. As Weiss quite correctly points out, the degree of a negotiator's cultural knowledge will influence strategies and tactics during the negotiation (Weiss 1994, p. 53). For example, a person with strong familiarity with the counterpart's language and culture may use the negotiation style and approach of his counterpart's culture, while a person with less familiarity may choose, as a strategy, to employ an agent or mediator from that culture to assist in the negotiations.

As international business transactions increasingly take the form of long-term relationships—what Gomes-Casseres (1996) has termed the "alliance revolution"—it is equally important to recognize that cultural learning continues long after the contract is signed. In effect, the dynamics of such long-term relationships between the parties are very much a continuing negotiation as the alliance partners shape the rules and practices of their business relationship.

Rule 2: Don't Stereotype

If rule one in international negotiation is "know the other side's culture," rule two is "avoid overreliance on that knowledge." As the survey indicates, not all Japanese evade giving a direct negative answer. Not all Germans will tell a counterpart specifically what they think of a proposal. In short, the negotiator who enters a foreign culture should be careful not to allow cultural stereotypes to determine his or her relations with local businesspersons. Foreign business executives and lawyers will be offended if they feel their counterparts are not treating them as individuals, but rather as cultural robots. In addition to giving offense, cultural stereotypes can be misleading. Many times the other side simply does not run true to the negotiating form suggested by books, articles, and consultants. The reason, of course, is that other forces besides culture may influence a person's negotiating behavior. Specifically, these forces may include the negotiator's personality, the organization he or she represents, and the context of the particular negotiation in question.

Rule 3: Find Ways to Bridge the Culture Gap

Generally, executives and lawyers who confront a culture different from their own in a negotiation tend to view it in one of three ways: as an obstacle, a weapon, or a fortress (Salacuse 1993). At the operational level, cultural differences are hardly ever seen as positive.

The conventional view among most American executives is that cultural differences are an obstacle to agreement and effective joint action. They therefore search for ways to overcome the obstacle. But a different culture in a business setting can become more than an obstacle; it can be seen as a weapon, particularly when a dominant party tries to impose its culture on the other side. For example, American lawyers' insistence on structuring a transaction "the way we do it in the United States" may be considered by their foreign counterparts as the use of American culture as a weapon.

Faced with a culture that it perceives as a weapon, a party to a business deal may become defensive and try to use its own culture as a fortress to protect itself from what it perceives as a cultural onslaught. The Japanese have often adopted this approach when confronted with American demands to open their markets. France's drive to limit the use of English in advertising is a defensive response to what it considered to be the weapon of "Anglo-Saxon" culture.

It may be helpful to try to think of cultural differences in yet another way. Differences in cultures tend to isolate individuals and groups from each other. In short, cultural differences create a gap between persons and organizations. Often the action that people take when confronted with cultural differences serves only to widen the gap—as, for example, when one side denigrates the other side's cultural practices.

Remembering the words of the English poet Philip Larkin, "Always it is by bridges that we live," effective international business negotiators should seek to find ways to bridge the gap caused by cultural difference. One way to build that bridge is by using culture itself. If culture is indeed the glue that binds together a particular group of people, the creative use of culture between persons of different cultures is often a way to link those on opposite sides of the culture gap. Basically, there are four types of cultural bridge building that one may consider when confronted with a culture gap in a negotiation:

1. *Bridge the gap using the other side's culture:* One technique for bridging the gap is for a negotiator or manager to try to assume some or all of the cultural values and characteristics of the foreign persons with whom he or she is dealing. In international business, negotiators often try to use or identify with the other side's culture in order to build a relationship. For example, when President Sadat of Egypt negotiated with Sudanese officials, he always made a point of telling them that his mother had been born in the Sudan. He was thus using a common cultural thread to build a relationship with his counterparts. In effect, he was saying, "Like you, I am Sudanese, so we have common cultural ties. I understand you and I value your culture. Therefore you can trust me." Similarly, an African American managing a joint venture in Nigeria stressed his African heritage to build relationships with Nigerian counterparts. And an Italian American negotiating a sales contract in Rome emphasized his Italian background as a way of bridging the cultural gap that he perceived.

2. *Bridge the gap using your own culture:* A second general approach to bridging the culture gap is to persuade or induce the other side to adopt elements of your culture. To implement this approach successfully requires time and education. For example, in order to give a common culture to a joint venture, an American partner incurred significant cost by sending executives of its foreign partner to schools and executive training programs in the United States and then assigning them for short periods to the U.S. partner's own operations.

3. *Bridge with some combination of both cultures:* A third approach to dealing with the culture gap is to build a bridge using elements from cultures of both sides. In effect, cultural bridging takes place on both sides of the gap and, with luck, results in the construction of a solid integrated structure. The challenge in this approach is to identify the most important elements of each culture and to find ways of blending them into a consistent, harmonious whole that will allow business to be done effectively. Sometimes a third person in the form of mediator or consultant can help in the process.

4. *Bridge with a third culture:* A final method of dealing with the culture gap is to build a bridge by relying on a third culture that belongs to neither of the parties. Thus, for example, in a difficult negotiation between an American executive and a Chinese manager, both discovered that they had a great appreciation of French culture since they had both studied in France in their youth. They began to converse in French, and their common love of France enabled them to build a strong personal relationship. They used a third culture to bridge the cultural gap between China and America. Similarly, negotiators from two different national cultures may use elements of their common professional cultures, as lawyers or as engineers, to bridge the gap between them.

Conclusion

Cultural bridging, like bridge construction, requires the cooperation of the parties at both ends of the divide. No negotiator will permit a bridge to be built if he or she feels threatened or sees the bridge as a long-term danger to security. Consequently, negotiators who want to build a bridge across the cultural divide to their counterpart must be concerned to strengthen the other side's sense of security, not weaken it as happens all too often in international business relationships.

References

Binnendijk, H. (ed.). (1987). *National Negotiating Styles.* Washington, DC: U.S. Department of State.

Bohannan, P. (1995). *How Culture Works.* New York: Free Press.

Campbell, N. C. G., et al. (1998). "Marketing Negotiations in France, Germany, the United Kingdom, and the United States," *Journal of Marketing* 52, pp. 49–62.

Faure, G. O., and G. Sjostedt. (1993). "Culture and Negotiation: An Introduction," in G.O. Faure and J. Z. Rubin (eds.), *Culture and Negotiation.* Newbury Park, CA: Sage Publications.

Fisher, G. (1980). *International Negotiation: A Cross-Cultural Perspective.* Yarmouth, ME: Intercultural Press.

Gomes-Casseres, B. (1996). *The Alliance Revolution.* Cambridge, MA: Harvard University Press.

Graham, J. L., et al. (1988). "Buyer–Seller Negotiations around the Pacific Rim: Differences in Fundamental Exchange Processes," *Journal of Consumer Research* 15, pp. 48–54.

Graham J. L., and R. A. Herberger. (1983). "Negotiators Abroad—Don't Shoot from the Hip: Cross-Cultural Business Negotiations," *Harvard Business Review* 61, pp. 160–83.

Hall, E. T. (1959). *The Silent Language.* New York: Doubleday.

Hall, E. T., and M. Reed Hall. (1990). *Understanding Cultural Differences.* Yarmouth, ME: Intercultural Press.

Hampden-Turner, C., and A. Trompenaars. (1993). *The Seven Cultures of Capitalism.* New York: Doubleday.

Hoebel, E. A. (1972). *Anthropology: The Study of Man* (4th ed.) New York: McGraw-Hill.

Hofstede, G. (1980). *Culture's Consequences: International Differences in Work-Related Values.* Newbury Park, CA: Sage Publications.

Hoppman, T. (1995). "Two Paradigms of Negotiation: Bargaining and Problem Solving," *Annals, AAPSS* 542, pp. 24–47.

Hughes, P., and B. Sheehan. (1993). "Business Cultures: The Transfer of Managerial Policies and Practices from One Culture to Another," *Business and the Contemporary World* 5, pp. 153–70.

Lewicki, R., et al. (1993). *Negotiation—Readings, Exercises, and Cases.* Burr Ridge, IL: McGraw-Hill.

Lublin, J. S., and B. O'Brian. (1997). "Merged Firms Often Face Culture Clash," *The Wall Street Journal,* February 14, 1997, p. A9A.

Mahbubani, K. (1995). "The Pacific Way," *Foreign Affairs* 74, pp. 100–11.

Moran, R. T., and W. G. Stripp. (1991). *Successful International Business Negotiations.* Houston: Gulf Publishing Company.

Pye, L. (1982). *Chinese Negotiating Style.* Cambridge, MA: Oelgeschlager, Gunn and Hain.

Salacuse, J. W. (1991). *Making Global Deals—Negotiating in the International Market Place.* Boston: Houghton Mifflin.

Salacuse, J. W. (1993). "Implications for Practitioners," in G. O. Faure and J. Z. Rubin (eds.), *Culture and Negotiation.* Newbury Park, CA: Sage Publications.

Weiss, S. E. (1994). "Negotiating with Romans," (parts 1 and 2), *Sloan Management Review* 35, pp. 51, 85.

Zartman, I. W. (1993). "A Skeptic's View," in G. O. Faure and J. Z. Rubin (eds.), *Culture and Negotiation.* Newbury Park, CA: Sage Publications.

Reading 5.3

Tales of the Bazaar: Interest-Based Negotiation across Cultures

Jeffrey M. Senger

An American traveling abroad can experience negotiation in a vast array of cultures, some of which approach a state of nature. Particularly in developing countries, many people negotiate for just about everything. While the fixed-price system of commerce is typical in the United States and Western Europe, it simply does not exist in many other parts of the world. Even the simplest things we take for granted, such as a meter in a taxicab, are nowhere to be found, and negotiation is forced into almost every transaction.

As a teacher of negotiation, as well as a lifelong student of it, I have found overseas travel to provide an amazing education in the field. Both my background and my current practice center largely on "interest-based negotiation" (Fisher, Ury, and Patton, 1991). My formal training is in the legal profession, where I first studied negotiation under Roger Fisher. I now conduct negotiation and mediation training programs for the U.S. Justice Department, and I have led courses in a number of other countries for the U.S. State Department. These programs emphasize interest-based principles, where negotiators work to identify underlying interests on both sides, explore creative options for mutual gain, and use legitimate standards to determine the best possible solutions.

The interest-based approach to negotiation is hardly universal, however. As is immediately obvious when one leaves Cairo, Illinois, for Cairo, Egypt, people negotiate differently in other cultures. While sellers always want to get as much as they can and buyers always want to pay as little as possible, the strategies people use to reach these goals vary dramatically.

In this article, I will describe negotiation methods observed over a series of trips to more than two dozen countries. I have found the interest-based approach to be reasonably robust around the world. At the same time, however, there is far more that can be learned from negotiating with people who have never even heard of *Getting to YES*.

Interest-Based Negotiation Around the World

This first section will discuss ideas of interest-based negotiation, as popularized in the United States, that work well all over the world. It is interesting that many negotiators from other countries who have not studied these theories nonetheless have developed similar approaches on their own. These concepts clearly have existed around the world for a long time. The discussion will cover five main themes of interest-based negotiation: relationship, interests, options, criteria, and alternatives.

Source: From *Negotiation Journal* 18, no. 3 (July 2002), pp. 233–50.

Relationship

The interest-based approach to negotiation begins with developing the relationship between the parties. Effective negotiation is enhanced when the parties have a positive relationship with each other. Travel in different parts of the world shows that this is indeed a universal element of effective negotiation. Many negotiators around the world have mastered this concept instinctively.

Relationships Built on Hospitality   Shopkeepers in other countries go out of their way to welcome customers to their stores. They often offer something to drink, typically tea. If it is a slow day, they will even sit down and drink tea with a customer themselves. I have encountered merchants who insisted on giving me a tour of their houses (which are often adjacent to their shops) before we began negotiations. One took me up on his roof to show me the view. One insisted we play a friendly game of backgammon before setting about negotiating over the price of the backgammon set. Others have introduced me to their children. Another even had me meet the animals the family owned, including a cow and several chickens.

These gestures are always made with great warmth and hospitality: "Please have some tea. I insist." "Come, come—you must meet my family. We can talk business later." The overtures change the essential nature of the relationship. Before these interactions, I have felt like a foreign customer. Afterward, I'm almost like a long-lost relative. This approach materially improves the relationship and makes negotiation easier. Perhaps as important, it also makes the customer more likely to want to purchase something.

Relationships Built on Favors   Other overseas salespeople foster a relationship by doing the customer a favor. In one shopping mall in India, I asked a storekeeper where the nearest pay phone was located, and he suggested I use his cell phone instead. I offered to pay him for the call. He waved this off and said, "Please, it is my pleasure." Of course, once I finished the call, he said, "Here, my friend, come look at a few things." It seemed the least I could do was to look at some products in the man's store after he had graciously offered his telephone.

In another city in India, I asked a man on the street where a store was located. He offered to drive me there on his motor scooter. He was both friendly and insistent. As there were no cabs in the area, I took him up on his offer. He refused to let me pay for the ride. However, I did notice he had a brief, private conversation with the storekeeper after we arrived. It is quite likely they negotiated a percentage that the store would pay my driver as a "finder's fee," based on my purchases at the store. It is equally likely the store owner passed along this fee to me through increased prices. Thus I ended up paying for my transportation in another form.

The "finder's fee" arrangement is common overseas. Often it is centered on the relationship between the seller and others in the local community. By making friends with others in the area, a seller can build a network that will greatly increase access to customers. For example, hotel clerks will recommend particular stores, giving a business card to take to the store for a "10 percent discount." The store will give the discount (from a wildly inflated marked price), but the customer will still end up paying enough extra to cover a kickback to the hotel clerk. Tour guides will similarly refer people to certain stores. Sometimes tour guides will schedule a stop at a store (ostensibly for a demonstration of local craft techniques or even for a bathroom break). Others will end a tour directly in front of a store. All of these arrangements, built on local relationships, result in increased business for the store and kickbacks for the other parties.

Interests

While traditional bargaining focuses on positions (one party wants this, the other party wants that), interest-based negotiation suggests instead that parties work to identify the interests that underlie their positions. If negotiators understand what is behind each others' demands, they are better able to craft solutions that give both parties what they need.

At first this advice seems to have limited applicability to a traveler, who appears to have only one interest—to pay as little money as possible for things. However, negotiators in other countries have discovered there can be many more interests than meet the eye even in the simplest purchase. These negotiations are not solely about money. Indeed, people living in other parts of the world have developed a remarkable assortment of ingenious methods for identifying and even creating interests.

Identifying Interests   At the most basic level, merchants in other countries have a talent for discovering what they have that interests a customer. The seller will watch a buyer's eyes intently from the moment the buyer enters the store. The owner knows that when people scan over the wares in the store, their eyes will stop for a moment on items they like. The store owner pays keen attention to this, and will often pull an item a customer noticed down from the shelf, polish it, and hand it to the person.

Creating Interests by Involving the Buyer   Sellers use other tactics that are effective at creating interests in buyers. In the ritual described in the previous paragraph, notice how the seller involves the buyer in the process by handing over the item and asking the buyer to hold it. Often the merchant will increase participation further by adding something like, "feel the silkiness of the material" (if it's cloth) or "notice how heavy it is" (if it's metal). While the effect is subtle, most people have a slightly increased interest in keeping something after they have it in their own hands and have examined it closely. After people have spent some time with an item, they have a new interest in not seeing that time go to waste.

The Interest in Repaying a Favor   Other techniques involve sellers who create an interest in a buyer to repay a favor or avoid feeling guilty. There is often a fine line between serving the customer's needs and attempting to make the customer feel indebted. Some sellers who vigorously polish an item for a customer are, no doubt, hoping this will make a few customers slightly more inclined to return the favor by going through with the purchase.

I noticed this effect when shopping for a carpet in Xian, China. As soon as I entered a store, the owner greeted me, unrolled five rugs, and then asked my feelings about each. I had only intended to browse around the store, but I told him which patterns and colors I preferred. After hearing my responses, he brought over another six carpets. Some of these were tied with string, which he cut open. He unrolled these carpets on top of the original five. Again he asked what I liked, and I told him. He eagerly went to obtain four more carpets to meet my taste, this time climbing a ladder to pull some down from an upper shelf.

At this point, I began feeling a little uncomfortable at all the effort that he had expended for me. Fifteen carpets had now been unrolled for my viewing. I realized that he was going to have to reroll all these carpets, tie some back up with string, and place others back up on the high shelf. I had not asked for this (indeed, it was not what I had in mind when I came into the store). On the other hand, I had not stopped him from getting the carpets for me, and I had even answered his follow-up questions knowing what he was going to do. I had a new interest in purchasing a carpet that had not existed when I entered the store—the interest in avoiding feeling guilty about all his work on my behalf. This technique is not going to sell a rug every time, but if it is used with a large number of customers, some may buy a rug who otherwise would not have.[1]

Sometimes merchants are light-hearted about this approach. In one store in Cairo, Egypt, a seller asked me to have tea with him. I declined because I had no intention of purchasing anything and did not want to feel indebted to him (though the custom is that the buyer incurs no obligation merely by accepting tea). The store owner recognized my hesitation, and said, "Please, you must have tea with me—in Egypt we believe that if you do not have tea with me after I offer it, my daughter will not marry!" He said this with a sparkle in his eye, indicating he did not really believe I was responsible for the marriage of his daughter. Nonetheless, it was a creative way to encourage me to accept his hospitality.

The Interest in Feeling Good about Yourself   International shopkeepers have a myriad of techniques for making a customer feel good about buying something. They often compliment a customer's taste in selecting an item to examine: "You have made an excellent choice, sir. This is indeed one of the finest things in my store." This approach develops a customer's interest in feeling sophisticated and discerning. Customers are a little more likely to purchase something that has been recognized as an example of their cultivation and eye for quality.

A related approach was taken by a salesman in Khajuraho, India. He started by asking where I was from. When I said I was from the United States, he replied, "America! You are from the richest country in the world! Your country has so much money!" I wasn't certain what this was all about until several minutes later, when we started negotiating over the price of an item. Then I recognized that his comment made it feel somewhat ungracious for me to haggle too competitively given that I was from such a wealthy place, especially compared to India. I shrugged this off, however, and continued to negotiate with the man. He then asked me what I did for a living, and I said I was a lawyer. He replied, "And you are a lawyer! You must be such a powerful and rich man!" Then he smiled broadly, adding, "How can you argue with me over a few rupees? They must mean nothing to you!"

This was effective, even though it was transparent. He was right, and we both knew it. The amount of money over which we differed was tiny in American terms. He had created an interest in me to feel magnanimous. The least I could do as a guest in his country was to share my good fortune by giving something that meant so little to me and yet so much to him.

Other store owners take the opposite approach. Rather than building up the customer, they emphasize how pathetic they are themselves. On a weekend, shopkeepers will implore, "Please buy something from me—it is a Sunday." The first time I heard this, I had to ask what it meant. The shopkeeper explained, "It means I would not be here unless I needed money very badly—Sunday is our day of rest!" Another owner even showed me his electric bill, pleading that he did not have enough money to pay it. Ignoring these gambits becomes easier upon learning that shopkeepers often work weekends because sales are particularly good then, and they are frequently among the wealthiest of local townspeople.

I was able to turn the tables on a shopkeeper with this approach in a recent trip in West Africa. He looked prosperous, so I asked if he owned the store himself. When he said he did, I replied, "This is a large and wonderful store—you must be a very successful man!" He looked somewhat sheepish. I continued by asking him if he had traveled. He said that several years ago he had been to America to visit relatives. I replied, "And you have even been able to travel to the United States! You are obviously thriving and prosperous!" He appeared vaguely uncomfortable as we negotiated, as if he had been disarmed, and the price I obtained was quite favorable.

Options

Once both sides have identified their interests, interest-based negotiators work to identify as many potential options for resolution as possible. Many people assume that there are few choices available to negotiators, and thus a benefit for one side necessarily means a loss for the other. In contrast, the idea behind option generation is to reduce the fighting about who gets more by working creatively to increase the value of the deal to both sides. Most of the time, negotiations overseas are routine, one-time transactions. Nonetheless, there are situations with a surprising number of options available.

Options with Form of Payment   Even simple negotiations over price in a craft market, for example, have options in terms of how a customer purchases a product. Often local currency is a seller's preference because no conversion is necessary for the seller to spend it later. In some countries, however, sellers prefer U.S. dollars because the dollar is a hard currency that tends to keep its value. In these countries, local currency is repeatedly devalued, and merchants want to minimize the amount of it they possess. Traveler's checks are another option. From the perspective of the seller, these have the advantage of being in hard currency. On the other hand, they must be converted into cash to be used. Further, unlike dollar bills, traveler's checks can generally only be converted at banks. This adds an additional administrative burden that makes them less attractive for most sellers. Finally, a seller can accept payment by credit card. This is frequently the least attractive option for a merchant because credit cards charge the seller a commission of at least 3 percent on all purchases.

These options can create flexibility in the price of an item. If a buyer has no preference in the form of payment, allowing the seller to make this choice can often shave money off the price. If both the buyer and the seller have conflicting preferences, this presents an opportunity for further negotiation (as when sellers seek to pass along to buyers the commission for the use of a credit card). Sometimes a buyer can negotiate for a price in an unattractive form of payment, such as a credit card, and then agree to pay cash at the last minute in an attempt to sway the seller. After a seller refuses an offer of $100 via credit card, for example, buyers have succeeded by placing five crisp $20 bills in front of the seller in place of their MasterCard.

Options with Combined Purchases   Other options exist when making multiple purchases. A customer willing to buy more than one item at the same store can usually negotiate a discount. It is thus often worthwhile to locate a single store that stocks many items, rather than buy them piecemeal in different stores throughout a town. Similarly, the price of a taxi ride seems at first to be a single-issue and zero-sum negotiation, but it can have some flexibility. The main option here is based on the taxi driver's interest in reducing the risk of not getting future customers. The price of a trip to a destination often decreases if the same driver is hired for the return trip. Hiring the driver for a morning or an entire day reduces the per-trip cost even further.

Options with Defective Products   Another option is locating an item that is less than perfect and asking for a discount. Even in a fixed-price store in Kyoto, Japan, a country where bargaining is rare, I saved several thousand yen on the price of a metal dragon sculpture by noting that the brass plaque on the front was slightly off-center. There must be a genuine flaw in the product, however. Merchants are well schooled in this tactic and are not fooled by an attempt to point out a "defect" that is insignificant or is merely a sign that a product has been made by hand.

Options with Additional Services   The rate for a hotel room also appears to be a simple transaction that would have little room for creativity, but this is not always the case. For example, after walking off the plane and into the terminal at some overseas airports, travelers can find themselves surrounded by a swarm of hotel touts. In these situations, often much can be negotiated in addition to the room rate. I have persuaded hotel representatives to give me free breakfast, drinks, and even occasionally dinner. Sometimes these are one-time offers, and other times the hotel provides them for the duration of the stay. Some hotels will offer free transportation from the airport, and others will transfer you to the airport at the end of the stay as well. Sometimes a hotel will agree to pay the room tax. Prices also vary depending upon the size of the room and whether it requires sharing a bath. Staying more than one night can lower the per-night cost.

Obviously, a number of factors contribute to the availability of these options, though it is surprising what can be obtained just by asking for it. Things are more negotiable at a hotel that has a large number of vacancies because it has fewer options for getting customers. Waiting until later in the day, when it is clear a room will go unoccupied otherwise, can improve the buyer's bargaining position. Negotiating in an airport setting where several hotel representatives are competing for business can work well. Often they can be played off against each another by telling hotel X what hotel Y just offered and asking if they can beat it.

Criteria

In addition to identifying interests and options, interest-based negotiators examine objective criteria to determine an appropriate result. The reliance on standards leads to both a fairer process and a fairer outcome. Rather than fight about who has more power, with both sides grinding each other down until one submits, interest-based negotiators work to settle a dispute through the application of legitimate criteria.

The value of criteria to an overseas traveler outside the United States may seem limited. The only criterion of interest to a seller may be getting as much money as possible, and for a buyer, paying as little as possible. Further, how can negotiators agree upon objective criteria when they grew up thousands of miles apart, in completely different countries with unique cultural backgrounds? However, a look at negotiation in other parts of the world reveals that the use of criteria is more extensive than might be expected.

Criteria as Pricing Categories   One major use of criteria in overseas negotiation is the application of different pricing categories. In these cases, the criteria being applied have nothing to do with the inherent value of the good. Rather, the criteria are used to determine an appropriate price given the willingness or ability of certain classes of customers to pay.

For example, overseas taxi drivers recognize that they can charge much higher rates to travelers. The price of a taxi procured at the front door of a five-star hotel often is several times higher than it would otherwise be. Similarly, on the way back, a passenger going to an expensive hotel will be quoted a much higher price. Some travelers will simply walk a block away from their hotels before hailing a cab, and on the way back will ask to be driven to a location adjacent to the hotel. While it is often still obvious they are tourists, at least they fall into the average-tourist criterion, not the five-star one.

Similarly, the tourist rate at local attractions can be much higher than the rate charged to natives. The most egregious example of this I have found was in Jordan, where admission to the ruins at Petra costs travelers 20 times as many dinar as natives.

A foreign service officer posted in Abuja, the capital city of Nigeria, told me the difference between the tourist and local rate is one of the most important considerations for him when he negotiates with native residents. The first thing I saw him do when bargaining for an item was to tell the seller, "I'm not a JJC, so give me a reasonable price." I asked him what a "JJC" was, and he said it meant "Johnny Just Come," a local expression for a person who had recently arrived in the city. By using the local vernacular, almost like speaking a shibboleth, he made it clear he would not be susceptible to wild overpricing.

Some travelers have been able to turn pricing criteria to their advantage. At the Great Pyramids at Giza, travelers can be swarmed with locals asking for money. One Egyptian tour guide told me that tourists from Russia are often the least generous. He said they frequently gave him nothing or "pencils and other things I cannot use." Thus he has stopped soliciting Russians. Apparently this reaction is typical in Egypt, as it is possible to escape haranguing by Egyptians by responding, "Ya Russki." This means, "I am Russian," and it can drive the Egyptians away (Humphreys 1999).

Appeal to Criteria as a Negotiating Tactic   Sometimes an appeal to criteria can advance one side's negotiation position. In India, while visiting a smaller temple near the Taj Mahal, I came upon a man kneeling with a live cobra in a basket in front of him. In his left hand, he held a leash with a live mongoose. In his mouth was a brightly colored red and yellow flutelike instrument. He was evoking the famous story of Rikki-Tikki-Tavi by Rudyard Kipling, which I enjoyed, so I took a picture. The moment the shutter snapped, the man stuck his hand out, demanding money. He was claiming that the criterion of customary practice in the area required me to pay him. Upon further reflection, I probably should have known that it is unlikely a man would post himself in front of a temple with a live mongoose and cobra for spiritual fulfillment alone. Thinking the service the man had performed was slight, I handed him a small number of rupees. He scowled and suggested that the going rate was much higher. I had no idea whether his alleged criterion was fair or not. However, it was a small amount of money, and I had no interest in an extended negotiation with a man who spoke little English and was scowling at me, so I accepted his proffered standard.

Alternatives

Interest-based negotiation also involves considering the alternatives to making a deal. Before negotiating, parties determine their best alternatives to a negotiated agreement. Armed with this information, negotiators are better prepared to know which offers are worth accepting and which should be rejected.

Alternatives and Power   Many times the party with the best alternative to negotiation has the most power in the interaction. For example, on a trip to India, I wanted to buy a statuette of the Hindu god Ganesha. Without looking at the situation closely, it might appear that I had more power in a negotiation for this idol than an Indian man who sells them on the street. Certainly I had more of the conventional attributes of power (money, education, etc.). However, when it came to the negotiation, this mattered very little.

The reason I had so little power was that the Indian merchant had a superior command of his alternatives to an agreement. Based on years of experience, he knew quite accurately what he could get another customer to pay for a Ganesha idol if he did not sell it to me. In contrast, I had a poor grasp of my alternatives. I wanted an idol, and I had never seen one before my arrival in India. If anybody was going to get taken advantage of in this transaction, I was.

Strengthening Alternatives   When confronted with weak alternatives, a negotiator's first response is to seek to improve them. In this case, the obvious approach is to expand my alternatives. If I can find other merchants with similar statuettes, I may find one who will sell for less. When I know my options in other stores, I can negotiate the best possible price from a seller.

Weakening the Other Side's Alternatives   A more aggressive approach is to weaken the other side's alternatives. In this particular negotiation, I learned about a belief among Indian merchants that the first sale of the day has special importance. The idea is that a merchant who makes a sale to the first customer will have good fortune the rest of the day. If the merchant fails to complete the deal, however, he will have poor luck until the following day. Upon discovering this, I woke up early one morning to ensure I would be the first customer and walked to the market. I was fascinated to see the effectiveness of this method. Many merchants told me they would give me a special "morning price" in order to win my business. One even chased after me when I left his store without a purchase, pleading with me to buy anything at all, just so that he would have good luck.

Manipulation of Interest-Based Negotiation

The examples used thus far have illustrated situations where interest-based negotiation has been used in good faith by both buyers and sellers to achieve their ends. This approach clearly has wide application, as shown by its value in all of these disparate negotiations. However, there are other situations where negotiators use the concepts in bad faith. This section will discuss situations where overseas bargainers used the ideas of interest-based negotiation to their advantage in a more manipulative way.

Misrepresentation of Relationship   In some cases, people push the idea of relationship beyond the good faith model suggested by interest-based negotiation. These negotiators build a relationship in order to take advantage of it. For example, while I was reading a guidebook in Old Delhi, India, a man approached me and asked where I was going. I made the mistake of answering his question. He then simply began following me, on the pretense of showing me the way. I shook my head and told him firmly I did not need his help because I knew where I was going. Still, he would not leave. I attempted to ignore him, but he persisted in walking next to me, chatting about his family and life in general. I tried to shake him by entering a huge outdoor Moslem temple, the Jama Masjid. This is the largest mosque in India, with a massive courtyard that can accommodate as many as 25,000 people for prayer sessions. Even better for my purposes, there is a small fee for admission, which my "guide" did not want to pay. When I entered, I thought I had finally eluded him. Eventually the *azan* (call for prayer) began, and tourists were required to leave. To my dismay, I discovered he had simply waited for me, for about an hour, outside the exit. The moment he saw me, he walked over and clung to me once again, nattering on. He made it clear that he was looking for a tip for his "guide services," and that if one was forthcoming, he would leave me alone.

This example is a bizarre twist on the use of relationship to further negotiation goals. While hard bargainers in the United States often demand concessions from parties who want to maintain the relationship, this negotiator actually created a distasteful relationship with me in order to persuade me to pay him to end it. The only way to give up the relationship, which I wanted very much to do, was to pay money.

Manipulation of Interests   A questionable appeal to my emotional interests in a negotiation took place on a trek in the Mount Everest National Park in Nepal. Rather than travel with a tourist group, I decided to engage a Sherpa and go on my own. I hired Bacchu, the same person that had traveled with a friend of mine named Stanley. The price I negotiated with Bacchu's agency explicitly included all of his expenses, including room and board. As the trip progressed, I found him to be a friendly, knowledgeable, and capable guide. However, he was also rather assertive in asking me to buy extra things for him.

The entire trek took 11 days, and Bacchu escalated his requests as time went on. At first we would have a drink at one of the small tea houses along the route. When the bill arrived, it was clear he expected me to pick it up, which I was willing to do. Later, he started dropping hints that he would like me to buy dinner for him as well. I told him I understood his meals were included in the rate negotiated with his agency. He replied that the amount the allotted for him was small. I resisted, because I did not want to feel I was paying twice for his meals.

Bacchu then started making references to how my friend Stanley, who had traveled with him earlier, would buy him all sorts of things. At one place, he said, "When we came here, Stanley bought me dinner." At another, he pointed out all of the individual things on the menu he said Stanley paid for. He said Stanley even gave him shirts and a pair of hiking boots. The tactic began to work, as I started to buy him things too, in order not to be outdone by my friend.

After a little while, I told Bacchu I did not like his comparing me to my friend in order to get more money than agreed in the contract. He responded that where earning money for his family was involved, he would do whatever he had to do. (This was a noble enough response, but I recall he spent a fair amount of this "family" money getting drunk on chhang and rakshi.) Because he was a good guide and an enjoyable fellow (when he wasn't entreating me for money), I bought him a reasonable number of meals and gave him a tip at the end.

This example shows yet another nonmonetary interest that an overseas negotiator effectively identified and exploited—my interest in wanting to seem as generous as my friend had been. I later asked Stanley about his experiences with Bacchu. Stanley said he did end up buying Bacchu many things, as had been reported, but he did so only because Bacchu hounded him endlessly about it. He hadn't appreciated it any more than I had. I told Stanley I wish he'd told me this earlier.

Misrepresentation of Alternatives   I was initially impressed with the power of worsening the other side's alternatives by getting up early to become an Indian seller's first customer of the day, as noted earlier. However, the luster of the "first sale of the day" dimmed somewhat when I later found merchants who told me that the "last sale of the day" was particularly important to them. They said completing this sale would give them luck for the following day. Still others told me that sales on Sunday would be especially favorable, offering their special "Sunday price." On further trips, I discovered that the importance of the "first sale of the day" is not really a Hindu belief, as merchants also talk about it in China, Nepal, and Turkey, among other countries. It seems that instead of being an article of religious faith, the "first sale of the day" is a shrewd negotiating ploy that merchants around the world use to manipulate customers.

This tactic is manipulative because the sellers are misrepresenting their alternatives in negotiation. By sharing an invented vulnerability, pleading that bad luck will befall them without a sale, they are appealing to the sympathy of the customer. The approach works by creating an interest on the part of the customer to be magnanimous to improve the merchant's luck. The merchant also exploits the interest shared by all travelers in getting a good deal. If customers believe a merchant is making special price concessions for them that are not offered to others, they are more likely to purchase things. Everyone wants to feel like a savvy shopper.

Violation of the Principles of Interest-Based Negotiation

Sometimes overseas negotiators directly violate the tenets of interest-based negotiation. In these situations, the concepts have limited applicability and can seem inadequate.

Extreme Opening Offers   One time in India, I stepped into a store with a wide selection of masks. The store owner noticed my interest in one particular mask, took it down, and started talking about its unusual quality and my exceptional discernment in selecting it. He asked what I would offer him, and I said I really wasn't interested. He said the usual price was $110, but he would offer me a discount. I said I could only offer a very low amount and did not want to insult him by offering so little for such a fine piece of art. He persisted, insisting that I make him an offer no matter how low it was.

In such situations, the traditional advice is to offer about half of the store owner's opening price and bargain up from there, ending at roughly two-thirds of the original price. I did not want to pay that much for the mask. However, the man was so insistent that I decided at least to offer him something, if only to show how a sale was impossible. I decided I was willing to offer $25, which was less than one-quarter of his original price. The merchant smiled at me and said, "Sold." The mask was worth $25 to me, and since it is very bad form to withdraw an offer once made, I went through with the transaction.

While this example does not involve tactics that were illegal, the store owner was acting in bad faith. Merchants customarily price items in reasonable relation to their worth, and this seller intentionally violated this practice to mislead me as to the item's value. I later did some comparison shopping in other nearby markets and found out the going rate for similar masks was indeed about $25.

Taking What You Want   In India, many people travel by means of the "auto-rickshaw." This is a three-wheeled motorized vehicle with a seat for the driver in front and a small seat for one or two people in the back. The sides of the vehicle are open to the air, making it something of a cross between a motorcycle and a subcompact car. The pollution from auto-rickshaws makes for a noxious ride, the noise is excruciating, and the owners are notorious for unbelievably reckless driving. Nonetheless, many people use them because they are readily available and inexpensive.

Determining price for an auto-rickshaw ride can be the trickiest part of the whole experience. Few have working meters. Some of the meters that do work have been rigged by the driver to overstate the price. Even if a vehicle has an unbiased meter, confusing local customs exist such as doubling the metered price and then adding another one-half fare to that figure. To minimize problems, most travelers learn to agree on a price in advance.

I found that even this approach has limitations, however. In one case, the driver and I agreed on a certain number of rupees for a trip within town. Once we arrived, however, the driver said the fare was 50 percent more than we had agreed. He refused to acknowledge the earlier agreement and insisted on the higher price. This appeared to me to be fraudulent, as our negotiation had been quite clear, and the trip was short enough that memory problems were unlikely.

In another situation, I did not have the necessary small bills to pay our agreed fare, so I handed the driver a larger bill and asked for change. He returned an insufficient amount. It is possible he made an simple arithmetic mistake, but this is unlikely because auto-rickshaw drivers are a seasoned lot. I stared at him, indicating my displeasure, and he looked back at me sheepishly. He was willing to look old and pathetic if it would get him more money.

There was a fundamental difference between these two examples. In the first case, I had leverage. We had arrived at the destination, so I had already obtained the service I needed. I merely handed the driver the originally agreed-upon fare and walked off. In the second case, however, I could not walk away because the driver was in possession of the larger bill I had given him. Quite possibly because of this difference, I decided that he may have been including a small tip for himself when he calculated the change, and I let it go.

Escalating Demands   Entrance to the lost city of Petra, in Jordan, requires traveling through a canyon known as the Siq. Rather than walk down the Siq, some visitors choose to make the journey on the back of a camel. Persistent young Jordanian boys encourage this option, saying, "air-conditioned taxi, mister?" The price for this ride is highly negotiable.

Upon reaching the end of the journey, many are surprised to find the negotiation is not over after all. Still high above the ground sitting on top of their camel, they hear their guide inform them that there is an additional "dismount fee." The guide patiently explains that the original negotiation was the "ride fee." In order to get off the camel, more dinar will be required. Sometimes the guides add that the dismount fee is "for the camel." Upon payment of this fee, the guide prompts the camel to lower itself down to the ground, making it possible to step off. As there is no way to get the camel to do this without the guide's assistance, paying the fee is unavoidable. This type of tactic is of course fraudulent, and would probably be actionable if it didn't take place in the middle of a desert.[2]

Scams   Sometimes negotiation itself seems inappropriate regardless of the reasonableness of the price being offered. The center of New Delhi, India, is a series of roads arranged in the form of concentric rings. A leftover from the days of British imperialism, the area is known as Connaught Circus. It is so overwhelmingly crowded that the easiest way to get from one part to another is to take underground tunnels that go beneath the mayhem. Walking through one of these tunnels, I encountered a young Indian boy who offered to clean my left shoe. He pointed up to a couple of birds roosting in the tunnel and then noted I had bird droppings on my shoe. The price he offered for the cleaning was eminently affordable, less than a dollar in rupees. However, I realized that the droppings had not arrived on my shoe directly from a bird. About 30 seconds earlier, a compatriot of his had placed the droppings there and scooted off, hoping to be undetected in the crush of people. I had barely seen him scamper away. The scam almost worked, as I very much wanted the droppings off my shoe. Still, I found myself simply refusing to reward this behavior. We were not negotiating only over the cost of a shoe cleaning, but also over whether I would validate this subterfuge. I found this too high a price to pay.

Interest-Based Negotiation in an Imperfect World

In a perfect world where everyone followed its precepts, interest-based negotiation could be an ideal approach. In practice, while it is often a valuable tool, it is not an infallible one. This section will discuss one situation in more depth to analyze the virtues and limitations of the approach.

Upon arrival in Accra, Ghana, I asked an attendant at a small traveler information counter at the airport how to get to Elmina, 100 miles away, where I had hotel reservations for the night. She said that at this time in the late afternoon the only choice would be a taxi. She handed me a tariff sheet that printed taxi fares in cedis, the local currency, from the airport to various destinations. Elmina was on the list.

I crossed the street from the airport to the taxi park, whereupon several dozen taxi drivers immediately clamored for my attention. The one who reached me first asked where I was going. I replied, "Elmina," and he smiled broadly (the main city of Accra is only five miles away, so a trip to Elmina represents a much larger than usual fare). I asked him how much he would charge, and he opened the car door, saying "Get in, and we will discuss the fare on the way." It is not necessary to be a student of negotiation to realize this is a poor idea. Once seated in the vehicle, the passenger loses all bargaining power. I merely smiled at him and said, "Let's talk price first."

The driver quoted me a fare that was several multiples of what I had hoped to pay. As there were so many drivers, I figured I would just approach others until I got a better fare. However, the next driver, who had overheard the first, replied with the exact same figure, as did several more. It became clear the drivers had found an effective response to comparison shopping—they had formed a cartel, all backing the price of the first driver to make an offer.

At this point I took out the tariff sheet from the airport and presented it to one of the drivers, insisting the fare should be what was listed on this document. The driver shook his head dejectedly as if I had defeated him and pointed reluctantly to a number printed on the form adjacent to Elmina. This price was about half of the original quoted fare. He said, "It is Ok, get in and we will go."

However, I looked at the tariff sheet more closely and noted there were two numbers next to Elmina, one about double the other. The driver had pointed to the higher figure. Although the text was in the Ga language and unreadable to me, it appeared that the first figure was for a one-way journey and the second was the round-trip rate. I showed this to the driver, who feigned ignorance, as if he had no idea what the first number meant. I began using hand signals to indicate the difference between traveling one-way and round-trip. It quickly became clear he knew full well what the numbers meant and just had been hoping I would not notice the difference. I insisted that the one-way fare was appropriate for a one-way trip.

The driver then tried another approach. "This is a very, very old tariff," he said. "This tariff is no longer valid." I responded that it had just been handed to me by the airport official moments earlier. He continued, "This tariff is out of date. Petrol costs twice as many cedis as when this was printed." I pointed out that the sheet was dated only six weeks earlier, but we were at a standoff.

It was starting to get dark outside when one of the more boisterous drivers finally took me over to a quiet taxi driver parked in a corner by himself. I asked the quiet one whether he would drive me to Elmina for the printed fare, and he said he would. When we arrived in Elmina several hours later, I tipped him handsomely.

While this negotiation ended happily, things easily might not have worked out so well. This example shows some significant limitations of the interest-based approach.

Unclear Criteria   It can be far from clear what criteria are legitimate. The driver first attempted to use the round-trip standard (rather than one-way). This might have worked had I not looked more closely at the form. The driver even might have argued legitimately that a round-trip fare was appropriate because, given the lateness of the day, he would be unable to locate a paying passenger for the trip back. The driver also said that gas prices had risen, and I had no way to determine the validity of this claim.

In many negotiations, each side offers its own criteria in support of its position. Indeed, clever negotiators can be very creative in devising legitimate-sounding reasons for their offers. Sometimes these criteria are not good faith suggestions but are merely negotiating ploys.

One interest-based response is to look for an objective way to choose among the possible criteria. Sometimes there will be a valid reason that one criterion is more appropriate than another. However, many times this is not so easy. Even people negotiating in good faith will not always agree on which standards should be used. For an American at Kotoka Airport in Accra (or any negotiator who is a newcomer to a situation), clear standards can be hard to come by.

The Ultimate Hard Bargaining   Even more fundamental limitations of the principled approach became clear at the point when the sun began setting in the taxi lot and I still had no driver. I continued insisting on the legitimacy of my criteria, but I was a hundred miles from where I was to spend the night. I may have had principle on my side, but that would not get me to Elmina. If the taxi drivers had continued to exercise raw power, in the form of their absolute control over the market for transportation to Elmina, I would have had to give up my criteria and pay their price.

Critics of interest-based negotiation note that it sometimes seems to "overlook the ultimate hard bargaining." (White 1984, p. 116). If the other side refuses to participate, there is sometimes little that an interest-based negotiator can do.

Nonetheless, it is worth remembering that in this case things did not get that far, and criteria ended up saving me a considerable amount of money. When I first arrived at the taxi park, I was quoted a fare much higher than what I ultimately paid. The use of criteria, in the form of a single sheet of paper, was powerful enough to cut the cost of my trip by 75 percent.

The power of principle is recognized in many parts of the world and by many different cultures. It is noteworthy that the Ghanaians did not dismiss the tariff sheet out of hand. Instead, they responded to it on its merits. Indeed, it changed the entire dynamic of the negotiation, turning the discussion from how much I was going to have to pay, to how much was fair.

Some Concluding Thoughts

Interest-based negotiation is extremely valuable in many cases and less relevant in some others. Overall, it is a useful framework for analyzing negotiation, and it provides helpful tools for approaching most situations. While not universal, it may have more to offer than any other established theory of negotiation.

At the same time, world travel also teaches that negotiation is not all there is to life. Following are two final ideas along these lines.

Money Isn't Everything   An easy mindset to adopt in negotiation is the idea that money is the ultimate goal. Some people find themselves doing everything possible to squeeze the last cent out of every seller they encounter. It is necessary to step back for a moment to realize that money isn't everything in negotiation or in life.

In India, men in their seventies make their living pedaling people to places in bicycle rickshaws. These men line up in front of fancy hotels and wait for hours for their turn to get a customer. Then they pedal their bicycle, pulling the heavy passenger carriage behind them, up hills in the 100-degree sun. They do this for 20 or 30 rupees a ride (considerably less than a dollar). They may only get a few passengers a day. Nonetheless, Western tourists find themselves negotiating fiercely to shave five rupees off the price of the ride.

The process of negotiation can bring out the worst in people. As the focus of negotiation is often to obtain the lowest price possible, there can be a tendency for negotiators to blind themselves to all other considerations. In other settings, this phenomenon is not as prevalent. For example, a restaurant customer legally could lower the price of every meal by never leaving a tip. Yet few people would consider doing this just to save a few dollars. People can lose this perspective in the negotiation context. The competitive aspects of the process can make people forget their better natures.

Negotiation for Enjoyment   Finally, people who live in countries where much of daily life involves negotiation often have a much healthier perspective on it. Many local merchants and customers seem to treat the process as a game and even to relish it. Both sides can have a little fun with themselves, like competitors in a sport or actors in a play. They may raise their voices, wave their arms angrily, and otherwise act offended with each other, but once they reach a deal, they are back to being the best of friends. Indeed, they seem entertained and amused by the process, and they look at it not as a chore but as a bit of an adventure. Ultimately, this may be the best negotiation approach of all.

Endnotes

The author wishes to thank Roger Fisher, Frank Sander, Pete Steenland, Aloma Shaw, David Shapiro, Rajib Chanda, Chris Honeyman, Rick Senger, Jon Gould, Jody Lee, and an anonymous Negotiation Journal reviewer for their assistance with this article.

1. Guy Olivier Faure (1991) gives a fascinating account of other challenges one can face when buying a carpet in the Orient.

2. Robert McKersie (1997a and 1997b) describes several possible responses to this problem, though none seems particularly likely to be effective, in my opinion.

References

Faure, G.O. 1991. Negotiating in the Orient: Encounters in the Peshawar bazaar, Pakistan. *Negotiation Journal* 7(3), pp. 279–90.

Fisher, R., W. Ury, and B. Patton. 1991. *Getting to YES: Negotiating agreement without giving in.* 2nd ed. New York: Penguin Books.

Humphreys, A., et al. 1999. *Lonely Planet Egypt.* Oakland: Lonely Planet Publications.

McKersie, R.B. 1997a. What would you do—on the back of a camel? *Negotiation Journal* 13(1), pp. 13–15.

———. 1997b. What would you do—on the back of a camel?—Part 2. *Negotiation Journal* 13(2), pp. 109–18.

White, J. (1984). The pros and cons of *Getting to YES. Journal of Legal Education* 34, pp. 115–20.

Reading 5.4

American Strengths and Weaknesses
Tommy T. B. Koh

American Strengths and Qualities

Two caveats are appropriate for any discussion of national negotiating styles. First, there may not necessarily be a definable negotiating style for each country or people. Good and effective negotiators, irrespective of their national or cultural background, have certain common skills. Second, although it is probably possible to say impressionistically that the American people possess certain character and personality traits, there are many exceptions to the rule, and a person's negotiating style is inevitably affected by his character, temperament, and attitude toward people.

American negotiators have many strengths and qualities. If distance makes the heart grow fonder, my perception of Americans may be unrealistically favorable and idealized, since Singapore is located 12,000 miles away from the United States.

First, U.S. negotiators are usually well prepared. They arrive at negotiations with their homework completed, and they are armed with facts, figures, maps, and charts. They usually know what their national interests are and what their negotiating objectives are. This is not always the case among Third World negotiators.

Second, American negotiators tend to speak clearly and plainly. As someone who was educated in the Anglo-Saxon legal tradition, I regard this as a virtue, not a liability. However, the American preference for plain speaking can sometimes cause unintended offense to other negotiators whose national culture prefers indirectness, subtlety, and avoidance of confrontation. There are, of course, exceptions to this rule.

Third, U.S. negotiators tend to be more pragmatic than doctrinaire. They focus on advancing their country's interests rather than principles that they cherish. The Reagan administration, however, was a clear exception to this rule, and at the Third U.N. Conference on the Law of the Sea decided, for rational and arguable reasons, that principles were more important than interests.

Fourth, American negotiators generally do not regard negotiations as a zero-sum game. A good U.S. negotiator is even prepared to put himself in the place of his negotiating adversary. A good U.S. negotiator is prepared to admit that his adversary, like himself, has certain irreducible, minimum national interests. A good U.S. negotiator is prepared to engage in a process of give and take, and he believes that the successful outcome of a negotiation is not one in which he wins everything and his adversary loses everything, but rather one in which there is a mutuality of benefits and losses, in which each side has a stake in honoring and maintaining the agreement.

Fifth, a U.S. negotiator's opening position is never his final position. He expects his opponent to make a counterproposal or a counteroffer. He is anxious to reach an agreement and will, therefore, make concessions to his opponent, expecting—not unreasonably—that

Source: Reprinted from *International Negotiation* 1 (1996), pp. 313–17. Used with permission

his adversary will behave in like manner. Americans are sometimes completely exasperated at international forums when their adversaries do not behave as they do.

Sixth, the American people are very candid and straightforward, and this is reflected in their negotiating style. Americans are not usually perceived as cunning or devious. In only one incident have I found American negotiators to be devious, and that was shocking. This incident occurred in July 1981 when the United Nations sponsored an international conference on Cambodia. The conference was initiated by the ASEAN (Association of Southeast Asian Nations) countries, which proposed a framework for the resolution of the Cambodian situation. All Cambodian factions were invited to participate in the conference, including, of course, the Khmer Rouge. Vietnam was invited, but boycotted the meeting. At the conference General Alexander Haig, then U.S. Secretary of State, staged a dramatic walkout, accompanied by the entire U.S. delegation, when the Khmer Rouge leader approached the rostrum to speak. The picture of this walkout appeared on the front page of *The New York Times.*

On a subsequent day, the ASEAN countries and the People's Republic of China (PRC) were locked in a ferocious confrontation over the future role of the Khmer Rouge in any postsettlement Cambodia. The ASEAN countries argued that in light of the massacres and atrocities that the Khmer Rouge had committed, it would be morally and legally impermissible to allow them to return to power. We demanded a public election to be organized and supervised by the United Nations. To ensure free elections, we insisted that all armed elements be disarmed or sequestered in camp. The Chinese fought against all these points. The negotiating group was composed of 25 delegations, but the dynamics of the discussions revolved around the PRC, the ASEAN countries, and Pakistan as a middleman. Pakistan, however, was not an honest broker and basically submitted a series of amendments to dilute the ASEAN position. I assumed that Pakistan, because of its proximity to the PRC, was "fronting" for the Chinese, and was shocked to learn later that they were actually fronting for the Americans. Although the American delegation had publicly walked out of the negotiations, they were privately supporting China for geostrategic reasons. This is the only example of devious behavior by American negotiators of which I am aware, but I will remember it.

Weaknesses and Idiosyncrasies

One problem in negotiating with Americans is that American delegations usually suffer from serious interagency rivalries. During the U.N. Law of the Sea Conference the American delegation met every morning, and sometimes their internal meetings lasted longer than the other meetings in the conference.

A second problem in negotiating with the United States is the separation of power between the administration and the Congress. One has to be very careful if one is negotiating an agreement that is subject to ratification by the U.S. Senate. It is important to always keep in touch with U.S. senators as the negotiating process continues in order to obtain their independent inputs, be aware of their sensitivities, and recognize vested domestic interests and blocking constituencies.

A third special characteristic is the influence of the U.S. private sector and private interest groups on negotiations. During the Law of the Sea Conference I made it a point to meet not only with the official U.S. delegation and members of the Congress, but also to meet with representatives from the seabed mining industry, the petroleum industry, the fishing industry, the marine scientific community, the environmental lobby, and individuals who have an affection for marine mammals. The reality of political life in America is that even one of these many lobbies can block ratification of a treaty. Foreign negotiators must understand the domestic political process in the United States and must, in some way, interfere in American internal affairs to ensure the success of their mission.

A fourth problem—the role of U.S. media—is a problem more for U.S. negotiators than for their counterparts. This is a problem because somehow the good nature of Americans and their propensity to candor makes it very difficult even for negotiators to keep confidences. And in the midst of a sensitive negotiation it is sometimes very counterproductive for the media to report on issues that are under negotiation. In a speech to the House Foreign Affairs Committee, Secretary of State George Shultz recounted with great frustration an occasion when the United State and U.S.S.R. were engaged in bilateral negotiations. The negotiation had reached a critical point, and he had that day drafted a cable giving his final instructions. He said he found to his horror at breakfast the next morning that *The New York Times* had reported the content of his cable. Members of the U.S. media should be asked whether they should exercise more discretion and self-restraint. Do they not feel an allegiance as American citizens to the advancement and protection of American national interests? Should not the right of the public to know and the freedom of the press sometimes be modulated by competing and larger interests? The extent to which the United States exposes its flank makes it easier for others to win at the negotiating table.

A fifth weakness is impatience. Americans suffer from an "instant-coffee complex." They do not have time, as Europeans and Asians do, to buy coffee beans, grind them every day, brew the coffee, enjoy the aroma, and savor every sip. Americans are always in a rush and are extremely frustrated when there is a lack of progress. Americans are result-oriented. Jeane Kirkpatrick had a shock several years ago when she visited the ASEAN capitals and met the foreign ministers of the six ASEAN countries. To each she asked, "Do you think there are prospects for settling the Cambodian conflict?" All six ASEAN foreign ministers said yes. She said, "Do you think it will be soon?" They all said, "Oh yes, very soon." She said, "Well, how soon?" They said, "Oh, about five years' time." She was shocked because to an American five years' time is certainly not soon.

A sixth weakness is cultural insensitivity. Everyone is guilty of this, not only Americans. Everyone assumes that others have similar cultures, customs, and manners. Singaporeans are "the barbarians of Southeast Asia." We are "the least sensitive and least subtle people in the region." But if one is a professional negotiator, then part of the preparation for an effective negotiation is to learn enough about the culture of one's adversary to at least avoid simple errors of behavior, attribution, and body language.

Finally, it is surprising that in many recent multilateral forums the United States has been represented by amateur rather than professional negotiators. Given that the United States is so rich in human resources and has a foreign service studded by superstars, it is amazing how inadequately the United States is represented at important international negotiations.

Conclusion

In conclusion, a good negotiator, whether an Indian, an American, a Canadian, English, Ghanian, or whoever, is a person with certain definable skills, aptitudes, and temperaments. His character and personality have an impact on his effectiveness. Some American negotiators put people off; others readily win people's confidence. In choosing a negotiator, select someone who does not bristle like a porcupine but who can win the trust and confidence of his negotiating partners. What are these qualities that attract people's confidence and trust? These are moral qualities, qualities of leadership. If a negotiator is a leader, a person who acquires a reputation for competence, reliability, and trustworthiness, then others will trust him with leadership roles. The word *charisma* is not useful because it does not accurately portray the quality that bestows leadership on certain negotiators and not others. Henry Kissinger is not charismatic; he is dominating and impassive and has an exceptional intellect and a monotonous voice. In 1976, when the Law of Sea Conference was deadlocked between industrialized and developing countries, Kissinger, who was then secretary of state and had no background in the law of the sea and knew nothing about seabed mining, spent one morning in New York meeting with the U.S. delegation. In the afternoon he met with other leaders of the Group of 77, and by the end of the day presented an innovative scheme for reconciling the competing ambitions and claims of the different countries.

There probably is an American negotiating style, and this partakes of the qualities, attitudes, customs, conventions, and reflexes that have come down through U.S. history, culture, and political institutions. On the whole, American negotiators have very positive qualities, being well prepared, reasonable, competent, and honorable. Even more than this, some, like Elliott Richardson, will take it upon themselves to be an honest broker and help to settle a conflict between two other groups in which they are a totally disinterested party. This graciousness and willingness to help are positive attributes as well.

Resolving Differences

Reading 6.1

Doing Things Collaboratively: Realizing the Advantage or Succumbing to Inertia?

Chris Huxham
Siv Vangen

The project has worked out, but oh boy, it has caused pain.
   —Senior health promotion officer, health promotion partnership

Decisions are made by the alliance executive, but they keep procrastinating over big decisions . . . you can't afford to procrastinate over spending a million pounds.
   —Information manager, retail property development alliance

Multi-agency work is very slow . . . trying to get people moving collectively rather than alone is difficult.
   —Project officer, young offender community organization

I am under partnership attack from my colleagues.
   —Operations manager, engineering supply chain

The long catalog of failed JVs—lcatel/Sharp, Sony/Qualcomm, Lucent/Philips—demonstrates the enormous difficulties in pulling companies like these together.
   —A Gartner analyst quoted in the *Financial Times,* December 10, 2002, p. 8

Not everyone who works daily in collaborative alliances, partnerships, or networks reports such negative experiences as these. Indeed the *Financial Times* (June 24, 2003, p. 14) reports a Nokia executive as saying that their linkages are paying off. Others talk similarly enthusiastically about their partnership experiences:

When it works well you feel inspired . . . you can feel the collaborative energy.

However, very many do express frustration. There has been much rhetoric about the value of strategic alliances, industry networks, public service delivery partnerships, and many other collaborative forms, but reports of unmitigated success are not common. In this article we explore the nature of *the practice of collaboration,* focusing in particular on some of the reasons why collaborative initiatives tend to challenge those involved.

Source: From *Organizational Dynamics* 33, no. 2 (2004), pp. 190–201. Published by Elsevier, Inc.

Two concepts are central to this exploration. The first is *collaborative advantage*. This captures the synergy argument: To gain real *advantage* from collaboration, something has to be achieved that could not have been achieved by any one of the organizations acting alone. This concept provides a useful "guiding light" for the purpose of collaboration. The second concept, *collaborative inertia*, captures what happens very frequently in practice: The output from a collaborative arrangement is negligible, the rate of output is extremely slow, or stories of pain and hard grind are integral to successes achieved.

Clearly there is a dilemma between advantage and inertia. The key question seems to be this:

> If achievement of collaborative advantage is the goal for those who initiate collaborative arrangements, why is collaborative inertia so often the outcome?

To address this question, and the question of what managers can do about it, we will present a set of seven overlapping perspectives on collaborative management. This is extracted from the theory of collaborative advantage, which has derived from extensive action research over 15 years. We have worked with practitioners of collaboration, in the capacity of facilitators, consultants, and trainers, in a wide variety of collaborative situations. We have kept detailed records about the challenges and dilemmas faced by managers, and of comments they make in the course of enacting their collaborative endeavors. Many such statements are reproduced as illustrative examples in this article.

Perspective 1: We Must Have Common Aims But We Cannot Agree on Them

Agreement on aims is an appropriate starting point because it is raised consistently as an issue. *Common wisdom* suggests that it is necessary to be clear about the aims of joint working if partners are to work together to operationalize policies.

Typically individuals argue for common (or at least compatible), agreed, or clear sets of aims as a starting point in collaboration. *Common practice,* however, appears to be that the variety of organizational and individual agendas that are present in collaborative situations makes reaching agreement difficult. For example, a board member of an alliance of 120 charities commented on the difficulty of reconciling members' interests. Invariably someone would call to say, "We don't want you to do that."

The reasons behind the struggles for agreement may not be obvious. Organizations come together bringing different resources and expertise to the table, which in turn creates the potential for collaborative advantage. Yet organizations also have different reasons for being involved, and their representatives seek to achieve different outputs from their involvement. Sometimes these different organizational aims lead to conflicts of interest. Furthermore, for some organizations the joint purpose for the collaboration is perceived as central to achieving organizational purposes, whereas others are less interested and perhaps only involved (reluctantly) as a result of external pressure. Tensions often arise, therefore, because some organizations are very interested in influencing and controlling the joint agenda, and some are reluctant to commit resources to it, and so on. Similarly, individuals too will join the collaboration with different expectations, aspirations, and understandings of what is to be achieved jointly. It follows that while at first glance it may appear that partners need be concerned only with the joint aims for the collaboration, in reality organizational and individual aims can prevent agreement because they cause confusion, misunderstanding, and conflicts of interest. In addition, while some of these various aims may be explicit, many will be taken for granted (assumed) by one partner but not necessarily recognized by another, and many will be deliberately hidden:

> My company is really most interested in having access to, and experience of, the Chinese business environment and cares little for the formally declared purpose of the alliance.

On reflection then it is not so surprising that reaching agreement can be very difficult.

Managing Aims in Practice

Figure 1 is a simplified version of a framework of aims in collaborative situations. Its purpose is to facilitate a better understanding of the motivations of those involved, and the ways in which multiple and (sometimes even) conflicting aims can prevent agreement and block progress. In turn, this sort of understanding can help in finding ways of addressing the concerns of all involved. The framework distinguishes between the various types of aims mentioned and emphasizes that some aims will be assumed rather than explicitly acknowledged, and many will be deliberately hidden.

This framework can be used as an effective tool for gaining insight about the motivations of members of a collaboration—even of one's own! Obviously it is not possible to know others' hidden agendas, but it is possible to speculate on the possibility that they might have some—and even guess at what they might be. Trying to "fill in" each of the cells of the framework for each other partner can be enlightening, whether it is done quickly, "back of an envelope" style, or as a major investigative exercise. Gaining this kind of insight into partners' expectations and aspirations can be very helpful in understanding and judging how best to work with them.

At the general level, the obvious conclusion to be drawn from the framework is that it is rarely going to be easy in practice to satisfy fully the common wisdom. Therein lies the dilemmas—clarity of purpose provides much needed direction, yet open discussion

FIGURE 1 | A Framework for Understanding Aims in Collaboration

(One Participant's Perspective)	Explicit	Assumed	Hidden
Collaboration Aims	The purpose of the collaboration.		By definition these are perceptions of joint aims and so cannot be hidden.
Organization Aims	What each organization hopes to gain for itself via the collaboration.		
Individual Aims	What each individual hopes to gain for him/herself via the collaboration.		

can unearth irreconcilable differences! Difficulties that arise out of the need to communicate across different professional and natural languages and different organizational and professional cultures are unlikely to assist the negotiation process. Likewise, concerns about accountability of participants to their own organizations or to other constituents are unlikely to make it easy for individuals to make compromises. Often the only practical way forward is to get started on some action without fully agreeing on the aims. In the words of the manager of an urban regeneration partnership engaged in writing a bid for funding, the task for managers can be to

> find a way of stating the aims so that none of the parties can disagree.

Perspective 2: Sharing Power Is Important, But People Behave As If It's All in the Purse Strings

As with the previous perspective, the "pain" associated with issues of power is often raised by practitioners of collaboration. *Common wisdom* is that "the power is in the purse strings," which suggests that those who do not have control of the financial resource are automatically deprived of power. Viewed dispassionately, these perceptions quite often seem at odds with "reality" since most parties do, minimally, have at least the "power of exit." A manager in an automotive industry joint venture commented,

> The balance of power was seemingly with the U.K. company, who had a majority shareholding; but in reality it was with the U.S. company, who knew how closely the investment analysts were watching the joint venture. The threat of pulling out was always in the background.

However, the *common practice,* unsurprisingly, is that people act as though their perceptions are real and often display defensiveness and aggression.

Looking more closely at where power is actually used to influence the way in which collaborative activities are negotiated and carried out, it is possible to identify different *points of power.* Many of these occur at a micro level in the collaboration, and would often not be particularly obvious to those involved. One example of a point of power is the naming of the collaboration, since this is likely to influence what it does. Those who are involved in the naming process are therefore in a powerful position at that time. Other examples concern invitations to join a collaboration; those who choose whom to involve are obviously powerful, but those who choose the process of whom to involve are even more so.

Many points of power relate to communication media and processes. One set of examples concerns the arrangements for meetings. Clearly, any person taking the role of chair or facilitator in a meeting is in a position of power while the meeting is in place, but those who get to choose which facilitator to appoint are more subtly and perhaps more significantly powerful. Those who choose the location of a meeting may be in a powerful position, particularly in terms of determining whether it will be on the premises of one of the participants. Those who choose the timing of the meeting are also powerful. It is possible to identify many more points of power that typically are present during collaborative activities.

An important characteristic of points of power is that they are not static. In collaborative situations, power continually shifts. At the macro level, for example, in a pre–start-up phase those who get to draw up contracts, write bids for funding, or have direct access to a customer may be powerful. In a start-up phase, however, once money is available, those who are given the task of administering the collaboration may be highly powerful in determining many parameters concerned with direction and ways of working. It may be only at later stages that the actual members become active and have the chance to exert power.

Less obvious, but very significant, are the continuous shifts of power at a micro level during all phases. For example, network managers are often in powerful positions between meetings because they are the only people formally employed by the network—and hence the only people who have its agenda as their main concern. They may also have access to the network funds. During meetings, however, members can shift many of the points of power in significant ways, often determining new members, times, and locations of meetings as well as influencing agreements about action. Those less centrally involved, such as facilitators or consultants, can be in powerful positions for short periods of time. External influences, such as those from government, can sometimes be extremely powerful in a short-term way as they make demands for reports or responses to initiatives.

Managing Power in Practice

Issues concerned with control of purse strings are significant, but there are many other points at which power is, in practice, enacted in collaborative settings. All participants have power at one time or another and may frequently have the option to empower themselves. Understanding and exploring the points of power can enable assessment of where and when others are unwittingly or consciously exerting power, and where and when others may view them as exerting power. It also allows for consideration of how and when deliberately to exert power. Responding to these insights, however, requires a willingness to accept that manipulative behavior is appropriate, which some would argue is against the spirit of collaborative working. We will return to this point later.

Perspective 3: Trust is Necessary for Successful Collaboration, But We Are Suspicious of Each Other

Issues relating to trust are also commonly raised by participants. The *common wisdom* seems to be that trust is a precondition for successful collaboration. However, while the existence of trusting relationships between partners probably would be an ideal situation, the *common practice* appears to be that suspicion, rather than trust, is the starting point. Often participants do not have the luxury to choose their partners. Either imposed (e.g., government) policy dictates who the partners must be or, as expressed by the business development manager of the Far East operation of a major oil producer, the pragmatics of the situation dictate that partners are needed where trust is weak:

> You may have to jump into bed with someone you don't like in order to prevent a competitor coming into the market.

This suggests that it is appropriate to pay attention to trust *building* between partners.

One way of thinking about trust building is through the loop depicted in Figure 2. This argues that two factors are important in getting started in a trusting relationship. The first is concerned with the formation of expectations about the future of the collaboration; these will be based either on reputation or past behavior, or on more formal contracts and agreements. Given the earlier remarks about the difficulty of agreeing on aims in collaborative settings, this in itself is a nontrivial starting point. The second starting point involves risk taking. The argument is that partners need to trust each other *enough* to allow them to take a risk to initiate the collaboration. If both of these initiators are possible, then the loop argues that trust can gradually be built through starting with some modest but realistic aims that are likely to be successfully realized. This reinforces trusting attitudes between partners and provides a basis for more ambitious collaboration.

Managing Trust in Practice

The practical conclusion from the trust-building loop is very similar to that concerning the management of aims: Sometimes it is better to get started on some small but tangible action and then to allow trust to develop slowly. This incremental approach to trust building would obviously not be relevant if an immediate need to attain a major objective is paramount. In those situations, expectation forming and risk taking would have to be managed simultaneously and alongside other trust-building activities. However, in other situations building trust incrementally is, in principle, appealing. We shall return to it later.

Perspective 4: We Are Partnership-Fatigued and Tired of Being Pulled in All Directions

In this perspective it is not so much the common wisdom but the *taken for granted assumptions* that are to be challenged. One of the most surprising observations about collaborative situations is the frequency with which clarity about who the collaborators

FIGURE 2 | The Trust Building Loop

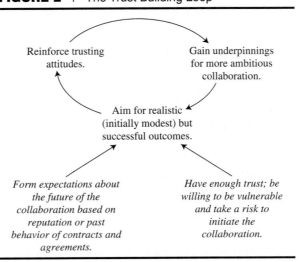

are is lacking. Different members often list different partners from each other, and staff who are very centrally involved in managing collaborations often cannot name partners without referring to formal documentation. Reasons for this include the different statuses or commitment that people or organizations have with regard to the network

> They were only involved to provide the financial support . . . (rather than as a proper member)

and ambiguity about whether people are involved as individuals or on behalf of their organizations:

> Members were invited to join because of their ethnic background, but the organizations they worked in (which were not specifically concerned with ethnicity issues) then became partners.

The lack of clarity about who partners are is often compounded by the complexity of collaborative arrangements in practice. The sheer scale of networking activities is one aspect of this. Many organizations are involved in multiple alliances. One major electronics manufacturer, for example, is said to be involved in around 400 strategic alliances. Clearly, even with the most coherent alliance management practices, no individual manager is likely to know which partner organizations are involved. Clearly also, multiple alliances must pull the organization in a variety of different directions. As one senior manager in a division of a multinational computer hardware manufacturer put it,

> We have separate alliances with two companies (worldwide operating system providers) that are in direct competition with each other . . . there is a lot of conflict within the company over these alliances . . . the people involved try to raise the importance of theirs.

The same issue arises in the public-sector context, with ever increasing numbers of partnerships and interagency initiatives appearing in localities. In this case, however, the problem that is most commonly voiced is "partnership fatigue," with individuals often regularly attending meetings of five or six collaborative schemes. More extreme cases occur in this sector too. For example, a manager from a community-based career guidance organization commented,

> When I heard of the person attending meetings of five partnerships, I thought "Is that all?!" . . . My organization is involved in 56 partnerships.

There are many other consequences of these multiple initiatives apart from fatigue. One is that some participants try to link agendas across the initiatives; but the links they see relate to the particular combinations of initiatives that they are involved in, which generally do not overlap precisely, if at all, with involvements of other members. Another is that it is hard for any individual to judge when another is inputting the views of their employing organization or bringing an agenda from another partnership.

In addition to the volume of relationships, there is frequently complexity in the networks of relationships between organizations. For example, the complexity of interacting supply chain networks—in which every supplier has multiple customers, every customer has multiple suppliers, and suppliers have suppliers and customers have customers—is potentially infinite. Many networks of collaborations are, in addition, hierarchical in the sense that collaborations are members of other collaborations. For example, a local government organization may be a member of a regeneration partnership but also a member of several community collaborations, which are in turn members of a community "umbrella group," which is in turn a member of the regeneration partnership. Similarly, joint ventures may be members of strategic alliances, trade associations may represent their members in policy networks, and so on.

Managing Ambiguity and Complexity in Practice

Clearly, it is hard for managers to agree on aims, build mutual understanding, and manage trust and power relationships with partners if they do not unambiguously know who their partners are. Equally, it is difficult to manage collaborative working in complex systems in which different elements must be affecting each other but there is little clarity on the nature of the interrelationships.

Diagramming techniques can help in mapping the structure of partnerships. Figure 3 provides two possible ways of doing this. Obviously this cannot remove the ambiguity and uncertainty completely, but it is generally enlightening at the point of construction and useful as a long-term reminder. As with the aims framework, this exercise can be done in more or less detail.

At a general level, learning how to identify, live with, and progress despite ambiguity and complexity is probably the key challenge of this perspective. A careful approach to nurturing relationships must be an essential aspect of this.

Perspective 5: Everything Keeps Changing

Collaborative structures are commonly talked about as though stability of membership can be *taken for granted,* at least for a tangible period. The ambiguity and complexity indicated in the previous section would be difficult enough for participants to cope with if that were the case. In practice, however, policy influences, which may be internal but are frequently imposed externally, often generate restructuring of member organizations. Mergers and demergers, new start-ups and closures, acquisitions and sell-offs, and restructurings are all commonplace. In turn, these imply a necessary restructuring of any collaboration in which they participated.

Equally, policy changes in the individual organizations or the collaboration affect the purpose of the collaboration. These may be generated internally—for example, as the result of a revision of strategic direction. Or they may be generated externally—for example, as a result of government policy or major market disturbances. Either way, this in turn implies a shift in the relevance of the collaboration to its members. New members may join and others may leave, and sometimes such changes are imposed:

> The problem isn't that their collaboration is not working, but that because of the new policy we are asking them to work differently, which means breaking up established successful and effective working relationships and building new ones.

FIGURE 3 | Example Diagramming Methods for Mapping the Complexity of Collaborative Structures

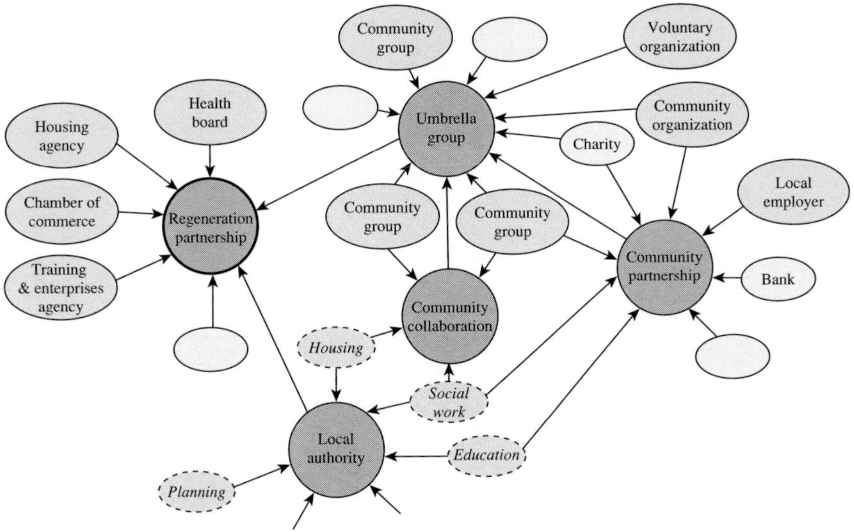

Hierarchies of collaboration.

Key:
Circles represent collaborations.
Arrows indicate members of collaborations.

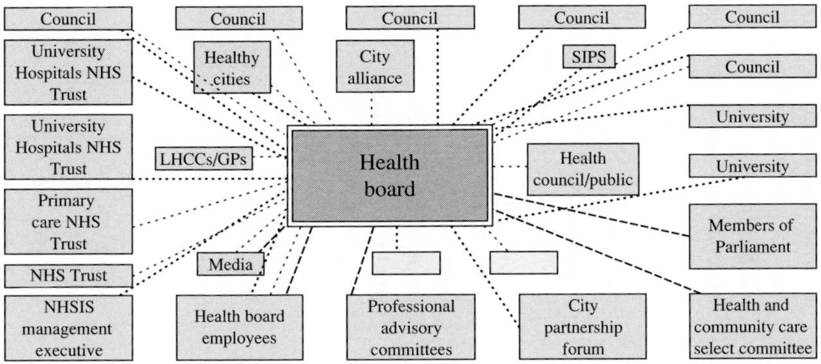

Mapping an organization's partnerships.

Key:
Center box represents the organization.
All other boxes represent parties with
which it has collaborative relationships.

Another source of dynamic change comes with individual movements. The manager of a company that was delivering a major service for an alliance partner, for example, commented that the relationship with the partner organization had been both helped and hindered because

> . . . the chief executive in the partner organization was, until recently, my boss in my own organization.

The relationships between individual participants in collaborations are often fundamental to getting things done. This makes collaborations highly sensitive to changes in individuals' employment, even if these are simply role changes within one of the participating organizations. Finally, even if all of these factors stood still there is often an inherent dynamic. If an initial collaborative purpose is achieved, there will usually be a need to move to new collaborative agendas, and these are likely to imply different membership requirements.

All organizations are dynamic to the extent that they will gradually transform. However, collaborations are sensitive to transformations in *each of* the partner organizations and therefore may change very quickly. In one example, a collaborative group with an ambiguous structure involving many partners went through three identifiable reincarnations over a three-year period and ended up as a very controlled partnership between two organizations. Its final stated purpose was related to, but definitely not the same as, the original one. It would be reasonable to argue that the final partnership was a different one from the original collaborative group, but it is possible to trace a clear lineage from one to the other.

Managing Collaborative Dynamics in Practice

One obvious conclusion that derives from recognition of the dynamic nature of collaborations is that the appealing trust-building loop (Figure 2) is inherently extremely fragile. Effort put into building mutual understanding and developing trust can be shattered, for example, by a change in the structure of a key organization or the job change of a key individual. A practical conclusion, therefore, for those who want to make collaboration work is that *the nurturing process must be continuous and permanent*. No sooner will gains be made than a disturbance, in the form of a change to one of the partners, will shatter many of them.

Perspective 6: Leadership Is Not Always in the Hands of Members

Given the inherent difficulties with collaborative forms that have been discussed so far, the issue of leadership seems highly relevant. Because traditional hierarchies do not exist in collaborative settings, it is appropriate to consider leadership in a general sense, rather than as specifically the realm of senior executives or prominent public figures. Here we consider leadership as being concerned with *the mechanisms that lead to the actual outcomes of a collaboration*. Put simply, we are concerned with what "*makes things happen*" in a collaboration. More formally, this concern is with the formation and implementation of the collaboration's policy and activity agenda.

Looked at from this perspective, leadership, interestingly, becomes something that is not enacted only by people. Structures and processes are as important in leading agendas as are the participants involved in the collaboration. Thus, for example, a structure in which only two organizations are involved in partnership should allow both organizations good access to the agenda, but clearly excludes others. To take an extreme contrast, a collaboration in which any organization that wants to be a member may send a representative allows wide access to the agenda in principle, but it can be difficult for any individual to have much influence in practice. Similarly, in the context of collaborative processes, a collaboration for which a major form of communication is through open meetings is going to allow a very different form of access to the agenda from one whose principal mode of communication is through e-mail and/or telephone. Thus agendas may be led by the type of structure that is in place and the type of processes used. Once again, this challenges a *taken for granted* presumption about the nature of leadership. Agendas can, of course, also be led by participants, though generally these are emergent, informal leaders rather than those who lead from a position of authority.

Structures, processes, and participants can be thought of as different *media* through which collaborative leadership is, in practice, enacted. An important point about these media is that all three are largely not controlled by *members* of the collaboration. Structures and processes are sometimes imposed externally—for example, by government, a corporate headquarters, or a funding body. Even if this is not the case, they often emerge out of previous action rather than being explicitly designed by members. Even in the context of "participants" as the leadership medium, leadership is not solely the role of *members* of the collaboration. External stakeholders such as customers or local public figures often strongly direct the territory of a partnership or alliance. A strong lead is often also given by support staff who are not strictly members. For example, the information manager of a retail property development alliance commented about his role in moving the alliance members toward agreement about action:

> I find that attrition helps . . . I am a stubborn old devil.

Managing Leadership Media

This perspective demonstrates the ease with which collaborations can move out of the control of their membership. Recognizing the at least partial inevitability of this and working around it is part of the practical response required. Diagramming techniques such as those in Figure 3 may be helpful in exploring the nature of the structure as a first step toward gaining an understanding of its leadership consequences.

For managers who wish to lead more actively, the implication appears to be that part of their activity must be concerned with the design of structures and processes that are effective for the particular purpose, and with monitoring their performance and evolution. We look further at active leadership in the final perspective.

Perspective 7: Leadership Activities Continually Meet with Dilemmas and Difficulties

Despite the strong contextual leadership derived from structures and processes, participants (whether or not they actually are members) do carry out *leadership activities* in order to move a collaboration forward in ways that they regard as beneficial. In carrying out these activities, they do affect the outcomes of collaborative initiatives. However, they are frequently thwarted by difficulties, so that the outcomes are not as they intend. For example, despite his war of attrition, the information manager quoted earlier was continuously thwarted in his attempts to create events in which key members of the partnering organizations would jointly consider their modes of thinking and working. Several dates set aside for group workshops were ultimately used for other kinds of meetings, as issues needing immediate attention emerged.

In practice, much of what is done by those who aim to take a lead in moving a collaboration forward may be said to be fundamentally *within the spirit of collaboration.* Activities of this sort are highly facilitative and are concerned with embracing, empowering, involving, and mobilizing members. However, the same people are also engaged in activities that, on the face of it, are much less collaborative. Many of them are adept at manipulating agendas and playing the politics. We have characterized these kinds of activities as being *toward collaborative thuggery* after the member of a city partnership who told us that a partnership that he was involved with had been successful:

> . . . because the convenor is a thug . . . if people are not pulling their weight he pushes them out.

He appeared to be arguing that this was a positive and effective mode of leadership.

Managing Leadership Activities

Does this, then, suggest a dilemma between the ideology of collaborative working and the pragmatism needed to get things done? Not necessarily. One way of thinking about this is to consider the nature of nurturing. Nurturing is often talked about in the context of the gentle care required for fragile plants. However, rather more decisive tactics have to be taken if the object is to nurture an overgrown garden back to health. Chopping down of excess growth and pulling up of weeds are likely to be key activities, in addition to the nurturing back to health of individual plants that have become overpowered by others. While it is not possible to produce hard evidence of this, those who lead more successfully seem to operate from both perspectives—the *spirit of collaboration* and *toward collaborative thuggery*—and to continually switch between them, often carrying out both types of leadership in the same act.

Realizing Collaborative Advantage

Our aim here has been to convey some of the complexity that underlies collaborative situations in a way that should seem real to those involved. Obviously the set of seven perspectives does not, in itself, provide any precise recipes for managerial action. It does, however, provide a dual basis for thoughtful action.

The first basis is through legitimizing the pain and addressing the isolation that people often feel when trapped in collaborative inertia:

> I have been working in a health education partnership . . . for about a year, and it is a relief and a reassurance to see that the "pain and grind" of partnership work exists in other partnerships, not just my situation.

Like this person, many managers are empowered simply by understanding that the problems they are experiencing are inevitable. This is partly because this awareness increases self-confidence, and partly because it immediately highlights the need to tackle the problem at a different level. Legitimizing a degree of manipulative and political activity through the notion of *collaborative thuggery* can also be helpful in this respect.

The second, and perhaps more significant, basis for action is through the conceptual handles that the perspectives provide. As presented here in summary, the combined picture gives a sense of the kinds of issues that have to be managed (a more detailed version of each perspective is available). Like the summary, the detailed perspectives do not provide a recipe for good practice, because to do so would be to oversimplify. Rather, they are intended to alert managers to challenges of collaborative situations that will need active attention and nurturing if problems of collaborative inertia are to be minimized. Each perspective provides a particular view on this, and can be used in isolation to stimulate thinking about that in particular. However, the issues raised by each perspective overlap with those raised by others, so the combination of perspectives always needs to be in the background, even if the focus at a particular time is a specific one. Many of the challenges are inherent, and there are often tensions between directly opposed possible ways of tackling them. This approach to practical support regards the action to be taken as a matter for managerial judgment. This includes making informed judgments about the resource that needs to be available to support the nurturing activities.

Don't Work Collaboratively Unless You Have to

One definite conclusion can, however, be drawn: Making collaboration work effectively is highly resource-consuming and often painful. The strongest piece of advice to managers (and policy makers) that derives from the discussed perspectives, therefore, is "don't do it unless you have to." Put rather more formally, the argument is that unless potential for real collaborative advantage is clear, it is generally best, *if there is a choice,* to avoid collaboration. It is worth noting, however, that collaborative advantage sometimes comes in nonobvious forms and may be concerned with the process of collaborating— for example, from the development of a relationship with a partner—rather than the actual output.

Selected Bibliography

This article draws on the *theory of collaborative advantage,* which we have developed gradually from extensive research with practitioners of collaboration over the last 15 years. The notions of collaborative advantage and collaborative inertia are central to this theory. *Collaborative advantage* was first used in this way in the early 1990s. See for example, C. Huxham and D. Macdonald, "Introducing Collaborative Advantage," *Management Decision* 30 (3) (1992), pp. 50–56. Rosabeth Moss Kanter used the term differently in her 1994 article "Collaborative Advantage: The Art of Alliances," *Harvard Business Review* 72 (4), pp. 96–108. *Collaborative inertia* was introduced in C. Huxham, "Advantage or Inertia: Making Collaboration Work," in R. Paton, G. Clark, G. Jones, and P. Quintas (eds.), *The New Management Reader* (London: Routledge, 1996), pp. 238–54.

Theory relating to the aims framework of perspective one can be found in C. Eden and C. Huxham, "The Negotiation of Purpose in Multi-Organizational Collaborative Groups," *Journal of Management Studies* 38 (3) (2001), pp. 351–69. A detailed discussion on the points of power in perspective two can be found in C. Huxham and N. Beech, "Points of Power in Interorganizational Forms: Learning from a Learning Network," *Best 10%, Proceedings of the Academy of Management Conference,* 2002. The development of the trust-building loop and its implication for the management of trust in perspective three is explored in S. Vangen and C. Huxham, "Nurturing Collaborative Relations: Building Trust in Interorganizational Collaboration," *Journal of Applied Behavioral Science* 39 (1) (2003), pp. 5–31. A detailed exposition of perspectives four and five can be found in C. Huxham and S. Vangen, "Ambiguity, Complexity, and Dynamics in the Membership of Collaboration," *Human Relations* 53 (6) (2000), pp. 771–806. For a detailed discussion on the conceptualization and enactment of leadership in perspectives six and seven see C. Huxham and S. Vangen, "Leadership in the Shaping and Implementation of Collaboration Agendas: How Things Happen in a (Not Quite) Joined Up World," *Academy of Management Journal (Special Forum on Managing in the New Millennium* 43 (6) (2000), pp. 1159–75; and S. Vangen and C. Huxham, "Enacting Leadership for Collaborative Advantage: Dilemmas of Ideology and Pragmatism in the Activities of Partnership Managers," *British Journal of Management* 14 (2003), pp. 61–74.

Reading 6.2

Taking steps toward "Getting to Yes" at Blue Cross and Blue Shield of Florida

Bridget Booth
Matt McCredie

Never before has there been a more opportune time for Blue Cross and Blue Shield of Florida, Inc., (BCBSF) to benefit from the concepts of principled negotiation outlined in the book *Getting to Yes*.

BCBSF is the industry leader in Florida, providing health benefit plans and health-related services. The company and its subsidiaries serve more than 6 million people. However, maintaining a market leadership position is difficult in light of the many challenges facing today's health care marketplace.

Factors such as rising health care costs, increased competition, consumerism, and shifting demographics have caused the company to search for new and different ways of doing business as customers' health care needs expand. Inherent in these new and different business models is the need for more collaborative business practices, such as those outlined in *Getting to Yes*.

Different Times Call for Different Approaches

Today's health care marketplace is becoming increasingly consumer driven. Consumers expect the same level of service and convenience from health organizations that they receive from other companies, such as online retailers, banks, and investment firms. The Institute of the Future predicts that by the end of 2010, the health market will be an innovative economy demanding nontraditional offerings such as wellness, food, cosmetics, fashion, health information, and even biosecurity.[1] Developing alliances with other organizations is one way the company is positioning itself for the health industry of the future. BCBSF's Alliance Group, a small department formed in 2001, enables business areas to develop strategic relationships with other entities.

Capitalizing on business opportunities through alliances enables BCBSF and other companies to pursue the risks and rewards of mutually compatible goals that would be difficult to achieve alone. Alliances include outsourcing partnerships, joint operating agreements, and joint ventures. These alliances provide the companies with access to new markets, capabilities, knowledge, and capital, along with the ability to share development and acquisition costs. Alliances also enable each party to bring products to market quickly in a cost-effective manner, which is critical in today's health care industry.

BCBSF's Alliance Group is experiencing positive outcomes by applying concepts outlined in *Getting to Yes* and is helping to move the organization more toward the management concepts of principled negotiation. Historically, however, businesses have not formally practiced or rewarded employees for these types of behaviors. For example, contract negotiations between companies often focus on each individual organization

Source: From *Academy of Management Executive* 18, no. 3 (2004), pp. 109–12.

championing its own positions without considering the other's interests. Rewards are often linked to how well an organization's position is defended or "won" without giving thought to what bigger solutions could emerge by focusing on mutual gains.

To expand beyond this type of traditional mind-set, BCBSF is seeking out ways to indoctrinate the concepts of principled negotiation throughout the entire organization. Principled negotiation, according to *Getting to Yes,* involves looking at issues based on their merits rather than defending steadfast positions. Its goal is to meet the underlying concerns of the parties. Shifting behavior away from a contest of wills toward this type of collaborative mind-set can be challenging. To help make the transition, BCBSF is emphasizing three major steps: top-level executive support; a disciplined, programmed approach to alliance management; and reinforcement of desired behaviors and related outcomes.

BCBSF is further embracing the concepts of principled negotiation by working with Vantage Partners, a consulting firm that partners with leading companies to institutionalize the capability to negotiate, build, and manage critical relationships effectively. Initially, BCBSF was seeking external perspectives for establishing superior alliance management capabilities. As part of that process, the company was introduced to mutual-gains behavior as a necessary component of developing successful alliances and other collaborative relationships. Vantage, founded by *Getting to Yes* coauthor Roger Fisher, helps its clients incorporate concepts from the book into their daily management practices. BCBSF has been working with Vantage Partners for approximately two years and has experienced increased trust and alignment with business associates as a result of implementing *Getting to Yes* concepts.

Putting the Concepts into Practice

On a daily basis, BCBSF is learning firsthand about the benefits of applying principled negotiation concepts in its alliances, as well as the pitfalls of what happens when the concepts are not applied consistently.

The company's movement toward applying *Getting to Yes* concepts is illustrated by the formation and management of a strategic alliance with a key competitor. Availity, LLC, a joint venture between subsidiaries of BCBSF and Humana, Inc., was conceived out of a desire to lower health costs, improve efficiencies, and provide more timely service to physicians and hospitals. Humana is one of the nation's leading publicly traded health benefits companies, with approximately 7 million medical members in 19 states and Puerto Rico. The company offers coordinated health insurance coverage and related services to employer groups, government-sponsored plans, and individuals. Both Humana and BCBSF were trying to reach the same goal of improving the manner in which hospitals and physicians conducted business with their organizations.

The resulting joint venture, Availity, is an Internet-based solution that streamlines administrative workflow and improves communication between physicians, hospitals, payers, and pharmacies. Through a secure Web site, physicians can submit requests for payments, check the status of payments for services, verify patients' coverage and eligibility, and receive authorizations for referrals and other medical services online. This streamlined process replaces time-consuming manual interactions such as phone calls and paperwork.

Currently, there are more than 9,000 physician offices, 208 hospitals, and more than 27,000 physicians in Florida using the Availity platform to process routine transactions.

The challenges of managing a joint venture with a key competitor could be daunting, if not impossible, without a shift in behavior by both parties to think of the other as a partner. Adding to the complexity are the organizations' differing corporate cultures, due in part to their structures: Humana is a for-profit publicly traded company, while BCBSF is a private, not-for-profit policyholder-owned mutual company. In addition, Humana serves a national market, while BCBSF primarily serves Florida. The change in mind-set to be collaborative versus competitive in the development of this solution was critical to the formation and ongoing success of the joint venture.

Separating the People from the Problem

Although BCBSF had not yet institutionalized *Getting to Yes* concepts during the early formation of Availity, the company became more deliberate in following the concepts after the alliance was operational and the organization became more aware of the benefits of principled negotiation. Looking back, despite a lack of formal training in *Getting to Yes* concepts, the company unconsciously implemented some of the concepts during the formation of Availity, which helped greatly in building the alliance.

As outlined in the book, separating the people from the problem requires emphasizing relationships by dealing directly with perceptions. BCBSF looked for ways to demonstrate its desire to collaborate by coming to the table with a sincere intent to build a relationship and determine common interests. Although it was not formally stated that the concepts of principled negotiation would be followed, the negotiators realized that forming a successful joint venture would require a collaborative approach. Both parties approached initial discussions in an open manner by listening rather than trying to debate or persuade. The two parties invested substantial amounts of time at the executive level to build the relationship. As the book says, prevention works best—and building this type of personal relationship "cushioned the people on each side against the knocks of negotiation." A strong relationship at the senior level continues to benefit the alliance today through subsequent governance activities.

Once Availity was established and operational, BCBSF began to interact with Availity as a business associate. This new relationship benefited from additional collaborative negotiation skills.

A significant challenge in implementing the concept of separating the people from the problem was the complex nature of the multiple relationships inherent in the Availity alliance. On the surface, it seemed as though only one relationship existed: the two initial owners. A closer look revealed several different relationships between BCBSF and Availity, ranging from BCBSF having an ownership interest in Availity, to BCBSF being the largest customer of Availity, to BCBSF being a vendor for Availity for technical development. Similarly, Humana has multiple relationships with Availity.

Many of the people involved in the formation had multiple accountabilities reflecting different aspects of the relationship. These multiple relationships and their corresponding accountabilities made it difficult to understand a person's perspective on a given issue. By mapping out the different relationships and corresponding accountabilities, ambiguity was reduced and problem solving improved. The exercise helped the parties understand the various perspectives and clarified accountabilities. Mapping out accountabilities in alliances is an approach that BCBSF is adopting, which is starting to result in more favorable outcomes in learning to separate people from problems. In addition, when individuals have several roles, the organization is learning the value of having those individuals clearly communicate which role they are representing.

Focus on Interests, Not Positions

During initial discussions, Humana and BCBSF laid the groundwork to understand each other and see the situation from the other's perspective. General discussions about how each party viewed the industry, the future of health care, opportunities for collaboration, and anticipated future challenges helped both parties to identify and understand the other's interests regarding electronic connectivity. At later stages—for example, during the testing phase—this exercise served as a strong foundation in helping the parties to separate people from problems because there was an understanding of the other's viewpoints.

One challenge in focusing on interests rather than positions had to do with the two organizations having different approaches to testing the various capabilities of Availity. One party was accustomed to using a prescribed methodology for testing the various capabilities. The other, being a new organization, had processes that were still under development. The "positions" had to do with which organization's testing procedures to follow, but the underlying interests for both parties were identical: for Availity to be up and running error-free.

After holding a number of brainstorming sessions, it became evident that the parties could combine components of their methodologies to create a joint solution. By focusing on interests rather than positions, the parties realized that testing did not have to follow a certain methodology; it just had to result in error-free operations. By shifting the focus to interests rather than the positions, a new solution involving leveraging existing resources in a more effective manner was designed. A joint testing approach was agreed upon to meet mutual interests, and the parties were able to learn from each other in creating the solution.

Inventing Options for Mutual Gain

Getting to Yes says, "Skill at inventing options can be one of your most useful assets." This was especially evident in the formation of Availity. Before Availity was conceived, Humana and BCBSF came together and identified their interests regarding electronic connectivity. Both parties wanted to improve relationships with hospitals and physicians, reduce health care industry costs for consumers, and improve workflow for hospitals, physicians, and payers. The solution resulted in the joint venture that became Availity, which mutually benefited both organizations.

To assure that options for mutual gain were being sought throughout the development of Availity, relationship manager responsibilities were assigned to individuals to keep the best interests of the alliance in the forefront. Each party had someone who functioned in this capacity, which helped with the overall success of the alliance. Relationship manager roles are now included in many of BCBSF's alliances to serve as objective arbitrators between the parties and to look for options for mutual gain.

Additional Lessons Learned

BCBSF has learned a number of lessons about how to develop collaborative and productive alliance relationships.

In general, the company's experience has been that applying the concepts from *Getting to Yes* came more naturally at the executive/strategic level and required much more deliberation at subsequent levels. When alliance parties moved away from the conceptual level and into daily operations, implementing *Getting to Yes* concepts became more challenging. There are several reasons for this, including the experience levels of those involved, challenges with establishing strategic alignment throughout all levels, and varying reward systems at different levels of the organization. Among the steps that BCBSF is taking to address these challenges are establishing alliance specialists at the middle management level, and providing training regarding principled negotiation concepts at all levels of the organization.

Many of the lessons learned involve setting clear expectations in the beginning of the alliance formation. One is the importance of being deliberate in establishing ground rules for interacting with others early in the relationship before negotiation begins. Agreed-upon methods for communicating, making decisions, and handling conflicts, although somewhat awkward to create, are critical in relationship building and can help the parties to separate people from problems, especially when conflicts arise and emotions are high.

Along the same lines, a documented business plan that defines the market opportunity, product or service, sales and promotion approach, as well as validates financial forecasts, can prove beneficial. The business plan is not only an effective tool for guiding the alliance; it also clarifies the interests and expectations of the parties.

In addition to a business plan, the alliance parties have found benefits in clearly defined strategies with supporting organizational goals. In addition, the company is establishing metrics that measure not only the business results of alliances but the quality and strength of the relationships as well.

Establishing early on what each party will contribute in terms of capital, resources, and revenue is also a lesson that the company has learned in forming successful alliances. Without this foundation, the parties may have differing viewpoints of what the other is contributing, which often lead to misunderstanding and can prevent the alliance from progressing smoothly.

Perhaps the biggest reward for implementing the concepts from *Getting to Yes* is being able to see firsthand the benefits—meeting business goals, spending less time defending positions, creating a less stressful business environment, and meeting the underlying interests of both parties. The concepts have helped the company discover new ways of doing business—opening a new world of possibilities never imagined before.

Endnote

1. *The Emerging Health Economy: A Special Report,* SR-787 B 2003. Menlo Park, CA: Institute for the Future.

Taking the Stress Out of Stressful Conversations
Holly Weeks

We all get caught in conversations fraught with emotion. Usually, these interactions end badly—but they don't have to, thanks to a handful of techniques you can apply unilaterally.

We live by talking. That's just the kind of animal we are. We chatter and tattle and gossip and jest. But sometimes—more often than we'd like—we have stressful conversations, those sensitive exchange that can hurt or haunt us in ways no other kind of talking does. Stressful conversations are unavoidable in life, and in business they can run the gamut from firing a subordinate to, curiously enough, receiving praise. But whatever the context, stressful conversations differ from other conversations because of the emotional loads they carry. These conversations call up embarrassment, confusion, anxiety, anger, pain, or fear—if not in us, then in our counterparts. Indeed, stressful conversations cause such anxiety that most people simply avoid them. This strategy is not necessarily wrong. One of the first rules of engagement, after all, is to pick your battles. Yet sometimes it can be extremely costly to dodge issues, appease difficult people, and smooth over antagonisms because the fact is that avoidance usually makes a problem or relationship worse.

Since stressful conversations are so common—and so painful—why don't we work harder to improve them? The reason is precisely because our feelings are so enmeshed. When we are not emotionally entangled in an issue, we know that conflict is normal, that it can be resolved—or at least managed. But when feelings get stirred up, most of us are thrown off balance. Like a quarterback who chokes in a tight play, we lose all hope of ever making it to the goal line.

For the past 20 years, I have been teaching classes and conducting workshops at some of the top corporations and universities in the United States on how to communicate during stressful conversations. With classrooms as my laboratory, I have learned that most people feel incapable of talking through sensitive issues. It's as though all our skills go out the window and we can't think usefully about what's happening or what we could do to get good results.

Stressful conversations, though, need not be this way. I have seen that managers can improve difficult conversations unilaterally if they approach them with greater self-awareness, rehearse them in advance, and apply just three proven communication techniques. Don't misunderstand me: There will never be a cookie-cutter approach to stressful conversations. There are too many variables and too much tension, and the interactions between people in difficult situations are always unique. Yet nearly every stressful conversation can be seen as an amalgam of a limited number of basic conversations, each with its own distinct set of problems. In the following pages, we'll explore how you can anticipate and handle those problems. But first, let's look at the three basic stressful conversations that we bump up against most often in the workplace.

Source: From *Harvard Business Review*, July–August 2001, pp. 113–19.

"I Have Bad News for You"

Delivering unpleasant news is usually difficult for both parties. The speaker is often tense, and the listener is apprehensive about where the conversation is headed. Consider David, the director of a nonprofit institution. He was in the uncomfortable position of needing to talk with an ambitious researcher, Jeremy, who had a much higher opinion of his job performance than others in the organization did. The complication for David was that, in the past, Jeremy had received artificially high evaluations. There were several reasons for this. One had to do with the organization's culture: The nonprofit was not a confrontational kind of place. Additionally, Jeremy had tremendous confidence in both his own abilities and the quality of his academic background. Together with his defensive response to even the mildest criticism, this confidence led others—including David—to let slide discussions of weaknesses that were interfering with Jeremy's ability to deliver high-quality work. Jeremy had a cutting sense of humor, for instance, which had offended people inside and outside his unit. No one had ever said anything to him directly, but as time passed, more and more people were reluctant to work with him. Given that Jeremy had received almost no concrete criticism over the years, his biting style was now entrenched and the staff was restive.

In conversations like this, the main challenge is to get off to the right start. If the exchange starts off reasonably well, the rest of it has a good chance of going well. But if the opening goes badly, it threatens to bleed forward into the rest of the conversation. In an effort to be gentle, many people start these conversations on a light note. And that was just what David did, opening with, "How about those Red Sox?"

Naturally Jeremy got the wrong idea about where David was heading; he remained his usual cocky, superior self. Sensing this, David felt he had to take off the velvet gloves. The conversation quickly became brutally honest, and David did almost all the talking. When the monologue was over, Jeremy stared icily at the floor. He got up in stiff silence and left. David was relieved. From his point of view, the interaction had been painful but swift. There was not too much blood on the floor, he observed wryly. But two days later, Jeremy handed in his resignation, taking a lot of institutional memory—and talent—with him.

"What's Going On Here?"

Often we have stressful conversations thrust upon us. Indeed, some of the worst conversations—especially for people who are conflict averse—are the altogether unexpected ones that break out like crackling summer storms. Suddenly the conversation becomes intensely charged emotionally, and electricity flies in all directions. What's worse, nothing makes sense. We seem to have been drawn into a black cloud of twisted logic and altered sensibilities.

Consider the case of Elizabeth and Rafael. They were team leaders working together on a project for a major consulting firm. It seemed that everything that could have gone wrong on the project had, and the work was badly bogged down. The two consultants were meeting to revise their schedule, given the delays, and to divide up the discouraging tasks for the week ahead. As they talked, Elizabeth wrote and erased on the white board. When she had finished, she looked at Rafael and said matter-of-factly, "Is that it, then?"

Rafael clenched his teeth in frustration. "If you say so," he sniped.

Elizabeth recoiled. She instantly replayed the exchange in her mind but couldn't figure out what had provoked Rafael. His reaction seemed completely disconnected from her comment. The most common reaction of someone in Elizabeth's place is to guiltily defend herself by denying Rafael's unspoken accusation. But Elizabeth was uneasy with confrontation, so she tried appeasement. "Rafael," she stammered, "I'm sorry. Is something wrong?"

"Who put you in charge?" he retorted. "Who told you to assign work to me?"

Clearly, Rafael and Elizabeth have just happened into a difficult conversation. Some transgression has occurred, but Elizabeth doesn't know exactly what it is. She feels blindsided—her attempt to expedite the task at hand has clearly been misconstrued. Rafael feels he's been put in a position of inferiority by what he sees as Elizabeth's controlling behavior. Inexplicably, there seem to be more than two people taking part in this conversation, and the invisible parties are creating lots of static. What childhood experience, we may wonder, is causing Elizabeth to assume that Rafael's tension is automatically her fault? And who is influencing Rafael's perception that Elizabeth is taking over? Could it be his father? His wife? It's impossible to tell. At the same time, it's hard for us to escape the feeling that Rafael is overreacting when he challenges Elizabeth about her alleged need to take control.

Elizabeth felt Rafael's resentment like a wave and she apologized again. "Sorry. How do you want the work divided?" Deferring to Rafael in this way smoothed the strained atmosphere for the time being. But it set a precedent for unequal status that neither Elizabeth nor the company believed was correct. Worse, though Rafael and Elizabeth remained on the same team after their painful exchange, Elizabeth chafed under the status change and three months later transferred out of the project.

"You Are Attacking Me!"

Now let's turn our attention to aggressively stressful conversations, those in which people use all kinds of psychological and rhetorical mechanisms to throw their counterparts off balance, to undermine their positions, even to expose and belittle them. These "thwarting tactics" take many forms—profanity, manipulation, shouting—and not everyone is triggered or stumped by the same ones. The red zone is not the thwarting tactic alone but the pairing of the thwarting tactic with individual vulnerability.

Consider Nick and Karen, two senior managers working at the same level in an IT firm. Karen was leading a presentation to a client, and the information was weak and disorganized. She and the team had not been able to answer even basic questions. The client had been patient, then quiet, then clearly exasperated. When the presentation really started to fall apart, the client put the team on the spot with questions that made them look increasingly inadequate.

On this particular day, Nick was not part of the presenting team; he was simply observing. He was as surprised as the client at Karen's poor performance. After the client left, he asked Karen what happened. She lashed out at him defensively: "You're not my boss, so don't start patronizing me. You always undercut me no matter what I do." Karen continued to shout at Nick, her antagonism palpable. Each time he spoke, she interrupted him with accusations and threats: "I can't wait to see how you like it when people leave you flailing in the wind." Nick tried to remain reasonable, but Karen didn't wind down. "Karen," he said, "pull yourself together. You are twisting every word I say."

Here Nick's problem is not that Karen is using a panoply of thwarting tactics, but that all her tactics—accusation, distortion, and digression—are aggressive. This raises the stakes considerably. Most of us are vulnerable to aggressive tactics because we don't know whether, or how far, the aggression will escalate. Nick wanted to avoid Karen's aggression, but his insistence on rationality in the face of emotionalism was not working. His cool approach was trumped by Karen's aggressive one. As a result, Nick found himself trapped in the snare of Karen's choosing. In particular, her threats that she would pay him back with the client rattled him. He couldn't tell whether she was just huffing or meant it. He finally turned to the managing director, who grew frustrated, and later angry, at Nick and Karen for their inability to resolve their problems. In the end, their lack of skill in handling their difficult conversations cost them dearly. Both were passed over for promotion after the company pinned the loss of the client directly on their persistent failure to communicate.

Preparing for a Stressful Conversation

So how can we prepare for these three basic stressful conversations before they occur? A good start is to become aware of your own weaknesses to people and situations. David, Elizabeth, and Nick were unable to control their counterparts, but their stressful conversations would have gone much better if they had been more usefully aware of their vulnerabilities. It is important for those who are vulnerable to hostility, for example, to know how they react to it. Do they withdraw or escalate—do they clam up or retaliate? While one reaction is not better than the other, knowing how you react in a stressful situation will teach you a lot about your vulnerabilities, and it can help you master stressful situations.

Recall Nick's problem. If he had been more self-aware, he would have known that he acts stubbornly rational in the face of aggressive outbursts such as Karen's. Nick's choice of a disengaged demeanor gave Karen control over the conversation, but he didn't have to allow Karen—or anyone else—to exploit his vulnerability. In moments of calm self-scrutiny, when he's not entangled in a live stressful conversation, Nick can take time to reflect on his inability to tolerate irrational aggressive outbursts. This self-awareness would free him to prepare himself—not for Karen's unexpected accusations but for his own predictable vulnerability to any sudden assault like hers.

Though it might sound like it, building awareness is not about endless self-analysis. Much of it simply involves making our tacit knowledge about ourselves more explicit. We all know from past experience, for instance, what kinds of conversations and people we handle badly. When you find yourself in a difficult conversation, ask yourself whether this is one of those situations and whether it involves one of those people. For instance, do you bare your teeth when faced with an overbearing competitor? Do you shut down when you feel excluded? Once you know what your danger zones are, you can anticipate your vulnerability and improve your response.

Explicit self-awareness will often help save you from engaging in a conversation in a way that panders to your feelings rather than one that serves your needs. Think back to David, the boss of the nonprofit institution, and Jeremy, his cocky subordinate. Given Jeremy's history, David's conversational game plan—easing in, then when that didn't work, the painful-but-quick bombshell—was doomed. A better approach would have been for David to split the conversation into two parts. In a first meeting, he could have raised the central issues of Jeremy's biting humor and disappointing performance. A second meeting could have been set up for the discussion itself. Handling the situation incrementally would have allowed time for both David and Jeremy to prepare for a two-way conversation instead of one of them delivering a monologue. After all, this wasn't an emergency; David didn't have to exhaust this topic immediately. Indeed, if David had been more self-aware, he might have recognized that the approach he chose was dictated less by Jeremy's character than by his own distaste for conflict.

An excellent way to anticipate specific problems that you may encounter in a stressful conversation is to rehearse with a neutral friend. Pick someone who doesn't have the same communication problems as you. Ideally, the friend should be a good listener, honest but nonjudgmental. Start with content. Just tell your friend what you want to say to your counterpart without worrying about tone or phrasing. Be vicious, be timid, be sarcastically witty, jump around in your argument, but get it out. Now go over it again and think about what you would say if the situation weren't emotionally loaded. Your friend can help you because he or she is not in a flush of emotion over the situation. Write down what you come up with together because if you don't, you'll forget it later.

Now fine-tune the phrasing. When you imagine talking to the counterpart, your phrasing tends to be highly charged—and you can think of only one way to say anything. But when your friend says, "Tell me how you want to say this," an interesting thing happens: Your phrasing is often much better, much more temperate, usable. Remember, you can say what you want to say, you just can't say it *like that*. Also, work on your body language with your friend. You'll both soon be laughing because of the expressions that sneak out unawares—eyebrows skittering up and down, legs wrapped around each other like licorice twists, nervous snickers that will certainly be misinterpreted. (For more on preparing for stressful conversations, see the sidebar "The DNA of Conversation Management.")

Managing the Conversation

While it is important to build awareness and to practice before a stressful conversation, these steps are not enough. Let's look at what you can do as the conversation unfolds. Consider Elizabeth, the team leader whose colleague claimed she was usurping control. She couldn't think well on her feet in confrontational situations, and she knew it, so she needed a few hip-pocket phrases—phrases she could recall on the spot so that she wouldn't have to be silent or invent something on the spur of the moment. Though such a solution sounds simple, most of us don't have a tool kit of conversational tactics ready at hand. Rectifying this gap is an essential part of learning how to handle stressful conversations better. We need to learn communication skills in the same way that we learn CPR: well in advance, knowing that when we need to use them, the situation will be critical and tense. Here are three proven conversational gambits. The particular wording may not suit your style, and that's fine. The important thing is to understand how the techniques work, and then choose phrasing that is comfortable for you.

The DNA of Conversation Management

The techniques I have identified for handling stressful conversations all have tucked within them three deceptively simple ingredients that are needed to make stressful conversations succeed. These are clarity, neutrality, and temperance, and they are the building blocks of all good communication. Mastering them will multiply your chances of responding well to even the most strained conversation. Let's take a look at each of the components in turn.

Clarity means letting words do the work for us. Avoid euphemisms or talking in circles—tell people clearly what you mean: "Emily, from your family's point of view, the Somerset Valley Nursing Home would be the best placement for your father. His benefits don't cover it." Unfortunately, delivering clear content when the news is bad is particularly hard to do. Under strained circumstances, we all tend to shy away from clarity because we equate it with brutality. Instead, we often say things like "Well, Dan, we're still not sure yet what's going to happen with this job, but in the future we'll keep our eyes open." This is a roundabout—and terribly misleading—way to inform someone that he didn't get the promotion he was seeking. Yet there's nothing inherently brutal about honesty. It is not the content but the delivery of the news that makes it brutal or humane. Ask a surgeon; ask a priest; ask a cop. If a message is given skillfully—even though the news is bad—the content may still be tolerable. When a senior executive, for example, directly tells a subordinate that "the promotion has gone to someone else," the news is likely to be highly unpleasant, and the appropriate reaction is sadness, anger, and anxiety. But if the content is clear, the listener can better begin to process the information. Indeed, bringing clarity to the content eases the burden for the counterpart rather than increases it.

Tone is the nonverbal part of delivery in stressful conversations. It is intonation, facial expressions, conscious and unconscious body language. Although it's hard to have a neutral tone when overcome by strong feelings, *neutrality* is the desired norm in crisis communications, including stressful conversations. Consider the classic neutrality of NASA. Regardless of how dire the message, NASA communicates its content in uninflected tones: "Houston, we have a problem." It takes practice to acquire such neutrality. But a neutral tone is the best place to start when a conversation turns stressful.

Temperate phrasing is the final element in this triumvirate of skills. English is a huge language, and there are lots of different ways to say what you need to say. Some of these phrases are temperate, while others baldly provoke your counterpart to dismiss your words—and your content. In the United States, for example, some of the most intemperate phrasing revolves around threats of litigation: "If you don't get a check to me by April 23, I'll be forced to call my lawyer." Phrases like this turn up the heat in all conversations, particularly in strained ones. But remember, we're not in stressful conversations to score points or to create enemies. The goal is to advance the conversation, to hear and be heard accurately, and to have a functional exchange between two people. So next time you want to snap at someone—"Stop interrupting me!"—try this: "Can you hold on a minute? I want to finish before I lose my train of thought." Temperate phrasing will help you take the strain out of a stressful conversation.

The Gap between Communication and Intent

One of the most common occurrences in stressful conversations is that we all start relying far too much on our intentions. As the mercury in the emotional thermometer rises, we presume that other people automatically understand what we mean. We assume, for instance, that people know we mean well. Indeed, research shows that in stressful conversations, most speakers assume that the listener believes that they have good intentions, regardless of what they say. Intentions can never be that powerful in communications—and certainly not in stressful conversations.

To see what I mean, just think of the last time someone told you not to take something the wrong way. This may well have been uttered quite sincerely by the speaker; nevertheless, most people automatically react by stiffening inwardly, anticipating something at least mildly offensive or antagonistic. And that is exactly the reaction that phrase is always going to get. Because the simplest rule about stressful conversations is that people don't register intention despite words; we register intention through words. In stressful conversations in particular, the emphasis is on what is actually said, not on what we intend or feel. This doesn't mean that participants in stressful conversations don't have feelings or intentions that are valid and valuable. They do. But when we talk about people in stressful communication, we're talking about communication between people—and not about intentions.

Of course, in difficult conversations we may all wish that we didn't have to be so explicit. We may want the other person to realize what we mean even if we don't spell it out. But that leads to the wrong division of labor—with the listener interpreting rather than the speaker communicating. In all conversations, but especially in stressful ones, we are all responsible for getting across to one another precisely what we want to say. In the end, it's far more dignified for an executive to come right out and tell an employee, "Corey, I've arranged a desk for you—and six weeks of outplacement service—because you won't be with us after the end of July." Forcing someone to guess your intentions only prolongs the agony of the inevitable.

Honor thy partner.   When David gave negative feedback to Jeremy, it would have been refreshing if he had begun with an admission of regret and some responsibility for his contribution to their shared problem. "Jeremy," he might have said, "the quality of your work has been undercut—in part by the reluctance of your colleagues to risk the edge of your humor by talking problems through with you. I share responsibility for this because I have been reluctant to speak openly about these difficulties with you, whom I like and respect and with whom I have worked a long time." Acknowledging responsibility as a technique—particularly as an opening—can be effective because it immediately focuses attention, but without provocation, on the difficult things the speaker needs to say and the listener needs to hear.

Is this always a good technique in a difficult conversation? No, because there is never any one good technique. But in this case, it effectively sets the tone for David's discussion with Jeremy. It honors the problems, it honors Jeremy, it honors their relationship, and it honors David's responsibility. Any technique that communicates honor in a stressful conversation—particularly a conversation that will take the counterpart by surprise—is to be highly valued. Indeed, the ability to act with dignity can make or break a stressful conversation. More important, while Jeremy has left the company, he can still do harm by spreading gossip and using his insider's knowledge against the organization. The more intolerable the conversation with David has been, the more Jeremy is likely to make the organization pay.

Disarm by restating your intentions.   Part of the difficulty in Rafael and Elizabeth's "What's Going On Here?" conversation is that Rafael's misinterpretation of Elizabeth's words and actions seems to be influenced by instant replays of other stressful conversations that he has had in the past. Elizabeth doesn't want to psychoanalyze Rafael; indeed, exploring Rafael's internal landscape would exacerbate this painful situation. So what can Elizabeth do to defuse the situation unilaterally?

Elizabeth needs a technique that doesn't require her to understand the underlying reasons for Rafael's strong reaction but helps her handle the situation effectively. "I can see how you took what I said the way you did, Rafael. That wasn't what I meant. Let's go over this list again" I call this the clarification technique, and it's a highly disarming one. Using it, Elizabeth can unilaterally change the confrontation into a point of agreement. Instead of arguing with Rafael about his perceptions, she grants him his perceptions—after all, they're his. Instead of arguing about her intentions, she keeps the responsibility for aligning her words with her intentions on her side. And she goes back into the conversation right where they left off. (For a fuller discussion of the disconnect between what we mean and what we say, see the sidebar "The Gap between Communication and Intent.")

This technique will work for Elizabeth regardless of Rafael's motive. If Rafael innocently misunderstood what she was saying, she isn't fighting him. She accepts his take on what she said and did and corrects it. If his motive is hostile, Elizabeth doesn't concur just to appease him. She accepts and retries. No one loses face. No one scores points off the other. No one gets drawn off on a tangent.

Fight tactics, not people.   Rafael may have baffled Elizabeth, but Karen was acting with outright malice toward Nick when she flew off the handle after a disastrous meeting with the client. Nick certainly can't prevent her from using the thwarting tactics with which she has been so successful in the past. But he can separate Karen's character from her behavior. For instance, it's much more useful for him to think of Karen's reactions as thwarting tactics rather than as personal characteristics. If he thinks of Karen as a distorting, hostile, threatening person, where does that lead? What can anyone ever do about another person's character? But if Nick sees Karen's behavior as a series of tactics that she is using with him because they have worked for her in the past, he can think about using countering techniques to neutralize them.

The best way to neutralize a tactic is to name it. It's much harder to use a tactic once it is openly identified. If Nick, for instance, had said, "Karen, we've worked together pretty well for a long time. I don't know how to talk about what went wrong in the meeting when your take on what happened, and what's going on now, is so different from mine," he would have changed the game completely. He neither would have attacked Karen nor remained the pawn of her tactics. But he would have made Karen's tactics in the conversation the dominant problem.

Openly identifying a tactic, particularly an aggressive one, is disarming for another reason. Often we think of an aggressive counterpart as persistently, even endlessly, contentious, but that isn't true. People have definite levels of aggression that they're comfortable with—and they are reluctant to raise the bar. When Nick doesn't acknowledge Karen's tactics, she can use them unwittingly, or allegedly so. But if Nick speaks of them, it would require more aggression on Karen's part to continue using the same tactics. If she is at or near her aggression threshold, she won't continue because that would make her uncomfortable. Nick may not be able to stop Karen, but she may stop herself.

People think stressful conversations are inevitable. And they are. But that doesn't mean they have to have bad resolutions. Consider a client of mine, Jacqueline, the only woman on the board of an engineering company. She was sensitive to slighting remarks about women in business, and she found one board member deliberately insensitive. He repeatedly ribbed her about being a feminist and, on this occasion, he was telling a sexist joke.

This wasn't the first time that something like this had happened, and Jacqueline felt the usual internal cacophony of reactions. But because she was aware that this was a stressful situation for her, Jacqueline was prepared. First, she let the joke hang in the air for a minute and then went back to the issue they had been discussing. When Richard didn't let it go but escalated with a new poke—"Come on, Jackie, it was a *joke*"—Jacqueline stood her ground. "Richard," she said, "this kind of humor is frivolous to you, but it makes me feel pushed aside." Jacqueline didn't need to say more. If Richard had continued to escalate, he would have lost face. In fact, he backed down: "Well, I wouldn't want my wife to hear about my bad behavior a second time," he snickered. Jacqueline was silent. She had made her point; there was no need to embarrass him.

Stressful conversations are never easy, but we can all fare better if, like Jacqueline, we prepare for them by developing greater awareness of our vulnerabilities and better techniques for handling ourselves. The advice and tools described in this article can be helpful in unilaterally reducing the strain in stressful conversations. All you have to do is try them. If one technique doesn't work, try an other. Find phrasing that feels natural. But keep practicing—you'll find what works best for you.

Reading 6.4

Renegotiating Existing Agreements: How to Deal with "Life Struggling against Form"

Jeswald W. Salacuse

Renegotiation of existing agreements is constant in all areas of life. In this article, the author examines the nature and causes of renegotiation and offers guidance to persons involved in the renegotiation process. He identifies three distinct types of renegotiations—postdeal, intradeal, and extradeal renegotiation. Each of the three types poses particular problems and opportunities, and each requires different techniques to deal with those problems and opportunities.

Despite lengthy discussions, skilled drafting, and strict enforcement mechanisms, parties to solemnly signed and sealed agreements often find themselves returning to the bargaining table later on to "renegotiate" them. Thus a key challenge in negotiating any agreement is not just "getting to yes" but also staying there.

The renegotiation of existing agreements is a constant in all areas of life. Economic recessions or significant changes in prices invariably lead to restructurings and workouts of thousands of business arrangements made in better times. Companies facing financial crises sometimes try to find a solution to their problems by renegotiating their labor contracts. In the international arena, the world has witnessed the renegotiation of mineral and petroleum agreements of the 1960s and 1970s, often in the face of threatened host country nationalizations and expropriations; the loan reschedulings of the 1980s following the debt crisis in developing countries; and the restructuring of project and financial agreements as a result of the Asian financial crisis of the late 1990s. In 2001 the American government launched a major foreign policy initiative by asking Russia to renegotiate the Anti-Ballistic Missile Treaty so the United States could develop a missile defense system. Later this same year, the terrorist attacks in New York and Washington on September 11 inaugurated a new era of insecurity that has prompted the review and renegotiation of existing agreements in many domains.

Through renegotiation, business executives, lawyers, and government officials continually seem to be seeking either to alleviate a bargain that has become onerous or to hold onto a good deal that the other side wants to change. The examples are so numerous that renegotiating existing agreements seems as basic to human relations as is negotiating new agreements. Seventy years ago, Karl Llewellyn, a noted American legal scholar, captured the tension between negotiated agreements and subsequent reality in the conclusion of his thoughtful inquiry into the role of contract in the social order: "One turns from the contemplation of the work of contract as from the experience of Greek tragedy. Life struggling against form . . ." (Llewellyn 1931: 751). Renegotiation

Source: From *Negotiation Journal* 17, no. 4 (October 2001), pp. 311–31. Blackwell Publishers, Ltd.

is one of the most important theaters in which parties to existing agreements play out the continuing struggle of life against form.

The purpose of this article is to examine the phenomenon of renegotiation, to explore its nature and causes, and to offer advice on how best to conduct the renegotiation process.

The Three Types of Renegotiation

Discussions of renegotiation apply the term to three fundamentally different situations, each of which presents different problems that require different solutions. The three situations are postdeal renegotiations, intradeal renegotiations, and extradeal renegotiations.

Postdeal renegotiation takes place at the expiration of a contract when the two sides, though legally free to go their own way, nonetheless try to renew their formal relationship. For example, consider the case of a power company that has built an electrical generating station and entered into a 20-year contract to supply electricity to a state public utility. At the end of 20 years, when local law considers their legal relationship at an end, the power company and the public utility begin discussions on a second long-term electricity supply contract, thereby renegotiating their original relationship. While this second negotiation process—a postdeal renegotiation—may at first glance seem to resemble the negotiation of their original contract, it also has some notable differences that influence renegotiation strategies, tactics, and outcomes.

Intradeal renegotiation occurs when the agreement itself provides that, at specified times or as the result of specified events occuring during the term of the contract, the parties may renegotiate or review certain of its provisions. For example, the just-mentioned electricity supply contract might include a provision calling for the renegotiation of the agreement's pricing terms in the event of dramatic changes in fuel costs, which could occur over a 20-year period. Here renegotiation is anticipated as a legitimate activity in which both parties, while still bound to each other in a valid contract, are to engage in good faith. It is an intradeal renegotiation because it takes places within the legal framework established for the original transaction.

The most difficult, stressful, and emotional renegotiations are those undertaken in apparent violation of the contract or at least in the absence of a specific clause authorizing a renegotiation. These negotiations take place extradeal, for they occur outside the framework of the existing agreement. The negotiations to reschedule loans following the Third World debt crisis of the early 1980s, the effort by the American government to renegotiate the ABM Treaty with the Russians, and attempts by companies to secure changes in existing union contracts all fit within the category of extradeal renegotiations. In each case, one of the participants is seeking relief from a legally binding obligation without any basis for renegotiation in the agreement itself.

Renegotiation has thus become a constant and ever-present fact of contemporary life, whether it is postdeal, intradeal, or extradeal. Renegotiation can be distinguished from initial negotiations by three factors that significantly affect the renegotiation process itself. They are *increased mutual knowledge, increased transactional understanding,* and *increased mutual linkage.* First, as a result of working together during their first agreement, the parties know much more about each other than when they negotiated that first agreement. Second, many of the questions that they had about their contemplated transaction during the initial negotiation have now been answered. And third, as a result of their investments in the transaction during the first agreement, it may now be more costly to abandon renegotiations than it was to have walked away from the initial negotiations.

In each type of renegotiation, different relationships and process dynamics are taking place among the parties. These dynamics lead to possible strategies and tactics that are worthy of consideration by thoughtful negotiators. Let's examine the processes at work in the three kinds of renegotiation.

Postdeal Renegotiations

Although a postdeal renegotiation takes place when the original transaction has reached or is approaching its end, several factors distinguish it from a negotiation in first instance—factors that may also significantly affect the renegotiation process. First, by virtue of law, custom, or express or implied contractual commitments, the parties may have a legal obligation to negotiate in good faith with one another despite the fact that their original contract has terminated; consequently, their ability to refuse to engage in postdeal renegotiations may be limited. The existence and precise nature of such a duty will depend on the law governing the contract.

Anglo-American law traditionally has recognized a broad, unrestrained freedom of negotiation that permits a party to begin or end negotiation at any time for any reason (Farnsworth 1987: 220–21). The rationale for this rule is that a limitation on the freedom to negotiate might discourage persons from undertaking transactions in the first place. By contrast, the law in certain other countries is less liberal, holding that once the parties have commenced negotiations, they may have an obligation to negotiate in good faith (Litvinoff 1997: 1659–62).

But even in common-law countries, the parties may have an obligation to renegotiate an agreement in good faith at its end because of an express provision in the original contract; the prevailing practices and customs of the business concerned; or the conduct of the parties toward one another during the life of their agreement. In contrast, parties seeking to negotiate a transaction in first instance have no such obligation and can abandon negotiations at any time.

The precise content of the obligation to renegotiate in good faith an existing negotiated agreement varies from country to country. It may include a duty not to negotiate with a third person until postdeal negotiations with a party in the original transaction have failed. Or it may also require a party not to terminate renegotiations without reasonable cause and without having persevered for a reasonable length of time (Farnsworth 1987: 269–85). Failure by either side to fulfill its obligations to renegotiate in good faith may result in liability in damages.

Even if the applicable law imposes no legal obligation to renegotiate in good faith, the original contract, as well as current economic factors, may constrain the postdeal renegotiation process in ways not present in the original negotiations. For example, the 20-year electricity supply contract mentioned earlier might provide that, if the power company and the public utility fail to negotiate a second 20-year supply contract, the public utility company will be obligated to purchase the project company's electrical generating station according to a pricing formula specified in the original agreement.

Beyond the legal and contractual constraints, the parties' increased mutual knowledge, increased transactional understanding, and increased mutual linkage will significantly influence the course of negotiations. For example, in renegotiating the electricity supply agreement, the power company's approach will be more cautious and reluctant if the history of the first contact was plagued by late and contested payments than if the public utility had always paid on time and in full. Similarly, if over the first 20 years the price of power under the contract had proven to be much higher than competing forms of energy, the public utility would seek changes in the pricing formula during the renegotiation. Finally, the fact that the power company organized itself and trained its employees to provide electricity over the long term to a single specific purchaser will probably mean that, all other things being equal, the power company would prefer to enter into a new contract with the utility rather than to make an agreement with another purchaser, a course of action entailing significant new risks and costs. Then too, the public utility, having come to rely on the power company for a major portion of its electrical supply, may wish to avoid the costs of finding another supplier or creating its own electrical generating capacity.

In any negotiation, a party's actions at the negotiating table are influenced by its evaluation of available alternatives to the deal it is trying to negotiate. Rational negotiators will not ordinarily agree to a transaction that is inferior to their best alternative to a negotiated agreement, or BATNA (Fisher, Ury, and Patton 1991: 99–102). In a postdeal renegotiation, each party's evaluation of its BATNA will be heavily influenced by knowledge of the other side obtained during the first agreement, its understanding of the transaction gained during that time, and the extent of the investment that it has made in the relationship.

In general, the success of postdeal renegotiations will depend on the nature of the relationship that developed between the parties during the original contract. If that relationship was strong and productive, the atmosphere at the renegotiation bargaining table will be that of two partners trying to solve a common problem. However, if the relationship was weak and troubled during the term of the initial agreement, the prevailing mood will be that of two cautious adversaries who know each other only too well.

These factors give rise to three general principles that negotiators should consider as they structure and conduct the process of postdeal renegotiations.

1. *Provide for postdeal renegotiations in the original contract.*   In transactions in which the desirability or likelihood of postdeal renegotiations is high, the parties should specify in their original agreement the process and rules that they will follow in conducting a postdeal renegotiation. For example, among other similar provisions, the contract should specify such matters as how soon before the end of the contract term renegotiations are to begin; how long the renegotiations are to continue before either party may legally abandon them; where the renegotiations are to take place; and the nature of the information that each side is to provide the other. Recognizing that postdeal renegotiations may become problematic, the contract might also authorize the use of mediators or other third-party helpers in the process.

2.   *Individually and jointly review the history of the relationship during the original contract.*   As part of its preparation, each party to a postdeal renegotiation should review, carefully and thoroughly, the experience of working with the other side during the first contract. An understanding of the problems encountered during that period will enable each side to shape proposals to remedy them during a contemplated second agreement. To make that review an opportunity for creative problem solving rather than mutual acrimony over past mistakes, the parties should structure a joint review of past experience, perhaps with the help of a neutral facilitator, at the beginning of the postdeal renegotiation process. For example, as a first step in the renegotiation process, the power company and the public utility might give a review team consisting of executives from each side the task of preparing a mutually acceptable history of their relationship. Inevitably, during the course of postdeal renegotiations, each side will refer to past events. The renegotiation process will proceed more smoothly and efficiently if, at the beginning of the process, the parties have a common understanding of their history together than if they engage in a continuing debate throughout the renegotiation about the existence and significance of past events.

3.   *Understand thoroughly the alternatives to a renegotiated deal.*   Negotiators should not only evaluate their own alternatives to the deal that they are trying to make, but they should also try to estimate their counterparts' alternatives. In a postdeal renegotiation, these two tasks are often complicated by the fact that the parties may have conducted their activities in such a way during the first contract that few realistic alternatives to a second contract seem possible. For example, the power company that owns a generating facility may feel that it has few other options than to enter into a second contract with the state public utility. Or the public utility company, in time of energy shortage, may see no realistic alternatives to making a second electricity power purchase agreement with the project company. Rather than accept the inevitability of a second contract, each side, long before the termination of the first contract, should carefully examine all options and seek to develop possible new alternatives before entering into postdeal renegotiations with the other side. For example, the state public utility, perhaps several years in advance of the end of the first contract, should contact other potential project companies to determine their interest in developing electrical generation plants.

Intradeal Renegotiations

Contractual stability is a goal sought by all sides in any negotiation. Parties to a contract obviously need the assurance that the terms of their agreement will be respected in the future. At the same time, most parties know that unforeseen events may arise during a contract term that drastically change the balance of benefits originally contemplated by their agreement. Consequently, a fundamental challenge in contracting practice is to achieve contractual stability but, at the same time, allow the parties to deal with changing circumstances in the future. The traditional approach to resolving this dilemma is for the parties during their original negotiation to attempt to anticipate all possible contingencies and to provide solutions for them in their agreement. This approach rejects the idea of intradeal renegotiation.

Another solution to the problem of balancing the imperatives of stability and change is for the contract itself to authorize the parties to renegotiate key elements of their relationship, should specified events or circumstances occur. In view of the impossibility of predicting all possible future contingencies, the inclusion in the agreement of some type of intradeal renegotiation clause would appear to be a useful device to give needed flexibility to long-term agreements. In fact, however, Western organizations rarely use them.

The traditional reluctance to use renegotiation clauses stems from a variety of factors, both legal and practical. First is the concern among lawyers that renegotiation clauses are merely "agreements to agree" and therefore may be unenforceable (Carter 1999: 188). On the other hand, although English common law has tended to dismiss agreements to negotiate as unenforceable, the contemporary approach in most American courts is to enforce agreements to negotiate in good faith. According to one recent case from a U.S. federal district court, "the critical inquiry in evaluating the enforceability of an express or implied agreement to negotiate in good faith is whether the standard against which the parties' good-faith negotiations are to be measured is sufficiently certain to comport with the applicable body of contract law" (*Howtek, Inc. v. Relisys et al.* [1999]). It would seem that a specific renegotiation clause in an existing contract with definite terms as to how the parties are to conduct the renegotiation process would easily meet this standard of enforceability. The required certainty would be further satisfied by specifying the precise events that give rise to the obligation to renegotiate and by specifically providing for the timing, locale, and conditions of the renegotiation process, among others.

Practical considerations have also led Western executives to view renegotiation clauses with suspicion on grounds that they increase uncertainty and risk in transactions and offend Western concepts of the "sanctity" of contract. Their presence in a contract also creates a risk that one of the parties will use a renegotiation clause as a lever to force changes in provisions that, strictly speaking, are not open to revision. The challenge of drafting these provisions and the heightened risks to contractual stability by renegotiation clauses that have yet to be tested in the courts are additional factors that have deterred their use in long-term contracts.

Despite these potential pitfalls, the inclusion of a renegotiation clause may actually contribute to transactional stability in certain situations. First, in cases in which significant changes in circumstances may result in severe unexpected financial hardship, a renegotiation clause may permit the parties to avoid default, with the attendant risk of litigation and extradeal renegotiations. During the original negotiations, it may be wiser for the parties to recognize the risk of changed circumstances and create within the contract a process to deal with them rather than to try to predict all eventualities and then be subject to the uncertain decisions of courts when those predictions prove to be flawed.

A second situation in which a renegotiation clause may be helpful occurs in cases in which the parties, by virtue of their differing cultures, understand and perceive the basis of their transaction in fundamentally different ways. For example, Western notions of business transactions as being founded upon law and contract often clash with Asian conceptions of business arrangements as based on personal relationships (Salacuse 1998: 225–27). In some Asian nations, executives often consider the essence of a business deal to be the relationship between the parties, rather than the written contract, which in their view can only describe that relationship imperfectly and incompletely. They may also assume that any long-term business relationship includes an implicit, fundamental principle: In times of change, parties in a business relationship should decide together how to cope with that change and adjust their relationship accordingly.

However, the Western party may view the long-term business transaction as set in the concrete of a lengthy and detailed contract without the possibility of modification. This sharply contrasts with the Asian side viewing the transaction as floating on the parties' fluid personal relationships, which always have within them an implicit commitment to renegotiate the terms of the transaction in the event of unforeseen happenings.

In long-term transactions, such as joint venture projects between Asian and Western companies whose success depends on close and continuing cooperation, it may be wise to recognize this difference of view at the outset of negotiations and attempt to find some middle ground. A renegotiation clause may represent such middle ground between total contractual rigidity on the one hand and complete relational flexibility on the other. It recognizes the possibility of redoing the deal, but controls the renegotiation process. An intradeal renegotiation clause, then, may give stability to an arrangement whose long-term nature creates a high risk of instability.

The use of renegotiation clauses in long-term agreements seems to be on the increase in recent years (Carter 1999: 189). A variety of intradeal renegotiation clauses exist to cope with the challenge of balancing contractual stability with adaptation to change. The following are some of the principal types.

1. *The implicit minor renegotiation clause.*   Despite some lawyers' claims to the contrary, contracts in long-term arrangements, no matter how detailed, are not a kind of comprehensive instruction booklet that the parties follow blindly. At best, such agreements are *frameworks* within which the participants constantly adjust their relationship. Karl Llewellyn (1931: 736–37) underscored this point many years ago when he wrote,

> . . . the major importance of a legal contract is to provide a framework for well-nigh every type of group organization and for well-nigh every type of passing or permanent relation between individuals and groups, up to and including states—a framework highly adjustable, a framework which almost never accurately indicates real working relations, but which affords a rough indication around which such relations vary, an occasional guide in cases of doubt, and a norm of final appeal when the relations cease in fact to work.

Executives responsible for implementing long-term transactions have consistently confirmed Llewellyn's observation in similar terms: "Once the contract is signed, we put it in the drawer. After that, what matters most is the relationship between us and our partner, and we are negotiating that relationship all the time." What this view means in practice is that certain matters in the agreement, usually but not always of a minor nature, are subject to renegotiation by the parties as part of their ongoing relationship, despite the fact that their contract contains no specific renegotiation clause (Kolo and Walde 2000: 45).

One can therefore argue that an "implicit minor renegotiation clause" is part of any transaction agreement. For example, if a long-term supply agreement provides that the supplier make deliveries in a country on June 30 of each year, but the government of the country later declares a national holiday on that date, making it difficult for the public utility to accept delivery, the parties would renegotiate a more appropriate time for delivery.

2. Review clauses.   Long-term contracts, particularly in the oil and mineral industries, sometimes commit the parties to meet at specific times to review the operation of their agreement. For example, one mining agreement provided that the parties were to meet together every seven years "with a view to considering in good faith whether this agreement is continuing to operate fairly . . . and with a view further to discussing in good faith any problems arising from the practical operation of this agreement" (Peter 1995: 79). Although the words *negotiation* or *renegotiation* appear nowhere in this clause, one reasonable interpretation of the provision is that it carries an implicit obligation for the parties to resolve problems through good faith negotiation.

3. Automatic adjustment clauses.   Transaction agreements often contain certain terms, such as those concerning prices or interest rates, subject to automatic change by reference to specified indexes, such as a cost-of-living index or the London Interbank Offered Rate (LIBOR). For example, the electricity supply contract might link the price to be paid for the electricity by the public utility to variations in fuel costs or the local cost-of-living index. While the aim of such a provision is to provide for flexibility without the risks inherent in renegotiation, negotiation may still be necessary to apply the index in unanticipated situations or in the event that the index itself disappears or becomes inappropriate (Kolo and Walde 2000: 44).

4. Open-term provisions.   Because of the difficulties and risks inherent in trying to negotiate arrangements to take place far in the future, some transaction agreements specifically provide that certain matters will be negotiated at a later time, perhaps years after the contract has been signed and the transaction implemented. For example, a foreign investor seeking approval for a factory from a host government might agree to negotiate appropriate senior management training schemes after it has constructed the facility and begun to hire local managers. This type of provision might be called an *open-term* clause because the matter in question has been left open for negotiation at a later time (Farnsworth 1987: 250).

In a strict sense, of course, the subsequent negotiation of an open term is not really a renegotiation of anything, since the parties have not yet agreed on any elements of that provision. In a broader sense, however, the negotiation of an open term at a later time will have the effect of modifying the overall relationship among the parties. Moreover, it is not inconceivable that one or more of the parties could use the opportunity of negotiating the open term as an occasion to seek concessions or changes in other terms through the common negotiating device of linking issues. For example, the foreign investor might offer the host government a particularly attractive management training program if the government would agree to certain desired regulatory changes.

5. *Formal renegotiation clauses.* In an effort to balance the imperatives of contractual stability with flexibility, long-term agreements sometimes contain formal wording that obligates the parties to renegotiate specified terms affected by changes in circumstances or unforeseen developments, such as those concerning construction costs, governmental regulations, or commodity prices. For example, an oil exploration contract between the government of Qatar and a foreign oil company provided that the two sides would negotiate future arrangements for the use of natural gas not associated with oil discoveries if commercial quantities of such "nonassociated" gas were later found in the contract area (Carver and Hossain 1990: 311). In addition, renegotiation clauses in investment contracts often accompany stabilization clauses by which a host country promises that any changes in laws or regulations will not adversely affect the foreign investment project. The effect of the two clauses is to obligate the host government and the project company to enter into negotiations to restore the financial equilibrium that such new laws and regulations may have destroyed.

An intradeal renegotiation clause obligates the parties only to negotiate, not to agree. If the two sides have negotiated in good faith but fail to agree, that failure cannot justify liability on the part of one of the parties. In order to bring finality to the process of intradeal renegotiation, long-term agreements sometimes include a *contract adaptation clause,* which stipulates that when certain specified events occur, the parties will first seek to negotiate a solution and, failing that, refer their problem to a third party for either a recommendation or a binding decision, depending on the desire of the parties to the contract. Certain institutions, such as the International Chamber of Commerce, have developed rules and facilities to help carry out the contract adaptation process.

Extradeal Renegotiation

In an extradeal renegotiation, one party is insisting on renegotiating terms of a valid contract that contains no express provision authorizing renegotiation. Unlike negotiations for the original transaction, which are generally fueled by both sides' hopes for future benefits, extradeal negotiations usually begin with both parties' shattered expectations. One side has failed to achieve the benefits expected from the transaction, and the other is being asked to give up something for which it bargained hard and which it hoped to enjoy for a long time. And whereas both parties to the negotiation of a proposed new venture participate willingly, if not eagerly, one party always participates reluctantly, if not downright unwillingly, in an extradeal renegotiation.

Beyond mere disappointed expectations, extradeal renegotiations, by their very nature, can create bad feeling and mistrust. One side believes it is being asked to give up something to which it has a legal and moral right. It views the other side as having gone back on its word, as having acted in bad faith by reneging on the deal. Indeed, the reluctant party may even feel that it is being coerced into participating in extradeal renegotiations since a refusal to do so would result in losing the investment it has already made in the transaction.

In most cases, it is very difficult for the parties to see extradeal renegotiations as anything more than a process in which one side wins and the other side loses. While the negotiation of any transaction initially is usually about the degree to which each side will share in expected benefits, an extradeal renegotiation is often about allocating a loss. At the same time, because the parties are bound together in a legal and economic relationhip, it is usually much more difficult for one or both of them to walk away from a troubled transaction than it is for two unconnected parties to a proposed agreement in the first instance.

In most countries, the law does not oblige a party to enter into renegotiations, no matter how much conditions have changed or how heavy the costs incurred by the other side since the contract was originally made (Carter 1999: 185).[1] In general, a party being asked to renegotiate an existing agreement has a legal right to refuse to renegotiate and to insist on performance in accordance with the letter of the contract. On the other hand, requests—or in some cases, demands—for renegotiation of an existing agreement are often accompanied by express or implied threats, including governmental intervention, expropriation, a slowdown in performance, or the complete repudiation or cancellation of the contract itself.

Parties facing a demand for renegotiation usually have an available legal remedy to enforce their existing contract and will often threaten to go to court to assert it. However, a willingness to pursue a legal remedy to its conclusion, rather than renegotiate, will usually depend on the party's evaluation of that remedy in relation to the results it expects from renegotiation. To the extent that the net benefits (i.e., benefits minus costs) from renegotiation exceed the expected net benefits from litigation, a rational party will ordinarily engage in the requested renegotiation. But if either before or during the renegotiation, a party decides that the net benefits to be derived from litigation will exceed the net benefits to be gained in renegotiation, that party will normally pursue its legal remedies.

On its side, the party asking for renegotiation will be making its own cost–benefit analysis of the relative merits of contract repudiation and its probable fate in litigation. As long as this party believes that the net benefits of repudiating the contract are less than the net benefits of respecting it, the contractual relationship will continue. But when (for whatever reason) it judges the respective net benefits to be the opposite, the result will be a demand for renegotiation with the threat of eventual repudiation in the background. Figure 1 seeks to capture this dynamic.

A party's reluctance to agree to an extradeal renegotiation may be due to the impact of renegotiation not only on the contract in question but on other contracts and relationships as well. Renegotiation of a transaction with one particular party may set an undesirable precedent for other renegotiations with other parties. For example, concessions

FIGURE 1 | Assessing the Effects of Changing Circumstances

Events	increase / decrease	Agreement benefits		
Net benefits of no contract	<	Net benefits of contract	=	Acceptance
Net benefits of no contact	>	Net benefits of contract	=	Rejection

by a union to one employer may lead another employer to seek equal treatment by demanding extradeal renegotiations of its own labor agreements.

Although the causes of extradeal renegotiations in individual cases are numerous, they generally fall into one of two basic categories: (1) the parties' imperfect contract with respect to their underlying transaction; and (2) changed circumstances after they have signed their agreement.

1. *The parties' imperfect contract.*   The goal of any written contract is to express the full meaning of the parties' agreement concerning their proposed transaction. Despite lawyers' belief in their abilities to capture that agreement in lengthy and detailed contracts, in practice a written contract, particularly in long-term arrangements, can achieve that goal only imperfectly, largely for three reasons. First, the parties to long-term agreements are inherently incapable of predicting all of the events and conditions that may affect their transactions in the future because that would require perfect foresight. Second, the transaction costs of making contracts limit the resources that the parties are able to devote to the contracting process and thus further restrict the ability of the parties to make a contract that perfectly reflects their understanding (Talley 1999: 1206; Tracht 1999: 623–24). Third, even if the parties had the requisite foresight and resources to draft a perfect contract, they have no assurance that a court will interpret their contract exactly as they intended.

Adding even more complexity to the problem of accurately negotiating and articulating the parties' intent in a long-term international transaction are the parties' differing cultures, business practices, ideologies, political systems, and laws—factors that often impede a true common understanding and inhibit the development of a working relationship (Salacuse 1991).

2. *Changed circumstances.*   Changes in circumstances since the time of the original contract are a second major cause for postdeal renegotiations. A sudden fall in commodity prices, the outbreak of civil war, a terrorist attack, the development of a new technology, or the imposition of currency controls are examples of changes in circumstance that often force the parties back to the negotiating table. As Raymond Vernon argued over three decades ago with respect to foreign investment projects, a bargain once struck will inevitably become obsolete for one of the parties and issues once agreed upon will be reopened at a later time. Long-term agreements, in Vernon's words, are "obsolescing bargains" (Vernon 1971: 46).

Generally speaking, changes in circumstances can either increase or decrease the costs and benefits of the agreement to the parties. As Figure 1 shows, when a change in circumstances means that the cost of respecting a contract for one of the parties is greater than the cost of abandoning it, the result is usually rejection of the deal or a demand for its renegotiation. The notions of *costs* and *benefits* are not limited to purely economic calculations. Political and social costs and benefits must also be accounted for. For example, in one case involving an investment project to build a luxury resort near the Giza Pyramids in Egypt, the Egyptian government originally signed the agreement because it believed the economic benefits of the project to exceed its potential costs. But when public and international opposition became strong and persistent, the government canceled the project because it judged the political costs to outweigh the economic benefits to be derived from its construction.

Since the risk of extradeal renegotiation is always present in any agreement, negotiators should ask themselves two basic questions:

- How can the likelihood of extradeal renegotiations be reduced?
- When renegotiations actually occur, how should the parties conduct them to make the process as productive and fair as possible?

In answering these questions, negotiators need to distinguish actions they should take before and after the transaction has broken down and one party is demanding renegotiation or threatening to reject the deal entirely. Some renegotiation principles to follow before deal breakdown include the following.

1. *Recognize that a signed contract does not necessarily create a relationship.* For a long-term transaction to be stable and productive for both sides, it must be founded on a relationship, a complex set of interactions characterized by cooperation and trust. A relationship also implies a connection between the parties. It is the existence of a solid relationship between the parties to a transaction that allows them to face unforeseen circumstances and hardships in a productive and creative manner.

A contract, no matter how detailed and lengthy, does not create a business relationship. Just as a map is not a country, but only an imperfect description thereof, a contract is not a business relationship, but only an imperfect sketch of what the relationship should be. A contract may be a necessary condition for certain kinds of relationships, but it is usually not a sufficient condition.

While negotiators must be concerned about the adequacy of contractual provisions, they should also seek to determine that a solid foundation for a relationship is in place. Accordingly, a negotiator should also ask a variety of noncontractual questions during the negotiating process: How well do the parties know one another? What mechanisms are in place to foster communications between the two sides after the contract is signed? To what extent are there genuine links and connections between the parties to the agreement? Is the deal balanced and advantageous for both sides?

Regardless of culture, in most countries whenever one party fails to respect its contractual obligations to another party, the existence of a valuable relationship between the parties is more likely to facilitate a negotiated resolution of their dispute than if no such relationship exists. The reason for this phenomenon is that the aggrieved party views the relationship with the offending party as more valuable than the individual claim arising out of the failure to honor the contractual provision. Thus in a workout, a bank is often willing to renegotiate a loan with a delinquent debtor company or country when the bank considers that the prospect of future business with the debtor is likely. Bondholders of the same debtor, on the other hand, will generally be more resistant to renegotiation than banks since bondholders generally do not have the same opportunity for a profitable business relationship in the future.

2. *Building a relationship takes time, so don't rush initial negotiations.*   Negotiators who are concerned to lay the foundation for a relationship as well as to conclude a contract know that sufficient time is required to achieve this goal. While speed of negotiation may appeal to Americans as "efficient" and a recognition of the fact that "time is money," for other cultures a quick negotiation of a complicated transaction may imply overreaching by one of the parties, insufficient consideration of the public interest, or even corruption.

A negotiation done in haste invites renegotiation later on. For example, in one case that attracted significant media attention in the mid-1990s, the fact that Enron, a major American energy company, negotiated a memorandum of understanding with the Maharashtra state government in India to build a $2 billion power plant after just three days of discussions during Enron's first visit to the Indian state made the subsequent power purchase agreement vulnerable to challenges from many quarters. Ultimately, the two sides were only able to resolve their conflict through a lengthy extradeal renegotiation that changed important terms in the 20-year contract by which Enron's project was to sell electricity to the Maharashtra State public utility (Salacuse 2001: 1342–57).

3. *Provide for intradeal renegotiations in appropriate transactions.*   If the risk of change and uncertainty is constant in long-term agreements, how should deal makers cope with it? The traditional method is to write detailed contracts that seek to foresee all possible eventualities. Most modern contracts deny the possibility of change. They therefore rarely provide for adjustments to meet changing circumstances. This assumption of contractual stability has proven false time and time again.

As suggested earlier, rather than viewing a long-term transaction as frozen in the detailed provisions of a lengthy contract, it may be more realistic to think of a long-term agreement as a *continuing negotiation* between the parties as they seek to adjust their relationship to the rapidly changing environment in which they must work together. Accordingly, the parties should consider providing in their contract that, at specified times or on the happening of specified events, they will renegotiate or at least review certain of the contract's provisions.

In this approach, the parties deal with the problem of renegotiation before, rather than after, they sign their contract. Both sides recognize at the outset that the risk of changed circumstances is high in any long-term relationship and that at sometime in the future either side may seek to renegotiate or adjust the contract accordingly. Rather than dismiss the possibility of renegotiation and then be forced to review the entire contract at a later time in an atmosphere of hostility between the partners, it may be better to recognize the possibility of renegotiation at the outset and set down a clear framework to conduct the process.

4. *Consider a role for mediation or conciliation in the deal.*   A third party can often help the two sides with their negotiations and renegotiations. Third parties, whether called mediators, conciliators, or advisers, can assist in building and preserving business relations and in resolving disputes without resorting to litigation. Consequently, negotiators should consider the possibility of building into their transactions a role for some form of mediation. For example, the contract might provide that before either party can resort to litigation to settle a dispute, they must use the services of a mediator or conciliator for a specific period of time in an attempt to negotiate a settlement of their conflict.

* * * *

When one side has demanded renegotiation of the basic contract governing their relationship, how should one or both of the parties proceed? Following are some renegotiation principles after a deal has broken down.

1. *Resist the temptation to make belligerent or moralistic responses to a demand for renegotiation, but seek to understand the basis of the demand.*   A party facing a demand for extradeal renegotiations often counters it with hostile, belligerent, or moralistic objections. Such responses are hardly ever effective in persuading the other side to end its insistence on renegotiation since that party has already determined that its own vital interests require repudiation or renegotiation of the agreement. Normally, it is only by dealing with those interests that the two sides in a renegotiation can resolve the conflict. Moreover, the party asking for renegotiation almost always asserts equally moralistic arguments to justify its own demands: The contract is exploitative, the negotiators were corrupt, one side used duress, the other side was ignorant of all the underlying factors, or the basic circumstances of the deal have changed in a fundamental way.

While respect for agreements is indeed a norm in virtually all societies (and may even rise to the level of a universal principle of law), most cultures also provide relief, in varying degrees, from the binding force of a contract in a variety of circumstances. "A deal is a deal" (*pacta sunt servanda*) is certainly an expression of a fundamental rule of human relations, but so is the statement "things have changed" (*rebus sic stantibus*). While a request for extradeal renegotiations may provoke bad feelings in one party, an outright refusal to renegotiate may also create ill will on the other side, which will see it as an attempt to impose an unjust bargain.

One may also argue that in many transactions (particularly between parties from different cultures) there are, in effect, two agreements: the legal contract, which sets out enforceable rights and duties, and the parties' "foundation relationship," which reflects their fundamental understanding in all its dimensions, legal and nonlegal. An important implied aspect of this relationship is an understanding, given the impossibility of predicting all future contingencies, that if problems develop in the future the two sides will engage in negotiations to adjust their relationship in a mutually beneficial way.

2. *Evaluate the benefits of a legal proceeding against the benefits of a future relationship.*   The extent of a party's willingness to renegotiate an agreement will usually be in direct proportion to the value it attaches to its potential future relationship with the other side. If a party judges that relationship to be worth more than its claim for breach of contract, it will ordinarily be willing to engage in extradeal renegotiation. On the other hand, if the party concludes that its claim is worth more than the benefits from a continuing relationship, it will usually insist on its contractual rights to the point of using litigation to protect them.

For example, one of the factors that encouraged Enron to renegotiate with the Maharashtra government after the cancellation of its electricity supply contract was the prospect of undertaking numerous energy projects throughout India in the years ahead.

Enron clearly judged those potential relationships to be worth more than winning an arbitration award in a case that would certainly be a long protracted struggle. Looking forward, Enron therefore constantly remained open to renegotiation throughout its conflict with the state of Maharashtra.

Often an aggrieved party facing a demand for renegotiation cannot accurately evaluate the worth of its claim or the value of a renegotiated contract without first engaging in some kind of discussions with the other side. Moreover, satisfaction of its claim through litigation against the other side is almost always subject to long delays, a further inducement to enter into renegotiations. Indeed, one of the functions of the delays inherent in pursuing legal remedies is to give the parties an opportunity to negotiate an efficient solution to their conflict (Tracht 1999: 622).

3. *Look for ways to create value in the renegotiation.* A party facing a demand for renegotiation has a tendency to see the process as the worst kind of win–lose activity in which any advantage gained by the other side is an automatic loss to itself. As a result, an unwilling participant in an extradeal renegotiation tends to be intransigent, to quibble over the smallest issues, to voice recriminations, and generally to fight a rearguard action throughout the process. By pursuing this approach, the parties may fail to capture the maximum gains possible from their encounter.

Joint problem-solving negotiation and integrative bargaining are as applicable to an extradeal renegotiation as they are to the negotiation of the deal in the first instance. The challenge for both sides in a renegotiation is to create an atmosphere in which problem solving can readily take place. Even if a party feels forced into an extradeal renegotiation, it should approach the process as an opportunity to secure gains from the process. Thus in the renegotiations between Enron and the Maharashtra State government over their electricity supply contract, while Maharashtra State gained a reduced power tariff, Enron secured the right to increase the capacity of its power plant.

4. *The parties should fully understand the alternatives to succeeding in the renegotiation—especially their costs.* The alternative to a successful extradeal renegotiation in most cases is litigation in which the party seeking renegotiation will be the defendant and the party refusing it is the plaintiff. Litigation has risks and costs for both sides, and it is important that both sides understand them thoroughly as they approach the renegotiation process so they can accurately evaluate the worth of any proposal put forward.

Often the party demanding renegotiation has a tendency to undervalue the risks and costs of litigation while the party facing that demand tends to overvalue its benefits. It is therefore important for each side as part of its negotiating strategy to be sure that the other has a realistic evaluation of its BATNA.

Sometimes an aggrieved party may try to focus the other's attention on those costs by commencing a lawsuit while the renegotiation discussions are in progress. In the Enron case, at the time the Maharashtra government canceled the electricity supply agreement, it probably assumed that its action would entail relatively little cost. It also seemed to have assumed that other investors would be willing to take Enron's place or that it would be able to find indigenous solutions to the state's power shortage. Once those assumptions proved false and once Enron had begun an arbitration case in London with a claim of $300 million, the state of Maharashtra became, considerably more open to renegotiation than it was at the time it canceled the contract.

5. Involve, either directly or indirectly, all necessary parties in the renegotiation. A successful renegotiation may not only require the participation of the parties who signed the original agreement, but it may also necessitate the involvement of other parties who did not sign it but who gained an interest in the transaction afterward. Such secondary parties may include labor unions, creditors, suppliers, governmental departments, and in the case of diplomatic negotiations, other states.

For example, in the renegotiation of a loan between a bank and a troubled real estate developer with a partially completed office building, no new agreement can be reached without the participation, directly or indirectly, of the unpaid construction contractor whose lien on the property can block refinancing of the project. It is therefore important in organizing any renegotiation to determine all the parties, both primary and secondary, that should participate and then to decide whether they should be involved in the face-to-face renegotiations between the primary parties or dealt with in separate discussions.

6. Design the right forum and process for the renegotiation.   Both sides should think hard about the appropriate process for launching and conducting extradeal renegotiations. Renegotiations often emerge out of crisis characterized by severe conflict, threats, and high emotion. An appropriate process for the renegotiation may help to mollify the parties and reduce the negative consequences of the crisis on their subsequent discussions. An inappropriate process, on the other hand, may serve to heighten those negative consequences and impede the renegotiations.

The government of the state of Maharashtra, for example, after, receiving the recommendation of a cabinet subcommittee, canceled the contract with Enron and also declared publicly that it would not renegotiate the agreement. In that context, if renegotiations were ever to take place, the parties would need to create a process that would preserve the government's dignity and prestige. Ultimately, the government chose to appoint a "review panel" consisting of energy experts to reexamine the project. The panel met with Enron representatives, as well as project critics, and then submitted a proposal to the government, containing the terms of a renegotiated electricity supply agreement to which Enron had agreed. The use of a panel of experts to conduct what amounted to a renegotiation, rather than face-to-face discussions between the government and Enron, served to protect governmental dignity. Moreover, the panel's status as a group of independent experts, rather than politicians, tended to give its recommendations a legitimacy needed to persuade the public that the renegotiated agreement protected Indian interests.

In some cases, the way in which the parties frame the renegotiation may influence its success. For example, rather than use the label *renegotiation,* a term that conjures up negative implications of fundamental changes in the sanctity of contract, the parties may refer to the process as a *review, restructuring, rescheduling, modification,* or an effort to clarify ambiguities in the existing agreement, rather than to change basic principles.[2] This approach, at least formally, respects the sanctity of contract and thereby may avoid some of the friction and hostility engendered by demanding outright extradeal renegotiations.

Yet another way of framing a renegotiation is a time-sensitive waiver, an approach that respects the agreement yet enables the burdened party to obtain temporary relief from certain contractual obligations.

7. *Involve the right mediator in the renegotiation process.* In the stress and hostility often engendered by an extradeal renegotiation, a mediator or other neutral third person may be able to aid the parties to overcome the obstacles between them so as to reach a satisfactory renegotiated agreement. A mediator may make a positive contribution by helping design and manage the renegotiation process so that the parties will have the maximum opportunities to create value through their interaction; by assisting with the communications between the two sides in a way that will facilitate positive results from their interactions; and by suggesting substantive solutions to the problems that the parties encounter during the course of their extradeal renegotiation. To be effective, the mediator must have the blend of skills, experience, and confidence of the parties appropriate to the renegotiation in question. The wrong mediator, on the other hand, can make a difficult renegotiation impossible.

Concluding Thoughts

Many persons view a contract renegotiation in negative terms. For them, it is an aberration, a disreputable practice that evokes images of broken promises, disappointed expectations, and bargains made but not kept. From the viewpoint of anyone facing demands for an unwanted renegotiation, such a reaction is normal and understandable. But from the vantage of society, renegotiation plays a constructive role in human relations at all levels.

    If Karl Llewellyn is correct—that the work of agreements in society is a struggle of life against form—the function of renegotiation in the social order is to mediate that struggle, to allow life and form to adjust to one another over the long term at least cost.

Endnotes

1. Indeed, English common law at one time viewed renegotiated contracts under certain conditions as invalid since they lacked the legal requirement of consideration in those cases in which as a result of renegotiation a party was promising to do no more than it was already obligated to do under its original contract (Waddams 1999: 204).

2. In the economic slowdown of 2001, increasing numbers of borrowers in the United States have been unable to make regular mortgage payments on their homes. Instead of foreclosing on delinquent borrowers judged to have the potential to make payments at some point in the future, some banks have established *loan modification programs,* by which they renegotiate the terms of the loan to prevent default (for example, by adding the unpaid interest to the principal of the loan). The banks frame these loans as *modified,* not *renegotiated,* mortgage agreements. See "Pinched homeowners are finding shelter in modified loans," *The Wall Street Journal,* October 30, 2001, p. A1.

References

Carter, J.W. 1999. The renegotiation of contracts. *Journal of Contract Law* 13, pp. 185–98.

Carver, J., and H. Hossain. 1990. An arbitration case: The dispute that never was. *ICSID Review* 5, pp. 311–25.

Farnsworth, E. A. 1987. Precontractual liability and preliminary agreements: Fair dealing and failed negotiation. *Columbia Law Review* 87, pp. 217–94.

Fisher, R., W. Ury, and B. Patton. 1991. *Getting to YES: Negotiating agreement without giving in.* 2nd ed. New York: Penguin.

Howtek, Inc. v. Relisys et al. 1999. 958 F. Supp. 46 (D.N.H.)

Litvinoff, S. 1997. Good faith. *Tulane Law Review* 87, pp. 1645–74.

Llewellyn, K.N. 1931. What price contract? An essay in perspective. *Yale Law Journal* 40, pp. 704–51.

Kolo, A., and T. Walde. 2000. Renegotiation and contract adaptation in international investment projects. *The Journal of World Investment* 1, pp. 5–28.

Peter, W. 1995. *Arbitration and renegotiation in international investment agreements.* 2nd ed. The Hague and Boston: Kluwer Law International.

Salacuse, J. W. 1991. *Making global deals: Negotiating in the international marketplace.* Boston: Houghton Mifflin.

———. 1998. Ten ways that culture affects negotiation. *Negotiation Journal* 13, pp. 199–205.

———. 2001. Renegotiation international project agreement. *Fordham International Law Journal* 24, pp. 1319–70.

Talley, E. L. 1999. Renegotiation, mechanism design, and the liquidated damages rule. *Stanford Law Review* 46, pp. 1195–1242.

Tracht, M. E. 1999. Renegotiation and secured credit: Explaining the equity of redemption. *Vanderbilt Law Review* 52, pp. 599–643.

Vernon, R. 1971. *Sovereignty at bay: The international spread of U. S. enterprises.* New York: Basic Books.

Waddams, S. M. 1999. Commentary on "The renegotiation of contracts." *Journal of Contract Law* 13, pp. 199–205.

Reading 6.5

Negotiating with Problem People
Len Leritz

In the movie *Big* Tom Hanks stars as a kid locked inside an adult body. What makes the movie funny is that it strikes a chord with viewers. "I know someone like that," they think between fistfuls of popcorn.

There are a lot of people out there who look like adults on the outside but are thinking like kids on the inside. And when it's your job to negotiate with one of them, you've got trouble. Most of these problem people fall into one of five categories: bullies, avoiders, withdrawers, high rollers, or wad shooters.

- *Bullies* verbally or physically attack, use threats, demand, or otherwise attempt to intimidate and push others around. They say things like "That's a stupid thing to say!" "Do you expect me to respond to that?" "If you don't, I will . . . !" "I want it, and I want it now!" "Move it!" "You can't do that!" "You better shape up!"

- *Avoiders* physically avoid or procrastinate, hide out, or refuse to negotiate out of fear of losing. They say things like "I'll do it tomorrow." "We don't have anything to talk about." "I don't have time." "That's not my problem."

- *Withdrawers* emotionally withdraw, get confused, go dumb and numb, or become paralyzed with fear. You'll hear them say, "I don't understand." "That doesn't make sense." "I don't know."

- *High rollers* attempt to shock and intimidate their opposition by making extreme demands. "You have until five o'clock to comply." "I want $50,000 for my car." "I want it all done by noon."

- *Wad shooters* assume an all-or-nothing, take-it-or-leave-it stance. "That's my bottom line." "If you don't want it, forget it." "Either you agree to all five points or I'm leaving."

What to Do with Them

The behavior of these different types of "enforcers" tends to be uncomplicated and obvious. Consequently, the following responses work effectively with most of them.

1. *Get their attention.* This step is especially important when you're up against bullies. Until you get their attention, you are wasting your time. You need to shock them out of their self-centered mind-set and let them know with no uncertainty that you intend to be taken seriously. You need to make them feel your presence.

The way to get their attention is to draw a boundary. The intention is not to punish the other person but simply to let them know what you will and will not tolerate. You want to create a negative consequence that will outweigh whatever benefit they are deriving from their current behavior.

Source: Reprinted from *Working Woman*, October 1988, pp. 35–37. Used with permission of the publisher.

How you draw your boundary will differ in each situation. You need to ask yourself what it is that will get the other person's attention—what is important to them. You may do it by physical action, by shouting at them, by walking out, by initiating legal procedures, or by telling them in a quiet and firm voice what you will and won't accept.

The key is that you have to mean it. The other person almost always knows whether you are serious about your boundary. No one crosses your boundary when you mean it.

Here is an example of what I call the "skillet approach" to dealing with enforcers. I once had a client who had been physically abused by her husband for years. She had threatened to leave him many times, but he knew that she didn't really mean it.

One night she finally decided to mean it. He had pushed her around earlier in the evening. She waited until he went to sleep and then went to the kitchen and got her biggest cast-iron skillet. She woke him up while holding the skillet over his head. "If you ever hit me again, I'll kill you in your sleep," she told him.

This time she meant it, and he believed her. Though he had trouble sleeping for a while, the abuse stopped. The woman had gotten her husband's attention by creating a consequence (the skillet), and she meant it.

Ask yourself what "skillet" you need to use—and mean it when you use it. When you don't mean it you are reinforcing the behavior you don't want.

2. *Call a spade a spade.*   Identify the enforcer's behavior and invite her to do something more constructive. Explaining to a bully, for example, that she's being a bully helps her become conscious of what she's doing and will often take the power out of it. This is especially true if others are involved and the enforcer feels embarrassed.

Suggesting other options at this point will help the person save face and will keep the negotiations moving. For example, you might say something like "Your repeated attacks are not getting us any closer to an agreement. I'd like to suggest that we each try to explain what we need, then work together to brainstorm some ways that we might both get what we need."

3. *Put their fears to rest.*   This step is particularly important when you're dealing with avoiders or withdrawers. You need to help them feel safer so that their capacities expand and they can move into more cooperative behaviors.

Here are some suggestions:

- Don't be defensive. Instead, look behind their behavior to their underlying needs and interests: "Would you be more comfortable if we met in your office?" "What conditions will make you willing to stay here and talk this out?"

- Respond to the needs of the internal kid: "I can see how you feel frustrated."

- Actively listen to them so they feel understood: "What I hear you saying is . . ."

- Be aware of who their constituency is, who it is they need to impress: "I want you to be able to go back to your department and feel proud of what we accomplished," you might say.

- Don't counterattack. When dealing with aggressive enforcers, such as bullies, the usual rule is the more aggressive, the more frightened the internal kid. Helping bullies feel safer may seem counterintuitive, but it's exactly what you need to do to get them on your level.

4. *Insist on playing by the rules.* Bullies, high rollers, and wad shooters will attempt to force you to accept unreasonable agreements. But you should refuse to be pressured. Instead, insist on fair criteria for both the process and the final settlement. You might say, "I refuse to be pressured into an agreement. I am willing to continue the negotiation only if we can agree to some fair procedures that we will both honor." Or if, for example, you feel a price the other person is asking is too high, you might say, "Let's check with some other suppliers and see what they are charging."

5. *Put the ball in their court.* When the other person takes extreme stands and makes unreasonable demands, ask her to explain how she arrived at her position. Point out that you need to understand her underlying needs better. You might say, "In order to understand your demands, I need to hear more from you about how you arrived at those points." Or "Your price is a little higher than I expected. I want to pay you fairly for your work. Explain to me what you will need to do to complete the job." When she answers you, demands that cannot be justified lose their power.

6. *Use the silent treatment.* Silence can be one of your most powerful strategies, especially with wad shooters. When the other person is being aggressive or unreasonable, try just looking at them calmly. Silence gives them nothing to push against.

Calm silence communicates power. The other person will feel uncomfortable with the power of your silence and will probably begin to fill it in—often by backtracking and becoming more reasonable.

A variation of using silence is to walk away. "I'm willing to talk about this whenever you are willing to stop attacking me. Until then, we have nothing to talk about."

7. *Do the sidestep.* Sidestepping or ignoring a statement can be an effective response if someone is making a personal attack, an extreme demand, or a take-it-or-leave-it challenge. Instead of responding directly, act as if you didn't hear what it was the person said. Change the topic and/or refocus the discussion on the underlying problem or conflict at hand.

For example, a corporate attorney says angrily to an opposing attorney, "I can't believe they pay you a professional salary." The opposing attorney might calmly respond, "I think we still have four issues we have not settled. Let's look at them one at a time." Or a film supplier says to a production manager, "The price is $10,000 per segment. Take it or leave it." The manager would answer, "How many segments did you say you had?" or "Your tone of voice sounds angry. Do you feel as if we have not been fair to you in our past dealings?"

8. *Meet the enemy head-on.* Don't be defensive. Justifying your position or needs encourages the other party to step up their attack. If you become defensive, the other person knows that she has you on the run. Invite her to give her criticism, then refocus it as an attack on the problem at hand. Ask her to explain how her comments will help solve the problem.

For example, the account supervisor at an advertising agency says to the creative director, "If you were committed to this new ad, you would have been here last week." A defensive response from the creative director would be, "I couldn't help it. I was burned out and needed the time off." A better reply would be "I know you are under pressure and last week was frustrating. What do we need to do so we don't get caught in that kind of last-minute bind in the future?"

9. *Refuse to be punished.* Anyone has a right to be angry from time to time, but no one has the right to punish you. You do not deserve to be punished. You will know that you are being punished when the other person keeps repeating her attack or the person vents her anger but refuses to tell you how she wants your behavior to change in response.

Draw a boundary by asking the other person what they want from you. If their response is "I don't know," inform them that you are willing to continue the discussion when they do know. In the meantime, you're not willing to be punished.

10. *Ask questions.* Taking a stand may make the other person defensive. Instead, ask questions. Asking questions doesn't give them an object to attack; it invites them to justify their position or to vent their feelings. It gives you more information about them.

When asking your questions, ask "what" questions rather than "why" questions. "What" questions invite factual responses. "Why" questions are usually sneaky judgments that make the other party defensive. "What" questions will keep the negotiation moving. "Why" questions will tend to lead you to battle positions. For example:

- Why did you think you could do that? (attacking)
- What was your motivation for doing that? (information seeking)
- Why did you do that? (attacking)
- What are the assumptions behind your actions? (information seeking)

11. *Point out the consequences.* When the other person refuses to agree to a reasonable settlement, show them the ramifications of their actions. Try to present it as a statement of inevitable consequences rather than as a threat: "The reality is, if our company shows a loss again in the fourth quarter due to the strike, we will have no choice but to lay off 500 union workers."

Armed with the right approach, you can convince any bully or withdrawer on the block that a rational, well-negotiated settlement is in everyone's best interest.

Reading 6.6

When and How to Use Third-Party Help
Roy J. Lewicki
Alexander Hiam
Karen Wise Olander

It may be that in spite of your best efforts to move the negotiations back on track, the two sides are still stuck, unable to go anywhere. In that case, you should consider asking a third party to step in. A third party is someone who is not directly involved in your negotiation or dispute, but who can be helpful in resolving it. This impartial party may be a friend, in the case of a simple negotiation, or it may be a neutral person whom both parties know and invite to assist, or it might even be someone with professional credentials whose job it is to intervene in such cases.

A third party is likely to use a number of conflict resolution techniques, engaging you and the other party in activities designed to reduce tension, improve communication, change the options, adjust the number of players or issues, or help find common ground. With outside help, the disputing parties may be able to move back on track and bring the negotiation to conclusion and closure.

When to Ask a Third Party to Intervene

In general, it is best to try everything you can to remedy the situation before you move to third-party intervention. However, when conflict escalates in negotiation, the parties often become suspicious of each other's motives, intentions, and behavior. One of the parties may try to use the tactics in a "partisan" way, with a bias toward achieving a specific outcome. Moreover, even when that party implements the practices in good faith, the other party doesn't see the efforts as genuine. Instead, he or she sees it as a ruse, a ploy, a tactic, or a way for the other to gain advantage. If the parties just cannot find a way to become "unstuck," then both parties should agree on the need for a third party. Although third parties can be very helpful, negotiators often resist using them because they feel they are decreasing the likelihood of achieving their preferred outcome.

Sometimes a third-party intervention will be imposed by an outside group that has the power or authority to do so and is anxious to resolve the matter. In an intrafamily dispute, when two children are fighting, a parent may intervene. In other cases, an intervention may be imposed by a constituency or higher-level authority, or it may result from a rule or legal procedure. For example, a number of warranties and contracts now specify that if there is a question as to liability or fault, the dispute will automatically go to an arbitrator or mediator.

Source: Reprinted from *Think Before You Speak* (New York: John Wiley & Sons, 1996) by Roy J. Lewicki, Alexander Hiam, and Karen Wise Olander, pp. 177–97. Copyright © 1996 by John Wiley & Sons, Inc. Reprinted by permission of the publisher.

When two negotiating parties invite the third party to intervene, then the intervention is usually friendly and progresses smoothly. If the intervention is imposed by an outside authority, then the relationship between the disputing parties and the third party may not necessarily be friendly, and the negotiating environment may become even more hostile.

Reasons to Use a Third Party

You may want to consider using third-party help if[1]

- The emotional level between the parties is high, with lots of anger and frustration.
- Communication between the parties is poor or has completely broken down, or the parties appear to be talking "past" each other.
- Stereotypic views of each other's position and motives are preventing resolution.
- Behavior is negative (e.g., there is intense anger or name-calling).
- The parties have serious disagreements about what information is necessary, available, or required.
- The parties disagree on the number, order, or combination of issues.
- Differences in interests appear to be irreconcilable.
- Values differ greatly, and the parties disagree about what is fundamentally right.
- There are no established procedures for resolving the conflict, or the procedures have not been followed.
- Negotiations have completely broken down and there is an impasse.

There can be several objectives in bringing in a third party to achieve a resolution. First, the parties want to resolve the dispute; they care about the *outcome* dimension. A second reason is to smooth, repair, or improve the *relationship* between the parties—to reduce the level of conflict and the resultant damages. Finally, third parties are often used simply to stop the dispute—to get the parties to separate and not fight any more, or to make sure that they have as little future interaction as possible (e.g., when the United Nations intervenes in conflicts around the world, its first objective is often to stop warring groups from fighting). Depending on which type of objective is most important—resolving the dispute, repairing the relationship, or separating the parties—different types of third parties with different skills may be needed. The type of third party selected will focus on some or all of these objectives, and it is important to know which ones are most important and in what order they should be pursued.

Each type of third party has advantages and disadvantages, depending on the situation. Which type you choose will depend not only on the situation, but also on what services are available, who specifically is available, and, if applicable, what may be required by rules and regulations that govern the conflict and its resolution (e.g., laws, contracts, documents, precedents). After we discuss the types of interventions, we will look at how to select the appropriate one for your circumstances.

The term *ADR* is used in the literature and elsewhere in reference to third-party resolution of disputes. ADR stands for *A*lternative *D*ispute *R*esolution. ADR procedures are alternatives to taking the conflict into the court system, hiring an attorney, and pursuing litigation. Since the early 1980s, there has been a major social movement to take *civil* disputes (where there is no criminal violation of law) out of the courts and, instead, refer them to third parties. There are a number of reasons for this: The parties have more control over what happens, the process is often quicker and less costly, and it keeps the court system from becoming hopelessly overburdened, particularly when key issues of law are not in question.

There are many people who perform ADR services, including the more formal labor arbitrators, divorce mediators, community mediators, and process consultants. Dispute resolution is also performed informally by ombudspersons, fact finders and referees, ministers, social workers, teachers, managers, or even friends of the disputing parties. There are also quasi-substitutes for formal court proceedings, such as summary jury trials and minitrials, judicial reference, court-annexed arbitration, settlement conferences, tribunals, and judicial committees.

In this reading we will define and discuss the formal and informal processes of arbitration, mediation, and process consultation. We will discuss what these people do and how they work to resolve disputes. These methods are separate from the arena of actual litigation, which will not be discussed here, but which will be used as a point of comparison. For example, all the preceding processes are generally of shorter duration and less costly than a court trial.

Advantages and Disadvantages of Using a Third Party

Some of the advantages of employing a third party to assist in resolving a dispute are

- The parties gain time to cool off as they break their conflict and describe the problem to the third party.
- Communication can be improved because the third party slows the communication down, helps people be clear, and works to improve listening.
- Parties often have to determine which issues are really important because the third party may ask for some prioritizing.
- The emotional climate can be improved as the parties discharge anger and hostility and return to a level of civility and trust.
- The parties can take steps to mend the relationship, particularly if this work is facilitated by the third party.
- The time frame for resolving the dispute can be established or reestablished.
- The escalating costs of remaining in conflict can be controlled, particularly if continuing the dispute is costing people money or opportunity (paying fees for attorneys becomes very costly).
- By watching and participating in the process, parties can learn how the third party provides assistance and in the future may be able to resolve their disputes without this help.
- Actual resolutions to the dispute and closure may be achieved.

FIGURE 1 | Different Types of Third-Party Involvement in Disputes

		Level of Third-Party Control over Outcome	
		High	Low
Level of Third-Party Control over Process	High	"Inquisition"	Mediation Process consultation
	Low	Arbitration	Negotiation

Disadvantages of ADR include

- The parties potentially lose face when the third party is called in, since there may be an image that the parties are somehow incompetent or incapable of resolving their own fight (this is true when those who are judging the negotiators are others who can publicly criticize them or move to have them replaced).
- There is also a loss of control of the process or the outcome or both, depending on which type of third party is called in to help. Relative to what they think they could have achieved had they "held out longer" or "fought harder," parties may be forced to accept less than 100 percent of their preferred target.

In general, when you bring a third party into the negotiations, the two contending parties will have to give up control over one or both aspects of the negotiation: the *process* and the *outcome*. The process is how the negotiation is conducted; the outcome is the result of the negotiation. As we discuss each type of third-party intervention, we will point out what the parties gain or lose in terms of process and outcome. Figure 1 depicts types of third-party involvement.

In negotiation without a third party, the opposing parties maintain control over both process and outcome. If they move to mediation, they give up control of the process but maintain control of the outcome. If they move to arbitration, they give up control of the outcome but retain control of the process. The fourth area in the diagram reflects a situation where the parties have control of neither process not outcome—and no negotiation occurs. We now consider the major types of third-party behavior individually.

Arbitration

Arbitration[2] is the most common form of third-party dispute resolution. When an arbitrator is called into a situation, the negotiators retain control of the process, but the arbitrator takes control of shaping and determining the outcome. Each party presents its position to the arbitrator, who then makes a ruling on either a single issue or on a package of issues.[3] This depends on the rules of the arbitration process, if any, and the request of the parties, if applicable. The arbitrator's ruling (decision) may be voluntary or binding, according to laws or a previous commitment of the parties.

The arbitrator can arrive at a recommended outcome in several ways. Usually the arbitrator selects one side's position or the other's ("rules" in favor of one party or the other's preferred settlement). But sometimes third parties may also offer an entirely different resolution. The arbitrator may suggest a "split" between the two parties' positions, in essence creating a compromise between their positions. In formal proceedings that are governed by law and contract agreements, such as labor and management negotiations, there is usually a very clear and strict set of policies about how arbitration rulings are to be made.

Arbitration is used in business conflicts, disputes between business and union workers, labor relations, contracts (usually in the public sector), and grievances. In the case of grievances, the arbitrator is bound to decide how the grievance should be resolved, whether consistent with the labor–management contract or current labor law.

Advantages of Arbitration

The major advantages of arbitration are:

1. A clear solution is made available to the parties (though it may not be one or both parties' choice).

2. The solution may be mandated on them (they can't choose whether to follow it or not).

3. Arbitrators are usually selected because they are wise, fair, and impartial, and therefore the solution comes from a respected and credible source.

4. The costs of prolonging the dispute are avoided. It is interesting to note that arbitrators' decisions tend to be consistent with judgments received from courts.[4] In a sense, they are "judges without robes," and their decisions are usually governed by public law or contract law.

Disadvantages of Arbitration

There are some disadvantages to arbitration.[5]

1. The parties relinquish control over shaping the outcome; thus the proposed solution may not be one that they prefer or are even willing to live with.

2. The parties may not like the outcome, and it may impose additional costs, sacrifices, or burdens on them.

3. If the arbitration is voluntary (they have a choice whether to follow the recommended solution or not), they may lose face if they decide not to follow the arbitrator's recommendation.

4. There is a *decision-acceptance effect*—there is less commitment to an arbitrated resolution, for at least two reasons: They did not participate in the process of shaping the outcome, and the recommended settlement may be inferior to what they preferred. If parties are less committed to an outcome, they will be less likely to implement it. (As we will see when we discuss mediation, there is better

commitment to a resolution and its implementation because the parties are fully involved in making the decision.) For example, when divorce proceedings go to arbitration—particularly regarding alimony or child custody issues—the party who "loses" is often uncommitted to the settlement and refuses to follow the mandate, and the parties wind up back in court.

5. Research on arbitration has often shown that it has a *chilling effect.*[6] During negotiation, the parties may behave differently if they expect that the dispute will have to go to arbitration. During the negotiation, they may hold back on compromises so they do not lose anything in arbitration, particularly when they anticipate that the arbitrator will "split the difference." In essence, you might get a better settlement if you refuse to make any concessions, because if the arbitrator splits the difference, you can do better than if you made concessions and then the arbitrator split the difference. So negotiators may take a hard-line position. To avoid this, parties who expect to go to arbitration often use a method called *final-offer arbitration.* In this procedure, the arbitrator asks the parties to make their "best final offer," and then the arbitrator rules for one side or the other with no split. This in effect forces the parties to make the best deal they can during a negotiation, which reduces the distance between them as they approach arbitration. The more extreme the final offer, the less likely the arbitrator may be to rule in favor of it.

6. In the *narcotic effect,*[7] parties with a history of recurring arbitration tend to lose interest in trying to negotiate, become passive, and grow very dependent on the third party for helping them move toward resolution. Their attitude is, "We're not going to be able to agree, and a settlement is going to be imposed anyway, so why should I work hard to try to negotiate?" Thus parties become "addicted" to arbitration and take less responsibility for themselves and resolving their own conflict. Further, a party with a strong-willed constituency may be uncompromising and unyielding during negotiation, and then blame the arbitrator for any compromises that have to be made in arbitration.

7. In the *half-life effect,*[8] the results of more and more arbitration are less and less satisfaction with the outcomes. Because the parties have become passive in the process and have less control over the outcomes as well, arbitration frequently becomes ritualistic and simply loses its effectiveness. Eventually the parties refuse to participate, take their case elsewhere, or remove themselves completely.

8. In the *biasing effect,* the arbitrators may be perceived not to be neutral and impartial, but to be biased. This is most likely to occur when an arbitrator makes a whole sequence of decisions that favors one side over the other. Interestingly, parties in strong conflict often try to bias the third party, and then reject the third party for being biased. (Witness the harassment that referees and umpires receive in most sporting events!) This shows how insidious and problematic destructive conflict can become. If an arbitrator is seen as biased, the parties will move toward selecting another arbitrator who will be neutral, or preferably, will favor their position.

Mediation

Formal mediation[9] is based on established rules and procedures. The objective of the mediator is to help the parties negotiate more effectively. The mediator does not solve the problem or impose a solution. He or she helps the disputing parties to develop the solution themselves and then to agree to it.[10] Thus the mediator takes control of the process, but not the outcome.

A major concern for the mediator is to assist the parties in areas of communication. The intent is to improve the parties' skills so they will be able to negotiate more effectively. The assumption in mediation is twofold. First, the parties can and will come up with a better solution than one that is invented by a third party; and second, the relationship is an important one, and the parties want to develop their ability to problem-solve about their conflict.

How Mediation Works[11]

There are a number of variations on the mediation process, but in general it tends to follow a reasonably common process. First, the mediator needs to be selected. The mediator can be a member of a professional mediation center or service, or can be acting informally as a mediator while in some other capacity (minister, manager, social worker, teacher, counselor, etc.).

The mediator begins by taking an active role. Usually, the mediator invites both sides to attend a meeting. The mediator sets ground rules by which the mediation will occur:

- The parties agree to follow a procedure set forth by the mediator.
- The parties agree to listen to each other and follow some rules of civility and respect toward each other.
- The role of the mediator is not to solve the parties' dispute, but to work with the parties to achieve a "negotiated" outcome.

As actual mediation starts, the mediator then takes on a more passive role. He or she meets with each party to listen to them and learn about the dispute. In most cases, the mediator does this with the other party in the room, so that each can hear how the other sees the dispute. However, if the parties cannot be candid in front of the other, or conflict is likely to erupt, the mediator may hold these meetings with each party separately. Through active listening and questions, the mediator tries to identify and understand the issues. The mediator looks for underlying interests, priorities, and concerns, and finds areas for potential collaboration or compromise.

In the next stage, the parties agree on the agenda—the key issues to be discussed, and the order for discussion. The mediator will help them prioritize and package their proposals and counterproposals as needed.

The mediator brings the parties together and encourages exploration of possible solutions, trade-offs, or concessions. These are designed to help communication flow more freely, reduce tension, and so forth. The mediator may invent proposals or suggest possible solutions, but will not impose any of these on the parties.

The final stage is agreement, which may be made public with an announcement of the settlement. There may be a written agreement, and it may or may not be signed. Many mediators push for some form of written agreement, to help the parties be clear about who is going to do what, and to enhance their commitment.

A long time may be involved in the mediation process, depending on the nature and degree of difficulty between the two parties. However, mediation is still less costly than going to court. The length of the stages may vary. For example, in divorce mediation, the preference is usually for both parties to begin meeting together as soon as possible, rather than having long individual meetings with the mediator. The objective is to move the parties toward communicating and working out their problems, but it will depend on the degree of cooperation of the parties and the skills of the mediator.

How Mediators Help

In addition to facilitating the negotiation process, mediators can help the parties save face when they need to make concessions. They can assist in resolving internal disagreements and help parties deal with their constituencies (e.g., by explaining the agreement to the constituency, or helping the negotiator save face with the constituency by portraying the negotiator as tough, fair, and effective). They may offer the parties incentives for agreement or concession, or offer negative incentives for noncooperation.

Mediators maintain control if the parties are unable to do so, largely by controlling the process (e.g., making sure the conflict between the parties does not escalate again, or that one side does not take undue advantage of the other). Mediators push when needed, and move into the background when the negotiators seem to be able to move forward themselves.

When Mediation Can Be Helpful

Mediation may be used in labor relations, or as a precursor to arbitration in grievance and contractual negotiations. It has also been used successfully in settling malpractice suits, tort cases, small claims, consumer complaints, liability claims, divorce,[12] civil and community disputes,[13] business disputes,[14] business and government cases involving the environment,[15] and international[16] disputes. It is increasingly being used in communities to resolve disputes between landlords and tenants or merchants and customers, and on college campuses to resolve conflicts in residence halls or between students of different genders, ethnic groups, and nationalities.

Most of these types of disputes are self-explanatory. What is interesting is to see the variety of ways that mediation can be taught and used. For example, children are being taught, as early as elementary school age, the art of mediation, and then taught how to use it to resolve conflicts in the classroom, on the playground, and in the home. While the techniques taught to children are probably not as sophisticated as they would be in a major international negotiation, the principles are exactly the same, and the dispute resolution skills children learn at an early age can carry over into their adult lives.

Factors Necessary for Success in Mediation

First, mediators *need to be seen by the disputants* as neutral, impartial, and unbiased. This is critical, because if mediators are seen by one or both disputants as "biased" toward one side or having a preferred outcome, then their actions will not be trusted. It is not enough for mediators themselves to believe they are neutral or can act in an unbiased manner—the acid test is that the *parties must see them as unbiased.*

Second, mediators may need to be expert in the field where the dispute occurs, although mediation requires less expertise than arbitration. An arbitrator has to know the key laws or contract issues in the area, and usually has to make a decision that is consistent with previous rulings. In contrast, as long as a mediator is neutral and smart enough to understand the key issues and arguments of both sides, he or she can be effective. Sometimes, in fact, naive mediators have so few biases about the dispute in question that they may discover helpful approaches that experts in this area have become blind to. Expertise is especially important to industrial conflicts, where industry-specific knowledge may be important. In divorce mediation, a knowledge of marital law is helpful. (For an agreement to be legally binding, a lawyer probably has to write the document, but parties can achieve fundamental agreements in principle with almost any kind of a mediator.) It is also useful for the mediator to have experience in mediating similar disputes.

Although it is not required by law, certification of mediation training enhances the mediator's credibility. The Federal Mediation and Conciliation Service of the U.S. Department of Labor is one group that certifies mediators. There are also local mediation services and dispute settlement centers that "certify" mediators by having them participate in a mandatory training program, as well as an apprenticeship with an experienced mediator. Mediation centers can assist disputing parties in finding a mediator.

Successful mediation depends to a large degree on timing. Mediation cannot be used as a technique for dispute resolution if the parties do not agree that they need help, or are so angry and upset at each other that they cannot even civilly sit in the same room together. Mediation also depends on the willingness of the parties to make some concessions and find a compromise solution. If they are so committed to their point of view that no compromise is even possible—a problem we see in attempting to mediate value-based disputes around issues like abortion and environmental management—then mediation is doomed to fail. If the parties are not both willing to accept mediation, then it is unlikely that other techniques will work until the parties soften their views.

Success

Mediation tends to be successful in 60 to 80 percent of cases, according to statistics. Success of using mediation as an ADR technique is most likely when[17]

- The conflict is moderate but not high.
- The conflict is not excessively emotional and polarized.
- There is a high motivation by both parties to settle.
- The parties are committed to follow the process of mediation.
- Resources are not severely limited.
- The issues do not involve a basic conflict of values.
- The power is relatively equal between the parties.
- Mediation is seen as advantageous relative to going to arbitration (or no agreement).

- The bargainers have experience and understand the process of give-and-take, and the costs of no agreement.[18]

In successful mediation, negotiators tend to be committed to the agreement that is generated.[19] Thus the implementation rate is high.

Disadvantages

Mediation is not effective or is more difficult to use when

- The bargainers are inexperienced and assume that if they simply take a hard line, the other party will eventually give in.
- There are many issues, and the parties cannot agree on priorities.
- The parties are strongly committed to their positions (and are held to them by an uncompromising constituency).
- There is very strong emotion, passion, and intensity to the conflict.
- A party has an internal conflict and isn't sure what to do.
- The parties differ on major social values.
- The parties differ greatly on their expectations for what is a fair and reasonable settlement.
- The parties' resistance points do not overlap—the most one party will give is still much less than the minimum the other will accept.

Mediation can be more time-consuming than arbitration. The parties have to take a lot of time explaining the dispute to the third party, and then participating in the process of searching for a resolution. Also, because mediation is not binding, there is no impetus for the parties to commit to the settlement or even to settle at all. Thus there is always the potential for the dispute to reappear and continue—perhaps even for a long time. And it is always possible that the dispute will escalate.

Combining Mediation and Arbitration

Some who monitor third-party interventions have suggested that even better than mediation, in some cases, may be requiring a sequence of dispute resolution events, such as mediation followed by arbitration. This sequence seems to minimize the liabilities of each type of ADR (arbitration and mediation) and to obtain better compromises.[20] If the parties expect that they will have to progress to arbitration, they may be more willing to modify their positions in mediation to improve their chances of ruling in favor of their side. On the other hand, the expectation of arbitration may make the parties "lazy" in mediation, particularly if they think the arbitrator will ultimately rule in their favor.

Assisting the Mediator

Mediators succeed when both parties are agreeable to the mediation. Further, there are ways you can help the process.

You can help a mediator to help you negotiate by being cooperative and giving clear information. Tell the mediator what is important to you and why you want it. If you do not understand something, speak up. Express your concerns if necessary. Remember that the mediator is there to assist in the negotiation process, not to remake it. Finally, be willing to make concessions or problem solve. The objective of mediation is to move the dispute from a competitive solution to a compromise or collaborative solution, and this requires the work of all parties. Ultimately, the success of the negotiation is your responsibility. You and the other party need to find, select, and implement a workable outcome. The mediator will assist you in this endeavor, but will not do the work for you.

Process Consultation

Another way of getting help with a stalled negotiation is to use a process consultant. Process consultants serve as counselors who focus on the *process* of negotiation, as their title would suggest. They assist parties in improving communication, reducing the emotionality of the proceedings, and increasing the parties' dispute resolution skills. Their objective is to enable parties to solve their own disputes in the future. Process consultants are thus useful if the relationship between the opposing parties is a long-term one.

A process consultant is somewhat like a mediator in that he or she helps with the steps in the process. But this person differs from the mediator in that there is no discussion of the specific issues or any attempt to solve them. Thus process consultants are often more like counselors who help the parties to get along better so that they can engage in better negotiation and problem solving.

The Process

Process consultants (PCs) first interview the parties individually. Then they design a schedule of structured meetings for the parties. At these meetings, the PCs have the disputing parties discuss their past conflicts and perceptions of each other. The PCs remain neutral, guiding the parties as needed. They keep people on track, keep the emotional level from escalating, and move the parties toward problem-solving behavior. Their objective is to change the conflict management climate, improve communication, promote constructive dialogue, and create the capacity for people to act as "their own third party."

PCs have expertise in the areas of conflict and emotions. They provide emotional support to their clients. They confront and diagnose problems while remaining neutral and unbiased. They must also be authoritative to keep the process moving. They control and manage the agenda of how the parties engage each other, but not what actually happens.

Process consultation is used in marital therapy, family therapy, organizational development, and team building. It is also used in labor–management disputes and international conflict where there are ethical, political, and cultural difficulties to contend with.

Process consultation is less likely to work in the following circumstances:

- There are severe, polarized disputes over large issues.
- The relationship is short-term and the parties have no stake in improving it.
- The issues are fixed (competitive rather than collaborative negotiation).
- The party's constituency is not supportive of improving the relationship.
- One or both parties are intent on revenge or retribution.

Other, Less Formal Methods of Dispute Resolution

"Ombuds" and Others

Ombudspersons, fact finders, and referees are employed by various organizations to deal with matters before they turn into disputes. In many cases, their job is to hear and investigate conflicts between employees, or between an individual employee and "the system" (the rules, practices, and policies of the organization). At NCR,[21] as at other companies, ombuds are trained in problem solving, dispute avoidance, negotiation, and dispute resolution.

Their mission is to limit and resolve problems quickly and informally. They usually are not part of the chain of command in an organization and may report directly to the CEO rather than to a specific department. They often have links with the legal and human resources departments, so they can discuss trends in compliance or legal issues. But it is essential for ombuds to be impartial, and hence they are often unattached to the organizational hierarchy.

When an employee takes a problem to an ombud or the equivalent, the ombud engages in confidential fact-finding, then informs both sides of their rights and the opportunities for resolving the conflict. The ombud may use a combination of counseling, conciliation, negotiation, and mediation. If the complaint involves corporate policy, salary, promotion, tenure, discharge, liability, discriminatory treatment, or the like, the ombud may recommend a settlement, but usually management is involved in the final decision.

The main reason for using an ombudsperson is to make sure the process is fair and that the individual employees, with very little power, have a way to get a fair investigation and hearing about their concerns. If you are negotiating within a system or organization, an ombud can make sure you know the channels that are available to you, your rights, and what kind of outside help you may need. Ombuds can often act as "change agents," pushing an organization to change its rules and policies to deal with unfair treatment practices.

Advantages and Disadvantages of Ombuds

Using an ombud or other type of counselor can be to your advantage if the power between the two disputing parties is out of balance. This is particularly true when a lower-level employee tries to challenge his or her employer and doesn't want to get fired simply for asking questions or raising concerns about "fairness" and "rights." As with other third-party practices, however, the final outcome may not be what you hoped for.

Some organizations specify a formal process for expressing and hearing problems and disputes in this system. They may require a staged approach, where the first step is an ombud, the next is mediation, and the final step is arbitration.

Managers as Third Parties

Finally, we turn to managers, supervisors, and others whose jobs do not consist primarily of mediating disputes, but who nevertheless often must intervene to get work done or deal with unproductive conflicts in the workplace. It is estimated that managers spend 20 percent of their time in conflict management.[22] Their methods tend to be informal since most work environments do not have established rules or guidelines for how to mediate a dispute. Few managers have any formal training in settling disputes, and many are uncomfortable with conflict. But they need to know that some conflict is all right[23] and to seek assistance themselves if they often find themselves refereeing employee disputes.

Styles

Managers tend to solve disputes along the lines we discussed for other types of interventions—high or low process control, high or low outcome control.[24] The style used will depend on the manager's tolerance for conflict, the time frame, and, to some degree, the personalities of the parties involved.

High Control of Both Process and Outcome   If a manager wants to maintain control of both the process and the outcome (which is the most typical scenario), the manager's style will be inquisitorial or autocratic. The manager behaves more like a judge in a European court, or like the infamous judge on the TV show *The People's Court*. The manager runs his or her own investigation, and then makes a decision. The manager will listen to both parties' stories, structure the process as he or she pleases, asking questions to learn more information, and then will decide on the solution. This method tends to be the most common among managers. It is frequently used when the issues are minor, quick decisions are needed, or management needs to implement an unpopular action.[25]

High Outcome Control, Low Process Control   A manager who wants to retain high control of the outcome, but low control of the process, will use passive listening and then will make a decision. This is most like the arbitration style described earlier. This is somewhat like the "high–high" method, except that the manager listens to both sides; he or she makes little effort to gather more information, ask questions, or structure the process other than to render a decision after hearing the arguments.

High Process Control, Low Outcome Control   This approach is most like mediation. More managers are learning to use this approach, although not as much as would be hoped. In many disputes, the manager considers the outcome more important than the process and wants to have some control over it, so this method is used less than it might be.

Low Process and Outcome Control   If the manager does not care about controlling either process or outcome, he or she will either ignore the dispute and let the parties deal with it by themselves, or tell the disputing employees, "You solve the problem yourselves, or I will impose a solution that probably neither of you will like." This may sound like a parent acting as intervener between two arguing children.

Factors Affecting the Choice of Method

The choice of dispute resolution method will often be based on the time frame. Because outcome control methods are believed to be quicker by the third party (hence often ignoring a lot of the "disadvantages" of arbitration and outcome control), high outcome control methods are used when efficiency and saving time are high priorities. Other factors that affect the choice of resolution method are

- The objectivity (neutrality) of the manager.
- The relationship of the parties (long-term or short-term).
- The effect of how this confrontation is resolved on future negotiations.
- The expected ability of the parties to resolve conflicts for themselves in the future.
- The extent of training of the manager in conflict resolution techniques.

Keys for Managers Helping Employees with Conflict

- Select a neutral site for the meeting.
- Be empathetic; listen as well as you can, and practice listening skills.
- Be assertive, particularly about setting guidelines for how the parties should deal with each other in a more productive manner.
- Ask for cooperation and be cooperative yourself.
- Ask what the parties want you to do to help solve the problem.
- When there is a resolution, if appropriate, get it in writing.
- Help the parties plan for implementation. And do not forget follow-up.

ADR's Usefulness

Since 95 percent of all civil cases are settled out of court, there is room in the area of dispute resolution for ADR.[26] Alternative methods of dispute resolution can save time and money, reduce the number of cases on court dockets, and provide timely solutions to problems. In fact, about half of state court systems now require that certain civil complaints be referred to arbitration prior to trial. Thirty-three jurisdictions require that family disputes regarding custody and visitation be brought into mediation.[27]

At the federal level, the U.S. district courts increasingly order civil cases into mandatory arbitration or refer parties to moderated settlement conferences, minitrials, and summary jury trials. The U.S. Court of Appeals for the District of Columbia and the U.S. Court of Claims are also experimenting with mediation programs.

As an example of costs, a commercial suit with a $200,000 claim will cost parties almost that much in legal fees, discovery costs, and actual trial costs. Mediation for this situation would cost about $2,500, usually shared between the two parties. So it makes sense to use third-party intervention before taking a case to court. And, as stated previously, mediation has a good track record—70 to 80 percent of all cases are successfully mediated.

Many employers now include in contracts, employment agreements, and other related documents an ADR clause that defines the dispute resolution process. It may specify[28]

- The rules or laws that apply to the process.
- The ADR methods to use and in what order to apply them.

- The location for the ADR procedure.
- The official language of the ADR process.
- Whether the outcome will be binding.
- How the costs will be allocated among the parties.

In fact, at NCR, ADR is specified as the first, preferred method for dispute settlement.

However, ADR is not always the perfect solution. As an example, in the case of a rate-setting dispute with the Public Utilities Commission of Ohio (PUCO),[29] ADR appeared not to work well for this regulated utility, and was not a viable solution. There were several reasons. First, the intervention was not voluntary, so there was lower commitment to the process. Time constraints for public utilities prohibited the long periods of consideration that tend to be required in mediated situations. Resources were strained because the utility had to prepare for court at the same time as pursuing ADR, in case ADR failed. Statutory requirements added further constraints and costs. Utilities in dispute need to have mediators who are fully aware of industry-specific details (especially in the area of regulation) in order to be effective, and this was not true in this case.

How Some Organizations Solve Disputes

Many organizations follow a "line authority" approach to solving problems: First you go to a supervisor, then to a division supervisor, then to a panel of supervisors, and finally to top management. If one of the parties is a union, the fourth step is binding arbitration. But there are other, more effective, more proactive ways to solve problems.

One such plan is PGR—peer group resolution[30]—which is used by Northern States Power Company. The purpose of the process is to investigate, review, and resolve disputes; employee peer groups serve on the panel and execute the process. The PGR steps are very specific.

Step 1. The employee with a complaint completes a PGR form and submits a copy of it to the human resources department within 10 days of the incident. The employee gives the original form to the immediate supervisor, who completes a meeting with the employee within three working days. The supervisor writes a response to the problem on the form, and returns it to the employee within two working days. The employee then has two days to decide whether the response satisfies the complaint, or whether to progress to step 2.

Step 2. The employee's second-level supervisor schedules and completes a meeting with the employee within three working days of receiving the form. This person writes a response on the form, and returns it to the employee within two working days of meeting with the employee. The employee has two working days after receiving the written response to complete the appropriate section of the form, either indicating satisfaction with the response and sending it to human resources, or going to step 3.

Step 3. In this step, the employee can select from one of two options listed on the PGR form: Meet either with a third-level supervisor or with a peer group panel.

The supervisor meeting process is similar to that in step 2. If the employee selects the peer group panel, the human resources department coordinates the random selection of panel members and schedules a panel review. The peer group panel consists of five employees, randomly chosen from two panelist pools. If the employee is nonsupervisory, then five panelists are selected from the nonsupervisory pool and four panelists from the supervisory pool. If the employee is supervisory, five panelists come from the supervisory pool, and four from the nonsupervisory pool. In either case the employee chooses two names from each pool to discard, resulting in a total of five panelists.

Within 10 working days of the employee choosing the final option, the panel meets with the employee and reviews the documentation and facts. The panel reaches a decision by majority vote to grant, modify, or deny the remedy requested by the employee. The panelists sign the form, adding explanations as appropriate. Human resources distributes copies of the decision to the employee and supervisors. The decision reached in this manner is binding and cannot be appealed. All materials are kept confidential.

The program is successful in part because all who volunteer to be panelists receive a full day of training for this role. They practice reviewing sample cases using the role-play process.

The results of peer group resolution at Northern States Power Company have been rewarding. Many disputes have been resolved before they get to step 3. Accountability of management has improved. Communication and problem-solving skills have improved. Concerns can be voiced and dealt with before they become major problems or disputes. The process allows all parties to deal with conflict in an organized manner. Productivity and morale are higher because employees feel they can be heard. They also learn, as panelists, to better appreciate what goes into management decisions, and participate in a process of resolving disputes.

The company requires everyone to complete an evaluation form to assess the process, and this has provided positive feedback. In addition, each party with a grievance must be interviewed three months after settlement to ensure that there is no retaliation.

Finding Third-Party Help

There are many organizations for mediators, arbitrators, and other third-party professionals. Among them are the Federal Mediation and Conciliation Service and the American Arbitration Association. There are private organizations that provide professional services, such as Endispute. There are also local mediation services in many communities, as well as consumer protection services available through district attorneys' offices. In most communities, you can simply look up "Mediation Services" in your classified telephone directory, and find a list of individuals and organizations providing services.

If you are interviewing a potential candidate for third-party help, you may want to find out about availability, interests, and potential conflicts. Select someone who has a knowledge of the subject area that is the center of your dispute. Do not use a person who is likely to be partisan.[31]

Endnotes

1. C. Moore, *The Mediation Process: Practical Strategies for Resolving Conflict* (San Francisco, CA: Jossey-Bass, 1986).

2. See F. Elkouri and E. Elkouri, *How Arbitration Works,* 4th ed. (Washington, DC: BNA, 1985); P. Prasow and E. Peters, *Arbitration and Collective Bargaining: Conflict Resolution in Labor Relations,* 2nd ed. (New York: McGraw-Hill, 1983); and R. N. Corley, R. L. Black, and O. L. Reed, *The Legal Environment of Business,* 4th ed. (New York: McGraw-Hill, 1977).

3. C. Feigenbaum, "Final-Offer Arbitration: Better Theory Than Practice," *Industrial Relations 14* (1975), pp. 311–317.

4. D. Golann, "Consumer Financial Services Litigation: Major Judgments and ADR Responses," *The Business Lawyer* 48 (May 1993), pp. 1141–49.

5. T. A. Kochan, *Collective Bargaining and Industrial Relations* (Homewood, IL: Irwin, 1980).

6. G. Long and P. Feuille, "Final Offer Arbitration: Sudden Death in Eugene," *Industrial and Labor Relations Review* 27 (1974), pp. 186–203; F. A. Starke and W. W. Notz, "Pre- and Postintervention Effects of Conventional versus Final-Offer Arbitration," *Academy of Management Journal* 24 (1981), pp. 832–50.

7. V. H. Vroom, "A New Look at Managerial Decision Making," *Organizational Dynamics 1* (Spring 1973), pp. 66–80.

8. J. C. Anderson and T. Kochan, "Impasse Procedures in the Canadian Federal Service," *Industrial and Labor Relations Review* 30 (1977), pp. 283–301.

9. T. A. Kochan and T. Jick, "The Public Sector Mediation Process: A Theory and Empirical Examination," *Journal of Conflict Resolution* 22 (1978), pp. 209–40; T. A. Kochan, *Collective Bargaining and Industrial Relations* (Homewood, IL: Irwin, 1980).

10. P. J. D. Carnevale and D. G. Pruitt, "Negotiation and Mediation," in M. Rosenberg and L. Porter (eds.), *Annual Review of Psychology* 43 (Palo Alto, CA: Annual Reviews, 1992), pp. 531–582; J. A. Wall and A. Lynn, "Mediation: A Current Review," *Journal of Conflict Resolution* 37 (1993), pp. 160–94; R. J. Lewicki, S. Weiss, and D. Lewin, "Models of Conflict, Negotiation and Third Party Intervention: A Review and Synthesis," *Journal of Organizational Behavior* 13 (1992), pp. 209–52.

11. Carnevale and Pruitt, "Negotiation and Mediation."

12. See W. A. Donohue, *Communication, Marital Dispute and Divorce Mediation* (Hillsdale, NJ: Erlbaum, 1991); K. Kressel, N. Jaffe, M. Tuchman, C. Watson, and M. Deutsch, "Mediated Negotiations in Divorce and Labor Disputes: A Comparison," *Conciliation Courts Review* 15 (1977), pp. 9–12; O. J. Coogler, *Structural Mediation in Divorce Settlement: A Handbook for Marital Mediators* (Lexington, MA: Lexington Books, 1978).

13. K. Duffy, J. Grosch, and P. Olczak, *Community Mediation: A Handbook for Practitioners and Researchers* (New York: Guilford, 1991); P. Lovenheim, *Mediate, Don't Litigate: How to Resolve Disputes Quickly, Privately, and Inexpensively without Going to Court* (New York: McGraw-Hill, 1989); L. Singer, *Settling Disputes: Conflict Resolution in Business, Families, and the Legal System* (Boulder, CO: Westview Press, 1990).

14. R. Coulson, *Business Mediation: What You Need to Know* (New York: American Arbitration Association, 1987).

15. W. Drayton, "Getting Smarter about Regulation," *Harvard Business Review* 59 (July–August 1981), pp. 38–52; R. B. Reich, "Regulation by Confrontation or Negotiation," *Harvard Business Review* 59 (May–June 1981), pp. 82–93; L. Susskind and J. Cruikshank, *Breaking the Impasse: Consensual Approaches to Resolving Public Disputes* (New York: Basic Books, 1987).

16. R. Fisher, *International Mediation: A Working Guide* (New York: International Peace Academy, 1978).

17. Carnevale and Pruitt, "Negotiation and Mediation"; K. Kressel and D. Pruitt (eds.), *Mediation Research* (San Francisco, CA: Jossey-Bass, 1989).

18. T. A. Kochan and T. Jick, "The Public Sector Mediation Process: A Theory and Empirical Examination," *Journal of Conflict Resolution* 22 (1978), pp. 209–40.

19. C. Moore, The *Mediation Process: Practical Strategies for Resolving Conflict* (San Francisco, CA: Jossey-Bass, 1986).

20. Starke and Notz, "Pre- and Postintervention Effects"; D. W. Grigsby, *The Effects of Intermediate Mediation Step on Bargaining Behavior under Various Forms of Compulsory Arbitration,* paper presented to the Annual Meeting of the American Institute for Decision Sciences, Boston, MA, November 1981; D. W. Grigsby and W. J. Bigoness, "Effects of Mediation and Alternative Forms of Arbitration on Bargaining Behavior: A Laboratory Study," *Journal of Applied Psychology* 67 (1982), pp. 549–54.

21. T. B. Carver and A. A. Vondra, "Alternative Dispute Resolution: Why It Doesn't Work and Why It Does," *Harvard Business Review,* May–June 1994, p. 124.

22. M. A. Rahim, J. E. Garrett, and G. F. Buntzman, "Ethics of Managing Interpersonal Conflict in Organizations," *Journal of Business Ethics* 14 (1992), pp. 423–32.

23. Rahim, Garrett, and Buntzman, "Ethics of Managing Interpersonal Conflict."

24. B. H. Sheppard, "Managers as Inquisitors: Some Lessons from the Law," in M. Bazerman and R. J. Lewicki (eds.), *Negotiating in Organizations* (Beverly Hills, CA: Sage, 1983), pp. 193–213.

25. Rahim, Garrett, and Buntzman, "Ethics of Managing Interpersonal Conflict."

26. G. M. Flores, "Handling Employee Issues through Alternative Dispute Resolution," *The Bankers Magazine,* July/August 1993, pp. 47–50.

27. From American Bar Association material—Section of Dispute Resolution (1800 M Street, Washington, DC).

28. M. S. Lans, "Try an ADR and You'll Save Yourself a Court Date," *Marketing and the Law,* June 21, 1993, p. 14.

29. D. C. Bergmann, "ADR: Resolution or Complication?" *Public Utilities Fortnightly,* January 15, 1993, pp. 20–22.

30. D. B. Hoffman and N. L. Kluver, "How Peer Group Resolution Works at Northern States Power Co.," *Employment Relations Today,* Spring 1992, pp. 25–30.

31. J. Greenwald, "Resolving Disagreements: Alternative Market Finds ADR Works to Its Advantage," *Business Insurance,* June 7, 1993, p. 45.

The Manager as the Third Party: Deciding How to Intervene in Employee Disputes

A. R. Elangovan

Consider the following scenarios in an organization:

> Two days before major contract work was to begin at an important client site, a dispute had erupted between the director of operations (DO) and controller of a small emission-testing (pollution control) company regarding hiring temporary workers. The DO argued that the extra workers were necessary to carry out the work, and per company regulations she had the authority to do whatever was needed to complete a contract. The controller disagreed, saying that the company regulations allow the DO only to purchase equipment and materials and that adding employees to the payroll requires the final approval of the HR department and finance department. The dispute was brought to the attention of the president of the firm for a settlement.
>
> The marketing manager and the production manager of a manufacturing company were at odds over the issue of design changes. The production manager was upset about the current procedures, which allowed marketing to make frequent changes to product design of new products right up to the commencement of production runs in order to appease customers. Each change meant three days of work to alter the specifications of all interacting components, loss of production line time reserved earlier, and lower cost-effectiveness. The production manager wanted to limit last-minute changes by setting two weeks before production as the deadline for final design. The marketing manager argued that last-minute alterations were necessary to cope with competitors' changes, meet customer demands, and maintain market share in the tough global environment. The conflict had escalated to an extent that coordination between the groups was suffering and morale was being affected, which prompted the executive vice president to step in.

If you were the president in the first example and the vice president in the second, how would you intervene in the dispute? Would you facilitate the discussion and interaction between the two disputants but leave the final solution in their hands? Or would you listen carefully to both sides, analyze the issue, and come up with a good solution? Or would you impress upon the two disputants the importance of learning to handle such disputes on their own and urge them to do so quickly? Of course, this would not be a problem if there were an intervention strategy that worked well for all disputes. Unfortunately, research has been unable to pinpoint a "magic" strategy that would be effective in all disputes. Even the highly popular and much touted approach of mediation has not lived up to its reputation under empirical scrutiny. Thus managers are left with numerous options for intervention, and it is not always clear *how* they should intervene in a dispute between two subordinates to ensure maximum success in resolving it.

Source: Adapted from A. R. Elangovan, "Managerial Third-Party Dispute Intervention: A Prescriptive Model of Strategy Selection," *Academy of Management Review* 20 (1995), pp. 800–30. Used with author's permission.

Managers as Third Parties

Conflict is an undeniable and pervasive feature of life in modern organizations. While the presence of conflict per se is not a problem, it is important that such conflict be managed properly to ensure that it is beneficial to achieving the goals of the organizations. Managed effectively, conflict can enhance performance by challenging the status quo, furthering the creation of new ideas, promoting reassessment of unit goals and activities, increasing the probability that the unit will respond to change, relieving tension, and serving as a medium for airing problems. But who is responsible for ensuring that conflict is managed successfully in organizations? At one level, it can be argued that it is every employee's responsibility to deal with daily conflict in a constructive rather than destructive manner. While an organization may aspire to this goal, the fact remains that employees or groups or departments are often unable to resolve disputes through established procedures or on their own. Often the supervisor or manager at the next higher level intervenes in the dispute to help resolve it. Research has shown that managers frequently act as third parties in employee disputes concerning a wide range of issues such as failure to perform specified duties, usurpation of responsibility, disagreement over company policies, discrimination, and so forth.[1] Given the significance of these issues, it is important that the managers intervene in a manner that contributes to the effective functioning of the organization. But more often than not, these managers are informal third parties rather than highly trained professionals. Unlike professional mediators and arbitrators, these managers are not external to the organization or the dispute but have an ongoing relationship with the disputants. Their effort at intervening is often part of their day-to-day managing of the work unit with a history of interactions and relationships among the parties involved. This not only limits the applicability of the prescriptions from professional third-party research to managerial intervention, but it also highlights the difficulties managers have in trying to identify the most appropriate form of intervention to use when handling a dispute between subordinates. What is needed is a framework that will help managers select the right intervention strategy in a given dispute situation. In developing this framework, however, it is necessary to identify what constitutes a successful intervention, the different intervention strategies available to the manager, and the key situational factors that would influence the selection of the appropriate strategy. Linking these three components, then, would produce a framework that indicates the kind of strategy to be selected in a given situation to achieve a successful resolution.

Criteria for Evaluating the Success of an Intervention

What constitutes a successful intervention? Within the organizational context, research has identified a wide array of criteria for evaluating the quality of dispute interventions.[2] For example, it can be argued that for an intervention to be rated as successful it must address and resolve *all* the issues in the dispute. Similarly, a good case can be made for stating that a successful intervention should leave the disputants satisfied with the outcomes of the resolution. In addition, it is equally important that the intervention process be perceived as fair since that would affect the disputants' commitment to implementing the resolution. Although the criteria listed are important, they focus on only part of the picture. For example, would an intervention that satisfies all these criteria be considered successful if it used up an inordinate amount of time and resources and caused disruption? Probably not. In other words, the efficiency with which an intervention is undertaken also plays a role in determining the success of the intervention. Unfortunately, however, it is often extremely difficult, if not impossible, to have interventions that are concurrently high on effectiveness, efficiency, satisfaction, and fairness. Part of the problem lies with the counteracting nature of these criteria if taken together. For example, imposing a resolution on the disputants after quickly gathering information may increase efficiency but would negatively affect the satisfaction and perceived fairness criteria since disputants may not accept or feel ownership of the resolution. Similarly, spending a lot of time seeking input and facilitating discussions to arrive at a consensus may lead to increased satisfaction and perceptions of fairness but does not guarantee a high-quality decision that effectively addresses all the problems in the best interest of the organization (effectiveness). This suggests that for developing a prescriptive model of intervention strategy selection, we need to first identify the criteria that are the most critical. But which of the criteria listed are pivotal to the success of an intervention? And whose perspective should we adopt—the disputants', the intervening manager's, or the organization's?

Given the *prescriptive* nature of this model, it can be argued that it is the *organization's* perspective that matters rather than the personal interests of the disputants or third parties. After all, the aim here is to develop a set of prescriptions that will guide managers in successfully intervening in disputes to benefit and enhance organizational performance. Broadly speaking, therefore, a successful intervention would be one that satisfies three criteria: *settlement effectiveness, timeliness,* and *disputant commitment.* *Settlement effectiveness* refers to the extent to which the issues in the dispute are fully addressed to produce a settlement congruent with the goals of the organization. *Timeliness* refers to resolving the dispute before significant costs are incurred either in the form of resources, money, and time spent in squabbling and finger-pointing before actually dealing with the dispute, or in the form of a decline in productivity due to disruptions in operations or losses incurred due to missed deadlines. *Disputant commitment* refers to the extent to which disputants are motivated or determined to implementing the agreed-upon settlement, which, in turn, is contingent on their satisfaction with the resolution and perceptions of fairness. In sum, a successful intervention is one where (*a*) the issues are fully addressed to produce a settlement consistent with organizational objectives, (*b*) the resolution is timely, and (*c*) the disputants are committed to the resolution.

Managerial Dispute Intervention Strategies

What are the various intervention strategies available to the manager acting as the third party? As noted in the introduction to this article, the manager has plenty of choice: The options range from imposing a settlement to encouraging the disputants to settle on their own, with numerous variations in between. Rather than compile a long, unwieldy list of the specific strategies that are available (some of which vary only by name), it is more useful and practical to identifying the major *types* or categories of strategies that are significantly different from each other. This would also help in matching the different

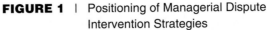

FIGURE 1 | Positioning of Managerial Dispute
Intervention Strategies

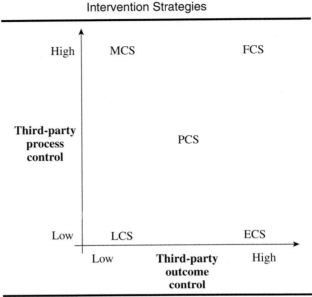

type of strategies to different disputes for achieving a successful resolution. One popular approach to classifying and understanding intervention strategies has been to use the degree of control wielded by the intervening third parties over the process (the procedures and activities involved in arriving at a settlement) and the outcome (the actual settlement to the dispute) of the resolution as two major dimensions.[3] Figure 1 presents a two-dimensional graph with the degree of third-party process control and the degree of third-party outcome control as the two axes.

Using these two axes, different intervention strategies can be "identified" by plotting various coordinates in the graph space. While numerous combinations varying by minute degrees of outcome and process control can be devised, for the sake of parsimony and applicability, only distinctly different combinations are considered here. Figure 1 shows five such combinations that are positioned into the corners and the center of the graph: *means control strategy* (MCS), *ends control strategy* (ECS), *full control strategy* (FCS), *low control strategy* (LCS), and *part control strategy* (PCS). These five combinations (intervention strategies) and the activities that are contained under each of these procedures are described in Figure 2. These descriptions capture the typical intervention procedures that fit under each combination. Variations of each combination can be included as long as they fit the basic description (e.g., mediation and conciliation are listed as examples under MCS).

So a manager using FCS to intervene in a dispute would control both the process and outcome of the resolution—that is, decide what information should be presented and how, ask specific questions, decide on a settlement, and impose it. When using MCS, however, the manager would control only the process and not the outcome. He or she would explain one disputant's views to the other, clarify issues, maintain order during

FIGURE 2 | Description of Managerial Dispute Intervention Strategies

MCS	*Means control strategy:* Manager intervenes in the dispute by influencing the process of resolution (i.e., facilitates interaction, assists in communication, explains one disputant's views to another, clarifies issues, lays down rules for dealing with the dispute, maintains order during talks) but does not attempt to dictate or impose a resolution (though he or she might suggest solutions); the final decision is left to the disputants; high on process control but low on outcome control (e.g., mediation, conciliation).
ECS	*Ends control strategy:* Manager intervenes in the dispute by influencing the outcome of the resolution (i.e., takes full control of the final resolution, decides what the final decision will be, imposes the resolution on the disputants) but does not attempt to influence the process; the disputants have control over what information is presented and how it is presented; high on outcome control but low on process control (e.g., arbitration, adjudication, adversarial intervention).
LCS	*Low control strategy:* Manager does not intervene actively in resolving the dispute; either urges the parties to settle the dispute on their own or merely stays away from the dispute; low on both process and outcome control (e.g., encouraging or telling the parties to negotiate or settle the dispute by themselves, providing impetus).
FCS	*Full control strategy:* Manager intervenes in the dispute by influencing the process and outcome (i.e., decides what information is to be presented and how it should be presented and also decides on the final resolution); asks the disputants specific questions about the dispute to obtain information and imposes a resolution; manager has full control of the resolution of the dispute; high on both process and outcome control (e.g., inquisitorial intervention, autocratic intervention).
PCS	*Part control strategy:* Manager intervenes in the dispute by sharing control over the process and outcome with the disputants (i.e., manager and disputants jointly agree on the process of resolution as well as strive for a consensus on the settlement decision); works with the disputants to help them arrive at a solution by facilitating interaction, assisting in communication, discussing the issues, and so on; in addition, takes an active role in evaluating options, recommending solutions, persuading the disputants to accept them, and pushing for a settlement; moderate on managerial process and outcome control (e.g., group problem solving, mediation–arbitration).

talks, and lay down rules for dealing with the dispute. In contrast, under ECS, the manager would let the disputants control the process (e.g., decide what information to present and how to present it), but the manager would take full control of the outcome by deciding final settlement and imposing it on the disputants. A manager using LCS would urge or tell the parties to settle the dispute on their own but would not actively intervene in the dispute. Finally, when using PCS, the manager would share control over the process and outcome with the disputants. The manager would jointly work toward a resolution with the disputants, facilitating interaction, clarifying issues, evaluating options, recommending solutions, and persuading the disputants to accept them (e.g., group problem solving).

Key Situational Factors That Affect Strategy Selection

Given the five strategies described, when should each strategy be used? In other words, how would the manager be able to determine that a certain dispute calls for a specific strategy to maximize intervention success? Obviously this entails assessing each dispute to identify some key characteristics or situational factors, which may then suggest that certain strategies are better suited for resolving that dispute than others. For example, if one of the distinguishing features of the dispute is time pressure (as in the first example in the introduction), it implies that speed is of essence and strategies that take longer to arrive at a settlement (e.g., PCS, MCS) may not be as appropriate as other strategies (e.g., FCS). Although one can focus on a plethora of factors to develop a profile of a dispute, it is both important and useful to zoom in on just the essential characteristics of the disputes that have significant bearing on the suitability and, hence, the probability of success of different intervention strategies. Described next are six factors that have been identified by prior research as being the critical ones and their implications for strategy selection:[4]

1. *Dispute importance:* How important is the dispute? A dispute is important if it is central to the survival or functioning of a group or organization. From a prescriptive standpoint, the manager should be more concerned about the dispute when the dispute importance is high than when it is low. When dispute importance is high, more care and control of outcome are needed, and therefore the intervening manager should not select a strategy that yields full outcome control to the disputants. This will ensure some managerial influence on the outcome and hence will lead to an organizationally beneficial solution. At the same time, however, to ensure commitment from the disputants, the manager should ensure that the process is orderly and not one-sided due to power and other differences between the disputants, and should make sure that the disputants feel that they have some influence in resolving the dispute (i.e., the manager should also retain some degree of process control).

2. *Time pressure:* Some disputes need to be settled more urgently than others. Since intervention strategies vary in how quickly they lead to a settlement, it is important to select the appropriate strategy to ensure intervention success. In general, when time pressure is high, the manager should not select a strategy that yields full control of the process and the outcome, in that order, to the disputants. Not acceding complete control of the process ensures that the manager can influence the speed at which the dispute is resolved. Not acceding complete control of the outcome ensures that the dispute will be resolved if disputants still cannot arrive at a settlement even when the process is speeded up.

3. *Nature of dispute:* Is the dispute about the interpretation, implementation, or execution of an existing rule, regulation, procedure, or operation within the existing organizational framework (dispute over "what is"), or is it about creating new or changing the existing procedures, operations, contracts, or systems (dispute over "what should be or would like it to be")? The label *dispute over privilege* (DOP) is used here to identify the "interpretive" disputes (where misunderstanding or ambiguity is at the root of the dispute), while the label *dispute over stakes* (DOS) is used to distinguish the "change" disputes (where the focus is on altering the system). For example, the dispute between a financial controller and a marketing manager regarding the interpretation of an expenses reimbursement clause is a DOP dispute. A dispute between the same individuals about increasing the maximum amount for client entertainment expenses is a DOS dispute. In a DOP dispute, the disputants are generally more open to, and might even expect, a

settlement from the third party because they were unable to, on their own, agree on an interpretation or application. This implies that an intervention strategy that gives the third party some degree of outcome control will be effective for a DOP dispute, and therefore the manager (third party) should not use strategies that limit his or her outcome control. In contrast, a DOS dispute reaches deeper to affect emotions and values, and it is imperative that disputants fully understand and accept any change in the system in order for them to be committed in the long run to the change. In such a situation, the manager should influence the process to ensure that it is orderly but leave the final settlement to the disputants; that is, for resolving a DOS dispute, the manager should not choose strategies that yield full process control but little outcome control to disputants.

4. *Nature of relations:* Are the disputants in a long-term relationship, or are they not likely to interact with each other after the dispute is resolved? This factor addresses the work group dynamics of the two disputants and is important because different intervention strategies have different effects on the relations between disputants. Since it is in the best interests of the organization to have a normal or positive working relationship between the parties, an intervention strategy that will further this objective should be selected for any given dispute. This implies that if the disputants are involved in a long-term relationship, then in the interest of long-term commitment and cooperation, the manager should ensure that the disputants have some degree of influence or control over the dispute settlement. So the manager should not choose an intervention strategy that limits the control disputants can have over the outcome. In addition, the manager should have some influence over the process to ensure that it is orderly and fair. On the other hand, when the disputants are not likely to interact with each other in the future on a regular basis, the manager can assume more control over the outcome, since the effect of the settlement on future relations is not much of a concern.

5. *Commitment probability:* This factor refers to the probability that the disputants will be committed to a settlement if it were to be decided unilaterally by the intervening manager. This, in turn, depends on the nature of the relationship between the manager and the disputants, including the degree of power the manager has and the subordinates' feelings of trust and loyalty. It is important to note that for long-term organizational effectiveness, it is not sufficient that the disputants merely indicate their acceptance of the settlement; they must honor the spirit of the settlement and not continue to harbor feelings of conflict or demonstrate reluctance in executing the resolution. This suggests that the manager must assess the commitment probability for imposing resolutions and select an intervention strategy accordingly. Low commitment probability implies that if the manager were to impose a settlement to a dispute then the disputants will not remain committed to it. In such cases, intervention strategies that do not accede control to disputants will be less effective than those that give disputants some control over the outcome. But if the manager perceives the commitment probability to be high, then he or she can assume more outcome control and impose a resolution whenever necessary (contingent on the status of the other attributes).

6. *Disputant orientation:* Disputant orientation addresses the question, What is the likelihood that the disputants will arrive at an organizationally appropriate settlement if given control over the resolution of the dispute (outcome control)? If disputant orientation is high, then the probability that the disputants will arrive at an organizationally compatible settlement is high; if disputant orientation is low, then the probability is low. Regarding strategy selection, if the manager views the disputants' orientation as being low, then he or she should not select intervention strategies that yield full outcome control to the disputing subordinates. This would ensure that the manager has some control and input into the final settlement and that the interests and goals of the organization are not compromised. On the other hand, if the disputant orientation is high, then the manager should select strategies that yield some degree of outcome control to the disputants to promote satisfaction and commitment.

In summary, the status of these six dispute factors has implications for the selection of strategies and helps satisfy one or more of the three intervention success criteria identified earlier. Each of these factors can be represented by a question that has two response options (high/low) (see Figure 3). A manager facing a particular dispute can diagnose the main situational demands by answering the six questions. The answers to the six questions provide the basis for selecting among the five intervention strategies.

Generating Decision Rules to Guide Strategy Selection

Next, the recommendations for the use or avoidance of outcome and process control for each factor (just discussed) indicate when different intervention strategies should be selected for successful intervention. This logic can be captured in a set of decision rules to direct the strategy selection process. Figure 4 presents the seven rules that underlie the proposed model. These rules are a series of "if . . . then . . ." statements that indicate for a certain status (high/low) of each factor the form of control (process, outcome) that should be retained by the intervening manager or given to the disputants to ensure the success of the intervention. This, in turn, implies that certain strategies may be dropped from the feasible full set of the five intervention strategies because of the risk they pose to a successful resolution of the dispute. For example, if the status of the commitment probability attribute is low (i.e., the likelihood that the disputants would be committed to a settlement imposed by the manager is low), then this suggests that the intervening manager should give the disputants some control over the outcome. For strategy selection purposes, this eliminates the two strategies that give the third party full outcome control (i.e., FCS and ECS) from the feasible set (Rule 5). For any given dispute, using the first six rules will lead to a feasible set of intervention strategies that would be most successful in resolving the dispute. The last rule, Priority Rule, guides the choice within the feasible set based on efficiency maximization. Each rule also contributes to protecting one or more of the three success criteria. The Dispute Importance, Nature of Dispute, and Disputant Orientation rules focus on who controls the outcome, thus ensuring *settlement effectiveness;* the Time Pressure and Priority rules focus on the need for expediency and the costs involved with delays, thus ensuring *timeliness;* and the Nature

FIGURE 3 | Key Situational Factors Influencing Strategy Selection

Question A	How important is this dispute to the effective functioning of the organization? (high/low)
Question B	How important is it to resolve the dispute as quickly as possible? (high/low)
Question C	Does the dispute concern the interpretation/application of existing rules, procedures, arrangements, and so on, or does it concern the alteration/change of existing rules, procedures, arrangements? (DOP/DOS)
Question D	What is the expected frequency of future work-related interactions between the disputants? (high/low)
Question E	If you were to impose a settlement on your subordinates (disputants), what is the probability that they would be committed to it? (high/low)
Question F	If you were to let your subordinates (disputants) settle the dispute, what is the probability that they would come to an organizationally compatible settlement? (high/low)

of Relations, Nature of Dispute, and Commitment Probability rules focus on ensuring acceptance and commitment of the disputants to the settlement, thus ensuring *disputant commitment*.

A Decision Tree for Selecting an Intervention Strategy

Figure 5 shows a decision tree developed using the five intervention strategies (Figure 2), the six questions pertaining to the situational factors of the dispute (Figure 3), and the seven rules with two status options (high/low) for each factor (Figure 4). To use the tree, a manager first identifies a dispute between subordinates that he or she has decided to help resolve. The manager starts at the extreme left of the decision tree and asks the first question. The answer, high or low, indicates the path to be taken to arrive at the next node signifying the next question. The process continues until the manager arrives at a terminal node or end point on the decision tree that indicates the optimal intervention strategy.

The model uses a choice elimination approach to arrive at the right strategy. Choices or intervention strategies that are not likely to result in a successful resolution are eliminated, thus narrowing the choice to the most appropriate intervention strategy for that specific dispute. Although six factors were identified as key dispute attributes, not all of them become relevant for all disputes. If the status of the attribute does not make a difference to the selection of an intervention strategy with regard to the success of the resolution for a particular dispute configuration, then it is not necessary to apply that rule. For example, when the dispute importance is low and time pressure is low, the manager need not be concerned with the status of the other attributes but can directly arrive at the appropriate intervention strategy without posing any risk to the dispute resolution success. Similarly, disputant orientation becomes relevant only when the status of other attributes suggest that the manager select an intervention strategy that yields full outcome control to the disputants. However, all six attributes are important and essential for the model as a whole to be valid and useful.

FIGURE 4 | Rules Underlying the Model

1. The Dispute Importance Rule: If the importance of the dispute is high, then the intervention strategy chosen should give the manager some degree of control on either or both dimensions. Accordingly, LCS is eliminated from the feasible set.

2. The Time Pressure Rule: If the time pressure associated with settling the dispute is high, then the intervention strategy chosen should give the manager some degree of process control. Accordingly, LCS and ECS are eliminated from the feasible set.

3. The Nature of Dispute Rule: If the dispute between subordinates is a DOP dispute, then the intervention strategy chosen should give the manager some degree of outcome control. Accordingly, LCS and MCS are eliminated from the feasible set. The only exception to the rule is when time pressure is low, commitment probability is low, but disputant orientation is high (MCS is the option). If the dispute between subordinates is a DOS dispute, then the manager should allow the subordinates some degree of control on either or both dimensions (process and outcome). Accordingly, FCS is eliminated from the feasible set. The only exception to the rule is when time pressure is high, commitment probability is high, and the disputants are not likely to interact frequently in the future.

4. The Nature of Relations Rule: If the subordinates (disputants) are likely to have a high frequency of interaction in the future, then the intervention strategy chosen should give the subordinates some degree of outcome control. Accordingly, FCS and ECS are eliminated from the feasible set. The only exception to the rule is when time pressure is low, commitment probability is high, and disputant orientation is low (ECS is the option).

5. The Commitment Probability Rule: If the probability that the subordinates (disputants) would be committed to a settlement imposed by the manager is low, then the intervention strategy chosen should give subordinates some degree of outcome control. Accordingly, FCS and ECS are eliminated from the feasible set.

6. The Disputant Orientation Rule: If the status of the dispute based on the previous five rules suggests choosing intervention strategies that yield full outcome control to subordinates (disputants), the manager should use disputant orientation as the final criterion. If disputant orientation is low, the intervention strategy chosen should give the manager some degree of outcome control. Accordingly, LCS and MCS are eliminated from the feasible set. If disputant orientation is high, the intervention strategy chosen should give subordinates some degree of outcome control. Accordingly, FCS and ECS are eliminated from the feasible set.

7. The Priority Rule: If the status of the dispute based on the previous six rules suggests more than one intervention as being equally effective, the following priority conditions must be observed to select one strategy. For high-importance disputes, when time pressure is low and commitment probability is low, the manager should choose the intervention strategy that allows him or her maximum process control (so that by ensuring an orderly and fair process the commitment can be increased); when time pressure is low and commitment probability is high, the manager should select the strategy that allows him or her maximum outcome control (so that the best interests of the organization are always protected) while giving the disputants at least some control over the resolution; when time pressure is high, the manager should choose the intervention strategy that requires the least amount of time to resolve the dispute without endangering commitment. For low-importance disputes, the manager should select the strategy that requires the least amount of resources (skills, time, etc.).

FIGURE 5 | A Model of Intervention Strategy Selection

DI   How important is this dispute to the effective functioning of the organization?

TP   How important is it to resolve the dispute as quickly as possible?

ND   Does the dispute concern the interpretation of existing rules, procedures, and arrangements or the changing of existing rules, procedures, and arrangements?

NR   What is the expected frequency of future work-related interactions between the disputants?

CP   If you were to impose a settlement on your subordinates (disputants), what is the probability that they would be committed to it?

DO   What is the orientation of the disputants? That is, if you were to let your subordinates (disputants) settle the dispute, what is the probability that they would come to an organizationally compatible settlement?

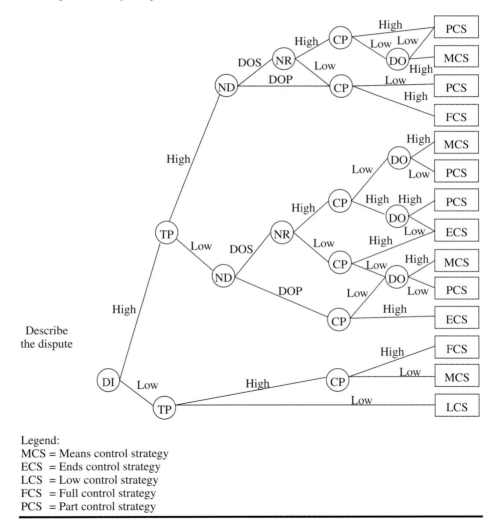

Legend:
MCS = Means control strategy
ECS = Ends control strategy
LCS = Low control strategy
FCS = Full control strategy
PCS = Part control strategy

Conclusion

Managing disputes in organizations is an important part of a manager's job. Often the success of the manager's interventions in these disputes has significant implications for the overall morale of the employees and their productivity. This article offers some guidelines for successful intervention by highlighting the key features of a successful intervention, classifying different intervention strategies, identifying the major situational factors that ought to be considered before selecting a strategy, generating a set of rules to guide the strategy selection process, and developing a decision tree model that can be used by practicing managers.

Endnotes

1.   See R. I. Lissak and B. H. Sheppard, "Beyond Fairness: The Criterion Problem in Research on Conflict Intervention," *Journal of Applied Social Psychology* 13 (1983), pp. 45–65; and B. H. Sheppard, "Third-Party Conflict Intervention: A Procedural Framework," in B. M. Staw and L. L. Cummings, (eds.), *Research in Organizational Behavior* 6 (1984), pp. 141–90 (Greenwich, CT: JAI).

2.   Sheppard, "Third-Party Conflict Intervention."

3.   See J. W. Thibaut and L. Walker, *Procedural Justice: A Psychological Analysis* (New York: Wiley, 1975); and R. Lewicki and B. Sheppard, "Choosing How to Intervene: Factors Affecting the Use of Process and Outcome Control in Third-Party Dispute Resolution," *Journal of Occupational Behavior* 6 (1985), pp. 49–64.

4.   See Sheppard, "Third-Party Conflict Intervention,"; R. Karambayya and J. M. Brett, "Managers Handling Disputes: Third-Party Roles and Perceptions of Fairness," *Academy of Management Journal* 32 (1989), pp. 687–704; R. Karambayya, J. Brett, and A. Lytle, "The Effects of Formal Authority and Experience on Third-Party Roles, Outcomes, and Perceptions of Fairness," *Academy of Management Journal* 35 (1992), pp. 426–38; and Lewicki and Sheppard, "Choosing How to Intervene."

Summary

Reading 7.1

Best Practices in Negotiation
Roy J Lewicki
David M. Saunders
Bruce Barry

Negotiation is an integral part of daily life, and the opportunities to negotiate surround us. While some people may look like born negotiators, negotiation is fundamentally a skill involving analysis and communication that everyone can learn. The purpose of this book is to provide students of negotiation with an overview of the field of negotiation, perspective on the breadth and depth of the subprocesses of negotiation, and an appreciation for the art and science of negotiation. In this final chapter we reflect on negotiation at a broad level by providing 10 "best practices" for negotiators who wish to continue to improve their negotiation skills (see Table 1).

1. Be Prepared

We cannot overemphasize the importance of preparation, and we strongly encourage all negotiators to prepare properly for their negotiations. Preparation does not have to be a time-consuming or arduous activity, but it should be right at the top of the best practices list of every negotiator. Negotiators who are better prepared have numerous advantages, including the ability to analyze the other party's offers more effectively and efficiently, to understand the nuances of the concession-making process, and to achieve their negotiation goals. Preparation should occur *before* the negotiation begins so that the time spent negotiating is more productive. Good preparation means understanding one's own goals and interests as well as possible and being able to articulate them to the other party skillfully. It also includes being ready to understand the other party's communication in order to find an agreement that meets the needs of both parties. Few negotiations are going to conclude successfully without both parties achieving at least some of their goals, and solid work up front to identify your needs and to understand the needs of the other party is a critical step to increasing the odds of success.

Source: From *Negotiation,* 5th ed., by Roy J. Lewicki, David M. Saunders, and Bruce Barry (McGraw-Hill/Irwin, 2005), Chapter 20, pp. 517–26.

TABLE 1 | Ten Best Practices for Negotiators

1. Be prepared.
2. Diagnose the fundamental structure of the negotiation.
3. Work the BATNA.
4. Be willing to walk.
5. Master paradox.
6. Remember the intangibles.
7. Actively manage coalitions.
8. Savor and protect your reputation.
9. Remember that rationality and fairness are relative.
10. Continue to learn from the experience.

Good preparation also means setting aspirations for negotiation that are high but achievable. Negotiators who set their sights too low are virtually guaranteed to reach an agreement that is suboptimal, while those who set them too high are more likely to stalemate and end the negotiation in frustration. Negotiators also need to plan their opening statements and positions carefully so they are especially well prepared at the start of negotiations. It is important to avoid preplanning the complete negotiation sequence, however, because while negotiations do follow broad stages, they also ebb and flow at irregular rates. Overplanning the tactics for each negotiation stage in advance of the negotiation is not a good use of preparation time. It is far better that negotiators prepare by understanding their own strengths and weaknesses, their needs and interests, the situation, and the other party as well as possible so that they can adjust promptly and effectively as the negotiation proceeds.

Finally, it is important to recognize and prepare for the effects of the broader context of the negotiation, such as the nature of existing relationships, the presence of audiences, opportunities for forming coalitions, and negotiation within or between teams, as well as for the effects of cross-cultural differences. Negotiators need to consider how these broad contextual factors will influence the negotiation.

2. Diagnose the Fundamental Structure of the Negotiation

Negotiators should make a conscious decision about whether they are facing a fundamentally distributive negotiation, an integrative negotiation, or a blend of the two, and choose their strategies and tactics accordingly. Using strategies and tactics that are mismatched will lead to suboptimal negotiation outcomes. For instance, using overly distributive tactics in a fundamentally integrative situation will almost certainly result in reaching agreements that leave integrative potential untapped because negotiators tend not to share readily the information needed to succeed in integrative negotiations in response to distributive tactics. In these situations, money and opportunity are often left on the table.

Similarly, using integrative tactics in a distributive situation may not lead to optimal outcomes either. For instance, one of the authors of this book was recently shopping for a new car, and the salesman spent a great deal of time and effort asking questions about the author's family and assuring him that he was working hard to get the highest possible value for his trade-in. Unfortunately, requests for clarification about the list price of the car and information about manufacturer incentives described in a recent newspaper advertisement were met with silence or by changing the topic of conversation. This was a purely distributive situation for the author, who was not fooled by the salesman's attempt to bargain "integratively." The author bought a car from a different dealer who was able to provide the requested information in a straightforward manner—and whose price was $1,500 lower than the first dealer for the same car!

Negotiators also need to remember that many negotiations will consist of a blend of integrative and distributive elements and that there will be distributive and integrative phases to these negotiations. It is especially important to be careful when transitioning between these phases within the broader negotiation because missteps in these transitions can confuse the other party and lead to impasse.

Finally, there are also times when accommodation, avoidance, and compromise may be appropriate strategies. Strong negotiators will identify these situations and adopt appropriate strategies and tactics.

3. Identify and Work the BATNA

One of the most important sources of power in a negotiation is the alternatives available to a negotiator if an agreement is not reached. One alternative, the best alternative to a negotiated agreement (BATNA), is especially important because this is the option that likely will be chosen should an agreement not be reached. Negotiators need to be vigilant about their BATNA. They need to know what their BATNA is relative to a possible agreement and consciously work to improve the BATNA so as to improve the deal. Negotiators without a strong BATNA may find it difficult to achieve a good agreement because the other party may try to push them aggressively, and hence they may be forced to accept a settlement that is later seen as unsatisfying.

For instance, purchasers who need to buy items from sole suppliers are acutely aware of how the lack of a positive BATNA makes it difficult to achieve positive negotiation outcomes. Even in this situation, however, negotiators can work to improve their BATNA in the long term. For instance, organizations in a sole supplier relationship have often vertically integrated their production and started to build comparable components inside the company, or they have redesigned their products so they are less vulnerable to the sole supplier. These are clearly long-term options and are not available in the current negotiation. However, it may be possible to refer to these plans when negotiating with a sole supplier in order to remind them that you will not be dependent forever.

Negotiators also need to be aware of the other negotiator's BATNA and to identify how it compares to what you are offering. Negotiators have more power in a negotiation when their potential terms of agreement are significantly better than what the other negotiator can obtain with his or her BATNA. On the other hand, when the difference between your terms and the other negotiator's BATNA is small, then negotiators have less room to maneuver. There are three things negotiators should do with respect to the other negotiator's BATNA: (1) Monitor it carefully in order to understand and retain your competitive advantage over the other negotiator's alternatives; (2) remind the other negotiator of the advantages your offer has relative to her BATNA; and (3) in a subtle way, suggest that the other negotiator's BATNA may not be as strong as he or she thinks it is (this can be done in a positive way by stressing your strengths or in a negative way by highlighting competitors' weaknesses).

4. Be Willing to Walk Away

The goal of most negotiations is achieving a valued outcome, not reaching an agreement per se. Strong negotiators remember this and are willing to walk away from a negotiation when no agreement is better than a poor agreement or when the process is so offensive that the deal isn't worth the work. While this advice sounds easy enough to take in principle, in practice, negotiators can become so focused on reaching an agreement that they lose sight of the real goal, which is to reach a good outcome (and not necessarily an agreement). Negotiators can ensure that they don't take their eye off the goal by making regular comparisons with the targets they set during the planning stage and by comparing their progress during their negotiation against their walkaway and BATNA. While negotiators are often optimistic about goal achievement at the outset, they may need to reevaluate these goals during the negotiation. It is important to continue to compare progress in the current negotiation with the target, walkaway, and BATNA and to be willing to walk away from the current negotiation if their walkaway or BATNA becomes the truly better choice.

Even in the absence of a good BATNA, negotiators should have a clear walkaway point in mind where they will halt negotiations. Sometimes it is helpful if the walkaway is written down or communicated to others so that negotiators can be reminded during difficult negotiations. When in team negotiations, it is important to have a team member monitor the walkaway point and be responsible for stopping the negotiation if it appears that a final settlement is close to this point.

5. Master the Key Paradoxes of Negotiation

Excellent negotiators understand that negotiation embodies a set of paradoxes—seemingly contradictory elements that actually occur together. We will discuss five common paradoxes that negotiators face. The challenge for negotiators in handling these paradoxes is to strive for *balance* in these situations. There is a natural tension between choosing between one or the other alternative in the paradox, but the best way to manage paradox is to achieve a balance between the opposing forces. Strong negotiators know how to manage this tension.

Claiming Value versus Creating Value

All negotiations have a value *claiming* stage, where parties decide who gets how much of what, but many negotiations also have a value *creation* stage, where parties work together to expand the resources under negotiation. The skills and strategies appropriate to each stage are quite different; in general terms, distributive skills are called for in the value claiming stage and integrative skills are useful in value creation. Typically the value creation stage will precede the value claiming stage, and a challenge for negotiators is to balance the emphasis on the two stages and the transition from creating to claiming value. There is no signpost to mark this transition, however, and negotiators need to manage it tactfully to avoid undermining the open brainstorming and option-inventing relationship that has developed during value creation. One approach to manage this transition is to publicly label it. For instance, negotiators could say something like "It looks like we have a good foundation of ideas and alternatives to work from. How can we move on to decide what is a fair distribution of the expected outcomes?" In addition, research shows that most negotiators are overly biased toward thinking that a negotiation is more about claiming value rather than creating value, so managing this paradox will likely require an overemphasis on discussing the creating value dynamics.

Sticking by Your Principles versus Being Resilient to the Flow

The pace and flow of negotiations can move from an intense haggle over financial issues to an intense debate over deeply held principles about what is right or fair or just. These transitions often create a second paradox for negotiators. On the one hand, effective negotiation requires flexible thinking and an understanding that an assessment of a situation may need to be adjusted as new information comes to light; achieving any deal will probably require both parties to make concessions. On the other hand, core principles are not something to back away from easily in the service of doing a deal. Effective negotiators are thoughtful about the distinction between issues of principle, where firmness is essential, and other issues where compromise and accommodation are the best route to a mutually acceptable outcome. A complex negotiation may well involve both kinds of issues in the same encounter. And it is not enough for the negotiator to know in her own mind that an unwavering commitment on issue X is grounded in some deep personal value or principle; good negotiators know that it is critical to convey that principle to the other party so that he or she will not misread firmness based on principle as hostility or intransigence.

Sticking with the Strategy versus Opportunistic Pursuit of New Options

New information will frequently come to light during a negotiation, and negotiators need to manage the paradox between sticking with their prepared strategy and pursuing a new opportunity that arises during the process. This is a challenging paradox for negotiators to manage because new "opportunities" may in fact be Trojan horses harboring unpleasant surprises. On the other hand, circumstances do change, and legitimate "one-time," seize-the-moment deals do occur. The challenge for negotiators is to distinguish phantom opportunities from real ones; developing the capacity to recognize the distinction is another hallmark of the experienced negotiator.

Strong preparation is critical to being able to manage the "strategy versus opportunism" paradox. Negotiators who have prepared well for the negotiation and who understand the circumstances are well positioned to make this judgment. We also suggest that negotiators pay close attention to their intuition. If a deal doesn't feel right, if it "seems too good to be true," then it probably *is* too good to be true and is not a viable opportunity. If negotiators feel uneasy about the direction the negotiation is taking, then it is best to take a break and consult with others about the circumstances. Often explaining the "opportunity" to a colleague, friend, or constituent will help to distinguish real opportunities from Trojan horses.

We are not suggesting that negotiators become overly cautious, however. There frequently are genuinely good opportunities that occur during a negotiation, legitimately caused by changes in business strategy, market opportunities, excess inventory, or a short-term cash flow challenge. Negotiators who have prepared well will be able to take full advantage of real opportunities when they arise and reduce the risk presented by Trojan horses.

Honest and Open versus Closed and Opaque

Negotiators face the *dilemma of honesty:* How open and honest should I be with the other party? Negotiators who are completely open and tell the other party everything expose themselves to the risk that the other party will take advantage of them. In fact, research suggests that too much knowledge about the other party's needs can actually lead to suboptimal negotiation outcomes. On the other hand, being completely closed will not only have a negative effect on your reputation, but it is also an ineffective negotiation strategy because you don't disclose enough information to create the groundwork for agreement. The challenge of this paradox is deciding how much information to reveal and how much to conceal, both for pragmatic and ethical reasons.

Strong negotiators have considered this paradox and understand their comfort zone, which will likely vary depending on the other party. We suggest that negotiators should remember that negotiation is an ongoing process. As the negotiators make positive progress, they should be building trust and feeling more comfortable about revealing more information to the other party. That said, there is some information that should probably not be revealed (e.g., the bottom line in a distributive negotiation) regardless of how well the negotiation is progressing.

Trust versus Distrust

As a mirror image of the dilemma of honesty, negotiators also face the *dilemma of trust:* how much to trust what the other party tells them. Negotiators who believe everything the other party tells them make themselves vulnerable to being taken advantage of by the other party. On the other hand, negotiators who do not believe anything the other party tells them will have a very difficult time reaching an agreement. As with the dilemma of honesty, we suggest that negotiators remember that negotiation is a process that evolves over time. First, as we noted, trust can be built by being honest and sharing information with the other side, which hopefully will lead to reciprocal trust and credible disclosure by the other side. Moreover, there will be individual differences in trust. Some negotiators will start off by being more trusting, but become less trusting if information comes to light showing that the other party is not trustworthy. Other negotiators will be more comfortable having the other party "earn their trust" and will be more skeptical early in negotiations. There is no right or wrong approach to managing this dilemma. Strong negotiators are aware of this dilemma, however, and constantly monitor how they are managing this challenge.

6. Remember the Intangibles

It is important that negotiators remember the intangible factors while negotiating and remain aware of their potential effects. Intangibles frequently affect negotiation in a negative way, and they often operate out of the negotiator's awareness. Intangibles include winning, avoiding loss, looking tough or strong to others, not looking weak, being fair, and so on. For instance, if the other party is vying with his archrival at the next desk for a promotion, he may be especially difficult when negotiating with you in front of his boss in order to "look tough." It is unlikely that the other negotiator will tell you this is what he is doing, and in fact he may not even be aware of it himself. The best way to identify the existence of intangible factors is to try to "see what is not there." In other words, if your careful preparation and analysis of the situation reveals no tangible explanation for the other negotiator's behavior—adamant advocacy of a certain point, refusal to yield another one, or behavior that just doesn't "make sense"—then it is time to start looking for the intangibles driving his behavior.

For example, several years ago one of the authors of this book was helping a friend buy a new car, and the price offered from the dealer was $2,000 less than any other dealer in town. The only catch was that the car had to be sold that day. On the surface this looked like a trick (see the previous discussion of strategy versus opportunism), but there was no obvious tangible factor that explained this special price. The friend had never purchased from the dealer before, the car was new and fully covered by a good warranty, and the friend had visited several dealers and knew this price was substantially lower than at other dealers. As we continued to discuss the potential deal, the salesman became more and more agitated. Sweat was literally falling from his brow. The friend decided to purchase the car, and as soon as he signed the salesman was simultaneously relieved and excited. He asked for a moment to telephone his wife to share with her some good news. It turned out that the salesman had just won a complicated incentive package offered by the dealer, and the prize was a two-week all expenses paid Caribbean vacation for his family of four. The incentive package required that a total of 10 vehicles be sold in a month, and that one of each category of vehicles at the dealership be sold. The salesman specialized in selling trucks, and the friend was buying a sports car, so you can imagine the pressure the salesman felt when he had given a huge discount to secure the deal and the friend was hesitating.

The intangible factor of trying to win the vacation package explained the salesman's behavior in this example. The buyer learned of this only when the salesman could no longer contain his excitement and shared the good news with his family. Often negotiators do not learn what intangible factors are influencing the other negotiator unless the other chooses to disclose them. Negotiators can "see" their existence, however, by looking for changes in the other negotiator's behavior from one negotiation to another, as well as by gathering information about the other party before negotiation begins. For instance, if you find out that the other party has a new boss that she doesn't like and she is subsequently more difficult to deal with in the negotiation, the intangible of the new boss may be to blame.

There are at least two more ways to discover intangibles that might be affecting the other. One way to surface the other party's intangibles is to ask questions. These questions should try to get the other party to reveal why he or she is sticking so strongly to a given point. It is important to remember that strong emotions and/or values are the root of many intangibles, so surfacing intangibles may result in the discussion of various fears and anxieties. The question-asking process should also be gentle and informal; if the questioning is aggressive, it may only make the other defensive, adding another intangible to the mix and stifling effective negotiations! A second way is to take an observer or listener with you to the negotiation. Listeners may be able to read the other's emotional tone or nonverbal behavior, focus on roadblock issues, or try to take the other's perspective and put themselves in the other's shoes (role reversal). A caucus with this listener may then help refocus the discussion so as to surface the intangibles and develop a new line of questions or offers.

Negotiators also need to remember that intangible factors influence their own behavior (and that it is not uncommon for us to not recognize what is making us angry, defensive, or zealously committed to some idea). Are you being particularly difficult with the other party because he "does not respect you"? Are you "trying to teach a subordinate a lesson"? Or do you want to "win" this negotiation to "look better" than another manager? Without passing judgment on the legitimacy of these goals, we strongly urge negotiators to be aware of the effect of intangible factors on their own aspirations and behavior. Often talking to another person—a sympathetic listener—can help the negotiator figure these out. Strong negotiators are aware of how both tangible and intangible factors influence negotiation, and they weigh both factors when evaluating a negotiation outcome.

7. Actively Manage Coalitions

Coalitions can have very significant effects on the negotiation process and outcome. Negotiators should recognize three types of coalitions and their potential effects: (1) coalitions against you, (2) coalitions that support you, and (3) loose, undefined coalitions that may materialize either for or against you. Strong negotiators assess the presence and strength of coalitions and work to capture the strength of the coalition for their benefit. If this is not possible, negotiators need to work to prevent the other party from capturing a loose coalition for their purposes. When negotiators are part of a coalition, communicating with the coalition is critical to ensuring that the power of the coalition is aligned with their goals. Similarly, negotiators who are agents or representatives of a coalition must take special care to manage this process.

Successfully concluding negotiations when a coalition is aligned against a negotiator is an extremely challenging task. It is important to recognize when coalitions are aligned against you and to work consciously to counter their influence. Frequently this will involve a "divide and conquer" strategy, where negotiators try to increase dissent within the coalition by searching for ways to breed instability within the coalition.

Coalitions occur in many formal negotiations, such as environmental assessments and reaching policy decisions in an industry association. Coalitions may also have a strong influence in less formal settings, such as work teams and families, where different subgroups of people may not have the same interests. Managing coalitions is especially important when negotiators need to rely on other people to implement an agreement. It may be possible for negotiators to forge an agreement when the majority of people influenced are not in favor, but implementing the outcomes of that agreement will be very challenging. Strong negotiators need to monitor and manage coalitions proactively, and while this may take considerable time throughout the negotiation process, it will likely lead to large payoffs at the implementation stage.

8. Savor and Protect Your Reputation

Reputations are like eggs—fragile, important to build, easy to break, and very hard to rebuild once broken. Reputations travel fast, and people often know more about you than you think that they do. Starting negotiations with a positive reputation is essential, and negotiators should be vigilant in protecting their reputations. Negotiators who have a reputation for breaking their word and not negotiating honestly will have a much more difficult time negotiating in the future than those who have a reputation for being honest and fair. Consider the following contrasting reputations: "tough but fair" versus "tough and underhanded." Negotiators prepare differently for others with these contrasting reputations. Negotiating with a tough but fair negotiator means preparing for potentially difficult negotiations while being aware that the other party will push hard for her perspective but will also be rational and fair in her behavior. Negotiating with a tough but underhanded other party means that negotiators will need to verify what the other says, be vigilant for dirty tricks, and be more guarded about sharing information.

How are you perceived as a negotiator? What is your reputation with others at this point? What reputation would you like to have? Think about the negotiators you respect the most and their reputation. What is it about their behavior that you admire? Also think about the negotiators that have a bad reputation. What would it take for them to change your image of them?

Rather than leaving reputation to chance, negotiators can work to shape and enhance their reputation by acting in a consistent and fair manner. Consistency provides the other party with a clear set of predictable expectations about how you will behave, which leads to a stable reputation. Fairness sends the message that you are principled and reasonable. Strong negotiators also periodically seek feedback from others about the way they are perceived and use that information to strengthen their credibility and trustworthiness in the marketplace.

9. Remember That Rationality and Fairness Are Relative

Research on negotiator perception and cognition is quite clear: People tend to view the world in a self-serving manner and define the "rational" thing to do or a "fair" outcome or process in a way that benefits themselves. First, negotiators need to be aware of this tendency in both themselves and the other party. Negotiators can do three things to manage these perceptions proactively. First, they can question their own perceptions of fairness and ground them in clear principles. Second, they can find external benchmarks and examples that suggest fair outcomes. Finally, negotiators can illuminate definitions of fairness held by the other party and engage in a dialogue to reach consensus on which standards of fairness apply in a given situation.

Moreover, negotiators are often in the position to collectively define what is right or fair as a part of the negotiation process. In most situations, neither side holds the keys to what is absolutely right, rational, or fair. Reasonable people can disagree, and often the most important outcome that negotiators can achieve is a common, agreed-upon perspective, definition of the facts, agreement on the right way to see a problem, or standard for determining what is a fair outcome or process. Be prepared to negotiate these principles as strongly as you prepare for a discussion of the issues.

10. Continue to Learn from the Experience

Negotiation epitomizes lifelong learning. The best negotiators continue to learn from experience—they know there are so many different variables and nuances when negotiating that no two negotiations are identical. These differences mean that for negotiators to remain sharp, they need to continue to practice the art and science of negotiation regularly. In addition, the best negotiators take a moment to analyze each negotiation after it has concluded, to review what happened and what they learned. We recommend a three-step process:

- Plan a personal reflection time after each negotiation.
- Periodically "take a lesson" from a trainer or coach.
- Keep a personal diary on strengths and weaknesses and develop a plan to work on weaknesses.

This analysis does not have to be extensive or time-consuming. It should happen after every important negotiation, however, and it should focus on *what* and *why* questions: What happened during this negotiation, why did it occur, and what can I learn? Negotiators who take the time to pause and reflect on their negotiations will find that they continue to refine their skills and that they remain sharp and focused for their future negotiations.

Moreover, even the best athletes—in almost any sport—have one or more coaches on their staff, and stop to "take a lesson." Negotiators have access to seminars to enhance their skills, books to read, and coaches who can help refine their skills. This book should be seen as one step along the way to sharpening and refining your negotiation skills, and we encourage you to continue to learn about the art and science of negotiation. We wish you the best of luck in all of your future negotiations!

Exercise 1

The Subjective Value Inventory (SVI)

Introduction

This exercise is designed to help you explore the psychological outcomes of a negotiation, including satisfaction, trust, rapport, and self-impressions. It involves completing a questionnaire following a simulated or actual negotiation. Your instructor will tell you which negotiation to use as the basis for filling it out.

Instructions for Completing the SVI

For each question, please circle a number from 1 to 7 that most accurately reflects your opinion. You will notice that some of the questions are similar to one another; this is primarily to ensure the validity and reliability of the questionnaire. Please answer each question independently, without reference to any of the other questions.

Important: If you encounter a particular question that is not applicable to your negotiation, simply circle "NA." Even if you did not reach agreement, please try to answer as many questions as possible.

1. How satisfied are you with your own outcome—that is, the extent to which the terms of your agreement (or lack of agreement) benefit you?

1	2	3	4	5	6	7	NA
Not at all satisfied			Moderately satisfied			Perfectly satisfied	

2. How satisfied are you with the balance between your own outcome and your counterpart(s)'s outcome(s)?

1	2	3	4	5	6	7	NA
Not at all satisfied			Moderately satisfied			Perfectly satisfied	

3. Did you feel like you forfeited or "lost" in this negotiation?

1	2	3	4	5	6	7	NA
Not at all			A moderate amount			A great deal	

4. Do you think the terms of your agreement are consistent with principles of legitimacy or objective criteria (e.g., common standards of fairness, precedent, industry practice, legality)?

1	2	3	4	5	6	7	NA
Not at all			Moderately			A great deal	

Source: Developed by Jared R. Curhan, Hillary A. Elfenbein, and Heng Xu. Copyright © 2005 by Curhan, Elfenbein, & Xu. Used here with permission.

5. Did you "lose face" (i.e., damage your sense of pride) in the negotiation?

1	2	3	4	5	6	7	NA
Not at all			Moderately			A great deal	

6. Did you feel as though you behaved appropriately in this negotiation?

1	2	3	4	5	6	7	NA
Not at all			Moderately			A great deal	

7. Did this negotiation make you feel more or less competent as a negotiator?

1	2	3	4	5	6	7	NA
It made me feel *less* competent.			It did not make me feel more or less competent.			It made me feel *more* competent.	

8. Did you behave according to your own principles and values?

1	2	3	4	5	6	7	NA
Not at all			Moderately			A great deal	

9. Do you feel your counterpart(s) listened to your concerns?

1	2	3	4	5	6	7	NA
Not at all			Moderately			A great deal	

10. Would you characterize the negotiation process as fair?

1	2	3	4	5	6	7	NA
Not at all			Moderately			A great deal	

11. How satisfied are you with the ease (or difficulty) of reaching an agreement?

1	2	3	4	5	6	7	NA
Not at all satisfied			Moderately satisfied			Perfectly satisfied	

12. Did your counterpart(s) consider your wishes, opinions, or needs?

1	2	3	4	5	6	7	NA
Not at all			Moderately			Very much	

13. How satisfied are you with your relationship with your counterpart(s) as a result of this negotiation?

1	2	3	4	5	6	7	NA
Not at all satisfied			Moderately satisfied			Perfectly satisfied	

14. What kind of overall impression did your counterpart(s) make on you?

1	2	3	4	5	6	7	NA
Extremely *negative*			Neither negative nor positive			Extremely *positive*	

15. Did the negotiation make you trust your counterpart(s)?

1	2	3	4	5	6	7	NA
Not at all			Moderately			A great deal	

16. Did the negotiation build a good foundation for a future relationship with your counterpart(s)?

1	2	3	4	5	6	7	NA
Not at all			Moderately			A great deal	

Pemberton's Dilemma

Introduction

This exercise creates a situation in which you and the other person(s) will be making separate decisions about how to manage your firm. In this situation, the outcomes (profits and losses) are determined not only by what you do, but also by a number of other factors such as the goals and motives that you and the other party have and the communication that takes place between you and them.

Read the background information for Pemberton's Dilemma that follows. In this exercise, you will represent your store in discussions with the other store about the hours that each store should open on Sundays. You and the other store will be making decisions simultaneously, and your profits will be directly affected by these decisions.

Background Information

Pemberton is a quaint little town located in the heartland of our great country. Although it is only a 30-minute drive to a major metropolitan center, most of the townsfolk prefer to do their shopping at one of the two general stores located in Pemberton. At these stores, one can buy a variety of goods, ranging from groceries to hardware equipment. Both establishments boast a soda fountain, which is quite popular among both the younger and older generations as well.

Like most small towns, Pemberton is proud of the fact that it has been able to preserve its many traditions, some of which date back to the 1890s. One of these grand traditions, which became official in 1923 when the Town Hall passed a resolution to this effect, is the cessation of all commercial activity on Sunday. Times have changed, however, and "Sunday shoppers" are becoming more and more prevalent. In fact, every Sunday there is a mass exodus to the nearby metropolitan center, where Sunday shopping has been permitted for years.

You are a member of the management team from one of the two general stores in Pemberton. Both the Country Market and the Corner Store have been consistently losing potential profit as Sunday shopping becomes more popular. Your management team, as well as the team from the competing general store, has recently contemplated opening the store on Sunday, in spite of the municipal resolution that prohibits this.

The ramifications of such decisions are important, since the profitability of such an action will depend on the decision made by the competing store. For instance, if neither store decides to open on Sunday, it will be business as usual, and both stores will make a profit of $20,000 in a given week.

Source: Written in collaboration with Gregory Leck.

If only one store decides to open on Sunday, that particular store would enjoy the patronage of all those Sunday shoppers and would manage to make a $40,000 profit for the week. Unfortunately, the store that decided to remain closed on that Sunday would actually incur a loss of $40,000 that week. This would be due to various reasons, most notably the preference of customers to continue to do their shopping throughout the week at the store that remained open on Sunday.

If both stores decided to stay open on Sunday, adverse consequences would be faced by both establishments. Although Town Hall may be able to turn a blind eye to one store violating the municipal resolution, two stores would be looked upon as a conspiracy against the traditionalists of Pemberton. Artemus Hampton, Pemberton's mayor and a direct descendant of one of the town's founders, would no doubt pressure Town Hall into levying the highest possible fine allowable by law. In this case, the penalty would be so excessive that both stores would incur losses of $20,000 each for the week. While your lawyers have suggested that the municipal resolutions prohibiting Sunday shopping in Pemberton might be overturned in a court case, this too would be a costly option. In either case, if both stores open on Sunday, they will each incur losses of $20,000 for the week.

Keeping this information in mind, your team is to decide each week, for the next 12 weeks, whether your store is to remain open on the Sunday of that week. The decision made for the first week must be made without prior consultation with the management team of the competing store. Subsequent decisions may be made after consulting with your competitors. Both teams shall reveal their decisions simultaneously. *Remember, the goal is to maximize profits over the next 12-week period.*

Familiarize yourself with the following profit chart. There will be 12 one-minute rounds where the stores will either open or close. Each round represents one Sunday, and every *fourth* Sunday is part of a long weekend. A three-minute planning session separates each Sunday. *There may not be any communication between the stores during the planning sessions.*

The exercise begins when representatives from the stores (one from each) meet and indicate with a card if their store will open or close on the first Sunday. Each team will record the outcome of each Sunday on their profit chart. The time periods between each Sunday are fixed and may not be altered. Each team will complete a total of 12 moves. Profits and losses are calculated after each Sunday and are cumulative for the 12 weeks (see the accompanying sample profit chart).

		Country Market			
		Close Sunday		**Open Sunday**	
Corner Store	**Close Sunday**	Corner:	+$20,000	Corner:	−$40,000
		Country:	+$20,000	Country:	+$40,000
	Open Sunday	Corner:	+$40,000	Corner:	−$20,000
		Country:	−$40,000	Country:	−$20,000

Profit Chart				
			Profit	
	Corner Store's Choice	**Country Market's Choice**	**Corner Store**	**Country Market**
First 15-minute planning period				
1.				
2.				
3.				
4. **Double** profit/loss, *this round only*				
Five-minute negotiation period				
5.				
6.				
7.				
8. **Triple** profit/loss, *this round only*				
Five-minute negotiation period				
9.				
10.				
11.				
12. **Quadruple** profit/loss, *this round only*				

The Commons Dilemma

Introduction

This is a simulation about the dynamics of competition and cooperation in a situation where there are multiple actors. The entire class will participate, with each individual student making a series of decisions over the course of several class periods. At each decision point, your outcomes will be determined by what everyone else does as well as by your own action. At the end of the simulation, when all decisions have been made, you will receive an overall score that can be converted into a grade for the exercise. Although the instructor will not discuss or debrief this exercise until after the final decision has been made, you and your fellow students are free to discuss it as you wish.

Source: This version of the Commons Dilemma was developed by Michael Morris; it is based on a presentation made by Gary Throop at the 1990 Organizational Behavior Teaching Conference. Used with permission.

Exercise 4

The Used Car

Introduction

The scenario for this role-play involves a single issue: the price of a used car that is for sale. While there is a great deal of other information that may be used to construct supporting arguments or to build in demands and requests in addition to the price, the sale price will ultimately be the indicator used to determine how well you do in comparison to other role-play groups.

Background Information

You are about to negotiate the purchase/sale of an automobile. The seller advertised the car in the local newspaper. (*Note:* Both role-players should interpret "local" as the town in which the role-playing is occurring.) Before advertising it, the seller took the car to the local Volkswagen dealer, who has provided the following information:

1998 Volkswagen Jetta GL sedan, four-cylinder, automatic transmission, power steering, air conditioning, front-wheel drive, dual air bags, cruise control.

Black with gray interior, power door locks, power windows, and AM/FM/CD stereo.

Mileage: 73,500 miles; steel-belted radial tires expected to last another 30,000 miles.

Fuel economy: 24 mpg city, 31 mpg highway; uses regular (87 octane) gasoline.

No rust; dent on passenger door barely noticeable.

Mechanically perfect except exhaust system, which may or may not last another 10,000 miles (costs $300 to replace).

Blue book (2005) values: retail, $6,600; trade-in, $5,125; loan, $4,625.

Car has been locally owned and driven (one owner).

Source: Revised version of an original role-play that was developed by Professor Leonard Greenhalgh, Dartmouth College. Used with permission.

Statement of Agreement for Purchase of the Automobile

Price: _____

Manner of payment: _____

Special terms and conditions: _____

_____

_____

_____

_____

We agree to the terms above:

_____   _____

              Seller   Buyer

* *

Who made the first offer? _____

Initial Settlement Proposals

Seller: _____

_____

Buyer: _____

_____

_____

Knight Engines/Excalibur Engine Parts

Introduction

The process of negotiation combines economic transactions with verbal persuasion. A great deal of what transpires during a negotiation is the verbal persuasion—people arguing for and supporting their own preferred position, and resisting similar arguments from the other party. At the same time, underlying this layer of persuasive messages is a set of economic transactions—bids and counterbids—that are at the economic core of the negotiation process.

The purpose of this exercise is to provide some experience with combining the economic transactions and the persuasive messages to support preferred economic outcomes. You will be assigned the role of Knight Engines or Excalibur Engine Parts for this exercise. Your objective is to negotiate a deal that is most advantageous to you and your company.

Source: Written in collaboration with Gregory Leck.

Exercise 6

GTechnica—AccelMedia

Introduction

The scenario for this simulation is a negotiation between a supplier of electronic components and a computer hardware maker over the price of a processor needed for the manufacture of a computer graphics accelerator adapter. The role-play information you will be given by your instructor provides details about the context of the negotiation that may help you to understand the situation, develop a bargaining strategy, and form arguments or demands to implement that strategy. Ultimately, however, how well you do in this negotiation in relation to other negotiating groups is determined by the final sale price for the part, if you are able to reach an agreement.

When you read your role information and are preparing to negotiate, keep these guidelines in mind:

- Use any plan or strategy that will help you achieve your objectives.
- If you are negotiating in a team, you may call a caucus at any time to evaluate your strategy or the opponent's strategy.
- Reach an agreement by the end of the specified time period, or conclude that you are not able to agree and that buyer and seller will explore other alternatives.
- Complete the negotiation outcome form as directed by your instructor. Be sure to write down any additional terms or conditions that were agreed to.

Exercise 7
_____

Planning for Negotiations

Introduction

This exercise asks you to focus on either an upcoming role-play negotiation or a real negotiation that will occur within your life within the next several weeks or months. In this exercise, your objective is to develop a plan for that negotiation.

Here you will find 10 question areas that can be used as a planning guide for this negotiation. These questions reflect the important elements to consider when you prepare to negotiate. Not all of these questions will be relevant to every negotiation, so you may not have a specific answer for every question. The purpose of the planning process is to make sure you consider all of the major factors that may impact the upcoming negotiation, and assemble information, arguments, or analysis so that you can be more effective in achieving your goals in that negotiation. The detailed questions are presented next, and a blank abbreviated planning guide is available after the questions for you to complete about your own upcoming negotiation. The readings in this book may offer additional help in considering how to plan most effectively.

If you are using this planning guide as part of a class exercise, your instructor may give you additional instructions on how to use the guide.

Planning Questions

Here are the major dimensions you should address in planning for a negotiation:

1. Understanding the issues—that is, what is to be negotiated.

2. Assembling the issues and defining the bargaining mix:

    - Which issues are most important and which issues are less important?
    - Which issues are linked to other issues, and which are separate or unconnected?

3. Defining the interests: What are the other's primary underlying interests?

4. Defining limits:

    - What is our walkaway point on each issue—that is, what is a minimally acceptable settlement for each issue or the issues as a package?
    - If this negotiation fails, what is our best alternative settlement (BATNA)?

5. Defining targets and openings:

    - What will be our preferred settlement in each issue?
    - What will be our opening request for each issue?
    - Where are we willing to trade off issues against each other in the bargaining mix?

6. Constituencies: To whom is the other accountable for the solution—that is, to whom does he or she report or have to explain or defend the outcome? Does this party also have to be involved in issue definition and goal setting?

Source: Developed by Roy J. Lewicki and John W. Minton.

7. Opposite negotiators: Who is the other party (or parties) in the negotiation?

   - What information do we have about them?
   - What issues will they have?
   - What priorities are they likely to have for their issues?
   - What are their interests?
   - What has been my past relationship with them? What future relationship do I need to have, or would I like to have with them?
   - What is their reputation and style, and how should I take this into consideration?

8. Selecting a strategy:

   - What overall negotiation and strategy do I want to select? How important are the outcome and the relationship with the other?
   - What strategy do I expect the other will be selecting?

9. Planning the issue presentation and defense:

   - What research do I need to do on the issues so that I can argue for them convincingly and compellingly?
   - Do I have (or can I prepare) graphs, charts, and figures that will clearly communicate my preferences?
   - In what order and sequence should I present the information?
   - What arguments can I anticipate from the other party, and how am I going to counteract their arguments?
   - What tactics will I use to present my arguments or defend against the other's arguments?
   - What tactics will I use to try to move us toward agreement?
   - What roles will different people play in the negotiation?

10. Protocol:

    - Where will we negotiate? Do we wish to influence the choice of location?
    - When will we negotiate? Do we wish to influence the time and length of negotiation?
    - Who will be at the actual negotiation meeting? Do we want to bring other parties to serve a particular purpose (e.g., an expert or an observer)?
    - Do we have an agenda? How can we help to either create the agenda or participate in its development?
    - What will we do if the negotiation fails?
    - Who will write down and confirm the agreement? Do we need to have the contract reviewed by a professional (e.g., attorney, accountant, agent)?

One member of each group should record the results of the group's work and be able to report the plan back to the group (you may wish to use large paper, overhead transparencies, or a written handout).

Planning Guide

This planning guide may be completed for any important upcoming negotiation:

1. What are the issues to be negotiated? _____
   _____
   _____

2. What are the priorities among the issues in the bargaining mix? _____
   _____
   _____

3. What are the primary underlying interests? _____
   _____
   _____

4. What are my limits on each issue—walkaway points and BATNAs?_____
   _____
   _____

5. What are my target points and opening requests on these issues? _____
   _____
   _____

6. Who are the important constituencies to whom I am accountable? _____
   _____
   _____

7. What do I know about the other negotiator's interests, negotiating style, and personal reputation? _____
   _____
   _____

8. What overall strategy do I want to pursue?_____
   _____
   _____

9. What do I need to assemble—research, documents, charts and graphs, and so on—to make the most effective presentation on what I want to achieve? What tactics will I use to present my arguments or defend against the other negotiator's arguments? _____
   _____
   _____

10. What protocol is important for this negotiation: where we negotiate, when we negotiate, who is present for the negotiation, agenda to be followed, note taking? Also, what is our backup plan if this negotiation fails? _____
   _____
   _____

Exercise 8

The Pakistani Prunes

Introduction

In many work settings it is not possible for people to work independently as they pursue their work goals. Often we find ourselves in situations where we must obtain the cooperation of other people, even though the other people's ultimate objectives may be different from our own. Getting things done in organizations requires us to work together in cooperation, even though our ultimate objective may be only to satisfy our own needs. Your task in this exercise is to learn how to work together more productively with others.

Source: Adapted by Roy J. Lewicki and John W. Minton.

Universal Computer Company I

Introduction

In this exercise you will play the role of a plant manager who has to negotiate some arrangements with another plant manager. You will be in a potentially competitive situation where cooperation is clearly desirable. Your task is to find some way to cooperate, when to do so might seem to put you at a disadvantage.

Read the background information section and the role information that the instructor has provided. Do not discuss your role with other class members. Plan how you will handle the forthcoming meeting with the other plant manager. Record your initial proposal on the Initial Settlement Proposal form. Do not show this to the other party you are negotiating with until after the negotiations are completed.

Background Information

The Universal Computer Company is one of the nation's major producers of computers. Plants in the company tend to specialize in producing a single line of products or, at the most, a limited range of products. The company has considerable vertical integration. Parts made at one plant are assembled into components at another, which in turn are assembled into final products at still another plant. Each plant operates on a profit center basis.

The Crawley plant produces computer chips, modules, cable harnesses, and terminal boards, which are shipped to other company plants. In addition to numerous computer chips, the Crawley plant makes more than 40 different modules for the Phillips plant. The two plants are about five miles apart.

The Quality Problem

Production at the Phillips plant has been plagued by poor quality. Upon examination it has been found that a considerable portion of this problem can be traced to the quality of the modules received from the Crawley plant.

The Crawley plant maintains a final inspection operation. There has been considerable dispute between the two plants as to whether the Crawley plant is to maintain a 95 percent overall acceptance level for all modules shipped to the Phillips plant, or to maintain that standard for *each* of the 42 modules shipped. The Phillips plant manager has insisted that the standard has to be maintained for each of the 42 individual modules produced. The Crawley plant manager maintains that the requirements mean that the 95 percent level has to be maintained overall for the sum of modules produced. Experience at the Phillips plant shows that while some module types were consistently well above the 95 percent acceptance level, 12 types of modules had erratic quality and would often fall far below the 95 percent level. As a result, while individual types of modules might fall below standard, the quality level

---

Initial Settlement Proposal

_____ Plant

How do you propose that the following expenses and repairs should be handled?

Expense of repairing all faulty modules: _____

_____

Expense of repairing faulty modules other than the 12 types that fall below the 95 percent level:

_____

_____

Expense of repairing the faulty modules of the 12 types that fall below the 95 percent level:

_____

_____

How to handle the repair of the faulty modules of the 12 types that fall below the 95 percent level:

_____

_____

How to handle the repair of the modules other than the 12 types that fall below the 95 percent level:

_____

_____

---

for all modules was at or above the 95 percent level. This raised serious problems at the Phillips plant, since the quality of its products is controlled by the quality of the poorest module.

The Interplant Dispute

The management of the Phillips plant felt that the quality problem of the modules received from the Crawley plant was causing them great difficulty. It caused problems with the customers, who complained about the improper operation of the products that contained the Crawley modules. As a result, the Phillips plant operation had earlier added secondary final inspection of its completed products. More recently it had added an incoming inspection of 12 poor-quality modules received from the Crawley plant. There were times when the number of modules rejected was large enough to slow or even temporarily stop production. At those times, to maintain production schedules, the Phillips plant had to work overtime. In addition, the Phillips plant had the expense of correcting all the faulty units received from the Crawley plant.

Ideally, the management of the Phillips plant would like to receive all modules free of defects. While this was recognized as impossible, they felt that the Crawley plant should at least accept the expense of repairs, extra inspections, and overtime required by the poor quality of the parts.

Since installing incoming inspection procedures on the 12 modules, the Phillips plant had been rejecting about $15,000 of modules a week. For the most part, these had been put into storage pending settlement of the dispute as to which plant should handle

---

Final Settlement Agreement

How, exactly, did you agree that the following expenses and repairs would be handled?
Expense of repairing all faulty modules: _____

_____

Expense of repairing faulty modules other than the 12 types that fall below the 95 percent level:

_____

_____

Expense of repairing the faulty modules of the 12 types that fall below the 95 percent level:

_____

_____

How to handle the repair of the faulty modules of the 12 types that fall below the 95 percent level:

_____

_____

How to handle the repair of the modules other than the 12 types that fall below the 95 percent level:

_____

_____

_____   _____
Representative, Phillips Plant   Representative, Crawley Plant

---

repairing them. Occasionally, when the supply of good modules had been depleted, repairs were made on some of the rejected units to keep production going. The Phillips plant had continued to make repairs on the remaining 30 types or modules as the need for repairs was discovered in assembly or final inspection.

From its perspective, the Crawley plant management felt that it was living up to its obligation by maintaining a 95 percent or better quality level on all its modules shipped to the Phillips plant. Further, they pointed out that using sampling methods on inspection meant that some below-standard units were bound to get through and that the expense of dealing with these was a normal business expense that the Phillips plant would have to accept as would any other plant. They pointed out that when buying parts from outside suppliers it was common practice in the company to absorb the expenses from handling the normal level of faulty parts.

The Phillips plant management argued that the Crawley plant management was ignoring its responsibility to the company by forcing the cost of repairs onto their plant, where only repairs could be made—rather than having the costs borne by the Crawley plant, where corrections of faulty processes could be made.

Exercise 10

Universal Computer Company II

Introduction

In this exercise you will play the role of a plant manager who has to negotiate the price of a new A25 computer chip. You will be in a potentially competitive situation where cooperation is clearly desirable. Your task is to find some way to cooperate, when to do so might seem to put you at a disadvantage.

Prior to negotiating, read the background information section and the role information that the instructor has provided. Do not discuss your role with other class members. Plan how you will handle the forthcoming meeting with the other plant manager.

Background Information

The Universal Computer Company is one of the nation's major producers of computers. Plants in the company tend to specialize in producing a single line of products or, at the most, a limited range of products. The company has considerable vertical integration. Parts made at one plant are assembled into components at another, which in turn are assembled into final products at still another plant. Each plant operates on a profit center basis.

The Crawley plant produces computer chips, modules, cable harnesses, and terminal boards, which are shipped to other company plants. In addition to numerous computer chips, the Crawley plant makes more than 40 different modules for the Phillips plant. The two plants are about five miles apart.

The A25 Computer Chip

Phillips purchases over 30 different computer chips from Crawley. Computer chip A25 represents the most advanced engineering and manufacturing technologies available at the Crawley plant, and is an important advance in multimedia hardware design for personal computers. Phillips will integrate the A25 chip into its motherboards, and in turn will sell the motherboards to Universal Computer (the parent company) and to other computer companies. Since the prices on all purchases between Phillips and Crawley have been previously negotiated, the price of the A25 chip is currently the only computer chip up for negotiation.

Twin Lakes Mining Company

Introduction

In this role-play you will have the opportunity to negotiate a serious problem—a conflict between a mining company and the government of a small city regarding an environmental cleanup. While the issues in this scenario have been simplified somewhat for the purpose of this role-play, such conflicts between industry and governmental groups are typical throughout the country. Try to introduce as much realism into this situation as you can, based on your own personal experiences.

Background Information

The Twin Lakes Mining Company is located in Tamarack, Minnesota, in the northern part of the state. It was established there in 1961. The city of Tamarack has a year-round population of approximately 18,000. Although there is a growing revenue that accrues to the city as a result of heavy summer tourism (summer homes, fishing, etc.) and several cottage industries, Tamarack is basically a one-industry city. Twenty-five hundred people, 60 percent of whom live within city limits, work for the Twin Lakes Mining Company; 33 percent of the city's real estate tax base of about $5 million consists of Twin Lakes Mining Company property and operations. Both in terms of direct tax revenue and indirect contribution to the economic stability of the local population, Tamarack is strongly dependent on the continued success of the Twin Lakes Mining Company.

The Twin Lakes Mining Company is an open-pit, iron ore mine. Open-pit mining consists of stripping the topsoil from the ore deposit with the use of power shovels. Train rails are then laid, and most of the ore is loaded into railroad cars for transportation to a central collecting point for rail or water shipment. As mining operations progress, rails are relaid or roads constructed to haul ore by truck. The ore is transported to a "benefication plant" located on the outskirts of Tamarack. Benefication of ore involves crushing, washing, concentration, blending, and agglomerating the ore. In the early days of ore production, such treatment was unnecessary; however, benefication is necessary today for several reasons. First, transportation costs of rejected material (gangue) are minimized. The crude ore may lose as much as one-third of its weight in grading, and, in addition, impurities are removed at a much lower cost than if removed during smelting. Second, ores of various physical and chemical properties can be purified and blended during this process. Finally, fine ore materials, which previously may have been rejected as a result of smelting problems, can now be briquetted and pelletized to increase their value. After the ore proceeds through this process of cleaning and agglomerating into larger lumps or pellets, it is shipped by railroad car to steel mills throughout the Midwest. Rejected materials are returned to "consumed" parts of the mine, and the land is restored.

Twin Lakes' benefication plant is located approximately five miles outside of Tamarack. As a result of the expansion of the residential areas of the city, summer home development, and various Twin Lakes operations, the plant has become a major problem for local citizens. For years, the Tamarack City Council has been pressing the company to clean up the most problematic operations.

While most of these discussions have been amicable, Twin Lakes has done little or nothing to remedy the major concerns. Now, as a result of more stringent environmental laws and regulations, Twin Lakes has come under pressure from both the state of Minnesota and the federal government for environmental cleanup. Both the state and the federal Environmental Protection Agency have informed Twin Lakes that the company is in major violation of water and air pollution quality standards, and that immediate action must be taken. Twin Lakes' estimates indicate that total compliance with the cleanup regulations will cost the company over $36 million. Because Twin Lakes is now mining relatively low-grade ore and because foreign competition in the steel market has significantly eroded the demand for ore, environmental compliance may seriously influence the profitability of the company. Many local citizens, as individuals and through the local chapter of the United Mineworkers Union, are putting significant pressure on the City Council to help the Twin Lakes Company in its environmental cleanup operations.

The imposition of the environmental controls on Twin Lakes, and the resulting pressure from all segments of the community, have led to renewed discussions between company officials and the City Council. As a result of these discussions, the following environmental issues have emerged:

1. *Water quality:* The Twin Lakes plant requires large amounts of water to wash the crushed ore. In addition, much of the highest-quality ore is reduced to an almost powderlike texture after washing and is being lost in the washing operation. As a result, the company has built a series of settlement recovery ponds alongside Beaver Brook near the plant. Water that has been used for washing ore is allowed to stand in these ponds; they are periodically drained and the ore recovered. Nevertheless, granules of iron ore and other impurities continue to wash downstream from the plant. The environmental agents have insisted that the effluent from the plant and the ponds be cleaned up. Estimates for the cost of a filtration plant are $20 million. Twin Lakes claims that it cannot afford to build the plant with its own revenue. Since Tamarack has periodically talked about Beaver Brook as a secondary water source for the city (and residential development makes this a more pressing concern in two to three years), the Twin Lakes officials hope that they might interest Tamarack in a joint venture.

2. *Air quality:* The entire process of mining, transporting, and crushing ore generates large amounts of dust. This has significantly increased the levels of particulates in the air. In addition, during the dry summer months, the operation of many large trucks along dirt roads intensifies the problem considerably. Twin Lakes believes that it can control a great deal of the dust generated immediately around the plant at a cost of approximately $8 million. The most significant debate with the city has been over a series of roads around the city outskirts. Approximately half of the roads are city owned; the rest have been specially constructed for the transportation of ore and material. Estimates for paving all the roads are $4.8 million, with a yearly maintenance cost of $600,000; periodic oil spraying of the roads, to

keep down the dust, would run approximately $800,000 annually, but an agreement to do this as a short-term measure may not satisfy the environmental agencies.

3. *Taxation of company land:* The land for the mine itself is outside city limits. However, the plant lies within city boundaries, and current taxes on the city land are $800,000 annually. The company has always felt that this taxation rate is excessive. In addition, several of the railroad spurs used to move ore into the plant, and out to the major railway line, cross city land. The city has continued to charge a flat rate of $400,000 annually for right-of-way use. It has occasionally offered the land for sale to the company at rates varying from $2.2 million to $2.4 million. Again, the company has felt that this rate is excessive.

Both the company and the city believe that if some resolution could be obtained on these three major issues, the remaining problems could be easily resolved, and Twin Lakes would agree to keep the mine open.

Exercise 12

City of Tamarack

Introduction

In this role-play, you will have the opportunity to negotiate a serious problem—a conflict between a mining company and the government of a small city regarding an environmental cleanup. Conflicts between community, government, and industry groups are very common, particularly around environmental management issues. The issues in this simulation may be similar to environmental cleanup, development, or management problems ongoing in your own community.

Background Information

The largest regional office of the Twin Lakes Mining Company is located in Tamarack, Minnesota, in the northern part of the state. It was established there in 1941. The city of Tamarack has a population of approximately 18,000. Although there is a growing revenue that accrues to the city as a result of heavy summer tourism (summer homes, fishing, etc.) and several cottage industries, Tamarack is basically a one-industry city. Two thousand five hundred people, 60 percent of whom live within city limits, work for the Twin Lakes Mining Company; 33 percent of the city's real estate tax base consists of Twin Lakes property and operations. Both in terms of direct tax revenue and indirect contribution to the economic stability of the local population, Tamarack is strongly dependent on the continued success of the Twin Lakes Company.

The primary activity of the Twin Lakes Mining Company consists of mining iron ore from open-pit mines. Open-pit mining consists of stripping the topsoil from the ore deposit with the use of a power shovel. Train rails are then laid, and most of the ore is loaded into railroad cars for transportation to a central collecting point for rail or water shipment. As mining operations progress, rails are relaid or roads constructed to haul ore by truck. The ore is transported to a plant located on the outskirts of Tamarack, where it is crushed, washed, concentrated, blended, and agglomerated into larger lumps or pellets. After the ore proceeds through this process of cleaning and agglomerating, it is shipped by railroad car to steel mills throughout the Midwest. Rejected materials are returned to parts of the mine where the mining process has been completed. Mines that are no longer in use are called *consumed* mines.

Twin Lakes' plant is located approximately five miles outside Tamarack. As a result of the expansion of the residential areas of the city, summer home development, and various Twin Lakes operations, the plant has become an environmental problem for local citizens. The primary problem is that the mining operations pollute the air with dust. For years, the Tamarack City Council has been pressing the company to clean up the most problematic operations. Although several discussions between the city and the company have occurred, Twin Lakes has done little to remedy the major concerns. Now, as a

Source: This exercise was written by Jeff Polzer. Used with permission.

result of more stringent environmental laws and regulations, Twin Lakes has come under pressure from the state of Minnesota and the federal government for environmental cleanup. Both the state and the federal Environmental Protection Agency have informed Twin Lakes that it is in major violation of air pollution quality standards and that immediate action must be taken. Because Twin Lakes is now mining relatively low-grade ore and because foreign competition in the steel market has significantly eroded the demand for ore, the high cost of environmental compliance might force the company to shut down its Tamarack operations. Many local citizens, as individuals and through the local chapter of the United Mineworkers Union, are putting significant pressure on the City Council to help the Twin Lakes Company in its environmental cleanup operations.

The imposition of the environmental controls on Twin Lakes, and the resulting pressure from all segments of the community, have led to renewed discussions between company and city officials about the future of Twin Lakes in the Tamarack area. As a result of these discussions, the following major issues, including environmental issues and others, have emerged:

Air quality—paving dirt roads: The entire process of mining, transporting, and crushing ore generates large amounts of dust. This has significantly increased the levels of particulates in the air. During the dry summer months, the operation of many large trucks along dirt roads intensifies the problem considerably.

Twin Lakes believes that it can control a great deal of the dust generated immediately around the plant and is planning to incur this expense without help from Tamarack. The most significant debate with the city has been over a series of roads around the outskirts of the city. They need to be paved to reduce the dust in the air to acceptable levels. Many of the roads are city-owned, and some have been specially constructed by the company for the transportation of ore and material. Almost all of the roads, including those constructed by the company, are used frequently by tourists. All of the roads have to be paved for Twin Lakes to comply with the environmental regulations and stay in business.

Air quality—road maintenance: The roads in question currently require a minimal amount of maintenance. They will require a much higher degree of maintenance if they are paved, however, especially because the harsh winters tend to break up paved roads. To keep the roads in an acceptable condition, the city and company will have to agree on who will maintain them.

Site of next mine: Twin Lakes has been testing several locations in the Tamarack area to determine the extent of iron ore deposits. Several of the locations have enough ore to be profitable, and Twin Lakes would like to open a new mine. Although the actual mining may not begin immediately, the decision concerning the location of a new site has to be made now to allow time for both the company to plan for a new mine and the city to plan its expansion around any new mining site.

Restoration of consumed mines: The consumed mines that are no longer used by the company are outside city limits. Some of these mines lie alongside main roads leading into the city from the most popular resort areas on local lakes. The city considers the consumed mines unsightly and is afraid that tourists may be repelled by the mines. The company has restored the land to the extent required by law, but the city would like to see further restoration.

Tax rate on company land: The land for the mine currently in operation is outside city limits. However, the plant lies within city boundaries, and Twin Lakes pays a substantial amount of money in taxes. The company has always felt that the Tamarack taxation rate is excessive.

Both the company and the city believe that if some resolution could be obtained on these major issues, the remaining problems could be easily resolved, and Twin Lakes would agree to keep its operations in the Tamarack area in business. Toward this end, a formal negotiation has been arranged between the City of Tamarack and the Twin Lakes Mining Company.

Island Cruise

Introduction

In this exercise you will participate in a negotiation about a cruise ship and its rights to visit a tropical island. You will role-play this negotiation as either the director of the cruise ship or the mayor of the island. The issues to be discussed during the negotiation include the number of visits per year that the ship can make, the length of individual visits, and the volume of passengers allowed to disembark from the ship on each day when it visits. This simulation provides a rich context for a business negotiation in which economic, cultural, and ecological factors all come into play.

Background Information

The *Island Queen* is a privately owned and operated luxury cruise ship. Cruise ship passenger demand has steadily fallen over the past few years due to the poor economy, fear of worldwide terrorism, and recurring cases of the Norwalk virus on cruise ships. "Norwalk-like viruses, which afflicted more than 1,500 passengers on several cruise ships in recent months, cause diarrhea, stomach pain, and vomiting for up to 48 hours" (Briscoe 2003). The *Island Queen's* operations department has decided that adding a new exotic destination to the standard 16-day itinerary will help stimulate passenger demand. While many islands in the region are possible candidates, Tropical Island is its first choice due to the island's reputation as an exotic and pristine locale.

Tropical Island

Tropical Island is part of a chain of lush Pacific islands in one of the most remote spots on earth. At 10 miles wide by 38 miles long, the island is not large. However, it is home to an extensive array of rare and endangered plant and animal species, many found only on Tropical Island. The traditional rural and native culture of the island has remained relatively unchanged over time, earning it the nickname "The Last Unspoiled Island."

The island is a wonderful combination of rain forests, desert lands, waterfalls, and black- and white-sand beaches. Weather on the island is pleasant year round, with maximum daytime temperatures ranging from 88 degrees Fahrenheit in the summer (May to October) to 80 degrees in the winter (November to April). Nighttime temperatures rarely fall below 60 degrees. As a result, the island's tourism, though considered minimal, remains almost constant year-round, at about 70,000 visitors per year.

Approximately 60 percent of the island's 7,000 residents have true Pacific Island ancestry. This makes Tropical Island the only one in the region where true natives are

Source: This exercise was written by Jeff Peddie in collaboration with Lisa Barron. Copyright © 2003 by Jeff Peddie. Used with permission.

the majority. These natives continue to practice the region's old traditions while trying to minimize the influence of the rampant commercialism found on other islands. The two closest islands are more than 25 miles away and are far more commercialized than Tropical Island.

Compared to the other islands in the region, Tropical Island is a quiet and pristine world of breathtaking beauty, where one can easily escape to peaceful solitude or participate in a myriad of outdoor activities. In addition, prices on the island are generally lower than on surrounding islands. As a result, many visitors are actually repeat customers, reimmersing themselves in the idyllic lifestyle they know they will find on the island.

Typical island activities include surfing, kayaking, fishing, and hiking. Snorkeling and scuba diving are especially spectacular due to the abundance of giant sea turtles. The island is also home to the longest barrier reef in the region, which stretches 28 miles. Guided hiking tours of the island's extensive rain forests allow visitors to learn about the flora and fauna unique to the region. For the less sure-footed, guided mule rides down the highest oceanfront cliffs in the world offer dramatic views of the unspoiled coastline.

With only one movie theater, one public restroom, and no stoplights, the island takes pride in its lack of development. A weekly Saturday morning farmer's market offers a vibrant taste of the rich local heritage. In addition, the island's macadamia nut farm, coffee plantation, and kite factory provide abundant opportunities to explore the island's unique character. Dining options cover the full spectrum from inexpensive eateries to extravagant gourmet feasts, complete with traditional native entertainment.

In addition to tourism, major industries on the island include fishing, farming, and retail sales. With the collapse of the sugar and pineapple industries in the 1990s, the island has moved to replace these once dominant industries with more diversified aquaculture and agriculture.

Tropical Island is governed by an autonomous council. Residents elect a mayor, who serves a three-year term with a two-term limit, and an eight-member island council with two-year terms. The island council, with current mayor Gil Egan as its representative, is responsible for making all decisions regarding the island community. Decisions are made by majority vote of the council. The mayor performs the function of "tie-breaker" when necessary.

There are five public and two private schools on the island serving 2,000 students from kindergarten through twelfth grade. Residents seeking a college-level education typically move off the island for the duration of their studies. These students rarely return to live permanently on the island. This has been a major concern of the islanders, who wish to reduce the loss of native residents. Therefore, construction of a local community college is under consideration.

Current means for tourists to access the island include small aircraft and small sea vessels. There are also two inter-island flights per day between Tropical Island and the surrounding islands, with each flight carrying about 50 passengers. On any given day, about 200 tourists arrive or depart Tropical Island, with a total of 500 tourists on the island at any given time. Electric cart rentals are available at the airport for transportation around the island.

Marine ecological studies performed on Tropical Island by the United Nations' International Maritime Organization Agency indicate that for each day a cruise ship operates in Tropical Island's sensitive coastal waters, at least two weeks of undisturbed marine environment must be maintained afterward to avoid permanent ecological damage. Each additional day of operation requires two additional weeks of recovery. The ecosystem, however, is not able to sustain more than five consecutive days of abuse. These figures assume no intentional damage to the ecosystem, such as removal of coral or wildlife as a result of cruise ship–related tourism.

During the time that a cruise ship is anchored near the island, and for four days following its departure, local residents are advised not to fish or swim within a two-mile radius of where the cruise ship had been anchored because of potential health hazards. The island's only natural harbor is the best location for anchoring cruise ships. Unfortunately, this two-mile-wide bay is also the island's most productive fishing spot.

The *Island Queen*

At 971 feet in length and weighing 91,000 tons, the $400 million *Island Queen* is the largest cruise ship ever to service the Tropical Island region. It accommodates 2,200 passengers and 1,100 crew members. Operation of the *Island Queen* is handled through Island Queen, Inc., a private corporation. Captain Stuart (Stu) Bing is the director of cruise ship operations for the *Island Queen*. While he has sole responsibility for negotiating all contracts governing the vessel's operation, he ultimately answers to the CEO and the board of directors of Island Queen, Inc., regarding all corporate matters.

With 10 distinctive restaurants and 14 separate lounges and bars, the *Island Queen* has a venue for the most discriminating guest. Passengers who desire the excitement of gambling will enjoy the lavish Grand Casino with its glass elevators, floating staircases, stained glass domes, and ocean view windows. The magnificent Riviera Deck, adorned with sparkling pools, bars, hamburger grill, ice cream bar, gymnasium, and spa, is the perfect spot for outdoor activities and food. The *Island Queen* sets a new standard for luxury cruise ships with its unique alternative 24-hour dining in the panoramic Horizon Court, two theaters, computerized golf, and a library featuring "listening chairs" for music and for books on tape. Industry standard venues and amenities such as buffet meals, theaters, and gyms are included in the price of the cruise. Dining in the more exclusive restaurants and some personal services such as massages and beauty treatments are an additional expense billed separately to the passenger.

The standard *Island Queen* cruise is 16 days and 15 nights. The itinerary consists of five days sailing to the island region, six days visiting various tropical islands, and five days returning to its home port. An island visit generally involves passengers disembarking at 8 a.m. and returning to the ship by 8 p.m. On more popular islands, the ship will remain in port for two days. At these ports, passengers may elect to spend the night on the island, but they must return to the ship by 8 p.m. the following evening when the ship sets sail for the next port.

Island Queen, Inc., has provided luxury cruises to the island region for over 20 years, but Tropical Island has never allowed cruise ships to visit. For economic reasons, Tropical Island is now considering offering exclusive visitation rights to a cruise line company. Though other cruise line companies are vying for the right to add Tropical Island to their itinerary, the *Island Queen* is the most luxurious prospect. An agreement with the *Island Queen* is expected to provide greater income per tourist for the island then an agreement with any of the other cruise lines because of the *Island Queen*'s wealthier clientele.

During one-day port visits, about half of the ship's passengers typically disembark. As the length of stay increases, fewer passengers disembark per day. Those who remain on the ship are an important revenue source as they continue to patronize onboard facilities including the casino, shops, and restaurants. Island disembarkation agreements are negotiated in increments of 100 passengers. Thus an agreement for 500 passengers per day would include any number of visitors up to 500. There are currently no island visits longer than two days because this would not leave enough time to visit all the other popular ports. However, a visit longer than two days is certainly possible given sufficient demand.

Because there is no suitable deepwater dock on Tropical Island, cruise ships will have to anchor in the ecologically sensitive coastal waters surrounding the island. A smaller vessel must then make multiple trips ferrying passengers back and forth between the ship and the island. The island's harbor area is considered the best location for anchoring cruise ships due to its proximity to the main island community.

Tropical Island and *Island Queen* Concerns

Large cruise ships, like the *Island Queen,* can severely impact the local marine ecology during their stay. According to one environmental group, typical cruise ships "produce massive volumes of waste, including sewage, nonsewage wastewater or gray water, ballast water, oily bilge water, air pollution, solid waste, and hazardous waste, each of which may harm sensitive marine ecosystems like the island's through the addition of harmful pathogens and chemicals, or the introduction of alien species" (Moriwake 2003).

There are, however, international environmental standards under which cruise lines must operate. According to the International Council of Cruise Lines,

> Cruise lines operate within a comprehensive scheme of international environmental standards set out by the International Maritime Organization (IMO), an agency of the United Nations which is based in London. These standards are set forth in international conventions, including the *International Convention for the Prevention of Pollution from Ships (MARPOL 73/78)*. MARPOL sets strict standards for all commercial vessels, including passenger vessels, to prevent ship-generated pollution from oil, garbage, and waste. MARPOL has been ratified by some 90 nations, including the United States and most other maritime nations of the world.

Still, the island community has strong reservations about allowing cruise-based tourism because of the industry's dismal record of environmental compliance and poor enforcement of laws regarding ship pollution.

There is also concern that a sudden increase in tourism will adversely affect the social makeup of the quiet rural island. Environmentalists note that "many small islands and towns in Alaska and the Caribbean are finding their local lifestyle, culture, and economy crowded out by foreign businesses and visitors" (Moriwake 2002). The island council's community plan defines its primary economic focus as agricultural industries. Tourism is to be limited to a level that will not adversely affect the community's traditional, social, economic, and environmental characteristics. An agreement between the

Island Queen and Tropical Island must take into account the impact it will have on the traditional lifestyle and customary rights of the native inhabitants.

The main reason cruise ship companies have been hesitant to add Tropical Island to their itinerary has been the lack of island infrastructure to support the needs of a typical cruise ship visit. Too many cruise tourists descending upon the island all at once may overwhelm existing island facilities, resulting in an unpleasant experience for everyone. The fact that there is only one public restroom on the island is enough to dissuade even the most optimistic tour operator. Limiting the number of tourists disembarking will help preserve the island's natural character and benefit the cruise ship since remaining passengers will spend their money onboard the ship.

Conclusion

Traditional island culture and mores, as well as island law, forbid council members, and Mayor Gil Egan as their representative, from accepting any form of financial incentives, such as bribes, from the cruise lines to gain commercial access to Tropical Island. A respectful and mutually beneficial relationship between Tropical Island and the *Island Queen* is desirable.

Any agreement between Tropical Island and the *Island Queen* should take into account the current economic environment, existing resources and infrastructure, expected tourism income for both parties, and any damage to local ecology and native culture resulting from added cruise line tourism. International maritime law requires that any agreement between the parties remain in force for six years following its adoption, so it is important to consider anticipated trends with any agreement since renegotiating in the near term will be very difficult, if not impossible.

Bibliography

007Cruise.Com. 2002. http://www.007cruise.com/oceanprincess.htm.

Briscoe, David. 2003. "Princess Cruise Hit By Virus" (Honolulu: The Associated Press, February 5, 2003), http://www.cbsnews.com/stories/2002/11/20/health/main530128.shtml.

International Council of Cruise Lines, Federal and State Pollution Standards for Cruise Ships, http://www.iccl.org/policies/environment.cfm.

Moriwake, Isaac. 2002. "Moloka'i Citizens Sue for Environmental Review of Cruise Ship Visits" (Earthjustice, December 3, 2002), http://www.earthjustice.org/news/display.html?ID=503.

Ronan, Courtney. 2000. "Moloka'i: The 'Most Hawaiian' Island," *Realty Times,* Real Estate Update (May 22, 2000), http://realtytimes.com/rtnews/nlpages/20000522_molokai.htm.

Thrifty Travel Inc. 2002. PRINCESS cruisecenter.com, http://www.princesscruisecenter.com.

Travel Creations. Norwegian Cruise Line: Norwegian Star and Princess Cruises: Sun Princess, http://www.travelcreations.net/weddings.asp.

Exercise 14

Salary Negotiations

Introduction

In this simulation, you will play the role of either a manager or subordinate in a negotiation over the subordinate's salary. Both in securing employment as well as promotions, we are frequently in a position to negotiate with our superiors over salary. Moreover, once we achieve managerial rank, we do the same with subordinates. This is one of the most common and, at the same time, most personal forms of negotiation. For many people, it is also the most difficult. Since salary can be a means of satisfying many needs— economic, recognition, status, or competitive success measure—it naturally leads to complex negotiations.

Source: Developed from examples used by John Tarrant, *How to Negotiate a Raise* (New York: Van Nostrand Reinhold, 1976).

Exercise 15

Job Offer Negotiation:
Joe Tech and Robust Routers

Introduction

The scenario for this simulation is a negotiation over a job offer that has been extended by a technology company to an MBA student nearing graduation. The background information introduces the principals involved, recaps their prior relationship, and presents a detailed summary of the terms of the offer that the firm has extended to the student. For the negotiation simulation, you will be assigned to assume the role of either the student or a representative of the hiring company. The role-play information that your instructor will then provide gives details about the specific interests and objectives of the party to which you are assigned.

In many ways, negotiations about job offers are just like any other negotiation: Parties try to pursue their own interests while keeping an eye on relationship concerns and seeking areas of common ground that might allow them to bridge compatible interests. In other ways, however, job offer negotiations may be perceived as distinctive because of the stakes involved: For the job seeker, they involve the negotiation of one's personal circumstances, often with an opponent who is someone you will have to "live with" on a day-to-day basis for what could be a long time to come. As you read your role information and prepare for the encounter, think about how the pursuit of your goals—whether you are in the role of the hiring firm or the job-seeking student—may or should be affected by the unique context involved when one is negotiating about employment.

Background Information

Joe Tech, an MBA student in the final semester before graduation, has an offer (see Offer Letter, p. 529) for permanent employment from Robust Routers (RR), and the deadline for accepting the offer is next week. Joe spent the summer before his final year in the MBA program working for RR in Mountain View, California. His boss during the summer internship was Leigh Bultema, the product manager for RR's flagship product—a new terabit router. Leigh is the person at RR with whom Joe will speak to negotiate the terms of the offer.

Economic and Industry Conditions

At the time of the job offer, the U.S. economy has leveled off following a prolonged upswing. Economic growth is significantly lower than it was just a couple of years ago. The good news for MBA students, however, is that the unemployment rate remains

Source: This simulation was developed by Jorge Ferrer, Andy Lauman, Fred Smith, and Tobey Sommer. It is adapted and used here with permission.

modest, and the job market for new MBA graduates has remained strong. In recent years, "traditional" MBA employers such as investment banks have felt pressure to compete with aggressive technology companies recruiting top MBA prospects with potentially lucrative stock options. More recently, the stock market entered a period of high turbulence, dampening the outlook for smaller technology firms. Even the most promising and profitable tech companies have seen their share prices come under pressure. Companies like RR, which make Internet "backbone" equipment, operate with extraordinary profit margins, and yet even their shares have fallen.

Just last week, however, there was a rebound in tech share prices, in large measure due to the resolution of a strike at Horizon Communications. Horizon settled its labor dispute and reaffirmed its commitment to capital spending, which Wall Street analysts had predicted would slow over the next two years. That potential slowdown would have eroded the stock valuations of network infrastructure manufacturers in general, and market leader RR in particular. Now Horizon has reaffirmed its capital expenditure plans and announced a multiyear purchase of RR's high-end terabit routers.

Company Background

Robust Routers (RR) was started in the mid-1980s by several enterprising graduate business students who had helped their university tie its computer lab machines together into a local area network. Anticipating a market for networking devices, the two borrowed money from friends and family, maxed out their credit cards, and started a company. Two years later they sold their first network router.

Originally targeting universities, RR by 1990 had expanded its marketing to include large and medium-sized corporations. As an early player with a proven track record, RR had a head start when the market for network routers took off in the early 1990s. RR's sales lept from $1 million in 1989 to $30 million in 1992. The company went public in 1993. Since then, RR has acquired several niche players in the market and currently has a market capitalization of $70 billion, a significant accomplishment for a company its age.

The computer hardware networking industry consists of companies designing, developing, and manufacturing products that provide connectivity solutions for multiuse computing environments, local area networks, and wide area networks. Network hardware products include PC cards, routers, hubs, remote access servers, switches, and adapters. At the time of Joe Tech's job offer, RR controls more than two-thirds of the global market and offers the industry's broadest range of products used to form information networks and power the Internet.

RR sells in approximately 75 countries through a direct sales force, distributors, value-added resellers, and system integrators. RR continues to purchase companies at a frenzied pace—it has made close to 10 acquisitions per year during the last two years. RR serves customers in three target markets: (1) enterprises—large organizations with complex networking needs, including corporations, government agencies, utilities, and educational institutions; (2) service providers—firms providing information services, including telecommunications carriers, Internet service providers, cable companies, and wireless communication providers; and (3) small/medium businesses—firms with a need for data networks of their own, as well as connection to the Internet and/or to business partners.

Joe Tech's Internship Experience at RR

Joe worked at RR during the summer between the first and second years of graduate school. He was fortunate to have secured an internship at the leading router company because they don't normally recruit from his school. He contacted an alumnus who worked for Horizon (one of RR's largest customers), who put him in touch with a friend at RR. Joe and Leigh Bultema hit it off from the initial exchange of e-mails, and after a fast-track series of telephone interviews, Joe had his internship set up for the summer.

Leigh Bultema began working at RR eight years ago, when the company took the market and really began to pull away from its competition. She was in the right place at the right time. RR had proprietary technology that promised to revolutionize the telecom industry, and Leigh had drive, ambition, and brains. Leigh rose through the ranks at RR quickly, working in positions in sales, marketing, manufacturing, and business development activities. A proven performer, Leigh has been assigned to pivotal and vital roles within RR during her tenure. RR has identified product management of the new terabit router as a priority function, and the CEO personally placed Leigh in this crucial role.

When he landed the summer internship, Joe expressed an interest in working in business development. However, because he did not enter RR through traditional recruiting channels from a top five MBA program, the business development internships were already filled. There were 50 MBA interns working at RR over the summer. They were spread out among marketing, strategic alliances, technical development, business development, treasury, and corporate marketing. Joe worked on product management for Leigh during the summer. The internship exposed Joe to senior management and different groups within the company, including the business development group for which Joe hoped to work after completing his MBA. Business development maintained all key business relationships at RR and was considered one of the preeminent functions within the firm. Joe received accolades from very senior executives on his internal product presentations of the terabit router.

The internship ended on a high note for the company and for Joe Tech. RR received an order from Horizon for its terabit router, and Joe received an offer letter from RR. The offer came from Leigh Bultema's product management group, not the business development group Joe was targeting. However, job assignments at RR changed frequently. At the end of the summer, Leigh assured Joe that if his interest truly lay with business development, all he had to do was perform well within product management and he could write his own ticket internally. Leigh herself had performed well in her initial job assignment within RR, and subsequently found herself courted by executives from several different internal groups who wanted her on their teams.

Although the permanent job offer was tendered back in August at the conclusion of the internship, RR told Joe that the offer would remain available until March 1. The specific terms of the offer are shown in the offer letter. Now it is February 20, and Joe has arranged to speak with Leigh to discuss the offer before making a decision.

Offer Letter

Robust Routers, Inc.
One Robust Center
555 Silicon Way

Mountain View, CA 94201

August 25, 2005

Joe Tech
401 Owen Way
Nashville, TN 37220

Dear Joe,

On behalf of Robust Routers, Inc., I am delighted to confirm our offer to you of the position of Associate Product Manager. Your appointment will be effective June 1, 2006. The specifics of this offer are as follows:

Position: Associate Product Manager, Terabit Router Group

Salary: Starting salary will be $88,000 annually, paid monthly.

Signing bonus: You will receive a signing bonus of $10,000, paid as a lump sum within 30 days after you accept the offer in writing.

Options: You will receive 1,000 stock options at a strike price equal to the share price of RR on the date of employment. Additionally, you will be eligible to receive a minimum grant of 500 incentive options after your first year of employment, and on each subsequent employment anniversary, provided your performance fully meets expectations and that you are an active employee on the subsequent grant date. The strike price for these options is set by company management and ratified by the board of directors annually. Options vest over a three-year period (33.3% per year).

Benefits: Robust Routers provides a comprehensive benefit plan to its employees. You will be entitled to the benefits detailed in the applicable plan document in effect at the time you join the company. Current benefits include health insurance, basic life insurance, dependent life insurance, long-term disability coverage, and immediate participation in Robust Router's matched savings plan for retirement. The Human Resources Department will send details on these benefits, along with specifics regarding paid sick leave, vacation leave, and holiday leave, under separate cover.

Relocation: You will receive a lump sum cash payment of $5,000 to help defray expenses associated with moving to Silicon Valley. Upon acceptance of our offer, you will receive a relocation handbook, which will provide detailed instructions regarding relocation benefits and information on the local area provided by several real estate firms.

Robust Routers is offering you a position with the understanding that you are not a party to a written agreement containing either a noncompete or nonsolicitation clause. Our corporation conducts routine employment checks on prospective employees. Your employment is contingent upon the successful completion and satisfactory results of these checks.

This offer remains in force until March 1, 2006. If you choose to accept the offer, please sign and return a copy of this offer letter on or before that date. Should you have any questions, the appropriate point of contact is the hiring manager, Leigh Bultema.

We are impressed with your background and experience, and we look forward to having you join the Robust Router team in June.

Sincerely,

Keith Hernandez
Managing Director
Product Management Group

cc: Leigh Bultema
       Human Resources

The Employee Exit Interview

Introduction

This exercise involves a negotiation between the managing director of a small, privately held consulting firm and an employee who wishes to leave the firm for personal reasons. There are two main issues under discussion: (1) back pay for sick days, and (2) stock that the employee wishes to sell back to the firm under its stock buyback plan.

Source: This exercise was written by G. Richard Shell and is used with permission.

Exercise 17

Newtown School Dispute

Introduction

In this simulation, you will play a member of either a school board or teachers' association bargaining team. You and the other members of your team, and the members of the other team, are negotiators representing constituencies. You will deal with a complex mix of bargaining issues; these issues have differing preference functions for each side. Finally, you will be subject to a variety of pressures during the negotiations.

Background Information

It is now September 10, the opening day of the school year in Newtown. The contract between Newtown School District and the Newtown Teachers' Association expired on June 30. Since then, the Board of Education and representatives of the Teachers' Association have met on several occasions in an attempt to finalize a contract, but these attempts have not been successful.

Prior to June 30 and during the summer months, there was increasing talk among the membership of the Teachers' Association of the desirability of calling a strike if the contract was not finalized by opening day. However, the leadership of the Teachers' Association agreed, for the benefit of the community, to resume normal operations throughout the system (without a contract) on opening day *on a day-to-day basis*. This is in response to parent pressures to resume normal operations. Parents have been placing pressure on both teachers and the board to keep the schools operating, but voters have twice defeated referendums for increased taxes to cover unavoidable budgetary increases. Due to decreases in enrollment and income from local taxes and state and federal aid, as well as increased costs, maintenance of the school budget at par with the previous year would produce a 3.95 percent budgetary shortfall, which the board feels would begin to exhaust budgetary categories beginning in the coming April. Therefore, the board feels that programs and personnel must be cut while, at the same time, productivity (workload) of teachers must be increased if the system is to function effectively within its budgetary constraints to the end (June 30) of the current fiscal year. The district is mandated by state law to provide 190 instructional days during the school year.

The Board of Education is caught between the Teachers' Association and community pressure groups. The board believes that it must satisfy these pressure groups, while at the same time keeping the teachers on the job with a contract that is acceptable to the bargaining unit's membership. The board is concerned that if it fails to respond appropriately to community pressures for cost reductions, it may be removed. The board's primary objective, therefore, is to cut costs while retaining as many programs as possible. It hopes to do so through cutbacks in teaching personnel and increases in teacher productivity (workload). The board also wishes to eliminate certain existing agreements in order to increase productivity. In this connection, the board

Source: Revised version of material originally developed by Frank W. Masters. Used with permission.

wants to negotiate a three-year contract that will "stabilize" the situation by creating orderly and predictable budgetary needs that will be less likely to be seen as excessive by various community groups. In contrast, the Teachers' Association wants to obtain a one-year contract to maintain flexibility.

The Teachers' Association also feels caught between community pressure groups, who want to avert a strike, and the board's apparent unwillingness to fight for increased budget allocations to run the system. The teachers feel the board has not faced up to the community's unwillingness to accept increased taxation to pay for education, and that the board is simply responding to community unwillingness by passing the burden along to teachers.

Newtown is a relatively settled and stable upper-middle-income community, with a strong interest in quality education, but is disinclined to increase its already burdensome tax rate. The Newtown School District consists of 12 schools: 9 elementary schools (K–8) and 3 senior high schools. The student population is 12,000, with 8,000 elementary and 4,000 high school students. The bargaining unit, representing 95 percent of all teachers, consists of 250 elementary teachers in all categories and 120 high school teachers in all categories.

Both sides wish to conclude an agreement to avert a strike. However, the Teachers' Association bargaining team is adamantly committed to improving the lot of its membership, and the board is just as committed to keeping its costs as low as possible. Nevertheless, each side feels it has some room to move on certain issues.

		Newtown School District Teachers' Salary Schedule				
Step	**Amount**	**Last Year's Number of Teachers**	**Cost**	**This Year's Number of Teachers**	**Cost**	
1 (Entry)	$28,500	20	$ 570,000	0	$ 0	
2	29,000	20	580,000	20	580,000	
3	30,000	28	840,000	20	600,000	
4	31,000	31	961,000	26	806,000	
5	32,000	30	960,000	28	896,000	
6	33,500	23	770,500	26	871,000	
7	34,500	24	828,000	23	793,500	
8	35,500	15	532,500	22	781,000	
9	37,000	16	592,000	15	555,000	
10	38,000	18	684,000	16	608,000	
11	39,000	19	741,000	18	702,000	
12	41,000	21	861,000	18	738,000	
13	42,000	20	840,000	19	798,000	
14	44,000	22	968,000	20	880,000	
15	45,000	18	810,000	21	945,000	
16	47,000	19	893,000	18	846,000	
17	48,000	16	768,000	18	864,000	
18	50,000	17	850,000	16	800,000	
19	51,000	14	714,000	15	765,000	
20	53,000	9	477,000	11	583,000	
Totals		400	$15,240,000	370	$14,411,500	

Current School Year, July 1–June 30, Projected Budget

1. Income

   1.1 Local tax (same rate as last year will continue,
       $5.85 per $1,000. No significant increase in
       property values expected.) $23,891,904

   1.2 State (formula yield per pupil will remain the
       same. Legislature may meet and possibly raise
       formula for next year.)   8,470,000

   1.3 Federal   1,369,500

       Total $33,731,404

Note: This is a decrease of $851,716 (−2.46%) from the previous year's income.

2. Expenditures

   2.1 Administration

       2.1.1 Professional salaries $2,030,000

       2.1.2 Clerical/secretaries   497,000

       2.1.3 Other   470,000

       Total $2,997,000

   2.2 Instruction

       2.2.1 Teacher salaries $14,411,500[a]

             Fringes   2,824,654

       2.2.2 Aides   2,047,000

       2.2.3 Materials/supplies   2,053,400[b]

       Total $21,336,554

   2.3 Plant operation/maintenance

       2.3.1 Salaries $2,312,400

       2.3.2 Utilities   2,023,000[c]

       2.3.3 Other   500,000[d]

       Total $4,835,400

   2.4 Fixed charges

       2.4.1 Retirement $2,111,200[e]

       2.4.2 Other   783,000

       Total   2,894,200

   2.5 Debt service $1,763,782[f]

   2.6 Transportation

       2.6.1 Salaries $631,060

       2.6.2 Other   660,370[g]

       Total $1,291,430

       Grand total $35,118,366

Notes:

Total number of pupils = 12,000

Total number of teachers = 370

Per pupil expenditure = $2,927

[a]Thirty teachers did not return to the system due to either retirement or other reasons.

[b]Costs of materials and supplies will be up 46 percent over last year's cost based largely on the rising cost of paper.

(continued)

Current School Year, July 1–June 30, Projected Budget (*concluded*)

cCost of utilities is expected to increase by approximately 65 percent due to rate increases and overdue, deferred maintenance.

dCost projections indicate a 13 percent increase in this category.

eTeacher retirement is up 5 percent due to increases mandated by the legislature to pay for new benefits. This was partially offset by attrition.

fDebt service is up 22 percent due to increased difficulty in floating bonds.

gOther transportation costs are up 31 percent due to increases in operating and maintenance costs.

Last School Year, July 1–June 30, Actual Audit

1. Income		
1.1	Local tax ($5.85 per $1,000 worth assessed real property. Assessment is at full value.)	$24,743,620
1.2	State (based on an equalization formula, improved during the last legislative session. Yielded $621.28 per pupil in administration last year.)	8,475,354
1.3	Federal	1,368,150
	Total	$34,587,124
2. Expenditures		
2.1	Administration	
	2.1.1 Professional salaries	$2,077,359
	2.1.2 Clerical/secretarial	513,529
	2.1.3 Other	454,972
	Total	$3,045,860
2.2	Instruction	
	2.2.1 Teacher salaries	$15,240,000
	Fringes	2,987,040
	2.2.2 Aides	2,277,451
	2.2.3 Materials/supplies	1,400,313
	Total	$21,904,804
2.3	Plant operations/maintenance	
	2.3.1 Salaries	$2,386,327
	2.3.2. Utilities	1,224,255
	2.3.3 Other	441,788
	Total	$4,052,370
2.4	Fixed charges	
	2.4.1 Retirement	$2,039,280
	2.4.2 Other	787,906
	Total	2,827,186
2.5	Debt service	$1,444,370

(*continued*)

Last School Year, July 1–June 30, Actual Audit (*concluded*)	
2.6 Transportation	
2.6.1 Salaries	$729,878
2.6.2 Other	582,656
Total	$1,312,534
Grand total	$34,587,124

Notes:

Total number of pupils = 12,800

Total number of teachers = 400

Per pupil expenditure = $2,702

Last year, the year of the audit on this page, there were 12,800 students in the public school system.

The current year's projected enrollment is 12,000.

Initial Offer Form

Board of Education _____ Teachers' Association _____

Item	Bottom-Line Position	Desired Settlement	Opening Offer
Salary	_____	_____	_____
Reduction in staff	_____	_____	_____
Workload	_____	_____	_____
Evaluation of teachers	_____	_____	_____
Binding arbitration	_____	_____	_____
Benefits	_____	_____	_____

Final Settlement Form

Board of Education _____ Teachers' Association _____

Item	Settlement
Salary	_____
Reduction in staff	_____
Workload	_____
Evaluation of teachers	_____
Binding arbitration	_____
Benefits	_____

Exercise 18

Bestbooks/Paige Turner

Introduction

This situation involves a negotiation between two representatives: one for an author, Paige Turner, and the other for a publishing company, Bestbooks. This is clearly a competitive situation, but some cooperation is also required. Your challenge is to get the best contract possible for your side.

Read the private material that your instructor has provided, and prepare your strategy for the negotiations. Each dyad of representatives will conduct its meeting trying to reach a new contract between Paige Turner and Bestbooks. When an agreement is reached, write down the settlement on the final settlement agreement form. Agreement must be reached on all eight issues in order for a final agreement to be struck.

Final Agreement Settlement Form	
Issue	**Settlement Point**
Royalties	_____
Signing bonus	_____
Print runs	_____
Weeks of promotion	_____
Number of books	_____
Advance	_____
Countries distributed	_____
Book clubs	_____

Source: Written in collaboration with Gregory Leck.

Exercise 19

Strategic Moves and Turns

Introduction

This exercise involves two short vignettes about negotiation situations within organizations. In each situation, the protagonist has a challenging negotiation that involves getting the other person to negotiate seriously. In the first one, a health care agency director is negotiating with her CEO for a promotion. In the second one, a pharmaceutical company executive is negotiating with an executive from a partner company about a joint venture in South America. Both situations involve challenges associated with overcoming resistance and getting one's proposals heard.

Vignette #1: Cynthia's Challenge[1]

Cynthia is a program director in a large home health care agency. She has worked there for five years and received salary increases as she has been promoted. With the resignation of the vice president, Cynthia is now one of the most senior people in the agency in terms of responsibility, but not in terms of salary. At the same time she has been taking on added responsibilities because of turnover and finds herself working more than 80 hours a week and picking up the slack from the vice president's departure. She knows that others with less responsibility are paid more than she is, and that eats at her. She also wants the vice president position. She's been essentially doing the job in an "acting" role and wants it to be official. She's always been on good terms with George, the CEO, helping him out when he needed it. Recently she oversaw an audit of the agency where she worked around the clock, making sure it was successful, and it was. Deciding the time was right, she planned to see George about a promotion to the vice president position with an increase in pay the job merited.

Cynthia had a negotiation with George about salary a year ago. Although she ultimately got a raise, the negotiations were difficult and she felt she deserved more. George praised her, telling her how much he valued her contributions to the organization. But when she raised the salary issue, he became angry and accused her of being inconsiderate and irresponsible in bringing the issue up. Cynthia did not want this situation to be repeated.

Vignette #2: Marjorie's Mandate[2]

As the newly appointed vice president of global joint ventures for ABCO, a large pharmaceutical company, Marjorie is responsible for monitoring and managing the firm's portfolio of joint venture projects. Always a vocal supporter of ABCO's emerging markets division, she was excited when Jim Drake, the CEO, gave her the opportunity to head this new function in the business. She knew that Jim, a risk-averse fellow, was

---

[1]This vignette was developed by Deborah M. Kolb, Deloitte Ellen Gabriel Professor for Women and Leadership, Simmons School of Management, 2002. Used with permission.

[2]This vignette was written by Fleur Weigert under the direction of Deborah M. Kolb, 2000. Used with permission.

skeptical about how profitable some of the joint ventures in South America and Asia would turn out to be. Marjorie's mandate was to analyze the existing joint ventures worldwide. Based on this analysis, the firm would invest in the profitable ventures, but "clean house," meaning disband the unprofitable ones. Jim, however, was prone to sending mixed messages. Over her 10 years at ABCO, Marjorie had learned that even with clear evidence that a project was a losing proposition, he hated to kill it.

Marjorie's recent challenge was a struggling marketing initiative in Chile that ABCO had undertaken with one of its South American partners—Sorso, Inc. Despite the losses mounting on the venture's books, Sorso was requesting an additional infusion of capital. Although other joint venture initiatives with Sorso continued to be reasonably successful in other countries in South America, this three-year-old project had problems from the beginning. Based on her current numbers and financial modeling, she saw further deterioration ahead. Additional funding, Marjorie decided, was not warranted until the political and economic climate in the region improved.

Dick Cortez headed ABCO's operations in South America. Although Marjorie had complete faith in Dick's abilities, she was concerned that he was not on top of this problem. The picture was not altogether clear, however, since Dick reported to Greg— the vice president of the International Division and Marjorie's peer—and not to her. Further, Dick had generally had free reign in how he managed operations in his area.

Marjorie began to push Dick hard on cutting back in Chile. "Dick believed the currency crunch was a temporary setback," she said. "Although he agreed that revenues had been slow to materialize, he pointed out that we had invested significant sums in building distribution channels in the region. These would be put at risk were we to scale back." Marjorie thought that Dick was too heavily involved with Sorso on other ventures to be able to see the benefits of shutting this losing proposition down. Moreover, Dick handled only South America. "He didn't want his budget sliced. I, on the other hand, had overall responsibility for these distribution arrangements, and I, not Dick, would be held accountable for poor performance."

CEO Jim Drake, impatient with Dick's foot-dragging, told Marjorie to get a handle on the Chilean joint venture. Although Dick thought that he should control what happened in his area, Marjorie decided she needed to intervene directly in the negotiations with Sorso in order to dismantle the project. Under pressure from Jim, she felt she had to move quickly and planned to travel to South America within the next few months to negotiate the venture's dissolution. Since the other South American joint ventures with Sorso would be continued, she hoped that Dick wouldn't see this decision as a harbinger of things to come, but rather as the phasing out of one unsuccessful experiment within a larger operation.

At her first meeting with Sorso, Marjorie learned that Dick had already been negotiating with them without telling her. Their understanding was that Dick was ABCO's chief negotiator with Sorso based on the excellent working relationship they had established. Marjorie proposed several options for ending the Chilean joint venture, but they responded that Dick had assured them the venture would continue. After the meeting, Marjorie confronted Dick about these private and unauthorized negotiations. He was nonchalant and told her not to get so excited. He was simply trying to maintain the good working relations that he had spent so long setting up with Sorso. He assured her that he would take care of it and that she shouldn't worry. This arrangement was not agreeable to Marjorie.

Elmwood Hospital Dispute

Introduction

In this exercise you will be dealing with a very complex negotiation situation. In contrast to earlier exercises, where there may have been a single opponent and one or two clearly defined issues, this simulation creates a negotiation between larger groups with less clearly defined issues—and perhaps stronger emotions. The key roles played by mediators are also introduced in this simulation.

Background Information

The situation described here is a composite, with some data drawn from a number of similar disputes, and other information constructed specifically for this training exercise. The scenario is not to be interpreted as an account of any actual dispute. This simulation is one of several developed and tested by the Institute for Mediation and Conflict Resolution in New York, and adapted with permission by the Community Conflict Resolution Program.

Elmwood is a medium-sized, 450-bed private hospital in a southwestern city of approximately 600,000. It is well equipped for inpatient care and has an open-heart surgery team that is a matter of special pride to the board of trustees and the hospital's director. None of the trustees live in the hospital's immediate neighborhood, though some of their parents once did. Most of them are professionals or businesspeople, and one of their main functions as trustees is to help in fund-raising for the hospital.

Until 10 years ago, Elmwood was in the middle of a white, middle-class community. Now, however, it is on the eastern edge of an expanding low-income neighborhood, which has moved across the nearby expressway and is continuing to grow eastward. A good part of the low-income community is served by West Point Hospital, back on the western side of the expressway. People on the east, however, are turning to Elmwood. There are very few private physicians left in the Elmwood area, and the hospital, through its outpatient clinic, is the main source of medical care for the newer residents.

These newer residents, who now make up approximately 65 percent of the service area, are a mix of relatively recent newcomers to the city, some from other parts of the United States and others from various foreign countries. Most are in low-paying service jobs. Many are on public assistance. Infant mortality is three times as high as in the rest of the city. Malnutrition is a problem, as are tuberculosis, lead poisoning, and other diseases associated with a slum environment. Most of these new residents cannot afford to be admitted to the hospital when sick and rely instead on outpatient treatment in what is now an overburdened facility at Elmwood.

Source: Adapted from an activity developed for the Institute of Mediation and Conflict Resolution, 1972.

Like most hospitals, Elmwood is in a financial squeeze. In addition, it has become increasingly difficult to attract new interns and residents and harder to retain present professionals. Although the hospital director is somewhat sympathetic to the medical care problems of the community, he sees his first priority as building the hospital's institutional strength by such measures as increasing intern- and resident-oriented research opportunities and adding facilities that would induce the staff to stay on rather than go elsewhere. He has apparently given some thought to sponsoring a neighborhood health center, but it has been put off by location problems. He has also heard about some heated conflicts over control of services at other hospitals in the state that took state and federal health grants. Right now, the director apparently intends to put these matters on the back burner until he gets the other things going.

Residents of the low-income community have organized a Concerned Community Coalition (CCC). The community has been asking the hospital to increase its almost nonexistent efforts in preventive medical care, improve and expand outpatient facilities, establish a satellite health center with day care facilities, and train a roving paraprofessional health team to administer diagnostic tests throughout the community. Elmwood is their neighborhood hospital, and to them, this is what a neighborhood hospital should be doing for the residents.

Two weeks ago, the CCC sent a letter to the director asking that the hospital initiate these efforts and requesting that he meet with them to discuss how the community and the hospital could work together. Although the community is deeply concerned about its medical problems and resents the fact that a city institution has not acted before this of its own volition, the letter was not unfriendly.

To date, the letter has not been answered.

Three days ago, the director and the chairman of the board announced the acquisition of a site about 15 blocks from the hospital on which it said it would build a heart research facility, a six-story nurses' residence, and a staff parking lot, with shuttle bus service to the hospital grounds.

On learning of the plans, the leaders and members of the CCC were incensed. They decided to sit in at the director's office until the hospital met their needs.

The day before yesterday, about 50 CCC supporters took over the director's office, vowing not to leave until the hospital agreed to meet the following demands:

1. Replacement of the board of trustees with a community-controlled board.

2. A 100 percent increase in outpatient facilities.

3. Establishment of a neighborhood health center and a day care facility on the newly acquired site.

4. Establishment of a preventive diagnostic mobile health team, consisting of neighborhood residents chosen by the CCC.

5. Replacement of the director by one chosen by the community.

While the hospital director indicated that he would be glad to meet with the group's leader to discuss the matters raised in its letter, he also stated quite forcefully that he considered the new demands arrogant and destructive and that, in any event, he would not meet under duress (i.e., as long as the sit-in continued).

The CCC said it would not leave until a meeting took place and the demands were accepted.

The sit-in began two days ago. This morning the hospital's lawyers moved to get an injunction against the sit-in. The CCC, aided by a legal services attorney, resisted.

The judge reserved decision, stating that to grant an injunction might only make the situation worse. He noted that both the hospital and the CCC would have to learn to live together for their own joint best interest. He therefore instructed the parties to meet to try to work out the problems between them, and has appointed a mediator to assist them. The mediator is a staff member of the city's Human Rights Commission, a unit of the municipal government.

At the judge's suggestion, the sides have agreed to meet with the mediator in the hospital library. The meeting has been scheduled for later today.

The Power Game

Introduction

The concept of *power* is a complex, elusive, and almost paradoxical one. It is complex because there is a wide variety of definitions of what constitutes power, and how it is effectively accumulated and used. It is elusive because there seems to be very little consensus about the definitions, or the best way to describe power and talk about it in action. Finally, power is paradoxical because it doesn't always work the way it is expected to; sometimes those who seem to have the most power really have the least, while those who may appear to have the least power are most in control.

This simulation offers an opportunity to experience power in a wide variety of forms and styles. During the activity, you may become aware of your own power and the power of others. Your objective will be to determine who has power, how power is being used, and how to use your own power to achieve your goals. This type of analysis is essential to effective negotiations when power relationships have not been well defined.

Source: Adapted from an exercise developed by Lee Bolman and Terrence Deal, Harvard Graduate School of Education, and published in *Exchange: The Organizational Behavior Teaching Journal.* Used with permission.

Coalition Bargaining

Introduction

The word *coalition* may be loosely defined as a group of individuals or subgroups who assemble to *collectively* exert influence on another group or individual. In an environment where there are many individuals, there are often many different points of view (different interests). Each individual views things differently, and each individual would like to have the "system" represent his or her views. In a dictatorship, the system usually represents the views of the dictator; but in a democratic environment, the views that are represented are usually those of a subgroup who have agreed to work together and collectively support one another's views in exchange for having a stronger impact on the system than each individual could have alone.

Many of us are familiar with the work of coalitions. The patterns of influence in national politics, governments, and communities provide us with some excellent examples. Whether it be the coalitions that are formed along traditional party ties (Democrats or Republicans) or along the concerns of special interest groups (Common Cause, the Sierra Club, the AFL–CIO, the National Rifle Association, the National Organization for Women, or hundreds of others), each group is attempting to influence the direction of the larger system by effectively pooling its resources, working together as a team, and persuading those who have control of the current system.

Coalitions are a common phenomenon in organizations as well. We have seen a significant emergence of coalitions in the business sector. In earlier times, these may have been no more than cooperative agreements and licensing between companies, or efforts to work together to influence political and economic policy. But the demands for increased business competitiveness have spawned a significant number of mergers, partnerships, and strategic alliances between companies, as they attempt to compete in the international marketplace or move into new markets, product lines, and spin-off businesses. Organizations are a complex web of cross-pressures among various subgroups, each one striving to have its own priorities adopted as the primary goals of the total organization. Those who are initiating and leading these efforts must have excellent strategic skills to assess the "power dynamics" that each party brings to this game and sophisticated negotiating skills to forge and manage the relationships between the parties.

The purpose of this exercise is to help you understand the different sources and expressions of power, or *leverage*, that individuals and groups can use in multiparty decision making. In this exercise, you will see people use power and influence in a variety of different ways. See if you can determine what kind of power is being used,

Source: Adapted from Roy J. Lewicki and Joseph Litterer, *Negotiation: Readings, Exercises, and Cases,* 1st ed. (Homewood, IL: Richard D. Irwin, 1985) and from Donald D. Bowen, Roy J. Lewicki, D. T. Hall, and F. Hall, *Experiences in Management and Organizational Behavior,* 2nd and 4th eds. (New York: John Wiley, 1996). Copyright © 1981 by John Wiley & Sons, Inc. Reprinted by permission of John Wiley & Sons, Inc.

and how effective that power is at gaining the other's compliance or cooperation. In addition, this exercise will help you explore the dynamics of trust and cooperation in a strongly competitive situation.

Rules of the Game

Objective

The objective is to form a coalition with another team in order to divide the stake. The coalition must also decide on a way of dividing the stake so as to satisfy both parties.

The Stake

Each team has unequal resources. In spite of the fact that you each contributed $X, you will receive a different stake, depending on the coalition you form. The following table should be filled in with information provided by the group leader (the individual pay-offs are determined by the number of participants in the activity and the total money collected):

> If an AB coalition forms, it will receive a stake of $_____.
>
> If an AC coalition forms, it will receive a stake of $_____.
>
> If a BC coalition forms, it will receive a stake of $_____.

The Strategy

Each team will meet separately to develop a strategy before the negotiations. You should also select a negotiator.

Rules for Negotiation

1. All members on a team may be present for negotiations; however, only the negotiator may speak.
2. Notes may be passed to negotiators if desired.
3. A team may change its negotiator between conversations.
4. At the termination of the game, the stake will be allocated only if a coalition has been formed.
5. Only one formal coalition is permitted.
6. A coalition will be recognized by the group leader only if (*a*) no two teams are permitted to receive the same amount of money, and (*b*) neither team in the coalition is allowed to receive zero.
7. If no coalition is reached, no funds are allocated.
8. Negotiations will be conducted in the following fixed order, and for the following fixed periods of time:

Order of Negotiation	Time for First Round of Negotiation	Time for Second and Third Rounds of Negotiation
Teams A and B	5 minutes	4 minutes
Teams A and C	5 minutes	4 minutes
Teams B and C	5 minutes	4 minutes

9. The team *not* in negotiations—that is, while the other two teams are negotiating—must leave the negotiation room. Other members of the companies who are *not* in the negotiating teams may not speak with any of the negotiators.

10. There cannot be any conversation between team members and observers at any time.

Valid Coalitions

1. A coalition will be recognized by the group leader only if (*a*) no teams are permitted to receive the same amount of money, and (*b*) neither team in the coalition is allowed to receive zero.

2. After negotiations, all three teams are given the opportunity to submit a written statement in the following form: "Team X has a coalition with Team Y, whereby Team X gets $X.xx and Y gets $Y.yy." When written statements meeting these requirements from any two teams agree, a valid coalition has been formed.

End of the Game

The group leader will ask each team to meet separately and to submit a ballot stating the coalition that they believe was formed. A blank ballot may be distributed by the referee, or should be written on a blank sheet of paper, in the following format:

Team (*your team*) has a coalition with Team _____, whereby Team _____ receives _____ (dollars or points) and Team _____ receives _____ (dollars or points).

Put your own team letter (A, B, or C) on the ballot.

Each team brings its written statement to the negotiating room. The group leader will announce whether a valid coalition has been formed (two ballots agree); the money is then distributed as specified on the ballots. If a coalition has not been formed, or if the coalition that has formed does not use up all of the initial stake, a problem will arise as to what to do with the funds.

The Connecticut Valley School

Introduction

In this situation you must allocate a limited capital budget among seven competing projects. Three parties are involved in the negotiation: the headmaster, the faculty budget committee, and the board of trustees. While the issues in this exercise appear straightforward, the parties do not necessarily perceive the budget process in the same manner.

Read the background information for the Connecticut Valley School; then read the role information that the instructor has provided for you. Participants who have been assigned to the same team (faculty budget committee, board of trustees, headmaster) will meet separately to decide how to manage the upcoming meeting.

The different parties will meet together to negotiate an agreement about the capital projects that will be funded. The chairperson of the board of trustees will chair this meeting. Participants will leave this meeting with an agreement about the priority of the capital spending projects. If no agreement is reached, each team should have a record of their final rankings and where they are willing to make further concessions.

Background Information

The Connecticut Valley School (CVS) is a private boarding school in Massachusetts. Headmaster John Loring has just submitted his annual recommendations for capital spending to the board of trustees. Capital spending will be funded from two sources: new debt and the accumulated interest on the school's endowment. Since the school is approaching its debt capacity and trustees are committed not to draw on the principal of the endowment, the school can afford to spend only $450,000 to $500,000 on capital improvements over the next year. The seven major projects under consideration are described briefly here:

1. *Swimming pool*

   Cost: $320,000   Expected life: 15 years

   Currently the school rents a local facility for $30,000 per year. In addition, the school pays $5,000 per year to bus students to the facility. If the school owned a pool, it could rent out pool time to local organizations for $15,000 per year. The headmaster feels that more students would use the pool if it were located on campus.

2. *Buses*

   Cost: $135,000 (3 buses)   Expected life: 6 years

   Salvage value: Nil

Source: Written by Peter Nye, University of Washington at Bothell. Used with permission.

CVS owns two campuses several miles apart. A private bus company transports students between campuses at a cost of $90,000 per year. If the school owns and operates its buses, it will incur $40,000 in operating expenses each year.

3. *New roof for hockey rink*

   Cost: $30,000

   A new roof is essential to prevent further damage to the rink and to the arena's infrastructure. The project could be delayed one year; but due to the additional damage that would result, total repair costs would jump to $60,000.

4. *Wood chip heating system*

   Cost: $400,000   Expected life: 15 years

   Cold New England winters and the high cost of fuel oil have been draining the school's operating funds. This new heating system could save the school between $70,000 and $80,000 per year over the next 15 years.

5. *Renovation of fine arts building*

   Cost: $150,000

   The faculty and trustees agree that an improved fine arts program is critical to the school's liberal arts mission. The renovated fine arts building would include a photography lab, a pottery shop, and art studios, as well as a small gallery. The building would not generate any incremental revenues or cost savings. However, a wealthy benefactor (after whom the building would be named) has offered to contribute $75,000 to subsidize the project. In addition, the facility would provide some marketing benefits, as a strong arts program attracts quality students.

6. *Renovations to women's locker room*

   Cost: $20,000

   The women's locker room has not been renovated since it was built 33 years ago for visiting men's teams. Many of the women have complained that the facility is dirty, depressing, and overcrowded. Some women refuse to use the facility. The headmaster insists that these complaints are unfounded. The renovations would generate no incremental revenues or cost savings.

7. *Upgrading the computer lab*

   Cost: $60,000

   Over the past eight years computer equipment has been purchased on a piece-meal basis with surplus operating funds. To support curricular goals, the school needs state-of-the-art computers and more workstations. The director of computing has proposed that the equipment be upgraded over three years. The first stage of this plan would require spending $60,000 on personal computers in the coming year. An additional $80,000 would be spent over the following two years.

   The school uses a 12 percent annual discount rate to evaluate all cost-saving investment projects.

Since not all of these projects can be undertaken, they must be prioritized. In his report to the trustees, Headmaster Loring ranked the seven projects as follows:

1. Swimming pool $320,000
2. Hockey rink roof $30,000
3. Buses $135,000
4. Heating system $400,000
5. Fine arts building $75,000
6. Women's locker room $20,000
7. Computer lab $60,000

He recommended that this year's capital funds be spent on the construction of a swimming pool, repairs to the roof of the hockey rink, and the purchase of three buses. These projects would require a total expenditure of $485,000. Loring's rankings were based on his subjective evaluation of cost–benefit trade-offs.

While the trustees must make the final decision, they have solicited advice from the faculty. The faculty is in touch with the day-to-day operations of the school and with the needs of the students. In addition, many faculty members feel that they were closed out of the decision process last year and that the ultimate allocation of funds was inconsistent with the school's objectives. In an attempt to improve the decision process, the trustees appointed a faculty budget committee to advise them on capital spending priorities. A meeting of the trustees, the budget committee, and the headmaster has been scheduled. The purpose of this meeting is to prioritize capital spending projects. It is expected to be a lively and productive session.

Bakery–Florist–Grocery

Introduction

This is a negotiation involving three parties. Representatives of three retail businesses—a bakery, a florist, and a grocery—will be meeting to negotiate details regarding a proposed joint market that would house all three of them. The tentative plan is to open a large market together in which each of the three shops will be located in a separate space, but in which there will also be shared market space. The idea is to make this joint space look attractive by furnishing it with benches, fountains, and plants, and by installing facilities such as an automatic bank teller machine (ATM). The goal is to make it possible for customers to shop in a pleasant and convenient way in a roofed-in shopping area, which (they hope) should eventually lead to increased sales.

The owner of each shop has appointed someone as a representative to participate in this negotiation. Your instructor will assign you to one of the three shop roles and provide detailed instructions for that role. In the negotiation, there will be three issues to be jointly decided: store design, temperature, and distribution of rental costs.

Source: This simulation was developed by Bianca, Beersma, who adapted the "Towers Market" case (see L. R. Weingart, R. J. Bennett, and J. M. Brett, "The Impact of Consideration of Issues and Motivational Orientation on Group Negotiation Process and Outcome," *Journal of Applied Psychology* 78 [1993], pp. 504–17) in order to fit a three-person negotiation context. It is used here with permission.

Exercise 25

The New House Negotiation

Introduction

Many negotiations involve only two parties—a buyer and a seller. However, there are many other negotiations in which the parties are represented by agents. An agent is a person who is hired to negotiate on behalf of the buyer or seller and usually collects some fee or commission based on these services.

The purpose of this negotiation is to gain experience by negotiating through agents. The negotiation simulates the sale and purchase of a piece of real estate, a transaction which is normally conducted through agents. Some of you will play the role of agents; others will play the role of buyers and sellers. This experience should provide a simple but rich context in which to observe the ways that negotiation can very quickly become highly complex.

The House

The property in question is a three-bedroom, two-bath, one-story house. It was listed in the local real estate multiple listings service two weeks ago at $225,000. The house has the following features:

- 2,100 square feet.
- Six years old (one owner prior to current owner).
- Two-car garage.
- Contemporary styling (back wall of house is basically all glass, with sliding draperies).
- Half-acre lot (no flooding problems).
- Brick exterior.
- Built-in range, dishwasher, garbage disposal, and microwave.
- Electric cooling and gas heat.
- Fireplace and ceiling fan in the family room.
- No fence.
- Assumable FHA loan.

Source: This simulation was developed by Conrad Jackson, College of Administrative Science, the University of Alabama at Huntsville. Adapted and used with permission.

EXHIBIT 1

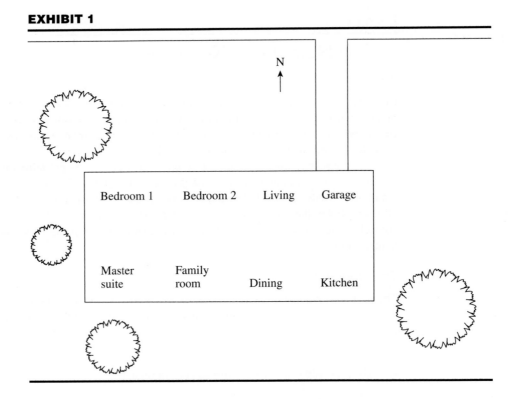

Exercise 26

Eurotechnologies, Inc.

Introduction

This role-play brings three additional new features to your negotiating experience. First, the context of this negotiation is *inside* an organization. In this scenario, you will be asked to represent one of two groups: a management team or a group of scientists who are protesting against a major management decision. Second, this simulation is considerably less structured than others, in that there is a great deal more flexibility and opportunity for creative solutions. Finally, the negotiation occurs in an international context, which may provide a new experience for many of you. We hope you find this simulation an interesting negotiating opportunity.

Eurotechnologies, Inc., General Information

Eurotechnologies, Inc. (ETI), is a Munich-area firm that employs about 900 people. It is a high-technology division of Mentor, whose corporate offices are in Paris. ETI's primary product is an elaborate bioelectronic detection system developed and manufactured under contract with a consortium of European governments. This system is used for detecting various types of life forms through radarlike procedures. Because of the highly classified nature of the manufacturing process and the need for manufacturing to occur in a relatively pollution-free environment, ETI has chosen to separate its manufacturing facilities from its main offices.

The manufacturing facilities are located in a remote area near Wasserburg, Germany, approximately 64 kilometers from downtown Munich. ETI has purchased several hundred acres of land that provide the adequate security and air quality for manufacturing and full-scale test operations. While it is a picturesque area far away from the congestion of the Munich area, it is not without its faults. Access to the plant requires travel over 16 kilometers of poor locally maintained road; manufacturing employees constantly complain of worn brakes, tire wear, and strain on their cars. The road is often rain-slicked, muddy, and treacherous in the winter. Most of the 630 workers (480 hourly, 140 staff, and 10 R&D personnel who run the test facility) employed in this plant commute from a 45–60 kilometer radius over this road into the plant; traffic congestion, particularly around the times of shift changes, makes travel and access a highly undesirable aspect of working for this plant.

The manufacturing facility itself is not air-conditioned and hence frequently hot in the summer and stuffy in the winter. The closest town, Wasserburg, is 16 kilometers away. The Wasserburg plant has a cafeteria, but the food is cooked elsewhere and reheated at the plant. The menu is limited and expensive.

Source: This role-play is developed by Robert Reinheimer, adapted from a scenario developed by Robert Reinheimer and Roy Lewicki. Used with permission. The case and role-play have been prepared for class discussion rather than to illustrate effective or ineffective handling of an administrative situation.

There are two groups of support personnel at Wasserburg. One group (approximately 110 employees) is directly connected with the manufacturing operations as supervisors, shipping and receiving, plant operation and maintenance, stock and inventory, clerical, and so on. The remainder (30 employees) are professional engineers responsible for providing technical support and quality maintenance for manufacturing. Facilities for this support staff are somewhat better than for hourly employees; office space and lighting are adequate and the building is air-conditioned. There is no separate cafeteria, and no place to entertain visitors; staff alternate between bringing their lunch, occasionally purchasing the cafeteria food and taking it back to their offices to eat, or carpooling for the 20-minute drive down to Wasserburg. Dissatisfaction and low morale among the professional staff are rampant.

The Downtown Location

The executive staff offices, the government liaison offices, and the research and development laboratory are located in suburban Munich, just north of the city center. Also, there are test facilities on a one-tenth scale for ongoing research and development programs. All administrative services are conducted from here: employment, payroll, security, data processing and system analysis, and research engineering and design. The buildings are spacious, clean, and air-conditioned and boast two cafeterias: one for hourly workers and one for research personnel and executive officers. Employees can also go out for lunch, and many good restaurants are nearby. Working hours are more flexible, and the environment is more relaxed with less visible pressure. While the normal starting time is 8:00 a.m., professional staff drift in as late as 9:30 and often leave early in the afternoon; working at home is frequent. On the other hand, when deadlines or schedules have to be met, it is not unusual to find them working 60 hours a week. The work environment is more informal and displays casualness similar to a university setting.

As the majority of the Munich-based employees are professional people, they consider themselves a cut above the manufacturing and technical service employees at Wasserburg. While they will acknowledge the value of the revenue generated by Wasserburg, they are convinced that it is really the Munich area group that carries the company. Without their high-level technical advances, ETI would not have the outside reputation it has for premium-quality products. Inside ETI, however, the rivalries between various engineering and scientific personnel led to the creation of "domains" or "kingdoms." The primary split is between Wasserburg and Munich, and over the years it has fostered extensive duplication of efforts. Each group (testing, maintenance, etc.) has been able to procure tools and equipment for itself that normally would be shared if the two locations were closer. The Munich technical divisions have even subcontracted certain testing and development operations to suppliers who are competitors of ETI, due to their basic lack of respect for in-house capabilities at Wasserburg and the red tape and expense of having to work through their own planning and scheduling staffs.

Additionally, the Munich R&D group has taken consulting contracts from other firms and has consistently failed to involve any Wasserburg personnel in those projects.

The Contract Bidding History

In recent years, ETI has put out numerous competitive bids for civilian and military contracts, but few projects have been forthcoming. Analysis of failures revealed that rejections have been due to excessive cost estimates rather than weak technical capabilities. ETI is considered to be one of the top 10 quality-based manufacturing firms of its kind on the continent. However, its overhead costs are prohibitive. The cost of operating two sites, duplication of effort, overstaffing, and a blurring of goals for corporate growth and expansion have caused the overhead rate to be 30–40 percent higher than that of competitors. For example, the United Kingdom had recently issued a request for bids on the development of a new bioelectronic system, similar to ETI's current product. The development contract alone was worth 12.25 million euros; and production of these units would be worth 73.35 million euros. ETI was positive it would get the contract. However, when the government evaluated the bids from five different companies, ETI came in first in the technical aspect of the bidding and fifth in the cost aspect; the company did not get the contract.

The Alternatives

Top management's reaction to this setback was to propose a 20 percent cost reduction plan. Many high-salaried technical and engineering personnel were destined to be laid off. The housecleaning was overdue; some deadwood and duplication of effort was eliminated. But after six months, it became a hard, cold fact that further reductions in overhead costs would be necessary in order to continue to be competitive.

ETI owned the Munich-area facility, and top management believed the most obvious way to achieve this reduction was to close it, move all of the Munich-area employees to the Wasserburg facility, and lease out the vacated buildings. The leases would be excellent tax shelters and an additional source of revenue. This consolidation was expected to reduce much of the duplication of effort, as well as provide better coordination on existing and future projects.

In thinking through how the proposed move might be accomplished, top management considered features designed to make it as palatable as possible. First, they proposed to spread the relocations over one full year. Each employee could either accept the move or reject it and accept termination from the company. ETI management would go as far as possible with those employees who rejected the relocation. They would offer a liberal time-off policy to those involved so the employee could seek other employment, provide a special bonus of one month's salary for relocation expenses, notify other companies in the Munich area of the names and résumés of terminating employees, and set up employment interviews with these companies. They also would notify all placement agencies in the area and pay all placement agency fees.

It was clear to management that even with the generous plan they had outlined, the move would be hugely painful for the organization and would represent some very real costs in terms of overall effectiveness. Yet they saw no alternative but to proceed with studying the proposed consolidation.

When the details of the proposal leaked, the plan was met with a massive reaction of hostility and despair. Almost all the Munich-area professional employees felt that a transfer to Wasserburg would mean a sharp decline in status with their peers in similar industries. Most had their homes close to Munich, and the drive to Wasserburg would increase their commuting time and cause wear and tear on their automobiles. The company thus knew that a certain percentage of employees would terminate because of the relocation. It estimated that a "safe level" of termination was 22 percent; if it reached 35 percent in any occupational group, it could be considered a critical problem. Management informally surveyed employees and found that among the administrative staff, the termination rate was likely to be near 25 percent.

The strongest reaction came from the company's research and development staff. They had grown used to having their laboratory and test facilities in the Munich area and drew heavily on informal relationships with faculty at the area's most prestigious universities for ideas and information. Their view was that being forced to move to Wasserburg, in addition to being undesirable, would cripple their ability to function effectively because of their loss of contact with other professionals. Of the 11 members of the research and development staff, only two expressed a willingness to consider the move to Wasserburg. The others claimed they would avail themselves of the many other employment opportunities their specialties commanded. They formally expressed their resistance in a letter to the company president (Exhibit 1).

The letter was written by a committee of R&D personnel formed to represent the group's interests regarding the proposed move. In the letter, they outlined their concerns and volunteered to take 20 percent salary cuts to contribute to the reduction of overhead costs. This reduction would total approximately 183,375 euros.

The committee members consisted of the following six employees:

- Axle Pederson, age 52. Oldest member of the group, but only one year at ETI. Previously worked with several environmental engineering firms in the Munich area. Moved to ETI because of the quality of the other people in the research group and because of interest in the projects that were being considered.

- Thomas Hoffmann, age 49. Most senior member of the ETI group (24 years), and a likely candidate to be the next vice president of research and development. Lived near Munich all his life, and currently lives a block away from Pieter Jensen, the president.

- Manfred Berkowitz, age 42. Fifteen years with ETI, and the most professionally aggressive of the group. Most active in research with high professional visibility.

- Volker Schmidt, age 47. Twenty-two years with ETI. Also very professionally active, second to Berkowitz. Schmidt has spent a number of years developing professional contacts in the Munich area and has been the most articulate in defending the richness of the professional stimulation to be derived from the area.

- Pieter van der Velden, age 36. Five years with ETI. Worked for two years at Wasserburg before being assigned to the Munich group. A definite up and comer in this group.

- Michael Blank, age 32. Four years with ETI. Strong research orientation, a close collaborator with Berkowitz on several professional papers. Berkowitz also served as a mentor to Blank while Blank was completing his PhD at Heidelberg University.

EXHIBIT 1

Mr. Pieter Jensen, President
Eurotechnologies, Inc.
300 Reinstrasse
Munich, Germany

Dear Mr. Jensen:

Our committee, representing your research and development personnel, wishes to express its serious concern about the recent events which have affected our company. We believe that ETI's survival depends on our retaining our technical excellence. We are dismayed that you and your management team seem to be contemplating actions that could cripple that capability.

We have all been shocked by our recent loss of contracts. However, it is critical for you to note that we have never been faulted for our technical expertise. It is our cost structure that prevents us from winning these bids. But an action which addresses the cost problem, while destroying our ability to compete technically, simply trades one problem for a more disastrous one. Closing the Munich facility and consolidating operations at Wasserburg creates just such a trade, and that is unacceptable.

Although no formal announcement of management's response to the current situation has been provided, it is clear that consolidation is in the wind. We believe that forcing R&D to move to the Wasserburg location will ruin the professional network that is our (and the company's) treasured asset. Some alternative must be found and, if it is not, the members of our department will seek individual solutions to their personal problems.

It is time that management emerges from behind closed doors and asks vital members of the company team to become involved in this decision. If management intends to launch this consolidation effort, we believe it will have disastrous results and that it is unlikely that research and development personnel will remain with the company.

Our interest is in the company's survival. If it were necessary, the members of the committee would be willing to agree to a 20 percent salary reduction in return for being able to remain in the Munich-area network. We request an opportunity to speak with management about this vital decision which massively affects all of us.

Sincerely,
(signed by all members of the committee)

After reading the statement sent by the committee, the president of Eurotechnologies, Pieter Jensen, conferred with the vice president for research and development (and the immediate superior of the scientists) and the vice president for human resources. The three discussed the statement that they had received and agreed that the situation was serious. It was clear that the Wasserburg move created unforeseen, legitimate problems for the vital R&D personnel and that management had erred in not seeking wider input in considering their cost reduction alternatives.

The management team debated the alternatives. They understood the frustrations of the research and development staff but were faced with having to cut almost 6,500,000 euros from annual costs in order for ETI to remain competitive. Consolidation still seemed the obvious answer, but the problems were mounting with this employee disclosure.

EXHIBIT 2

(addressed to all committee members)
Research and Development
Eurotechnologies, Inc.
300 Reinstrasse
Munich, Germany

Dear (names):

I have given my most serious consideration to the points you raised in your recent letter. We share your interest in doing what is best for ETI and welcome your interest in contributing to that goal.

It is clear that our technical expertise is one of our greatest assets and that your work in research and development is a vital contributor to that expertise. We have no wish to reduce our technical competitiveness. Nevertheless, our failure to produce cost-competitive contract bids is a problem that requires a painful solution, and we have only 18 months to produce an effective response.

We acknowledge that we have begun to examine the consolidation of our operations at the Wasserburg facility. Such a consolidation would reduce duplication of facilities, equipment, and personnel. These reductions would contribute significantly to an overall cost saving. Page two of this letter is an exhibit of the ongoing cost savings we believe would result from such a move.

At the same time, we believe that this action would be unwise if it truly has the crippling effect on your effectiveness that you forecast. Our dilemma, as the management team for ETI, is to address the need for major, fast cost reduction while providing for the continuation of our technical excellence. We also believe that any proposal must be fair to the many employees who are a part of the Eurotechnologies family.

In response to your letter, I have ordered that further evaluation of the Wasserburg alternative be halted for the time being. I ask that your committee send some of its members to a meeting with myself and other members of the management team to discuss the situation as it has evolved. We share an interest in ETI's survival if we can develop a plan that is mutually acceptable in achieving that goal. I look forward to meeting with you.

Sincerely,
(signed, Pieter Jensen)

Jensen wrote a letter to the committee acknowledging their concerns and inviting the members of that group to come to a meeting with the president, the VP of research and development, the VP of human resources, and other senior company officials. Jensen was careful to make no commitments or promises in the letter; he simply invited them to come to a meeting (Exhibit 2).

ETI Expense Statement (in thousands of euros)

Overhead	Wasserburg	Munich	Totals Current	Totals Consolidated
Manufacturing	18,035			18,035
Administrative	2,662	5,406		2,906
R&D	483	4,343		4,531
Total	21,180	9,749	30,929	25,472
R&D Expenses				
Utilities	82	204		173
Computer lease		1,019		1,019
Supplies	212	449		492
Consulting		749		663
Total	294	2,421	2,715	2,347
Salaries and Benefits				
Professional	1,630	2,282		3,912
Benefits	245	342		587
Hourly	8,137	305		8,325
Benefits	813	31		824
Relocation				750*
Total	10,825	2,960	13,785	14,398
				13,648†
Facilities				
Debt service	815	2,630		815
Insurance/ maintenance/taxes	408	1,070		408
Total	1,223	3,700	4,923	1,223
Grand total: Current versus consolidated			52,352	42,656†

*One-time expense

†Ongoing total

Third-Party Conflict Resolution

Introduction

In addition to being involved in their own conflicts, managers are often called upon to intervene and to settle conflicts between other people. The two activities in this section are designed to explore how third parties may enter conflicts for the purpose of resolving them, and to practice one very effective approach to intervention. In the first activity, you will read about a manager who has a problem deciding how to intervene in a dispute, and you will discuss this case in class. Part 2 of this exercise contains a mediation guide.

Part 1: The Seatcor Manufacturing Company

You are senior vice president of operations and chief operating officer of Seatcor, a major producer of office furniture. Joe Gibbons, your subordinate, is vice president and general manager of your largest desk assembly plant. Joe has been with Seatcor for 38 years and is two years away from retirement. He worked his way up through the ranks to his present position and has successfully operated his division for five years with a marginally competent staff. You are a long-standing personal friend of Joe's and respect him a great deal. However, you have always had an uneasy feeling that Joe has surrounded himself with minimally competent people by his own choice. In some ways, you think he feels threatened by talented assistants.

Last week you were having lunch with Charles Stewart, assistant vice president and Joe's second in command. Upon your questioning, it became clear that he and Joe were engaged in a debilitating feud. Charles was hired last year, largely at your insistence. You had been concerned for some time about who was going to replace Joe when he retired, especially given the lack of really capable managerial talent on Joe's staff. Thus you prodded Joe to hire your preferred candidate—Charles Stewart. Charles is relatively young, 39, extremely tenacious and bright, and a well-trained business school graduate. From all reports he is doing a good job in his new position.

Your concern centers on a topic that arose at the end of your lunch. Charles indicated that Joe Gibbons is in the process of completing a five-year plan for his plant. This plan is to serve as the basis for several major plant reinvestment and reorganization decisions that would be proposed to senior management. According to Charles, Joe Gibbons has not included Charles in the planning process at all. You had to leave lunch quickly and were unable to get much more information from Charles. However, he did admit that he was extremely disturbed by this exclusion and that his distress was influencing his work and probably his relationship with Joe.

Source: Developed by Roy J. Lewicki. "The Mediation Guide" developed by Larry Ray, American Bar Association, and Robert Helm, Oklahoma State University. "The Seatcor Manufacturing Company" and "The Summer Interns" developed by Blair Sheppard, Duke Corporate Education. Used with permission.

You consider this a very serious problem. Charles will probably have to live with the results of any major decisions about the plant. More important, Joe's support is essential if Charles is to properly grow into his present and/or future job. Joe, on the other hand, runs a good ship and you do not want to upset him or undermine his authority. Moreover, you know Joe has good judgment; thus he may have a good reason for what he is doing.

How would you proceed to handle this issue?

Part 2: The Mediation Guide

This section presents a series of steps for effectively conducting a mediation. You may use this checklist and the flowchart depicted in Exhibit 1.

Step 1: Stabilize the Setting

Parties often bring some strong feelings of anger and frustration into mediation. These feelings can prevent them from talking productively about their dispute. You, as mediator, will try to gain their trust for you and for the mediation process. Stabilize the setting by being polite; show that you are in control and that you are neutral. This step helps the parties feel comfortable, so they can speak freely about their complaints, and safe, so they can air their feelings.

1. _____ Greet the parties.
2. _____ Indicate where each of them is to sit.
3. _____ Identify yourself and each party, by name.
4. _____ Offer water, paper and pencil, and patience.
5. _____ State the purpose of mediation.
6. _____ Confirm your neutrality.
7. _____ Get their commitment to proceed.
8. _____ Get their commitment that only one party at a time will speak.
9. _____ Get their commitment to speak directly to you.
10. _____ Use calming techniques as needed.

Step 2: Help the Parties Communicate

Once the setting is stable and the parties seem to trust you and the mediation process, you can begin to carefully build trust between them. Both must make statements about what has happened. Each will use these statements to air negative feelings. They may express anger, make accusations, and show frustration in other ways. But with your help, this mutual ventilation lets them hear each other's side of the story, perhaps for the first time. It can help calm their emotions, and can build a basis for trust between them.

1. _____ Explain the rationale for who speaks first.
2. _____ Reassure them that both will speak without interruption, for as long as necessary.
3. _____ Ask the first speaker to tell what has happened.

   a. _____ Take notes.

   b. _____ Respond actively; restate and echo what is said.

   c. _____ Calm the parties as needed.

   d. _____ Clarify, with open or closed questions, or with restatements.

   e. _____ Focus the narration on the issues in the dispute.

   f. _____ Summarize, eliminating all disparaging references.

   g. _____ Check to see that you understand the story.

   h. _____ Thank this party for speaking, the other for listening quietly.

 4. _____ Ask the second speaker to tell what has happened.

   a. _____ Take notes.

   b. _____ Respond actively; restate and echo what is said.

   c. _____ Calm the parties as needed.

   d. _____ Clarify, with open or closed questions, or with restatements.

   e. _____ Focus the narration on the issues in the dispute.

   f. _____ Summarize, eliminating all disparaging references.

   g. _____ Check to see that you understand the story.

   h. _____ Thank this party for speaking, the other for listening quietly.

 5. _____ Ask each party, in turn, to help clarify the major issues to be resolved.

 6. _____ Inquire into basic issues, probing to see if something instead may be at the root of the complaints.

 7. _____ Define the problem by restating and summarizing.

 8. _____ Conduct private meetings, if needed (explain what will happen during and after the private meetings).

 9. _____ Summarize areas of agreement and disagreement.

 10. _____ Help the parties set priorities on the issues and demands.

Step 3: Help the Parties Negotiate

Cooperativeness is needed for negotiations that lead to agreement. Cooperation requires a stable setting, to control disruptions, and exchanges of information, to develop mutual trust. With these conditions, the parties may be willing to cooperate, but still feel driven to compete. You can press for cooperative initiatives by patiently helping them to explore alternative solutions, and by directing attention to their progress.

 1. _____ Ask each party to list alternative possibilities for a settlement.

 2. _____ Restate and summarize each alternative.

 3. _____ Check with each party on the workability of each alternative.

 4. _____ Restate whether the alternative is workable.

 5. _____ In an impasse, suggest the general form of other alternatives.

6. _____ Note the amount of progress already made, to show that success is likely.

7. _____ If the impasse continues, suggest a break or a second mediation session.

8. _____ Encourage them to select the alternative that appears to be workable.

9. _____ Increase their understanding by rephrasing the alternative.

10. _____ Help them plan a course of action to implement the alternative.

Step 4: Clarify Their Agreement

Mediation should change each party's attitude toward the other. When both have shown their commitment through a joint declaration of agreement, each will support the agreement more strongly. For a settlement that lasts, each component of the parties' attitudes toward each other—their thinking, feeling, and acting—will have changed. Not only will they now *act* differently toward each other, but they are likely to *feel* differently, more positively, about each other and to *think* of their relationship in new ways.

1. _____ Summarize the agreement terms.

2. _____ Recheck with each party his or her understanding of the agreement.

3. _____ Ask whether other issues need to be discussed.

4. _____ Help them specify the terms of their agreement.

5. _____ State each person's role in the agreement.

6. _____ Recheck with each party on when he or she is to do certain things, where, and how.

7. _____ Explain the process of follow-up.

8. _____ Establish a time for follow-up with each party.

9. _____ Emphasize that the agreement is theirs, not yours.

10. _____ Congratulate the parties on their reasonableness and on the workability of their resolution.

EXHIBIT 1 | Steps in a Mediation Process

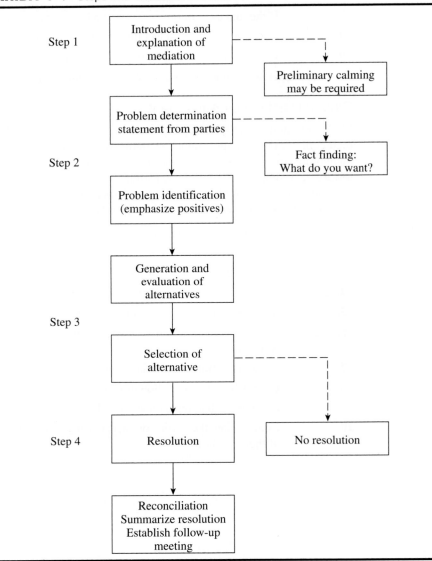

500 English Sentences

Introduction

This exercise involves a cross-cultural negotiation where there are several tangible and intangible factors at stake. You will play the role of either a Japanese teacher who is head of the English Department that is responsible for the publication of an English textbook, or an American assistant English teacher who has been asked to work on the book.

Source: This exercise was written by Laura Turek. Copyright 1996. Used with permission.

Sick Leave

Introduction

This exercise involves a cross-cultural negotiation where there are several tangible and intangible factors at stake. You will play the role of either a Japanese manager responsible for the supervision of several foreign assistant English teachers, or an American assistant English teacher.

Source: This exercise was written by Laura Turek. Copyright 1996. Used with permission.

Alpha–Beta

Introduction

In this situation you will negotiate a possible robot manufacturing and marketing agreement with another company. You will be a member of a team that represents either an electrical company in the nation of Alpha or a manufacturer of electrical machinery in the nation of Beta.

Background Information

Alpha

Alpha Inc. is a large, broadly diversified electrical company based in the nation of Alpha. The company is one of the leading makers of numerical control equipment and plans to become a leader in equipping the "factory of the future." It has recently spent hundreds of millions of dollars putting together a collection of factory automation capabilities ranging from robotics to computer-aided design and manufacturing. Alpha Inc. has been acquiring companies, investing heavily in new plants, and spending considerable sums on product development. Innovative robots, some equipped with vision, are being developed, but they have been a bit slow in making their way out of the company's R&D labs. To meet its objective of quickly becoming a major worldwide, full-service supplier of automation systems, Alpha Inc. has found it necessary to tie up, in various ways, with foreign firms that are further up the robotics learning curve.

Robotics in the Nation of Alpha

There are 30 robot manufacturers in Alpha, and big computer and auto firms have recently been entering the business. During 1980, use and production of robots in Alpha was only about 33 percent of what it was in the nation of Beta. One survey reported 4,370 robots in use in Alpha in 1980, mainly in the auto and foundry-type industries, and 1,269 produced. Robot sales in 1980 were estimated at $92 million, with a significant share accounted for by imports. The industrial automation market as a whole is growing at well over 20 percent a year, and the robotics portion of it is expected to become a $2 billion-a-year domestic market by 1990.

Beta

Beta Inc. is the leading manufacturer of integrated electrical machinery in the nation of Beta. Run by scientists since its founding, the company is Beta's most research-oriented corporation: It employs over 9,000 researchers, and its R&D spending equals 5.9 percent

Source: This exercise was first developed by Thomas N. Gladwin in 1984, and is copyrighted 1990–91 by Thomas N. Gladwin, Stephen E. Weiss, and Allen J. Zerkin. Used with permission.

of corporate sales. Beta Inc. started producing robots only in 1979 but plans within a few years to become the world's largest robot producer. To do so, it must double its manufacturing capacity and strongly push exports (to date, nearly all of its output has been sold at home). The company's deep commitment to robotics is reflected in the recent formation of a 500-person technical task force to develop a universal assembly robot with both visual and tactile sensors. Beta Inc. expects to be using the new robots for some 60 percent of its in-house assembly operations within three years.

Robotics in the Nation of Beta

Beta Inc. is only 1 of 150 companies making or selling robots in Beta, a nation with "robot fever" and a government that has declared automation a national goal. An estimated 12,000 to 14,000 programmable robots are already on the job in the nation, representing 59 percent of those in use worldwide. In 1980, Betan firms churned out nearly $400 million worth of robots (approximately 3,200 units, or 50 percent of world production). The nation exported only 2.5 percent of its production and imported fewer than 5 percent of its robots. Industry analysts see robot production in Beta rising to $2 billion in 1985 and to $5 billion in 1990.

Over the past five months, Alpha Inc. and Beta Inc. have held preliminary negotiations over a possible robot manufacturing and marketing tie-up. The two companies have reached the following tentative agreement:

1. The tie-up over seven years will proceed in two phases: (*a*) in years 1–4, Beta will supply Alpha with fully assembled Beta Inc. robots for sale under Alpha's brand name; (*b*) in years 5–7, Alpha will begin producing these robots themselves in Alpha, using Beta technology and key components.

2. The tie-up will focus on the robots that Beta Inc. currently has on the market.

3. The agreement will be nonexclusive; that is, Beta Inc. will be allowed to enter the Alphan market directly at any time and allowed to tie up with other Alphan firms.

The two companies' negotiation teams are now scheduled to meet for discussion of remaining issues. They include the following:

1. The number of different models involved.

2. The quantity of Beta Inc. units to be imported and/or produced under license by Alpha during each year.

3. The unit price to be paid to Beta.

4. Access to Alpha's vision technology.

5. The royalty rate to be paid to Beta.

Bacchus Winery

Introduction

This exercise is a three-party negotiation between representatives of three cultural groups: an American, a Japanese, and a Serbian. The American firm (Bacchus) produces a variety of wines; the Japanese firm (Tokyo Saki) produces saki and rice wines; the Serbian firm (Serbian Steins & Stems) produces fine decanters, wineglasses, and accessories. The three firms will discuss the terms of a possible merger/joint venture between them.

Source: Adapted by Roy J. Lewicki from an exercise developed by Judi McLean Parks, Washington University. Used with permission.

Exercise 32

Collecting Nos

Introduction

In all work settings, there comes a time when we need something from someone else. It might be an approval, it might be resources, or it might be some form of assistance. Whatever it might be, it is virtually impossible for us to get our work done without the cooperation of others. And the best way to get what you want from others is to ask them for it. Yet many people would rather do it themselves than ask someone else. One reason people are hesitant to ask for things is because they do not want to get a no.

A similar problem exists in negotiations. On the one hand, inexperienced negotiators often are afraid to ask for what they want or need because they are afraid to get a no. On the other hand, those who are asked will frequently *not* say no, in spite of their strong dislike of the request or having to fulfill it. Therefore, many negotiations are incomplete because the requester did not ask for enough, or the respondent actually gave more than he or she wanted to. Several negotiation experts have argued that negotiation only *begins* when the other party says no; if you do not get a no, you probably have not asked for enough!

The purpose of this exercise is to give you experience in making requests and dealing with others' objections. Your task in this exercise is to collect nos.

Part A

Continue to make requests until you have collected 10 nos. Keep a verbatim written record of *each* request you make, the response you receive to each request, and what meaning or interpretation you gave to the response (what thoughts or feelings you had in reaction to the response). Create the following table:

Request I Made	Response I Received	My Reaction to the Response
1.		
2.		
3.		
etc.		

Source: Developed by Professor Jeffrey Ford of the Fisher College of Business, The Ohio State University, for this volume. Used with permission.

Part B

Pick one of the requests for which you received a no, and make that same request of the same person a second time. If you receive another no, wait until later and make the same request yet a third time. Write down what the person says each time.

Part C

Pick at least one of the requests for which you received a no, and ask the person who said no, "What would have to happen for you to say yes to my request?" Write down what the person says. Your instructor will help you process these reactions in class.

Case 1

Capital Mortgage Insurance Corporation (A)

Frank Randall hung up the telephone, leaned across his desk, and fixed a cold stare at Jim Dolan.

> OK, Jim. They've agreed to a meeting. We've got three days to resolve this thing. The question is, what approach should we take? How do we get them to accept our offer?

Randall, president of Capital Mortgage Insurance Corporation (CMI), had called Dolan, his senior vice president and treasurer, into his office to help him plan their strategy for completing the acquisition of Corporate Transfer Services (CTS). The two men had begun informal discussions with the principal stockholders of the small employee relocation services company some four months earlier. Now, in late May 1979, they were developing the terms of a formal purchase offer and plotting their strategy for the final negotiations.

The acquisition, if consummated, would be the first in CMI's history. Furthermore, it represented a significant departure from the company's present business. Randall and Dolan knew that the acquisition could have major implications, both for themselves and for the company they had revitalized over the past several years.

Jim Dolan ignored Frank Randall's intense look and gazed out the eighth-floor window overlooking Philadelphia's Independence Square.

> That's not an easy question, Frank. We know they're still looking for a lot more money than we're thinking about. But beyond that, the four partners have their own differences, and we need to think through just what they're expecting. So I guess we'd better talk this one through pretty carefully.

Company and Industry Background

CMI was a wholly owned subsidiary of Northwest Equipment Corporation, a major freight transporter and lessor of railcars, commercial aircraft, and other industrial equipment. Northwest had acquired CMI in 1978, two years after CMI's original parent company, an investment management corporation, had gone into Chapter 11 bankruptcy proceedings. CMI had been created to sell mortgage guaranty insurance policies to residential mortgage lenders throughout the United States. Mortgage insurance provides banks, savings and loans, mortgage bankers, and other mortgage lenders with protection against financial losses when homeowners default on their mortgage loans.

Lending institutions normally protect their property loan investments by offering loans of only 70 percent to 80 percent of the appraised value of the property; the

Source: Capital Mortgage Insurance Company (A), 9-480-057. Copyright ©1980 by the President and Fellows of Harvard College.

This case was prepared by James P. Ware as a basis for class discussion rather than to illustrate either effective or ineffective handling of an administrative situation. Reprinted by permission of the Harvard Business School. This case written in 1979. For a variety of reasons, it is not possible to update the financial information or the fact pattern in the case. We contiune to use it in this book because of the teaching value of the case, in spite of its age.

remaining 20 to 30 percent constitutes the homeowner's down payment. However, mortgage loan insurance makes it possible for lenders to offer so-called high-ratio loans of up to 95 percent of a home's appraised value. High-ratio loans are permitted only when the lender insures the loan; although the policy protects the lender, the premiums are paid by the borrower, as an addition to monthly principal and interest charges.

The principal attraction of mortgage insurance is that it makes purchasing a home possible for many more individuals. It is much easier to produce a 5 percent down payment than to save up the 20 to 30 percent traditionally required.

CMI had a mixed record of success within the private mortgage insurance industry. Frank Randall, the company's first and only president, had gotten the organization off to an aggressive beginning, attaining a 14.8 percent market share by 1972. By 1979, however, that share had fallen to just over 10 percent even though revenues had grown from $18 million in 1972 to over $30 million in 1979. Randall attributed the loss of market share primarily to the difficulties created by the bankruptcy of CMI's original parent. Thus he had been quite relieved when Northwest Equipment acquired CMI in January 1978. Northwest provided CMI with a level of management and financial support it had never before enjoyed. Furthermore, Northwest's corporate management had made it clear to Frank Randall that he was expected to build CMI into a much larger, diversified financial services company.

Northwest's growth expectations were highly consistent with Frank Randall's own ambitions. The stability created by the acquisition, in combination with the increasing solidity of CMI's reputation with mortgage lenders, made it possible for Randall to turn his attention more and more toward external acquisitions of his own. During 1978 Randall, with Jim Dolan's help, had investigated several acquisition opportunities in related insurance industries, with the hope of broadening CMI's financial base. After several unsuccessful investigations, the two men had come to believe that their knowledge and competence was focused less on insurance per se than it was on residential real estate and related financial transactions. These experiences had led to a recognition that, in Frank Randall's words, "we are a residential real estate financial services company."

The Residential Real Estate Industry

Frank Randall and Jim Dolan knew from personal experience that real estate brokers, who play an obvious and important role in property transactions, usually have close ties with local banks and savings and loans. When mortgage funds are plentiful, brokers often steer prospective home buyers to particular lending institutions. When funds are scarce, the lenders would then favor prospective borrowers referred by their favorite brokers. Randall believed that these informal relationships meant that realtors could have a significant impact on the mortgage loan decision and thus on a mortgage insurance decision as well.

For this reason, CMI had for many years directed a small portion of its marketing effort toward real estate brokers. CMI's activities had consisted of offering educational programs for realtors, property developers, and potential home buyers. The company derived no direct revenues from these programs, but offered them in the interest of stimulating home sales and, more particularly, of informing both realtors and home buyers of how mortgage insurance makes it possible to purchase a home with a relatively low down payment.

Because he felt that real estate brokers could be powerful allies in encouraging lenders to use mortgage insurance, Randall had been tracking developments in the real estate industry for many years. Historically a highly fragmented collection of local, independent entrepreneurs, the industry in 1979 appeared to be on the verge of a major restructuring and consolidation. For the past several years many of the smaller brokers had been joining national franchise organizations in an effort to gain a brand image and to acquire improved management and sales skills.

More significantly, in 1979, several large national corporations were beginning to acquire prominent real estate agencies in major urban areas. The most aggressive of these appeared to be Merrill Lynch and Company, the well-known Wall Street securities trading firm. Merrill Lynch's interest in real estate brokers stemmed from several sources; perhaps most important were the rapidly rising prices on property and homes. Realtors' commissions averaged slightly over 6 percent of the sales price; *Fortune* magazine estimated that real estate brokers had been involved in home sales totaling approximately $190 billion in 1978, netting commissions in excess of $11 billion (in comparison, stockbrokers' commissions on all securities transactions in 1978 were estimated at $3.7 billion).[1] With property values growing 10 to 20 percent per year, commissions would only get larger; where 6 percent of a $30,000 home netted only $1,800, 6 percent of a $90,000 sale resulted in a commission well in excess of $5,000—for basically the same work.

There were also clear signs that the volume of real estate transactions would continue to increase. Although voluntary intercity moves appeared to be declining slightly, corporate transfers of employees were still rising. One of Merrill Lynch's earliest moves toward the real estate market had been to acquire an employee relocation company several years earlier. Working on a contract basis with corporate clients, Merrill Lynch Relocation Management (MLRM) collaborated with independent real estate brokers to arrange home sales and purchases for transferred employees. Like other relocation companies, MLRM would purchase the home at a fair market value and then handle all the legal and financial details of reselling the home on the open market. MLRM also provided relocation counseling and home search assistance for transferred employees; its income was derived primarily from service fees paid by corporate clients (and augmented somewhat by referral fees from real estate brokers, who paid MLRM a portion of the commissions they earned on home sales generated by the transferred employees).

Later, in September 1978, Merrill Lynch had formally announced its intention to acquire at least 40 real estate brokerage firms within three to four years. Merrill Lynch's interest in the industry stemmed not only from the profit opportunities it saw but also from a corporate desire to become a "financial services supermarket," providing individual customers with a wide range of investment and brokerage services. In 1978 Merrill Lynch had acquired United First Mortgage Corporation (UFM), a mortgage banker. And

---

[1]"Why Merrill Lynch Wants to Sell Your House," *Fortune,* January 29, 1979.

in early 1979 Merrill Lynch was in the midst of acquiring AMIC Corporation, a small mortgage insurance company in direct competition with CMI. As *Fortune* reported,

> In combination, these diverse activities hold some striking possibilities. Merrill Lynch already packages and markets mortgages through its registered representatives. . . . If all goes according to plan, the company could later this year be vertically integrated in a unique way. Assuming the AMIC acquisition goes through, Merrill Lynch will be able to guarantee mortgages. It could then originate mortgages through its realty brokerages, process and service them through UFM, insure them with AMIC, package them as pass-through or unit trusts, and market them through its army of registered representatives. (January 29, 1979, p. 89)

It was this vision of an integrated financial services organization that also excited Frank Randall. As he and Jim Dolan reviewed their position in early 1979, they were confident that they were in a unique position to build CMI into a much bigger and more diversified company. The mortgage insurance business gave them a solid financial base, with regional offices throughout the country. Northwest Equipment stood ready to provide the capital they would need for significant growth. They already had relationships with important lending institutions across the United States, and their marketing efforts had given them a solid reputation with important real estate brokers as well.

Thus Randall, in particular, felt that at least he had most of the ingredients to begin building that diversified "residential real estate financial services company" he had been dreaming about for so long. Furthermore, Randall's reading of the banking, thrift, and real estate industries suggested that the time was ripe. In his view, the uncertainties in the financial and housing industries created rich opportunities for taking aggressive action, and the vision of Merrill Lynch "bulling" its way into the business was scaring realtors just enough for CMI to present a comforting and familiar alternative.

The Metropolitan Realty Network

Frank Randall spent most of the fall of 1978 actively searching for acquisition opportunities. As part of his effort, he contacted David Osgood, who was the executive director of the Metropolitan Realty Network, a national association of independent real estate brokers. The association, commonly known as MetroNet, had been formed primarily as a communication vehicle so its members could refer home buyers moving from one city to another to a qualified broker in the new location.

Randall discovered that Osgood was somewhat concerned about MetroNet's long-term health and viability. Though MetroNet included over 13,000 real estate agencies, it was losing some members to national franchise chains, and Osgood was feeling increasing pressures to strengthen the association by providing more services to member firms. Yet the entrepreneurial independence of MetroNet's members made Osgood's task particularly difficult. He had found it almost impossible to get them to agree on what they wanted him to do.

One service that the MetroNet brokers *were* agreed on developing was the employee relocation business. Corporate contracts to handle transferred employees were especially attractive to the brokers because the contracts virtually guaranteed repeat business in the local area, and they also led to intercity referrals that almost always resulted in a home sale.

MetroNet brokers were also resentful of how Merrill Lynch Relocation Management and other relocation services companies were getting a larger and larger share of "their" referral fees. Osgood told Randall that he had already set up a committee of MetroNet brokers to look into how the association could develop a corporate relocation and third-party equity capability[2] of its own. Osgood mentioned that their only effort to date was an independent firm in Chicago named Corporate Transfer Services, Inc. (CTS), that had been started by Elliott Burr, a prominent Chicago broker and a MetroNet director. CTS had been formed with the intention of working with MetroNet brokers, but so far it had remained relatively small and had not met MetroNet's expectations.

As Randall explained to Osgood what kinds of activities CMI engaged in to help lenders and increase the volume of home sales, Osgood suddenly exclaimed, "That's exactly what *we're* trying to do!" The two men ended their initial meeting convinced that some kind of working relationship between CMI and MetroNet could have major benefits for both organizations. Osgood invited Randall to attend the next meeting of MetroNet's Third-Party Equity Committee, scheduled for March 1. "Let's explore what we can do for each other," said Osgood. "You're on," concluded Randall.

The Third-Party Equity Business

Randall's discussion with David Osgood had opened his eyes to the third-party equity business, and he and Jim Dolan spent most of their time in preparation for the March 1 committee meeting steeped in industry studies and pro forma income statements.

They quickly discovered that the employee relocation services industry was highly competitive, though its future looked bright. Corporate transfers of key employees appeared to be an ingrained practice that showed no signs of letting up in the foreseeable future. Merrill Lynch Relocation Management was one of the two largest firms in the industry; most of the prominent relocation companies were well-funded subsidiaries of large, well-known corporations. Exhibit 1 contains Jim Dolan's tabulation of the seven major relocation firms, along with his estimates of each company's 1978 volume of home purchases.

Dolan also developed a pro forma income and expense statement for a hypothetical firm handling 2,000 home purchases annually (see Exhibit 2). His calculations showed a potential 13.1 percent return on equity (ROE). Dolan then discovered that some companies achieved a much higher ROE by using a home purchase trust, a legal arrangement that made it possible to obtain enough bank financing to leverage a company's equity base by as much as 10 to 1.

Randall and Dolan were increasingly certain that they wanted to get CMI into the employee relocation services business. They saw it as a natural tie-in with CMI's mortgage insurance operations—one that could exploit the same set of relationships that CMI already had with banks, realtors, savings and loans, and other companies involved

---

[2]The term *third-party equity capability* derived from the fact that a relocation services company actually purchased an employee's home, freeing up the owner's equity and making it available for investment in a new home. Within the industry, the terms *third-party equity company* and *employee relocation services company* were generally used interchangeably.

EXHIBIT 1 | Major Employee Relocation Services Companies

Relocation Company	Parent Organization	Estimated 1978 Home Purchases	Estimated Value of Home Purchases*	Estimated Gross Fee Income[†]
Merrill Lynch Relocation	Merrill Lynch	13,000	$975,000,000	$26,800,000
Homequity	Peterson, Howell, & Heather	12,000	900,000,000	24,750,000
Equitable Relocation	Equitable Life Insurance	5,000	375,000,000	10,300,000
Employee Transfer	Chicago Title and Trust	5,000	375,000,000	10,300,000
Relocation Realty Corporation	Control Data Corporation	3,000	225,000,000	6,200,000
Executrans	Sears/Coldwell Banker	3,000	225,000,000	6,200,000
Transamerica Relocation	Transamerica, Inc.	3,000	225,000,000	6,200,000

*Assumes average home values of $75,000.

[†]Assumes fee averaging 2.75 percent of value of homes purchased.

EXHIBIT 2 | Hypothetical Employee Relocation Company Pro Forma Income Statement

Key assumptions

1. Annual purchase volume of 2,000 homes.
2. Assume average holding period of 120 days. Inventory turns over three times annually, for an average of 667 units in inventory at any point in time.
3. Average home value of $75,000.
4. Existing mortgages on homes average 50 percent of property value. Additional required capital will be 40 percent equity, 60 percent long-term debt.
5. Fee income from corporate clients will average 2.75 percent of value of properties purchased (based on historical industry data).
6. Operating expenses (marketing, sales, office administration) will average 1 percent of value of properties purchased (all costs associated with purchases, including debt service, are billed back to corporate clients).

Calculations	
Total value of purchases	
(2,000 units at $75,000)	$150,000,000
Average inventory value	50,000,000
Capital required	
Existing mortgages	25,000,000
New long-term debt	15,000,000
Equity	10,000,000
Fee income at 2.75%	4,125,000
Operating expenses at 1%	1,500,000
Net income	$2,625,000
Tax at 50%	(1,312,500)
Profit after tax	$1,312,500
Return on equity	13.1%

in the development, construction, sale, and financing of residential real estate. The two men felt that real estate brokers had a critically important role in the process. Brokers were not only involved in the actual property transactions, but in addition they almost always had local contacts with corporations that could lead to the signing of employee relocation contracts. Equally important, from Randall's and Dolan's perspective, was their belief that a close relationship between CMI and the MetroNet brokers would also lead to significant sales of CMI's mortgage insurance policies.

The March 1 meeting with MetroNet's Third-Party Equity Committee turned into an exploration of how CMI and MetroNet might help each other by stimulating both home sales and high-ratio mortgage loans. After several hours of discussion, Frank Randall proposed specifically that CMI build an operating company to handle the corporate relocation business jointly with the MetroNet brokers. As a quid pro quo, Randall suggested that the brokers could market CMI mortgage insurance to both potential home buyers and lending institutions.

The committee's response to this idea was initially skeptical. Finally, however, they agreed to consider a more formal proposal at a later date. MetroNet's board of directors was scheduled to meet on April 10; the Third-Party Equity Committee could review the proposal on April 9 and, if they approved, present it to the full board on the 10th.

As the committee meeting broke up, Randall and Dolan began talking with Elliott Burr and Thomas Winder, two of the four owners of Corporate Transfer Services, Inc. (CTS). Though Burr had been the principal founder of CTS, his primary business was a large real estate brokerage firm in north suburban Chicago that he operated in partnership with William Lehman, who was also a CTS stockholder.

The four men sat back down at the meeting table, and Randall mentioned that his primary interest was to learn more about how an employee relocation business operated. Burr offered to send him copies of contracts with corporate clients, sample financial statements, and so on. At one point during their discussion Burr mentioned the possibility of an acquisition. Randall asked, somewhat rhetorically, "How do you put a value on a company like this?" Burr responded almost immediately, "Funny you should ask. We've talked to an attorney and have put together this proposal." Burr reached into his briefcase and pulled out a two-page document. He then proceeded to describe a complex set of terms involving the sale of an 80 percent interest in CTS, subject to guarantees concerning capitalization, lines of credit, data processing support, future distribution of profits and dividends, and more.

Randall backed off immediately, explaining that he needed to learn more about the nature of the business before he would seriously consider an acquisition. As Jim Dolan later recalled,

> I think they were expecting an offer right then and there. But it was very hard to understand what they really wanted; it was nothing we could actually work from. Besides that, the numbers they were thinking about were ridiculously high—over $5 million. We put the letter away and told them we didn't want to get specific until after the April 10 meeting. And that's the way we left it.

Preparation for the April 10 Meeting

During the next six weeks Randall and Dolan continued their investigations of the employee relocation industry and studied CTS much more closely.

One of their major questions was how much additional mortgage insurance the MetroNet brokers might be able to generate. Frank Randall had CMI's marketing staff conduct a telephone survey of about 25 key MetroNet brokers. The survey suggested that most brokers were aware of mortgage insurance, although few of them were actively pushing it. All of those questioned expressed an interest in using CMI's marketing programs, and were eager to learn more about CMI insurance.

By early May a fairly clear picture of CTS was emerging. The company had been founded in 1975; it had barely achieved a break-even profit level. Annual home purchases and sales had reached a level of almost 500 properties, and CTS had worked with about 65 MetroNet brokers and 35 corporate clients. Tom Winder was the general manager; he supervised a staff of about 25 customer representatives and clerical support staff. Conversations with David Osgood and several MetroNet brokers who had worked with CTS suggested that the company had made promises to MetroNet about developing a nationwide, well-financed, fully competitive organization. To date, however, those promises were largely unfulfilled. Osgood believed that CTS's shortage of equity and, therefore, borrowing capacity, had severely limited its growth potential.

Jim Dolan obtained a copy of CTS's December 1978 balance sheet that, in his mind, confirmed Osgood's feelings (see Exhibit 3). The company had a net worth of only $420,000. Three of the four stockholders (Elliott Burr, William Lehman, and Michael Kupchak) had invested an additional $2 million in the company—$1.3 million in short-term notes and $700,000 in bank loans that they had personally guaranteed. While CTS owned homes valued at $13.4 million, it also had additional bank loans and assumed mortgages totaling $9.8 million. Furthermore, the company had a highly uncertain earnings stream; Frank Randall believed the current business could tail off to almost nothing within six months.

During late March both Randall and Dolan had a number of telephone conversations with Burr and Winder. Their discussions were wide ranging and quite open; the CTS partners struck Randall as being unusually candid. They seemed more than willing to share everything they knew about the business and their own company. On one occasion, Burr asked how much of CTS Randall wanted to buy and how Randall would feel

EXHIBIT 3 | CTS Balance Sheet

CORPORATE TRANSFER SERVICES, INC.
Unaudited Balance Sheet
December 1978

Assets	($ 000)
Cash	$ 190
Homes owned	13,366
Accounts and acquisition fees receivable	665
Other (mainly escrow deposits)	143
	$14,364

Liabilities	
Client prepayments	$ 1,602
Notes payable to banks	4,161
Assumed mortgages payable	5,670
Loan from stockholders	700
Advance from MetroNet	300
Other liabilities	211
	$12,644

Capital	
Subordinated debenture due stockholder (April 1981)	1,300
Common stock	450
Deficit	(30)
	$14,364

about the present owners retaining a minority interest. Burr's question led Randall and Dolan to conclude that in fact they wanted full ownership. They planned to build up the company's equity base considerably and wanted to gain all the benefits of a larger, more profitable operation for CMI.

In early April, Randall developed the formal proposal that he intended to present to MetroNet's board of directors (see Exhibit 4). The proposal committed CMI to enter negotiations to acquire CTS and to use CTS as a base for building a third-party equity company with a capitalization sufficient to support an annual home purchase capability of at least 2,000 units. In return, the proposal asked MetroNet to begin a program of actively supporting the use of CMI's insurance on high-ratio loans.

Randall and Dolan met again with the Third-Party Equity Committee in New York on April 9 to preview the CMI proposal. The committee reacted favorably, and the next day MetroNet's board of directors unanimously accepted the proposal after discussing it for less than 15 minutes.

Formal Negotiations with Corporate Transfer Services

On the afternoon of April 10, following the MetroNet board meeting, Randall and Dolan met again with Elliott Burr and Tom Winder. Now that CMI was formally committed to acquisition negotiations, Burr and Winder were eager to get specific and talk numbers. However, Randall and Dolan remained very cautious. When Burr expressed an interest in discussing a price, Randall replied, "We don't know what you're worth. But we'll entertain any reasonable argument you want to make for why we should pay more than your net worth." The meeting ended with a general agreement to firm things up by April 25. Later, reflecting on this session, Jim Dolan commented,

> Our letter of agreement committed us to having an operating company by July 12, so the clock was running on us. However, we know that after the April 10 board meeting they would be hard pressed not to be bought, and besides they were obviously pretty eager. But at that point in time we had not even met the other two stockholders; we suspected the high numbers were coming from them.

Further Assessment of CTS

Even though the April 10 meeting had ended with an agreement to move ahead by April 25, it quickly became evident that a complete assessment of CTS and preparation of a formal offer would take more than two weeks. Other operating responsibilities prevented both Randall and Dolan from devoting as much time as they had intended to the acquisition, and the analysis process itself required more time than they had expected.

During the first week of May, Jim Dolan made a "reconnaissance" trip to Chicago. His stated purpose was to examine CTS's books and talk with the company's local bankers. He also scrutinized the office facilities, met and talked with several office employees, observed Tom Winder interacting with customers and subordinates, and generally assessed the company's operations. Dolan spent most of his time with Winder, but he also had an opportunity to have dinner with William Lehman, another of CTS's

EXHIBIT 4 | Letter of Intent

Board of Directors
The Metropolitan Realty Network
New York, NY

April 9, 1979

Gentlemen:

It is our intention to enter negotiations with the principals of Corporate Transfer Services, Inc., for the acquisition of the equity ownership of this Company by Capital Mortgage Insurance Corporation.

In the event Capital Mortgage Insurance Corporation is successful in the acquisition of Corporate Transfer Services, Inc., it is our intention to capitalize this Company to the extent required for the development of a complete bank line of credit. The initial capital and bank line of credit would provide the MetroNet association members an annual equity procurement of 1,500–2,000 units. In addition, we would be prepared to expand beyond this initial capacity if the MetroNet Association volume and profitability of business dictate.

We are prepared to develop an organizational structure and support system that can provide a competitive and professional marketing and administrative approach to the corporate transfer market.

Our intentions to enter negotiations with Corporate Transfer Services, Inc., are subject to the following:

1. The endorsement of this action by you, the board of directors of MetroNet, for Capital Mortgage Insurance Corporation to acquire this organization.

2. The assurance of the MetroNet Association for the continuation of their support and use of CTS. Upon completion of the acquisition, the MetroNet Association would agree to sign a Letter of Agreement with the new owners of Corporate Transfer Services.

3. The assurance of the MetroNet Association to cooperate in the development of a close working relationship with CMI for the influence and control they may provide when seeking high-ratio conventional mortgage loans using mortgage insurance.

Capital Mortgage Insurance will need the support of expanded business by the MetroNet Association, due to the heavy capital commitment we will be required to make to CTS to make this acquisition feasible. In this regard, CMI is prepared to offer the MetroNet nationwide members a range of marketing programs and mortgage financing packages that will help earn and deserve the mortgage insurance business and expand the listings, sales, and profitability of the MetroNet members.

Upon receiving the endorsement and support outlined in this letter from the board of directors of MetroNet, we will proceed immediately with the negotiations with Corporate Transfer Services, Inc. It would be our intention to have the acquisition completed and the company fully operational by the time of the MetroNet national convention in San Francisco in July 1979.

Sincerely,

Franklin T. Randall
President and Chief Executive Officer

stockholders. Dolan returned to Philadelphia with a generally favorable set of impressions about the company's operations and a much more concrete understanding of its financial situation. He reported to Randall, "They're running a responsible organization in a basically sensible manner." At the same time, however, Dolan also reported that CTS was under increasing pressure from its bankers to improve its financial performance.

Dolan's trip also provided him with a much richer understanding of the four men who owned CTS: Elliott Burr, William Lehman (Burr's real estate partner), Michael Kupchak (a private investor), and Tom Winder. Of these four, only Winder was actively involved in the day-to-day management of the company, although Elliott Burr stayed in very close touch with Winder and was significantly more involved than either Lehman or Kupchak. From their meetings and telephone conversations, Randall and Dolan pieced together the following pictures of the four men:

- *Elliott Burr,* in his middle 50s, had been the driving force behind Corporate Transfer Services. He was a classic real estate salesman—a warm, straightforward, friendly man who enthusiastically believed in what he was doing. An eternal optimist, he had been an early advocate of MetroNet's getting into the employee relocation business. Burr knew the relocation business extremely well; he personally called on many of the large Chicago corporations to sell CTS's services.

  Burr appeared to be very well off financially. Burr and Lehman Real Estate was one of the largest realty firms on Chicago's North Shore, and Burr was held in high regard by local bankers. One banker had told Dolan, "Burr's word is his bond."

- *William Lehman,* Burr's real estate partner, was in his mid-60s. He appeared to be much more of a financial adviser and investor than an operating manager. Lehman personally owned the shopping center where Burr and Lehman Real Estate was located, as well as the office building where CTS was leasing space.

  Dolan characterized Lehman as an "elder statesman—a true gentleman." Dolan recalled that when he had had dinner with Lehman during his visit to Chicago, Lehman had kept the conversation on a personal level, repeatedly expressing concern about Dolan's plane reservations, hotel accommodations, and so on. He had hardly mentioned CTS during the entire dinner.

- *Michael Kupchak* was the third principal stockholder. Kupchak, about 50, had been a mortgage banker in Chicago for a number of years. Recently, however, he had left the bank to manage his own investments on a full-time basis.

  Dolan met Kupchak briefly during his Chicago visit, and characterized him as a "bulldog"—an aggressive, ambitious man much more interested in financial transactions than in the nature of the business. He had apparently thought Dolan was coming to Chicago to make a firm offer and had been irritated that one had not been forthcoming. Frank Randall had not yet met Kupchak face-to-face, although they had talked once by telephone.

- *Thomas Winder,* 44, had spent most of his career in real estate–related businesses. At one time he had worked for a construction company, and then he had joined the mortgage bank where Michael Kupchak worked.

Kupchak had actually brought Winder into CTS as its general manager, and the three original partners had offered him 25 percent ownership in the company as part of his compensation package.

Winder was not only CTS's general manager, but its lead salesperson as well. He called on prospective corporate clients all over the country, and he worked closely with MetroNet. That activity primarily involved appearing at association-sponsored seminars to inform member brokers about CTS and its services.

It was obvious to Jim Dolan that CTS had become an important source of real estate sales commissions for the Burr and Lehman partnership. Most of CTS's clients were in the Chicago area, and a large portion of the real estate transactions generated by CTS were being handled by Burr and Lehman Real Estate.

Dolan also inferred that the three senior partners—Burr, Lehman, and Kupchak—were close friends socially as well as professionally. The men clearly respected each other and valued each other's opinions. On one occasion Burr had told Dolan, "It's because of Bill Lehman that I have what I have today. I can always trust his word." Tom Winder was also woven into the relationship, but he was apparently not as closely involved as the other three. Randall and Dolan both sensed that Elliott Burr was the unofficial spokesman of the group. "I have the impression he can speak for all of them," commented Dolan.

In late April, Randall obtained a copy of a consultant's report on the employee relocation industry that had been commissioned by MetroNet's Third-Party Equity Committee. The report estimated that there were more than 500,000 homeowner/employees transferred annually, generating over 1 million home purchases and sales. However, fewer than 55,000 of these transfers were currently being handled by relocation services companies. Dolan's own analysis had projected a 10–15 percent annual growth rate in the use of relocation companies, leading to industry volume estimates of 60,000 in 1979, 67,000 in 1980, and 75,000 by 1981. The consultant's report stressed that success in the relocation business depended on a company's ability to provide services to its corporate clients at lower cost than the clients could do it themselves. In addition, profitability depended on a company's ability to turn over its inventory of homes quickly and at reasonable prices. Dolan's own financial projections showed a potential return on equity of over 30 percent by 1983, assuming only an 8 percent share of the market. And that return did not include any incremental profits resulting from new sales of CMI mortgage insurance policies generated by MetroNet brokers. Randall in particular was confident that the close ties between CMI and MetroNet would result in at least 5,000 new mortgage insurance policies annually—a volume that could add over $400,000 in after-tax profits to CMI's basic business.

On May 10, Randall and Dolan attended a Northwest Equipment Corporation financial review meeting in Minneapolis. Prior to their trip west Randall had prepared a detailed analysis of the CTS acquisition and the employee relocation industry. The analysis, in the form of a proposal, served as documentation for a formal request to Northwest for a capital expenditure of $9 million. Randall had decided that he was willing to pay up to $600,000 more than the $420,000 book value of CTS's net worth; the remaining $8 million would constitute the initial equity base required to build CTS into a viable company. The financial review meeting evolved into a lengthy critique of the acquisition proposal. Northwest's corporate staff was initially quite skeptical of the financial projections, but Randall and Dolan argued that the risks were relatively low (the homes could always be sold) and the potential payoffs, both economic and strategic, were enormous. Finally, after an extended debate, the request was approved.

Formal Negotiations with CTS

When Randall and Dolan returned from Minneapolis, they felt it was finally time to proceed in earnest with the acquisition negotiations. Randall sensed that at present CTS was limping along to no one's satisfaction—including Elliott Burr's. The company was sucking up much more of Burr's time and energy than he wanted to give it, and its inability to fulfill MetroNet's expectations was beginning to be an embarrassment for Burr personally.

In spite of these problems, Randall remained interested in completing the acquisition. Buying CTS would get CMI into the relocation business quickly, would provide them with immediate licensing and other legal documentation in 38 states, and would get them an experienced operations manager in Tom Winder. More important, Randall knew that Elliott Burr was an important and respected MetroNet broker, and buying CTS would provide an effective, influential entry into the MetroNet "old boy" network. Though he couldn't put a number on the value of that network, Randall believed it was almost more important than the acquisition of CTS itself. Randall was convinced that the connection with the MetroNet brokers would enable him to run CTS at far lower cost than the established relocation companies, and he also expected to realize a significant increase in CMI's mortgage insurance business.

May 21, 1979

Now, as Randall and Dolan sat in Randall's office on May 21, they discussed the draft of a formal purchase offer that Dolan had prepared that morning (see Exhibit 5 for relevant excerpts). The two men had decided to make an initial offer of $400,000 more than the $420,000 book value of CTS's net worth, subject to a formal audit and adjustments depending on the final sales prices of all homes owned by CTS as of the formal purchase date. This opening bid was $200,000 below Randall's ceiling price of $600,000 for the firm's goodwill. The offer was for 100 percent of the ownership of the company. The $2 million in outstanding notes would pass through to the new company owned by Randall and Dolan. The offer also included a statement of intent to retain Tom Winder as CTS's general manager and to move the company to CMI's home office in Philadelphia.

As Randall and Dolan reviewed their plans, it was clear that they were more concerned about how to conduct the face-to-face negotiations than with the formal terms themselves. In the telephone call he had just completed, Randall had told Elliott Burr only that they wanted to meet the other stockholders and review their current thinking. At one point during the conversation Jim Dolan commented,

> I really wonder how they'll react to this offer. We've been putting them off for so long now that I'm not sure how they feel about us anymore. And our offer is so much less than they're looking for.

EXHIBIT 5 | Draft of Purchase Letter

The Board of Directors and Stockholders
Corporate Transfer Services, Inc.
Chicago, IL

May 24, 1979

Gentlemen:

Capital Mortgage Insurance Corporation (the "Purchaser") hereby agrees to purchase from you (the "Stockholders"), and you, the Stockholders, hereby jointly and severally agree to sell to us, the Purchaser, 100 percent of the issued and outstanding shares of capital stock of Corporate Transfer Services (the "Company") on the following terms and conditions.

Purchase Price. Subject to any adjustment under the following paragraph, the Purchase Price of the Stock shall be the sum of $400,000.00 (four hundred thousand dollars even) and an amount equal to the Company's net worth as reflected in its audited financial statements on the closing date (the "Closing Date Net Worth").

Adjustment of Purchase Price. The Purchase Price shall be reduced or increased, as the case may be, dollar-for-dollar by the amount, if any, by which the net amount realized on the sale of homes owned as of the Closing Date is exceeded by, or exceeds, the value attributed to such homes in the Closing Date Net Worth.

Continuation of Employment. Immediately upon consummation of the transaction, the Purchaser will enter into discussion with Mr. Thomas Winder with the intent that he continue employment in a management capacity at a mutually agreeable rate of pay. Mr. Winder will relocate to Philadelphia, Pennsylvania, and will be responsible for the sale of all homes owned by the Company at the Closing Date.

Covenant-Not-to-Compete. At the closing, each Stockholder will execute and deliver a covenant-not-to-compete agreeing that he will not engage in any capacity in the business conducted by the Company for a period of two years. If the foregoing correctly states our agreement as to this transaction, please sign below.

Very truly yours,

CAPITAL MORTGAGE INSURANCE
CORPORATION

The foregoing is agreed to and accepted.   By _____
President

Randall replied,

I know that—but I have my ceiling. It seems to me the real question now is what kind of bargaining stance we should take, and how to carry it out. What do you think they are expecting?

Discussion Questions

1. Prepare, and be ready to discuss, a negotiation strategy for Randall and Dolan.
2. What should CMI be expecting from CTS?

Pacific Oil Company (A)

For the discussion of Pacific Oil Company, please prepare the following:

1. As background information, read the appendix to this case: "Petrochemical Supply Contracts: A Technical Note" (p. 607).

2. Read the Pacific Oil Company case.

3. Prepare the following questions for class discussion:

   a. Describe the problem that Pacific Oil Company faced as it reopened negotiations with Reliant Chemical Company in early 1985.

   b. Evaluate the styles and effectiveness of Messrs. Fontaine, Gaudin, Hauptmann, and Zinnser as negotiators in this case.

   c. What should Frank Kelsey recommend to Jean Fontaine at the end of the case? Why?

The Pacific Oil Company

"Look, you asked for my advice, and I gave it to you," Frank Kelsey said. "If I were you, I wouldn't make any more concessions! I really don't think you ought to agree to their last demand! But you're the one who has to live with the contract, not me!"

Static on the transatlantic telephone connection obscured Jean Fontaine's reply. Kelsey asked him to repeat what he had said.

"OK, OK, calm down, Jean. I can see your point of view. I appreciate the pressures you're under. But I sure don't like the looks of it from this end. Keep in touch—I'll talk to you early next week. In the meantime, I will see what others at the office think about this turn of events."

Frank Kelsey hung up the phone. He sat pensively, staring out at the rain pounding on the window. "Poor Fontaine," he muttered to himself. "He's so anxious to please the customer, he'd feel compelled to give them the whole pie without getting his fair share of the dessert!"

Kelsey cleaned and lit his pipe as he mentally reviewed the history of the negotiations. "My word," he thought to himself, "we are getting completely taken in with this Reliant deal! And I can't make Fontaine see it!"

Background

Pacific Oil Company was founded in 1902 as the Sweetwater Oil Company of Oklahoma City, Oklahoma. The founder of Sweetwater Oil, E.M. Hutchinson, pioneered a major oil strike in north central Oklahoma that touched off the Oklahoma "black gold" rush

Source: Case prepared by Roy J. Lewicki.

Although this case is over 20 years old, the editors of this volume believe that it presents valuable lessons about the negotiation process.

of the early 1900s. Through growth and acquisition in the 1920s and 1930s, Hutchinson expanded the company rapidly and renamed it Pacific Oil in 1932. After a period of consolidation in the 1940s and 1950s, Pacific expanded again. It developed extensive oil holdings in North Africa and the Middle East, as well as significant coal beds in the western United States. Much of Pacific's oil production is sold under its own name as gasoline through service stations in the United States and Europe, but it is also distributed through several chains of independent gasoline stations. In addition, Pacific is also one of the largest and best-known worldwide producers of industrial petrochemicals.

One of Pacific's major industrial chemical lines is the production of vinyl chloride monomer (VCM). The basic components of VCM are ethylene and chlorine. Ethylene is a colorless, flammable, gaseous hydrocarbon with a disagreeable odor; it is generally obtained from natural or coal gas, or by "cracking" petroleum into smaller molecular components. As a further step in the petroleum cracking process, ethylene is combined with chlorine to produce VCM, also a colorless gas.

VCM is the primary component of a family of plastics known as the vinyl chlorides. VCM is subjected to the process of polymerization, in which smaller molecules of vinyl chloride are chemically bonded together to form larger molecular chains and networks. As the bonding occurs, polyvinyl chloride (PVC) is produced; coloring pigments may be added, as well as "plasticizer" compounds that determine the relative flexibility or hardness of the finished material. Through various forms of calendering (pressing between heavy rollers), extruding, and injection molding, the plasticized polyvinyl chloride is converted to an enormous array of consumer and industrial applications: flooring, wire insulation, electrical transformers, home furnishings, piping, toys, bottles and containers, rainwear, light roofing, and a variety of protective coatings. (See Exhibit 1 for a breakdown of common PVC-based products.) In 1979, Pacific Oil established the first major contract with the Reliant Corporation for the purchase of vinyl chloride monomer. The Reliant Corporation was a major industrial manufacturer of wood and petrochemical products for the construction industry. Reliant was expanding its manufacturing operations in the production of plastic pipe and pipe fittings, particularly in Europe. The use of plastic as a substitute for iron or copper pipe was gaining rapid acceptance in the construction trades, and the European markets were significantly more progressive in adopting the plastic pipe. Reliant already had developed a small polyvinyl chloride production facility at Abbeville, France, and Pacific constructed a pipeline from its petrochemical plant at Antwerp to Abbeville.

The 1979 contract between Pacific Oil and Reliant was a fairly standard one for the industry and due to expire in December of 1982. The contract was negotiated by Reliant's purchasing managers in Europe, headquartered in Brussels, and the senior marketing managers of Pacific Oil's European offices, located in Paris. Each of these individuals reported to the vice presidents in charge of their companies' European offices, who in turn reported back to their respective corporate headquarters in the States. (See Exhibits 2 and 3 on pages 592 and 593 for partial organization charts.)

EXHIBIT 1 | Polyvinyl Chloride Major Markets, 1982 (units represented in
MM pounds)

Market	MM Pounds	Percentage of Market Share
Apparel		
Baby pants	22	0.6
Footwear	128	3.2
Miscellaneous	60	1.5
	210	5.3
Building and construction		
Extruded foam moldings	46	1.2
Flooring	428	10.8
Lighting	10	0.3
Panels and siding	64	1.6
Pipe and conduit	720	18.5
Pipe fittings	78	2.0
Rainwater systems	28	0.7
Swimming pool liners	40	1.0
Weather stripping	36	0.9
Miscellaneous	50	1.2
	1,500	38.2
Electrical		
Wire and cable	390	9.9
Home furnishings		
Appliances	32	0.8
Miscellaneous	286	9.8
	318	10.6
Housewares	94	2.4
Packaging		
Blow molded bottles	64	1.6
Closure liners and gaskets	16	0.4
Coatings	16	0.4
Film	124	3.2
Miscellaneous	80	2.0
	300	7.6
Recreation		
Records	136	3.4
Sporting goods	46	1.2
Miscellaneous	68	1.7
	250	6.3
Transportation		
Auto mats	36	0.9
Auto tops	32	0.8
Miscellaneous	164	4.2
	232	5.9

(continued)

EXHIBIT 1 | (concluded)

Market	MM Pounds	Percentage of Market Share
Miscellaneous		
Agriculture (including pipe)	106	2.6
Credit cards	24	0.4
Garden hose	40	1.0
Laminates	44	1.1
Medical tubing	42	1.1
Novelties	12	0.3
Stationery supplies	32	0.8
Miscellaneous	12	0.3
	312	7.6
Export	146	3.7
Miscellaneous	98	2.5
	244	6.2
Total	3,850	100.0

The 1982 Contract Renewal

In February 1982, negotiations began to extend the four-year contract beyond the December 31, 1982, expiration date. Jean Fontaine, Pacific Oil's marketing vice president for Europe, discussed the Reliant account with his VCM marketing manager, Paul Gaudin. Fontaine had been promoted to the European vice presidency approximately 16 months earlier after having served as Pacific's ethylene marketing manager. Fontaine had been with Pacific Oil for 11 years and had a reputation as a strong up-and-comer in Pacific's European operations. Gaudin had been appointed as VCM marketing manager eight months earlier; this was his first job with Pacific Oil, although he had five years of previous experience in European computer sales with a large American computer manufacturing company. Fontaine and Gaudin had worked well in their short time together, establishing a strong professional and personal relationship. Fontaine and Gaudin agreed that the Reliant account had been an extremely profitable and beneficial one for Pacific and believed that Reliant had, overall, been satisfied with the quality and service under the agreement as well. They clearly wanted to work hard to obtain a favorable renegotiation of the existing agreement. Fontaine and Gaudin also reviewed the latest projections of worldwide VCM supply, which they had just received from corporate headquarters (see Exhibit 4, p. 593). The data confirmed what they already knew—that there was a worldwide shortage of VCM and that demand was continuing to rise. Pacific envisioned that the current demand–supply situation would remain this way for a number of years. As a result, Pacific believed that it could justify a high favorable formula price for VCM.

Fontaine and Gaudin decided that they would approach Reliant with an offer to renegotiate the current agreement. Their basic strategy would be to ask Reliant for their five-year demand projections on VCM and polyvinyl chloride products. Once these projections were received, Fontaine and Gaudin would frame the basic formula price that

EXHIBIT 2 | Partial Organization Chart—Pacific Oil Company

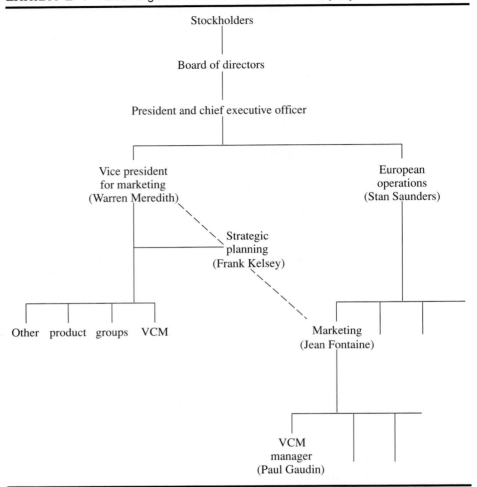

they would offer. (It would be expected that there would be no significant changes or variations in other elements of the contract, such as delivery and contract language.) In their negotiations, their strategy would be as follows:

1. To dwell on the successful long-term relationship that had already been built between Reliant and Pacific Oil, and to emphasize the value of that relationship for the success of both companies.

2. To emphasize all of the projections that predicted the worldwide shortage of VCM and the desirability for Reliant to ensure that they would have a guaranteed supplier.

3. To point out all of the ways that Pacific had gone out of its way in the past to ensure delivery and service.

EXHIBIT 3 | Partial Organization Chart—Reliant Chemical Company

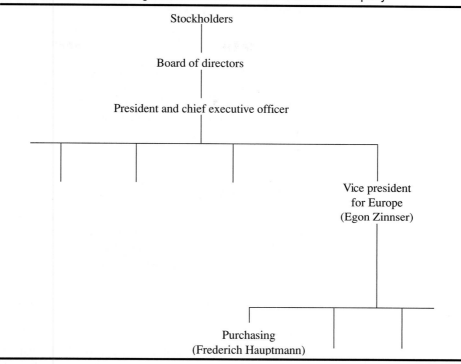

EXHIBIT 4 | Memorandum, January 17, 1982

TO: All VCM Marketing Managers
FROM: F. Kelsey, Strategic Planning Division
RE: Worldwide VCM Supply–Demand Projections
DATE: January 17, 1982
CONFIDENTIAL—FOR YOUR EYES ONLY

Here are the data from 1980 and 1981, and the five-year projections that I promised you at our last meeting. As you can see, the market is tight, and is projected to get tighter. I hope you will find this useful in your marketing efforts—let me know if I can supply more detailed information.

Year	Total Projected Demand (in MM pounds)	Supply Plant Capacities	Operating Rates to Meet Demand (percent)
1980	4,040	5,390	75%
1981	4,336	5,390	80
1982	5,100	6,600	77
1983	5,350	6,600	81
1984	5,550	6,600	83
1985	5,650	7,300	75
1986	5,750	7,300	78

4. To use both the past and future quality of the relationship to justify what might appear to be a high formula price.

5. To point out the ways that Pacific's competitors could not offer the same kind of service.

Over the next six months, Gaudin and Fontaine, independently and together, made a number of trips to Brussels to visit Reliant executives. In addition, several members of Pacific's senior management visited Brussels and paid courtesy calls on Reliant management. The net result was a very favorable contract for Pacific Oil, signed by both parties on October 24, 1982. The basic contract, to extend from January 1983 to December 1987, is represented as Exhibit 5 on page 595.

A Changed Perspective

In December of 1984, Fontaine and Gaudin sat down to their traditional end-of-year review of all existing chemical contracts. As a matter of course, the Reliant VCM contract came under review. Although everything had been proceeding very smoothly, the prospects for the near and long-term future were obviously less clear, for the following reasons:

1. Both men reviewed the data that they had been receiving from corporate headquarters, as well as published projections of the supply situation for various chemicals over the next 10 years. It was clear that the basic supply–demand situation on VCM was changing (see Exhibit 6 p. 599). While the market was currently tight—the favorable supply situation that had existed for Pacific when the Reliant contract was first negotiated—the supply of VCM was expected to expand rapidly over the next few years. Several of Pacific's competitors had announced plans for the construction of VCM manufacturing facilities that were expected to come on line in 20–30 months.

2. Fontaine and Gaudin knew that Reliant was probably aware of this situation as well. As a result, they would probably anticipate the change in the supply–demand situation as an opportunity to pursue a more favorable price, with the possible threat that they would be willing to change suppliers if the terms were not favorable enough. (Although rebuilding a pipeline is no simple matter, it clearly could be done, and had been, when the terms were sufficiently favorable to justify it.)

3. Fontaine was aware that in a situation where the market turned from one of high demand to excess supply, it was necessary to make extra efforts to maintain and re-sign all major current customers. A few large customers (100 million pounds a year and over) dominated the marketplace, and a single customer defection in an oversupplied market could cause major headaches for everyone. It would simply be impossible to find another customer with demands of that magnitude; a number of smaller customers would have to be found, while Pacific would also have to compete with spot market prices that would cut profits to the bone.

EXHIBIT 5 | Agreement of Sale

This Agreement, entered into this *24th* day of *October, 1982,* between *Pacific Oil Company,* hereinafter called Seller, and *Reliant Chemical Company of Europe,* hereinafter called Buyer. WITNESSETH:

Seller agrees to sell and deliver and Buyer agrees to purchase and receive commodity (hereinafter called "product") under the terms and conditions set forth below.

1. Product: Vinyl Chloride Monomer

2. Quality: ASTM requirements for polymer-grade product

3. Quantity: 1983: 150 million pounds

             1984: 160 million pounds

             1985: 170 million pounds

             1986: 185 million pounds

             1987: 200 million pounds

4. Period: Contract shall extend from January 1, 1983, until December 31, 1987, and every year thereafter, unless terminated with 180 days' prior notification at the end of each calendar year, but not before December 31, 1987.

5. Price: See Contract formula price.

6. Payment Terms:

   a. Net 30 days.

   b. All payments shall be made in United States dollars without discount or deduction, unless otherwise noted, by wire transfer at Seller's option, to a bank account designated by Seller. Invoices not paid on due date will be subject to a delinquency finance charge of 1 percent per month.

   c. If at any time the financial responsibility of Buyer shall become impaired or unsatisfactory to Seller, cash payment on delivery or satisfactory security may be required. A failure to pay any amount may, at the option of the Seller, terminate this contract as to further deliveries. No forbearance, course of dealing, or prior payment shall affect this right of Seller.

7. Price Change:

The price specified in this Agreement may be changed by Seller on the first day of any calendar *half-year* by written notice sent to the Buyer not less than thirty (30) days prior to the effective date of change. Buyer gives Seller written notice of objection to such change at least ten (10) days prior to the effective date of change. Buyer's failure to serve Seller with written notice of objection thereto prior to the effective date thereof shall be considered acceptance of such change. If Buyer gives such notice of objection and Buyer and Seller fail to agree on such change prior to the effective date thereof, this Agreement and the obligations of Seller and Buyer hereunder shall terminate with respect to the unshipped portion of the Product governed by it. Seller has the option immediately to cancel this contract upon written notice to Buyer, to continue to sell hereunder at the same price and terms which were in effect at the time Seller gave notice of change, or to suspend performance under this contract while pricing is being resolved. If Seller desires to revise the price, freight allowance, or terms of payment pursuant to this agreement, but is restricted to any extent against doing so by reason of any law, governmental decree, order, or regulation, or if the price, freight allowance, or terms of payment then in effect under this contract are nullified or reduced by reason of any law, governmental decree, order, or regulation, Seller shall have the right to cancel this contract upon fifteen (15) days' written notice to purchaser.

8. Measurements:

Seller's determinations, unless proven to be erroneous, shall be accepted as conclusive evidence of the quantity of Product delivered hereunder. Credit will not be allowed for shortages of

(*continued*)

EXHIBIT 5 | (*continued*)

1/2 of 1 percent or less of the quantity, and overages of 1/2 of 1 percent or less of the quantity will be waived. The total amount of shortages or overages will be credited or billed when quantities are greater and such differences are substantiated. Measurements of weight and volume shall be according to procedures and criteria standard for such determinations.

9. Shipments and Delivery:

Buyer shall give Seller annual or quarterly forecasts of its expected requirements as Seller may from time to time request. Buyer shall give Seller reasonably advanced notice for each shipment which shall include date of delivery and shipping instructions. Buyer shall agree to take deliveries in approximately equal monthly quantities, except as may be otherwise provided herein. In the event that Buyer fails to take the quantity specified or the pro rata quantity in any month, Seller may, at its option, in addition to other rights and remedies, cancel such shipments or parts thereof.

10. Purchase Requirements:

a. If during any consecutive three-month period, Buyer for any reason (but not for reasons of force majeure as set forth in Section 12) takes less than 90 percent of the average monthly quantity specified, or the prorated minimum monthly quantity then applicable to such period under Section 12, Seller may elect to charge Buyer a penalty charge for failure to take the average monthly quantity or prorated minimum monthly quantity.

b. If, during any consecutive three-month period, Buyer, for any reason (but not, however, for reasons of force majeure as set forth in Section 12) takes Product in quantities less than that equal to at least one-half of the average monthly quantity specified or the prorated minimum monthly quantity originally applicable to such period under Section 12, Seller may elect to terminate this agreement.

c. It is the Seller's intent not to unreasonably exercise its right under (*a*) or (*b*) in the event of adverse economic and business conditions in general.

d. Notice of election by Seller under (*a*) or (*b*) shall be given within 30 days after the end of the applicable three-month period, and the effective date of termination shall be 30 days after the date of said notice.

11. Detention Policy:

Seller may, from time to time, specify free unloading time allowances for its transportation equipment. Buyer shall be liable to the Transportation Company for all demurrage charges made by the Transportation Company, for railcars, trucks, tanks, or barges held by Buyer beyond the free unloading time.

12. Force Majeure:

Neither party shall be liable to the other for failure or delay in performance hereunder to the extent that such failure or delay is due to war, fire, flood, strike, lockout, or other labor trouble, accident, breakdown of equipment or machinery, riot, act, request, or suggestion of governmental authority, act of God, or other contingencies beyond the control of the affected party which interfere with the production or transportation of the material covered by this Agreement or with the supply of any raw material (whether or not the source of supply was in existence or contemplated at the time of this Agreement) or energy source used in connection therewith, or interfere with Buyer's consumption of such material, provided that in no event shall Buyer be relieved of the obligation to pay in full for material delivered hereunder. Without limitation on the foregoing, neither party shall be required to remove any cause listed above or replace the affected source of supply or facility if it shall involve additional expense or departure from its normal practices. If any of the events specified in this paragraph shall have occurred, Seller shall have the right to allocate in a fair and reasonable manner among its customers and Seller's own requirements any supplies of material Seller has available for delivery at the time or for the duration of the event.

(*continued*)

EXHIBIT 5 | *(concluded)*

13. Materials and Energy Supply:

If, for reasons beyond reasonable commercial control, Seller's supply of product to be delivered hereunder shall be limited due to continued availability of necessary raw materials and energy supplies, Seller shall have the right (without liability) to allocate to the Buyer a portion of such product on such basis as Seller deems equitable. Such allocation shall normally be that percentage of Seller's total internal and external commitments which are committed to Buyer as related to the total quantity available from Seller's manufacturing facilities.

14. Disclaimer:

Seller makes no warranty, express or implied, concerning the product furnished hereunder other than it shall be of the quality and specifications stated herein. Any implied warranty of FITNESS is expressly excluded and to the extent that it is contrary to the foregoing sentence; any implied warranty of MERCHANTABILITY is expressly excluded. Any recommendation made by Seller makes no warranty of results to be obtained. Buyer assumes all responsibility and liability for loss or damage resulting from the handling or use of said product. In no event shall Seller be liable for any special, indirect, or consequential damages, irrespective of whether caused or allegedly caused by negligence.

15. Taxes:

Any tax, excise fee, or other charge or increase thereof upon the production, storage, withdrawal, sale, or transportation of the product sold hereunder, or entering into the cost of such product, imposed by any proper authority becoming effective after the date hereof, shall be added to the price herein provided and shall be paid by the Buyer.

16. Assignment and Resale:

This contract is not transferable or assignable by Buyer without the written consent of Seller. The product described hereunder, in the form and manner provided by the Seller, may not be assigned or resold without prior written consent of the Seller.

17. Acceptance:

Acceptance hereof must be without qualification, and Seller will not be bound by any different terms and conditions contained in any other communication.

18. Waiver of Breach:

No waiver by Seller or Buyer of any breach of any of the terms and conditions contained in this Agreement shall be construed as a waiver or any subsequent breach of the same or any other term or condition.

19. Termination:

If any provision of this agreement is or becomes violate of any law, or any rule, order, or regulation issued thereunder, Seller shall have the right, upon notice to Buyer, to terminate the Agreement in its entirety.

20. Governing Law:

The construction of this Agreement and the rights and obligations of the parties hereunder shall be governed by the laws of the State of New York.

21. Special Provisions:

BUYER: SELLER:

                                              PACIFIC OIL CORPORATION
_____

(firm)

By: _____   By: _____

Title: <u>Senior Purchasing Manager</u>   Title: <u>Marketing Vice President</u>

Date: _____   Date: _____

4. In a national product development meeting back in the States several weeks prior, Fontaine had learned of plans by Pacific to expand and diversify its own product line into VCM derivatives. There was serious talk of Pacific's manufacturing its own PVC for distribution under the Pacific name, as well as the manufacture and distribution of various PVC products. Should Pacific decide to enter these businesses, not only would they require a significant amount of the VCM now being sold on the external market, but Pacific would probably decide that, as a matter of principle, it would not want to be in the position of supplying a product competitor with the raw materials to manufacture the product line, unless the formula price were extremely favorable.

As they reviewed these factors, Gaudin and Fontaine realized that they needed to take action. They pondered the alternatives.

A New Contract Is Proposed

As a result of their evaluation of the situation in December 1984, Fontaine and Gaudin decided to proceed on two fronts. First, they would approach Reliant with the intent of reopening negotiation on the current VCM contract. They would propose to renegotiate the current agreement, with an interest toward extending the contract five years from the point of agreement on contract terms. Second, they would contact those people at corporate headquarters in New York who were evaluating Pacific's alternatives for new product development, and inform them of the nature of the situation. The sooner a determination could be made on the product development strategies, the sooner the Pacific office would know how to proceed on the Reliant contract.

Gaudin contacted Frederich Hauptmann, the senior purchasing manager for Reliant Chemicals in Europe. Hauptmann had assumed the position as purchasing manager approximately four weeks earlier, after having served in a purchasing capacity for a large German steel company. Gaudin arranged a meeting for early January in Hauptmann's office. After getting acquainted over lunch, Gaudin briefed Hauptmann on the history of Reliant's contractual relationships with Pacific Oil. Gaudin made clear that Pacific had been very pleased with the relationship that had been maintained. He said that Pacific was concerned about the future and about maintaining the relationship with Reliant for a long time to come. Hauptmann stated that he understood that the relationship had been a very productive one, too, and also hoped that the two companies could continue to work together in the future. Buoyed by Hauptmann's apparent enthusiasm and relative pleasure with the current agreement, Gaudin said that he and Jean Fontaine, his boss, had recently been reviewing all contracts. Even though the existing Pacific–Reliant VCM agreement had three years to run, Pacific felt that it was never too soon to begin thinking about the long-term future. In order to ensure that Reliant would be assured of a continued supply of VCM, under the favorable terms and working relationship that was already well established, Pacific hoped that Reliant might be willing to begin talks now for contract extension past December 31, 1987. Hauptmann said that he would be willing to consider it but needed to consult other people in the Brussels office, as well as

EXHIBIT 6 | Memorandum, December 9, 1984

TO: All VCM Marketing Managers
FROM: F. Kelsey, Strategic Planning Division
RE: Worldwide VCM–Supply–Demand Projections
DATE: December 9, 1984
CONFIDENTIAL—FOR YOUR EYES ONLY

This will confirm and summarize data that we discussed at the national marketing meeting
last month in Atlanta. At that time, I indicated to you that the market projections we made several years ago have changed drastically. In early 1983, a number of our competitors announced their intentions to enter the VCM business over the next five years. Several facilities
are now under construction, and are expected to come on line in late 1986 and early 1987.
As a result, we expect a fairly significant shift in the supply–demand relationship over the
next few years.

I hope you will give this appropriate consideration in your long-range planning effort.
Please contact me if I can be helpful.

Year	Total Projected Demand (in MM pounds)	Supply Plant Capacities	Operating Rates to Meet Demand (percent)
1982	5,127 (actual)	6,600	78%
1983	5,321 (actual)	6,600	81
1984	5,572 (rev. 11/84)	6,600	84
1985	5,700	7,300	78
1986	5,900	8,450	70
1987	6,200	9,250	64
1988	6,500	9,650	67
1989	7,000	11,000	63

senior executives at corporate headquarters in Chicago. Hauptmann promised to contact
Gaudin when he had the answer.

By mid-February, Hauptmann cabled Gaudin that Reliant was indeed willing to
begin renegotiation of the current agreement, with interest in extending it for the future.
He suggested that Gaudin and Fontaine come to Brussels for a preliminary meeting in
early March. Hauptmann also planned to invite Egon Zinnser, the regional vice president of Reliant's European operations and Hauptmann's immediate superior.

March 10

Light snow drifted onto the runway of the Brussels airport as the plane landed. Fontaine
and Gaudin had talked about the Reliant contract, and the upcoming negotiations, for
most of the trip. They had decided that while they did not expect the negotiations to be a
complete pushover, they expected no significant problems or stumbling points in the deliberations. They thought Reliant negotiators would routinely question some of the coefficients
that were used to compute the formula price as well as to renegotiate some of the minimum
quantity commitments. They felt that the other elements of the contract would be routinely discussed but that no dramatic changes should be expected.

After a pleasant lunch with Hauptmann and Zinnser, the four men sat down to review the current VCM contract. They reviewed and restated much of what Gaudin and Hauptmann had done at their January meeting. Fontaine stated that Pacific Oil was looking toward the future and hoping that it could maintain Reliant as a customer. Zinnser responded that Reliant had indeed been pleased by the contract as well but that it was also concerned about the future. They felt that Pacific's basic formula price on VCM, while fair, might not remain competitive in the long-run future. Zinnser said that he had already had discussions with two other major chemical firms that were planning new VCM manufacturing facilities and that one or both of these firms were due to come on line in the next 24–30 months. Zinnser wanted to make sure that Pacific could remain competitive with other firms in the marketplace. Fontaine responded that it was Pacific's full intention to remain completely competitive, whether it be in market price or in the formula price.

Zinnser said he was pleased by this reply and took this as an indication that Pacific would be willing to evaluate and perhaps adjust some of the factors that were now being used to determine the VCM formula price. He then presented a rather elaborate proposal for adjusting the respective coefficients of these factors. The net result of these adjustments would be to reduce the effective price of VCM by approximately 2 cents per pound. It did not take long for Fontaine and Gaudin to calculate that this would be a net reduction of approximately $4 million per year. Fontaine stated that they would have to take the proposal back to Paris for intensive study and analysis. The men shook hands, and Fontaine and Gaudin headed back to the airport.

Throughout the spring, Gaudin and Hauptmann exchanged several letters and telephone calls. They met once at the Paris airport when Hauptmann stopped over on a trip to the States and once in Zurich when both men discovered that they were going to be there on business the same day. By May 15, they had agreed on a revision of the formula price that would adjust the price downward by almost one cent per pound. Gaudin, relieved that the price had finally been established, reported back to Fontaine that significant progress was being made. Gaudin expected that the remaining issues could be closed up in a few weeks and a new contract signed.

May 27

Hauptmann contacted Gaudin to tell him that Reliant was now willing to talk about the remaining issues in the contract. The two men met in early June. Gaudin opened the discussion by saying that now that the formula price had been agreed upon, he hoped that Reliant would be willing to agree to extend the contract five years from the point of signing. Hauptmann replied that Reliant had serious reservations about committing the company to a five-year contract extension. He cited the rapid fluctuations in the demand, pricing structure, and competition of Reliant's various product lines, particularly in the construction industry, as well as what appeared to be a changing perspective in the overall supply of VCM. Quite frankly, Hauptmann said, Reliant didn't want to be caught in a long-term commitment to Pacific if the market price of VCM was likely to drop in the foreseeable future. As a result, Reliant wanted to make a commitment for only a two-year contract renewal.

Gaudin tried to give Hauptmann a number of assurances about the continued integrity of the market. He also said that if changing market prices were a concern for Reliant, Pacific Oil would be happy to attempt to make adjustments in other parts of the contract to ensure protection against dramatic changes in either the market price or the demand for Reliant's product lines. But Hauptmann was adamant. Gaudin said he would have to talk to Fontaine and others in Paris before he could agree to only a two-year contract.

The two men talked several times on the telephone over the next two months and met once in Paris to discuss contract length. On August 17, in a quick 45-minute meeting in Orly Airport, Gaudin and Hauptmann agreed to a three-year contract renewal. They also agreed to meet in early September to discuss remaining contract issues.

September 10

Hauptmann met Gaudin and Fontaine in Pacific's Paris office. Hauptmann stressed that he and Zinnser were very pleased by the formula price and three-year contract duration that had been agreed to thus far. Fontaine echoed a similar satisfaction on behalf of Pacific and stated that they expected a long and productive relationship with Reliant. Fontaine stressed, however, that Pacific felt it was most important to them to complete the contract negotiations as quickly as possible, in order to adequately plan for product and market development in the future. Hauptmann agreed, saying that this was in Reliant's best interest as well. He felt that there were only a few minor issues that remained to be discussed before the contract could be signed.

Fontaine inquired as to what those issues were. Hauptmann said that the most important one to Reliant was the minimum quantity requirements, stipulating the minimum amount that Reliant had to purchase each year. Gaudin said that based on the projections for the growth of the PVC and fabricated PVC products over the next few years, and patterns established by past contracts, it was Pacific's assumption that Reliant would want to increase their quantity commitments by a minimum of 10 percent each year. Based on minimums stipulated in the current contract, Gaudin expected that Reliant would want to purchase at least 220 million pounds in year 1, 240 million pounds in year 2, and 265 million pounds in year 3. Hauptmann responded that Reliant's projections were very different. The same kind of uncertainty that had led to Reliant's concern about the term of the contract also contributed to a caution about significantly overextending themselves on a minimum quantity commitment. In fact, Reliant's own predictions were that they were likely to take less than the minimum in the current year (*underlifting,* in the parlance of the industry) and that, if they did so, they would incur almost a $1 million debt to Pacific. Conservative projections for the following year (1987) projected a similar deficit, but Reliant hoped that business would pick up and that the minimum quantities would be lifted. As a result, Hauptmann and Zinnser felt that it would be in Reliant's best interest to freeze minimum quantity requirements for the next two years—at 200 million pounds—and increase the minimum to 210 million pounds for the third year. Of course, Reliant *expected* that, most likely, they would be continuing to purchase much more than the specified minimums. But given the uncertainty of the future, Reliant did not want to get caught if the economy and the market truly turned sour.

Fontaine and Gaudin were astonished at the conservative projections Hauptmann was making. They tried in numerous ways to convince Hauptmann that his minimums were ridiculously low and that the PVC products were bound to prosper far more than Hauptmann seemed willing to admit. But Hauptmann was adamant and left Paris saying he needed to consult Zinnser and others in Brussels and the States before he could revise his minimum quantity estimates upward. Due to the pressure of other activities and vacation schedules, Gaudin and Hauptmann did not talk again until late October. Finally, on November 19, the two men agreed to a minimum quantity purchase schedule of 205 million pounds in the first year of the contract, 210 million pounds in the second year, and 220 million pounds in the third year. Moreover, Pacific agreed to waive any previous underlifting charges that might be incurred under the current contract when the new contract was signed.

October 24

Jean Fontaine returned to Paris from meetings in New York and a major market development meeting held by senior Pacific executives at Hilton Head. After a number of delays due to conflicting market research and changes in senior management, as well as the general uncertainty in the petroleum and chemical markets, Pacific had decided not to develop its own product lines for either PVC or fabricated products. The decision was largely based on the conclusion—more gut feel than hard fact—that entry into these new markets was unwise at a time when much greater problems faced Pacific and the petro-chemicals industry in general. Fontaine had argued strenuously that the VCM market was rapidly going soft, and that failure to create its own product lines would leave Pacific Oil in an extremely poor position to market one of its basic products. Fontaine was told that his position was appreciated but that he and other chemical marketing people would simply have to develop new markets and customers for the product. Privately, Fontaine churned on the fact that it had taken senior executives almost a year to make the decision, while valuable time was being lost in developing the markets; but he wisely decided to bite his tongue and vent his frustration on 36 holes of golf. On the return flight to Paris, he read about Pacific's decision in the October 23 issue of *The Wall Street Journal* and ordered a double martini to soothe his nerves.

December 14

Fontaine and Gaudin went to Brussels to meet with Hauptmann and Zinnser. The Pacific executives stressed that it was of the utmost importance for Pacific Oil to try to wrap up the contract as quickly as possible—almost a year had passed in deliberations, and although Pacific was not trying to place the "blame" on anyone, it was most concerned that the negotiations be settled as soon as possible.

Zinnser emphasized that he, too, was concerned about completing the negotiations quickly. Both he and Hauptmann were extremely pleased by the agreements that had been reached so far and felt that there was no question that a final contract signing was imminent. The major issues of price, minimum quantities, and contract duration had been solved. In their minds, what remained were only a few minor technical items in contract language. Some minor discussion of each of these should wrap things up in a few weeks.

Fontaine asked what the issues were. Zinnser began by stating that Reliant had become concerned by the way that the delivery pipeline was being metered. As currently set up, the pipeline fed from Pacific's production facility in Antwerp, Belgium, to Reliant's refinery. Pacific had built the line and was in charge of maintaining it. Meters had been installed at the exit flange of the pipeline, and Reliant was paying the metered amount to Pacific. Zinnser said that some spot-checking by Reliant at the manufacturing facility seemed to indicate that they may not be receiving all they were being billed for. They were not questioning the integrity of the meters or the meter readers, but felt that since the pipe was a number of years old, it may have developed leaks. Zinnser felt that it was inappropriate for Reliant to absorb the cost of VCM that was not reaching its facility. They therefore proposed that Pacific install meters directly outside of the entry flange of Reliant's manufacturing facility and that Reliant only be required to pay the meter directly outside the plant.

Fontaine was astonished. In the first place, he said, this was the first time he had heard any complaint about the pipeline or the need to recalibrate the meters. Second, if the pipeline was leaking, Pacific would want to repair it, but it would be impossible to do so until spring. Finally, while the meters themselves were not prohibitively expensive, moving them would mean some interruption of service and definitely be costly to Pacific. Fontaine said he wanted to check with the maintenance personnel at Antwerp to find out whether they could corroborate such leaks.

Fontaine was unable to contact the operating manager at Antwerp or anyone else who could confirm that leaks may have been detected. Routine inspection of the pipeline had been subcontracted to a firm that had sophisticated equipment for monitoring such things, and executives of the firm could not be reached for several days. Fontaine tried to raise other contract issues with Zinnser, but Zinnser said that this was his most important concern, and this issue needed to be resolved before the others could be finalized. Fontaine agreed to find out more about the situation and to bring the information to the next meeting. With the Christmas and New Year holidays approaching, the four men could not schedule another meeting until January 9.

January Meetings

The January 9 meeting was postponed until January 20, due to the death of Hauptmann's mother. The meeting was rescheduled for a time when Hauptmann needed to be in Geneva, and Gaudin agreed to meet him there.

Gaudin stated that the investigation of the pipeline had discovered no evidence of significant discharge. There were traces of *minor* leaks in the line, but they did not appear to be serious, and it was currently impossible to determine what percentage of the product may be escaping. The most generous estimate given to Gaudin had been 0.1 percent of the daily consumption. Hauptmann stated that their own spot monitoring showed it was considerably more and that Reliant would feel infinitely more comfortable if the new metering system could be installed.

Gaudin had obtained estimates for the cost of remetering before he left Paris. It was estimated that the new meters could be installed for approximately $20,000.

Tracing and fixing the leaks (if they existed) could not be done until April or May and might run as much as $50,000 if leaks turned out to be located at some extremely difficult access points. After four hours of debating with Hauptmann in a small conference room off the lobby of the Geneva Hilton, Gaudin agreed that Pacific would remeter the pipeline.

Hauptmann said that as far as he was concerned, all of his issues had been settled; however, he thought Zinnser might have one or two other issues to raise. Hauptmann said that he would report back to Zinnser and contact Gaudin as soon as possible if another meeting was necessary. Gaudin, believing that Pacific was finally beginning to see the light at the end of the tunnel, left for Paris.

January 23

Hauptmann called Gaudin and said that he and Zinnser had thoroughly reviewed the contract and that there were a few small issues of contract language which Zinnser wanted to clarify. He said that he would prefer not to discuss them over the telephone and suggested that since he was going to be in Paris on February 3, they meet at the Pacific offices. Gaudin agreed.

Fontaine and Gaudin met Hauptmann on February 3. Hauptmann informed them that he felt Reliant had been an outstanding customer for Pacific in the past and that it probably was one of Pacific's biggest customers for VCM. Fontaine and Gaudin agreed, affirming the important role that Reliant was playing in Pacific's VCM market. Hauptmann said that he and Zinnser had been reviewing the contract and were concerned that the changing nature of the VCM market might significantly affect Reliant's overall position in the marketplace as a purchaser. More specifically, Reliant was concerned that the decline in market and price for VCM in the future might endanger its own position in the market, since Pacific might sign contracts with other purchasers for lower formula prices than were currently being awarded to Reliant. Since Reliant was such an outstanding customer of Pacific—and Fontaine and Gaudin had agreed to that—it seemed to Reliant that Pacific Oil had an obligation to write two additional clauses into the contract that would protect Reliant in the event of further slippage in the VCM market. The first was a "favored nations" clause, stipulating that if Pacific negotiated with another purchaser a more favorable price for VCM than Reliant was receiving now, Pacific would guarantee that Reliant would receive that price as well. The second was a "meet competition" clause, guaranteeing that Pacific would willingly meet any lower price on VCM offered by a competitor, in order to maintain the Reliant relationship. Hauptmann argued that the "favored nations" clause was protection for Reliant, since it stipulated that Pacific valued the relationship enough to offer the best possible terms to Reliant. The "meet competition" clause, he argued, was clearly advantageous for Pacific since it ensured that Reliant would have no incentive to shift suppliers as the market changed.

Fontaine and Gaudin debated the terms at length with Hauptmann, stressing the potential costliness of these agreements for Pacific. Hauptmann responded by referring to the costliness that the absence of the terms could have for Reliant and suggesting that perhaps the Pacific people were truly *not* as interested in a successful long-term relationship as they had been advocating. Fontaine said that he needed to get clearance from senior management in New York before he could agree to these terms and that he would get back to Hauptmann within a few days when the information was available.

Frank Kelsey's View

Frank Kelsey was strategic planning manager, a staff role in the New York offices of the Pacific Oil Corporation. Kelsey had performed a number of roles for the company in his 12 years of work experience. Using the chemistry background he had achieved in college, Kelsey worked for six years in the research and development department of Pacific's Chemical Division before deciding to enter the management ranks. He transferred to the marketing area, spent three years in chemical marketing, and then assumed responsibilities in marketing planning and development. He moved to the strategic planning department four years ago.

In late 1985, Kelsey was working in a staff capacity as an adviser to the executive product vice president of Pacific Oil Company. Pacific had developed a matrix organization. Reporting relationships were determined by business areas and by regional operating divisions within Pacific Oil. Warren Meredith, the executive vice president, had responsibility for monitoring the worldwide sale and distribution of VCM. Jean Fontaine reported to Meredith on all issues regarding the overall sale and marketing of VCM and reported to the president of Pacific Oil in Europe, Stan Saunders, on major issues regarding the management of the regional chemicals business in Europe. In general, Fontaine's primary working relationship was with Meredith; Saunders became involved in day-to-day decisions only as an arbiter of disputes or interpreter of major policy decisions.

As the negotiations with Reliant evolved, Meredith became distressed by the apparent turn that they were taking. He called in Frank Kelsey to review the situation. Kelsey knew that the VCM marketing effort for Pacific was going to face significant problems. Moreover, his dominant experience with Pacific in recent years had been in the purchasing and marketing operations, and he knew how difficult it would be for the company to maintain a strong negotiation in VCM contracts.

Meredith asked Kelsey to meet with Fontaine and Gaudin in Paris and review the current status of negotiations on the Reliant contract. While Kelsey could act only in an advisory capacity—Fontaine and Gaudin were free to accept or reject any advice that was offered, since they were the ones who had to live with the contract—Meredith told Kelsey to offer whatever services the men would accept.

Kelsey flew to Paris shortly after New Year's Day 1986. He met with Fontaine and Gaudin, and they reviewed in detail what had happened in the Reliant contract negotiations over the past year. Kelsey listened, asked a lot of questions, and didn't say much. He felt that offering advice to the men was premature and perhaps even unwise; Fontaine and Gaudin seemed very anxious about the negotiations and felt that the new contract would be sealed within a month. Moreover, they seemed to resent Kelsey's visit and clearly didn't want to share more than the minimum amount of information. Kelsey returned to New York and briefed Meredith on the state of affairs.

When Fontaine called Meredith for clearance to give Reliant both "favored nations" and "meet competition" clauses in the new contract, Meredith immediately called Kelsey. The two of them went back through the history of events in the negotiation and realized the major advantages that Reliant had gained by its negotiation tactics.

Meredith called Fontaine back and advised against granting the clauses in the contract. Fontaine said that Hauptmann was adamant and that he was afraid the entire negotiation was going to collapse over a minor point in contract language. Meredith said he still thought it was a bad idea to make the concession. Fontaine said he thought he needed to consult Saunders, the European president of Pacific Oil, just to make sure.

Two days later, Saunders called Meredith and said that he had complete faith in Fontaine and Fontaine's ability to determine what was necessary to make a contract work. If Fontaine felt that "favored nations" and "meet competition" clauses were necessary, he trusted Fontaine's judgment that the clauses could not cause significant adverse harm to Pacific Oil over the next few years. As a result, he had given Fontaine the go-ahead to agree to these clauses in the new contract.

March 11

It was a dark and stormy night, March 11, 1986. Frank Kelsey was about to go to bed when the telephone rang. It was Jean Fontaine. Kelsey had not heard from Fontaine since their meeting in Paris. Meredith had told Kelsey about the discussion with Saunders, and he had assumed that Fontaine had gone ahead and conceded on the two contract clauses that had been discussed. He thought the contract was about to be wrapped up, but he hadn't heard for sure.

The violent rainstorm outside disrupted the telephone transmission, and Kelsey had trouble hearing Fontaine. Fontaine said that he had appreciated Kelsey's visit in January. Fontaine was calling to ask Kelsey's advice. They had just come from a meeting with Hauptmann. Hauptmann and Zinnser had reported that recent news from Reliant's corporate headquarters in Chicago projected significant downturns in the sale of a number of Reliant's PVC products in the European market. While Reliant thought it could ride out the downturn, they were very concerned about their future obligations under the Pacific contract. Since Reliant and Pacific had already settled on minimum quantity amounts, Reliant wanted the contractual right to resell the product if it could not use the minimum amount.

Kelsey tried to control his emotions as he thought about this negative turn of events in the Reliant negotiations. He strongly advised against agreeing to the clause, saying that it could put Pacific in an extremely poor position. Fontaine debated the point, saying he really thought Reliant might default on the whole contract if they didn't get resale rights. "I can't see where agreeing to the right to resale is a big thing, Frank, particularly given the size of this contract and its value to me and Pacific."

KELSEY: Look, you asked for my advice, and I gave it to you. If I were you, I wouldn't make any more concessions. Agreeing to a resale clause could create a whole lot of unforeseen problems. At this point I think it's also the principle of the thing!

FONTAINE: Who cares about principles at a time like this! It's my neck that's on the line if this Reliant contract goes under! I'll have over 200 million pounds of VCM a year to eat in an oversupplied market! It's my neck that's on the line, not yours! How in the world can you talk to me about "principle" at this point?

KELSEY: Calm down, Jean! I can see your point of view! I appreciate the pressures on you, but I really don't like the looks of it from this end. Keep in touch—let me ask others down at the office what they think, and I'll call you next week.

Kelsey hung up the telephone, and stared out of the windows at the rain. He could certainly empathize with Fontaine's position—the man's neck was on the block. As he mentally reviewed the two-year history of the Reliant negotiations, Kelsey wondered how they had gotten to this point and whether anyone could have done things differently. He also wondered what to do about the resale clause, which appeared to be the final sticking point in the deliberations. Would acquiescing to a resale clause for Reliant be a problem to Pacific Oil? Kelsey knew he had to take action soon.

APPENDIX Petrochemical Supply Contracts: A Technical Note

Supply contracts between chemical manufacturing/refining companies and purchasing companies are fairly standard in the industry trade. They are negotiated between supplier and purchaser in order to protect both parties against major fluctuations in supply and demand. Any purchaser wishing to obtain a limited amount of a particular product could always approach any one of a number of chemical manufacturing firms and obtain the product at *market price*. The market price is controlled by the competitive supply and demand for the particular product on any given day. But purchasers want to be assured of a long-term supply and do not want to be subject to the vagaries of price fluctuation; similarly, manufacturers want to be assured of product outlets in order to adequately plan manufacturing schedules. Long-term contracts protect both parties against these fluctuations.

A supply contract is usually a relatively standard document, often condensed to one page. The major *negotiable* elements of the contract, on the *front side* of the document, include the price, quantity, product quality, contract duration, delivery point, and credit terms (see Exhibit 1A for a sample blank contract). The remainder (*back side*) of the contract is filled with traditionally fixed legal terminology that governs the conditions under which the contract will be maintained. While the items are seldom changed, they may be altered or waived as part of the negotiated agreement.

The primary component of a long-term contract is the price. In the early years of the petrochemical industry, the raw product was metered by the supplier (either in liquid or gaseous form) and sold to the purchaser. As the industry became more competitive, as prices rose rapidly, and as the products developed from petrochemical supplies (called *feedstocks*) became more sophisticated, pricing became a significantly more complex

EXHIBIT 1A | Agreement of Sale

This Agreement, entered into this _____ day of _____, _____, between *Pacific Oil Company,* hereinafter called Seller, and _____, hereinafter called Buyer.

WITNESSETH:

Seller agrees to sell and deliver and Buyer agrees to purchase and receive commodity (hereinafter called "product") under the terms and conditions set forth below.

1. Product:
2. Quality:
3. Quantity:
4. Period:
5. Price:
6. Payment Terms:
    a. Net _____.
    b. All payments shall be made in United States dollars without discount or deduction, unless otherwise noted, by wire transfer at Seller's option, to a bank account designated by Seller. Invoices not paid on due date will be subject to a delinquency finance charge of 1% per month.
    c. If at any time the financial responsibility of Buyer shall become impaired or unsatisfactory to Seller, cash payment on delivery or satisfactory security may be required. A failure to pay any amount may, at the option of the Seller, terminate this contract as to further deliveries. No forbearance, course of dealing, or prior payment shall affect this right of Seller.
7. Price Change:

    The price specified in this Agreement may be changed by Seller on the first day of any calendar _____ by written notice sent to the Buyer not less than thirty (30) days prior to the effective date of change. Buyer gives Seller written notice of objection to such change at least ten (10) days prior to the effective date of change. Buyer's failure to serve Seller with written notice of objection thereto prior to the effective date thereof shall be considered acceptance of such change. If Buyer gives such notice of objection and Buyer and Seller fail to agree on such change prior to the effective date thereof, this Agreement and the obligations of Seller and Buyer hereunder shall terminate with respect to the unshipped portion of the Product governed by it. Seller has the option immediately to cancel this contract upon written notice to Buyer, to continue to sell hereunder at the same price and terms which were in effect at the time Seller gave notice of change, or to suspend performance under this contract while pricing is being resolved. If Seller desires to revise the price, freight allowance, or terms of payment pursuant to this agreement, but is restricted to any extent against doing so by reason of any law, governmental decree, order, or regulation, or if the price, freight allowance, or terms of payment then in effect under this contract are nullified or reduced by reason of any law, governmental decree, order, or regulation, Seller shall have the right to cancel this contract upon fifteen (15) days' written notice to purchaser.

8. Measurements:

    Seller's determinations, unless proven to be erroneous, shall be accepted as conclusive evidence of the quantity of Product delivered hereunder. Credit will not be allowed for shortages of 1/2 of 1% or less of the quantity and overages of 1/2 of 1% or less of the quantity will be waived. The total amount of shortages or overages will be credited or billed when quantities are greater and such differences are substantiated. Measurements of weight and volume shall be according to procedures and criteria standard for such determinations.

(continued)

EXHIBIT 1A | (*continued*)

9. Shipments and Delivery:

Buyer shall give Seller annual or quarterly forecasts of its expected requirements as Seller may from time to time request. Buyer shall give Seller reasonably advanced notice for each shipment which shall include date of delivery and shipping instructions. Buyer shall agree to take deliveries in approximately equal monthly quantities, except as may be otherwise provided herein. In the event that Buyer fails to take the quantity specified or the pro rata quantity in any month, Seller may, at its option, in addition to other rights and remedies, cancel such shipments or parts thereof.

10. Purchase Requirements:

a. If during any consecutive three-month period, Buyer for any reason (but not for reasons of force majeure as set forth in Section 12) takes less than 90 percent of the average monthly quantity specified, or the prorated minimum monthly quantity then applicable to such period under Section 12, Seller may elect to charge Buyer a penalty charge for failure to take the average monthly quantity or prorated minimum monthly quantity.

b. If, during any consecutive three-month period, Buyer, for any reason (but not, however, for reasons of force majeure as set forth in Section 12) takes Product in quantities less than that equal to at least one-half of the average monthly quantity specified, or the prorated minimum monthly quantity originally applicable to such period under Section 12, Seller may elect to terminate this agreement.

c. It is the Seller's intent not to unreasonably exercise its rights under (*a*) or (*b*) in the event of adverse economic and business conditions in general.

d. Notice of election by Seller under (*a*) or (*b*) shall be given within 30 days after the end of the applicable three-month period, and the effective date of termination shall be 30 days after the date of said notice.

11. Detention Policy:

Seller may, from time to time, specify free unloading time allowances for its transportation equipment. Buyer shall be liable to the Transportation Company for all demurrage charges made by the Transportation Company, for railcars, trucks, tanks, or barges held by Buyer beyond the free unloading time.

12. Force Majeure:

Neither party shall be liable to the other for failure or delay in performance hereunder to the extent that such failure or delay is due to war, fire, flood, strike, lockout, or other labor trouble, accident, breakdown of equipment or machinery, riot, act, request, or suggestion of governmental authority, act of God, or other contingencies beyond the control of the affected party which interfere with the production or transportation of the material covered by this Agreement or with the supply of any raw material (whether or not the source of supply was in existence or contemplated at the time of this Agreement) or energy source used in connection therewith, or interfere with Buyer's consumption of such material, provided that in no event shall Buyer be relieved of the obligation to pay in full for material delivered hereunder. Without limitation on the foregoing, neither party shall be required to remove any cause listed above or replace the affected source of supply or facility if it shall involve additional expense or departure from its normal practices. If any of the events specified in this paragraph shall have occurred, Seller shall have the right to allocate in a fair and reasonable manner among its customers and Seller's own requirements any supplies of material Seller has available for delivery at the time or for the duration of the event.

13. Materials and Energy Supply:

(*continued*)

EXHIBIT 1A | *(concluded)*

If, for any reasons beyond reasonable commercial control, Seller's supply of product to be delivered hereunder shall be limited due to continued availability of necessary raw materials and energy supplies, Seller shall have the right (without liability) to allocate to the Buyer a portion of such product on such basis as Seller deems equitable. Such allocation shall normally be that percentage of Seller's total internal and external commitments which are committed to Buyer as related to the total quantity from Seller's manufacturing facilities.

14. Disclaimer:

Seller makes no warranty, express or implied, concerning the product furnished hereunder other than it shall be of the quality and specification stated herein. Any implied warranty of FITNESS is expressly excluded and to the extent that it is contrary to the foregoing sentence; any implied warranty of MERCHANTABILITY is expressly excluded. Any recommendation made by Seller makes no warranty of results to be obtained. Buyer assumes all responsibility and liability for loss or damage resulting from the handling or use of said product. In no event shall Seller be liable for any special, indirect or consequential damages, irrespective of whether caused or allegedly caused by negligence.

15. Taxes:

Any tax, excise fee, or other charge or increase thereof upon the production, storage, withdrawal, sale, or transportation of the product sold hereunder, or entering into the cost of such product, imposed by any proper authority becoming effective after the date hereof, shall be added to the price herein provided and shall be paid by the Buyer.

16. Assignment and Resale:

This contract is not transferable or assignable by Buyer without the written consent of Seller. The product described hereunder, in the form and manner provided by the Seller, may not be assigned or resold without prior written consent of the Seller.

17. Acceptance:

Acceptance hereof must be without qualification, and Seller will not be bound by any different terms and conditions contained in any other communication.

18. Waiver of Breach:

No waiver by Seller or Buyer of any breach of any of the terms and conditions contained in this Agreement shall be construed as a waiver or any subsequent breach of the same or any other term or condition.

19. Termination:

If any provision of this agreement is or becomes violate of any law, or any rule, order, or regulation issued thereunder, Seller shall have the right, upon notice to Buyer, to terminate the Agreement in its entirety.

20. Governing Law:

The construction of this Agreement and the rights and obligations of the parties hereunder shall be governed by the laws of the State of _____.

21. Special Provisions:

BUYER: SELLER:

_____   _____
                (firm)   (firm)

By: _____   By: _____

Title: _____   Title: _____

Date: _____   Date: _____

process. Most contemporary contract prices are determined by an elaborate calculation called a *formula price,* composed of several elements:

1. *Feedstock characteristics:* Petrochemical feedstock supplies differ in the chemical composition and molecular structure of the crude oil. Differences in feedstocks will significantly affect the refining procedures and operating efficiency of the refinery that manufactures a product, as well as their relative usefulness to particular purchasers. While some chemical products may be drawn from a single feedstock, large-volume orders may necessitate the blending of several feedstocks with different structural characteristics.

2. *Fuel costs:* Fuel costs include the price and amount of energy that the manufacturing company must assume in cracking, refining, and producing a particular chemical stream.

3. *Labor costs:* Labor costs include the salaries of employees to operate the manufacturing facility for the purpose of producing a fixed unit amount of a particular product.

4. *Commodity costs:* Commodity costs include the value of the basic petrochemical base on the open marketplace. As the supply and demand for the basic commodity fluctuate on the open market, this factor is entered into the formula price.

A formula price may therefore be represented as a function of the following elements:

$$\text{Formula price} = \text{Feedstock cost} + \text{Energy cost} + \text{Labor cost} + \text{Commodity cost (per unit)}$$

If only one feedstock were used, the chemical composition of the feedstock would determine its basic cost and the energy, labor, and commodity costs of producing it. If several feedstocks were used, the formula price would be a composite of separate calculations for each particular feedstock, or a weighted average of the feedstock components, multiplied by the cost of production of each one.

Each of the elements in the formula price is also multiplied by a weighting factor (coefficient) that specifies how much each cost will contribute to the determination of the overall formula price. The supplier generally sets a *ceiling price,* guaranteeing that the formula price will not exceed this amount. Below the ceiling price, however, the supplier endeavors to maximize profits while clearly specifying the costs of production to the purchaser, while the purchaser attempts to obtain the most favorable formula price for himself. Since basic cost data and cost fluctuations are well known, negotiations typically focus on the magnitude of the coefficients that are applied to each element in the formula. Hence the actual formula computation may be represented as follows:

$$\begin{aligned}\text{Formula price} = &\ (\text{Weighting coefficient} \times \text{Feedstock cost}) \\ &+ (\text{Weighting coefficient} \times \text{Energy cost}) \\ &+ (\text{Weighting coefficient} \times \text{Labor cost}) \\ &+ (\text{Weighting coefficient} \times \text{Commodity cost})\end{aligned}$$

A fairly typical ratio of the weighting coefficients in this formula would be 70 percent (0.7) for feedstock cost, 20 percent (0.2) for energy costs, 5 percent (0.05) for labor costs, and 5 percent (0.05) for commodity costs. Multiple feedstocks supplied in a particular contract would be composed of a different set of costs and weighting elements for each feedstock in the supply.

The computation of a formula price, as opposed to the determination of a market price, has a number of advantages and disadvantages. Clearly, it enables the supplier to pass costs along to the purchaser, which minimizes the risk for both parties in the event of rapid changes in cost during the duration of the contract. The purchaser can project directly how cost changes will affect his supply costs; the supplier is protected by being able to pass cost increases along to the purchaser. However, when the market demand for the product is very high, the formula price constrains the seller in the ceiling price he can charge, hence curtailing potential profit for the product compared to its value on the open marketplace. Conversely, when market demand is very low, the contract may guarantee a large market to the supplier, but at a price for the product that could be unprofitable compared to production costs.

Quantity

Formula prices are typically computed with major attention given to quantity. Costs will fluctuate considerably based on the efficiency with which the production plant is operated, number of labor shifts required, and so on. Hence, in order to adequately forecast demand, attain particular economies of scale in the manufacturing process, and plan production schedules, suppliers must be able to determine the quantities that a particular customer will want to acquire. (Because of the volumes involved, no significant inventory is produced.) Quantities will be specified in common units of weight (pounds, tons, etc.) or volume (gallons, etc.).

Quantity specifications are typically treated as minimum purchase amounts. If a purchaser desires significantly more than the minimum amount (*overlifting*) in a given time period (e.g., a year), the amount would be sold contingent on availability and delivered at the formula price. Conceivably, *discount* prices or adjustments in the formula price could be negotiated for significant purchases over minimum quantity. Conversely, underpurchase of the minimum amount (*underlifting*) by a significant degree typically results in penalty costs to the purchaser. These are typically referred to as *liquidated damages* in the industry and may be negotiated at rates anywhere from a token fine of several thousand dollars to as much as 30 percent of the formula price for each unit underlifted. Faced with the possibility of underlifting (due to market or product demand changes that require less raw material in a given time period), purchasers typically handle underlifting in one of several ways:

1. Pay the underlifting charges (liquidated damages) to the supplier, either as stated or according to some renegotiated rate.

2. Not pay the liquidated damages, under the assumption that the supplier will not want to press legal charges against the purchaser at the expense of endangering the entire supply contract.

3. Resell the commodity to another purchaser who may be in need of supply, perhaps at a discounted price. Such action by the purchaser could cause major

instability in the market price and in supply contracts held at the original manufacturer or other manufacturers. For this reason, sellers typically preclude the right of the purchaser to resell the product as part of the standard contract language.

Quality

The quality of the product is related to the particular feedstock from which it is drawn, as well as the type and degree of refining that is employed by the supplier. Standard descriptions for gradations of quality are common parlance for each major chemical product.

Delivery

Most contracts specify the method of delivery, point of delivery, and way that the quantity amounts will be measured as the product is delivered. Gases are typically metered and delivered by direct pipeline from the manufacturer to the purchaser; liquids and liquefied gases may be sold by pipeline or shipped via tank truck, railroad tank car, tank barges, and tank ships.

Contract Duration

Most typical supply contracts extend for a period from one to five years; significantly longer or shorter ones would probably only be negotiated under extreme circumstances. Negotiations for contract renewal are typically begun several months prior to contract expiration.

Payment Terms

Payment terms are determined by the credit ratings and cash flow demands of both parties. Typical contracts specify payment within 30 days of delivery, although this time period may be shortened to payment on delivery or lengthened to a period of three months between delivery and payment.

Contract Language

As can be determined from Exhibit 1A, there are a number of elements in the contract that delineate the conditions under which the parties agree to bind themselves to the contract, or to deviate from it. Terminology and agreements are typically standard unless altered by negotiation prior to contract signing. These elements include the following:

1. *Measurements:* A mechanism for specifying how quantity amounts will be determined and how disputes over differences in delivered quantity will be resolved.

2. *Meet competition:* The seller agrees to meet competitive market prices for the product if they become substantially lower than the current negotiated formula price.

3. *Favored nations:* The supplier agrees that if he offers a better price on the product to any of the purchaser's competitors, he will offer the same price to this buyer.

4. *Purchase requirements:* The purchase requirements govern the conditions and terms under which liquidated damages may be invoked.

5. *Force majeure:* The force majeure clause exempts the parties from contract default in the event of major natural disasters, strikes, fires, explosions, or other events that could preclude the seller's ability to deliver the product or the buyer's ability to purchase.

6. *Disclaimers:* The disclaimers protect both buyer and seller against unreasonable claims about the product or its quality.

7. *Assignability:* The assignability clause limits the right of either party to assign the contract to another purchaser or supplier if they so desire.

8. *Notifications:* The notifications section specifies the lead time during which one or both parties must notify the other party of any change in the contract or its renewal.

9. *Other clauses:* Other clauses include conditions under which the product may be assured delivery, application of taxes, provisions for resale, definitions of contract breach and termination, the legal framework used to enforce the contract (in the event of cross-state or cross-national agreements), and methods of notification of one party to the other.

Contract Management and Maintenance

While a supply contract is a legally binding document that attempts to articulate the way two companies will work together, it more commonly stands as the cornerstone of a complex long-term social relationship between buyer and seller. This relationship requires constant monitoring, evaluation, and discussion by representatives of both organizations. Thus, while similar supply contracts may exist between a particular manufacturer and three different buyers, there may be major differences in the day-to-day interactions and quality of relationships between the manufacturer and each buyer. Experienced sales representatives have defined a good seller–buyer relationship as meeting the following criteria:

- *The purchaser can be counted on to live up to the terms and conditions of the contract as negotiated.* The purchaser accepts a fair formula price in price negotiations and does not attempt to push the supplier into an artificially low price. The purchaser lifts as much of the product per time period as he agreed to lift under the contract. The purchaser is trustworthy and follows a course of action based on sound business ethics.

- *The purchaser does not attempt to take advantage of fluctuations or aberrations in the spot market price to gain advantage.* He accepts the fact that a formula price has been negotiated and that both parties agree to live up to this price for the duration of the contract. He does not seek contract price changes as the market price may drop for some time period.

- *When there is a mutual problem between seller and purchaser, it can be openly discussed and resolved between the two parties.* Problems resulting from the continued inability of the supplier to provide the product, and/or the continued inability of the buyer to consume the product, can be openly addressed and resolved. Problems in the quality of the product, labor difficulties resulting in problems in manufacturing, loading, shipping, unloading, cleanliness of the shipping equipment, and so on can be promptly explored and resolved to mutual satisfaction. Finally, changes in the business projections of one or both parties can be shared, so that difficulties anticipated by the supplier in providing all of the product, or difficulties anticipated by the purchaser in consuming all of the product, can lead to amicable and satisfactory resolutions for both parties. Ability to resolve these problems requires mutual trust, honesty, open lines of communication, and an approach to problem solving that seeks the best solution for both sides.

Case 3

A Power Play for Howard
Bill Brubaker
Mark Asher

Nothing less than the future of the Washington Bullets hung in the balance on the evening of July 11 when Juwan Howard, the club's all-star free agent forward, arrived at agent David Falk's headquarters in Chevy Chase Pavilion to solicit $100 million contract offers from National Basketball Association team executives.

Outside, on Wisconsin Avenue NW, the Bullets held a We-Love-Juwan rally for rabid fans desperate to keep their young star in Washington—a city that hasn't had a winning NBA team in nine years. Inside, in Falk's private office—adorned with Michael Jordan–autographed basketballs and other client memorabilia—Howard braced himself for a long night of high-stakes negotiating.

Bullets General Manager Wes Unseld got first crack at Howard—a courtesy Falk said he was extending to the club as "the incumbents." It soon became clear, however, that incumbency, like loyalty, had limited value in professional sports. Shortly after 7 p.m. Unseld offered a seven-year, $78.4 million contract. Lucrative as it was—the offer amounted to more than $136,000 per game through the 2002–2003 season—Howard considered the proposal far below his market value. He loved playing and living in Washington, and the thought of leaving brought tears to his eyes even as he dismissed Unseld's offer.

Yet leave he would. By dawn, Howard had begun seriously contemplating a move south to play for the Miami Heat, which ultimately trumped the Bullets with a seven-year, guaranteed $100.8 million deal—the biggest in the history of team sports, garnished with luxury hotel suites and limousine service for the 23-year-old Howard during road trips. The Bullets' most promising player in a generation was gone, and with him hopes of resuscitating the club's fortunes.

But Howard's tears would prove premature and the Heat's huge offer only the opening gambit in one of the most intricate and controversial episodes in recent sports history. Over the next 30 days, Howard would sign with Miami only to have the contract invalidated by the league, triggering a bitter sequence of threats, legal maneuvers, and shifting alliances. The final outcome would prove a colossal windfall for the Bullets: When Washington opens its 1996–97 season Friday in Orlando, Juwan Howard will be wearing his familiar No. 5 on a red, white, and blue Bullets uniform.

This turbulent saga—recounted here following extensive interviews with Howard, agents, league officials, union representatives, and team executives—illuminates the extent to which pro sports have become a tangle of emotion and fiscal logic, on-court talent and off-court financial calculation.

The unprecedented case also featured an unusual collaboration between two traditional adversaries, the NBA and the players' union, the National Basketball Players

Association. It featured the repudiation, first by the league and then by Howard, of one of basketball's most charismatic, cunning, and successful coaches, Pat Riley, who is also the Heat's president. By taking strong and decisive action against Riley and Heat owner Micky Arison, the NBA may have brought Washington's franchise back from the dead—a critical development for a club that will change its name to the Wizards next year and move into a new, 20,600-seat downtown arena, the MCI Center.

During a summer in which free agent bidding took the never-never land of NBA salaries to new heights, Howard's odyssey ultimately became the story of a favorite son who briefly sought his fortune elsewhere but ended up returning to the fold—perhaps wiser and certainly much, much richer. Buoyed with a nine-figure contract from the Bullets, Howard celebrated by buying a $230,000 Ferrari sports car and a luxury suite at MCI Center and by contemplating his dream house: a Washington-area mansion with eight bedrooms, indoor and outdoor swimming pools, a bowling alley, theater, and basketball court. "I want elevators inside my house," Howard would explain. "That's always has been a dream of mine."

"This was about bucks," Unseld said in his office next to USAir Arena, a computer printout of NBA player salaries by his side. "No matter how you want to put it, I think that's eventually what it came down to."

A Sour Start

Howard's summer of 1996 "fiasco," as he has called it, had its roots in the summer of 1994 when the Bullets drafted the 6-foot-9-inch University of Michigan junior. Howard wanted a six-year, $24 million deal, considered the going rate for the fifth player chosen in that year's draft. By agreeing, the Bullets could have locked Howard into a long-term contract.

But during negotiations in the sunroom of Bullets owner Abe Pollin's house in Bethesda, John Nash, then the club's general manager, essentially told Howard he wasn't worth it. Nash (who resigned under pressure in April) later offered Howard an 11-year, $37.5 million deal with the option of becoming a free agent after his second season, in 1996. Howard considered the below-market offer "totally unfair," but he accepted it and soon established himself as a valuable NBA commodity, averaging 19.8 points, 8.3 rebounds, and 3.6 assists per game over the two seasons.

Howard's game was more than statistics, however. With a positive attitude and strong work ethic, he became a guiding light for less disciplined teammates. Off court, he donated time and money to charitable causes and community projects. Polite and soft-spoken, Howard was untouched by controversy until this May, when a Detroit woman filed a paternity suit alleging he is the father of her 4 1/2-year-old son. Howard has denied the allegation. A blood test taken by Howard indicated there is a greater than 99.99 percent probability he is the child's father, according to a lab report filed in court by the woman's attorneys.

Knowing that Howard would become a free agent this year, players from opposing teams playfully began recruiting him during games last season. "Grant Hill was recruiting me, telling me what Detroit had," Howard said in an interview earlier this month. "Alonzo [Mourning of the Heat] and Patrick [Ewing of the New York Knicks] were recruiting me at the All-Star Game. I just laughed, man. I just said, 'Yo, this seems like college recruiting all over again.' It felt good to feel wanted."

Howard insisted that he wanted to remain a Bullet. "He's theirs to lose," said agent Falk, 46, a George Washington University law school graduate whose client list at Falk Associates Management Enterprises (FAME) includes Jordan, Mourning, and Ewing. In a half-page ad in *The Washington Post,* Pollin promised Bullets fans, "We will do everything we can to keep Juwan with us in Washington. . . . We love Juwan Howard." Howard and his agents could not open negotiations with clubs until a new collective bargaining agreement (CBA) was signed this summer. In early July, with the moratorium still in effect, Falk deliberately sent the Bullets a signal by telling a *Washington Post* reporter he expected Howard would sign for $15 million to $20 million a year ($105 million to $140 million over seven years, the maximum term allowed under the new CBA).

One minute after the new labor agreement was finalized at 4:59 p.m. on July 11, the NBA's free agent marketplace officially opened. So began a competition that in tone and tension resembled a cross between a television game show and a Turkish bazaar. That evening, a parade of free agents and team officials converged on FAME's eighth-floor headquarters at Chevy Chase Pavilion. Offers for various players were scrutinized by Falk's 36-year-old partner and fellow lawyer, Curtis Polk, in what the agents called their "War Room"—an inner sanctum with a computer main-frame, three laptops, and six telephone lines. But most of the action would unfold in Falk's private office, watched over by a framed *Sports Illustrated* magazine cover featuring Falk and Jordan.

Between 5 and 7 p.m. Falk quickly negotiated a one-year, $30 million contract that would keep Jordan playing for the Chicago Bulls. Then he turned to Howard.

Unseld, a wide-bodied, 6-foot-7 Hall of Famer who led Washington to its only NBA title in 1978, immediately notified Howard, Falk, and Polk that he alone would represent the Bullets. Howard and his agents asked for assurances that the Bullets' coaching staff, headed by Jim Lyman, would be retained. Unseld said it would. Howard also asked how the Bullets intended to improve a team that hadn't made the NBA playoffs for eight years. Unseld disclosed that he was trying to acquire Rod Strickland, one of the NBA's top point guards.

Unseld, who had replaced Nash as the Bullets' general manager only two months earlier, then offered Howard a seven-year, $78.4 million contract. The proposal stirred little enthusiasm among Howard or his agents, and after Unseld left Falk's office, Polk said there was no chance Howard would play again in a Bullets uniform. The assessment, with its ring of cold finality and implication of abrupt change, was upsetting to Howard, who began to cry.

But the press of business beckoned. Between 8 and 10 p.m. the Detroit Pistons' top basketball executive, Rick Sund, discussed his interest in Howard, followed at 11 p.m. by Knicks General Manager Ernie Grunfeld, who had flown to Washington in the team's Gulfstream jet. Neither made a firm offer that evening.

At 2 a.m., Howard slipped off to take a nap. As he dozed, the Heat, represented by Riley, a club lawyer and two vice presidents, negotiated with Mourning, their prized, 6-foot-10, free agent center. Of 160 free agents on the market, the Heat rated Mourning and Howard third and fourth most desirable, respectively, after Jordan and the Orlando Magic's Shaquille O'Neal, who ended up with the Los Angeles Lakers.

Riley asked Mourning to sign a one-year contract at less than market value to help the Heat create more room under the salary cap. Mourning dismissed the proposal.

Riley said he then assured Mourning that after "taking care of some business" with other players, "I will make you the highest-paid player on the team."

At that moment, the seeds of controversy were planted.

Under the CBA, club officials are forbidden to make undisclosed agreements, promises, "representations, commitments, inducements . . . or understandings of any kind" with players. The prohibition aimed to prevent clubs from circumventing the rules of the league's salary cap, which limits spending on players to keep teams competitive with one another; in general terms, the cap restricts teams' payrolls to $24.3 million for the 1996–97 season. The CBA also requires teams to report immediately all player contracts—oral or written—to the league.

Riley would later contend, bitterly, that his pledge to Mourning was proper because it contained no specific dollar figures—an interpretation of the CBA supported by the players' union but disputed by the league.

Shortly before 3 a.m. Mourning left the room and Howard walked in. "All the guys were very tired," Riley recalled, "and it was very, very serious in there. We all knew we were going to be talking about a lot of money." Riley tried to lighten the mood by recalling how his brother had represented him in his first negotiation as an NBA player in 1967. "Before going into the room, my brother looked me in the eye and said, 'Just think, Pat! You're going to earn $17,000 a year!' " Riley told Howard and his agents.

The Heat's opening bid for Howard was $84 million over seven years. For several hours the two sides haggled. By the time the session broke up around 6 a.m. on Friday, July 12, Riley had increased his offer to $91 million plus $3.5 million in bonuses and some perks. The Heat executives shuffled off to breakfast, then to their hotel, the ANA, on M Street NW.

At noon, Howard returned to Falk's office to review the offers. The Bullets initially were eliminated from consideration; Howard had been impressed by Riley, who had won four NBA championships as the Lakers' coach. But Howard could not easily shrug off his feelings for the Washington club, and it was decided to give the team another chance, what Falk called "the court of appeals." Howard asked to meet Pollin at his house in Bethesda.

At 5 a.m. Howard, Falk, and Polk joined Pollin, Unseld, and club president Susan O'Malley in the sunroom where Howard had his first negotiation with the Bullets in 1994. Pollin announced to his guests that Unseld would make one last offer, and warned that the Bullets wouldn't exceed that "by a dime."

The Bullets executives left the room for a few minutes to confer. When they returned, Unseld increased his seven-year offer from $78.4 million to $84 million. "Wes and Susan said they had studied the numbers and . . . this is what they could afford," Falk said. "They had given Juwan an ultimatum." (Pollin declined to be interviewed for this article.)

The meeting broke up before 6 p.m. Back at FAME's offices Howard again cried as he considered the take-it-or-leave-it negotiation at Pollin's house, which echoed his first contract talks two years earlier. Regret gave way to irritation. "I couldn't believe this was happening again . . . despite that I gave 100 percent on and off the floor for the franchise," Howard said. "Abe Pollin had made that promise to the people that he would do anything it took—anything possible—to make sure Juwan Howard stays in Washington."

Howard told Falk and Polk that Miami was his top choice, but he wanted the Heat to up the ante. Within an hour Riley was back in Falk's office. The Heat now offered $95.2 million plus $6 million in bonuses, but Howard wanted more perks. Riley agreed to the hotel suites and limos, as well as an extra $5,000 to help Howard sponsor a summer basketball camp.

Still, Howard's agents pressed for more.

"You've got to stop this," an exasperated Riley finally demanded. "Every time I walk out of the room and come back in there is something else. Please. It's over with, OK? This is the final offer."

Riley left around 8:30 p.m. Falk and Howard phoned Unseld at his Baltimore home. Do the Bullets have any room to compromise? Howard wanted to know. For three hours, Unseld floated various suggestions for increasing the value of his offer, such as deferred payments. But Falk would have none of it.

"Can you do any more?" Howard finally asked.

Unseld was out of ideas. "No," he said.

"OK," Howard said, "I guess there's no more to talk about. Thank you for two great years. And good luck to you guys."

Howard hung up and turned to Falk. "Call Pat Riley," he told the agent.

Miami Bound

Around 1 a.m. on July 13, the phone again rang in Riley's room at the ANA Hotel. Howard was on the phone.

"Coach," he told Riley. "I'm coming to Miami."

Howard reviewed the Heat's offer, point by point, with an elated Riley. The final deal would amount to $100.8 million in cash, plus perks. "Then they began to ask for a little bit more," Riley later recalled. "Silly things. I said, 'You need [more game] tickets? OK, we'll give you a couple more tickets. But let's move on, OK?' "

In Falk's office, Howard exchanged champagne toasts with new teammate Mourning and FAME staffers. Falk declined to disclose FAME's cut for negotiating the Howard deal other than to say it was less than the maximum 4 percent agents can charge under the labor agreement.

Yet an apparently ironclad deal still seemed to have some wiggle room. Unseld talked to Falk by phone that afternoon.

"Is it a done deal?" the Bullets executive said he asked. Falk said no.

Later, Falk phoned Unseld again. "Falk gave me a figure and says, 'If you guys did this . . . ' " Unseld recalled. "And I thought that was strange because I thought it was finished with us."

Falk said later he never suggested Howard was open to new offers, and Unseld concedes he may have misinterpreted Falk's signals. Nevertheless, Unseld phoned Pollin at his Virginia farm, and the Bullets' owners agreed to increase the club's offer from $84 million to $94.5 million.

Unseld said he then phoned Falk only to have the new offer rejected. But Falk said he recalls no new bid on the afternoon of July 13, and he accused the Bullets of using "spin control . . . to make it look like they were really close" to signing Howard.

The next day, the Bullets renounced their rights to Howard—conditional on him having a valid contract with the Heat—in order to have room under the salary cap to sign free agent forward Tracy Murray. In the coming days the Bullets also would acquire free agent forward center Lorenzo Williams and, in a trade with the Portland Trail Blazers, point guard Strickland and forward Harvey Grant. But the club was being lambasted by Washington fans and media for losing Howard.

On July 17, Howard flew to Miami in a private jet to sign his new contract. At a news conference that evening, Howard called his new contract a "blessing" and his relationship with the Heat "like a marriage." The signing, he said, was the most important day of his life, after graduation day in Ann Arbor, Michigan, last year.

The Unraveling

Riley had little time to celebrate: NBA investigators were heading his way. In an interview on July 16 on ESPN, Mourning left the impression that he had an agreement with the Heat. Asked if his new deal was for "$100 million plus," Mourning said, "Yeah, it is."

If Mourning had such an agreement, the Heat had not notified the NBA as required. A new Mourning agreement would have dramatically shrunk the room Miami had under the salary cap to sign Howard. And that would jeopardize the validity of Howard's contract. Riley and Falk again insisted no deal had been finalized. (Mourning declined to be interviewed for this story.)

The NBA hired Robert Del Tufo—a former New Jersey attorney general who also had once prosecuted mobsters and Russian spies as a U.S. attorney—to determine if the Heat had circumvented salary cap rules. Had the team made an undisclosed deal with Mourning, possibly as early as last November, when the club obtained him in a trade with the Charlotte Hornets?

Del Tufo and two other lawyers flew to Miami to interview Heat executives on July 24. Riley insisted there were no undisclosed deals. But a week later, on July 31, the NBA's chief legal officer, Jeffrey Mishkin, phoned Arison, the Heat's owner, to tell him the NBA had disapproved Howard's contract because the club could not fit Howard's first-year base pay of $9 million under the salary cap. Mishkin told Arison the Heat had improperly made an undisclosed agreement with Mourning and used his previous, less lucrative contract to calculate the room the club had available to sign Howard. The team also had miscalculated the portion of incentive bonuses in two other free agent deals—for guard Tim Hardaway and forward P. J. Brown—that should have been counted against the cap, Mishkin asserted.

Under the CBA, a club can offer a player performance bonuses that are unlikely, in the club's estimation, to be achieved. "Unlikely" bonuses ultimately are not charged against the cap. The CBA defines "unlikely" bonuses as those based on achievements not attained the previous season by a player or his team. The CBA also gives the NBA commissioner authority to contest any "unlikely" bonus he considers to be, in fact, probable.

Riley had given Brown and Hardaway "unlikely" bonuses. One incentive, for example, would pay Brown $1.5 million if the Heat won either 27 home games or 43 total games this season. The Heat deemed that "unlikely" because the franchise never had won more than 26 home games or 42 total games in its eight-year history.

But the league, noting that the Heat had significantly improved its prospects by signing Howard, disagreed. Mishkin told Arison that those bonuses, now deemed "likely," shaved $2.5 million from the Heat's payroll ceiling, thus invalidating the Howard deal.

Riley was stunned by the news. He denounced the ruling as "unconscionable," one that "dismantled" his team. As a "partner" of the Heat, he asserted that the NBA had a "fiduciary responsibility" to alert the club if the Howard deal was in jeopardy. "Every team in this league pushes the envelope a little," Riley said. "And then you talk to the NBA and they say, 'You can't go that far.'"

Owner Arison, who had tangled with the league before, was equally upset. In 1995 the league had fined him $1 million—and taken his top 1996 draft choice—for recruiting Riley while he was under contract to the Knicks. Miami officials speculated that NBA Commissioner David Stern may have disallowed the Howard contract to punish the Heat's relentlessness or to bail out Pollin's flailing franchise.

"We're not mistake-free," Arison, who also owns Carnival Cruise Lines, said in an interview. "I don't think we made mistakes greater than many teams have made, and we're being punished greater than any team's ever been punished for similar mistakes."

The NBA office was unmoved. The league could not alert Miami to potential problems with the Howard deal, an NBA official said, because it only learned of the Brown and Hardaway details after their contracts were signed.

Stern, in his first public comments on the Howard case, said he judged the case solely on its merits. "We took our action because that's what the facts before us required us to do. . . . If the Heat is unhappy, get on line," he said in an interview last month.

"At a meeting of 29 owners you would get unanimity that I have it in for all 29 owners," Stern added. "If you're not prepared to have all of the teams mad at you, you're not doing your job."

Over the Cap: The Dispute between the NBA and the Heat		
Issue	**Miami's Version**	**NBA's Version**
Salary cap	$24.3 million	$24.3 million
All other Heat players	$4.26 million	$4.26 million
Alonzo Mourning	$6.84 million*	$9.4 million**
Tim Hardaway	$2 million	$3 million
$2 million salary	$2 million salary	$2 million salary
$2 million bonuses	$2 million unlikely bonuses	$1 million likely bonuses, $1 million unlikely
P. J. Brown	$1.7 million	$3.2 million
$1.7 million salary	$1.7 million salary	$1.7 million salary
$1.5 million bonuses	$1.5 million unlikely bonuses	$1.5 million likely bonuses
Juwan Howard	$9 million	$9 million
Total	$23.8 million	$28.86 million
	($500,000 *under* cap)	($4.56 million *over* cap)

*Heat's figure—representing 150 percent of Mourning's salary last season, in accordance with new collective bargaining agreement—was based on its contention that it had not made agreement with Mourning before making agreement with Howard.

**NBA's figure—representing salary league believed Mourning would receive in 1996–97—was based on league's decision that Heat had made undisclosed deal with Mourning before it made deal with Howard.

▨ Areas of dispute.

The Heat is Off

In a news release on July 31, the NBA stated that issues raised by the Howard matter would be resolved by arbitrators jointly selected by the league and union. The Heat, however, had at least as much at risk under arbitration as Juwan Howard. Under a worst-case scenario for the Heat, if an arbitrator and appeals panel upheld the NBA's allegations regarding the alleged Mourning agreement, the league could void Mourning's contract, fine the club $5 million, suspend Riley for a year, take away draft picks—and still leave the Heat without Howard.

While the NBA was disapproving his contract, Howard was en route to Miami to shop for a house in Coconut Grove, a picturesque community on Biscayne Bay. Howard planned to visit a Mediterranean-style house on the water—a location that would even let him take a boat to practice. But as Howard stepped into the airport terminal, one of his agents told him of the latest trouble.

Howard rushed to the Heat's downtown offices, where Riley assured him the NBA's allegations were false. "We'll fight these charges like hell because we've been wronged here," Riley told Howard.

With Arison looking on, Howard hugged Riley. "Coach," he later quoted himself as saying, "I'm behind you guys 100 percent."

That evening, Howard joined Riley at Paulo Luigi's, a trendy restaurant in Coconut Grove. But in the next several days the warm relationship between new player and new team quickly cooled. Howard concluded after discussions with Polk that if he backed Miami and the team lost a protracted fight with the league, other NBA clubs might have as little as $40 million or $50 million to offer him for seven years. In effect, he would take a $50 million pay cut and become, he said, "a laughingstock."

That house on Biscayne Bay suddenly lost its appeal. Riley found he couldn't get Howard to return his calls.

"I mean, this is a business," Howard later explained. "Yes, indeed, I believe in loyalty. But I believe in loyalty in the sense that it has to be done right and make sure that I don't lose in no kind of fashion."

Falk had gone to Europe and Israel on a long-planned family vacation, leaving Polk to sort out Howard's future. Polk tried to sort through the key issues. Could the Heat prevail in arbitration? Possibly, Polk believed, but it might take two months. But if the Heat lost the arbitration, Howard stood to lose tens of millions.

The Bullets could sign Howard only if the league restored the team's "Larry Bird rights." The CBA provision, named after the former Boston Celtics star, allowed teams to exceed the salary cap in order to re-sign their own players. The Bullets had lost their "Bird rights" to Howard when they renounced him. But if the rights were restored, the Bullets would have no limit on the sum of money they could pay Howard.

On August 1, the NBA declared Howard a free agent. Howard instructed Polk, "Wait for word on the Bullets before coming to an agreement with any team."

The next day, Unseld phoned Pollin, who was in Atlanta for the Olympics.

"If we can get Juwan, we could be a very good team," Unseld said.

"Do what you want to do," Pollin responded. "Do what you have to do."

Unseld had tried not to second-guess himself over the earlier Howard negotiations—the media and irate fans had done plenty of that. But now he had a chance to make amends. "I'm sure if I looked back on it," he subsequently said, "I would find plenty of mistakes. . . . I choose not to do that because if I did I would drive myself crazy."

The league was driving the Heat crazy. On August 2, NBA Deputy Commissioner Russ Granik told Arison by phone that based on his understanding of the CBA the Heat would be unlikely to regain Howard's services through arbitration. "You will not get Juwan Howard," Granik declared, according to Heat officials.

Later that day, the Heat obtained a temporary injunction prohibiting Howard from signing another contract unless it recognized the validity of the Miami deal. The injunction named the NBA and Howard as defendants. Howard was angry at the Heat for not forewarning him. "Where's the loyalty there?" he demanded.

The players' union agreed with the Heat that the Hardaway and Brown bonuses were "unlikely" and that Mourning did not have an undisclosed agreement. But the union disagreed with Miami over whether Howard should be allowed to re-sign with the Bullets.

On August 3, as the league and union were completing an agreement to restore the Bullets' Bird rights, Unseld prepared to negotiate his second-chance contract with Howard. Polk, concerned that Miami would impose further legal obstacles, phoned Howard in his hometown of Chicago and advised him to return to Washington. Howard arrived that night.

Monday, August 5, was triumphant for the Bullets, disastrous for the Heat. The league and union agreed that if a player signs a second contract after his first deal has been disapproved, the second contract is the valid one, making arbitration moot. The deal, which would apply first and foremost to Howard, was intended to protect players against financial losses in disputes between the NBA and its teams.

In Howard's case, the league and union also agreed to restore the Bullets' Bird rights and allow Murray and Williams to remain with the Bullets. If the club re-signed Howard, however, it would forfeit its 1997 first-round draft choice.

Riley, ever more furious, accused the league and union of "getting into bed together" in an "unholy alliance."

On the afternoon of August 5 Unseld phoned Polk. "We got our Bird rights restored. Why don't you come on over?" Unseld said, according to Polk.

Pollin agreed to match the terms of Howard's $100.8 million Miami deal—adding $4.2 million to cover Maryland taxes because Florida has no state income tax—even though Howard seemed to be in a decidedly weaker negotiating position. "We wanted a happy player," Unseld said.

Howard's seven-year, $105 million Bullets contract—contingent upon the resolution of the Heat's legal challenges—took but 30 minutes to negotiate. Unseld refused, however, to match Riley's offer of hotel suites and limos. "I didn't want him getting picked up in a limousine and everybody else getting on a bus. It's as simple as that," Unseld explained. "Everybody else in a regular room and one guy in a suite? I don't think it makes for the chemistry of a team."

Before signing the contract, Unseld took Howard aside. "He wanted to see where my head was at," Howard said. "He wanted to see, Did I have any grudges against him? . . . I told him, 'Hell, no.' Excuse my French. I said, 'No. You guys had to do what was best for the organization and make a bright business decision for yourselves. And I had to do the same thing for me.' "

Shortly after 10 p.m., Riley called Polk at his Rockville home. Though arbitration was now a remote possibility, Riley still hoped for a final meeting with Howard. "We needed Juwan to tell us, 'If I go down the road with you and you win [arbitration] I will come to Miami,' " Riley said.

Polk refused, and the conversation turned ugly. "Riley told me, 'You're a shrinking violet. . . . You're a coward,' " Polk said. Riley said he does not recall making those comments, but added, "We had some very, very heated discussions."

For Riley, the battle was over. Without Howard in his corner, he said, "we had nobody to fight for anymore. . . . And that's where you had to cut bait." Riley remained furious at the league for allowing Washington to recover from its mistake. "The league built a team in Washington, basically," he later charged.

Falk said the Heat fell victim to a league intent on "dealing very sternly, no pun intended" with clubs that pursued free agents too aggressively and to a union "not in a strong enough position to do battle with the league."

"The league had the whole thing wired; the league forced Miami to settle," Falk added. "The league presented the Heat with a plea bargain: If you go to an arbitrator, you'll go to jail for 100 years. If you don't, we'll let you off."

In the settlement, announced August 10, Howard's contract with the Bullets was approved. The NBA and Miami agreed to drop "the various legal proceedings between the parties," which meant the Heat would abandon its bid for a permanent injunction and the league would not pursue the alleged undisclosed Mourning agreement. The Heat signed Brown and Hardaway to new contracts, removing the issue of whether their bonuses were likely or not, and Mourning signed a seven-year, $105 million deal.

Two days later, Howard appeared at a news conference at USAir Arena.

"He's baaaaaack," Unseld said in introducing his once and future star.

"I look at this as a blessing—a blessing from God," Howard told reporters, echoing the same language he had used a few weeks earlier in Miami. "I could recall the time I graduated from college. That was the best day of my life, right there. I consider this behind that."

The "$205 Million Man"

In the end, Pat Riley said, he bears Howard no malice. "You know what? I wish Juwan the very best," Riley said one afternoon recently. "But I think deep down in his heart he will always wonder what it would have been like to play with Alonzo and this team down here. That's something he'll never know."

Riley paused, chuckling softly as he reconsidered. "Juwan will probably win championships in Washington," he said. "And he'll probably forget that this whole thing ever happened."

That, Howard said, is unlikely.

"I will never forget this," he said after a Bullets practice. "This is something I can tell my grandkids about. How I signed a $100 million contract. How I signed a $105 million contract. I'm the first guy this has ever happened to. This summer—Juwan Howard had the look of a man who had just accomplished something really big— "I was a $205 million man."

Also contributing to this story were *Washington Post* staff writers George Solomon in New York and J. A. Adande at the Bullets training camp in Shepherdstown, West Virginia.

Case 4

Collective Bargaining at Magic Carpet Airlines: A Union Perspective (A)

History of Magic Carpet Air

Magic Carpet Air (MCA) began operations in 1961, serving 2 cities, and grew to serve 18 cities by 1987. River City Airlines (RCA) began in 1969 with service to 4 cities and grew to serve 12 cities by 1987. In January 1987, Magic Carpet Air purchased River City Airlines and merged the two operations. The joining of these two regional airlines created a small "national" airline (defined as a carrier with sales between $100 million and $1 billion) with sales of $140,265,000 in 1987. Even so, the firm competed primarily in only one region of the country, and managers constantly compared it to other large regional airlines.

In May 1988, Magic Carpet Air entered into a marketing agreement with a major national carrier and became a "feeder" airline for that carrier (e.g., American Eagle is a feeder airline for American Airlines, United Express is a feeder for United Airlines). That is, MCA delivered passengers from small airports to larger ones, where passengers could make connections using that airline. Subsequently, no more reservations were given to the public as Magic Carpet Air; passengers believed that they bought tickets for the major carrier. The company also repainted all aircraft to make the public believe Magic Carpet Air was part of the major carrier.

Prior to 1989, the flight attendants at neither company were unionized. However, both MCA and RCA flight attendants worried about what they perceived as the arbitrary way that MCA management resolved personnel issues such as merging seniority lists. Such fears led several workers to contact the League of Flight Attendants (LFA), a union whose membership consisted solely of flight attendants. Despite opposition to unionization from MCA, the LFA won a union certification election with 82 percent of the vote.

Previous Contract Negotiations

Negotiations for the first MCA–LFA contract began in November 1989, and negotiators from both sides cooperated effectively. The committee borrowed language from other airline contracts (e.g., Piedmont Airlines). The committee also incorporated the past practices and working conditions that were used at River City Airlines. These rules had

Source: This case was prepared by Peggy Briggs and William Ross of the University of Wisconsin–LaCrosse and is intended to be used as a basis for class discussion rather than to illustrate either effective or ineffective handling of the situation. The names of the firms, individuals, and locations; dates; conversation quotations; and financial information have all been disguised to preserve the firm's and union's desire for anonymity.

An earlier version of this case was presented and accepted by the refereed Midwest Society for Case Research and appeared in *Annual Advances in Case Research, 1991.* All rights reserved to the authors and the MSCR.

not been written down but had been mutually acceptable past practices. Negotiators signed the final contract in August 1990. The contract was effective until August 1994.

Negotiations for the second contract also went smoothly. In terms of contract provisions, the second contract was basically an extension of the first, with a modest pay increase and one additional paid holiday. The agreement was effective until August 31, 1997.

What follows is a synopsis of the 1997 contract negotiations from a union negotiator's perspective.

League of Flight Attendants (LFA) Negotiating Team

Whenever an LFA carrier began negotiations, the National Office of LFA sent a national bargaining representative (NBR) to the scene. Dixie Lee, the NBR assigned to the MCA negotiations, met with the flight attendants' Master Executive Council (MEC) to select a negotiating team. The negotiating team prepared for negotiations and conducted the actual bargaining sessions. Once at the table, Dixie spoke for the committee. Using an NBR as the spokesperson lessened the likelihood that a flight attendant who was emotionally involved with an issue might say something inappropriate while trying to negotiate. Dixie had 14 years' experience and had also assisted with the 1994 MCA contract negotiations. Although Dixie was the spokesperson, the negotiating team was formally chaired by Ruth Boaz, LFA MEC president at Magic Carpet Air. Other members of the team included local LFA union presidents Peggy Hardy, Marie Phillips, and Jody Rogers.

Determining the Union's Bargaining Objectives

The LFA negotiating committee members first identified their bargaining objectives. For the 1997 contract, the LFA negotiating committee devised an opening offer based on the average working conditions and wage rates for flight attendants offered by other, similarly sized carriers. They looked at wage, unemployment, and cost-of-living data from government sources such as the *Monthly Labor Review*. The committee members knew the financial history of MCA and kept their proposals within financial reach of the company. They also used other employee groups (e.g., pilots, mechanics) within MCA as a guide—many of the LFA proposals were items that these other unions already had in their contracts. The LFA negotiating committee hoped to bring wages and work rules in line with the company's financial performance and industry standards (see Table 1). Finally, they looked at past grievances and arbitration cases to determine if contract wording needed changes.

Committee members also considered the wishes of the rank-and-file members. To do this, the committee mailed a survey to the 115 LFA members asking questions regarding wages, working conditions, and issues of concern to flight attendants. They received a 75 percent response rate; results are shown in Table 2.

After tallying the responses, negotiating team members discovered that the flight attendants' major concern was wage determination. MCA currently paid flight attendants for the time they were in the aircraft with it moving under its own power—they

TABLE 1 | 1996–97 Regional Airline Industry Comparisons

Airline	Starting Wage/Hour	Days off per Month	Duty Rig* as Airline (percentage of time)
A	$17.00	11	60%
B	$15.00	12	62%
C	$15.00	12	none
D	$14.00	13	none
E	$14.00	10	none
F	$13.50	10	33%
Magic Carpet	$13.00	10	none

*Duty rig is a pay calculation that is a certain percentage of the period of time which a flight attendant is on duty with the company. Duty time normally begins 45 minutes prior to first scheduled trip departure time and ends 15 minutes after final arrival time at the end of the day.

were not paid for the time spent sitting in airports waiting for flights. Union members wanted MCA to implement *duty rigs*. A duty rig paid the attendant a fixed percentage of the period of time he or she was on duty with the company.

For example, suppose an attendant worked a 15-hour day, but worked in moving aircraft for only six hours. Under the current system, MCA paid wages for six hours, plus one hour for preparation time (*duty time*) at the beginning of the day. However, if the duty rig pay rate was 67 percent, MCA would pay the attendant for 10 hours of work, plus 1 hour for duty time. Thus duty rigs would require the airline to pay a percentage of the wage for all time at work, whether flying or sitting.

TABLE 2 | Results of the Flight Attendant Survey

Questionnaires mailed: 115

Questionnaires returned: 86

Question: What was the flight attendant's top priority for the new contract?

Direct wages	40%
Job security	31%
Working conditions	26%
Other	3%

Question: How did the flight attendant want to receive her/his direct wages?

Duty rigs	47%
Hourly rate	34%
Holiday pay	15%
Other	4%

Question: How did the flight attendant want her/his job security?

Seniority protection	60%
Protection from layoffs	28%
Protection of contract	12%

Create Havoc Around Our System (CHAOS) program, where the union sought to enlist the aid of the public and employed creative tactics (e.g., intermittent strikes, informational picketing) to pressure management to resolve their contract dispute. The union also invited any member in good standing to attend any negotiation session.

Convincing the Company

The third strategy attempted to convince the company to take the LFA seriously. In a widely publicized move, negotiation team members did extensive research on both economic picketing and informational picketing, inquiring at all of their domicile cities as to what permits would be needed to picket. The union mailed their *Negotiation Update* newsletters to each manager's home address, informing managers of the LFA's preparations in the event of a future strike. Committee members hoped these actions would convince management that the LFA made serious proposals—and would strike if those proposals were not met.

Settling Issues

The fourth strategy was that the team would not proceed with an item without the entire team being in total agreement. All planning meetings and caucuses (meetings without the company team member present) during negotiations would involve every committee member.

Company Negotiating Team

The company negotiating team consisted of the following people:

*   Bill Orleans, director of labor relations.
*   Ross Irving, director of human resources.
*   Kristine Lamb, director of in-flight services.
*   Christian Andrew, executive vice president.
*   Willie Sanders, senior vice president of operations.
*   Tom Windham, chief executive officer (CEO) and president.

The company team was in a state of transition, and consequently seemed to suffer from much confusion. Bill Orleans had recently been demoted from director of human resources to director of labor relations—a move he resented. Ross Irving, the new director of human resources, hired from another firm, avoided the sessions; he seemed uncomfortable sitting next to his predecessor, particularly since Orleans had negotiated most of the union contracts at MCA. Finally, Lamb, who was used to giving orders to flight attendants, acted as if the negotiations reflected a lack of loyalty on the part of the workers and interference with her job on the part of management. Tom Windham was grooming Willie Sanders to take over upon Windham's retirement.

The Negotiating Process: Initial Positions

Airlines are governed under the Railway Labor Act of 1926, as amended. This act states that labor contracts never expire, but may be amended on their amendable dates. When the amendable date comes near, a letter is mailed by the party requesting changes in the contract to the counterparty in the contract. This letter allows contract talks to begin. Dixie mailed MCA such a letter on March 31, giving a full 60 days' notice of the flight attendants' intent to open talks for amending their current contract before September 1.

Inasmuch as the company would not meet in a neutral city, LFA negotiators agreed to an MCA proposal to meet at a hotel located near corporate headquarters. MCA paid for the meeting room. The first negotiation session was scheduled for May 29, 1997.

Everyone on the LFA committee had the jitters. It was the first time in negotiations for Marie, Jody, and Peggy. Dixie gave them some last-minute instructions:

> I don't want y'all to speak or use any facial expressions at the table. Instead, I want all of y'all to silently take notes. Draw a vertical line down the middle of each note page. Write whatever the managers say on the left side of the page and write whatever I say on the right-hand side of the page. Is it OK with y'all if I do the negotiating? I've found things go best if only one person talks at the bargaining table.

As the LFA negotiators filed into the conference room, they saw it was empty. Each of the managers arrived late. Twenty minutes later, Orleans still had not come. As everyone waited, CEO Tom Windham arrived. Small talk began as Windham glanced over his notes and spoke:

> You know that as a feeder airline we do not have full control over our own destiny; the marketing agreement with the major carrier restricts our flexibility. Even so, I am willing to give your flight attendant group a modest increase. I am not looking for any concessions. Also, my philosophy is that all the groups (pilots, agents, office personnel) should be treated equally. However, your union does have a good agreement right now—say, why don't we just agree to continue the present contract for another six years? It could save a lot of time!

As everyone chuckled at Windham's joke, Orleans arrived. The union negotiators could tell by the expression on his face that he was surprised and embarrassed to see Tom Windham there. Windham stood up, wished everyone good luck, and left.

The Union's Initial Position

Dixie spent the first day describing problems with the current contract. At 4:15 p.m., the union presented the company with its neatly typed contract proposal. Dixie had written "change," "new," "clarification," and so on in the margin next to each paragraph that had been changed in any way from the 1994 contract.

ORLEANS: This is a "wish book"! Do I look like Santa Claus?

LEE: Stop fidgeting, Mr. Orleans. Let me explain why we are insisting on these changes.

Dixie read only about one-third of the provisions in the union's contract proposal. Two additional sessions were necessary to read through the entire proposal. The major changes are summarized in Table 3.

TABLE 3 | Changes in the Magic Carpet Air–League of Flight Attendants Contract

Contract Provision	1994–97 Contract	Union Proposal
Compensation		
Base wage	$13.00	$15.45
Wage after five years	$20.20	$25.55
Duty rig pay	None	1 hour pay per 2 hour duty (50%)
Daily guarantee	3.25 hours	4.5 hours
Holiday pay	None	8 holidays at double-time rate
Job security		
Successorship	None	Contract will still be binding
Protection of seniority rights in the event of a merger	None	Arbitrator combines MCA seniority list with that of the other airline
Working conditions		
Trip trading lead time	5 days	24 hours
Shoe allowance	None	$100/year
Winter coat	None	Total cost
Uniform maintenance	$16/month	$20/month

Management's Initial Position

On the fourth day, company representatives presented their initial offer to the union. Orleans handed each of the LFA committee members a book in a binder. As they leafed through the book, members were puzzled. They did not see any notations indicating changes from the current contract. Orleans talked quickly, summarizing the provisions in the contract; most of the proposed provisions included some type of union concessions, but he did not highlight these.

> LEE: Is this a serious proposal? The union presented a realistic proposal using industry standards, and your opener (opening offer) is totally unreasonable.

> ORLEANS: Don't get your panties in a wad. The party has just begun and there is lots of time to dance. Why, we didn't even list any wages in our proposal—we were hoping you would work for free, ha ha.

Orleans then gave a long, patronizing sermon regarding MCA's poor financial health and how the company could be bankrupt at any time. However, in the history of Magic Carpet Air, the company had never shown a loss on its financial statement.

A recess was called for lunch. As the union members caucused, Peggy looked depressed. Marie sat with fists clenched.

> MARIE: I can't eat anything! I am furious at Mr. Orleans—he has some nerve!

> JODY: The others were not much better. Did you hear their snide remarks about us when they went to lunch?

> PEGGY: What are we going to do? They have asked for concessions on everything! And Mr. Windham promised us just the opposite.

DIXIE: Now girls, just relax. It is still the first week of negotiations. I suggest that we just work from our initial contract proposal and ignore theirs. It can't be taken seriously anyway, in my opinion.

MARIE: Well, you'll have to carry on without me tomorrow; I have to work. Management won't let me rearrange my schedule to negotiate. At least I won't have to watch Mr. Orleans chain smoke!

Talks resumed after lunch break. Dixie summarized each section of the LFA proposal. Orleans fidgeted and kept saying "No." Nothing was settled that day.

By noon the next day, it became obvious that not much was getting accomplished. Finally, the union moved to sections where it did not propose any changes and the managers tentatively agreed to keep those intact. It seemed like a mountain had been climbed just to get the company to agree to those "no changes." Negotiations were adjourned for the day.

LEE: When can we meet? Monday, at 8:30?

SANDERS: No good for me. I have important meetings that day.

LEE: How about Tuesday?

ANDREW: I can't make it. Every day next week is bad.

ORLEANS: The following week I will be out of town. Sorry!

LEE: OK, y'all tell us when y'all's schedules are free.

ORLEANS: We'll have to caucus. We'll get back to you.

Instead of caucusing and deciding when they could next meet, the managers simply went home, leaving the union negotiating team to wonder when—or if—bargaining would continue.

Round 2

On Wednesday, July 16, Ruth Boaz got a letter from management asking for a meeting two days later. Ruth quickly scheduled a planning session for Thursday night, where the LFA team members reviewed their objectives and the progress to date. Negotiations with MCA resumed Friday.

July 18: Grievances and Uniforms

Irving proposed using the same language for a revised grievance procedure as that printed in the pilot's contract. The union caucused. Ruth telephoned the pilot's union and, once she was satisfied that the pilots were happy with their grievance procedure, convinced the union negotiating team to agree.

The discussion moved to the section on uniforms. After some countering back and forth on various issues, a winter coat was added as an optional item; however, who would pay the cost was still an issue. The union wanted MCA to pay the total cost.

ORLEANS: Unacceptable. You'll have to buy your own coats. We already give $16 per month for uniform cleaning.

LEE: But a winter coat is expensive. Surely y'all recognize that a poor little ol' flight attendant couldn't be expected to shoulder the entire cost of a new coat. Mr. Orleans, have a heart.

ORLEANS: I do have a heart; fortunately, it is not attached to my wallet, ha ha. OK, we will allow $40 every five years to buy a coat.

LEE: According to my research, a new coat costs $120. And it costs $10 per month to clean.

ORLEANS: How often does someone dry-clean a coat she only wears three months of the year? She doesn't clean it 12 times! (*Pause.*) OK, if you drop this silly request for free shoes, then we'll raise the combined uniform and coat maintenance allowance to $16.50 per month.

LEE: But, Mr. Orleans, shoes are a part of our uniform, too. You expect us to all wear the same type of shoes, don't you? You pay for the other parts of our uniforms, so it is only reasonable that MCA should also pay for shoes. Our research shows that two pairs of standard shoes cost, on average, $100.

ORLEANS: However, you can wear the shoes when you are not on duty, too. You probably wouldn't do that with other parts of your uniforms. So we're not paying for shoes you can wear other places.

BOAZ: Mr. Orleans, I can assure you that we don't wear our uniform shoes when we go dancing on the weekends. (Everyone laughed.)

ORLEANS: If we pay $25 for shoes and $45 for a coat, then we will pay $17.50 per month for uniform maintenance.

LEE: Good, but not good enough.

(Both sides sat in silence for nearly four minutes. Mr. Orleans was obviously uncomfortable with this period of silence.)

ORLEANS: Let's see . . . *(fumbling with a pen and paper)* we'll split the cost of the new coat, so that is $60 and we'll pay $25 for shoes. Good enough now?

LEE: Raise the combined uniform and coat maintenance to $18 per month and you have a deal.

LEE: *(As they were writing the agreed-upon section.)* Why don't we make it one new coat for the life of the three-year contract, instead of one new coat every five years? That makes it so much easier for everyone to keep track of.

Orleans rolled his eyes and nodded in acquiescence. The meeting then adjourned for the weekend. At last the union team felt that some progress was being made.

Case 5

The Ken Griffey Jr. Negotiation
Background Note

This case is a journalist's account (originally published in *Sports Illustrated*) of negotiations surrounding a professional baseball player in the United States named Ken Griffey Jr. that took place during the winter of 2000. For readers unfamiliar with Griffey, the sport of baseball, or the nature of U.S. major league baseball teams, contracts, and negotiations, this introductory note will provide some basic details that will help you follow the case. You do not need to be particularly knowledgeable about baseball to understand and analyze what went on, but it does help to know a little bit about the context in which negotiations over Griffey's future took place.

Who Is Ken Griffey Jr.?

Griffey (also known as "Junior") is generally regarded as one of the premier professional baseball players in the two North American leagues collectively known as Major League Baseball. Consequently, at the time the events in the case took place, many other teams coveted his talents and would have liked to have signed him. For those who care to know the baseball-related details, he is an outfielder who has proven to be both an excellent hitter and a superb fielder over a career of several years. But despite his experience, he was at the time of the dispute only 30 years old in a game where players can be very successful into (and occasionally beyond) their late 30s.

What Was Going on at the Time of the Case?

As the negotiations opened, Griffey played for a team called the Seattle Mariners. His contract with Seattle was to end following the 2000 season (which started in April and ended in October 2000). If Griffey stayed in Seattle for the 2000 season and let his contract run out, he could have become a free agent who could sell his talents and services to any other team in baseball, and the Seattle ballclub would get nothing if Griffey signed with another team. But if the Seattle team could trade him (at the time of the case, during the winter preceeding the season), they could get something for him. Because Griffey is a first-rate talent, a trade would presumably bring Seattle several very good players in return.

Couldn't Seattle Have Kept Griffey?

They could have tried to sign him to a new contract, either before or after his existing contract ran out. But it was widely known that Griffey was unhappy in Seattle for a

Source: The case is drawn from Tom Verducci, "Home Economics," *Sports Illustrated,* February 21, 2000, pp. 31–40. Copyright © 2000, Time Inc. All rights reserved. Used here with permission. The box titled "Who the Mariners Got" came from *USA Today Baseball Weekly,* February 16, 2000, p. 7, by Paul White. Copyright © 2000. Reprinted with permission. The background note that precedes the case was written by Bruce Barry.

variety of reasons (some of which are mentioned in the case). It also says in the case that Seattle offered Griffey a new eight-year, $138 million contract in July 1999, which Griffey met "with indifference." As a result, it was in Seattle's interest to try to trade him, rather than waiting, which would have brought the risk that they would lose him with no compensation if his contract ran out at the end of the 2000 season and he became a free agent and signed with another team.

What Control Did Griffey Have over His Fate?

In most cases, a player can be traded without his consent. Teams trade players for all kinds of reasons: to get rid of an expensive player with declining skills; to attract talent at some other position; bad fit in team chemistry and so on. Griffey, however, met a league threshold—10 years playing, and the past 5 with his current team—that gives a player the right to veto any trade. Of course, even for players who do not have this veto, trading them near the end of their contract means the new team will soon have to sign them to a new contract. The player might not have the contractual right to formally veto a trade, but he can signal his preferences by indicating which teams would find him more or less cooperative in agreeing to a new contract.

Home Economics

Aloft in a $35 million Falcon 900 jet, Ken Griffey Jr. told the story of recently playing golf with Jack Nicklaus for the first time. Nicklaus, his son Mike, and Mark O'Meara, a PGA Tour pro and friend of Griffey's, smacked their drives off the first tee down the middle of the fairway. Griffey, hitting last, could feel his knees trembling as he stood over the ball. He didn't know Nicklaus well, and the golfing legend had said almost nothing to him. Griffey promptly sent an ugly slice screeching far into the rough. "So Jack walks by me," Griffey said, "and as he's walking, he says to me, 'In my sport we play the foul balls.' "

Griffey howled with laughter, as did the rest of the passengers, including his wife, Melissa; his son, Trey, 6; his daughter, Taryn, 4; and a few Reds executives and members of their families. This went on for two hours—Griffey, the life of the party, telling one funny story after another. Never had a man seemed so ebullient upon signing away the next 10 years of his career for about half his market value.

What mattered more than selling himself short was that Griffey, Cincinnati Moeller High class of '87, son of Reds coach Ken and Birdie Griffey of Cincinnati, was heading home. Reds majority owner Carl Lindner had approved the trade with the Seattle Mariners and Griffey's new contract and then had provided his jet to make the sentimental journey possible. Considering his status as one of the game's greatest players now and forever, Griffey accepted such a huge discount that commissioner Bud Selig greeted the news of his signing by yelling, "Thank you! Thank you very much!" and nearly weeping.

Griffey is guaranteed $116.5 million over the next nine years, with the Reds holding an option for a 10th season. Although Griffey's salary will be $12.5 million a year (plus a $4 million buyout for the 10th year), the deal is worth only about $89 million in present-day dollars because Griffey agreed to defer $57.5 million of that total at 4 percent interest. Those payments are stretched between 2010 and 2025, when Griffey will be 56 years old.

Griffey agreed to those terms one day after the Mariners finally blinked following four months of talking and posturing about a trade with the Reds. Seattle agreed to take right-handed starter Brett Tomko, outfielder Mike Cameron, and two minor leaguers, right-hander Jake Meyer and infielder Antonio Perez.

Lindner, a Cincinnati financier who has a controlling interest in Chiquita Brands International Inc. and Amtrak, among other holdings, sent his jet to Orlando, where Griffey lives, to bring him to Ohio in style for the posttrade news conference. Two thousand people greeted the Falcon 900 as it touched down. A Rolls-Royce and two limousines pulled up while two news choppers with searchlights hovered above. Lindner told Griffey to hop in the front seat of the Rolls—with the 80-year-old Lindner driving—and told Junior's wife and kids to sit in the back. The rest of the traveling party jumped into the limos. As the vehicles crawled out of the airport, fans swarmed the cars, popping the flashes of their cameras, banging on the hoods and windows, and yelling, "Welcome home!"

Lindner, in the lead car, slowly steered the Rolls free from the knot of people; the sleeves of his jacket slid back enough to reveal a pair of gold cuff links he wears every day that read ONLY IN AMERICA. As the caravan gathered speed onto Kellogg Avenue, something happened that seemed serendipitous—that is, if you hadn't known how well-connected Lindner is in Cincinnati. Every one of the traffic lights on the avenue switched to flashing yellow, affording Griffey an unimpeded trip downtown to Cinergy Field, where a burst of fireworks welcomed him.

Unimpeded? If only the trip had been so easy from the beginning. Griffey wound up in Cincinnati only after the Mariners alienated him with their curious trade tactics; only after the Reds twice pulled out of the talks, including as recently as three days before the actual trade; only after Griffey's agent illegally jump-started discussions; and only after Griffey was snubbed by his first choice, the Atlanta Braves, who wanted his teammate, shortstop Alex Rodriguez, instead. According to several insiders familiar with the deal, this is the story of how Griffey came home.

The first sign of trouble in Seattle came in July, when the Mariners offered Griffey (who was scheduled to become a free agent after the 2000 season) $138 million over eight years and were met not with a counterproposal but with indifference. Griffey, whose Mariners salary was $8.5 million, had no problem with the money—though he didn't tell Seattle that at the time—but he wasn't sure if he wanted to stay. His children were reaching school age, and that had made him ponder more often the idea of playing closer to Orlando. "We'll think about it," his agent, Brian Goldberg, told Seattle.

Later that month the Mariners opened Safeco Field, a resplendent $517 million stadium with a sliding canopy that keeps out the Northwest rain but not the chill. Between one wall of the Mariners' clubhouse and Griffey's locker the club did not install the three other lockers that would have fit there. This area was designed specifically for Griffey, who in that space could store his personal travel trunk for his bats, as well as the assortment of gadgets, boxes, and other equipment he accumulates during a season.

Griffey showed his appreciation for this custom-made jewel of a park by saying nothing. The franchise player who made the team's continued existence in Seattle possible refused to comment on Safeco Field. He would explain later that he did so to avoid misleading people about his future. If he praised the place, people might think he was staying. If he ripped it, people might think he was leaving. But the silence was ominous. His private grumblings were worse. The ball had jumped in the Kingdome, his old, indoor home stadium. Safeco was, in the words of one of his teammates before the final price was toted up, "a $450 million icebox. He knows it might cost him the home run record." Balls hit in the air died. Centerfield, in particular, was a graveyard; the Mariners couldn't hit balls out even in batting practice.

One night, after yet another of his well-struck fly balls had died in an opposing outfielder's glove, Griffey called Woody Woodward, the Seattle general manager at the time, from a dugout telephone. In front of his teammates Griffey screamed through the phone at Woodward, "Get me out of this place! Trade me right now!"

"That wasn't why he left," Goldberg said last Friday, referring to Safeco Field. "It was one piece in the puzzle. There was no one thing, no one event. I want to emphasize [that] what happened was not anyone's fault. Things just kind of went sideways."

Griffey's mood darkened on August 12. That's when his wife and children returned to Orlando in preparation for the school year. A few days later he told friends that he was leaning toward playing for the Braves or the Houston Astros, contending teams with spring training sites within minutes of his home. (The Mariners train in Arizona.) Griffey liked the idea of gaining five weeks at home with his family during the school year. "What can the Mariners offer me that nobody else can?" he said. "Nothing."

Griffey's season deteriorated. He hit just .255 after the All-Star break, including .212 in the final month, and finished at .285, albeit with 48 homers and 134 RBIs. Teammates noticed how he'd skip batting practice and stretching exercises for weeks at a time, preferring to linger in the clubhouse. The Mariners lost 83 games, failing to make the postseason for the ninth time in his 11 seasons with the club.

Woodward retired after the season, remaining true to the words he repeated to Cincinnati general manager Jim Bowden on the three or four occasions every season when Bowden would ask, "When are you going to trade me Griffey?" Woodward would say, "I'm not going to be remembered as the guy who traded Ken Griffey Jr."

That distinction would fall to 62-year-old Pat Gillick, Woodward's successor. In November, Gillick and Mariners CEO Howard Lincoln flew to Orlando to meet with Griffey. The outfielder did not want any more offers. He wanted out. He told Gillick and Lincoln he preferred to be traded rather than play the last season of his contract in Seattle. As a player with 10 years of major league service, including at least the past 5 with his current team, Griffey had the right to veto any trade. He gave the Mariners a list of four teams he would consider playing for. He listed them in his order of preference: Braves, Reds, Astros, and New York Mets.

Gillick made a request before leaving Orlando: Would it be OK with Griffey if he talked to teams not on his list? Gillick wanted to gain some leverage by expanding the market. Griffey gave his approval.

Over the next month that tactic blew up on Gillick. The GM seemed to Goldberg and Griffey to be spending more time talking with clubs not on the list than with those on the list. Gillick tried to cut deals with the Cleveland Indians, New York Yankees, Pittsburgh Pirates, St. Louis Cardinals, and Tampa Bay Devil Rays, each time asking

Goldberg if Griffey would accept a trade based on what were supposed to be only diversionary talks. Gillick was also telling baseball people that Griffey had 20 teams on his approval list—every team that trains in Florida. "After a month of that, it was starting to wear on Junior," Goldberg says. The idea of coming back to Seattle for one last season became more remote.

Privately, Gillick had been told by Seattle executives that Griffey was known to change his mind easily. So Gillick didn't assume the list of four teams was written in stone. Meanwhile, that list was quickly sliced in half. The Braves told Gillick they might have interest in Griffey as a free agent, but they would not trade for him. Atlanta did, however, want to talk about a trade for Rodriguez, who will be a free agent after the 2000 season. Gillick passed, explaining that he had to resolve the Griffey matter first. The Astros also dropped out; owner Drayton McLane already had worries about his payroll, with second baseman Craig Biggio, outfielders Derek Bell and Carl Everett, and left-handed starter Mike Hampton all entering the last year of their contracts. (All but Biggio, who signed an extension, were eventually traded.)

That left the Reds and the Mets. Talks with Cincinnati got off to an awful start at the general managers' meetings on November 19. Sitting in an ocean-view suite at the Ritz Carlton in Laguna Niguel, California, Gillick made his first offer to Bowden: Griffey for four frontline players—second baseman Pokey Reese, first baseman Sean Casey, left-handed starter Denny Neagle, and right-handed closer Scott Williamson—and one player from a list of the five best prospects in the Cincinnati system. Bowden nearly fell out of his chair. His club had won 96 games last season. All his plans were aimed at building a winning team in 2003, when the Reds are scheduled to open a new ballpark. A deal like this would decimate the team and his plans. Before leaving the room, he recovered enough to tell Gillick firmly, "Casey and Reese are not going to be in this deal."

Gillick and Bowden exchanged many proposals in the ensuing weeks without getting close to a trade. One of Bowden's earliest pitches included Cameron, a speedy outfielder with a 240 career average. Gillick said he didn't want Cameron. Bowden drew up a secret list of 11 players, including prospects, that he wouldn't trade. At the top of that list was Reese, a natural shortstop and the player Gillick demanded as a hedge against Rodriguez's leaving by trade or free agency. Also, as a condition of any deal, Bowden insisted that the Mariners pay Griffey's entire 2000 salary of $8.5 million and allow Cincinnati a window to sign him to an extension; Seattle refused on both counts.

Once, after Bowden faxed a proposal to Seattle, Gillick left a voice mail for Bowden: "Jim, you may have a problem. Someone used your letterhead and signed your name to the most ridiculous proposal for Ken Griffey Jr. that's ever been made. If I were you, I would order an investigation to find out what's going on."

Bowden called back and left his own voice mail for Gillick: "Pat, we checked with security about the faxed proposal. You're right. It is ridiculous. I would never give up that much for Ken Griffey Jr."

That was one of the few light moments between Gillick, the old-school, close-mouthed veteran, and Bowden, who at 38 still hadn't outgrown his reputation as a whiz kid with an affinity for reporters, TV cameras, and Austin Powers. Both of them knew Gillick's hand was growing weaker, and the tension between them escalated.

Bowden tried to turn up the heat on Gillick on December 9, the eve of the winter meetings in Anaheim, by publicly announcing that he was going to bring Griffey home. The next day, though, Reds managing executive John Allen told Bowden the chase was over; Lindner had decided the Reds could not afford to trade for and sign Griffey. Allen ordered Bowden to announce that the Reds were out of it.

Bowden couldn't do that . . . not yet, anyway. It would mean all the spadework of the past month had been a public sham. No, instead Bowden scheduled a meeting with Gillick for the morning of December 11 in Gillick's suite. When Gillick began the session by asking for Reese again, Bowden wasted no time. He shot up from his chair, "That's it!" he yelled. "I told you we weren't trading Pokey Reese, and you continue to insist on Pokey Reese! We have nothing more to talk about! We're finished!" He wheeled and hustled out of the room, making sure Gillick had no chance to respond. Bowden called a news conference to announce that the Reds were finished trying to get Griffey because of the Mariners' intractable demand for one player, Reese. It was a masterpiece of showmanship.

Now Bowden was worried about the Mets, especially when one New York executive told him at the winter meetings, "We're going to step up and do it." Mets general manager Steve Phillips agreed to send right-handed starter Octavio Dotel, outfielder Roger Cedeño, and one other player to Seattle for Griffey, but the two teams could not agree on the third player. Gillick wanted right-handed closer Armando Benitez, but Phillips wasn't biting. Deadlocked, the general managers decided they would see if Griffey would approve a deal to the Mets before they tried to settle on the third player.

At 11:15 p.m. EST, Mariners president and COO Chuck Armstrong, who was in Hawaii, telephoned Goldberg at his Cincinnati home and asked if Griffey would accept a trade to New York. "I'm going to dinner in 15 minutes," Armstrong said. "We need to have an answer as soon as possible, because if the answer is no, the Mets need to get on to other things as early as tomorrow morning."

Goldberg called Griffey at home with the news. Griffey talked it over with his wife and mother. By this time he was annoyed at Gillick's games of thrust and parry. Now he had to decide his future in 15 minutes? (Armstrong later explained that he did not mean to imply that the deadline was a mere 15 minutes.) Besides, even though the Mets were on Griffey's list, they were a weak fourth. He had listed them because they were a contending club that trained in Florida, and a part of him was intrigued with the idea of tweaking George Steinbrenner, the Yankees' owner, who Griffey claims once had him chased from the clubhouse when his father played for New York. Griffey's desire to play for the Reds far surpassed his vague interest in the Mets. He called Goldberg back, "I don't feel right about this," he said. "I feel cornered. Tell them no."

Now only the Reds were left—and by this time Griffey was sure he didn't want to return to the Mariners. Some fans had peppered his Web site with hate messages, and a letter from Seattle threatening his family had arrived at his Orlando home. The idea of playing in the town where his parents and grandmother lived looked better and better.

Bowden, sensing his strengthened bargaining position, took it upon himself to quietly reopen talks with Seattle in January. The Mariners wavered about what to do:

Midway through that month Gillick decided he'd rather have his team play the season with Griffey than cave in and make a bad trade; Lincoln preferred to honor Griffey's request rather than bring back a hostile star. The talks continued to go nowhere, but Bowden couldn't stop himself from dropping hints about them in public. He held a panel discussion about the possible trade at a Reds publicity event on January 28. One fan asked him, "How about Tomko, [left-handed reliever Dennys] Reyes, and [out-fielder Dmitri] Young for Griffey?" Responded Bowden, "I like that one. I'd do that one." Then he laughed. In fact, Bowden had made that exact proposal earlier that morning.

On January 30, after two more days of no movement, Bowden presented this idea to Gillick: "Forget about the issues of the 2000 salary and the long-term contract. Let's just see if we can make a baseball trade, and we'll let Chuck Armstrong and John Allen negotiate the dollars." On February 5 Mariners vice president Roger Jongewaard called Bowden with a new proposal, this one without Reese: Seattle wanted Perez, Reyes, Tomko, and catcher Jason LaRue (one of the 11 players on Bowden's secret list and the only top young catcher in Bowden's system). Bowden couldn't part with LaRue. Perez was also on the list of 11, but with Reese, veteran shortstop Barry Larkin, and shortstop prospect Travis Dawkins in the organization, Bowden felt deep enough in the middle infield to make him expendable.

When Jongewaard ended the conversation by saying, "Where are you going to be tomorrow?" Bowden detected the scent of urgency. After he hung up the phone, Bowden said softly to himself, OK, we're Jason LaRue away from getting Griffey. I can find a way to make this deal.

Bowden dialed Allen. "John, we've agreed on three players," he said. "I feel I can make this deal tomorrow. Do I have the OK?"

"I'll call Mr. Lindner and call you back," Allen said.

Not until 6:30 the next evening, just as Bowden sat down to dinner, did Allen call back. "Jim, I've got some bad news for you," Allen said. "You're going to have to pull out. It can't work financially. I want you to release a statement tomorrow."

Bowden drove the next morning, Monday, February 7, with his wife, Amy, to the airport for a flight to Florida to prepare for two arbitration hearings, conveniently post-poning work on the statement. He randomly pulled into a parking spot in the lot. He and Amy looked at each other. The car was parked in section D-30 (Griffey Sr.'s number), row 24 (Junior's Seattle number). "It's going to happen," Amy said. On Tuesday morning Armstrong telephoned Goldberg. "We heard the Reds are going to release a statement pulling out of trade talks," Armstrong said. "We're giving you permission to contact the Reds."

The Mariners had no authority to grant Goldberg such permission—that lies only with the commissioner's office—but Goldberg didn't know that. He called Allen. "Junior's willing to commit to a long-term deal with the Reds in the event of a trade," Goldberg said. "He's willing to work with terms that are very reasonable, less than market value."

(A high-ranking Major League Baseball source says that an investigation did confirm that the contact was illegal but that baseball considered it not serious enough to jeopardize the deal because the Mariners had endorsed the contact and no third team was harmed. Another source familiar with the investigation says that baseball officials are so pleased to see Griffey in Cincinnati under such reasonable contract terms that "they're willing to look the other way on this one" and may choose only to levy a small fine on each club.)

With that phone call the endgame had begun. Suddenly Griffey was affordable. Allen telephoned Lindner, who immediately gave a green light to make the deal. Allen called Bowden and said, "Mr. Lindner has had a change of heart. You have permission to go make a baseball deal. Whatever money you can get them to include in the deal will help, but Mr. Lindner is not putting any financial restrictions on you."

Bowden called Gillick. They agreed to a 4 p.m. conference call the next day, February 9. Gillick said he and Armstrong needed to be somewhere at 8 p.m. Fine, Bowden thought, a deadline. It'll be done by eight.

Bowden started the conference call where they had left off: Perez, Reyes, and Tomko, and let's talk about the fourth player. "Wait," Gillick said. "We want Pokey Reese in it. Now that you're considering Griffey long-term, the price has gone up."

Executives from the two clubs alternately argued and caucused for the next hour. The Mariners gave in. They asked for Cameron instead of Reese. Bowden coyly refused. He offered to get outfielder Jim Edmonds from the Anaheim Angels and pass him on to the Mariners. Gillick didn't want Edmonds, who could be a free agent at the end of the season and who, the Mariners already knew, would not sign a long-term deal with them.

Bowden came back with another offer: Tomko and Cameron for Griffey. Gillick insisted on Reyes and Perez, as well. "You're not getting Reyes and Perez," Bowden exclaimed. "No way. We don't want to do it, but we'll put Perez in. That's it. No more. And this deal is off the table tomorrow. Let's make it or not right now."

Said Gillick, "Are you going to let Dennys Reyes keep you from trading for Ken Griffey, and are you willing to live with that for the rest of your life?"

Bowden shot back, "Are you willing to lose Ken Griffey for nothing and live with that for the rest of your life?"

It was 7:55 p.m. The conference call ended abruptly. The Mariners hung up without so much as a goodbye. Bowden sat in silence by the phone. They hadn't said goodbye, he thought. That's a good sign. Maybe they'll call back.

His telephone rang at 8:21 p.m. One of the lower-level Mariners executives said they had to have a fourth player. What about Meyer, a relief pitcher the Reds had left unprotected in the December Rule V draft? That was it. The deal was done.

Beginning at 9 p.m. and only now with the proper blessing of Major League Baseball, the Reds had 72 hours to work out a deal with Griffey and Goldberg. "I don't want to be an albatross around anybody's neck," Griffey told Goldberg. "I don't want to take up such a huge part of somebody's payroll that they can't do other things. They should still have money to get a player at the [trading] deadline if they need one."

The contract came together quickly. "The secret to the deal working is the amount of deferred money," Allen says. "This is a return to fiscal responsibility." Actually, the deal is an anomaly. Griffey had limited his own market value by announcing he wanted to play for one team—a team with limited resources, at that. Neither he nor Goldberg, an attorney and longtime family friend who represents no other ballplayer, had a history of playing hardball at negotiating tables.

Other agents reacted with as much horror as Selig did glee. Surely, they figured, the deal must include some form of income escalation, such as a guarantee that Griffey would always be the highest-paid Red, or an attendance clause similar to what Mark McGwire has with the Cardinals. But none exists.

It took only a few hours for Griffey to begin to have the effect on Cincinnati that McGwire had on St. Louis after the slugging first baseman's trade there in July 1997. The Cinergy Field switchboard was overwhelmed with incoming calls for tickets. The only way to reach anyone in the Reds office was on a cell phone. So many people showed up to buy season tickets that they had to take numbers in the lobby and wait to be called into a room to buy them—and even then Reds employees couldn't get an open phone line to run charge cards. An advertising agency called to offer free billboard space with a picture of Griffey to hawk season tickets.

The rest of the National League celebrated, too, now that it can promote dates featuring Griffey, McGwire, and the Chicago Cubs' Sammy Sosa, probably the three greatest drawing cards in the game today. The only three players still alive to have hit more than 55 home runs in a season all play in the National League Central, which gives teams such as Selig's own cash-strapped Milwaukee Brewers 18 dates to sell the Big Three. Look for special ticket packages—the 18-game Power Pack—at a National League ballpark near you.

Remember this, though: Griffey, McGwire, and Sosa hit 176 home runs among them last year, yet all played for losing teams that finished a combined 67½ games out of first place. Beyond the glamour of the home run race, the success of the Reds, Cardinals, and Cubs will depend mostly on pitching, which none have in abundance.

Bowden will try to deal from his surplus of outfielders to find another starter to join Neagle, Pete Harnisch, Steve Parris, and Ron Villone, though Bowden's history suggests he will do so in July. (He has picked up Dave Burba, Juan Guzman, Mark Portugal, and David Wells in deadline deals.) He postponed any such thoughts, though, on the jet ride back to Florida last Thursday night. This was a time to celebrate, especially when Lindner's son Craig popped the corks on the Dom Pérignon.

It was also a time to reflect. Bowden thought about his seven years with the Reds, all but the last in the employ of the penurious Marge Schott, whom Lindner replaced as the majority owner. He thought about how Schott wouldn't provide the offices and clubhouse with bottled water. (That's why we have water fountains, she reasoned.) Now here he was sipping champagne and sinking softly into the cushioned leather upholstery of a private jet that cost nearly as much as his team's entire 1999 payroll, surrounded by fresh food, a DVD player, a big-screen television, and one of the 50 greatest players of the 20th century. Only two others, he figured, had changed teams in their youthful primes: Babe Ruth and Rogers Hornsby.

He saw Griffey laughing with his children, and he knew the fit was right. Junior last wore a Cincinnati uniform when he was eight years old and his father was an All-Star outfielder with the Reds. The kids beat their dads 12–0 in the player–family game. Junior would relish victories by his father's teams because after them he could grab "red pop and bubble gum" from the clubhouse. He'd cry after losses because that's when children weren't allowed in. Now Trey and Taryn can scamper around the same places he did, only this time at the feet of their father *and* grandfather.

Bowden had felt a tightness in his gut ever since he'd hung up the phone at 8:30 the night before. That and a sense of decorum were all that kept him from yelping with joy as loud as he could. Yes, sir. He was flying.

Who the Mariners Got

Mike Cameron: If this deal ever is to be perceived as "close to" an even swap, Cameron is the key. The 27-year-old is on the verge of developing into an impact player. The Reds realized last year he was miscast as a leadoff hitter despite his speed and a significant improvement in his willingness to take walks. Those walks and a leap to 21 home runs and 34 doubles make his still-high strikeout rate palatable as long as he's batting in an RBI position. Cameron is much faster than Ken Griffey Jr. and runs the bases extremely well. The Mariners will notice little drop-off defensively. How much higher Cameron can push his batting average (280–290?) and power numbers (30–35 home runs a year?), while inevitably and unfairly being compared to Griffey, will determine how much sting Seattle fans will feel.

Brett Tomko: The big right-hander has been on the trading block since early last season, from about the time the Reds concluded he doesn't pitch big. That is, for a guy who throws in the low 90s, his command has been slipping and he's become homer prone. Despite falling out of favor by May, Tomko actually pitched better during the second half of the season. And he's not much more than a year removed from being considered a future front-of-the-rotation starter. Unless the Mariners trade another pitcher in the meantime, Tomko won't be asked to slot in any higher than number 5.

Antonio Perez: His (Class A) Midwest League numbers last season are good, albeit indicative of how raw the infielder is. But when you realize he didn't turn 18 until late July, the stats are more than promising. He's fast—35 steals—but still learning to run the bases—caught 24 times. He showed pop in his bat (20 doubles and seven homers) that is good for a teenager with time to build on his 5-11, 175-pound frame. He showed outstanding strikezone judgment in the 1998 Dominican Summer League. That slipped some when he was tossed in among older players last season. His 36 errors are not uncommon for a green shortstop, but he spent half the season at second base, which could turn out to be his better position. His on-base ability has been good from the beginning, so he projects as a solid candidate to eventually be at or near the top of a major league batting order.

Jake Meyer: He's the one you're least likely to see in the majors at any point. He has been close to a strikeout-an-inning man through his three minor league seasons, with a fastball scouts say is in the low- to mid-90s. Some folks around last year's Class A Rockford club claim it approached 100 mph at times. His control is the issue, and it took a noticeable dive when he reached Double-A for the first time midway through last season. The 5.96 ERA in 20 games at Chattanooga muddled future-closer thoughts created by his 2.54 ERA and 16 saves at Rockford. The biggest negative is that the UCLA product just turned 25 and hasn't yet proven himself in Double-A.

Bottom line for Mariners: Wait and see. First to learn if GM Pat Gillick has enough surplus, especially in pitching, to make another deal. It made more sense to make the trade with Cincinnati and then assess other possibilities rather than lock into a three-way deal. Cameron will be fine in center field, but this team needs a corner outfielder who is an offensive threat. Someone who could hit in or near the middle of the order would be nice, but a better fit would be someone who could keep Seattle from forcing Cameron or Brian Hunter into the leadoff spot. Anaheim's Jim Edmonds has been mentioned, as has Montreal's

(continued)

Who the Mariners Got (*concluded*)

Rondell White. The best fit might be Johnny Damon of the Royals, who have plenty of outfielders and need pitching. Of more long-term concern is whether all of this will have any effect on free-agent-to-be number 2, Alex Rodriquez. He's not going to sign during the season, but Gillick will have to gauge if there's any chance of luring him back next winter. If not, he needs to see if there's a reasonable trade package out there for him before August. Seattle's improved pitching thrusts it into contention. They could stay there with another deal that brings back some offense.

Bottom line for Reds: Getting a superstar without deleting anybody you need is the perfect trade. Cincinnati's biggest concern remains its starting pitching, but Tomko was nothing more than a fifth starter to them. Of course, the rest of the rotation is not without its concerns, most of them physical. Remember though, that the Reds added a 48-homer guy and the NL Central-champion Astros lost 22-game winner Mike Hampton. And the difference between the two clubs was just one game. It would appear the Reds have obliterated the gap. But have they made up the seven games between themselves and the Braves?

Case 6

Teotihuacan Murals

In 1993, from May through October, the Fine Arts Museums of San Francisco show-cased the exhibit *Teotihuacan: City of the Gods/Ciudad de los Dioses*. Over 200 objects had been assembled from collections throughout Mexico, Europe, and the United States to focus on the arts of the pre-Columbian Teotihuacan culture. According to Harry Parker, III, director of the Fine Arts Museums of San Francisco:

> *Teotihuacan; City of the Gods/Ciudad de los Dioses* is more than an exhibition. It is a re-markable artistic and cultural event. It grows from a special relationship between Mexico and the Fine Arts Museums of San Francisco.[1]

The exhibition was envisioned to serve many different objectives, including in-creased understanding of an ancient culture of great importance both to the people of Mexico and to the members of California's Mexican American community. In addition, it represented a symbol of goodwill between Mexico and the United States. According to Rodolfo Figueroa, Consul General de México in 1993,

> Teotihuacan siempre ha sido el alma y el corazón del pueblo mexicano. Representa la grandeza de la herencia prehispánica mexicana, el elemento vital de la historia nacional y de la identidad de México. . . . Creemos que eventos como éste, contribuyen en forma significativa a las buenas relaciones y la comprensión entre los pueblos de orígenes y naciones distintas.[2]
> [Teotihuacan has always been the heart and soul of the Mexican people. It represents the grandeur of pre-Columbian Mexican heritage, the lifeblood of Mexico's national history and identity. . . . We believe that events like this one contribute significantly to good rela-tions and understanding among people of different origins and nations.]

To Thomas K. Seligman, director of the Stanford University Museum of Art, the exhibition was of special significance. It represented, in large measure, the fruits of a successful negotiation that had begun more than 15 years earlier when he had been cu-rator in charge of the Art of Africa, Oceania, and the Americas (AOA) department at the Fine Arts Museums of San Francisco.

The Extraordinary Gift

In early 1976, Thomas Seligman received a telephone call from the probate depart-ment of Crocker National Bank. Harald Wagner, a San Francisco architect, had died on February 4, 1976, and his will bequeathed a collection of pre-Columbian murals

Source: This case was written by Professor Susan E. Brodt, E. Marie Shantz Associate Professor of Organi-zational Behavior at Queen's University, Canada (sbrodt@business.queensu.ca), with the assistance of Christy McCammon. It is based on interviews and additional documents including Thomas Seligman's essay, "An Unexpected Bequest and an Ethical Dilemma" (pp. 15–23) in K. Berrin (ed.), *Feathered Serpents and Flowering Trees: Reconstructing the Murals of Teotihuacan* (San Francisco: The Fine Arts Museums of San Francisco 1988). Although words cannot fully convey my appreciation, I thank Tom Seligman, Judy Teichman, Walter Newman, Ian White, and others who gave generously of their time to help create this case. Copyright 1995. Used with permission.

and other objects to San Francisco's M. H. de Young Museum. Although Seligman was not acquainted with Wagner or his collection, as AOA curator at the Fine Arts Museums of San Francisco (which included the de Young Museum) it was his responsibility to examine and possibly take possession of these objects. Seligman referred the bank to Judith Teichman, deputy city attorney for the city and county of San Francisco, which was the customary procedure for bequests.

Two months later Seligman met with an officer of the bank at Wagner's house. Seligman was astounded by what he found. Sections of colorful painted murals, ranging in size from a few inches (10 cm) to 14 feet (4.27 meters) in length, were lying on the floor and on tables, and other pieces were mounted on the walls of the living room. Many more mural fragments were in the dining room and basement—over 70 mural fragments in total. Seligman stood speechless as he surveyed the collection; he knew immediately that the murals were from the pre-Columbian culture of Teotihuacan, famous for its large pyramids of the sun and moon just north of present-day Mexico City. They were undoubtedly very important cultural objects. There were more pre-Columbian murals in the Wagner house than Seligman had ever seen in one place.

The murals were, however, in various states of deterioration; some had been framed in cork while others had been glued to pieces of plywood. Several had little protection other than the cardboard boxes in which they rested. Seligman noticed that amateurish efforts had been made to preserve many of the murals by filling cracks with plaster, and overpainting or waxing some original surfaces. It was obvious that the murals were badly damaged, easily fragmented, and in immediate need of protection.

"What have we gotten into?" Seligman thought to himself as he considered the cultural importance of the murals and their fragile condition. He was also aware of his museum's lack of experience in dealing with murals such as these. At the same time, though, he felt a responsibility to protect these precious objects and mitigate the effects of amateur restoration and mountings presumably performed by Wagner.

Seligman knew that to preserve and protect the murals, the issues surrounding the murals' ownership and the probate of the estate needed to be settled quickly. Moreover, he realized that he might need to convince the other legatees to renounce any possible claims to the murals.

The bank was eager to begin the process of setting the estate, but several issues first needed to be resolved. For example, there was some question about who would pay the taxes and cost of administering the estate (approximately $250,000[3]). Because the probate of Wagner's estate might be lengthy, and because of the fragile state of the murals, Seligman recommended that the murals be stored immediately to prevent further deterioration.

The murals were moved from the Wagner mansion and stored in the basement of the de Young Museum for safekeeping while the estate was being probated. The museum contracted with Crocker Bank to store the murals (at the estate's expense). The murals, weighing almost 3,400 pounds (1,542 kg), were packed in 10 crates. The museum's largest storeroom had been cleared to make room for these treasures. The murals were to be stored only temporarily, and Seligman knew that he and the Fine Arts Museums needed to investigate all of the issues and decide on a proper course of action. Of primary concern were ownership, curatorship of the collection, relations with Mexico (particularly his Mexican colleagues in the museum community), and the Fine Arts Museums' policy regarding bequests.

Based upon his experience as a curator, Seligman realized that proper curatorship of the collection required that the interrelationships among the mural fragments be established and the fragile fragments be protected, preserved, and ultimately displayed in the best possible way. Beyond the proper curatorship, the issue of ownership, and relations with Mexico, raised an even broader question.

Seligman learned from his initial research that the murals were exceptionally rare and that their restoration would require special expertise. Mexico's National Institute of Anthropology and History of Mexico (Instituto Nacional de Antropología e Historia)—INAH—the governmental department responsible for all archaeology and most museums in Mexico, had a notable conservationist center experienced in dealing with Teotihuacan murals. After consulting with conservators, Seligman also discovered that an estimated $500,000 and approximately three years of conservation work would be required to restore the Wagner murals. (See Exhibit 1 for a breakdown of the cost estimate.)

Seligman was aware that in recent years many countries (particularly developing countries) had sought restitution for the artifacts of their past civilizations that had been looted to supply the international art market. Museums and collectors throughout the United States had long been criticized for leading the worldwide pillaging of such artifacts. It was very possible that adding Wagner's Teotihuacan murals to the Fine Arts Museums' collection would cause a backlash from Mexico. In addition, Teichman had informed Seligman that under the constitution and laws of the state of California, repatriating the murals would require "just compensation" to the city for it to be considered a valid transaction.[4] (In essence, the California Constitution prohibits public entities or officers from giving away public property.)

There were also policy issues to consider, starting with the Fine Arts Museums' acquisition policy, which was broadly worded. The Teotihuacan murals would provide the first concrete case of the policy's application and might well set an example for the museum community at large.

Seligman thought about the broader implications that the bequest might have in setting a precedent for other U.S. museums. He hoped that UNESCO's (United Nations Educational, Scientific, and Cultural Organization) Convention on the Means of Prohibiting and Preventing the Illicit Import, Export, and Transfer of Ownership of Cultural

EXHIBIT 1 | Restoration Estimates

Stage I:	Undoing previous restorations	$50,000
Stage II:	Stabilizing the surfaces of the murals; includes removing overpainting and adhesives	$150,000
Stage III:	Creating the proper support systems	$300,000

Restoration allows murals to be displayed vertically, which protects the fragments and preserves the impression of "pieces of walls." Estimate includes custom-made aluminum frame.

It is projected that the process will take at least three years to complete, with two to three conservators working on the project.

Property (November 14, 1970) might provide useful insights. Thirty-eight nations had already signed the convention. Seligman thought that it might serve as a useful guide.

Finally, Seligman knew immediately that his primary interest was in preserving the murals and the cultural heritage they represented. Even though he was an administrator (i.e., Deputy Director of Education and Exhibitions), he was still curator of the Museums' AOA collection, which was the reason that the Wagner collection had been brought to his attention.

To begin addressing these issues, Seligman solicited input from his colleagues in the museum community. He listened carefully to their widely divergent perspectives. The overwhelming sentiment was to avoid contacting anyone from the government of Mexico because of the potential political implications. Mexican involvement, many predicted, would lead to a bitter political and legal battle. However, Seligman thought that Mexico's consul general in San Francisco, Señor Sierra-Becarra, might be an important resource. Many of Seligman's colleagues cautioned him against approaching Señor Sierra-Becarra. They also advised Seligman that it would be impossible for him to deal directly with INAH (i.e., professional-to-professional) because INAH was part of the Mexican government.

For almost two years Seligman conducted a careful study of the situation. During this same period, an important event occurred: Mexico requested that the United States institute legal proceedings against the city and county of San Francisco for possession of the murals under a 1971 bilateral agreement of cooperation between the two countries. In July 1978 the U.S. Attorney filed an action on behalf of Mexico to transfer the Wagner probate proceedings to the federal district court. The city and county of San Francisco objected to the transfer of the case, and a federal judge agreed that such a transfer would be inappropriate, thereby returning the matter to the state probate court. According to Mexican law, however, the murals were still considered to be the property of Mexico.

It was now the fall of 1978, over two years after he had first learned of Wagner's bequest, and Seligman knew it was time to move forward. Probate of the estate had almost been completed with the murals preliminarily distributed to the de Young Museum (although without prejudice to any right to title or possession, which Mexico might validly present). Furthermore, the condition of the murals had become critical. Their fragile state had been painfully revealed when U.S. Customs agents inspected the murals in mid-1977. Two murals, which had been packed by specialists in packing art, were found in crumbled pieces. Clearly, the preservation of the murals was at stake and the time to act was at hand. To preserve the murals, Seligman knew that he needed the cooperation and, more important, the collaboration of his museum colleagues in Mexico.

The Museums' board of directors was eager to know what Seligman proposed to do with the murals. Mexico, the museum community, and the general public also awaited word as to the Fine Arts Museums' plans. Seligman thought about the role of his museum, its responsibility to itself, to Mexico, to the museum community, and to the San Francisco community (including the Mexican American community), all of whom would be affected by his actions. Whatever he decided to do, Seligman would need to convince the director of the Museums, Ian White, and the board of trustees as to the benefits of his plan.

The Fine Arts Museums of San Francisco

In 1972 two museums owned by the city and county of San Francisco—the M.H. de Young Memorial Museum and the California Palace of the Legion of Honor—merged to create the Fine Arts Museums of San Francisco. The Museums served the combined population of the Northern California counties of close to 10 million people and the hundreds of thousands of tourists who visited San Francisco each year. The Museums had been particularly important because of the limited number of major museums on the West Coast. A membership roster of 30,000 people, among the largest for U.S. art museums, highlighted the Museums' popularity.

Overseeing a combined collection of 200,000 objects valued at approximately $200–300 million, the Fine Arts Museums' four curatorial departments provided a comprehensive view of art history, from ancient times through the 20th century. As shown in Exhibit 2, the departments were European Art; American Art; Textiles, Prints and Drawings; and Art of Africa, Oceania, and the Americas. The Africa, Oceania, and Americas (AOA) department had been established with a permanent gallery in 1973. In 1976, when the Wagner murals were bequeathed to the museum, the collection's holdings were far less extensive than the holdings of any of the other three departments and were valued at approximately $10–20 million. The AOA collection consisted of traditional arts of Africa (primarily West Africa), Oceania (primarily

EXHIBIT 2 | The Fine Arts Museums Organizational Chart

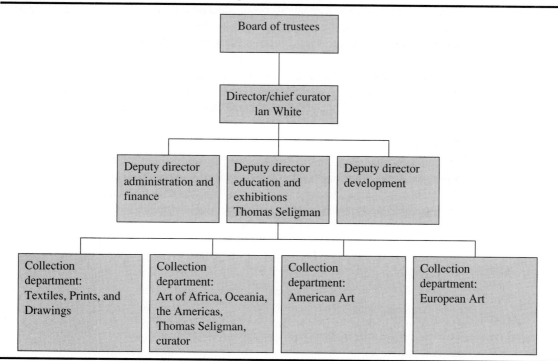

Melanesia, Micronesia, and Polynesia), Mesoamerica (especially Mexico, Central America, and Peru), and Native Americans.

In his roles as curator in charge of AOA and as deputy director in charge of education and exhibitions, Seligman reported to the director of the Fine Arts Museums, Ian White. The museum's director and the board of trustees had ultimate decision-making authority regarding policy decisions.

The president of the board of trustees was Walter Newman, a well-known businessman and civic leader. Newman was concerned with the service side of the Museums' business: Specifically, he stressed ways to improve the service that the museums provided to the community. For instance, he was responsible for computerizing the museums' ticketing systems so that the public could be scheduled to see exhibitions at certain showing times to prevent the problem of bottlenecks and people waiting on the street for hours for popular exhibits. He also played an important role as president of the board, ensuring that the Museums' finances were secure; Newman set policies to ensure the Museums' longevity.

Ever since Seligman had begun working at the de Young Museum in 1971, he had worked closely and amicably with Ian White, Walter Newman, and the rest of the board of trustees. The environment had been collegial, and he enjoyed interacting with all the members of the senior administration. However, Seligman had never been faced with anything as potentially controversial as the Wagner murals.

The Teotihuacan Murals

The collection of Teotihuacan murals bequeathed by Harald Wagner to the de Young Museum was by far the largest single collection of Teotihuacan murals outside of Mexico. Mexico had approximately 500 murals from the Teotihuacan that were in storage at INAH, on display at the museum at Teotihuacan, or at the Churubusco Conservation Center (INAH's restoration facility for all cultural and historic material). There were also an untold number of murals that had not yet been unearthed at the site of the Teotihuacan, since only 10 percent of the eight square miles had been excavated.

Valuation

Typically, the auction market was the instrument that established the value of art objects; however, there had been no auction history associated with any of the pieces in the Wagner collection. Although other Teotihuacan murals had been offered for sale in the past,[5] private collectors and most museums had shied away from such murals because they were fragile, subject to crumbling, and difficult to display given their thick and uneven backing. Essentially, collectors were offered a chunk of wall that was heavy and awkward. There were many difficulties involved with transporting, displaying, and preserving them.

American museums had shown more interest than private collectors, but only three institutions had made outright purchases: the Cleveland Museum of Art, the Art Institute of Chicago, and the Denver Art Museum. Because these purchases included only small fragments and not entire murals, the prices paid by these museums were of limited relevance to the Wagner collection. Nine other U.S. museums accepted Teotihuacan murals as permanent donations between 1967 and 1979. The handful of murals that were in the United States could not, however, be considered of the same magnitude or significance as the Wagner collection because of the latter's enormity, uniqueness, and iconographic breadth.

New York dealer Edward Merrin, who appraised the murals, estimated their value to be approximately $5 million in light of the environment for pre-Columbian art. A 3-foot (.91 meters) by 4-foot (1.22 meters) Mayan stelae that was in excellent condition could garner between $1million and $2 million; it was not unreasonable, therefore, to assume that a restored Teotihuacan mural from the same era might be worth 30 to 50 percent less. With 30 semicomplete murals in the Wagner Collection, an estimate of $5 million had seemed likely. If there were absolute certainty that the murals would not be returned to Mexico (i.e., if they were "clean"), they would be even more valuable.

From a museum's point of view, an important factor in the Teotihuacan murals' value was the revenue that they might provide in terms of exhibition. Special exhibitions typically brought in between $100,000 and $400,000 during a four-month period, and a museum held about 10 exhibitions per year. A blockbuster exhibit, such as the King Tut exhibit held at the de Young in 1979, could bring in as much as $2.5 million. An exhibition of Wagner's collection of Teotihuacan murals would have tremendous draw due to several factors: (1) the magnificence and exceptional quality of the collection, (2) the strong Hispanic cultural heritage of California, and (3) the small number of such murals outside of Mexico. Before any exhibit could be mounted, however, the murals needed to be restored, preserved, and housed properly (which involved significant costs).

The History of Teotihuacan

Teothiuacan, Mexico's foremost archaeological zone and one of its national symbols, is located about an hour's drive from Mexico City; it is often referred to as "the pyramids" by visitors because of the impressive pyramids that dominate the landscape. The pyramids, once believed to be of Aztec origin, actually predated the Aztec people; the Aztecs arrived in A.D. 1350 to find the abandoned temples 600 years after the collapse of Teotihuacan. The Aztecs named the site Teotihuacan, or "City of the Gods," because it appeared to them that the gods had created these awesome structures.

Tourists typically visit only the heart of Teotihuacan's ceremonial complex. They climb the huge stepped pyramids, roughly the size of the Egyptian pyramids, and tour the museum and other major religious and civic structures. The area of Teotihuacan covers eight square miles surrounding the ceremonial center. Much of the remains of the civilization is still underground, however, and awaits the archaeologist. In fact, it has been estimated that as of 1994 less than 10 percent of Teotihuacan has been excavated.

The Teotihuacan era lasted for over 700 years (begun before AD I) and at its peak had approximately 150,000 people living within eight square miles. In AD 500 it was the size that Paris would be in the 17th century. Throughout its history, Teotihuacan was the most populous and influential city in Mesoamerica. The cultural achievements of the Teotihuacan had indeed been so important that pre-Columbian art or history cannot be understood without reference to this great civilization.

The Wagner Collection

The Wagner collection of Teotihuacan murals may quite possibly represent an important link in our understanding of that ancient civilization. Little is known about the Teotihuacan culture in a practical sense, perhaps because the spectacular pyramids and major ceremonial buildings have long stolen attention from the more basic questions about the culture (e.g., social organization and agronomy). Although scholars have not yet discovered an organized system of writing used by the people, many of the Wagner murals reveal important glyphs that may provide new and valuable evidence about the civilization. According to Teotihuacan specialist Arthur Miller of the University of Pennsylvania's University Museum,

> Not only are many of the murals of outstanding quality, but a study of them could confirm many stylistic and iconographic patterns, perhaps even supply missing links, in the lexicon of Teotihuacan painting.[6]

However fascinating the murals were, even the most experienced art dealers were not interested in purchasing them when they entered the market in the early 1960s. Most dealers and collectors were not interested in wall art on fragile four-inch-thick adobe backing, which made them subject to crumbling. This had been true for all collectors except Harald Wagner.

Harald Wagner was a successful architect in San Francisco who enjoyed buying buildings, restoring them, and then selling them for profit. Wagner also had great sympathy for certain artists and supported them whenever possible; he greatly admired the work of Arthur and Lucia Mathews, for example, important artists of the California decorative style. Arthur Mathews is known as one of California's greatest muralists. Wagner bequeathed his personal collection of Mathews's art to the Oakland (California) Art Museum.

Wagner also loved Mexico and its people, which led him to purchase and renovate an 18th century hacienda in Mexico, which he lived in during part of the year. It was not surprising, therefore, that Wagner might have appreciated the Teotihuacan murals in light of his fascination with the Mexican culture and his adoration of the California decorative style. The Teotihuacan murals and the California decorative style both placed primary attention on the architectural context, and placed secondary emphasis on a love of the decorative, an interest in flat patterns, and an appreciation of exotic natural forms with an emphasis on allegory, abstraction, and symbolism.

Furthermore, Wagner may have enjoyed the challenge of reconstructing the crumbling murals, visualizing the dramatic result once restored. Wagner's limited efforts to sell the murals after they were assembled had been unsuccessful, however, although his efforts later provided evidence that Wagner had brought the frescoes into the United States sometime *before* the effective date of the U.S.–Mexico bilateral treaty of cooperation (i.e., March 24, 1971). It was unknown why he had selected the de Young Museum in his will.

The Museum Community and Cultural Patrimony

Within the museum community, a climate of concern had developed surrounding cultural patrimony; the concern erupted in 1969 with Clemency Coggin's article "Illicit Traffic in Pre-Columbian Antiquities" published in *Art Journal* that documented the despoliation of Mayan sites. In addition, there had been several celebrated cases of U.S. museums or dealers repatriating objects of cultural importance. Repatriation involves the voluntary return of culturally significant objects to the country of origin without monetary remuneration.

For example, an Afo-A-Kom statue that was acquired by a Madison Avenue dealer's shop in 1973 had been repatriated to Africa. The statue had strong religious and cultural significance to the Kom, a tribe in French Cameroon, and after wide publicity and international outcry, the statue was returned.

As a result of the concern about cultural claims to art objects, the Association of Art Museum Directors (AAMD) published *Professional Practices in Art Museums* (1971), which confirmed and elaborated on the profession's concerns about illicit removal of cultural property. In addition, the American Association of Museums (AAM) published *Museum Ethics* (1978), which set forth a code of professional ethics and encouraged museums to adopt acquisition policies designed to prevent the support, especially indirect support, of the illicit removal of cultural property from other nations.

The Fine Arts Museums' policy on acquisitions and collections did not cover cultural patrimony specifically; it provided a broadly stated prohibition against "acquiring objects in violation of the laws of the USA or the laws of the country of origin."[7] Documentation, such as valid titles and export permits, was required to make a determination. Like the code of professional conduct outlined in *Museum Ethics,* the policy was very broad, yet its general premises supported the notion that the museums should not participate in the illicit removal of cultural property.

The most specific guidance that seemed relevant to the Wagner murals (and which addressed the issue of repatriation) appeared in the soon-to-be-published study conducted by the International Council of Museums (ICOM) titled "Study on the Principles, Conditions, and Means for the Restitution or Return of Cultural Property in View of Reconstituting Dispersed Heritages." The study noted the specific circumstances under which countries should be subject to requests for restitution or the return of cultural property. ICOM specified "objects that are indispensable to people in understanding their origin and culture" (section 10) and "which have an essential sociocultural value" (section 12). The general finding was that requests for repatriation or restitution should be the exception; in fact, according to section 31:

> . . . it would thus be preferable that the transfer of property *remain relatively exceptional,* [emphasis added] given, on the one hand, the serious legal and practical difficulties involved in this procedure, and on the other hand, the availability of technical methods which are much more flexible and easier to implement at the simple level of museum institutions, and which lead to practically identical results . . .[8]

Only under special conditions, therefore, could countries request repatriation or restitution, and the usual practice was not to return cultural property.

The Role of a Museum

According to *Professional Practices in Art Museums,* museums' functions include "the acquisition, preservation, and presentation of the collections, as well as the scholarship and interpretation related to them."[9] Some museums feature their role as collectors and preservers of art (and culture) and venues for research and scholarship, whereas others emphasize their role in educating the public. All museums have a responsibility to themselves, however, and must maintain their existence (e.g., financial and organizational health).

Museum as Collector or Preserver

Museums collect and preserve works of art. In this role they are repositories of priceless artifacts, and they afford protection from the elements and the usual deterioration that occurs with the passage of time. In addition, careful attention to preservation can improve the quality and condition of works and extend their longevity. Preservation efforts require the talents of researchers and technicians. The role of collector and preserver emphasizes the value and importance of the works, their significance in history, and their role in research and scholarship. It also suggests a commitment to the proper storage and display of the works to the public where they can be appreciated and admired. In this capacity, museums provide an expertise in caring for objects and ensuring their long-lasting preservation.

Museum as Educator

Museums are educational institutions—that is, places where people can learn about ancient and modern civilizations through preserved works of art. Museums provide a window to past worlds that helps many individuals understand their own roots, especially in the multicultural society in the United States where many people cannot afford to visit their ancestors' homeland. In California, for example, where a significant percentage of the population is of Mexican origin, the Teotihuacan murals inform many citizens of their cultural heritage.

In addition to educating the public through exhibitions, many museums educate scholars by providing direct access to collections. Scholars may specialize in preservation, social history, agronomy, or periods in history or parts of the world.

Sustaining the Organization

Most museums sustain themselves by carefully managing their existing resources, securing grants from funding agencies, and soliciting funds and donations from the public (e.g., corporations, individuals).

Ethical and Political Climate

In 1976 the climate in the United States was highly charged. During the Nixon era, "art-for-drug interdiction" was an unfortunate reality. As a result, many members of the museum community preferred to be uninvolved in government activities; for example, the recommendation that Seligman not involve the U.S. or Mexican governments was representative of the museum community's sentiment. His colleagues feared that the Wagner collection might become a "political football" between the U.S. and Mexico. The fear was that art objects would be used as barter in other agendas such as drug trafficking or illegal immigration.

In the international arena, the United Nations formed the United Nations Educational Scientific and Cultural Organization (UNESCO) in 1946 with a general commitment to preserve, protect, and promote the world's cultures. Equal dignity of national cultures and the conception of cultural values as the heritage of the people as a whole were its central tenets. The founders of UNESCO recognized that world peace could not be established through political and economic arrangements alone, but had to be based on human spiritual, intellectual, moral, and cultural cooperation.

In 1970 UNESCO passed the Convention on the Means of Prohibiting and Preventing the Illicit Import, Export, and Transfer of Ownership of Cultural Property. This general framework for international cooperation was designed to curb the illicit movement of looted antiquities and stolen art and was adopted in response to the concern of many groups of archaeologists, anthropologists, historians, museum professionals, and developing nations over objects that were improperly removed from their countries of origin. The most notorious example was the pillaging of Mayan sites documented in the 1969 article by Coggin in *Art Journal.*

The United States supported UNESCO's efforts, and the U.S. Senate gave its advice and consent for ratification in 1972; by 1978, however, the United States had not yet adopted the measure. The Senate Committee on Finance supported UNESCO's approval because it was seen as critical for foreign relations as well as the preservation of the cultural heritage of humankind. The Senate Committee on Finance elaborated:

> An expanding worldwide trade in objects of archaeological and ethnological interests has led to wholesale depredations in some countries, resulting in the mutilation of ceremonial centers and archaeological complexes of ancient civilizations and the removal of stone sculptures and reliefs. The governments which have been victimized are disturbed by the outflow of these objects to foreign lands, and the appearance in the United States of these objects has given rise to outcries and urgent requests for return by other countries.[10]

The primary opposition was the American Association of Dealers in Ancient, Oriental, and Primitive Art, who viewed the convention as unfairly penalizing their business. Their well-funded opposition sparked a heated debate. Many young, small museums also opposed the policy as it could impose a significant disadvantage to museums that had not yet established full collections. The opposition's argument was that certain cultural objects were better off in the United States, where they would receive the care of museums that would preserve and protect the objects, while at the same time providing a conduit for education and scholarship.

A related controversy concerned ownership. By the 1970s, many populations occupied land that was originally the homeland of other people (e.g., the United States). Questions about whether current inhabitants have rightful ownership to cultural objects from previous cultures still spark heated discussion and debate.

Some museum professionals questioned the protection that developing countries could afford for precious objects. They reasoned that developing countries might be tempted by the lucrative market value associated with objects, particularly in light of a country's pressing economic needs. In addition, some people believed that the technological capabilities of developed countries should be preferred over the less available technology in developing countries. Because of the age and fragile condition of many cultural artifacts, technology was believed to be a critical factor in terms of an object's preservation.

Finally, some U.S. museums opposed UNESCO's efforts, arguing that they would not be able to compete in the international arena; no industrialized countries had adopted the treaty so far, and there was no indication that they would do so in the near future.

The arguments for and against UNESCO's convention were heartfelt and heated. As of 1978, the convention did not dictate what museums should do with cultural artifacts; it helped inform and guide museum managers in their decisions, however.

The Legal Environment in the United States

In the summer of 1977, the U.S. Customs Service asked to inspect the Wagner murals. It was not clear how they had learned of them. Upon viewing the murals, one Customs agent expressed an interest in returning the murals to Mexico. As Customs had no basis for such action, it was prevented from doing so by the Museums' attorneys.

Shortly thereafter, the Mexican government formally requested the assistance of the U.S. Attorney General to recover the murals under the 1971 "Treaty of Cooperation . . . Providing for the Recovery and Return of Stolen Archaeological, Historical, and Cultural Properties" between the United States and Mexico. According to this treaty, each government would cooperate in the effort. The treaty defines archaeological property as "art objects and artifacts of the pre-Columbian cultures . . . of outstanding importance to the national patrimony" (Article 1, section Ia). An action was instituted by the U.S. Attorney on behalf of Mexico to transfer the Wagner estate to federal district court. Although the climate at the time was such that the United States supported Mexico's attempts to reclaim pre-Columbian artwork, the action was resolved in favor of the city and county of San Francisco primarily because Mexico was not "a defendant" in the probate proceeding, and only defendants could seek a transfer from state to federal court. Furthermore, the "Treaty of Cooperation" was not retroactive. Wagner's documents included receipts dated in the 1960s for the purchase of the murals in Mexico. Also, there was evidence that Wagner had offered the murals for sale to a Los Angeles museum during the late 1960s.

Despite this setback, Mexico stood fast in its belief that the murals should be returned. Javier Moctezuma, former cultural attaché at the Mexican Embassy in Washington, D.C., stated Mexico's position:

> Mexico will never give up the rights to these murals. But, as a last resort, museums can negotiate among themselves, since there is a conflict of national laws.[11]

Mexico's Interests

Officials in the Mexican government felt strongly about the return of the Teotihuacan murals. The murals were important components of the national cultural heritage, and they engendered considerable pride among the people of Mexico. It was common knowledge among members of the museum world that Joaquín García-Bárcena,

Director of Pre-Hispanic Monuments at INAH, advocated Mexico's reclamation of pre-Columbian objects.

To the people of Mexico, Teotihuacan has special meaning:

> Teotihuacan has to some extent become the collective heart and soul of Mexico, a national symbol bound to the national identity and history of the Mexican people. . . . To many Mexican intellectuals Teotihuacan is the lifeblood of their national history and identity, past and present—mysterious, unresolved, but indestructible—a solid core whose presence always has been and always will be there, in spite of Mexico's many struggles and omnipresent poverty.[12]

In addition to the emotional ties, Mexican law proclaims ownership to the Teotihuacan murals. Ley Federal Sobre Monumentos y Zonas Arqueológicas, Artísticas e Históricas (Law Concerning Monuments and Archaeological, Artistic, and Historical Zones) vests Mexico with the ownership of all art and artifacts found or to be found in Mexico. Similarly, the United States claims title to all cultural property found on federal lands.

Next Steps

Seligman had studied the complex set of issues surrounding the extraordinary bequest and needed to take action. In representing the Fine Arts Museums, he had an obligation to the people of San Francisco. As a curator, he was concerned about the preservation of the murals. As a member of the international museum community, he respected the opinions of colleagues, many of whose own countries' cultural heritage had been pillaged. Mexico's reaction and INAH's cooperation would also be important considerations. Finally, Seligman felt obligated to uphold the principles set forth by ICOM and UNESCO.

Whatever he decided, Seligman knew that his decision should reflect the best interests of the Fine Arts Museums. It must also lead to a consensus among the senior administrators of the institution (namely, the board of trustees, chaired by Walter Newman, and the director of the museum, Ian White) and the deputy city attorney, Judith Teichman.

Seligman thought to himself, "My most important consideration, first and foremost, is the preservation of these objects." It was imperative that he act quickly because the preservation of the murals was at stake. Restoration and housing of these treasures needed to be resolved before more damage was done.

Endnotes

1. *Teotihuacan: City of the Gods/Ciudad de los Dioses,* p. 48. Guide published by the Fine Arts Museums of San Francisco to accompany the exhibit.

2. *Ibid.,* p. 48

3. All amounts are listed in U.S. dollars, unless otherwise noted.

4. According to Judith Teichman, deputy city attorney, the "Charitable Trust" law of the city and county of San Francisco states that no property can be given away without "just compensation" (personal communication, December 21, 1993).

5. Many murals had been looted from the site in the early 1960s and appeared on the market.

6. A. Miller, *The Wall Paintings of Teotihuacan* (Washington, DC: Dumbarton Oaks, 1973).

7. Acquisition Policy of the Fine Arts Museums of San Francisco (Section 3). October 23, 1975.

8. "Study on the Principles, Conditions, and Means for the Restitution or Return of Cultural Property in View of Reconstituting Dispersed Heritages," International Council of Museums (ICOM), 1979.

9. *Professional Practices in Art Museums,* p. 12 (Association of Art Museum Directors, 1971).

10. L. DuBoff, *Art Law, Domestic and International* (South Hackensack, NJ: F.B. Rothman, 1975).

11. B. Braun, "Subtle Diplomacy Solves a Custody Case," *Art News,* Summer 1982, p. 101.

12. K. Berrin, "Reconstructing Crumbling Walls: A Curator's History of the Wagner Murals Collection." In K. Berrin (ed.), *Feathered Serpents and Flowering Trees: Reconstructing the Murals of Teotihuacan,* p. 26 (San Francisco: Fine Arts Museums of San Francisco, 1988).

Case 7

___

Midwestern:: Contemporary Art

(A) Who Is in Charge?

The Midwestern::Contemporary Art (MCA) museum is one of the nation's largest facilities devoted to modern art, exhibiting some of the most compelling and thought-provoking works of art created since 1945. The MCA documents contemporary visual culture through painting, sculpture, photography, video, film, and performance arts. The museum is located in a new facility near the historic White Tower in the heart of the city of Great Lakes, and boasts a gift shop, bookstore, restaurant, 300-seat theater, terraced sculpture garden, and spectacular view of Lake Michigan. Under the leadership of several directors over four decades, the MCA was transformed from an insignificant art showroom in a converted bakery into what is known today as a major shrine to contemporary art. MCA's continued success can be attributed to the vision of its leaders, succinctly captured in the museum's mission statement:

> The mission of MCA is to be an innovative center of contemporary art where the public can directly experience the work and ideas of living artists as well as understand the historical, social, and cultural context of the art of our time.
>
> The museum boldly interweaves exhibitions, performances, collections, and educational programs to form a challenging, refreshing, and exciting atmosphere for our visitors. In addition, we take pride in providing insights into the creative process for our public viewers.
>
> MCA aspires to attract a broad and diverse audience, create a sense of community, and act as a venue for contemplation and discussion about contemporary art and culture.

Peter and Catherine Smith

Peter and Catherine Smith met when they were teenagers. Friends of the couple said the two functioned as a unit. The couple was not well known among the downtown crowd of collectors until they became involved with contemporary art in the 1970s. Thereafter, the Smiths tended to shy away from the social limelight.

Both Smiths had careers in the legal sector—Peter graduated from an Ivy League school and became the assistant to the chairman of a national retailer headquartered in Great Lakes. He later served as a municipal judge. Catherine graduated from a Great Lakes law school and became the first female lawyer in the state attorney's office, handling cases in child and spousal abuse.

The couple began collecting art after Catherine experienced cerebral vascular spasms in the late 1960s and was forced to give up her legal career. In an assessment of her life, Catherine told her husband that she would be unable to fulfill three of her lifelong dreams: raising their daughters, breeding horses, and acquiring a collection of

Source: Research assistant Rudolph Ng and professor Matthew Liao-Troth prepared this case as a basis for class discussion rather than to illustrate effective or ineffective handling of an administrative situation. Jane Lee assisted with preliminary work on this case and made suggestions for the teaching notes.

art. Upon Catherine's unexpected recovery, the couple dedicated more time to their children, invested in a horse, and made their first art purchases.

A visit to New York's Museum of Modern Art in the early 1970s prompted the couple's interest in works created by contemporary artists. After much research and first-hand observations at galleries, the Smiths began to purchase works of art in the minimalist genre, along with examples of new realist paintings and conceptual art. Such works had not been acquired in depth by Great Lakes collectors, but by 1980 the Smiths' intense collecting activity was recognized by supporters of the MCA.

In June of 1981, Peter was invited to be a member of the MCA board of trustees. Catherine recalled later,

> Board President Heidi Goldman visited us, saying, "I have good news and bad news. You have been asked onto the board, and we need a check for $10,000." I admired that directness.

Peter Smith joined the board and began pushing his desire that MCA would attract more artists and a broader base of audience to appreciate contemporary art. He and his wife were prepared to donate more money to make MCA a better museum with a facility larger than the three-story townhouse it then occupied. In 1989 Peter Smith was elected the board chairman. He then devoted more time to managing the MCA with the hope that his business acumen could make MCA a more nationally prominent museum.

Keith Schmidt

Keith Schmidt was hired as MCA's executive director at the start of 1989. Before that, Schmidt served as director of the Seaside Art Museum on the West Coast. Prior to that, he was director of the Southern Museum of Art. At both museums, Schmidt successfully instigated novel building programs, including plans for a new museum building in Seaside and the design and construction of a 70,000-square-foot, $12.1 million adaptive reuse project of historic National Register buildings for the Southern Museum of Art.

During his first month at MCA, Schmidt showed that his reputation was well earned. One of the first things he did at MCA was to set goals for the museum. He wanted the museum to be the best in the Midwest and among the top five across the nation in five years. To achieve such an ambitious objective, he realized the necessity of large donations and media attention. Henceforth his time was split among fund-raising, recruiting the best curators, and obtaining and showing the best artwork.

The Conflict between the Chairman and Director

During the two-year overlap of Smith's chairmanship and Schmidt's term as executive director, the two men often had intense debates at board meetings. These confrontations were rooted in a number of areas: what artifacts to show, which artist to invite to forums, and when to hold exhibitions. However, the most heated arguments occurred over the direction and speed of MCA's expansion.

John Stuart, a former board member and chairman of the museum's budget committee, commented on the differences between Smith and Schmidt:

> I remember a specific meeting when Peter challenged Keith. We were coming out of a rough time—having funded some very expensive exhibitions—and were just about to break

even financially. Keith wanted to rent extra office space and hire more staff. Peter asked why we were moving so quickly, but he didn't give orders or intimidate anyone. Besides, any good board chairman had to ask, and it was his responsibility to make intelligent business decisions. During the first six months of 1990, Peter asked a lot of questions. He wanted to proceed in a conservative manner and be assured that there was a backup plan if we didn't continue the plans with the new building. Yet Keith proceeded, racing ahead like a wild bull and perhaps without authority to take such action. There was no question that Keith and Peter disagreed on a number of financial issues. However, each year, we always ended up with a balanced budget, and so I feel that Schmidt acted very responsibly in dealing with fiscal matters.

By October 1991, tension between the two had become very visible to others in the museum. Smith approached his friend and fellow board member, Jennifer Lee, for advice. At a loss for how to handle the aggressive style of Schmidt, Smith expressed his frustration:

> Jennifer, I don't know how other folks on the board feel, but I'm pretty darn sure about my duties and responsibility as a chairperson. You know, they didn't put me in this position without a charge. I'm here to oversee the museum's operation, and Keith's exceedingly ambitious agenda isn't financially sound. I feel that as the board chairman, I should have the final say on this serious matter.

On the other hand, Keith Schmidt also sought to build coalition support from board members. He approached Richard Lang, counsel to the board, and told him his problem with the chairman:

> Throughout my 12-year experience as an art museum director in three other places, I have never had so much interference from the board and chairpersons. I always thought that if the board hired me, then they must trust my ability as a leader and manager of their institution. Rarely had previous chairpersons or board members questioned or objected to my proposals since they had faith in my professional knowledge. After all, my recommendations and proposals have almost always resulted in prosperity and development of their institutions. However, sometimes at MCA, some members of the board, and especially Peter, seem to be downright intrusive and skeptical of my day-to-day management.

In November 1991, the board decided to vote on whether to go with Schmidt's advice to rapidly expand MCA or to adhere to Smith's conservative policy. Although most members were somewhat skeptical about Schmidt's aggressive plan to develop the museum, most of them felt that they should take the risk. After the vote, Smith was reasonably upset since his opinion was not supported by the majority. Soon after, Peter and Catherine Smith disappeared from the Chicago art community, and repeated phone calls from MCA were not returned. At this point, the board elected a new chairperson for MCA.

Discussion Questions for Part (A)

1. Is Peter Smith micromanaging Keith Schmidt?
2. What type of conflict are they experiencing?

3. What can an organization do structurally to reduce conflict resulting from role ambiguity?

4. How should Peter Smith react when his advice is not followed by the board?

5. How are the roles of board chairman and an executive director different in an organization such as MCA?

(B) The Decision

It is now the fall of 1997. Peggy Fischer, who earlier this year was elected chair of the Midwestern::Contemporary Art (MCA) board, pored over the messages that her secretary had left on her desk. Almost immediately, Fischer's attention turned to a message marked "urgent" on the very top of the stack. Bob Hatchs, the museum's treasurer, had left a memo stating that the MCA was currently facing a very critical financial situation because a $5 million pledge to the museum had not been honored. After reading Hatchs's memo, Fischer realized the gravity of MCA's financial situation—without the $5 million promised by Peter Smith, the museum's ability to fulfill its mission and attract important exhibits to its state-of-the-art facility would be jeopardized. The new chairperson was determined to resolve the issue as soon as possible in order to preserve both her and the museum's reputation in the art world as well as the local community.

Peggy Fischer

As a modern art enthusiast, Peggy Fischer collected a wide variety of artifacts ranging from postmodernist paintings to surrealist sculptures. In 1980 her friends in the Chicago art community suggested that she join MCA, and after several financial contributions to the museum she became a board member. In 1989, after Peter Smith became chairman of MCA's board and Schmidt became the director, Fischer, like other members, often noticed that there were conflicts between two strong-willed men. Nevertheless, she chose to remain quiet as the heated debates between the two escalated. After Smith left the MCA board and Avery Truman replaced him, Fischer was chosen as the next chairperson because of her ability to establish excellent interpersonal relationships among board members.

Fischer knew that Peter Smith and his wife Catherine had been long-time supporters of MCA until museum director Keith Schmidt was hired in 1989. After a series of explicit heated debates and covert power struggles between Peter Smith and Keith Schmidt, the Smiths disappeared from the Chicago art scene at the end of 1991 and missed all payments on their $5 million pledge toward the planned new building for the museum.

Like many nonprofit organizations, MCA typically does not receive the full amount of pledges. Some donors are unable to fulfill pledges because of unexpected financial hardship. Others simply change their giving priorities between the time they sign the letter of intent to give and the point where payment becomes due. Normally a nonprofit would defer obligations based on such a pledge until it was realized, but at the time the Smiths' pledge failed to materialize, MCA was in a fiscal bind: Construction funding depended on that pledge. In addition, in 1995 while construction was under way, a revision of accounting rules by the Financial Accounting Standards Board (FASB) had big implications for how MCA could treat the pledge.

The New Building for MCA

After receiving promises and pledges from a variety of board members and other donors, the MCA board went ahead with construction of a new building for the institution starting in 1993. Not only was the new MCA to be the first project designed in the United States by architect Mattias Lee Bollinger, but it would also be the first building made specifically for MCA's use since the institution's founding in 1967. With almost seven times the square footage of the museum's previous facility, the new home of MCA would provide space for installing both temporary exhibitions and works from the permanent collection. The building also would give MCA a terraced outdoor sculpture garden, a museum store for books and design objects, a café and special events area, and a 15,000-volume art library. In addition, there was to be room for the Gibbons Education Center, which incorporates studio classrooms—or a space suitable for symposia and performances—and a 300-seat auditorium. The new MCA facility opened in mid-1996, about six months before Peggy Fischer became chair of the museum's board.

In 1995, while construction was in progress, revisions to FASB accounting rules forced many nonprofit organizations across the nation to record pledges as income at the time of the pledge. This impacted MCA greatly because in the past, pledges were not recorded until the actual transfer of money from donor to museum occurred. The new rule forced the MCA to take greater action in enforcing pledges; they needed to keep their accounts receivables low for financial purposes, such as construction loans or bond issuance, while constructing the new facility. Because of this FASB rule revision, lawsuits to collect unpaid pledges became a hot topic among nonprofit organizations across the United States. Edward Able, head of the American Association of Museums representing 8,000 institutions, told reporters,

> We fought the changes made by the FASB to no avail, and the issue has been highly charged for nonprofit groups since that time. We have not polled our members to determine the amounts of the suits or their frequency, but people throughout the art community are hard pressed to cite any instances of museums suing over large pledges.

Today's Board Meeting

Now, in late 1997, MCA finds itself in a financial crisis because of a high debt load resulting from construction and because of the Smiths' unfulfilled pledge, which by now was to have been fully paid. At a meeting today of the MCA board, Peggy Fischer sought advice from the board about how to proceed The board's chief counsel, board member Richard Lang, suggested that Fischer take legal action against Peter Smith. Lang explained his reasoning:

> From a legal standpoint, we have every reason to believe that the lawsuit will proceed in our interests. In 1990, Peter Smith made a written pledge on behalf of himself and his wife to give an endowment that would help build a new MCA facility. The pledge is legally

binding since we relied on his donations for our financial security and had reasonable expectation that he would indeed fulfill his pledge. We would not have proceeded with the construction of the new building without his pledge. In the court of law, we can make a plea of the reliance damages[1] that we have suffered and, thus, seek remedies from the Smiths.

Lang also cited a high-profile 1994 case involving the Philadelphia Museum of Art. Like the MCA situation, the Philadelphia Museum of Art received a $5 million pledge from one of its donors that was not honored. The donor in question passed away before the transfer of funds, and his estate refused to honor the pledge. Subsequently, the Philadelphia Museum sued the estate, and the two parties reached "an amicable settlement." He recalled another similar case in 1996 where the University of California–Irvine won a lawsuit against a donor who refused to pay up his $1 million pledge. Lang argued that even though MCA may never receive the $5 million in its entirety, the lawsuit would send a strong message to its prospective donors that the museum takes pledges seriously and relies on them.

Andrew Whitehorse, another board member, agreed with Lang's suggestion. Whitehorse pointed out that it was unlikely for MCA to gain other financial resources because a stagnant economy and stock market would not benefit the endowment fund and the amount of donations. "How are we supposed to pay for the new building and MCA's continuous exhibitions?" Whitehorse asked. He further expressed his concern that the board's long-standing prestige might be hurt if the financial crisis was not handled properly and swiftly.

On the other hand, Rich Steiner, a member on the board, objected to Lang's proposed legal strategy, and contended that the crisis would be best resolved through nonlegal avenues. Steiner argued that resorting to lawsuits will increase MCA's financial burden due to enormous legal fees from prolonged legal proceedings or failed attempts to win court cases. Jennifer Lee, a longtime MCA board member, concurred:

> The lawsuit will not only irritate and anger the Smiths to the point that they will never voluntarily donate money to us again, but it will also cause other potential donors to view our actions as being insensible. Furthermore, we the MCA—a nonprofit organization— should not behave like all other greedy businesses that resort to the court of law whenever there is a conflict. We can't be so shortsighted as to focus exclusively on the $5 million. Besides, how would other donors perceive our legal actions? Would they think twice in the future before placing their trust in us? What kind of image will we be sending out to the community?

Another MCA board member and friend of the Smiths, John Stuart, sided with Lee and Steiner by asserting that it would be callous to sue the couple at this time. He explained,

> Although it's Peter and Catherine's moral responsibility to honor their pledge, we should not sue them. This is strictly confidential, but I have recently learned that Peter has been

---

[1]*Reliance damages* are contract damages placing the injured party in as good a position as he would have been in had the contract terms been met.

diagnosed with terminal cancer and is undergoing a series of chemotherapy treatments. Peter is now too weak to walk, and Catherine is physically and emotionally distressed to see her husband suffer. I strongly believe that it would be unwise and very insensitive to file a lawsuit against the Smiths. I am sure that they can be reasoned with; now is just not the time to approach them.

After the board meeting, Fischer reviewed the situation and became uncomfortable with several aspects of the legal route. Although she was concerned that the financial crisis may result in the museum's bankruptcy, Fischer feared the implications of a possible lawsuit against the Smiths. Fischer was unable to predict the consequences of taking the legal actions because, with the exception of Philadelphia Museum of Art, no lawsuit involving such a large amount of money had ever been filed by a nonprofit organization (the Philadelphia Museum signed a secrecy agreement barring both parties from discussing their settlement). Furthermore, even though Fischer was not a very close friend of the Smiths, she did work with them for a significant period of time, and was not particularly comfortable with the notion of filing a lawsuit against the couple during such an unfortunate time. Nonetheless, the financial pressure posed by the construction of the new facility was magnifying, and without income, the new facility might be unable to remain open.

As this intense day drew to a close, Fischer glanced at her calendar and noticed that the next board meeting was in five days. She knew that she had to make a decision by the next meeting, but Fischer suspected that decision making was only the first step in handling the situation.

Discussion Questions for Part (B)

1. What alternative approaches could Peggy Fischer use to collect the unfulfilled pledge?

2. Should Fischer involve the board in further discussions leading to a decision about whether or not to file a lawsuit? Or should she formulate a recommendation on her own for the board's next meeting?

3. Do you think the museum should sue the Smiths? Why or why not?

500 English Sentences

Scott sat looking out the window, watching a group of boys playing baseball in the school yard. Poor kids, he thought, they are the real losers in all of this. He looked down at a copy of *500 English Sentences* and the endorsement letter on his desk. He glanced at the clock and realized that he had to have an answer for Mr. Honda within the hour. He was feeling very frustrated and stressed from the events of the past 10 days. He decided that he would go to the karate school after work, something that always made him feel better. He sighed as he thought about what he had to do next.

Scott

Scott was 26 years old and had been living in Japan for 18 months. He was born in Auburn, Massachusetts, and had spent most of his life in the United States. Scott's father was a successful entrepreneur who believed that hard work and good old-fashioned principles were the ingredients to success. He always taught his children to stand up for what they believed in and to never sacrifice their values in order to get ahead. Scott's mother was a housewife who took care of the family home and the children. She loved to travel and encouraged Scott's father to take the family abroad every year so that their children would have a better understanding of the world around them.

Scott was a very disciplined student. He was an English major and had been on the dean's honor role for every semester throughout his four years at college. During his senior year, Scott worked as a teaching assistant, grading papers and tutoring students.

Scott started studying karate when he was a junior in high school. He enjoyed the physical workout and the disciplinary aspect of the sport and continued to train throughout his undergraduate years. By the time he was ready to graduate, Scott had earned a third-degree black belt.

> It was through karate that I first became interested in Japan. I thought it would be enlightening to experience Japanese culture and learn more about their ways of thinking. My goal was to one day go over to Japan and train in a Japanese karate dojo (school) and learn from a real karate sensei. My biggest problem was to figure out how to go about doing this. I knew that I didn't have the luxury of just moving to Japan to study karate, and since I didn't speak the language I figured that my chances of working for a company in Japan were about nil.

In the fall of his senior year, Scott saw a poster for the Japan Exchange and Teaching (JET) Program at school that advertised teaching jobs in Japan. He had heard of other students going over to Japan to teach English but had never given any serious thought to a career in teaching, even if only for a short time. To work as an assistant

Source: This case was written by Laura Turek. Copyright ©1996 by Laura Turek. Used with permission. This case was prepared as a basis for classroom discussion, not to illustrate either the effective or ineffective management of an administrative situation.

English teacher on the JET program, applicants had to have a bachelor's degree and an interest in Japan. Knowledge of Japanese language or a degree in education were not listed as requirements. This was what Scott had been hoping for: an opportunity to go over to Japan to continue his karate under a Japanese instructor as well as a chance to put his English degree to good use. He wrote the address in his notebook and sent for an application that very night.

The Japan Exchange and Teaching (JET) Program

Before the JET Program

The origins of the JET program can be traced back to 1982. In that year, the Japanese Ministry of Education (Monbusho) initiated a project known as the Monbusho English Fellows (MEF) Program, which hired Americans to work at the local boards of education in order to assist Japanese English teaching consultants who acted as advisers to the Japanese teachers of English in the public schools. The task of the MEFs was to oversee the junior and senior high school English teachers and to assist them with their training. In 1983, the British English Teachers Scheme (BETS) was inaugurated by the Ministry of Education. However, from the outset the British teachers were stationed at schools, and the goals of the program did not only concern English instruction but also sought to increase mutual understanding and improve friendly relations between the peoples of Japan and Britain. While there were some differences between the two programs, both shared a common goal: inviting native English speakers to Japan to assist in improving foreign language instruction.

The Birth of the JET Program

The realization that Japan must open itself more fully to contact with international society began to foster an awareness of the importance of promoting internationalization and international exchange at the local level. This brought about not only expanded English instruction, but also a rapid increase in exchange programs. Taking these new circumstances into account, the Japanese Ministry of Home Affairs in 1985 released a paper titled "Plans for International Exchange Projects" as part of its priority policy of local governments for the following year. In the paper, the Ministry of Home Affairs proposed a definite course for the internationalization of local governments, which ideally would lead to smoothly functioning cultural exchanges. All of these ideas were finally implemented in a concrete project: the Japan Exchange and Teaching (JET) Program.

The Ministry of Home Affairs abolished the two projects currently in effect (MEF and BETS) and created a new one that was entrusted simultaneously to three ministries: the Ministry of Foreign Affairs, the Ministry of Education, and the Ministry of Home Affairs. However, the concept of appointing local authorities to implement the program and act as host institutions was preserved. While discussions were held with each of the local authorities to work out the details and ensure the smooth implementation of such a massive program, the formation of a cooperative organization for all local governments was expedited.

The Creation of CLAIR

CLAIR, originally the Conference of Local Authorities for International Relations, was established in October 1986 by the *Todofuken* (the 47 prefectures of Japan) and the *Seireishiteitoshi* (the [then] 10 designated cities) as a cooperative organization responsible for implementing the JET program in conjunction with the three Japanese ministries just named.

CLAIR's Role in the JET Program

To ensure smooth implementation of the JET program, the three ministries, the local authorities, and CLAIR were all given specific functions. The functions that the conference attempted to fulfill for implementing the JET program were as follows:

1. Advice and liaison during recruitment and selection.
2. Placement of participants.
3. Participant orientation, conferences.
4. Guidance for local authority host institutions.
5. Participant welfare and counseling.
6. Travel arrangements for participants coming to Japan.
7. Liaison with related groups and institutions.
8. Publications and reference materials.
9. Publicity for the program.

The larger goal behind these functions of the conference was the promotion of international exchange at the local level. Independent of this development, the Council of Local Authorities for International Relations (a publicly endowed foundation) was inaugurated in July 1987. The council's main duty was to study and survey participating nations' local authorities overseas with the ultimate objective being to support local government programs for the promotion of internationalization. By fostering international exchange at the regional level, the council came to assume the same duties as the Conference of Local Authorities for International Relations. It was suggested that both organizations merge since they held information relevant to each other's work and shared the goals of improving work efficiency and performing their tasks more effectively. Moreover, the annual growth of the JET program led to an increased number of interrelated duties and tasks. Thus it was necessary to strengthen the structure of the Conference of Local Authorities for International Relations.

It was decided that the operations and financial assets of the conference would be assumed by the council, and in August 1989 they were amalgamated, under the acronym of CLAIR, to form a joint organization of local public bodies in Japan to support and promote internationalization at the regional level.

Scott's Acceptance

Scott reviewed the JET information he had received. There were two different positions available: (1) the coordinator for international relations (CIR) and (2) the assistant language teacher (ALT). The first position, although it sounded interesting, was out of the question since knowledge of Japanese was a requirement. Scott applied for the second position because as an English major he felt that he was qualified to assist in the teaching of English. Scott was chosen for an interview and was successful in obtaining an offer to teach English in Japan.

> The JET program and CLAIR were very good at trying to prepare the participants for their stay in Japan. I attended several workshops and orientations concerning my job in Japan as well as seminars on what to expect living in such a different culture from my own. I remember thinking some of the potential situations they were preparing us for seemed a bit unrealistic and that I would probably never encounter them, but I found out soon enough that Japan and the United States are culturally a world apart, and I was glad to have received the predeparture training. Without it, I would have thought that I had arrived in Wonderland with no idea on how to behave at the tea party.

Scott's Situation in Japan

Scott was sent to a small village on the northern island of Hokkaido, where he taught English at Naka High School. At first, Scott had some difficulties adjusting to living in such a remote place. The people were friendly, yet since they were not accustomed to seeing many foreigners, Scott always felt that he was on display, or that his every move was under scrutiny.

> It was strange being the only non-Japanese person living in the town. I was there to do my job, and study karate, but somehow ended up as the town celebrity. Everyone in town knew everything about me. They all knew where I lived, when I entertained guests. I felt like my every move was monitored. It got so bad that I even had to hang my wash inside my house because people started to tell me that they liked my colorful boxer shorts.
>
> People not only watched what I did, but how I did it. Everyone wanted to know how the American talked, walked, and ate. People asked me daily if I could eat with chopsticks. I made a conscious effort very quickly to blend in as much as I could. It was either that or get angry, and I don't think people were being malicious, they were just overly curious.

The biggest problem that Scott encountered from the start was feelings of incompetence and frustration. The only people in the whole village with whom he could speak without much difficulty were the Japanese English teachers at the high school. If he ran into problems at the bank or supermarket, he was forced to rely on a mixture of basic Japanese and English accompanied by an elaborate display of sign language which more often than not ended in frustration. To overcome the communication problems, Scott began studying Japanese every night at home. He also found a Japanese language teacher at the high school who agreed to tutor him.

> Until I moved to Japan, I never realized how frustrating life can be when you cannot even do the simplest tasks for yourself like read your electric bill or use an automated teller machine. I felt pretty helpless a lot of the time, and no one seemed to understand what I was going through. Whenever I had a problem involving a language or cultural misunderstanding, I would go see Mr. Honda, the head of English, not only because his

English was the best of all of the teachers, but also because he had lived abroad in England and Australia, and I figured that he would be able to understand what I was going through.

Mr. Honda

Mr. Honda was the head of English at Naka High School. He was 46 years old and had been teaching English at various schools in the prefecture for more than 22 years. In his youth, Mr. Honda had studied English at Oxford and had spent two summers in Australia on homestays. His command of spoken English and his vocabulary were quite remarkable. Mr. Honda acted as a mentor to Scott. He considered Scott as his *kohai* (junior) and believed that as a good Japanese manager, it was his duty to guide the young foreigner throughout his stay in Japan. Mr. Honda showed this same kind of paternalistic concern for all of the junior English teachers and counseled them on everything from lesson planning to when they should think about marrying. None of the younger teachers in the English department made any decision without the approval of Mr. Honda. Scott thought that this was a waste of talent and initiative. He knew a couple of young teachers who were very dynamic and had some creative teaching ideas, yet were forced to use the dated teaching methods of Mr. Honda because he was their superior.

Although he never expressed it openly, Mr. Honda did not really like dealing with these young ALTs. He found it insulting to work with such young foreigners, who more often than not had no formal training as English teachers yet were hired to tell him how to do his job better. He did not share in the opinion that these foreign assistants were experts in English teaching just because they could speak the language fluently. Mr. Honda, as well as the other teachers on the staff, had trouble adjusting to the ALTs since they were hired on a yearly contract basis, which was renewable only to a maximum of three years. This left the school barely enough time to get to know an ALT before he or she left and another took over. Mr. Honda also didn't like the fact that these young assistant teachers were earning nearly the same salary as he each month, despite his 22 years of experience.

In spite of his feelings for ALTs in general, Mr. Honda liked Scott. He not only felt that Scott was qualified to be doing the job but also thought that Scott was adapting very well to the Japanese style of management.

> Scott works very hard. He shows great enthusiasm for teaching English at our school. He is very pleasant to work with and is making a big effort to learn the Japanese language and ways. It is a pleasure to have such a good teacher on our staff.

Acceptance in the Group

Scott joined the local karate school and began training every night after work.

> I felt very much at ease at the karate dojo. Despite the fact that I had no idea what my karate teacher and the other men were saying to me, we seemed to get along very well because we were all there for a common goal: to study karate. I think the other members

accepted me into their group because I showed them that I was serious about the sport and had a determination to learn. At first, I saw the other members only at the karate school, but after a few months, they started inviting me to dinners and other social gatherings. Sometimes we even went out drinking after practice. It was good to feel like I was a part of something. I was tired of being treated like the "funny *gaijin*" all the time.

For the first few months, Scott felt isolated at work. Excluding the English teachers, many of his coworkers did not talk to him at all, which made him feel unwelcome at the school. It wasn't until he asked a young English teacher about the situation that she told Scott how several of the teachers were afraid to speak to him because they felt that their English skills were too weak. Scott told the young teacher that it was he who should be embarrassed for not speaking Japanese. After that, Scott made an effort to speak in Japanese, even though his mistakes often made him feel ridiculous and self-conscious. The other teachers slowly began to warm up to Scott and started to converse more with him at school.

Scott went out of his way to get involved at school. He not only taught his courses but also became involved with many of the clubs after school. He ran the English-speaking club and helped coach the karate club. He was also willing to come in on weekends when there was a special event going on at the school.

I got involved with extracurricular activities at school, not necessarily for altruistic reasons, but I guess because aside from karate, there was really not much for me to do in such a remote place where I could barely speak the language. I guess the other teachers thought that I was different from some of the other foreigners who had worked at Naka High because I was putting in extra time and work. Whatever the reason, they began to treat me like one of the group.

The Move

Scott had been in Japan almost a year and made the decision to renew for another. He asked to be transferred to Satsuki, the capital city of the prefecture, because his girlfriend back in the United States was thinking of coming over to Japan and there would be no work for her in such a small town as the one he was in. The teachers at Naka High were sad to see Scott leave and gave him a huge farewell party at which everyone made speeches saying how they would miss him.

It was kind of sad to leave Naka High. Once I got to know them, the teachers at Naka were quite a down-to-earth group who treated me like I was one of the family. The problem was that life in such a small town no longer offered what I needed. My girlfriend wanted to come over to Japan and I knew that she could get a job in Satsuki. My karate sensei also told me that if I wanted to test for my fourth-degree black belt, I would get better training at one of the bigger karate dojos in the city, and this was the reason that I came to Japan in the first place.

The city was quite a change for Scott. Since many foreigners lived there—English teachers, university students, and businesspeople—he did not receive the same attention as he had in the village. Compared to the small town, it was like living back in the

United States. Nishi High, the school where Scott was assigned, was not at all like Naka High. Instead, it was a large academic high school where there was a particular emphasis placed on preparing for the rigorous university entrance exam. Only students who scored in the very top percentile were admitted to the best universities in the country, and Nishi prided itself on the number of students who were accepted to Tokyo University, the best in the country.

Scott was not the only foreigner working at this school. John, a 22-year-old from Australia, had just been hired to replace a Canadian woman who had spent two years teaching at the school. John had just graduated with a degree in chemistry, but he had studied Japanese for about seven years before moving to Japan.

One surprise Scott encountered was that Mr. Honda had also been transferred to Nishi High to head their English department. Mr. Honda spoke very highly of Scott to the teachers at Nishi and, as a result, Scott was put in charge of the advanced English class, which was cramming for the university entrance exams.

The English department used a textbook titled *500 English Sentences,* which had been written approximately 10 years before by members of Nishi's staff. The book had become a standard and was used by virtually every high school in the prefecture. The teachers who wrote it were all subsequently promoted to work as advisers at the Satsuki Board of Education. Scott had tried the book in his classes, but thought that it was an inferior text riddled with grammatical inconsistencies, spelling mistakes, and archaic usages of the English language. Although this book was part of the curriculum, Scott refused to use it and instead taught from the other texts. Scott assumed this was not a problem since none of the other teachers ever mentioned the fact that he did not use the text in his classes.

In the Limelight

After three months of working at Nishi, Scott found out that there was going to be a prefecturewide English teachers' convention held at the school. Scott was surprised when the English staff asked him to conduct a demonstration class for one of the seminars. He was told that, in total, about 200 teachers were expected to attend.

Despite initial misgivings and stage fright, Scott's demonstration class was a huge success, and Nishi High received outstanding commendations from all the teachers who attended and from the board of education. The English teachers at Nishi praised Scott for bringing honor to their school. Scott was glad that everything had gone well, but he did not think that he deserved the only credit.

> For various reasons, I was awarded much of the credit for the outstanding commendations, though I felt most of the work had been done by the regular English staff. Anyway, at this point I had built an excellent relationship with the school's staff, and found that this made the whole working situation function much easier, made getting things done possible, and kept me "part of the loop" in decisions in the English department.

Scott began to receive more and more responsibilities at work. The English staff would consult with him on problems big or small concerning the teaching of English. Although Scott and John both arrived at Nishi High at the same time, Scott was considered *sempai* (the senior). Scott attributed this to a combination of his age and the fact that he had already worked one year at another school in Japan.

> It was a bit unnerving that I was given more authority than John, I had been in Japan one year longer than he had and was a few years older, but he was able to speak their language fluently and was a capable teacher. The Japanese English teachers treated me as though I were John's superior and often put me in an awkward position by making John answer to me.

The Dilemma

One afternoon while Scott was sitting at his desk in the staff room, he was approached by several of the Japanese English teachers, including Mr. Honda. Mr. Honda began by inquiring after Scott's health and complimenting him on his students' recent test scores. After several minutes of small talk, Mr. Honda cleared his throat and got to the point. He laid a copy of *500 English Sentences* on Scott's desk and smiled at him. Scott thought that Mr. Honda and the other teachers had finally come to ask him to use the text in his class. "Yes, it's a textbook, and a humdinger at that," said Scott. Scott's comment was met with confusion, nervous laughs, and several coughs. "No," replied Mr. Honda, "We were hoping that you would be so kind as to help us in repairing any errors there might be in this text for republication by the prefecture." Mr. Honda continued saying that Nishi High had been assigned the duty of editing the text and resubmitting it to the publisher for printing. He said that Scott's help would be greatly appreciated since he had been an English major at university and the Japanese teachers already knew that he was a more capable teacher. Mr. Honda also said that they desired Scott's help because he was a native English speaker and he would have an excellent grasp of both current and colloquial usage of the language, something which none of the Japanese English teachers had.

Scott agreed to help them with the project and asked Mr. Honda how soon he wanted the manuscript returned. Again Mr. Honda cleared his throat and said, "Very soon."

"How soon is very soon?" asked Scott. Mr. Honda replied that the manuscript had to be into the publisher within 10 days. Ten days seemed unreasonably short to Scott, so he asked Mr. Honda how long he had known about the project. Mr. Honda replied that the school had been asked to do the project more than six months ago. Not wanting to ask why the English teachers took so long to begin working on the manuscript, Scott took the project and promised to have it back within a few days. Mr. Honda smiled and thanked Scott. Scott went home that night and started working on the project.

> I was glad to have the opportunity to do something productive and lasting. I had hated this text since I had first seen it and had secretly ridiculed the foolish foreigner whose name and recommendation graced its inner cover. I exalted in the opportunity to finally dismember the text and replace the reams of errors with actual functional English.

Scott worked on the manuscript every night for four nights, putting in an average of eight hours of work each night. He returned the text to Mr. Honda on the fifth day, full of red ink: corrections, sample replacement sentences, and explanations as to why the changes were necessary. To Scott's surprise, Mr. Honda did not thank him for the work. Instead, he looked very uncomfortable and smiled nervously as he flipped through the marked pages of the manuscript.

Two days later, Mr. Honda returned to Scott's desk. He praised Scott for his work and reminded him of their mutual indebtedness. He talked about the weather, asked Scott how his karate training was progressing, and inquired about Scott's girlfriend's health. Eventually, Mr. Honda turned the discussion to the manuscript. Apologetically, he said, most of the corrections could not be used. Scott was confused and asked why. Mr. Honda revealed that he had given the corrected manuscript to John to look at and that John had disagreed with some of the corrections. Scott became concerned and asked to see the manuscript to see the contended corrections. Upon reviewing the manuscript, Scott noted three places where John had marked disagreement. John had also noted that the differences with these three sentences were probably due to usage in Australia compared with the United States and that since he was not an English major, like Scott, Scott was probably correct. Mr. Honda agreed that Scott's corrections were valid and went back to his desk.

Mr. Honda returned an hour later to say that despite their earlier conversation all of the corrections could not be used because it was so late in the process and that it would be very troublesome for the publisher to make so many changes.

> By now I was getting frustrated. I told Mr. Honda that he should have thought of this six months ago when he first learned about the project and then asked him which was more important to him, the publisher or the students?

That night, one of the junior members of the Japanese English staff offered Scott a ride home. They discussed various topics, including how much Scott liked living in Japan. The young teacher then told Scott a story involving a junior member of the staff who tried to be helpful by correcting a memo that his boss had written. Since the memo had already been circulated once, the subsequent recirculation with the corrections resulted in a great loss of face for the boss. This resulted in strained relations, even though no offense was intended. By the time the teacher finished his anecdote, they had already arrived at Scott's house. He thanked the teacher for the ride, then got out of the car.

The next day, Scott did not discuss the topic of the manuscript and the situation seemed to have resolved itself. He assumed that Mr. Honda would go ahead and not use his changes, but he was unsure of what he could do about it.

After a few days of silence between Scott and the English teachers, Mr. Honda and the same group of English teachers came over to Scott's desk. This time they looked extremely nervous and spoke in very polite *keigo* (extremely respectful Japanese) that Scott could barely follow. Upon reaching some sort of consensus among themselves, they presented Scott with a single sheet of paper. On it was the verbatim endorsement of the previous issue of *500 English Sentences* with a blank line and Scott's name typed under the blank. "Would you be so kind as to sign this?" asked Mr. Honda. Scott was shocked. He thought the issue was closed when he had made a fuss about the corrections.

> I looked at the group and plainly and directly said that there was no way that I would sign such a statement since I felt that the text was substandard and that my integrity as a teacher would be compromised by signing the statement.

Scott suggested that Mr. Honda ask John to sign the endorsement, but Mr. Honda replied that due to his seniority, English degree, and good association with Nishi High, the board of education had personally asked for Scott's signature. Mr. Honda then added that he needed to send it in to the publisher by 5:00 p.m. that same day.

What to Do

Mr. Honda went back to his own desk, and Scott sat thinking about what he should do. All he could think about was having his name endorsing a text that he considered to be substandard. He didn't see how he could knowingly sign his name to a project that he knew was flawed.

Sick Leave

Kelly tried to control her anger as she thought about her supervisor. She couldn't understand why he was being so unreasonable. Maybe to him it was only a couple days of paid leave and not worth fighting over, but to her it meant the difference between being able to go on vacation during Golden Week[1] or having to stay home. She looked at her contract and the phone number of CLAIR on her desk. She wasn't the only person in the office affected by this. She sat and thought about how she should proceed.

Kelly

Kelly was 22 years old and had been working for the past six months at the Soto Board of Education office in Japan. This was her first job after graduating from college with a degree in management, and she was really excited to finally be in the real world.

Kelly was born in Calgary and had spent most of her life in Alberta, Canada. Kelly's father was a successful lawyer in Calgary, and her mother was a high school English teacher. Kelly had an older sister, Laurel, 27, who had just passed the bar exam and was working for a corporate law firm in Edmonton.

Kelly had studied Japanese in high school and in university and spoke and wrote the language quite well. When she was 15 years old, Kelly spent four months in Japan on a school exchange. She had enjoyed the time she spent there and always planned to return one day. Upon graduating from high school, Kelly went to the University of Alberta, in Edmonton, to study management.

During her final year at the university, Kelly heard some of her friends talking about the Japan Exchange and Teaching (JET) Program. She was told that it was quite easy to get accepted—all an applicant needed was a university degree and an interest in Japan—and that it would be a great way to make money and see another part of the world. Kelly would have her degree by the end of the year and thought that having lived in Japan and knowing the language showed enough interest to have her application considered. Kelly thought that a year or two in Japan after her management degree would improve her Japanese and give her more of a competitive advantage when she returned to Canada to begin her career. She also thought that it would be a great way to make money and have some fun before she came home to start a real job. She asked her friend how she could apply to the program and returned home that night to work on her résumé.

Source: This case was written by Laura Turek. Copyright ©1996 by Laura Turek. Used with permission. This case was prepared as a basis for classroom discussion, not to illustrate either the effective or ineffective management of an administrative situation.

[1]Golden Week is the period from April 29 to May 5, in which there are four Japanese national holidays. Many Japanese employees and their families take advantage of this period to go on vacation.

The Japan Exchange and Teaching (JET) Program

Before the JET Program

The origins of the JET program can be traced back to 1982. In that year, the Japanese Ministry of Education (Monbusho) initiated a project known as the Monbusho English Fellows (MEF) Program, which hired Americans to work at the local boards of education in order to assist Japanese English teaching consultants who acted as advisors to the Japanese teachers of English in the public schools. The task of the MEFs was to oversee the junior and senior high school English teachers and to assist them with their training. In 1983, the British English Teachers Scheme (BETS) was inaugurated by the Ministry of Education. However, from the outset the British teachers were stationed at schools, and the goals of the program did not only concern English instruction but also sought to increase mutual understanding and improve friendly relations between the peoples of Japan and Britain. While there were some differences between the two programs, both shared a common goal: inviting native English speakers to Japan to assist in improving foreign language instruction.

The Birth of the JET Program

The realization that Japan must open itself more fully to contact with international society began to foster an awareness of the importance of promoting internationalization and international exchange at the local level. This brought about not only expanded English instruction, but also a rapid increase in exchange programs. Taking these new circumstances into account, the Japanese Ministry of Home Affairs in 1985 released a paper titled "Plans for International Exchange Projects" as part of its priority policy of local governments for the following year. In the paper, the Ministry of Home Affairs proposed a definite course for the internationalization of local governments, which ideally would lead to smoothly functioning cultural exchanges. All of these ideas were finally implemented in a concrete project: the Japan Exchange and Teaching (JET) Program.

The Ministry of Home Affairs abolished the two projects currently in effect (MEF and BETS) and created a new one that was entrusted simultaneously to three ministries: the Ministry of Foreign Affairs, the Ministry of Education, and the Ministry of Home Affairs. However, the concept of appointing local authorities to implement the program and act as host institutions was preserved. While discussions were held with each of the local authorities to work out the details and ensure the smooth implementation of such a massive program, the formation of a cooperative organization for all local government was expedited.

The Creation of CLAIR

CLAIR, originally the Conference of Local Authorities for International Relations, was established in October 1986 by the *Todofuken* (the 47 prefectures of Japan) and the *Seireishiteitoshi* (the [then] 10 designated cities) as a cooperative organization responsible for implementing the JET program in conjunction with the three Japanese ministries just named.

CLAIR's Role in the JET Program

To ensure smooth implementation of the JET program, the three ministries, the local authorities, and CLAIR were all given specific functions. The functions that the conference attempted to fulfill for implementing the JET program were as follows:

1. Advice and liaison during recruitment and selection.
2. Placement of participants.
3. Participant orientation, conferences.
4. Guidance for local authority host institutions.
5. Participant welfare and counseling.
6. Travel arrangements for participants coming to Japan.
7. Liaison with related groups and institutions.
8. Publications and reference materials.
9. Publicity for the program.

The larger goal behind these functions of the conference was the promotion of international exchange at the local level. Independent of this development, the Council of Local Authorities for International Relations (a public endowed foundation) was inaugurated in July 1987. The council's main duty was to study and survey participating nations' local authorities overseas with the ultimate objective being to support local government programs for the promotion of internationalization. By fostering international exchange at the regional level, the council came to assume the same duties as the Conference of Local Authorities for International Relations. It was suggested that both organizations merge since they held information relevant to each other's work and shared the goals of improving work efficiency and performing their tasks more effectively. Moreover, the annual growth of the JET program led to an increased number of interrelated duties and tasks. Thus it was necessary to strengthen the structure of the Conference of Local Authorities for International Relations.

It was decided that the operations and financial assets of the conference would be assumed by the council, and in August 1989 they were amalgamated, under the acronym of CLAIR, to form a joint organization of local public bodies in Japan to support and promote internationalization at the regional level.

Counseling System of JET (Figure 1)

1. *Role of the host institution:* Basic problems that JET participants faced during their stay in Japan were addressed by the host institution. If a JET had a complaint or a problem at work or in his or her private life, the JET could alert his or her supervisor, who took up the matter and attempted to solve it.

2. *Role of CLAIR:* Problems or difficulties that JET program participants faced were as a rule dealt with by host institutions. However, if the issues were difficult to solve at this level, or if they concerned grievances between the JET participant and the host institution, CLAIR employed a number of non-Japanese program coordinators who would intervene and respond directly to participants' needs.

FIGURE 1 | Counseling System

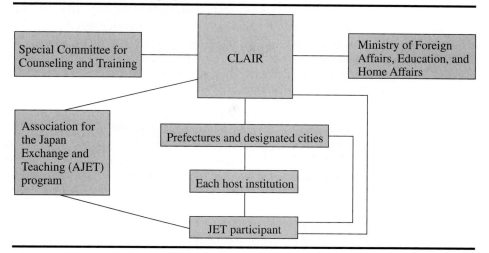

CLAIR would then step in on behalf of the JET participant and work to solve the problems with the host institution.

3. *The Special Committee for Counseling and Training:* The Special Committee for Counseling and Training consisted of the staff members of the three ministries (Foreign Affairs, Home Affairs, and Education), embassies of the participating countries, and host institutions. It took charge of orientation, conferences, public welfare, and counseling. If necessary, it answered the questions and concerns of the JET participants.

AJET

The Association for the Japan Exchange and Teaching (AJET) Program was an independent, self-supporting organization created by JET program participants, whose elected officers were all volunteers. Membership in AJET was also voluntary. AJET provided members with information about working and living in Japan and provided a support network for members at the local, regional, and national levels. Many Japanese and JETs considered AJET to be the union of the JET program participants.

The First Job

Kelly looked over the information she received from JET. There were two different positions available: (1) the coordinator for international relations (CIR) and (2) the assistant language teacher (ALT). The first position sounded quite interesting to Kelly since applicants were required to have a functional knowledge of Japanese. ALTs, on the other hand, were not required to know any Japanese before arriving in Japan. She realized that her odds of getting accepted were greater if she applied to the second position since almost 600 ALTs were selected across Canada, compared with only 25 CIRs. Kelly was chosen for a CIR interview but in the end was offered a position as an ALT.

At first she was a little disappointed, but then she reminded herself that her original goal was to perfect her Japanese, and she started to look forward to her trip to Japan.

Kelly received a lot of information about working and living in Japan from CLAIR. CLAIR also offered several predeparture training sessions and orientations about life in Japan and its potential problems, but she decided not to attend because after four months in Japan she already knew what to expect.

The Placement

Kelly was sent to Soto, a medium-sized city on the island of Shikoku. Kelly found the area a far cry from Osaka, where she had stayed the previous time she was in Japan. Soto was, in Kelly's opinion, "a small provincial town, stuck in the middle of nowhere." She had enjoyed the activity and nightlife of Osaka and, except for sports, her only entertainment options in Soto were one movie theater, several pachinko[2] parlors, and scores of karaoke bars. Kelly very quickly developed the habit of going away on the weekends to tour different parts of the island. She would also use her holidays to take advantage of visiting parts of Japan that she might never again get a chance to see. After a few months, Kelly decided that Soto was at least a good place to improve her Japanese since not many people spoke English very well, and only a few other foreigners lived there.

Kelly worked at the board of education office three days a week and visited schools the other two days to help with their English programs. There were three other JET participants who worked in the same office: Mark, 27, another Canadian; Andrea, 26, an American; and Suzanne, 25, from Britain. Like Kelly, Suzanne had been in Japan for only the past six months, while Mark and Andrea had been working there for a year and a half. Kelly was on good terms with the other JETs in the office, although she was closest with Suzanne since they had both arrived in Japan at the same time and had met at their orientation in Tokyo.

Although Kelly had lived in Japan before, this was the first time she had worked in a Japanese office. She had learned about Japanese work habits in a cross-cultural management class at the university, yet she was still surprised at how committed the Japanese were to their jobs. The workday began each morning at 8:30 with a staff meeting and officially ended each night at 5:00 p.m., yet no one left the office before 7:00 or 8:00 p.m., The Japanese also came in on Saturdays, which Kelly thought was absurd since it left the employees with only one day a week to relax or spend time with their families.

Kelly and the other JETs in the office had a standard North American contract given to them by CLAIR which stipulated hours, number of vacation days, amount of sick leave, and so on (Figure 2). The contract stated that the JET participants only worked from Monday to Friday until 5:00 p.m. and did not mention working on Saturdays. Neither Kelly nor the other foreigners ever put in extra hours at the office, nor were they ever asked to do so.

Kelly's supervisor was Mr. Higashi. At first Kelly thought that he was very kind and helpful because he had picked her and Suzanne up from the airport and had arranged

---

[2]*Pachinko* is a Japanese-style game of chance that resembles a cross between pinball and a slot machine. It is a very popular pastime among certain groups and, like any form of gambling, can be quite lucrative.

FIGURE 2 | Contract of English Teaching Engagement

Article 11: Paid Leave

Section 1

During the period of employment and with the approval of his/her supervisor, the JET participant may use 20 paid holidays individually or consecutively.

Section 2

When the JET participant wishes to make use of one of the above-mentioned paid holidays, he/she shall inform his/her supervisor three days in advance. Should the JET participant wish to use more than three paid holidays in succession, he/she is required to inform his/her supervisor one month in advance.

Article 12: Special Holidays

Section 1

The JET participant shall be entitled to special holidays under the following circumstances:

1. Sick leave—the period of serious illness or injury resulting in an acknowledged inability to work.
2. Bereavement—the period of 14 consecutive days, including Sundays and national holidays, immediately after the loss of father, mother, or spouse.
3. Natural disaster—the period the board of education deems necessary in the event of destruction of or serious damage to the JET participant's place of residence.
4. Transportation system failure—the period until the said problem has been resolved.

Section 2

Under the conditions of Article 12, Section 1 (1), above, the JET participant may take not more than 20 days of consecutive sick leave. Moreover, if the interval between two such periods of sick leave is less than one week, those two periods shall be regarded as continuous.

Section 3

The special holidays noted above in Article 12, Section 1, are paid holidays.

Article 17: Procedure for Taking (Sick) Leave

Section 1

When the JET participant wishes to make use of the special holidays/leave specified in Article 12, Section 1, he/she must apply and receive consent from his/her supervisor before taking the requested holidays. If circumstances prevent the JET participant from making necessary application beforehand, he/she should do so as soon as conditions permit it.

Section 2

In the event of the JET participant taking three or more consecutive days of sick leave, he/she must submit a doctor's certificate. The board of education may require the JET participant to obtain the said medical certificate from a medical practitioner specified by the board.

---

their housing before they arrived in Japan. Mr. Higashi even took the two women shopping to help them buy necessary items like bedding and dishes so they did not have to be without, even for one night.

Mr. Higashi

Mr. Higashi was born and had lived all of his life in Soto. He was 44 years old and had been teaching high school English in and around Soto for more than 20 years. Two years ago, Mr. Higashi was promoted to work as an adviser to all English teachers at the Soto

Board of Education. This was a career-making move, and one that placed him on the track to becoming a school principal.

This new position at the board of education made Mr. Higashi the direct supervisor over the foreign JET participants in the office, as well as making him responsible for their actions. He had worked with them before when he was still teaching in the schools, but since they only came once a week to his school, he had never had the chance to get to know any of them really well.

Mr. Higashi found it very difficult to work with JETs. Since they were hired on a one-year contract basis, renewable only to a maximum of three, he had already seen several come and go. He also considered it inconvenient that Japanese was not a requirement for the JET participants because, since he was the only person in the office who could speak English, he found that he wasted a lot of his time working as an interpreter and helping the foreigners do simple everyday tasks like reading electric bills and opening a bank account. Despite this, he did his best to treat the foreign assistants as he would any other *kohai,* or subordinate, by nurturing their careers and acting as a father to them, since he knew what was best for them. Mr. Higashi was aware that his next promotion was due not only to his own performance but also to how well he interacted with his subordinates, so he worked hard to be a good mentor.

Mr. Higashi took an instant liking to Kelly because she spoke Japanese well and had already lived in Japan. Although she was the youngest of the four ALTs, he hoped that she would guide the others and assumed that she would not be the source of any problems for him.

The ALTs' Opinion of Mr. Higashi

At first, Mr. Higashi seemed fine. All of the ALTs sat in two rows with their desks facing each other, as they used to do in grade school, with Mr. Higashi's desk facing Kelly's. The foreigners all agreed that Mr. Higashi acted more like a father than a boss. He continually asked Kelly and Suzanne how they were enjoying Japanese life and kept encouraging them to immerse themselves in Japanese culture. He left brochures on Kelly's desk for courses in flower arranging and tea ceremony and even one on Japanese cooking. At first Kelly found this rather amusing, but she soon tired of it and started to get fed up with this constant pressure to "sign up" for Japanese culture. What she resented the most was that Mr. Higashi kept insisting she try activities that were traditionally considered a woman's domain. Not that she had anything against flowers, but if she had been a man, she knew that Mr. Higashi would not have hassled her this much to fit in. She knew that Japanese society was a male-dominated one. On her first day at the office, Kelly had looked around and noticed that there were no Japanese women who had been promoted to such a senior level within the board of education. The only women who worked there were young and single "office ladies" or secretaries. Although they were all very sweet young women, Kelly was not about to become one of them and "retire" if and when she found a husband.

Kelly had been very active in sports back in Canada and bought herself a mountain bike when she arrived in Japan so that she could go for rides in the country. At Suzanne's encouragement, Kelly joined a local Kendo club. She had seen this Japanese style of fencing before back in Calgary, and had always been attracted to the fast movements and interesting uniforms. Kelly hoped that Mr. Higashi would be satisfied that she was finally getting involved in something traditionally Japanese and leave her alone.

On top of his chauvinistic attitudes, Kelly didn't think much of Mr. Higashi as a supervisor. If Kelly or any of the other foreigners had a problem or question concerning living in Japan, he would either ignore them or give them information that they later found out was incorrect. Andrea told Kelly that she stopped going to Mr. Higashi when she had problems and instead consulted the office lady, since she was always able to help her. Andrea had even joked that the office lady should be their supervisor because she was by far more effective than Mr. Higashi.

As far as Suzanne was concerned, Mr. Higashi was utterly exasperating. He was forever arranging projects and conferences for the ALTs to participate in, then changing his mind and canceling at the last minute without bothering to tell them. He would also volunteer the ALTs to work on special assignments over the holiday periods and then get angry when they told him that they had previous plans and were unable to go. Suzanne recalled that one week before the Christmas vacation, Mr. Higashi announced that he had arranged for her to visit a junior high school. Suzanne informed him that while she would love to go, it was impossible since she had already booked the time off and had arranged a holiday to Seoul, Korea. Mr. Higashi got angry and told her that he and the board of education would lose face if she didn't attend. Suzanne told Mr. Higashi that losing face would not have been an issue if he had told her about the visit in advance so she could have prepared for it. As a result, Suzanne lost all respect for Mr. Higashi as a manager and continually challenged his authority. Whenever a problem arose, she was quick to remind him that things were very different and much better in Britain.

Mark also had difficulties with Mr. Higashi. Mark was not much of a group player and resented Mr. Higashi's constantly telling him what to do. He preferred to withdraw and work on his own. He didn't like Mr. Higashi's paternalistic attitude. He just wanted to be treated like a normal, capable employee and be given free rein to do his work. As a show of his independence, Mark refused to join in on any of the "drinking meetings" after work.

The Japanese Opinion of the ALTs

The other Japanese employees in the office found it difficult to work with the ALTs because, as far as they were concerned, the ALTs were never there long enough to become part of the group. It seemed like just after they got to know one ALT, he or she left and was replaced by another. Another problem was that since the foreigners usually did not speak Japanese, communication with them was extremely frustrating.

The biggest problem that the employees at the board of education office had with the ALTs was that they were so young and inexperienced. All of the men in the office had worked a minimum of 20 years to reach this stage in their careers, only to find themselves working side by side with foreigners who had recently graduated from college. To make matters worse, these young foreigners were also hired to advise them how to do their jobs better. The employees were also aware that the ALTs earned practically the same salary as their supervisor each month.

The Japanese employees did not consider the ALTs to be very committed workers. They never stayed past 5:00 p.m. on weekdays, and never came to work on the weekends even though the rest of the office did. It seemed as though the ALTs were rarely at the office. The ALTs also made it very clear that they had a contract that allowed them vacation days, and they made sure that they used every single day. The Japanese employees, on the other hand, rarely ever made use of their vacation time and knew that if they took holidays as frequently as the foreigners, they could return to find that their desk had been cleared.

The Incident

Kelly woke up one Monday morning with a high fever and a sore throat. She phoned Mr. Higashi to let him know that she wouldn't be coming in that day and possibly not the next. Mr. Higashi asked if she needed anything and told her to relax and take care of herself. Before he hung up, Mr. Higashi told her that when she came back to the office, to make sure to bring in a doctor's note. Kelly was annoyed. The last thing she wanted to do was to get out of bed and go to the clinic for a simple case of the flu. As she was getting dressed she thought she was being treated like a schoolgirl by being forced to bring in a note.

Two days later, Kelly returned to the office with the note from a physician in her hand. Andrea informed her that Mark and Suzanne had also been sick and that she had been by herself in the office. She also said that Mr. Higashi was suspicious that the three of them had been sick at the same time and had commented that he knew that foreigners sometimes pretended to be sick in order to create longer weekends. Kelly was glad that she had gone to the doctor and got a note so she could prove that she was really sick. Kelly said good morning to Mr. Higashi and gave him her note. He took it from her without so much as looking at it and threw it onto a huge pile of incoming mail on his desk. He asked her if she was feeling better and then went back to his work.

At midmorning, the accountant came over to Kelly's desk and asked her to sign some papers. Kelly reached for her pen and started to sign automatically until she noticed that she was signing for two days of paid leave and not sick leave. She pointed out the error to the accountant, who told her that there had not been a mistake. Kelly told the accountant to come back later and went over to speak with Mr. Higashi. To her surprise, Mr. Higashi said that there had been no mistake and that this was standard procedure in Japan. He said that typical Japanese employees normally did not make use of their vacation time due to their great loyalty to the company. If an employee became sick, he often used his paid vacation first out of respect for his employers.

Kelly responded that this was fine for Japanese employees, but since she was not Japanese, she preferred to do things the Canadian way. Mr. Higashi replied that since she was in Japan, maybe she should start doing things the Japanese way. Kelly turned away and looked at Andrea, not believing what had just happened.

The next day, both Mark and Suzanne returned to the office only to find themselves in the same predicament as Kelly. Suzanne called Mr. Higashi a lunatic and Mark chose to stop speaking to him altogether. Kelly was furious that they were being forced to waste two of their vacation days when they were guaranteed sick leave. She threw the JET contract on Mr. Higashi's desk and pointed out the section that stipulated the number of sick days they were entitled to and demanded that he honor their contract as written.

Mr. Higashi looked extremely agitated and said that he had to go to a very important meeting and would discuss the situation later. The accountant reappeared with the papers for the three ALTs to sign, but they all refused. Suzanne started to complain about Mr. Higashi's incompetence, while Mark complained about the Japanese style of management. Suzanne said that it was a shame that none of them had bothered to join AJET, for wasn't this the kind of problem that unions were supposed to handle? Kelly stared at the contract on her desk and said that they could take it to a higher level and involve CLAIR. Andrea said that things could get ugly and people could lose face if it went that far. Kelly took her agenda out of her desk and started looking for CLAIR's phone number.

Discussion Questions

1. What should Kelly and the other ALTs do now?
2. Why did conflict occur? How could it have been prevented?

Questionnaire 1

The Personal Bargaining Inventory

Introduction

One way for negotiators to learn more about themselves, and about others in a negotiating context, is to clarify their own personal beliefs and values about the negotiation process and their style as negotiators. The questionnaire in this section can help you clarify perceptions of yourself on several dimensions related to negotiation—winning and losing, cooperation and competition, power and deception—and your beliefs about how a person "ought" to negotiate. Your instructor is likely to ask you to share your responses with others after you complete the questionnaire.

Advance Preparation

Complete the Personal Bargaining Inventory questionnaire in this exercise. Bring the inventory to class.

Personal Bargaining Inventory Questionnaire

The questions in this inventory are designed to measure your responses to your perceptions of human behavior in situations of bargaining and negotiation. Statements in the first group ask you about *your own behavior* in bargaining; statements in the second group ask you to judge *people's behavior in general*.

Part I: Rating Your Own Behavior

For each statement, please indicate how much the statement is *characteristic of you* on the following scale:

1 Strongly uncharacteristic
2 Moderately uncharacteristic
3 Mildly uncharacteristic
4 Neutral, no opinion
5 Mildly characteristic
6 Moderately characteristic
7 Strongly characteristic

Rate each statement on the seven-point scale by writing in one number closest to your personal judgment of yourself:

Rating	Statement
_____	1. I am sincere and trustworthy at all times. I will not lie, for whatever ends.
_____	2. I would refuse to bug the room of my opponent.
_____	3. I don't particularly care what people think of me. Getting what I want is more important than making friends.
_____	4. I am uncomfortable in situations where the rules are ambiguous and there are few precedents.

Source: Adapted from an exercise developed by Bert Brown and Norman Berkowitz.

Personal Bargaining Inventory Questionnaire (*continued*)

Rating	Statement
_____	5. I prefer to deal with others on a one-to-one basis rather than as a group.
_____	6. I can lie effectively. I can maintain a poker face when I am not telling the truth.
_____	7. I pride myself on being highly principled. I am willing to stand by those principles no matter what the cost.
_____	8. I am a patient person. As long as an agreement is finally reached, I do not mind slow-moving arguments.
_____	9. I am a good judge of character. When I am being deceived, I can spot it quickly.
_____	10. My sense of humor is one of my biggest assets.
_____	11. I have above-average empathy for the views and feelings of others.
_____	12. I can look at emotional issues in a dispassionate way. I can argue strenuously for my point of view, but I put the dispute aside when the argument is over.
_____	13. I tend to hold grudges.
_____	14. Criticism doesn't usually bother me. Any time you take a stand, people are bound to disagree, and it's all right for them to let you know they don't like your stand.
_____	15. I like power. I want it for myself, to do with what I want. In situations where I must share power I strive to increase my power base, and lessen that of my co–power holder.
_____	16. I like to share power. It is better for two or more to have power than it is for power to be in just one person's hands. The balance of shared power is important to effective functioning of any organization because it forces participation in decision making.
_____	17. I enjoy trying to persuade others to my point of view.
_____	18. I am not effective at persuading others to my point of view when my heart isn't really in what I am trying to represent.
_____	19. I love a good old, knockdown, drag-out verbal fight. Conflict is healthy, and open conflict where everybody's opinion is aired is the best way to resolve differences of opinion.
_____	20. I hate conflict and will do anything to avoid it—including giving up power over a situation.
_____	21. In any competitive situation, I like to win. Not just win, but win by the biggest margin possible.
_____	22. In any competitive situation, I like to win. I don't want to clobber my opponent, just come out a little ahead.
_____	23. The only way I could engage conscientiously in bargaining would be by dealing honestly and openly with my opponents.

Part II: Rating People's Behavior in General

For each statement, please indicate how much you agree with the statement on the following scale:

1 Strongly disagree

2 Moderately disagree

3 Mildly disagree

4 Neutral, no opinion

5 Mildly agree

6 Moderately agree

7 Strongly agree

Think about what you believe makes people effective negotiators. Rate each statement on the seven-point scale by writing in one number closest to your judgment of what makes an excellent negotiator:

Rating	Statement
_____	24. If you are too honest and trustworthy, most people will take advantage of you.
_____	25. Fear is a stronger persuader than trust.
_____	26. When one is easily predictable, one is easily manipulated.
_____	27. The appearance of openness in your opponent should be suspect.
_____	28. Make an early minor concession; the other side may reciprocate on something you want later on.
_____	29. Personality and the ability to judge people and persuade them to your point of view (or to an acceptable compromise) are more important than knowledge and information about the issues at hand.
_____	30. Silence is golden—it's the best reply to a totally unacceptable offer.
_____	31. Be the aggressor. You must take the initiative if you are going to accomplish your objectives.
_____	32. One should avoid frequent use of a third party.
_____	33. Honesty and openness are necessary to reach equitable agreement.
_____	34. It is important to understand one's values prior to bargaining.
_____	35. Be calm. Maintaining your cool at all times gives you an unquestionable advantage. Never lose your temper.
_____	36. Keep a poker face; never act pleased as terms are agreed upon.
_____	37. A good negotiator must be able to see the issues from the opponent's point of view.
_____	38. An unanswered threat will be read by your opponent as weakness.
_____	39. In bargaining, winning is the most important consideration.
_____	40. The best outcome in bargaining is one that is fair to all parties.
_____	41. Most results in bargaining can be achieved through cooperation.
_____	42. Principles are all well and good, but sometimes you have to compromise your principles to achieve your goals.
_____	43. You should never try to exploit your adversary's personal weakness.
_____	44. A member of a bargaining team is morally responsible for the strategies and tactics employed by that team.
_____	45. Good ends justify the means. If you know you're right and your goal is worthy, you needn't be concerned too much about *how* your goal is achieved.
_____	46. Honesty means openness, candor, telling all, and not withholding pertinent information, not exaggerating emotion. One should always be honest during bargaining.
_____	47. Imposing personal discomfort on an opponent is not too high a price to pay for success in negotiation.
_____	48. Regardless of personal considerations, team members should accept any role assigned to them by the bargaining team.
_____	49. There is no need to deal completely openly with your adversaries. In bargaining as in life, what they don't know won't hurt them.
_____	50. There is nothing wrong with lying to an opponent in a bargaining situation as long as you don't get caught.

The SINS II Scale

Introduction

The purpose of the SINS II scale is to inquire about your general disposition toward ethical issues in negotiation. It will help you determine your views on a range of ethical and unethical negotiation tactics. The instructor will explain how to score and interpret this questionnaire.

Advance Preparation

Complete the SINS II scale as specified by your instructor.

Incidents in Negotiation Questionnaire

This questionnaire is part of research study on how negotiators decide when certain strategies and tactics are ethical and appropriate in negotiations.

In completing this questionnaire, *please try to be as candid as you can about what you think is appropriate and acceptable to do.* You are being asked about tactics that are controversial; however, your responses on this questionnaire are completely anonymous, and no one will ever know your individual responses.

You will be asked to consider a list of tactics that negotiators sometimes use. You should consider these tactics in the context of a *situation in which you will be negotiating for something that is very important to you and your business*. For each tactic, you will be asked to indicate how appropriate the tactic would be to use in this situation. Then assign a rating to each tactic, evaluating how appropriate it would be to use this tactic in the context specified above, based on the following scale:

1	2	3	4	5	6	7
Not at all appropriate			Somewhat appropriate			Very appropriate

(If you have any need to explain your rating on a tactic, please do so in the margin or at the end of the questionnaire.)

Rating

---

1. Promise that good things will happen to your opponent if he/she gives you what you want, even if you know that you can't (or won't) deliver these things when the other's cooperation is obtained. ____

2. Get the other party to think that you like him/her personally despite the fact that you don't really. ____

3. Intentionally misrepresent information to your opponent in order to strengthen your negotiating arguments or position. ____

4. Strategically express anger toward the other party in a situation where you are not really angry. ____

SINS stands for Self-Reported Inappropriate Negotiation Strategies. Questionnaire developed by Robert Robinson, Roy J. Lewicki, and Eileen Donahue, 1998. Modified by Roy J. Lewicki, 2001, using items developed by Bruce Barry. Used with permission of the developers.

Incidents in Negotiation Questionnaire (*concluded*)

	Rating
5. Attempt to get your opponent fired from his/her position so that a new person will take his/her place.	____
6. Intentionally misrepresent the nature of negotiations to your constituency in order to protect delicate discussions that have occurred.	____
7. Express sympathy with the other party's plight although in truth you don't care about their problems.	____
8. Gain information about an opponent's negotiating position by paying your friends, associates, and contacts to get this information for you.	____
9. Feign a melancholy mood in order to get the other party to think you are having a bad day.	____
10. Make an opening demand that is far greater than what you really hope to settle for.	____
11. Pretend to be disgusted at an opponent's comments.	
12. Convey a false impression that you are in absolutely no hurry to come to a negotiated agreement, thereby trying to put time pressure on your opponent to concede quickly.	____
13. Give the other party the false impression that you are very disappointed with how things are going.	____
14. In return for concessions from your opponent now, offer to make future concessions which you know you will not follow through on.	____
15. Threaten to make your opponent look weak or foolish in front of a boss or others to whom he/she is accountable, even if you know that you won't actually carry out the threat.	____
16. Deny the validity of information which your opponent has that weakens your negotiating position, even though that information is true and valid.	____
17. Give the other party the (false) impression that you care about his/her personal welfare.	____
18. Intentionally misrepresent the progress of negotiations to your constituency in order to make your own position appear stronger.	____
19. Talk directly to the people whom your opponent reports to, or is accountable to, and tell them things that will undermine their confidence in your opponent as a negotiator.	____
20. Stimulate fear on your part so that the other party will think you are tense about negotiating.	____
21. Gain information about an opponent's negotiating position by cultivating his/her friendship through expensive gifts, entertaining, or "personal favors."	____
22. Pretend to be furious at your opponent.	____
23. Make an opening demand so high/low that it seriously undermines your opponent's confidence in his/her ability to negotiate a satisfactory settlement.	____
24. Guarantee that your constituency will uphold the settlement reached, although you know that they will likely violate the agreement later.	____
25. Gain information about an opponent's negotiating position by trying to recruit or hire one of the opponent's teammates (on the condition that the teammate bring confidential information with him/her).	____

The Influence Tactics Inventory

Introduction

The questionnaire in this exercise is designed to measure your predisposition to use different influence tactics at work. In responding to these questions, you will learn something about the influence tactics that you use, depending on whom you want to influence.

Procedure

Step 1

Identify three different people whom you have needed to influence at work. One should be a superior, one a subordinate, and the other a coworker.

Step 2

Work completely through the questionnaire for *each* of the three people you have chosen, keeping only one person in mind at a time. Use the following scale to respond to each of the statements that follow. Be sure to respond to all of the statements for each of the three people.

5 I usually use this tactic to influence him or her.

4 I frequently use this tactic to influence him or her.

3 I occasionally use this tactic to influence him or her.

2 I seldom use this tactic to influence him or her.

1 I never use this tactic to influence him or her.

Step 3

Your instructor will hand out a scoring key. Follow the key to score the questionnaire.

Superior	Subordinate	Coworker	Statement
_____	_____	_____	1. Kept checking up on him or her.
_____	_____	_____	2. Made him or her feel important ("only you have the brains, talent to do this").
_____	_____	_____	3. Wrote a detailed plan that justified my ideas.
_____	_____	_____	4. Gave no salary increase or prevented that person from getting a raise.
_____	_____	_____	5. Offered an exchange (e.g., if you do this for me, I will do something for you).

Source: Adapted from David Kipnis, Stuart M. Schmidt, and Ian Wilkinson, "Intraorganizational Influence Tactics: Explorations in Getting One's Way," *Journal of Applied Psychology* 65, pp. 440–52. Used with permission.

(concluded)

Superior	Subordinate	Coworker	Statement
———	———	———	6. Made a formal appeal to higher levels to back up my request.
———	———	———	7. Threatened to notify an outside agency if he or she did not give in to my request.
———	———	———	8. Obtained the support of coworkers to back up my request.
———	———	———	9. Simply ordered him or her to do what I requested.
———	———	———	10. Acted very humbly to him or her while making my request.
———	———	———	11. Presented him or her with information in support of my point of view.
———	———	———	12. Threatened his or her job security (e.g., hint of firing or getting him or her fired).
———	———	———	13. Reminded him or her of past favors that I had done for him or her.
———	———	———	14. Obtained the informal support of higher-ups.
———	———	———	15. Threatened to stop working with him or her until he or she gave in.
———	———	———	16. Had him or her come to a formal conference at which I made my request.
———	———	———	17. Demanded that he or she do what I requested.
———	———	———	18. Acted in a friendly manner prior to asking for what I wanted.
———	———	———	19. Explained the reasons for my request.
———	———	———	20. Promised (or gave) a salary request.
———	———	———	21. Offered to make a personal sacrifice if he or she would do what I wanted (e.g., work late, work harder, do his/her share of the work).
———	———	———	22. Filed a report about the other person with higher-ups (e.g., my superior).
———	———	———	23. Engaged in a work slowdown until he or she did what I wanted.
———	———	———	24. Obtained the support of my subordinates to back up my request.

The Trust Scale

Introduction

The purpose of the Trust Scale is to inquire about your general level of trust and distrust in another person before or after a negotiation. Your instructor will explain how to score and interpret this questionnaire.

Advance Preparation

Complete the Trust Scale as specified by your instructor.

Procedure

1. Complete the Trust Scale.

2. Your instructor will hand out a scoring key for the Trust Scale. Follow the key to score your questionnaire. A description of the questionnaire and what it measures will be provided by the instructor.

3. Be prepared to share your answers to the questions with others in a small group or class discussion.

Trust Scale

Identify a specific other person for whom you have some level of trust. Then rate that other person on the following five-point scale:

1	2	3	4	5
Strongly disagree		Undecided		Strongly agree

Rating

1. This person's behavior meets my expectations. _____
2. This person fears the consequences if he or she doesn't comply with our agreements. _____
3. This person will protect and defend me, even at his or her own expense. _____
4. I try to protect myself and my interests from this person. _____
5. This person does as he or she promises. _____
6. I can easily monitor what this person does to make sure he or she complies. _____
7. This person and I have the same basic values. _____
8. This person enjoys making my life miserable. _____
9. I communicate regularly with this person, and he or she keeps me informed about what he or she is doing. _____

Source: Questionnaire developed by Roy J. Lewicki. Please request permission if used for nonpedagogical purposes.

Trust Scale (*concluded*)

	Rating
10. If this person doesn't do as he or she promises, I can "get even."	_____
11. This person cares for me so much that he or she often does what is best for me even without asking me.	_____
12. I see this person more as a competitor and an opponent.	_____
13. I can check up on this person if I need to.	_____
14. This person knows that I have lots of ways of retaliating if he or she doesn't follow through.	_____
15. We identify with each other.	_____
16. I don't expect this person to make any sacrifices for me.	_____
17. I have interacted with this person a lot.	_____
18. This person knows what I will do if he or she violates a commitment.	_____
19. This person and I have the same fundamental views of the world.	_____
20. When I am with this person, the atmosphere is always tense.	_____
21. This person is honest with me.	_____
22. This person is aware that I will know if he or she breaks his or her word.	_____
23. This person will go out of his or her way to protect my interests if they are challenged or threatened.	_____
24. This person's value system is fundamentally different from my own.	_____
25. I think I can accurately predict what this person will do.	_____
26. This person knows that it is in his or her own best interest to do what he or she promises.	_____
27. This person and I really stand for the same basic things.	_____
28. Whatever happens, you can expect this person to take care of only himself or herself.	_____
29. In my experience, this person is very reliable.	_____
30. This person cares for me a great deal.	_____
31. If this person thought he or she could get away with it, he or she would take advantage of others.	_____
32. Everything I know about this person makes me cautious and suspicious.	_____

Discussion

In recent years, a great deal of research has been conducted on the nature of trust and the role it plays in critical social relationships. Trust is essential to productive social relationships with others, and it can play a critical role in negotiations, particularly integrative negotiations. High trust contributes to better negotiations, and more cooperative, productive negotiations are likely to enhance trust. Conversely, low trust may contribute to less productive negotiations, and less productive negotiations are likely to decrease trust.

There are many definitions of trust, reflecting different views about trust as either a core characteristic of one's personality or a set of perceptions, expectations, and judgments that are shaped by what we know about the other party and the situation in which our relationship with them takes place. In discussing trust here, we will define *trust* as "an individual's belief in, and willingness to act on the basis of, the words, actions, and decisions of another."

Recent research suggests that there are two different types of trust—calculus-based and identification-based trust. *Calculus-based trust* is based on consistency of behavior—that people will do what they say they are going to do. Behavioral consistency is sustained by offering either the promise of rewards for people to do what they say they are going to do, or the threat of punishment (e.g., loss of relationship) that will occur if consistency is not maintained—that is, people do *not* do what they say they will do. This type of trust is based on an ongoing, economic calculation of the value of the outcomes to be received by creating and sustaining the relationship relative to the costs of maintaining or severing it. Not only are these rewards and punishments given directly to the other, but we also can reward or punish the other by enhancing or destroying the other's reputation with friends, associates, and business partners if they honor or violate the trust.

Identification-based trust is based on complete empathy with or identification with the other party's desires and intentions. At this level, trust exists because each party effectively understands, appreciates, agrees with, empathizes with, and takes on the other's values because of the emotional connection between them—and thus can act for the other. Identification-based trust thus permits one to act as an "agent" for the other and substitute for the other in interpersonal transactions. The other can be confident that his or her interests will be fully protected, and that no surveillance or monitoring of the actor is necessary. A true affirmation of the strength of identification-based trust between parties can be found when one party acts for the other in a manner even more zealous than the other might demonstrate; the parties not only know and identify with each other, but understand what they must do to sustain the other's trust. One learns what "really matters" to the other and comes to place the same importance on those behaviors as the other does. When we watch very closely knit groups work together under pressure, such as jazz quartets, basketball teams, or very skilled work groups, we get to see identification-based trust in action.

In addition, research is beginning to confirm that distrust is fundamentally different from trust, rather than being more or less of the same thing. Although trust can be defined as "confident positive expectations regarding another's conduct," distrust can indeed be "confident negative expectations" regarding another's conduct. Moreover, research is confirming that there are two forms of distrust: calculus-based distrust and identification-based distrust.

Calculus-based distrust consists of confident negative expectations of another's conduct. Like calculus-based trust, it is also grounded in consistency of behavior—but consistency in that the other consistently *fails* to do as he or she says. This type of distrust is based on an ongoing, economically based calculation or what we stand to lose by maintaining the relationship with the other, relative to the costs of severing it or finding an alternative way to meet our needs. Distrust of the other can be enhanced or reduced based on the other's reputation with friends, associates, and business partners if they violate or honor the trust.

Similarly, *identification-based distrust* consists of confident negative expectations of another's conduct grounded in perceived incompatibility of closely held values, dissimilar or competing goals, or a negative emotional attachment. Identification-based distrust is based on a complete lack of empathy or lack of identification with the other party's desires and intentions. Such distrust is grounded in a visceral dissimilarity with and dislike for the other—we do not agree with or empathize with the other, and we hold very dissimilar values. We expect that we have little in common with the other and that in fact the other may be a committed adversary who is out to do us in.

There are many implications for understanding relationships as complex combinations of these two types of trust and distrust:

- First, and most important, a relationship with another party can have elements of both trust and distrust. Relationships with other people are complex; we come to know them in a variety of different situations and contexts, some of which create trust and some of which create distrust. While many of these relationships will be dominated by trust or distrust, some will contain elements of both; we characterize these relationships as ones laden with *ambivalence.*

- Trust and distrust build as we come to know another party and have direct and indirect experiences with them (i.e., we learn about them from both our own and other people's experience). As we gain more information about another, we draw a more complex and detailed picture of the other.

- Remarkably, most relationships do not start at zero trust. Research has tended to show that most people begin a relationship assuming that the other is reasonably trustworthy. Thus most relationships start with a moderately positive level of trust.

- A number of other factors will influence how much we trust or distrust another party. These include our own personality (individuals differ in the amount of trust they have for another party), our general motivation and disposition toward the other party (e.g., cooperative or competitive), the other's reputation and our judgments of his or her trustworthiness, and the context in which the trust judgments are occurring.

- When trust has been violated, rebuilding trust may not be the same as controlling or managing distrust. Rebuilding trust may require actions such as acknowledgment of responsibility for violating the trust, making an apology, or claiming responsibility for one's actions. However, managing distrust may require actions that bind or constrain any future harmful consequences from violating trust again. Being clear about expectations for the other's conduct, setting deadlines, explicitly specifying consequences for failing to comply, detailing procedures for monitoring and verifying the other's actions, and cultivating alternative ways to have one's needs met are all ways to manage distrust, but engaging in these actions does not necessarily rebuild trust.

Discussion Questions

1. Think about the person you rated in this questionnaire. How close and personal (or distant and impersonal) is your relationship with that person?

2. Experiment with the questionnaire by rating several different people. For example, rate

   - The person whom you trust the most.

   - A person whom you trust in a professional capacity (e.g., a doctor, counselor, adviser).

- A boss or colleague at work.
- A person whom you are very close to.
- A person whom you actively distrust.
- A person who has violated your trust.

How do your ratings differ for each? What does this say about the role of trust and distrust in your relationship with that person?

3. How do you build trust in order to make negotiation more effective? What kinds of things can you do to strengthen trust? What should you avoid if you do not want to damage existing trust?

4. What do you do to manage your relationship with someone you distrust? How are these actions different from trust building or trust rebuilding?

5. Think about the person who has violated your trust. What happened in this situation? Why do you no longer trust that person? What would it take to repair the relationship with that person?

Communication Competence Scale

Generally speaking, *communication competence* can be defined as the ability to enact both appropriate and effective messages in any communication setting. Appropriate communication conforms to the expectations and rules of a situation, while effective communication allows parties in an interaction to achieve their goals. Communication competence, then, is a broad construct that refers to the ability to accurately assess situations and other people and respond to them in ways that allow you to get what you want while still complying with social rules and expectations.

The scale here is a diagnostic tool to help you determine your current level of communication competence. Answer the questions as honestly as you can, thinking about what you actually do in most situations you encounter. Once you have completed the instrument, your instructor will help you interpret your score.

Directions

The following are statements about the communication process. Answer each as it relates to what you generally think about concerning social situations. Please indicate the degree to which each statement applies to you by placing the appropriate number (according to the scale below) in the space provided:

5 Always true of me

4 Often true of me

3 Sometimes true of me

2 Rarely true of me

1 Never true of me

Rating	Statement
_____	1. Before a conversation, I think about what people might be talking about.
_____	2. When I first enter a new situation, I watch who is talking to whom.
_____	3. During a conversation, I am aware of when a topic is going nowhere.
_____	4. After a conversation, I think about what the other person thought of me.
_____	5. Generally, I think about how others might interpret what I say.
_____	6. After a conversation, I think about my performance.
_____	7. During a conversation, I am aware of when it is time to change the topic.
_____	8. When I first enter a new situation, I try to size up the event.
_____	9. Before a conversation, I mentally practice what I am going to say.

Source: Adapted by Roy J. Lewicki from R.L. Duran and B.H. Spitzberg, "Toward the Development and Validation of a Measure of Cognitive Communication Competence," *Communication Quarterly* 43 (1995), pp. 259–75. Used with permission.

(*concluded*)

Rating	Statement
_____	10. After a conversation, I think about what I said.
_____	11. Generally, I think about the consequences of what I say.
_____	12. Before a conversation, I think about what I am going to say.
_____	13. Generally, I study people.
_____	14. After a conversation, I think about what I could have said.
_____	15. When I first enter a new situation, I think about what I am going to talk about.
_____	16. Generally, I think about how what I say may affect others.
_____	17. During a conversation, I pay attention to how others are reacting to what I am saying.
_____	18. Generally, I am aware of people's interests.
_____	19. During a conversation, I think about what topic to discuss next.
_____	20. After a conversation, I think about what I have said to improve for the next conversation.
_____	21. Generally, I think about the effects of my communication.
_____	22. During a conversation, I know if I have said something rude or inappropriate.

Endnotes

Reading 3.10

1. (Northcraft & Neale, 1991; Thompson, 1990)
2. (Personal communication, 1997)
3. (Cusumano, 1997; Guzzo & Shea, 1992; Katzenbach & Smith, 1993)
4. (Triandis, 1989)
5. (e.g., DeSanctis & Fulk, 1999; Lane & Beamish, 1990)
6. (Brodt, 1999; Brodt & Tuchinsky, 2000; O'Connor, 1997; Peterson & Thompson, 1997; Thompson, Peterson, & Brodt, 1996)
7. (Latane, 1981)
8. (Turner & Oakes, 1989)
9. (Hogg & Abrams, 1988)
10. (Thompson et al., 1996)
11. (Thompson, 1990)
12. (Hill, 1982; Hinsz, 1990; Maier, 1967; Stasser, 1988)
13. (Brodt & Dietz, 1999, 2000; Henry, 1995; Laughlin, VanderStoep, & Hollingshead, 1991; Stasser, Stewart, & Wittenbaum, 1995)
14. (Hinsz, Tindale, & Vollrath, 1997; Kerr, MacCoun, & Kramer, 1996)
15. (e.g., Diehl & Stroebe, 1987)
16. (Brodt & Tuchinsky, 2000; O'Connor, 1997; Peterson & Thompson, 1997; Thompson et al., 1996)
17. (Erev & Somech, 1996; Harkins & Szymanski, 1989; Petty, Harkins, & Williams, 1980; Weldon & Gargano, 1988)
18. (Thompson & Hastie, 1990)
19. (Hinsz, 1990; Laughlin, 1980; Shaw, 1932)
20. (Henry, 1995; Sniezek & Henry, 1989)
21. (Janis, 1982)
22. (Moscovici & Zavalloni, 1969; Myers, 1982)
23. (e.g., McGuire, Kiesler, & Siegel, 1987)
24. (e.g., intellective tasks; see Kaplan, 1987; Laughlin, 1980)
25. (Laughlin; Laughlin & Ellis, 1986)
26. (Kerr, 1992; Kerr et al., 1996; Myers & Lamm, 1976)
27. (Baumeister & Leary, 1995; Deutsch & Gerard, 1955)
28. (Moscovici, 1984; Tindale, Smith, Thomas, Filkins, & Sheffey, 1996)
29. (Insko et al., 1987; Insko & Schopler, 1987; Schopler & Insko, 1992)

30. (Brodt, 1994; O'Connor, 1997; Thompson et al., 1996)

31. (Brodt, 1994; see Thompson, 2001, for a review)

32. (Benton & Druckman, 1974; Carnevale, Pruitt, & Britton, 1979; Klimoski & Ash, 1974; see Pruitt & Carnevale, 1993, for a review)

33. (O'Connor, 1997; Pruitt & Carnevale; Thompson, 2001; Laughlin, 1980)

34. (Gelfand & Realo, 1999)

35. (Brodt & Tuchinsky, 2000; Hilty & Carnevale, 1993)

36. (Brodt & Dietz, 1999)

37. (Thompson et al., 1996)

38. (Moreland, Argote, & Krishnan, 1998; Wegner, 1987; Wegner, Erber, & Raymond, 1991)

39. (Moreland et al., 1998)

40. (Wegner, 1987; Wegner et al., 1991)

41. (Peterson & Thompson, 1997)

42. (Keenan & Carnevale, 1989)

43. (Fry, Firestone, & Williams, 1983; see Valley, Neale, & Mannix, 1995, for a review)

44. (Jehn & Shah, 1997)

45. (Latane, 1981)

46. (Insko et al., 1987; Insko & Schopler, 1987; Schopler & Insko, 1992)

47. (Carnevale et al., 1979; O'Connor, 1997; Pruitt & Carnevale, 1993)

48. (cf. Bazerman, Magliozzi, & Neale, 1985; Walton & McKersie, 1965)

49. (Brewer & Kramer, 1985; Tajfel, 1982)

50. (Thompson, 1993)

51. (Brewer & Kramer; Polzer, 1996; Wilder & Shapiro, 1991)

52. (Insko et al., 1987; Insko & Schopler, 1987; Schopler & Insko, 1992)

53. (Tajfel & Turner, 1979)

54. (Hogg & Abrams, 1988)

55. (Diekmann, Samuels, Ross, & Bazerman, 1997; Messick & Rutte, 1992; Messick & Sends, 1979)

56. (Karau & Williams, 1993)

57. (Lax & Sebenius, 1986)

58. (Thompson et al., 1996)

59. (Ross, Amabile, & Steinmetz, 1977)

60. (Jehn, Northcraft, & Neale, 1999)

61. (Latane, 1981)

62. (e.g., discontinuity effect; Insko et al., 1987)

63. (Hogg & Abrams, 1988; Turner & Oakes, 1989)

64. (Fortune & Brodt, 2000; Schweitzer, Brodt, & Croson, 2000; Valley, Moag, & Bazerman, 1998)

References

Reading 3.10

Baumeister, R., & Leary, M. (1995). The need to belong: Desire for interpersonal attachments as a fundamental human motivation. *Psychological Bulletin, 117,* 497–529.

Bazerman, M., Magliozzi, T., & Neale, M. (1985). The acquisition of an integrative response in a competitive market. *Organizational Behavior and Human Performance, 34,* 294–313.

Benton, A., & Druckman, D. (1974). Constituent's bargaining orientation and intergroup negotiations. *Journal of Applied Social Psychology, 4,* 141–150.

Brewer, M., & Kramer, R. (1985). The psychology of intergroup attitudes and behavior. *Annual Review of Psychology, 36,* 219–243.

Brodt, S. (1994). "Inside information" and negotiator decision behavior. *Organizational Behavior and Human Decision Processes, 58,* 172–202.

Brodt, S. (1999). *Group memory systems and their implications for negotiating teams and intergroup negotiation.* Durham, NC: Duke University, Fuqua School of Business.

Brodt, S., & Dietz, L. (1999). Shared information and information sharing: Understanding negotiation as collective construal. In R. Bies, R. Lewicki, & B. Sheppard (Eds.), *Research on negotiation in organizations* (Vol. 7, pp. 263–283). Greenwich, CT: JAI Press.

Brodt, S., & Dietz, L. (2000). *Knowing, caring and sharing: The effect of expertise and relational concern on group decision making.* Manuscript submitted for publication.

Brodt, S., & Tuchinsky, M. (2000). Working together but in opposition: An examination of the "good cop/bad cop" negotiating team tactic. *Organizational Behavior and Human Decision Processes, 81,* 155–177.

Carnevale, P., Pruitt, D., & Britton, S. (1979). Looking tough: The negotiator under constituent surveillance. *Personality and Social Psychology Bulletin 5,* 118–121.

Cusumano, M. (1997). How Microsoft makes large teams work like small teams. *Sloan Management Review, 39,* 9–20.

DeSanctis, G., & Fulk, J. (1999). *Shaping organization form: Communication, connection, and community.* Thousand Oaks, CA: Sage.

Deutsch, M., & Gerard, H. B. (1955). A study of normative and informational social influence upon individual judgment. *Journal of Abnormal and Social Psychology, 51,* 629–636.

Diehl, M., & Stroebe, W. (1987). Productivity loss in brainstorming groups: Toward the solution of a riddle. *Journal of Personality and Social Psychology, 53,* 497–509.

Diekmann, K. A., Samuels, S. M., Ross, L., & Bazerman, M. H. (1997). Self-interest and fairness in problems of resource allocation: Allocators versus recipients. *Journal of Personality and Social Psychology, 72,* 1061–1074.

Erev, M., & Somech, A. (1996). Is productivity loss the rule or the exception? Effects of culture and group-based motivation. *Academy of Management Journal, 39,* 1513–1537.

Fortune, A., & Brodt, S. (2000). *Face to face or virtually: The influence of task and media on trust and deception in negotiation.* Manuscript submitted for publication.

Friedman, R., & Podolny, J. (1992). Differentiation of boundary spanning roles: Labor negotiations and implications for role conflict. *Administrative Sciences Quarterly, 37,* 28–47.

Fry, W. R., Firestone, L., & Williams, D. (1983). Negotiation process and outcomes of stranger dyads and dating couples: Do lovers lose? *Basic and Applied Social Psychology, 4,* 1–16.

Gelfand, M., & Realo, A. (1999). Individualism collectivism and accountability in intergroup negotiations. *Journal of Applied Psychology, 84,* 721–736.

Guzzo, R., & Shea, G. (1992). Group performance and intergroup relations in organizations. In M. Dunnette & L. Hough (Eds.), *Handbook of industrial and organizational psychology, Vol. 3* (2nd ed., pp. 269–313). Palo Alto, CA: Consulting Psychologists Press.

Harkins, S., & Szymanski, K. (1989). Social loafing and group evaluation. *Journal of Personality and Social Psychology, 56,* 934–941.

Hastie, R. (1986). Experimental evidence on group accuracy. In B. Grofman & G. Owen (Eds.), *Decision research* (Vol. 2, pp. 129–157) Greenwich, CT: JAI Press.

Henry, R. (1995). Improving group judgment accuracy: Information sharing and determining the best member. *Organizational Behavior and Human Decision Processes, 62,* 190–197.

Hill, G. (1982). Group versus individual performance: Are N+1 heads better than one? *Psychological Bulletin, 91,* 517–539.

Hilty, J., & Carnevale, P. (1993). Black-hat/white-hat strategy in bilateral negotiation. *Organizational Behavior and Human Decision Processes, 55,* 444–469.

Hinsz, V. (1990). Cognitive and consensus processes in group recognition memory performance. *Journal of Personality and Social Psychology, 59,* 705–718.

Hinsz, V., Tindale, R. S., & Vollrath, D. (1997). The emerging conceptualization of groups as information processors. *Psychological Bulletin, 121,* 43–64.

Hogg, M., & Abrams, D. (1988). *Social identification.* London: Routeledge.

Insko, C, Pinkley, R., Hoyle, R., Dalton, B., Hong, G., Slim, R., Landry, P., Holton, B., Ruffin, P., & Thibaut, J. (1987). Individual-group discontinuity: The role of intergroup contact. *Journal of Experimental Social Psychology, 23,* 250–267.

Insko, C, & Schopler, J. (1987). Categorization, competition, and collectivity. In C. Hendrick (Ed.), *Group processes* (pp. 213–251). Beverly Hills, CA: Sage.

Janis, I. (1982). *Groupthink.* Boston: Houghton Mifflin.

Jehn, K., Northcraft, G., & Neale, M. (1999). Why diffs make a difference: A field study of diversity, conflict, and performance in workgroups. *Administrative Science Quarterly, 44,* 741–763.

Jehn, K., & Shah, P. (1997). Interpersonal relationships and task performance: An examination of mediating processes in friendship and acquaintance groups. *Journal of Personality and Social Psychology, 72,* 775–790.

Kaplan, M. (1987). The influencing process in group decision making. *Review of Personality and Social Psychology, 8,* 189–213.

Karau, S., & Williams, K. (1993). Social loafing: A meta-analytic review and theoretical integration. *Journal of Personality and Social Psychology, 65,* 681–706.

Katzenbach, J., & Smith, D. (1993). *The wisdom of teams: Creating the high-performance organization.* Cambridge, MA: Harvard Business School Press.

Keenan, P., & Carnevale, P. (1989). Positive effects of within-group cooperation on between-group negotiation. *Journal of Applied Social Psychology, 19,* 977–992.

Ken, N. (1992). Group decision making at a multialternative task: Extremity, interfaction, distance, pluralities, and issue importance. *Organizational Behavior and Human Decision Processes, 52,* 64–95.

Kerr, N., MacCoun, R., & Kramer, G. (1996). Bias in judgment: Comparing individual and groups. *Psychological Review, 103,* 687–719.

Klimoski, R., & Ash, R. (1974). Accountability and negotiation behavior. *Organizational Behavior and Human Performance, 11,* 409–425.

Lane, H., & Beamish, P. (1990). Cross-cultural cooperation behavior in joint ventures in LDCs. *Management International Review, 30,* 87–102.

Latane, B. (1981). The psychology of social impact. *American Psychologist, 36,* 343–356.

Laughlin, P. (1980). Social combination processes in cooperative problem-solving groups on verbal intellective tasks. In M. Fishbein (Ed.), *Progress in social psychology* (pp. 127–155). Hillsdale, NJ: Erlbaum.

Laughlin, P., & Ellis, A. (1986). Demonstrability and social combination processes on mathematical intellective tasks. *Journal of Experimental Social Psychology, 22,* 177–189.

Laughlin, P., VanderStoep, W., & Hollingshead, A. (1991). Collective versus individual induction: Recognition of truth, rejection of error, and collective information processing. *Journal of Personality and Social Psychology, 61,* 50–67.

Lax, D., & Sebenius, J. (1986). *The manager as negotiator.* New York: Free Press.

Maier, N. R. F. (1967). Assets and liabilities in group problem-solving: The need for an integrative function. *Psychological Review, 74,* 239–249.

McGuire, W., Keisler, S., & Siegel, J. (1987). Group and computer-mediated discussion effect in risk decision making. *Journal of Personality and Social Psychology, 52,* 917–930.

Messick, D., & Rutte, C. (1992). The provision of public good by experts: The Groningen study. In W. Liebrand, D. Messick, & H. Wilke (Eds.), *Social dilemmas: Theoretical issues and research findings* (pp. 101–109) Oxford, England: Pergamon Press.

Messick, D., & Sentis, K. (1979). Fairness and preference. *Journal of Experimental Social Psychology, 15,* 418–434.

Moreland, R., Argote, L., & Krishnam, R. (1998). Training people to work in groups. In R. S. Tindale, L. Heath, J. Edwards, E. J. Prosovac, F. B. Bryant, Y. Suarez-Balcazar, E. Henderson-King, & J. Myers (Eds.), *Theory and research on small groups* (pp. 37–60). New York: Plenum Press.

Moscovici, S. (1984). The phenomenon of social representations. In R. M. Farr & S. Moscovici (Eds.), *Social representations* (pp. 3–69) Cambridge, England: Cambridge University Press.

Moscovici, S., & Zavalloni, M. (1969). The group as a polarizer of attitudes. *Journal of Personality and Social Psychology, 12,* 125–135.

Myers, D. (1982). Polarizing effect of social interaction. In M. Brandstatter, J. Davis, & G. Stocker-Kreichgauer (Eds.), *Group decision processes* (pp. 125–161). New York: Academic Press.

Myers, D., & Lamm, H. (1976). The group polarization phenomenon. *Psychological Bulletin, 83,* 602–627.

Northcraft, G., & Neale, M. (1991). Dyadic negotiation. In M. Bazerman, R. Lewicki, & B. Sheppard (Eds.), *Research on negotiation in organizations* (Vol. 3, pp. 203–230). Greenwich, CT: JAI Press.

O'Connor, K. (1997). Groups and solos in context: The effects of accountability on team negotiation. *Organizational Behavior and Human Decision Processes, 72,* 384–407.

Peterson, E., & Thompson, L. (1997). Negotiation teamwork: The impact of information distribution and accountability on performance depends on the relationship among team members. *Organizational Behavior and Human Decision Processes, 72,* 364–383.

Petty, R., Harkins, S., & Williams, K. (1980). Effects of group diffusion of cognitive effort on attitudes: An info processing view. *Journal of Personality and Social Psychology, 38,* 81–92.

Polzer, J. (1996). Intergroup negotiations: The effects of negotiating teams. *Journal of Conflict Resolution, 40,* 678–698.

Pruitt, D., & Carnevale, P. (1993). *Negotiation in social conflict.* Pacific Grove, CA: Brooks/Cole.

Ross, L., Amabile, T., & Steinmetz, J. (1977). Social roles, social control, and biases in social-perception processes. *Journal of Personality and Social Psychology, 35,* 485–494.

Schopler, J., & Insko, C. (1992). The discontinuity effect in interpersonal and intergroup relations: Generality and mediation. In W. Stroebe & M. Hewstone (Eds.), *European review of social psychology* (pp. 121–151). Chichester, England: Wiley.

Schweitzer, M., Brodt, S., & Croson, R. (2000). *Visual access and context-dependent lies: The use of deception in videoconference and telephone mediated negotiations.* Manuscript submitted for publication.

Shaw, M. (1932). A comparison of individuals and small groups in the rational solution of complex problems. *American Journal of Psychology, 44,* 491–504.

Sniezek, J., & Henry, R. (1989). Accuracy and confidence in group judgment. *Organizational Behavior and Human Decision Processes, 43,* 1–28.

Stasser, G. (1988). Computer simulation as a research tool: The DISCUSS model of group decision making. *Journal of Experimental Social Psychology, 24,* 393–422.

Stasser, G., Stewart, D., & Wittenbaum, G. (1995). Expert roles and information exchange during discussion: The importance of knowing who knows what. *Journal of Experimental Social Psychology, 31,* 244–265.

Tajfel, H. (1982). *Social identity & intergroup relations.* Cambridge, England: Cambridge University Press.

Tajfel, H., & Turner, J. (1979). An integrative theory of intergroup conflict. In W. Austin & S. Worchel (Eds.), *The social psychology of intergroup relations* (pp. 33–50). Monterey, CA: Brooks/Cole.

Thompson, L. (1990). An examination of naive and experienced negotiators. *Journal of Personality and Social Psychology, 59,* 82–90.

Thompson, L. (1993). The impact of negotiation on intergroup relations. *Journal of Experimental Social Psychology, 29,* 304–325.

Thompson, L. (2001). *The mind and heart of the negotiator.* Upper Saddle River, NJ: Prentice Hall.

Thompson, L., & Hastie, R. (1990). Social perception in negotiation. *Organizational Behavior and Human Decision Processes, 47,* 98–123.

Thompson, L., Peterson, E., & Brodt, S. (1996). Team negotiation: An examination of integrative and distributive bargaining. *Journal of Personality and Social Psychology, 70,* 66–78.

Tindale, R. S., Smith, C, Thomas, L., Filkins, J., & Sheffey, S. (1996). Shared representations and asymmetric social influence processes in small groups. In E. Witte & J. Davis (Eds.), *Understanding group behavior: Consensual action by small groups* (Vol. 1, pp. 81–104). Hillsdale, NJ: Erlbaum.

Triandis, H. (1989). The self and social behavior in differing cultural contexts. *Psychological Review, 96,* 506–520.

Turner, J., & Oakes, P. (1989). Self-categorization theory and social influence. In P. Paulus (Ed.), *Psychology of group influence* (2nd ed., pp 233–275). Hillsdale, NJ: Erlbaum.

Valley, K., Moag, J., & Bazerman, M. (1998). A matter of trust: Effects of communication on the efficiency and distribution of outcomes. *Journal of Economic Behavior and Organization, 34,* 211–238.

Valley, K., Neale, M., & Mannix, E. (1995). Friends, lovers, colleagues, strangers: The effects of relationship on the process and outcome of negotiation. In R. Lewicki, B. Sheppard, & R. Bies (Eds.), *Research on negotiation in organizations* (Vol. 5, pp. 65–93). Hillsdale, NJ: Erlbaum.

Walton, R., & McKersie, R. (1965). *A behavioral theory of labor negotiations.* New York: McGraw-Hill.

Wegner, D. (1987). Transactive memory: A contemporary analysis of the group mind. In B. Mullen & G. Goethals (Eds.), *Theories of group behavior* (pp. 185–208). New York: Springer-Verlag.

Wegner, D., Erber, R., & Raymond, P. (1991). Transactive memory in close relationships. *Journal of Personality and Social Psychology, 61,* 923–929.

Weldon, E., & Gargano, G. (1988). Cognitive loafing: The effects of accountability and shared responsibility on cognitive effort. *Personality and Social Psychology Bulletin, 14,* 159–171.

Wilder, D., & Shapiro, P. (1991). Facilitation of outgroup stereotypes by enhanced ingroup identity. *Journal of Experimental Social Psychology, 27,* 431–452.

Title Index

Name Index

Names printed in **bold face** are of authors with selections in this volume, along with the appropriate page references.